HOW TO READ A FILM

OTHER BOOKS BY JAMES MONACO

HOW TO READ A FILM

The World of Movies, Media, and Multimedia

Language, History, Theory

Third Edition, Completely Revised and Expanded

James Monaco

with diagrams by David Lindroth

New York   Oxford
OXFORD UNIVERSITY PRESS
2000

Oxford University Press

Oxford   New York
Athens   Auckland   Bangkok   Bogotá   Buenos Aires   Calcutta
Cape Town   Chennai   Dar es Salaam   Delhi   Florence   Hong Kong   Istanbul
Karachi   Kuala Lumpur   Madrid   Melbourne   Mexico City   Mumbai
Nairobi   Paris   São Paulo   Singapore   Taipei   Tokyo   Toronto   Warsaw
and associated companies in
Berlin   Ibadan

First published in 2000 by Oxford University Press, Inc.
198 Madison Avenue, New York, New York 10016

Oxford is a registered trademark of Oxford University Press

Library of Congress Cataloging-in-Publication Data
Monaco, James.
How to read a film: the world of movies, media, and multimedia:
art, technology, language, history, theory / James Monaco:
with diagrams by David Lindroth.—3rd ed., completely rev. and expanded.
p. cm.
Includes bibliographical references and index.
ISBN 0-19-513981-X (Cloth)
ISBN 0-19-503869-X (Pbk.)
1. Motion pictures. 2000
PN1994.M59   1997   97-1832
791.43'01'5—dc21

Since this page cannot legibly accommodate all necessary credits, the following page
is regarded as an extension of the copyright page.

9 8 7 6 5 4 3 2 1
Printed in the United States of America
on acid-free paper

CREDITS

Design Director: David Lindroth.

General Editor English Edition: Curtis Church.

General Editor German Edition: Hans-Michael Bock.

Editorial Assistance: Richard Allen, Joellyn Ausanka, William D. Drennan, Kathleen Fitzpatrick, Joe Medjuck, James Pallot, Leonard Quart, Roger Rawlings, Anne Sanow, Jerrold Spiegel, Dan Streible, John Wright, Robert Wohlleben.

Production Assistance: Kate Collins, Nick Drjuchin, Suzanne Goodwin, Jo Imeson, Susan Jacobson, Charles Monaco, Margaret Monaco, Andrew Monaco, Greg Parker, Stephen Plumlee, Susan Schenker.

A NOTE ON THE TYPE

This edition of *How To Read a Film* is set in Adobe's release of Meridien. Designed in 1957 by Swiss typographer Adrian Frutiger for the French foundry Deberny & Peignot, Meridien's large x-height enhances legibility while its Latinesque serifs and flared stems give it a classical Roman elegance. One of the pioneers of "cold type" design, Frutiger is perhaps best-known for the influential Univers family. The display types are Bodoni and Trade Gothic. The captions are set in Trade Gothic Light.

The book was set by UNET 2 Corporation. Prepress by Jay's Publishers Services, Inc..

WWW.ReadFilm.com

For Susan
With love, still

In Memoriam

Lucille

CONTENTS

INTRODUCTION

What with one thing and another, almost twenty years have passed since the second edition of *How To Read a Film*. I have excuses, mind you. We raised a family, bought a house, made a living. We founded two companies in the process. Moreover, sales of the second edition kept increasing, year after year, thanks to a loyal group of readers and film professors. In the computer industry, there's a saying: "If it ain't broke, don't fix it."

The timing had been right for the book. The first edition was completed in 1977, just at the end of an exciting period of film history. The past twenty years have had their share of good films (and competent scholarship); Hollywood thrived during the eighties and nineties, as new distribution media made the economics of filmmaking more flexible. And independent filmmakers have both more freedom and cheaper technology at their command. But there have been no major movements since the seventies to alter radically our view of the medium or its history. The movie generation of the sixties has had a longer reign now than the generation of the thirties that preceded it. If you make a list of the important filmmakers of the late 1970s, it will serve—with only a few additions and deletions—as a list of the dominant personalities of the late 1990s. As the generation has, so the book has lasted.

Yet, in the past twenty years, the whole world has changed.

The new technology is pervasive, and its effect on the way we make not only movies but all media is about to become profound. The microcomputer revolution, which was beginning just as the first edition of *How To Read a Film* appeared, has thoroughly dominated the cultural and business history of the 1980s and 1990s. The way we process text, images, and sounds today is radically different from what it was twenty years ago. And the union of media, which the invention of movies foreshadowed a hundred years ago, is now nearly a reality. It's as if film, the defining medium of the twentieth century, was but prologue to the new media of the twenty-first. As the old technologies of chemistry and mechanics yield to digital electronics and photonics, filmmakers may rediscover the pioneer spirit. The medium is about to be reborn: now, if you can think it, you can film it.

The way we consume motion pictures has changed even more. In the 1970s, film buffs organized their lives around repertory-house schedules, and might travel 50 miles to catch a screening of a rare film. Today, even the most out-of-the-way town has a video store with four or five thousand titles in stock, ready for viewing at a moment's notice, and if you can't find it there, you can get it on the Internet. Twenty years ago, very few of us actually owned movies; today, even fewer of us do not. Films are a lot more like books, now (and books are about to become more cinematic). In the past twenty years our exposure to filmed entertainment has increased by a magnitude or more.

While the new technology is exciting and promising, the art that it serves has yet to share the spirit of revolution. That's not surprising: art imitates life, not technology, and our political concerns are just about the same as they were twenty years ago. The Cold War ended, not with a bang, but a series of whimpers, and ended too late to have the dramatic effect it should have had on most people's lives (except for the victims of the Eastern European ethnic wars). The world of politics is as postmodern as our popular culture. We don't invent, we don't react, we don't create. We simply repeat, and repeat, and repeat. Ideas and feelings that were heady, exciting, and full of promise for a few brief shining moments in the 1960s are still with us, now nagging responsibilities, long in the tooth, often distorted ("politically correct"). I don't know why this has happened (perhaps we were too busy trying to figure out how to get our computers to work), but it has. It seems clear, now, that the generation of the 1960s will have to leave to our children the work of reinventing social politics, restoring its humor, and rediscovering its joy. At least they have a fresh century at their disposal.

This fourth edition of *How To Read a Film* was conceived from the beginning as a multimedia production.[*] The book seemed to welcome this approach not only because of its subject, but also for its architecture, which was global rather than linear. The seven sections of the book stand independently; readers can use them (or ignore them) as they see fit. Now the additional "parts" on the disc are available for this do-it-yourself construction project. You can find out more about the multimedia edition at WWW.ReadFilm.com or by writing or calling UNET 2 Corporation, 80 East 11th Street, New York NY 10003; 800 269 6422.

When I began work on the third edition, it looked like a six-month project. But the work stretched out for years as we discovered more and more possibilities

---

[*] The third edition appeared only in German as *Film verstehen* (1995).

for exciting multimedia extensions to the basic text. The movies, additional texts, and vastly expanded opportunities for still illustrations were obvious from the start. But as the project developed, we realized the importance of interactive "laboratories," and became enamored of the possibilities for author's notes that commented on the text. As a writer who had always been much too fond of parentheses and footnotes, I found this opportunity to go off on tangents irresistible. Then, too, one of the difficulties of writing about film has always been that you don't have the same tools at your command as the people you write about. Multimedia restores the balance. Now we can show as well as tell.

I wrote the first edition of *How To Read a Film* on the Smith-Corona electric typewriter on which I had learned to type in college, and on which I had pounded out about 1.5 million words as a freelance writer in the 1970s. I rewrote it on a series of PowerBooks, working on files that had been retrieved from the digital typesetting for the second edition. The experience was fascinating. Writers' tools, like painters', can have a marked effect on the work. Henry James's novels doubled and tripled in length once he was earning enough to switch from handwriting to dictation. Ernest Hemingway wrote with a pencil. Standing up. You can feel it in his prose. The main advantage of word-processing software is the power to revise. As I worked my way through the then fifteen-year-old sentences of the second edition, I saw immediately how the craft had changed. Time and again in the old prose, I saw myself spinning wheels. Phrases, clauses, sometimes whole sentences existed only to pass the time, keep the rhythm going, while I figured out how to say what I had in mind. This is a function of typewriting. I've cleaned up a lot of this padding.

Being able to look at the paragraphs on the screen in an approximation of the font in which they will appear in the book was also instructive. You can see problems that aren't apparent in a double-spaced Courier typescript. (Yes, you could do this in the old days on galley proofs, but that was an expensive luxury for most writers.) The visual architecture of writing becomes more important. The typescript or manuscript bears as much relation to the printed book as pencil sketches do to finished paintings. Writers are now beginning to have the same control over the final product that painters have always had.

Perhaps even more important than the power of revision and increased control over the architecture of the text is the opportunity electronic publishing provides for real-time writing. Books have always been "batch-processed." Once a book goes to press it is finished. The economics of publishing make frequent editions difficult. Now we have the ability—and with it goes a responsibility—to keep the text fresh. Closely allied with this new facility is the interactivity of electronic text. I've always missed the other side of the conversation; now, I expect to hear at least a part of it. (Check the website at WWW.ReadFilm.com for updates.)

All these high-tech advantages are intriguing, but don't give up on the classic crafts of media too quickly. At a multimedia conference in Los Angeles in February 1995, I watched a demonstration of the new QuickTime VR technology. The large audience broke into spontaneous applause when they saw it in operation. The speaker then described how the VR team at Apple had first tried videotape as the source material for QuickTime VR, rejected it in favor of an expensive panoramic still camera, then finally settled on old-fashioned 35 mm still photography. "Film!" he exclaimed, "This stuff has incredible resolution!" The Hollywood professionals in the audience chuckled at the irony.

And just as the nineteenth-century film medium itself isn't likely to disappear anytime soon, so, too, the more time I spend with computers, the more I appreciate the ingenious device that is a book. Like the inclined plane or the wheel, the book is a simple machine of rugged versatility. No sensible person would prefer a computer screen to a well printed page for reading text (or looking at pictures). This stuff has incredible resolution. Moreover, sewing the pages together on one side provides an excellent search engine for many applications.

In the end, however, it is not the technical superiority of print on bound pages that will prove the lasting value of the book but rather its physical reality. It is only a matter of time before digital technology provides the resolution and visual power of print. What it can never provide is the "thingness" of a book. In an increasingly virtual and abstract world, these physical objects, with unique weight, feel, and smell, will be increasingly prized.

"No ideas but in things," Wallace Stevens told us.

The production of the fourth edition of *How To Read a Film* (both the book and the disc) has been very much a team effort. You'll find the members of the team listed in the credits; I'm grateful to them all. I especially want to thank Jo Imeson, Kate Collins, Joellyn Ausanka, and Curtis Church for their conscientious attention to detail. James Pallot, Jerrold Spiegel, Joe Medjuck, and Curtis Church all provided valuable critiques of the revision as it progressed. Richard Allen of NYU, Raymond Fielding of Florida State University, Annette Insdorf of Columbia University, Leo Braudy of the University of Southern California, Steven Reich, Richard Reisman, and Dan Streible of the University of Texas all provided valuable information. I'm grateful to numerous film teachers who thoughtfully provided feedback over the years. Richard Lorber of Winstar New Media and Bruce Ricker of Rhapsody Films provided materials as well as encouragement.

One of the plusses in revisiting *How To Read a Film* has been the chance to work again with David Lindroth and Hans-Michael Bock. As before, David Lindroth has provided creative and engaging diagrams—only now they are all digital. It was a pleasure to work with David again. Hans-Michael Bock, the general editor of the German edition, *Film verstehen*, has once again given a native Geist to that version that a simple translation never could have conveyed. (The work on *Film verstehen* has proceeded concurrently with the English-language edition.) Ludwig Moos of Rowohlt Verlag provided patient support during the process. To all, much thanks.

I'm also grateful to my wife and children. While it is traditional in acknowledgements of this kind to thank your family, in this case it is doubly appropriate. Not only did they offer the support, encouragement, and patience any writer needs, they also contributed directly. Their assistance in research, editing, production, and programming was invaluable. I hope they agree that this family project was more fun than any yard sale.

J. M.
Sag Harbor
August 1999

PREFACE
to the Second Edition

Is it necessary, really, to learn how to read a film?[*] Obviously, anyone of minimal intelligence over the age of four can—more or less—grasp the basic content of a film, record, radio, or television program without any special training. Yet precisely because the media so very closely mimic reality, we apprehend them much more easily than we comprehend them. Film and the electronic media have drastically changed the way we perceive the world—and ourselves—during the past eighty years, yet we all too naturally accept the vast amounts of information they convey to us in massive doses without questioning how they tell us what they tell. *How To Read a Film* is an essay in understanding that crucial process—on several levels.

In the first place, film and television are general mediums of communication. Certain basic interesting rules of perception operate: Chapter 3, "The Language of Film: Signs and Syntax," investigates a number of these concepts. On a more advanced level, film is clearly a sophisticated art—possibly the most important art of the twentieth century—with a rather complex history of theory and practice. Chapter 1, "Film as an Art," suggests how film can be fit into the spectrum of the more traditional arts; Chapter 4, "The Shape of Film History," attempts a brief survey of the development of the art of movies; Chapter 5, "Film Theory: Form and Function," surveys some of the major theoretical developments of the past seventy-five years.

Film is a medium and an art, but it is also, uniquely, a very complex technological undertaking. Chapter 2, "Technology: Image and Sound," is—I hope—a clear exposition of the intriguing science of cinema. Although film is dominant, the development of the electronic media—records, radio, tape, television, video—has proceeded in parallel with the growth of film during this century. The relationship between film and media becomes stronger with each passing year; Chapter 6 outlines a general theory of media (both print and electronic), discusses the equally complex technology of the electronic media, and concludes with a survey of the history of radio and television.

As you can see from this outline, the structure of *How To Read a Film* is global rather than linear. In each of the six chapters the intention has been to try to explain a little of how film operates on us psychologically, how it affects us politically. Yet these twin central dominant questions can be approached from a number of angles. Since most people think of film first as an art, I've begun with that

---

[*]   I have made no changes to this Preface. It was another time.

aspect of the phenomenon. Since it's difficult to understand how the art has developed without some knowledge of the technology, Chapter 2 proceeds immediately to a discussion of the science of film. Understanding technique, we can begin to discover how film operates as a language (Chapter 3). Since practice does (or should) precede theory, the history of the industry and art (Chapter 4) precedes the intellectualization of it here (Chapter 5). We conclude by widening the focus to view movies in the larger context of media (Chapter 6).

This order seems most logical to me, but readers might very well prefer to begin with history or theory, language or technology, and in fact the book has been constructed in such a way that the sections can be read independently, in any order. (This has resulted in a small number of repetitions, for which I ask your indulgence.) Please remember, too, that in any work of this sort there is a tendency to prescribe rather than simply describe the complex phenomena under investigation. Hundreds of analytical concepts are discussed in the pages that follow, but I ask that readers consider them just that—concepts, analytical tools—rather than given laws. Film study is exciting because it is constantly in ferment. It's my hope that *How To Read a Film* is a book that can be argued with, discussed, and used. In any attempt at understanding, the questions are usually more important than the answers.

How To Read a Film is the result of ten years spent, mainly, thinking, writing, and talking about film and media. Having tried in the pages that follow to set down a few ideas about movies and TV, I find I am most impressed with the number of questions that are yet to be answered. Appendix II gives a fair sense of the considerable amount of work that has already been done (mainly in the past ten years); there is much more yet to do. Had *How To Read a Film* included all the material I originally wanted to cover it would have been encyclopedic in length; as it is now, it is an admittedly hefty, but nevertheless still sinewy, introduction. More and more it seems to me movies must be considered in the context of media in general—in fact, I would go so far as to suggest that film is best considered simply as one stage in the ongoing history of communications. Chapter 6 introduces this concept. You will find some additional material on both print and electronic media in the Chronology.

A few miscellaneous notes: Bibliographical information not included in footnotes will be found in the appropriate section of Appendix II. Film titles are in English, unless the original foreign language titles are commonly used. In cases where halftones are direct enlargements of film frames, this has been noted in the captions; in most other cases, you can assume the halftones are publicity stills and may differ in slight respects from the actual images of the film.

I owe a very real debt to a number of people who have helped in various ways. *How To Read a Film* never would have been written without my invaluable experience teaching film at the New School for Social Research. I thank Allen Austill for allowing me to do so, Reuben Abel for taking a chance on a young teacher in 1967, and Wallis Osterholz for her unflagging encouragement and necessary help. I am especially grateful to my students at the New School (and the City University of New York) who, although they may not know it, gave at least as much as they got.

At Oxford University Press I have been particularly fortunate. Editor John Wright, with intelligence, savvy, and humor, has added immeasurably to whatever success the book might enjoy. Ellen Royer helped to make sense out of a manuscript that may have been lively, but was certainly sprawling and demanding. Dana Kasarsky designed the book with care and dealt efficiently with the myriad problems such a complex layout entails. Ellie Fuchs, Jean Shapiro, and Editor James Raimes at Oxford were consistently and dependably helpful. Curtis Church has overseen the production of the second edition with patience and great care. Thanks to all.

David Lindroth has drawn more than three dozen diagrams which I think add considerably to the effect of *How To Read a Film*. If I may say so, I think they are notably superior to comparable illustrations of this sort. David not only translated my scrawls into meaningful conceptions, he also added significantly to the realization of those conceptions. His input was invaluable.

Dudley Andrew and David Bombyk read the manuscript and commented upon it rigorously and in exceptionally useful detail. Their comments were enormously helpful. I also want to thank Kent R. Brown, Paul C. Hillery, Timothy J. Lyons, and Sreekumar Menon for reading and commenting upon the manuscript.

William K. Everson, Eileen M. Krest, and my brother Robert Monaco provided valuable information I was unable to discover for myself, as did Jerome Agel, Stellar Bennett (NET), Ursula Deren (BBC), Kozu Hiramatsu (Sony), Cal Hotchkiss (Kodak), Terry Maguire (FCC), Joe Medjuck (University of Toronto), Alan Schneider (Juilliard), and Sarah Warner (I.E.E.E.). Many thanks.

Marc Fürstenberg, Claudia Gorbman, Annette Insdorf, Bruce Kawin, and Clay Steinman, among others, made suggestions valuable for this revised edition.

Penelope Houston of *Sight and Sound* and Peter Lebensold of *Take One* graciously allowed me to draw on materials originally published in their journals.

Finally, I thank my wife, Susan Schenker, who read and commented on the manuscript, talked out difficulties with me, helped write the Appendices, and did so much more. (Acknowledgments are always such a faint reflection of real feelings.)

J.M.
New York City
January 1977
February 1981

1
FILM AS AN ART

The Nature of Art

If poetry is what you can't translate, as Robert Frost once suggested, then "art" is what you can't define. Nevertheless, it's fun to try. Art covers such a wide range of human endeavor that it is almost more an attitude than an activity. Over the years, the boundaries of the meaning of the word have expanded, gradually yet inexorably. Cultural historian Raymond Williams has cited art as one of the "keywords"—one that must be understood in order to comprehend the interrelationships between culture and society. As with "community," "criticism," and "science," for example, the history of the word "art" reveals a wealth of information about how our civilization works. A review of that history will help us to understand how the relatively new art of film fits into the general pattern of art.

The ancients recognized seven activities as arts: History, Poetry, Comedy, Tragedy, Music, Dance, and Astronomy. Each was governed by its own muse, each had its own rules and aims, but all seven were united by a common motivation: they were tools, useful to describe the universe and our place in it. They were methods of understanding the mysteries of existence, and as such, they themselves took on the aura of those mysteries. As a result, they were each aspects of religious activity: The performing arts celebrated the rituals; history recorded the story of the race; astronomy searched the heavens. In each of these seven classical arts we can discover the roots of contemporary cultural and scientific categories. History, for example, leads not only to the modern social sciences but also to prose narrative (the novel, short stories, and so forth). Astronomy, on the other hand, represents the full range of modern science at the same time as it suggests another aspect of the social sciences in its astrological functions of prediction and interpre-

Figure 1-1. THE ANCIENT MUSES. Calliope (epic poetry), Clio (history), Erato (love poetry), Melpomene (tragedy), Terpsichore (choral dancing), Polyhymnia (sacred music), Euterpe (lyric poetry), Thalia (comedy), and Urania (astronomy). The fellow in the middle is Apollo. (*Pitti Palace, Florence.*)

tation. Under the rubric of poetry, the Greeks and Romans recognized three approaches: Lyric, Dramatic, and Epic. All have yielded modern literary arts.

By the thirteenth century, however, the word "art" had taken on a considerably more practical connotation. The Liberal Arts curriculum of the medieval university still numbered seven components, but the method of definition had shifted. The literary arts of the classical period—History, Poetry, Comedy, and Tragedy—had merged into a vaguely defined mix of literature and philosophy and then had been reordered according to analytical principles as Grammar, Rhetoric, and Logic (the Trivium), structural elements of the arts rather than qualities of them. Dance was dropped from the list and replaced by Geometry, marking the growing importance of mathematics. Only Music and Astronomy remained unchanged from the ancient categories.

Outside the university cloisters, the word was even more flexible. We still speak of the "art" of war, the medical "arts," even the "art" of angling. By the sixteenth century, "art" was clearly synonymous with "skill," and a wheelwright, for example, was just as much an artist as a musician: each practiced a particular skill.

By the late seventeenth century, the range of the word had begun to narrow once again. It was increasingly applied to activities that had never before been included—painting, sculpture, drawing, architecture—what we now call the "Fine Arts." The rise of the concept of modern science as separate from and contradictory to the arts meant that Astronomy and Geometry were no longer regarded in the same light as Poetry or Music. By the late eighteenth century, the Romantic vision of the artist as specially endowed restored some of the religious aura that had surrounded the word in classical times. A differentiation was now made between "artist" and "artisan." The former was "creative" or "imaginative," the latter simply a skilled workman.

In the nineteenth century, as the concept of science developed, the narrowing of the concept of art continued, as if in response to that more rigorously logical activity. What had once been "natural philosophy" was termed "natural science"; the art of alchemy became the science of chemistry. The new sciences were precisely defined intellectual activities, dependent on rigorous methods of operation. The arts (which were increasingly seen as being that which science was not) were therefore also more clearly defined.

By the middle of the nineteenth century the word had more or less developed the constellation of connotations we know today. It referred first to the visual, or "Fine," arts, then more generally to literature and the musical arts. It could, on occasion, be stretched to include the performing arts and, although in its broadest sense it still carried the medieval sense of skills, for the most part it was strictly used to refer to more sophisticated endeavors. The romantic sense of the artist as a chosen one remained: "artists" were distinguished not only from "artisans" (craftspeople) but also from "artistes" (performing artists) with lower social and intellectual standing.

With the establishment in the late nineteenth century of the concept of "social sciences," the spectrum of modern intellectual activity was complete and the range of art had narrowed to its present domain. Those phenomena that yielded to study by the scientific method were ordered under the rubric of science and were strictly defined. Other phenomena, less susceptible to laboratory techniques and experimentation, but capable of being ordered with some logic and clarity, were established in the gray area of the social sciences (economics, sociology, politics, psychology, and sometimes even philosophy). Those areas of intellectual endeavor that could not be fit into either the physical or the social sciences were left to the domain of art.

As the development of the social sciences necessarily limited the practical, utilitarian relevance of the arts, and probably in reaction to this phenomenon, theories of estheticism evolved. With roots in the Romantic theory of the artist as prophet and priest, the "art for art's sake" movement of the late Victorian age celebrated form over content and once more changed the focus of the word. The arts were no longer simply approaches to a comprehension of the world; they were now ends in themselves. Walter Pater declared that "all art aspires to the condition of music." Abstraction—pure form—became the touchstone of the work of art and the main criterion by which works of art were judged in the twentieth century.[*]

The rush to abstraction accelerated rapidly during the first two-thirds of the twentieth century. In the nineteenth century the avant-garde movement had taken the concept of progress from the developing technology and decided that some art must perforce be more "advanced" than other art. The theory of the avant garde, which was a dominating idea in the historical development of the arts from the Romantic period until recently, expressed itself best in terms of abstraction. In this respect the arts were, in effect, mimicking the sciences and technology, searching for the basic elements of their "languages"—the "quanta" of painting or poetry or drama.

The Dada movement of the 1920s parodied this development. The result was the minimalist work of the middle of this century, which marked the endpoint of the struggle of the avant garde toward abstraction: Samuel Beckett's forty-second dramas (or his ten-page novels), Josef Albers's color-exercise paintings, John Cage's silent musical works. Having reduced art to its most basic quanta, the only choice for artists (besides quitting) was to begin over again to rebuild the structures of the arts. This new synthesis began in earnest in the 1960s (although the avant-garde abstractionists had one last card to play: the so-called conceptual art movement of the 1970s, which eliminated the work of art entirely, leaving only the idea behind).

The end of the avant-garde fascination with abstraction came at the same time that political and economic culture was, in parallel, discovering the fallacy of progress and developing in its place a "steady state" theory of existence. From the vantage point of the turn of the twenty-first century, we might say that art made the transition quicker and easier than politics and economics.

The acceleration of abstraction, while it is certainly the main factor in the historical development of the arts during the twentieth century, is not the only one. The force that counters this estheticism is our continuing sense of the political dimension of the arts: that is, both their roots in the community, and their power to explain the structure of society to us.

In Western culture, the power of this relevance (which led the ancients to include History on an equal footing with Music) has certainly not dominated, but it does have a long and honorable history parallel with, if subordinate to, the esthetic impulse toward abstraction. In the 1970s, when the first edition of this book appeared, it seemed safe to assume that as abstraction and reductionism faded away, the political dimension of art—its social nature—would increase in importance. Now, from the perspective of Y2K, it appears that it hasn't—at least not to the degree we expected. Instead, most of the arts, film chief among them, have settled down into a period of commercial calm. There is an evident increase in the political and social quotient of most contemporary arts: you can see it in the increasing prevalence of television docudramas and reality-based programming,

---

* I am indebted to Raymond Williams's essay in *Keywords: A Vocabulary of Culture and Society*, pp. 32, 34.

the mainstream influence of Rap music, and a renewed vigor in independent filmmaking. However, the politics that these arts reflect hasn't progressed much beyond the stage it had reached by 1970: more or less the same issues concern us now as then. "Don't kill the messenger" (and don't blame the artists). And, while the artists have understood and accepted the passing of the avant garde, the politicians haven't yet freed themselves from dependence on the Left–Right dialectic—now equally moribund—upon which that artistic movement depended.

So there is more politics in art—it's just poor quality politics. Moreover, the explosion in the technology of the arts since the mid-1970s, a subject we will discuss in some detail in Chapters 6 and 7, has overshadowed and often displaced the renewed relevance that we expected. This technology is the third basic factor that has determined the history of the arts during the past hundred years.

Originally, the only way to produce art was in "real time": the singer sang the song, the storyteller told the tale, the actors acted the drama. The development in prehistory of drawing and (through pictographs) of writing represented a quantum jump in systems of communication. Images could be stored, stories could be preserved, later to be recalled exactly. For seven thousand years the history of the arts was, essentially, the history of these two representative media: the pictorial and the literary.

The development of recording media, different from representative media in kind as well as degree, was as significant historically as the invention of writing seven thousand years earlier. Photography, film, and sound recording taken together shifted dramatically our historical perspective.

The representational arts made possible the "re-creation" of phenomena, but they required the complex application of the codes and conventions of languages. Moreover, those languages were manipulated by individuals and therefore the element of choice was and is highly significant in the representational arts. This element is the source of most of the esthetics of the pictorial and literary arts. What interests estheticians is not *what* is said but *how* it is said.

In stark contrast, the recording arts provide a much more direct line of communication between the subject and the observer. They do have their own codes and conventions, it's true: a film or sound recording is not reality, after all. But the language of the recording media is both more direct and less ambiguous than either written or pictorial language. In addition, the history of the recording arts has—until recently—been a direct progression toward greater verisimilitude. Color film reproduces more of reality than does black-and-white; sound film is more closely parallel to actual experience than is silent; and so forth.

This qualitative difference between representational media and recording media is very clear to those who use the latter for scientific purposes. Anthropologists, for example, are well aware of the advantages of film over the written word. Film does not completely eliminate the intervention of a third party between the

Figure 1-2. Josef Albers's *Homage to the Square: Silent Hall*, 1961, one of his more lively compositions, exemplifies mid-twentieth-century minimalism. (*Oil on composition board, 40' x 40", The Museum of Modern Art, New York. Dr and Mrs Frank Stanton Fund. Photograph © 1995, The Museum of Modern Art, New York.*)

subject and the observer, but it does significantly reduce the distortion that the presence of an artist inevitably introduces.

The result is a spectrum of the arts that looks like this:

❏ the performance arts, which happen in real time;
❏ the representational arts, which depend on the established codes and conventions of language (both pictorial and literary) to convey information about the subject to the observer;
❏ the recording arts, which provide a more direct path between subject and observer: media not without their own codes but qualitatively more direct than the media of the representational arts.

That is, until now. The application of digital technology to film and audio, which began to gather momentum in the late 1980s, points to a new level of discourse: one that is about to revolutionize our attitude toward the recording arts. Simply put, digital techniques like morphing and sampling destroy our faith in the honesty of the images and sounds we see and hear. The verisimilitude is still there—but we can no longer trust our eyes and ears. We'll discuss these remarkable developments in greater detail in Chapter 7.

Ways of Looking at Art

In order to understand how the recording arts established their place in the spectrum of art, it's necessary first to define some of the basic concepts of that spectrum. There is a wide variety of factors that interrelate to give each of the classical and modern arts its own particular personality, resulting in some elaborate esthetic equations. Two ordering systems, one mainly nineteenth-century in origin, the other more contemporary, suggest themselves immediately.

The Spectrum of Abstraction

The older of these systems of classification depends for its definition on the degree of abstraction of a particular art. This is one of the oldest theories of art, dating back to Aristotle's *Poetics* (fourth century B.C.). According to the Greek philosopher, art was best understood as a type of mimesis, an imitation of reality dependent on a *medium* (through which it was expressed) and a *mode* (the way the medium was utilized). The more mimetic an art is, then, the less abstract it is. In no case, however, is an art completely capable of reproducing reality.

A spectrum of the arts organized according to abstraction would look something like this:

Practical	Environmental	Pictorial	Dramatic	Narrative	Musical
design architecture		sculpture painting drawing graphics	—— stage drama ——	novel story nonfiction	poetry dance music

Diagram A

The arts of design (clothing, furniture, eating utensils, and so forth), which often are not even dignified by being included in the artistic spectrum, would be found at the left end of this scale: highly mimetic (a fork comes very close to thoroughly reproducing the idea of a fork) and least abstract. Moving from left to right we find architecture, which often has a very low esthetic quotient, after all; then sculpture, which is both environmental and pictorial; then painting, drawing, and the other graphic arts at the center of the pictorial area of the spectrum.

The dramatic arts combine pictorial and narrative elements in various measures. The novel, short story, and often nonfiction as well are situated squarely in the narrative range. Then come poetry, which although basically narrative in nature also tends toward the musical end of the spectrum (but sometimes in the other direction, toward the pictorial); dance, combining elements of narrative with music; and finally, at the extreme right of the spectrum, music—the most abstract and "esthetic" of the arts. Remember Walter Pater: "All art aspires to the condition of music."

Where do photography and film fit in? Because they are recording arts, they cover essentially the entire range of this classical spectrum. Photography, which is a special case of film (stills rather than movies), naturally situates itself in the pictorial area of the spectrum, but it can also fulfill functions in the practical and environmental areas to the left of that position.

Film covers a broad range, from practical (as a technical invention it is an important scientific tool) through environmental, on through pictorial, dramatic, and narrative to music. Although we know it best as one of the dramatic arts, film is strongly pictorial, which is why films are collected more often in art museums than in libraries; it also has a much stronger narrative element than any of the other dramatic arts, a characteristic recognized by filmmakers ever since D. W. Griffith, who pointed to Charles Dickens as one of his precursors. And because of its clear, organized rhythms—as well as its soundtrack—it has close connections with music. Finally, in its more abstract incarnations, film is strongly environmental as well: as display technologies mature, architects increasingly integrate filmed backgrounds into their more tangible structures.

This spectrum of abstraction is only one way to organize the artistic experience; it is not in any sense a law. The dramatic area of the spectrum could easily be subsumed under pictorial and narrative; the practical arts can be combined with the environmental. What is important here is simply to indicate the range of abstraction, from the most mimetic arts to the least mimetic.

(Let's remember that what we are doing here is more art than science. The abstract diagrams and dichotomies here—and throughout the book—should never be thought to carry the weight of law; they are simply ways of seeing, attempts at understanding. If you like these abstractions, please try some of your own; if you don't like them, move on to Chapter 2.)

The Modes of Discourse

The second, more modern way to classify the various arts depends on the relationships among the work, the artist, and the observer. This triangular image of the artistic experience directs our attention away from the work itself, to the medium of communication. The degree of abstraction enters in here, too, but only insofar as it affects the relationship between the artist and the observer. We are interested now not in the quality of the work itself, but in the mode of its transmission.

Organized this way, the system of artistic communication would look something like Diagram B. The vertical axis constitutes the immediate experience of an art; the horizontal, the transmission or narration of it. Artifacts, pictorial representations, and pictorial records (that area above the horizontal axis) occupy space rather than time. Performances, literature, and film records are more concerned with time than with space. (In Diagram A, the space arts occupy the left-hand side of the spectrum, the time arts the right.)

Note that any single art occupies not a point in Diagram B but rather an area. A painting, for example, is both an artifact and a representation. A building is not only an artifact but also partially a representation and occasionally a performance. (Architectural critics often use the language of drama to describe the experience of a building; as we move through it our experience of it takes place in time.) The recording arts, moreover, often use elements of performance and representation.

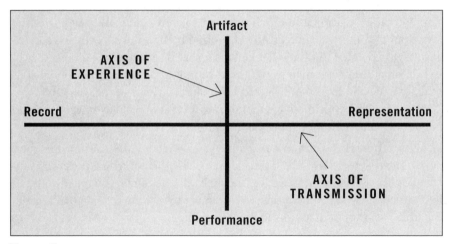

Diagram B

The spectrum in Diagram A gives us an index of the degree of abstraction inherent in an art; in other words, it describes the actual relationship between an art and its subject matter. The graph of Diagram B gives us a simplified picture of the various modes of discourse available to the artist.

The "Rapports de Production"

There is one final aspect of the artistic experience that should be investigated: what the French call "rapports de production" (the relationships of production). How and why does art get produced? How and why is it consumed? Here is the "triangle" of the artistic experience:

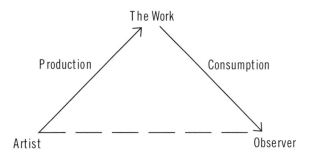

Diagram C

Examination of the relationship between the artist and the work yields theories of the production of art, while analysis of the relationship between the work and the observer gives us theories of its consumption. (The third leg of the triangle, artist–observer, has been until now potential rather than actual, although the heightened interest in interactive means of communication, which began in the early 1980s with the growth of online services, now opens up this relationship to some interesting new possibilities. For the first time, artist and observer have the technology to collaborate.)

Whether we approach the artistic experience from the point of view of production or of consumption, there is a set of determinants that gives a particular shape to the experience. Each of them serves a certain function, and each in turn yields its own general system of criticism. Here is an outline of the determinants, their functions, and the systems of criticism they support:

Determinant →	Sociopolitical	Psychological	Technical	Economic
Function →	utilitarian	expressive	art for art's sake	careerist product
System of criticism →	ethical/ political	psycho-analytical	esthetic/ formalist	infra-structure

Diagram D

These determinants of the rapports de production function in most human activities, but their operation is especially evident in the arts, since it is there that the economic and political factors that tend to dominate most other activities are more in balance with the psychological and technical factors.

Historically, the political determinant is primary: it is this factor that decides how an art—or work of art—is used socially. Consumption is more important here than production. Greek and Roman theories of art as an epistemological activity fit under this category, especially when the quest for knowledge is seen as quasi-religious. The ritualistic aspect of the arts as celebrations of the community

Figure 1-3. Edward Dayes's painting *Queen Square, London, 1786* offers striking similarities with…

is at the heart of this approach. The political determinant defines the relationship between the work of art and the society that nurtures it.

The psychological determinant, on the other hand, is introspective, focusing our attention not on the relationship between the work and the world at large, but on the connections between the work and the artist, and the work and the observer. The profound psychological effect of a work of art has been recognized ever since Aristotle's theory of catharsis. In the early twentieth century, during the great age of psychoanalysis, most psychological analysis centered on the connection between the artist and the work. The work was seen as an index of the psychological state of its author—sort of a profound and elaborate Rorschach test. Recently, however, psychological attention has shifted to the connection between the work and its consumer, the observer.

The technical determinant governs the language of the art. Given the basic structure of the art—the particular qualities of oil paint, for example, versus tempera or acrylics—what are the limits of the possibilities? How does the translation of an idea into the language of the art affect the idea? What are the thoughtforms of each particular artistic language? How have they shaped the materials the artist utilizes? These questions are the province of the technical determinant. The recording arts, because they are grounded in a much more complex technology than the other arts, are especially susceptible to this kind of analysis. Chapter 2 will discuss these factors in depth. But even seemingly untechnological arts like

Figure 1-4. … this landscape from Stanley Kubrick's *Barry Lyndon*, set in the eighteenth century. Film naturally draws on the historical traditions of the older arts. (*Frame enlargement.*)

the novel are deeply influenced by the technical determinant. For example, the novel could not exist in the form we know today without the invention of the printing press.

Finally, all arts are inherently economic products and as such must eventually be considered in economic terms. Again, film and the other recording arts are prime examples of this phenomenon. Like architecture, they are both capital-intensive and labor-intensive; that is, they involve large expenditures of money and they often require large numbers of workers.

These four determinants reveal themselves in new relationships at each stage of the artistic process. The technological and economic determinants form the basis for any art. The language of the art and its techniques exist before the artist decides to use them. Moreover, each art is circumscribed by certain economic realities. Film, because it is a very expensive art, is especially susceptible to the distortions caused by economic considerations. The elaborate economic infrastructure of film—the complex rules of production, distribution, and consumption that underlie the art—set strict limitations on filmmakers, a fact that is often ignored by critics. These economic factors, in turn, are related to certain political and psychological uses to which an art can be put. As an economic commodity, for example, film can often best be understood as selling a service that is essentially psychological in nature: we most often go to movies for the emotional effects they provide.

Artists, confronted with these various determinants, make choices within the set of established possibilities, occasionally breaking new ground, most often reorganizing and recombining existing factors.

As we move down the other leg of the artistic triangle, the determinants reveal themselves in new relationships. Once the work of art has been completed it has, in a sense, a life of its own. It is, first of all, an economic product to be exploited. This exploitation results in certain psychological effects. The end product, as the influence of the film spreads, is political. No matter how apolitical the work of art may seem, every work has political relevance, like it or not.

Historically, the political and psychological determinants have been recognized as important factors in the artistic experience since classical times. In his *Ars Poetica,* for example, Horace declared that the criteria for a work were that it be both utile et dulce, "useful" and "sweet," or "enjoyable." The utilitarian value of the work is governed by the political determinant, its enjoyability by the psychological.

Only recently, however, has serious attention been paid to the technical and economic determinants of the work of art. The approach of semiotics is to study the arts and media as languages or language systems—technical structures with inherent laws governing not only *what* is "said" but also *how* it is "said." Semiotics attempts to describe the codes and structural systems that operate in cultural phenomena. It does this by using a linguistic model; that is, the semiotics of film describes film as a "language."

Dialectical criticism, on the other hand, studies the arts in their economic context. Pioneered by the Frankfurt school of German philosophers in the 1930s and 1940s—especially Walter Benjamin, T. W. Adorno, and Max Horkheimer—dialectical criticism analyzes the direct relationships among the work, the artist, and the observer as they are expressed in terms of economic and political structures. The addition of these two modern approaches to the arts—semiotics and dialectics—gives us a fuller and more precise understanding of the complexities of the artistic experience.

It also allows us more freedom to define its limits. While the image of the artist as priest or prophet reigned, there was no way to disconnect the experience of the work from the production of it. Art depended on artists. But when we recognize the technical and linguistic roots of esthetics, we are more inclined to approach the artistic experience from the point of view of the consumer. In other words, we can liberate ourselves from artist/priests and develop a "protestant" theory of art. We have already admitted the practical arts of design into the pantheon. We can go further.

One of the most obvious candidates for admission to the spectrum of the arts is sports. Most sports activities adapt the basic dramatic structure of protagonist/antagonist and can therefore be viewed in dramatic terms. That the "plot" is not preordained simply increases its possibilities and the element of suspense. That the basic "theme" is repeated every time a game is played only reinforces the ritualistic aspects of the drama. Most sports activities share many of the values of dance. Media have not only permitted the recording of sports events for future study and enjoyment but have also significantly decreased the distance between athletes and observers and therefore have heightened our sense of the choreographic aspect of most sports.

Imagine a stranger totally unfamiliar with either dance or basketball being confronted with an example of each. There is no element of either human activity that would insist that we differentiate between them: Michael Jordan is at least the equal of Mikhail Baryshnikov. The difference between these masters' performances is like the difference between Jazz and Classical music. That sports are "unintentional" (that is, that they are not performed to make a point) simply increases the potential variety of our experience of them.

There are other areas of human endeavor that, like sports, take on new significance when we approach them from the point of view of consumption rather than production—consumables, for example. We experience food and drink (and perfume and possibly other sensual devices) in much the same way that we experience that most esthetic of arts, music. The metaphors we have used to describe the latter (ever since Shakespeare in *Twelfth Night* suggested that "music be the food of love") reinforce this close comparison.

True, the quantity of thought in food or drink is often exceedingly low; it is difficult to make a "statement" in, say, the language of green vegetables. But that is only to note that our senses of taste, smell, and touch are different in kind from our senses of sight and hearing. The element of craft in the creation of food or drink is no less sophisticated ideally than it is in music or drawing. And critics of wine and cooking often use metaphors that would not be out of place if we were to talk about literature or painting.

Let's turn this around: at least in part, we consume arts like music, film, and literature in the same way that we consume food. Like music, the art of food and drink comes close to a purely synesthetic experience. One sign of this is that our normal mode of experience of both differs in kind from the narrative arts. We consume music, like food, regularly and repeatedly. Having heard Mozart's Piano Concerto no. 23 once, having drunk a single bottle of Chassagne–Montrachet, we do not think that we have exhausted their possibilities. We also do not think to censure either the concerto or the wine because we cannot discover "meaning" in it. If the pure esthetic is a valid criterion for art, then consumables should be admitted to the spectrum.

What this theory of the art of food is meant to suggest, of course, is that the function of the observer or consumer in the process of art is every bit as important as the function of the artist/producer. If we do not admit wine or baseball to the spectrum of accepted arts, it is not the fault of the producers of those works, but rather a collective decision by consumers—a decision that can be rescinded.

There is a second corollary: If the sum total of the artistic experience includes the consumer as well as the producer, and if we express it as a product:

PRODUCTION x CONSUMPTION

then a novel way of increasing the sum presents itself. Heretofore, when evaluating a work of art, we have concentrated on the production factor. We have judged only the artist's contribution, usually measured against an artificial ideal:

$$\frac{\text{ACHIEVEMENT}}{\text{REQUIREMENT}}$$

a quotient that may have some value in judging other economic activities of a more practical nature (the production of floor waxes or screwdrivers, for example) but that is specious as a system of artistic evaluation, since it depends for its validity on the denominator, an arbitrary "requirement." But we can just as easily increase the experience of art by increasing the factor of consumption, both in quality and in quantity.

In quantitative terms, the more people who are exposed to a work of art, the more potential effect it has. In qualitative terms, the observer/consumer does have it within his power to increase the sum value of the work by becoming a more sophisticated, creative, or sensitive participant in the process. This is not a new idea in practice, although it may be so in theory. Indeed, film itself is especially rich in this sort of activity. Film buffs, after all, have trained themselves to discern the thematic, esthetic, even political values inherent in, say, the films of minor directors such as Jacques Tourneur or Archie Mayo. At best, such buffs are the cutting edge of criticism for general students of the subject; at worst, they have discovered a way to extract greater value from poor artistic ore than the rest of us. This is the new ecology of art.

Artists themselves are well aware of the potential of this new, responsive relationship. Found art, found poetry, aleatoric theater, musique concrète, all are based on an understanding of the potential power of the observer to multiply the value of artistic experience. What the artist does in each of these instances is to act as a preobserver, an editor who does not create, but chooses. The poet Denise Levertov has expressed the basis for this enterprise succinctly:

> I want to give you
> something I've made
>
> some words on a page—as if
> to say "Here are some blue beads"

or, "Here's a bright red leaf I found on
the sidewalk" (because

to find is to choose, and choice
is made).... *

In eight lines she describes not only the essential artistic drive but also the justi-
fication for approaching art not from the point of view of the producer but from
that of the consumer: "because to find is to choose, and choice is made."

This means not only that observers can increase their perception of made art
works, but also that they can act: making choices from the dramatic, pictorial,
narrative, musical, and environmental materials that present themselves day by
day: choice is made. Moreover, there is an ethical aspect to this new artistic equation, for it implies strongly that the observer is the equal of the artist. The word
"consumer," then, is misleading, for the observers are no longer passive but
active. They participate fully in the process of art.

The significance of this reappraisal of the roles of artist and observer cannot be
underestimated. The most difficult challenge the arts have had to sustain in their
seven-thousand-year history has been that posed by the techniques of mass production that grew up with the industrial revolution. While the advantage of mass
production has been that it makes art no longer an elite enterprise, it has also
meant that artists have had to struggle continuously since the industrial revolution to prevent their work from being turned into a commodity. Only the active
participation of the observer at the other end of the process is guarantee against
this.

Where once the work of art was judged purely according to arbitrary ideals
and artificial requirements, now it can be seen as "semifinished" material, to be
used by the observer to complete the artistic process rather than simply consumed.
The question now is not, "Does this art work meet the standards?" but rather,
"How can we use this art work best?" Of course, we are speaking of an ideal here.
In reality, most observers of art (whether popular or elite) still passively consume.
But the movement toward participatory artistic democracy is growing.

The new technology amplifies this new equality between artist and observer.
Now that the observer has the technological power to reshape the artist's work in
numerous ways, the artist would be foolish not to make allowances for the
observer's new-found freedom. Any sophisticated teenager with a Macintosh
today can "sample" a favorite CD just as easily as the recording artist who produced it. And most kids who spend more than an hour a day with MTV are aware
that there are multiple editions, or "mixes," for most popular songs, just as they
know that movies are released in several versions. The work of art is no longer

---

* From Denise Levertov, *Here and Now.* Copyright © 1957 by Denise Levertov.
Reprinted by permission of City Lights Books.

holy. Rather than producing a finished work, the artist now produces—like it or not—raw materials that we consumers can edit to our liking: "… choice is made."

The spectrum of abstraction, the modes of discourse, the range of determinants, the equation of producer and consumer (and its corollary, the democratization of the process)—these various approaches to the study of the arts, as we noted earlier, are not meant to carry the weight of scientific law, but simply as aids to an understanding of the artistic experience. As conceptual structures, they are useful, but there is a danger in taking them too seriously. These are ways of thinking. They are not derived inductively; rather, they are deduced from the artistic experience itself, and they are meant to set that experience in its proper context: as a phenomenon that is comparable at the same time as it appears unique. The experience of art comes first; abstract criticism of this sort is—or should be—a secondary activity.

Moreover, none of these conceptual structures exists in isolation. The elements are all in continual flux and their relationships are dialectical. The interest lies not in whether or not, say, architecture is an environmental or pictorial art but in the fact that these elements exist in a dialectical relationship with each other within the art. This is the central struggle that enlivens it. Likewise, it isn't so important whether we classify film as being in the mode of record or representation. (It does evince elements of representation—and of performance and artifact, as well). What counts is that the contrasts between and among these various modes are the source of power for the art of film.

Generally, the spectrum of abstraction describes the relationships of the arts to their raw material in reality; the system of modes of discourse explains something about the ways in which the arts are transmitted from artist to observer; the structure of determinants describes the main factors that define the shape of the arts; and the equation of artist and observer suggests new angles of critical approach to the phenomena of the arts.

Film, Recording, and the Other Arts

The recording arts comprise an entirely new mode of discourse, parallel to those already in existence. Anything that happens in life that can be seen or heard can be recorded on film, tape, or disc. The "art" of film, then, bridges the older arts rather than fitting snugly into the preexisting spectrum. From the beginning, film and photography were neutral: the media existed before the arts. "The cinema is an invention without a future," Louis Lumière is often quoted as having said. And indeed it might have appeared so in his day. But as this revolutionary mode of discourse was applied, in turn, to each of the older arts, it took on a life of its own. The earliest film experimenters "did" painting in film, "did" the novel, "did" drama, and so forth, and gradually it became evident which elements of those arts worked in filmic situations and which did not.

In short, the art of film developed by a process of replication. The neutral template of film was laid over the complex systems of the novel, painting, drama, and music to reveal new truths about certain elements of those arts. In fact, if we disregard for the moment the crudity of early recording processes, the majority of the elements of those arts worked very well in film. Indeed, for the past hundred years the history of the arts is tightly bound up with the challenge of film. As the recording arts drew freely from their predecessors, so painting, music, the novel, stage drama—even architecture—had to redefine themselves in terms of the new artistic language of film.

Film, Photography, and Painting

"Moving pictures" are at first glance most closely parallel to the pictorial arts. Until quite recently, film could compete directly with painting only to a limited extent; it wasn't until the late 1960s that film color was sophisticated enough to be considered more than marginally useful as a tool. Despite this severe limitation, the effects of photography and film were felt almost immediately, for the technological media were clearly seen to surpass painting and drawing in one admittedly limited but nevertheless vital respect: they could record images of the world directly. Certainly, the pictorial arts have other functions besides precise mimesis, but ever since the early Renaissance mimesis had been a primary value in pictorial esthetics. To people for whom travel was a difficult and risky business, the reproduction of landscape scenes was fascinating and the portrait an almost mystical experience. Inundated now by myriad snapshots, mug shots, newspaper photos, and picture postcards, we tend to downplay this function of the pictorial arts.

Very soon after the invention of a viable means of recording a photographic image was announced to the world on January 7, 1839, in a lecture by François Arago to the French Academy of Sciences, the portrait became its chief area of exploitation. The daguerreotype allowed thousands of ordinary people to achieve the kind of immortality that had hitherto been reserved to an elite. The democratization of the image had begun. Within a few years, thousands of portrait galleries had come into being.

But Louis Daguerre's invention was incomplete; it produced an image, but it could not reproduce itself. Only a month after the announcement of Daguerre's unique system, William Henry Fox Talbot described how an image could be reproduced by recording a negative photographic image in the camera and using that to produce, in turn, multiple positives. This was the second important element of the art of photography. When Frederick Scott Archer's collodion process replaced Talbot's rough paper negatives with film, the system of photography,

Figure 1-5A. There are two ways to spend exorbitant amounts of money on making movies. For *Apocalypse Now* Francis Ford Coppola reinvented the Vietnam War with the proverbial cast of thousands. The film cost upwards of $30 million in the mid-seventies....

which can both capture images and reproduce them infinitely and precisely, was complete.

Naturally, the new invention of photography was immediately applied to the task where it was most useful: the production of portraits. Painting responded in kind. The years of development and maturation of photography, roughly the 1840s to the 1870s, are just those years in which the theory of painting was quickly developing away from mimesis and toward a more sophisticated expression. Freed by the invention of photography from the duty to imitate reality, painters were able to explore more fully the structure of their art. There is certainly no simple cause-and-effect relationship between the invention of photography and these developments in the history of painting. Joseph Turner, for example, was producing "antiphotographic" landscapes thirty years before Daguerre perfected his invention. But their connection is more than coincidental.

More directly, the very quality of the photographic image seems to have had a direct effect on the thinking of painters like the Impressionists (Monet and Auguste Renoir, in particular), who worked to capture the immediate and seemingly accidental quality of the mechanically derived image. In moving away from the idea of a painting as an idealization and toward immediate scientific realism, the Impressionists produced images that must be understood as logically con-

Figure 1-5B. ... James Cameron spent most of his $90 million budget for *Terminator 2* (1991) on special effects, the cost of which dwarfed even Arnold Schwarzenegger's star salary. *T2* was the first major film to utilize digital special effects heavily. Within a few years, the cost of these effects had fallen precipitously, as morphing software dropped to the price level of video games.

nected with photography. Because the camera now existed, painters were motivated to rediscover the immediacy of the moment and the peculiar quality of light, two factors that loom large in the esthetic formula of still photography. When Monet put a number of these moments side by side, as in his series of paintings of cathedrals and haystacks at different times of the day, he took the next logical step: his painterly "flip-books" are intriguing precursors of the movies.

Still photographers themselves in the mid-nineteenth century also seem on occasion to be looking toward motion—the time element—as the fulfillment of their art. Not long after the portrait and the landscape had established the documentary value of photographs, experimenters like Oscar G. Rejlander and Henry Peach Robinson in England merged the two forms by staging elaborate tableaux not unlike those common in the popular theaters of the day. They used actors and often achieved their effects by painstakingly piecing together collages of negatives. Certainly these photographic dramas are a response to painters' ideas first (they are strongly reminiscent of pre-Raphaelite work), but with the benefit of hindsight we can discern in Rejlander's and Robinson's elaborate images the roots of the dramatic element that was to become paramount once pictures began to move. If Rejlander and Robinson were sentimental pre-Raphaelites, so, too, was D. W. Griffith.

Figure 1-6A. By the late 1960s, the "fine" arts had become tightly integrated into popular culture. Museums were no longer quiet refuges for intellectuals and students, but rather popular, crowded gathering places with long lines waiting for admission. More often than not, you couldn't see the paintings. But you could observe the people looking at the paintings. The change dates from the landmark exhibition of the *Mona Lisa* behind bulletproof glass at New York's Metropolitan Museum of Art in 1963. Here we see "People Not Looking at Manet's *Déjeuner sur l'Herbe*"...

There are many instances of these subtle interrelationships between the developing technology of photography and the established arts of painting and drawing in the nineteenth century, and the next major development in the esthetics of painting, in the early twentieth century, corresponded with the rise of the moving picture. Again, there is no way we can make a precise correlation. It's not as if Marcel Duchamp went to see a showing of *The Great Train Robbery,* cried, "Aha!" and next day sat down to paint *Nude Descending a Staircase.* But again, the coincidences cannot be ignored.

From one perspective, the movements of Cubism and Futurism can be seen as direct reactions to the increasing primacy of the photographic image. It's as if artists were saying: since photography does these things so well, we shall turn our attention elsewhere. Cubist painting deliberately eschewed atmosphere and light (the areas in which the Impressionists competed directly—and successfully—with the rising photographers) in order to break radically and irrevocably with the mimetic tradition of Western painting. Cubism marked a significant turning point in the history of all the arts; the artist was freed from a dependence on the existing patterns of the real world and could turn attention to the concept of a work of art that was, for the first time, separate from its subject.

From another perspective, Cubism was moving parallel with the development of film. In trying to capture multiple planes of perspective on canvas, Picasso,

Figure 1-6B. ... and "Crowds Accompanying Manet's *Odalisque*," both scenes from the Louvre, October 1976. (*JM*)

Braque, and others were responding directly to the challenge of film that, because it was a *moving* picture, permitted—even encouraged—complex, ever-changing perspectives. In this sense, *Nude Descending a Staircase* is an attempt to freeze the multiple perspectives of the movies on canvas. Traditional art history claims that the most important influence on Cubism was African sculpture and this is no doubt true, since the Cubists were probably more familiar with those sculptures than with the films of Edwin S. Porter or Georges Méliès, but structurally the relationship with film is intriguing.

One of the important elements of Cubism, for example, was the attempt to achieve on canvas a sense of the interrelationships among perspectives. This doesn't have its source in African sculpture, but it is very much like the dialectic of montage—editing—in film. Both Cubism and montage eschew the unique point of view and explore the possibilities of multiple perspective.

The theoretical relationship between painting and film continues to this day. The Italian Futurist movement produced obvious parodies of the motion picture; contemporary photographic hyperrealism continues to comment on the ramifications of the camera esthetic. But the connection between the two arts has never again been as sharp and clear as it was during the Cubist period. The primary response of painting to the challenge of film has been the conceptualism that Cubism first liberated and that is now common to all the arts. The work of mimesis has been left, in the main, to the recording arts. The arts of representation and artifact have moved on to a new, more abstract sphere. The strong challenge film presented to the pictorial arts was certainly a function of its mimetic capabilities, but it was also due to the one factor that made film radically different from painting: film moved.

In 1819, John Keats had celebrated the pictorial art's mystical ability to freeze time in an instant in his "Ode on a Grecian Urn":

> Thou still unravish'd bride of quietness,
> Thou foster child of silence and slow time...
> Heard melodies are sweet, but those unheard
> Are sweeter...
>
> Ah, happy, happy, boughs! that cannot shed
> Your leaves, nor ever bid the Spring adieu
> And, happy melodist, unwearied,
> For ever piping songs for ever new;
> More happy love! more happy, happy love!
> For ever warm and still to be enjoy'd,
> For ever panting, and for ever young...

There is something magical and intoxicating about the frozen moment of a still work of art that captures life in full flight. But there is an instructive irony in Keats's poem, for it is almost certain that the sort of urn he was hymning had friezelike illustrations, and friezes are among the major attempts of the still pictorial arts to tell a story, to narrate events—to exist, in short, in time as well as space.

In this sense, movies simply fulfill the destiny of painting. Richard Lester made this point nicely in the end credits of *A Funny Thing Happened on the Way to the Forum* in 1966. The film, based on a musical, based on a play by Plautus (thus the classical connection), ends with a shot of Buster Keaton as Erronius running confidently once again around the Seven Hills of Rome. The image gradually turns into an animated frieze against which the credits are projected. The ultimate freeze-frame ending! Keats's happy boughs, happy piper, and happy, happy lovers likewise in their original incarnation on the surface of the urn would move if they could.

Film and the Novel

The narrative potential of film is so marked that it has developed its strongest bond not with painting, not even with drama, but with the novel. Both films and novels tell long stories with a wealth of detail and they do it from the perspective of a narrator, who often interposes a resonant level of irony between the story and the observer. Whatever can be told in print in a novel can be roughly pictured or told in film (although the wildest fantasies of a Jorge Luis Borges or a Lewis Carroll might require a lot of special effects). The differences between the two arts, besides the obvious and powerful difference between pictorial narration and linguistic narration, are quickly apparent.

Figure 1-7. FOUND ART. Andy Warhol's eight-hour-long *Empire* (1964) consists of one image: the Empire State Building viewed through Manhattan smog. The office building as art-object. (*Frame enlargements, Warhol Enterprises.*)

First, because film operates in real time, it is more limited. Novels end only when they feel like it. Film is, in general, restricted to what Shakespeare called "the short two hours' traffic of our stage." Popular novels have been a vast reservoir of material for commercial films over the years. In fact, the economics of the popular novel are such now that recycling the material as a film is a prime consideration for most publishers. It almost seems, at times, as if the popular novel (as opposed to elite prose art) exists only as a first draft trial for the film.

But commercial film still can't reproduce the range of the novel in time. An average screenplay, for example, is 125 to 150 typescript pages in length; the average novel three times that. Almost invariably, details of incident are lost in the transition from book to film. Only the television serial can overcome this deficiency. It carries with it some of the same sense of duration necessary to the large novel. Of all the screen versions of *War and Peace,* for example, the most successful seems to me to have been the BBC's twenty-part serialization of the early 1970s; not necessarily because the acting or direction was better than the two- or six-hour film versions (although that is arguable), but because only the longform television serial could reproduce the essential condition of the saga—duration.

At the same time as film is limited to a shorter narration, however, it naturally has pictorial possibilities the novel doesn't have. What can't be transferred by incident might be translated into image. And here we come to the most essential difference between the two forms of narration.

Novels are told by the author. We see and hear only what he wants us to see and hear. Films are more or less told by their authors, too, but we see and hear a great deal more than a director necessarily intends. It would be an absurd task for a novelist to try to describe a scene in as much detail as it is conveyed in cinema. (The contemporary novelist Alain Robbe-Grillet has experimented in just this

Figure 1-8. "Mother and Daughter," a daguerreotype by William Shew, circa 1850. Although now
in poor condition, this portrait still shows the fine
detail and range of tones of which Daguerre's process was capable. (*Daguerreotype, sixth-plate, 3
1/8" by 2 5/8". Collection, The Museum of Modern Art, New York. Gift of Ludwig Glaeser. Copy
print © 1995, The Museum of Modern Art, New
York.*)

way in novels like *Jealousy* and *In the Labyrinth*.) More important, whatever the
novelist describes is filtered through his language, his prejudices, and his point of
view. With film we have a certain amount of freedom to choose, to select one
detail rather than another.

The driving tension of the novel is the relationship between the materials of
the story (plot, character, setting, theme, and so forth) and the narration of it in
language; between the tale and the teller, in other words. The driving tension of
film, on the other hand, is between the materials of the story and the objective
nature of the image. It's as if the author/director of a film were in continual conflict with the scene he is shooting. Chance plays a much larger part, and the end
result is that the observer is free to participate in the experience much more
actively. The words on the page are always the same, but the image on the screen
changes continually as we redirect our attention. Film is, in this way, a much
richer experience.

But it is poorer, as well, since the persona of the narrator is so much weaker.
There has only been one major film, for example, that tried to duplicate the first-
person narration so useful to the novel, Robert Montgomery's *Lady in the Lake*
(1946). The result was a cramped, claustrophobic experience: we saw only what
the hero saw. In order to show us the hero, Montgomery had to resort to a battery
of mirror tricks. Film can approximate the ironies that the novel develops in narration, but it can never duplicate them.

Naturally, then, the novel responded to the challenge of film by expanded
attention to just this area: the subtle, complex ironies of narration. Like painting,
prose narrative has in the twentieth century turned away from mimesis and
toward self-consciousness. In the process it has bifurcated. What was once in the

Figure 1-9. William Henry Fox Talbot's *Loch Katrine* (Talbottype, c. 1845). The rough paper negative of the Talbottype (or collotype, as it was also known) produced a texture in the image which was not always welcome. The later collodion process, using clear glass negatives, avoided this texture.

nineteenth century a unified experience, the main form of social and cultural expression, and the chosen art of the newly literate middle classes, has in the twentieth century divided into two forms: the popular novel (James Michener, Stephen King, Danielle Steele, et al.), which is now so closely connected with film that it sometimes begins life as a screenplay; and the elite novel (Donald Barthelme, Frederick Busch, Milan Kundera), where the "artistic" avant-garde work is being done.

This high art novel, since James Joyce, has developed along lines parallel to painting. Like painters, novelists learned from the experience of film to analyze their art and conceptualize it. Vladimir Nabokov, Jorge Luis Borges, Alain Robbe-Grillet, Donald Barthelme, and many others wrote novels about writing novels (as well as other things) just as many twentieth-century painters painted paintings about painting paintings. Abstraction progressed from a focus on human experience, to a concern for ideas about that experience, finally to an interest mainly in the esthetics of thought. Jean Genet, playwright and novelist, said: "Ideas don't interest me so much as the shape of ideas."

In what other respects has the novel been changed by film? Since the days of Defoe, one of the primary functions of the novel, as of painting, was to communicate a sense of other places and people. By the time of Sir Walter Scott, this travelogue service had reached its zenith. After that, as first still, then motion picture photography began to perform this function, the scenic and descriptive character of the novel declined. Moreover, novelists have learned to narrate their stories in the smaller units common to film. Like contemporary playwrights, they think now more often in short scenes than in longer acts.

Finally, one of the novel's greatest assets is its ability to manipulate words. Films have words, too, of course, but not usually in such profusion and never with the concrete insistence of the printed page. If painting under the influence of film has tended toward design, then the novel is approaching poetry as it redoubles its attention to itself and celebrates its material: language.

Film and Theater

On the surface, theatrical film seems most closely comparable to stage drama. Certainly the roots of the commercial film in the early years of this century lie there. But film differs from stage drama in several significant respects: it has the vivid, precise visual potential of the pictorial arts; and it has a much greater narrative capability.

The most salient difference between staged drama and filmed drama, as it is between prose narrative and film narrative, is in point of view. We watch a play as we will; we see a film only as the filmmaker wants us to see it. And in film we also have the potential to see a great deal more. It has become a truism that a stage actor acts with his voice, while a film actor uses his face. Even in the most intimate situation, an audience for a stage play (note the word we use—"audience," listeners—not spectators) has difficulty comprehending all but the broadest gestures. Meanwhile, a film actor, thanks to dubbing, doesn't even require a voice of his own; dialogue can be added later. But the face must be extraordinarily expressive, especially when it is magnified as much as a thousand times in close-ups. A film actor will often consider a day well spent if he's accomplished one good "look." When we consider in addition that films can be made with "raw material"—nonprofessional actors, even people who aren't aware they're being filmed—the contrasts between stage acting and film acting appear even greater.

Just as important as the difference in acting styles is the contrast between dramatic narration in film and on stage. In Shakespeare's time, the unit of construction for stagework was the scene rather than the act. A play consisted of twenty or thirty scenes rather than three to five much longer acts. By the nineteenth century, this had changed. As theater moved from the thrust stage to the proscenium arch, and as realism became an important force, the longer, more verisimilitudinous unit of the act took precedence. During a half-hour act, audiences could suspend their disbelief and enter into the lives of the characters; the shorter unit of the scene made this more difficult.

Film grew up just at the time this sort of stage realism was at its height. And just as painting and the novel had relinquished the function of mimesis to film, so did the stage. The scene returned as the basic unit of construction. Strindberg and others developed an expressionistic (at times almost Cubist) use of the stage

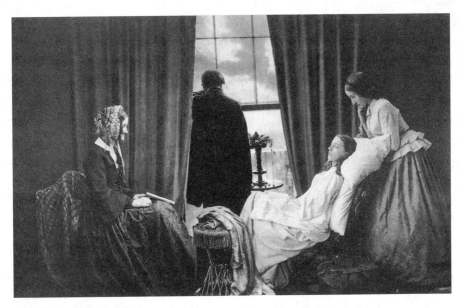

Figure 1-10. The composite photographs of photo-artists like Rejlander and Robinson were in part a response to the relative inflexibility of the medium in the nineteenth century. This particular composition, Henry Peach Robinson's *Fading Away* (1858), is a collage of five negatives. The system allowed the artist to capture foreground details as well as the back light through the window. The composite technique was a direct precursor of modern cinematic matte processes. (*International Museum of Photography, George Eastman House.*)

space. Pirandello analyzed the structure of stage art in detail, and in the process abstracted the experience of the stage for a generation of future playwrights.

By the late twenties, avant-garde theater was in a position to challenge the upstart film seriously. There was no point in realistic stage sets after the style of David Belasco when film could show real locations; no sense in subtlety of gesture when it couldn't be seen past the first row, and audiences could go around the corner to see silent actresses like Gish and Garbo do extraordinary and wonderful things with their faces without seeming to move a muscle. When sound and dialogue joined the image on the screen, film was even more closely comparable to stage drama.

But theater has one advantage over film, and it is a great one: theater is live. If it is true that film can accomplish a great many effects unknown in the theater simply because it is shot discontinuously, it is also true that the people who perform in film are, quite obviously, not in contact with their audience.

In their own ways, two very different theorists of theater made use of this incontrovertible fact. In the late twenties and thirties, both Bertolt Brecht and Antonin Artaud (still the most influential theorists of drama in the modern period) developed concepts of theater that depended on the continuing interac-

Figure 1-11. Marcel Duchamp's *Nude Descending a Staircase, no. 2.* (*1912, oil on canvas, 58" by 35". Philadelphia Museum of Art. Louise and Walter Annenberg Collection.*)

Figure 1-12. The visual conventions of Cubism were utilized by a number of avant-garde film artists. The theory of Cubism has been even more pervasive. Ingmar Bergman's 1966 film *Persona* was an eloquent example of Cubist perspective. The points of view of actress Elizabeth Vogler (Liv Ullmann, left) and her nurse (Bibi Andersson, right) are in such intense balance (as shown here) that at the climax of the film (in another shot) the images of their faces merge together on screen. (*Frame enlargement.*)

tion between audience and cast. Artaud's so-called Theater of Cruelty required a more demanding and intimate relationship between performer and observer than had ever before existed in the theater. Artaud's aim was to involve the audience deeply in a direct way, as they never could be in the cinema.

In his manifesto *The Theatre and Its Double* Artaud wrote:

> We abolish the stage and the auditorium and replace them by a single site, without partition or barrier of any kind, which will become the theater of the action. A direct communication will be re-established between the spectator and the spectacle [p. 93f].

Artaud conceived a kind of frontal assault on the spectator, a "total" theater in which all the forces of expression would be brought to bear. He redefined the language of the theater as consisting

> of everything that occupies the stage, everything that can be manifested and expressed materially on a stage and that is addressed first of all to the

senses instead of being addressed primarily to the mind as is the language
of words... such as music, dance, plastic art, pantomime, mimicry, gestic-
ulation, intonation, architecture, lighting, and scenery [pp. 38–39].

We can see here that the new language of the stage as conceived by Artaud is influenced by the language of film, even as it counters the rising dominance of the new
art. Film, because it had no set rules, no traditions, no academicians, had logically
and quickly discovered the value of each of the components Artaud suggests: plastic art, music, dance, pantomime, et cetera. Once again, one of the older arts finds
itself in a love–hate relationship with the new technology. But Artaud never lost
sight of his one significant advantage:

theater is the only place in the world where a gesture, once made, can
never be made the same way twice [p. 75].

Brecht took the opposite tack. His theory of Epic Theater is more complex—
and some would say more sophisticated—than Artaud's Theater of Cruelty. Recognizing the same basic value as Artaud—the immediacy and intimacy of the theatrical performance—Brecht thought to recreate the relationship between actor
and audience as a dialectic. No longer would the audience willingly suspend disbelief. That is so much easier in a movie theater.

Epic Theater, Brecht wrote,

turns the spectator into an observer, but arouses his capacity for action,
forces him to take decisions.... [In the old, dramatic theater] the spectator
is in the thick of it, shares the experience, the human being is taken for
granted, he is unalterable, [while in the new, Epic Theater] the spectator
stands outside, studies; the human being is the object of the inquiry, he is
alterable and able to alter.... [*Brecht on Theatre*, p. 37].

All this is accomplished by a device Brecht labeled the Estrangement Effect (die
Verfremdungseffekt), whose object, in Brecht's words, was to "alienate the social
gest underlying every incident. By social gest is meant the mimetic and gestural
expression of the social relationships prevailing between people" [p. 139]. This is
clearly more than just a theory of drama. Brecht's Epic Theater and its Verfremdungseffekt can be applied to a wide range of arts, not least of which is film itself.
And, indeed, Brecht's ideas have a major place in the development of film theory.

What Brecht did for the theater was to heighten the spectator's participation,
but in an intellectual way, whereas Artaud had specifically rejected intellectual
approaches in favor of theater as "a means of inducing trances." Both theories,
however, were distinctly antimimetic.

Because of their structural similarities, theater and film interact more often
than do other arts. If in France it is true that many of the more celebrated twentieth-century novelists were filmmakers (Alain Robbe-Grillet, Marguerite Duras),
in England, Italy, Germany, and the U.S. (to a lesser extent) people who work in

Figure 1-13. During the 1870s and 1880s, the experiments of Étienne Jules Marey in France and Eadweard Muybridge in America paved the way for the development of the motion picture camera. Muybridge was particularly interested in the movement of humans and animals. This plate, *Woman Kicking*, was shot with three cameras each with twelve taking lenses, all connected to an electrical clock mechanism switch. The three strips show the same action from side, front, and back views. (*Plate 367, from Animal Locomotion, 1887. Collotype, 7 1/2" by 20 1/4". Collection, Museum of Modern Art, New York. Gift of the Philadelphia Commercial Museum. Copy print © 1995, The Museum of Modern Art, New York.*)

film are more likely to split their careers between screen and stage. The stage (together with dance) is the only art that regularly uses film per se within its own context. The relationship has been fruitful. As the theories of Brecht and Artaud have matured over the past forty years, the theater has developed along the lines they forecast; no radically new theories of theater have superseded them. From Artaud's work, contemporary theater gets its renewed interest in the ritual aspect of the dramatic experience and the sense of communal celebration that has always been basic to theater.

Much of this is accomplished by the intense emphasis of contemporary dramatic theater on mise-en-scène as opposed to text. On the other hand, contemporary theater also looks toward the spoken word as a source of energy. British playwrights especially developed the concept of theater as conversation that has roots in Brecht. Harold Pinter, John Osborne, Edward Bond, and Tom Stoppard, among others, have created in the past forty years a theater of verbal performance that succeeded on an intimate stage as it never could have on film.

The close parallelism between the forms of theater and feature film could very well have meant disaster for the older art. Arts have "died" before: in the seventeenth century, the narrative or epic poem was superannuated by the invention of the novel, for example. But theater has responded to the challenge of film with a new vitality, and the interaction between the two forms of art has proved to be a major source of creative energy in the mid-twentieth century.

Film and Music

Film's relationship with music is altogether more complex. Until the development of the recording arts, music held a unique position in the community of arts. It was the only art in which time played a central role. Novels and theater exist in time, it is true, but the observer controls the "time" of a novel and, as important as rhythms are in the performing arts, they are not strictly controlled. A playwright or director can indicate pauses, but these are generally speaking only the crudest of time signatures. Music, the most abstract of arts, demands precise control of time and depends on it.

If melody is the narrative facet of music, and rhythm the unique, temporal element, then harmony may be the synthesis of the two. Our system of musical notation indicates this relationship. Three notes read from left to right form a melody. When they are set in the framework of a time signature, rhythms are overlaid on the melody. When we rearrange them vertically, however, harmony is the result.

Painting can set up harmonies and counterpoint both within a picture and between pictures, but there is no time element. Drama occasionally experiments with counterpoint—Eugène Ionesco's doubled dialogues are a good example—but only for minor effects. Music, however, makes a lot of interesting art out of

Figure 1-14. During the 1960s and 1970s, a kind of realist backlash took place among the older, nonrecording arts. The French "nouveau roman" had close links with cinema, just as American "hyperrealism" or "photo-realism" looked to photography for its esthetic base. Here, Phillip Pearlstein's *Female Model Reclining on Deck Chair* (*1978, oil on canvas, 48" by 60". Courtesy Frumkin/Adams Gallery, New York*).

the relationship between "horizontal" lines of melody, set in rhythms, and "vertical" sets of harmonies.

(No, I'm not sure how to fit Rap, or Hip-Hop, into this equation. While Rap grows out of a centuries-old and fertile tradition of spoken rhythmic art, and while it was probably the most innovative artform of the 1990s, its eschewal of both melody and harmony suggests that it is "music" only because it is distributed on CDs and appears on MTV. Maybe Rap makes the point that the one essential element of music is rhythm. Perhaps we should consider Rap, at least in one sense, as the last gasp of abstraction—ironically, the only truly popular expression of the avant-garde abstractionist tendency. Or maybe it's enough to think of Rap as the musicalization of poetry: "All art aspires to the condition of music"—and to its market.)

Abstractly, film offers the same possibilities of rhythm, melody, and harmony as music. The mechanical nature of the film medium allows strict control of the time line: narrative "melodies" can now be controlled precisely. In the frame,

Figure 1-15. Audrey Totter and Robert Montgomery in *Lady in the Lake*. "First-person" narration in film, strictly construed, must make ingenious use of mirrors if the narrator/hero is to be seen. (*Museum of Modern Art/Film Stills Archive.*)

events and images can be counterpoised harmonically. Filmmakers began experimenting with the musical potential of the new art very early on. Ever since René Clair's *Entr'acte* (1924) and Fernand Léger's *Ballet Mécanique* (1924–25), in fact, abstract or "avant-garde" film has depended on musical theory for much of its effect. Even before sound, filmmakers had begun to work closely with musicians. Hans Richter's *Vormittagsspuk* (*Ghosts Before Breakfast,* 1928) had a score by Hindemith, played live. Walter Ruttmann's *Berlin—Symphony of a City* (1927) had a live symphonic score as well.

Music had quickly become an integral part of the film experience; silent films were normally "performed" with live music. Moreover, the innovative filmmakers of the silent period were already discovering the musical potential of the image itself. By the late 1930s Sergei Eisenstein, for his film *Alexander Nevsky,* constructed an elaborate scheme to correlate the visual images with the score by the noted composer Prokofiev. In this film as in a number of others, such as Stanley Kubrick's *2001: A Space Odyssey* (1968), music often leads, determining images.

Because film is projected normally at a rate of twenty-four frames per second, the filmmaker has even more precise control over rhythms than the musician.

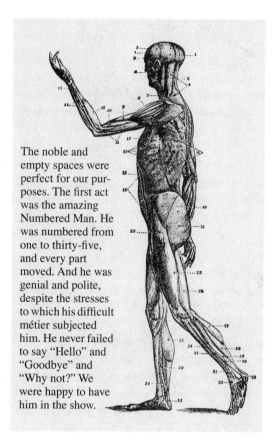

The noble and empty spaces were perfect for our purposes. The first act was the amazing Numbered Man. He was numbered from one to thirty-five, and every part moved. And he was genial and polite, despite the stresses to which his difficult métier subjected him. He never failed to say "Hello" and "Goodbye" and "Why not?" We were happy to have him in the show.

Figure 1-16. Donald Barthelme's "fictions" were not quite novels, not quite poems. He often experimented by integrating old lithographs and drawing with his texts. Here, a page from his story "Flight of Pigeons from the Palace" (*Sadness*, Farrar, Straus, & Giroux, 1972). Despite their abstraction, Barthelme's stories lent themselves to dramatization because they had a visual as well as narrative reality.

The shortest semihemidemiquaver that could be written in the Western system of notation would last 1/32 of a second—but it would be impossible to play live notes at that rate. The 1/24 of a second unit, which is the lowest common denominator of film, effectively exceeds the quickest rhythms of performed Western music. The most sophisticated rhythms in music, the Indian tals, approach the basic unit of film rhythm as an upper limit.

We are ignoring, of course, music that is produced mechanically or electronically. Even before systems of sound recording had matured, the player piano offered an opportunity to musicians to experiment with rhythmic systems that were impossible for humans to perform. Conlon Nancarrow's "Studies for Player Piano" (the earliest dating from 1948) were interesting explorations of these possibilities.

Film thus utilizes a set of musical concepts expressed in visual terms: melody, harmony, and rhythm are long-established values in film art. Although film itself has had a strong economic impact on music, providing a major market for musicians, it has had no particularly strong *esthetic* effect on music. The techniques of sound recording, however, have revolutionized the older art. The influence of the new technology was felt in two waves.

The invention of the phonograph in 1877 radically altered the dissemination of music. No longer was it necessary to attend a performance, a privilege that was, over the centuries, limited to a very small elite. Bach's *Goldberg Variations,* written as bedtime music for a single wealthy individual, Count Kaiserling, former Russian ambassador at the court of the Elector of Saxony, to be played by his personal harpsichordist, Johann Gottlieb Goldberg, were now accessible to millions of people who couldn't afford private musicians on twenty-four-hour call.

Recordings and, later, radio broadcasts quickly became powerful pervasive media for the dissemination of music, parallel with performance but superseding it. This had just as profound an effect on the nature of the art of music as the invention of both movable type and the printing press had on literature. The technology quickly dominated the art.

Just as the invention of movable type had opened up literature to the masses, so recordings democratized music. The historical significance cannot be underestimated. But there was a negative aspect to the mechanical reproduction of music, too. Folk music, the art people created for themselves in the absence of professional musicians, was greatly attenuated. In the end, this was a small price to pay for the vast new channels of dissemination and, in fact, the new musical literacy that recordings helped to create later redounded to the benefit of the popular musical arts, which have in the twentieth century become the focal point of the musical world as they never were in earlier times.

While the invention of the phonograph had a profound sociological effect on music, it had a very minor technical effect. There were good technological reasons for this, having to do with the limitations of Edison's system, which will be discussed in the next chapter. As a result, it was not until the late 1940s and early 1950s—when magnetic tape began to replace the phonograph record as the main means of recording, and electrical transcription yielded to electronic methods— that music technique came under the influence of the recording arts.

Again, the effect was revolutionary. Musicians had been experimenting with electronic instruments for years before the development of magnetic tape, but they were still bound by the limits of performance. Tape freed them, and allowed the possibility of editing music. The film soundtrack, which was optical rather than magnetic, had predated tape by twenty years, but in the context of film it had always been relegated to a supporting role; it was never an independent medium.

Once tape entered the recording studio, sound recording was no longer simply a means of preserving and disseminating a performance; it now became a main focus of creativity. Recording is now so much an integral part of the creation of music that even popular music (to say nothing of avant-garde and elite music)

Figure 1-17. "THE LOOK." John Wayne as J. B. Books in Don Siegel's 1976 Western, *The Shootist.* Even in this still photograph, the face speaks volumes.

has become since the early fifties a creature of the recording studio rather than performance. The Beatles' *Sergeant Pepper's Lonely Hearts Club Band* (1967), a milestone in the development of the practical recording arts, was not reproducible in performance. There had been many earlier examples of this shift of focus, dating back at least as early as the popular records of Les Paul and Mary Ford in the early fifties, but the Beatles' record is generally regarded as the coming of age of recording as one of the primary creative musical forces.

The balance has altered so radically now that "performances" of popular music (to say nothing of avant-garde performances) often integrate recordings, and much music simply can't be performed at all live. If the techniques of visual recording had had as great an effect on theater, then a standard popular theatrical performance today would consist in large part of film, and avant-garde theater would consist almost entirely of film!

Clearly, the relationship between sound recording and the musical arts is very complex. We have described only the bare outlines of the new dialectic here. It may be most significant that, unlike the technique of image recording, the technique of sound recording was quickly integrated with the art of music. Film was seen from the very beginning as a separate art from theater and painting and the novel; but sound recording even today is still subsumed under the category of music.

Partially, this is the result of the mode of recording—discs—that pertained until the 1960s. Unlike film, discs could simply record and reproduce their material, not re-create it. But the development of tape and electronic technology added an element of creativity to sound recording. If anything, sound recording is now more flexible and sophisticated than image recording. It may be only a matter of time before sound recording is seen as a separate art. If radio had survived the invention of television, this would have happened sooner, but coincidentally, just as sound recording was emerging as an art in its own right around 1950, radio art was being submerged by television. It is only now beginning to recover its flexibility.

Significantly, sound recording as an integral component of cinema also languished during those years and has itself only recently begun to reemerge. Ideally, sound should be the equal of image in the cinematic equation, not subservient, as it is now. In short, film has only begun to respond to the influence of the art of music.

Film and the Environmental Arts

If there is one category of art that has been relatively immune to the influence of film and the recording arts, it is architecture. Unlike the novel, painting, and music, the environmental arts have not responded directly to the new mode of discourse. In fact, we can discern a more fruitful relationship between drama and architecture than between film and architecture. Not only has the function of the theater as a building had a direct effect on the art produced inside it: architectural constructions themselves have become a part of performance. This phenomenon dates back at least as far as the Masques of the early seventeenth century, whose elaborate "strange devices"—especially those of the architect Inigo Jones—held pride of place. More recently, the movement toward environmental theater, with its concurrent theory that the audience should participate physically in the space of a production as well as in its narration, has led to an even more intimate union of drama and theatrical architecture.

But, as Brecht and Artaud understood, the Achilles heel of film art lies precisely here: we cannot enter into the world of the image physically. Images of film can surround us, overwhelm us psychologically, but we are still structurally separate. Even so-called Virtual Reality media beg the question: you still can't touch or feel the environment they create. We cannot interact with film. Meanwhile, architecture—more than any other art—insists on and requires interaction. Its function is to serve practical aims, and its form follows from that.

Until now, the relationship between film and the environmental arts has remained metaphorical rather than direct. Film can give us a record of architec-

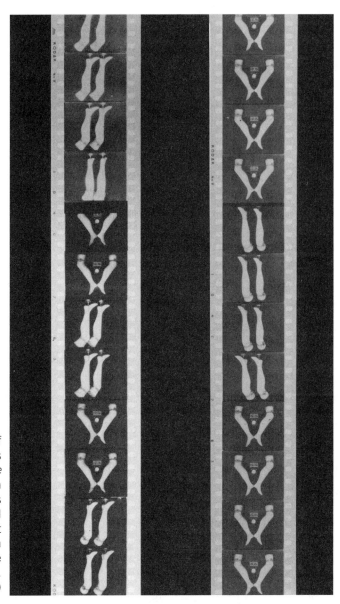

Figure 1-18. Strips of film from Léger's *Ballet Mécanique* (1924–25). Each group of four frames would last 1/6 second on screen. The effect would be of a rhythmic double exposure. (*MOMA/FSA*.)

ture (as it can give us a record of any of the other arts), but this hardly constitutes a dialectical relationship. The theory of film montage may have had some slight effect on architectural theory, but it's safe to say this influence was minimal, at best. Likewise, although our sense of film as a "constructed" work is strong, it is the metaphor of construction rather than the actual craft of building design that governs it.

But while this has been true in the past, the future may hold some surprises. "Pop" architecture—the Las Vegas esthetic—comes closer to comparing with the structure of cinema than does the kind of elite architecture with formal artistic intentions that has until recently occupied exclusively the attention of architectural critics and historians. As a social and political expression of the culture, architecture may be more closely parallel with film than it seems at first glance. In the late sixties (especially in *2 or 3 Things I Know About Her,* 1966) Jean-Luc Godard first explored these admittedly tenuous connections. In the 1970s and 1980s, architect/critics Robert Venturi, Denise Scott Brown, and Stephen Izenour approached the film/architecture connection from the opposite point of view. In an exhibition they designed called "Signs of Life: Symbols in the American City" (Renwick Gallery, Washington, D.C., 1976), the Venturis utilized a system of electronically controlled painting developed by the 3M Company to produce life-size, vividly realistic evocations of city scenes that they then integrated with actual constructions.

The ramifications of this technique could be considerable. Insofar as architecture is an art of environment rather than simply a system of construction, the objective visual component might very well be susceptible to photographic—and possibly cinematographic—production. Thomas Wilfred's landmark "lumia" light sculptures, as well as the "light shows" common as accompaniment to rock music performances in the late 1960s, also point to interesting applications of cinematic techniques to environmental situations.

In the early 1990s, Bill Gates, wealthy founder of the Microsoft corporation, built a large home for himself near his company's headquarters in Redmond, Washington. This sedate mansion was equipped with numerous large wall screens meant to display—electronically—great artworks for which Gates, separately, had acquired electronic distribution rights. The result? A kind of virtual Xanadu, the software mogul's answer to the press mogul's mansion 700 miles down the Pacific Coast Highway.

While it's hard to see how the integration of photography and architecture could lead to anything more than simple trompe-l'oeil effects, this growing concern with the artificiality of the visual environment has been foreshadowed by contemporary developments in what we might call "sound architecture." Just as architects have always been concerned with the physical environment we experience, usually as it is transmitted to us visually, so now the aural environment is drawing their attention.

The Muzak of 1960s and 1970s elevators, shopping centers, and office buildings was the first example of an aural environment. The "Environment" series of electronically constructed or modified recordings produced by Syntonic Research, Inc. in the early 1970s offered more elaborate examples. Computer-designed reconstructions of natural sounds such as ocean waves, rain, and birdsong, they provided the first psychologically affective aural backgrounds. Socially, the omnipresence of radio and many types of television perform a similar function: they serve as backgrounds, aurally and visually, against which we play out our everyday lives.

While the public experience of Muzak was in decline throughout the 1980s and 1990s, the private experience of the near-ubiquitous Walkman has taken its place. We now create our own individual, portable sound environments to carry with us wherever we go. If the Walkman was the first step to private virtual realities, the cellular phone was the second. Enough of these very private devices have been sold in the U.S. that it is conceivable that there could come a time soon when *absolutely no one will be listening to the real world.*[*] This possibility gives new meaning to the conundrum that asks, "If a tree falls in the forest, and there is no one there to hear it, does it make a sound?" and it raises some serious questions about the electronic society, which we will discuss in more detail in Chapter 7.

At present, the art of such cultural elements is of a very low grade: sound environments are more a problem than a feature of contemporary life. But eventually that problem will be confronted and architects, charged with responsibility for the effect of our artificial world, will become as deeply involved in the aural environment as the visual, and recordings of both will become integrated as a matter of course with the physical, concrete design of our environment.

The Structure of Art

Film, sound recording, and video, then, have had profound effects on the nature and development of nearly all the other, older arts and have in turn to a considerable extent been shaped by them. But while the spectrum of arts is wide, the domain of film and the recording arts is even wider. Film, records, and tapes are media: that is, agencies or channels of communication. While art may be the main use to which they are put, it is clearly not the only use. Film is also an important scientific tool that has opened up new areas of knowledge. It provides the first signifi-

---

[*] Perhaps with good reason: parallel to the growth of private listening devices has been the cacophonous explosion in automatic, uncontrollable public noise—nagging backup warnings, belligerent 175-watt auto sound systems, intrusive car alarms, pointless digital-watch alarms, teenagers' pagers. Sound pollution has increased so dramatically in the electronic age that Walkman earplugs may be the only answer. In 1993, some organizations for the deaf complained about new surgical techniques that gave a measure of hearing to the deaf: they were protesting the loss of "the gift of silence."

cant general means of communication since the invention of writing more than seven thousand years ago.

As a medium, film needs to be considered as a phenomenon very much like language. It has no codified grammar, it has no enumerated vocabulary, it doesn't even have very specific rules of usage, so it is very clearly not a language *system* like written or spoken English; but it nevertheless does perform many of the same functions of communication as language does. It would then be very useful if we could describe the way film operates with a degree of logical precision. In Chapter 5 we will discuss how the desire to describe a rational—even scientific—structure for film has been one of the main motivations of film theorists for more than half a century.

Since the 1960s, semiotics has presented an interesting approach to the logical description of the languagelike phenomenon of film and the other recording arts. The linguist Ferdinand de Saussure laid the groundwork for semiotics in the early years of this century. Saussure's simple, yet elegant, idea was to view language as simply one of a number of systems of codes of communication. Linguistics, then, becomes simply one area of the more general study of systems of signs—"semiotics" (or "semiology").

Film may not have grammar, but it does have systems of "codes." It does not, strictly speaking, have a vocabulary, but it does have a system of signs. It also uses the systems of signs and codes of a number of other communication systems. Any musical code, for instance, can be represented in the music of film. Most painterly codes, and most narrative codes, can also be represented in film. Much of the preceding discussion of the relationship between film and the other arts could be quantified by describing the codes that exist in those other arts that can be translated into film as opposed to those that cannot. Remember Frost: "Poetry is what gets lost in translation." So the genius of an art may be just those codes that don't work well in any other art.

Yet while the code system of semiotics goes a long way toward making possible a more precise description of how film does what it does, it is limited in that it more or less insists that we reduce film, like language, to basic discrete units that can be quantified. Like linguistics, semiotics is not especially well adapted to describing the complete, metaphysical effect of its subject. It describes the language, or system of communication, of film very well. But it does not easily describe the artistic activity of film. A term borrowed from literary criticism may be useful in this respect: "trope."

Generally, in literary criticism the term "trope" is used to mean "figure of speech": that is, a "turn" of phrase in which language is bent so that it reveals more than literal meanings. The concepts of code and sign describe the elements of the "language" of an art; the concept of trope is necessary to describe the often very unusual and illogical way those codes and signs are used to produce new, unexpected meanings. We are concerned now with the active aspect of art. "Trope," from the Greek *tropos* (via Latin *tropus*) originally meant "turn," "way," or "manner," so even etymologically the word suggests an activity rather than a static definition.

Rhythm, melody, and harmony, for example, are essential codes of music. Within each of these codes there are elaborate sets of subcodes. A syncopated beat, such as that essential to the idiom of jazz, can be considered as a subcode. But the exciting, idiosyncratic syncopations of Thelonious Monk's music are tropes. There is no way to quantify them scientifically; and that, precisely, is the genius of Thelonious Monk.

Likewise, in painting, form, color, and line are generally regarded as the basic codes. Hard edges and soft edges are subcodes. But the precise, exquisite lines of a painting by Ingres, or the subtle soft edges of a study by Auguste Renoir, are idiosyncratic tropes.

In stage drama, gesture is central to the art, one of its basic codes. The offering of a ringed hand for the kiss of devotion is a specific subcode. But the way Laurence Olivier performs this gesture in *Richard III* is very peculiarly his own: a trope.

The system of an art can generally be described in semiotic terms as a collection of codes. The unique activity of an art, however, lies in its tropes. Film can be used to record most of the other arts. It can also translate nearly all the codes and tropes common to narrative, environmental, pictorial, musical, and dramatic arts. Finally, it has a system of codes and tropes all its own, unique to the recording arts.

Its own codes and tropes stem from its complex technology—a new phenomenon in the world of art and media. For an understanding of how film is *un*like all the other arts—the second stage of our investigation—it is necessary to take a close look at that technology: this is the subject of Chapter 2.

Poetry is what you can't translate. Art is what you can't define. Film is what you can't explain. But we're going to try, anyway.

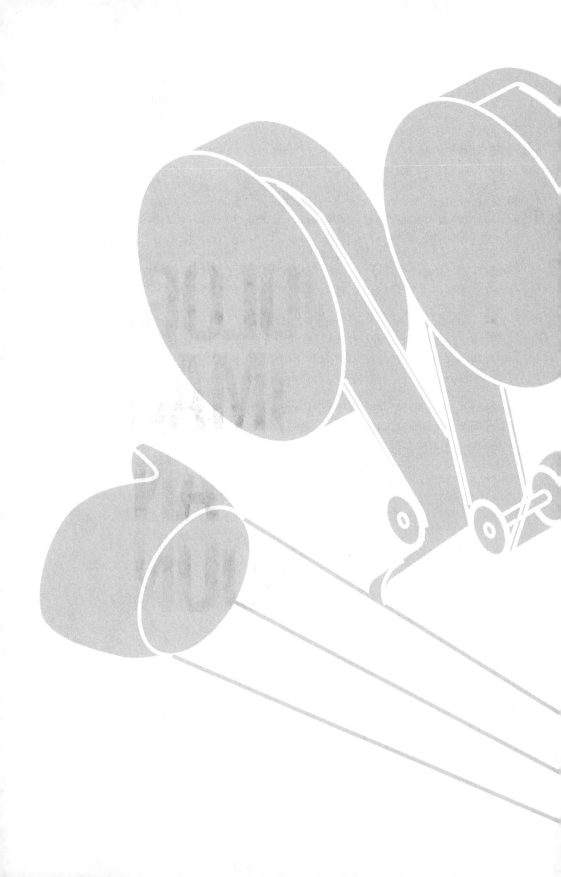

TECHNOLOGY: IMAGE AND SOUND

2

Art and Technology

Every art is shaped not only by the politics, philosophy, and economics of society, but also by its technology. The relationship isn't always clear: sometimes technological development leads to a change in the esthetic system of the art; sometimes esthetic requirements call for a new technology; often the development of the technology itself is the result of a combination of ideological and economic factors. But until artistic impulses can be expressed through some kind of technology, there is no artifact.

Usually the relationships are broad: the novel never could have come into being without the printing press, but the recent rapid increases in the technology of printing (discussed briefly in Chapter 6) have had little discernible effect on the esthetic development of the novel. What esthetic changes have occurred in its three-hundred-year history find their root causes in other historical factors, mainly the social uses of the art.

Stage drama was radically altered when new lighting techniques allowed it to be brought indoors and sheltered behind the proscenium arch, but the twentieth-century reversion to the thrust stage was mainly due not to developments in technology but to ideological factors. Bach played on the harpsichord of his own day sounds quite different from Bach performed on the modern "well-tempered clavier," but Bach is still Bach. The invention of oil paint provided painters with a medium of wonderful versatility, but if oil paint had never been invented, painters would have painted anyway.

In short, although there has been a communion between art and technology that consists of more than an occasional genius like Leonardo da Vinci combining

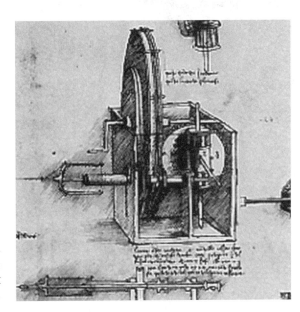

Figure 2-1. This da Vinci drawing suggests the bond between visualization and invention, art and technology.

good work in both fields, a communion that belies the modern conception of the two fields as mutually antagonistic, nevertheless one can study the history of painting without ever having gained any knowledge of how oils differ from acrylics, and students of literature can certainly succeed in mastering the basic history of literature without having studied the operation of the Linotype or the offset press.

This is not the case with film. The great artistic contribution of the industrial age, the recording arts—film, sound recording, and photography—are inherently dependent on a complex, ingenious, and ever more sophisticated technology. No one can ever hope to comprehend fully the way their effects are accomplished without a basic understanding of the technology that makes them possible, as well as its underlying science.

Image Technology

The invention of photography in the early nineteenth century marks an important line of division between the pretechnological era and the present. The basic artistic impulses that drive us to mimic nature were essentially the same both before and after that time, but the augmented technical capacity to record and reproduce sounds and images of the twentieth century presents us with an exciting new set of choices.

Previously we were limited by our own physical abilities: the musician created sounds by blowing or strumming or singing; the painter who captured real images depended entirely on his own eye to perceive them; the novelist and the

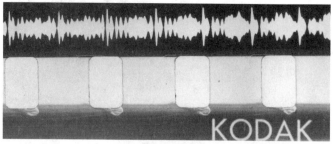

A. Soundtrack. Magnification: 4.9x

B. Record groove. Magnification: 1.8x

C. Audiotape.
Mag: 2.5x

D. Audio Compact Disc. Magnification: 3.5x

Figure 2-2. AURAL AND VISUAL RECORDING SYSTEMS. In order to record and reproduce sounds and images, recording technology must translate aural and visual information into physical or electronic "language-systems."

The variable-area soundtrack (A), an analogue system, translates the frequency (pitch) and amplitude (volume) of sounds into regular patterns of light. The loudest sound is represented by the widest light band. The variable-area soundtrack is an elegant visualization of wave mechanics. (See Chapter 6.)

Vinyl record grooves (B) translate audio information into analogous physical waveforms. This section of a 33 1/3 rpm disc is approximately 5 cm by 2 cm. Each groove section pictured carries about 1/4-second of music (in this case, Duke Ellington), and since this is a stereo record, each groove carries two channels of information, one on each side of the groove.

Magnetic audiotape (C) encodes information electromagnetically; as a result, the signal cannot be seen here as it can in A and B above. The visible lines are simply signs of wear. The section of professional reel-to-reel tape shown carries slightly more than 1/20 second of information at a normal speed of 7 1/2 inches per second. In normal stereo recording this 1/4-inch-wide tape might carry four parallel channels (two in each direction).

This 10-mm section of a contemporary digital audio compact disc (D) represents 208 seconds of stereo music (Susannah McCorkle), encoded as microscopic pits in the substrate. The CD format represents a significant advance in information density.

Visual information is far more complex than aural information and therefore more difficult to encode. Because there is vastly more information to represent, visual encoding is bit-oriented and often binary. In other words, the information is broken into discrete quanta ("bits") and each "bit" of information can have either of two values: "yes" or "no," "black" or "white."

The most flexible of the three common systems of visual encoding is photography. Figure E is an enlargement of a section of standard 8" x 10" black-and-white print, 15 mm high. The grain is clearly visible. Remember that in order to reproduce the photograph as you see it, a printer's halftone screen has had to be imposed.

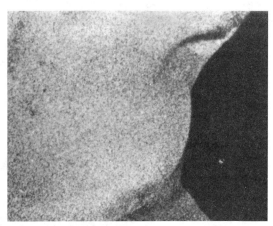

E. Photographic grain. Magnification: 4.5x

Figure F shows the same section of the same photograph as it was reproduced in a book. The halftone screen analyzes the variable information present in the photographic grain into black-and-white dot patterns. In this case, the screen size was 133 lines per inch. Notice that the white mark in the black area to the right (an imperfection in the photograph) has nearly disappeared in the halftone reproduction. Furthermore, in both Figure E and Figure F you are viewing this representation of a photograph with a halftone screen through the coarse filter of a computer screen. Although the resolution of your screen is most likely about 72 pixels per inch, so-called "dithering" or "anti-aliasing" techniques allow us to approximate the feel of the printed version. You may want to compare these illustrations to the actual printed versions.

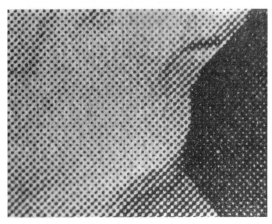

F. Halftone screen. Magnification: 6.4x

Figure G shows a section of color television screen. An NTSC standard American television screen is composed of 210,000 of these bits of information, red, green, and blue dots arranged in patterns of 30 to 90 lines per inch—much cruder than the halftone screen in E.

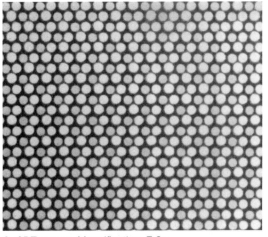

G. CRT screen. Magnification: 7.9x

Figure 2-3. This version of the camera obscura reflected the incoming light to a screen at the top of the box so that an artist could trace the image. If the pinhole is sufficiently small, an image will be projected. The optical principle is described in Figure 2-9. (*International Museum of Photography, George Eastman House.*)

poet, not engaged physically in their art, were limited in describing events or characters by their own powers of observation. Recording technology now offers us the opportunity of capturing a representation of sounds, images, and events and transmitting them directly to the observer without the necessary interposition of the artist's personality and talents. A new channel of communication has been opened, equal in importance to written language.

Although the camera did not come into practical use until the early nineteenth century, efforts to create such a magical tool, which would record reality directly, dated from much earlier. The camera obscura (Figure 2-3), the grandfather of the photographic camera, dates from the Renaissance. Da Vinci had described the principle, and the first published account of the usefulness of the invention dates from 1558, the year in which Giovanni Battista della Porta published his book *Natural Magic.* There are even references dating back as far as the tenth-century Arabic astronomer Al Hazen. The camera obscura (literally "dark room") is based on a simple optical rule, but it includes all the elements of the basic contemporary photographic camera except one: film, the medium on which the projected image is recorded.

Louis Daguerre is usually credited with the first practical development of such a medium in 1839, but his colleague Joseph Nièpce had done much valuable work before he died in 1833, and may be credited, as Beaumont Newhall has

Figure 2-4. The camera lucida consisted of a lens arrangement that enabled the artist to view subject and drawing paper in the same "frame," and thus simply outline the image that appeared to be projected on the paper. (*International Museum of Photography, George Eastman House.*)

noted, with the first "successful experiment to fix the image of nature" in 1827. William Henry Fox Talbot was working simultaneously along similar lines: modern photography has developed from his system of negative recording and positive reproduction. Daguerre, whose recording photographic plate was positive and therefore not reproducible (except through being photographed itself), had reached a deadend; the daguerreotype marked the end of a line of technological development, not the beginning of one. But Fox Talbot's negative permitted infinite reproductions. The paper negative was soon replaced by the flexible collodion film negative, which not only marked a distinct improvement in the quality of the image but also suggested a line of development for the recording of motion pictures.

Like the still camera, the motion picture camera was not without its antecedents. The Magic Lantern, capable of projecting an image onto a screen, dates from the seventeenth century and was quickly adapted to photographic use in the 1850s. The production of the illusion of motion was made possible in a very crude way by the so-called Magic Discs of the 1830s and the more sophisticated Zoetrope (Figure 2-6), patented in 1834 by William Horner (although precursors of the Zoetrope may date to antiquity). In the 1870s Eadweard Muybridge, working in California, and Étienne Jules Marey, in France, began their experiments in making photographic records of movement. Émile Reynaud's Praxinoscope

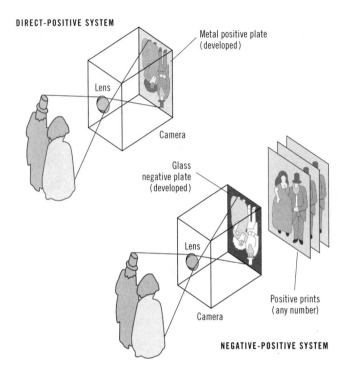

DIRECT-POSITIVE SYSTEM

Metal positive plate
(developed)

Lens

Camera

Glass
negative plate
(developed)

Lens

Camera

Positive prints
(any number)

NEGATIVE-POSITIVE SYSTEM

Figure 2-5. PHOTOGRAPHIC SYSTEMS. The negative–positive system (right) of the Talbot-type, Collotype, and modern photography permits infinite reproduction of the image. The direct positive system of the early Daguerreotype (left) creates a single, iconic image. Contemporary "instant photograph" systems such as Polaroid also produce direct positives and are therefore comparable to the Daguerreotype.

(1877) was the first practicable device for projecting successive images on a screen. In 1889 George Eastman applied for a patent on his flexible photographic film, developed for the roll camera, and the last basic element of cinematography was in place.

By 1895 all these elements had been combined, and movies were born.

Sound Technology

The technology of sound recording developed more rapidly. Edison's phonograph, which does for sounds what the camera/projector system does for images, dates from 1877. In many ways it is a more extraordinary invention than cinematography, since it has no antecedents to speak of. The desire to capture and reproduce still pictures predated the development of moving pictures by many years, but there is no such thing as a "still" sound, so the development of sound recording, of necessity, took place all at once.

Figure 2-6. THE ZOETROPE.
The cylinder was spun; the images on the inside of the drum were viewed through the slots opposite them, creating the illusion of motion. (*International Museum of Photography, George Eastman House.*)

Equally as important as the phonograph, although not often mentioned in histories of the recording arts, is Bell's telephone (1876). It presages the regular transmission of sounds and images whose technology provided us with radio and television but, more important, Bell's invention also shows how electrical signals can be made to serve the purposes of sound recording.

Edison's original phonograph was an entirely physical-mechanical invention, which gave it the virtue of simplicity but also seriously delayed technological progress in the field. In a sense, the purely mechanical phonograph, like Daguerre's positive photograph, was technically a deadend. It was not until the mid-1920s that Bell's theories of the electrical transmission of sound were united with the technology of the mechanical phonograph. At almost precisely the same time, sound recordings were united with image recordings to produce the cinema as we know it today.

It is interesting to conjecture whether there would have been any period of silent cinema at all had Edison not invented a mechanical phonograph: in that case it's quite possible that Edison (or another inventor) would have turned to Bell's telephone as a model for the phonograph and the electrical system of recording sound would have developed much earlier, more than likely in time to be of service to the first filmmakers.

It is worth noting that Thomas Edison himself conceived of his Kinetograph as an adjunct to the phonograph. As he put it in 1894:

> In the year 1887, the idea occurred to me that it was possible to devise an instrument which should do for the eye what the phonograph does for

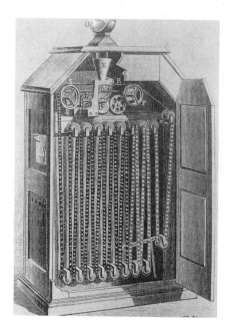

Figure 2-7. Edison's Kinetoscope was a private viewing machine. The film was formed in a continuous loop running around rollers in the base of the machine: no need to rewind before the next showing! (*MOMA/FSA.*)

the ear, and that by a combination of the two all motion and sound could be recorded and reproduced simultaneously.[*]

William Kennedy Laurie Dickson, an English assistant to Edison who did much of the development work, describes Edison's first conception of the Kinetograph as parallel in structure and conception with his successful phonograph:

> Edison's idea ... was to combine the phonograph cylinder or record with a similar or larger drum on the same shaft, which drum was to be covered with pin-point microphotographs which of course must synchronize with the phonograph record.

This configuration, of course, did not succeed, but the ideal union of sound and image was suggested. Indeed, after Dickson had turned to the new perforated Eastman continuous roll film, he continued to think of the moving pictures as necessarily joined with the sound record; his first demonstration of his success to Edison on October 6, 1889, was a "talkie." Dickson called this device a "Kineto-phone." Edison had just returned from a trip abroad. Dickson ushered him into

---

[*]   Quoted in W. K. L. Dickson, "A Brief History of the Kinetograph, the Kinetoscope, and the Kineto-Phonograph," in Raymond Fielding's *A Technological History of Motion Pictures and Television*, p.9.

Figure 2-8. Ladies and gentlemen amusing themselves at the Kinetoscope parlor at 28th Street and Broadway, circa 1895. That's a bust of the modest inventor, prominent in the foreground. (*MOMA/FSA.*)

the projecting room and started the machine. He appeared on the small screen, walked forward, raised his hat, smiled, and spoke directly to his audience:

> "Good morning, Mr. Edison, glad to see you back. Hope you like the Kinetophone. To show the synchronization I will lift my hand and count up to ten."

These words, less well known, should certainly rank with Bell's telephonic "Mr. Watson, come here, I want to see you" and Morse's telegraphic "What hath God wrought?"

Because of the technical problems posed by Edison's mechanical recording system—mainly synchronization—the effective marriage of sound and image did not occur until thirty years later, but the desire to reproduce sound and image in concert existed from the earliest days of film history.

By 1900, all the basic tools of the new technological arts had been invented: the painter had the alternative of the still camera; the musician the alternative of the phonograph; and novelists and theater folk were contemplating the exciting possibilities of motion pictures. Each of these records could be reproduced in large quantities and therefore reach large numbers of people. Although the technology of broadcasting was still a few years in the future, workable methods of instantaneous communication had been demonstrated by the telephone and the telegraph; in fact, we are now realizing, as cable technology develops, that wired transmission offers quite a few advantages over radio wave broadcasting, not least of which is addressability. Despite the saturation of the radio spectrum, there is much life left in radio wave broadcasting, as the development of cellular phone systems showed in the 1980s. From now on, however, broadcast and wired transmission must be considered as part of the same industry. The competition between the two technologies will provide much business-page drama in the early years of the twenty-first century.

This flowchart indicates the various stages of the process of film:

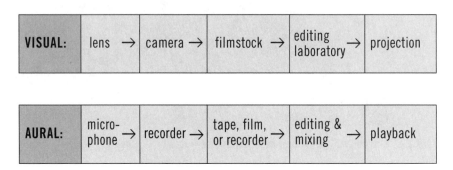

VISUAL:	lens →	camera →	filmstock →	editing laboratory →	projection

AURAL:	micro-phone →	recorder →	tape, film, or recorder →	editing & mixing →	playback

Diagram E

At any one of these stages variables can be introduced to give an artist more control over the process. Within each area of the chart there is a large number of factors, each of which has a discernible effect on the finished product, and these factors interact with each other, and between areas, to create an excitingly complex technology. Indeed, no small part of the appreciation of the activity of filmmaking as well as the product lies in an understanding of the technical challenges that filmmakers must surmount.

The Lens

The earliest of cameras, the camera obscura, consisted of a light-tight box with a pinhole in one side. Contemporary cameras, both still and motion picture, operate on the same principle: the box is more precisely machined; photosensitive, flexible film has replaced the drawing paper as the "screen" upon which the image falls; but the greatest changes have taken place in the pinhole. That crude optical device has evolved into a complex system of great technical sophistication. So much depends upon the glass eye of the lens through which we all eventually view a photograph or a film that it must be regarded as the heart of photographic art.

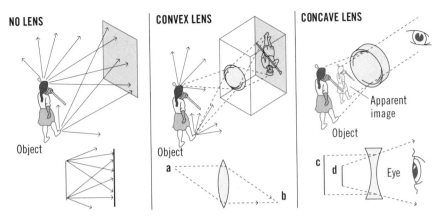

Figure 2-9. LENSES. If there is no lens to focus the rays of light coming from the subject, no image will be produced (left): all rays from all points will strike all parts of the photosensitive plate or film. The convex lens (center) bends the rays from each single point so that they converge on the "focus plane" a certain distance behind it. The image created is reversed right to left and top to bottom. (A transparent negative can then be turned to create the proper left-right orientation in the print.) A pinhole, if it is small enough, will act like a convex lens to give a rough focus. This is the elementary principle which led to the invention of the Camera Obscura (see Figure 2-3). The concave lens (right) causes the rays to diverge in such a way that an observer perceives an "apparent," or "virtual," image which seems smaller than the actual object. The diagrams below the drawings schematically indicate the principles.

Here is the basic idea of the technology of optics: Because light travels at different speeds in different mediums, light rays bend when they pass from one medium to another. Lenses made out of glass or other transparent materials can then focus those rays. While the lens of the human eye is continuously variable, changing in shape each time we unconsciously refocus from one object to another, photographic lenses can only perform the specific tasks for which they are painstakingly designed.

A photographer has three basic types of lenses available to him. These three general categories of lenses are usually classified according to their focal length: the distance from the plane of the film to the surface of the lens. Although a lens is usually chosen specifically for the subject it must photograph, there are various ancillary characteristics to each lens that have become valuable esthetic tools for the photographer. For cameras that use 35 mm film, the "normal" lens has a focal length roughly between 35 and 50 mm. This lens is the most common choice for the photographer because it distorts least and therefore most closely mimics the way the human eye perceives reality.

The wide-angle lens, as its name indicates, photographs a wide angle of view. A photographer finding himself in a cramped location would naturally use this lens in order to photograph as much of the subject as possible. However, the wide-angle lens has the added effect of greatly emphasizing our perception of depth and often distorting linear perception. The fish-eye lens, an extremely wide-angle lens, photographs an angle of view approaching 180°, with corresponding distortion of both linear and depth perception. Generally, for 35 mm photography, any lens shorter than 35 mm in focal length is considered a wide-angle lens.

The telephoto or long lens acts like a telescope to magnify distant objects, and this, of course, is its most obvious use. Although the long lens does not distort linear perception, it does have the sometimes useful effect of suppressing depth perception. It has a relatively narrow angle of view. Normally, any lens longer than 60 mm is considered a telephoto lens, the effective upper limit being about 1200 mm. If greater magnification were desired, the camera would simply be attached to a standard telescope or microscope.

It should be noted that these lenses are not simply solid pieces of glass, as they were in the eighteenth century, but rather mathematically sophisticated combinations of elements designed to admit the most amount of light to the camera with the least amount of distortion.

Since the 1960s, when they came into general use, zoom lenses, in which these elements and groups of elements are adjustable, have gained considerable popularity. The zoom lens has a variable focal length, ranging from wide-angle to telephoto, which allows a photographer to change focal lengths quickly between shots and, more important cinematographically, also to change focal lengths during a shot. This device has added a whole new set of effects to the vocabulary of the shot. Normal zoom lenses (which can have a focal length range from 10 to 100 mm) naturally affect the size of the field photographed as focal length is shifted (since longer lenses have a narrower angle of view than do shorter lenses), and this effect permits the zoom shot to compete with the tracking shot (see Figure 3-59).

Thanks to computer-aided design and manufacturing techniques and advances in the chemistry of optics, the photographic lens is now an instrument of considerable flexibility; we have reached a point where it has become possible to control individually most of the formerly interrelated effects of a lens. In 1975, for example, optics specialists at the Canon company developed their "Macro zoom lens" in which elements of the Macro lens (which allows closeup photography at extreme short ranges), combined with a zoom configuration, allow zooms that range in focus from 1 mm to infinity.

Only one major problem in lens technology remains to be solved. Wide-angle and telephoto lenses differ not only in angle of view (and therefore magnification) but also in their effect on depth perception. No one has yet been able to construct a lens in which these two variables can be controlled separately.

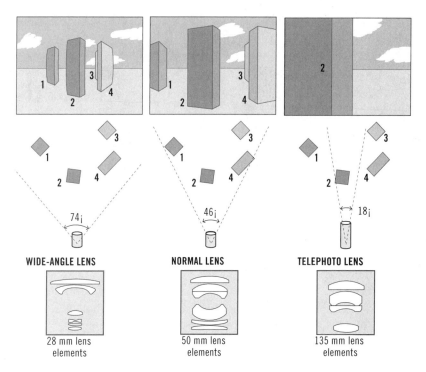

Figure 2-10. WIDE-ANGLE, "NORMAL," AND TELEPHOTO LENSES. Nearly all modern photographic lenses are more complicated than the simple lenses shown in Figure 2-9. Most are composed of sets of elements, such as those which are schematized at the bottom of this diagram. The 28 mm, 50 mm, and 135 mm lenses are common wide-angle, "normal," and "telephoto" lenses in 35 mm photography, whether motion picture or still. Each of the three lenses is seeing the same arrangement of four columns from the same distance and perspective. The frames at the top are exact visualizations of the various images of the scene each lens produces. The wide-angle lens image appears to be taken from a greater distance; the telephoto image is greatly magnified. Notice the slight linear distortion in the wide-angle image and the "flat" quality of the telephoto image. In 35 mm photography, the 50 mm lens is considered "normal" because it best approximates the way the naked eye perceives a scene. (Compare Figure 3-59.)

Alfred Hitchcock spent decades working on this problem before he finally solved it in the famous tower shot from *Vertigo* (1958) by using a carefully controlled zoom combined with a track and models. Hitchcock laid the model stairwell on its side. The camera with zoom lens was mounted on a track looking "down" the stairwell. The shot began with the camera at the far end of the track and the zoom lens set at a moderate telephoto focal length. As the camera tracked in toward the stairwell, the zoom was adjusted backwards, eventually winding up at a wide-angle setting. The track and zoom were carefully coordinated so that the size of the image appeared not to change. (As the track moved in on the center of

Figure 2-11. Providing an ultimate emblem for Hitchcock's life and work, the tower scene from *Vertigo* forged a union of technology and psychology. The camera tracks in and zooms out to distort our perception of depth without changing the range of the frame. (*Frame enlargements.*)

the image, the zoom moved out to correct for the narrowing field.) The effect relayed on the screen was that the shot began with normal depth perception which then became quickly exaggerated, mimicking the psychological feeling of vertigo. Hitchcock's shot cost $19,000 for a few seconds of film time.

Steven Spielberg used a similar combined track-and-zoom in *Jaws* (1975) to add to the sense of apprehension. Perhaps the most interesting application of this unusual technique was in the diner scene from *Goodfellas* (1990). Director Martin Scorsese used it through the tense scene between Robert De Niro and Ray Liotta to heighten the audience's sense of dread.

To summarize: the shorter the lens, the wider the angle of view (the larger the field of view), the more exaggerated the perception of depth, the greater the linear distortion; the longer the lens, the narrower the angle of view, the shallower the depth perception.

Standard lenses are variable in two ways: the photographer adjusts the focus of the lens (by varying the relationship between its elements), and he controls the amount of light entering the lens.

There are three ways to vary the amount of light that enters the camera and strikes the film:

❏   the photographer can interpose light-absorbing material in the path of the light rays (filters do this and are generally attached in front of the lens),

❏   he can change exposure time (the shutter controls this),

❏   or he can change the aperture, the size of the hole through which the light passes (the diaphragm controls this aspect).

Figure 2-12. WIDE-ANGLE DISTORTION. Anna Karina in Jean-Luc Godard's *Pierrot le fou* (1965). (*l'Avant-Scène. Frame enlargement.*)

Filters are generally used to alter the quality of the light entering the camera, not its quantity, and are therefore a minor factor in this equation. Aperture and exposure time are the main factors, closely related to each other and to focus.

The diaphragm works exactly like the iris of the human eye. Since film, more so than the retina of the eye, has a limited range of sensitivity, it is crucial to be able to control the amount of light striking the film. The size of the aperture is measured in f-stops, numbers derived by dividing the focal length of a particular lens by its effective aperture (the ratio of the length of a lens to its width, in other words). The result of this mechanical formula is a series of standard numbers whose relationship, at first, seems arbitrary:

$f1$	$f1.4$	$f2$	$f2.8$	$f4$	$f5.6$	$f8$	$f11$	$f16$	$f22$

Diagram F1

These numbers were chosen because each successive f-stop in this series will admit half the amount of light of its predecessor; that is, an f1 aperture is twice as "large" as an f1.4 aperture, and f2.8 admits four times as much light as f5.6. The numbers have been rounded off to a single decimal place; the multiplication factor is approximately 1.4, the square root of 2.

The speed of a lens is rated by its widest effective aperture. A lens 50 mm long that was also 50 mm wide would, then, be rated as an f1 lens; that is, a very "fast" lens that at its widest opening would admit twice as much light as an f1.4 lens and four times as much light as an f2 lens. When Stanley Kubrick decided that he wanted to shoot much of *Barry Lyndon* (1975) by the light of a few eighteenth-century candles, it was necessary that he adapt to movie use a special lens the

Figure 2-13. TELEPHOTO DISTORTION. A shot from Robert Altman's *Buffalo Bill and the Indians* (1976). Bill's posse is at least a half mile from the camera.

Zeiss company had developed for NASA for space photography. The lens was rated at f0.9, while the fastest lenses then in general use in cinematography were f1.2s. The small difference between the two numbers (0.3) is deceiving for, in fact, Kubrick's NASA lens admitted nearly twice as much light as the standard f1.2 lens.

Since the development of these ultrafast lenses filmmakers have had powerful new tools at their command, although only knowledgeable filmgoers might notice the new effects that are possible. Fast lenses are also important economically, since lighting is one of the most time-consuming and therefore expensive parts of filmmaking. Modern amateur cinematographers expect their Camcorders to record a decent image no matter what the light, and most do; only the professionals know how remarkable a technical feat this is. A contemporary CCD ("charge-coupled device") Camcorder is so effective at amplifying the light the lens transmits that it can serve as a night-vision scope, more efficient than the human eye.

The concept of the f-number is misleading, not only because the series of numbers that results doesn't vividly indicate the differences among various apertures, but also because, being a ratio of physical sizes, the f-number is not necessarily an accurate index of the actual amount of light entering the camera. The surfaces of

Figure 2-14. This frame enlargement from Godard's "Camera-Eye" (1967) clearly shows the effect of rapid zooming during the shot. The blurred lines aim toward the center of the image. Most zooms do not occur quickly enough to blur individual frames like this. (*l'Avant-Scène. Frame enlargement.*)

lens elements reflect small amounts of light, the elements themselves absorb small quantities; in complex multi-element lenses (especially zoom lenses) these differences can add up to a considerable amount. To correct for this, the concept of "T-number" was developed. The T-number is a precise electronic measurement of the amount of light actually striking the film.

Changing the size of the diaphragm—"stopping down"—because it effectively changes the diameter of the lens also changes the depth of field: the smaller the diameter of the lens opening, the greater the precision of focus. The result is that the more light there is available, the greater the depth of field. The phrase "depth of field" is used to indicate the range of distances in front of the lens that will appear satisfactorily in focus. If we were to measure depth of field with scientific accuracy, a lens would only truly be in focus for one single plane in front of the camera, the focus plane. But a photographer is interested not in scientific reality but in psychological reality, and there is always a range of distances both in front of and behind the focus plane that will appear to be in focus.

We should also note at this point that various types of lenses have various depth-of-field characteristics: a wide-angle lens has a very deep depth of field, while a telephoto lens has a rather shallow depth of field. Remember, too, that as

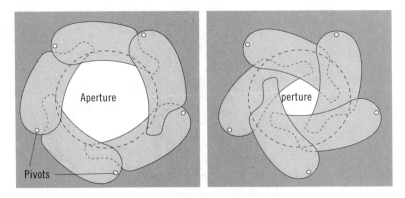

Figure 2-15. THE DIAPHRAGM. One of the simplest elements of the photographic system, as well as one of the most important, the diaphragm is constructed of wafer-thin, spring-loaded metal leaves—usually five or six in number—which overlap each other so that the size of the aperture can be accurately adjusted.

each particular lens is stopped down, as the aperture is narrowed, the effective depth of field increases.

Filmmakers and photographers are thus presented with a complex set of choices regarding lenses. The style of photography that strives for sharp focus over the whole range of action is called deep focus photography. While there are a number of exceptions, deep focus is generally closely associated with theories of realism in film while shallow focus photography, which welcomes the limitations of depth of field as a useful artistic tool, is more often utilized by expressionist filmmakers, since it offers still another technique that can be used to direct the viewer's attention. A director can change focus during a shot either to maintain focus on a subject moving away from or toward the camera (in which case the term is follow focus) or to direct the viewer to shift attention from one subject to another (which is called rack focus).

The Camera

The camera provides a mechanical environment for the lens, which accepts and controls light, and the film, which records light. The heart of this mechanical device is the shutter, which provides the second means available to the photographer for controlling the amount of light that strikes the film. Here, for the first time, we find a significant difference between still and movie photography. For still photographers, shutter speed is invariably closely linked with aperture size. If

Figure 2-16. Ten candles provided all the light for this scene from Kubrick's *Barry Lyndon* (1975). Murray Melvin and Marisa Berenson. (*Frame enlargement.*)

they want to photograph fast action, still photographers will probably decide first to use a fast shutter speed to "freeze" the action, and will compensate for the short exposure time by opening up the aperture to a lower f-stop (which will have the effect of narrowing the depth of field). If, however, they desire the effect of deep focus, still photographers will narrow the aperture ("stop down"), which will then require a relatively long exposure time (which will in turn mean that any rapid action within the frame might be blurred). Shutter speeds are measured in fractions of a second and in still photography are closely linked with corresponding apertures. For instance, the following linked pairs of shutter speeds and apertures will allow the same amount of light to enter the camera:

F-STOP:	$f1$	$f1.4$	$f2$	$f2.8$	$f4$	$f5.6$	$f8$	$f11$	$f16$
SHUTTER SPEED	$\frac{1}{1000}$	$\frac{1}{500}$	$\frac{1}{250}$	$\frac{1}{125}$	$\frac{1}{60}$ *	$\frac{1}{30}$	$\frac{1}{15}$	$\frac{1}{8}$ *	$\frac{1}{4}$

Diagram F2 (* approximately)

In motion picture photography, however, the speed of the shutter is determined by the agreed-upon standard twenty-four frames per second necessary to synchronize camera and projector speed. Cinematographers, therefore, are strictly limited in their choice of shutter speeds, although they can control exposure time

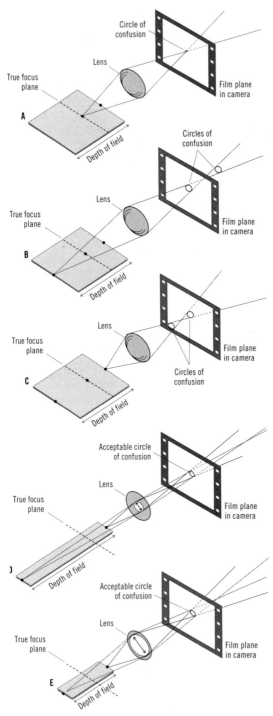

Figure 2-17. FOCUS AND DEPTH OF FIELD. Lenses bend light rays in such a way that only one plane in front of the lens is truly and accurately in focus. The dotted line in these five drawings represents that true focus plane. However, psychologically, a certain range of distances in front and in back of the focus plane will appear satisfactorily in focus. This "depth of field" is represented here by the shaded areas.

In A, an object point on the precise focus plane produces the narrowest "circle of confusion" on the film plane behind the lens. In B, an object point at the far end of the range of depth of field produces the largest acceptable circle of confusion. For objects beyond this point, the circle of confusion is such that the eye and brain read the image as being "out of focus." In C, an object point at the near boundary of depth of field produces a similarly acceptable circle of confusion. Objects nearer to the lens than this will produce an out-of-focus circle of confusion.

D and E illustrate the effect of aperture size (or diaphragm setting) on depth of field. The narrower aperture in D yields a greater depth of field, while the larger aperture in E limits the depth of field. In both illustrations, points at the near and far end of the depth of field range produce equal, acceptable circles of confusion.

In all five drawings depth of field has been slightly reduced for illustrative purposes. The calculation of the depth of field of a particular lens and aperture is a simple matter of geometry. Generally, depth of field extends toward infinity. It is much more critical in the near range than the far.

Figure 2-18. SHALLOW FOCUS. Characters are sharply in focus, background is blurred in this shot from Kubrick's *Paths of Glory* (1957). (*MOMA/FSA.*)

within narrow limits by using a variable shutter, which controls not the time the shutter is open, but rather the size of the opening. Clearly, the effective upper limit in cinematography is 1/24 second. Since the film must travel through the projector at that speed, there is no way in normal cinematography of increasing exposure time beyond that limit. This means that cinematographers are effectively deprived of one of the most useful tools of still photography: there are no "time exposures" in normal movies.

Focal length, linear distortion, distortion of depth perspective, angle of view, focus, aperture, depth of field, and exposure time: these are the basic factors of photography, both movie and still.

A large number of variables are linked together, and each of them has more than one effect. The result is, for example, that when a photographer wants deep focus he decreases the size of the aperture, but that means that less light will enter the camera so that he must add artificial light to illuminate the subject sufficiently, but that might produce undesirable side effects, so, to compensate, he will increase exposure time, but this means that it will be more difficult to obtain a clear, sharp image if either the camera or the subject is moving, so he may decide

Figure 2-19. DEEP FOCUS. One of the more extraordinary deep-focus shots photographed by Gregg Toland for Orson Welles's *Citizen Kane* (1941). The focus reaches from the ice sculptures in the near foreground to the furniture piled up behind the table at the rear. (*MOMA/FSA.*)

to switch to a wider-angle lens in order to include more area in the frame, but this might mean that he will lose the composition he was trying to achieve in the first place. In photography, many decisions have to be made consciously that the human eye and brain make instantly and unconsciously.

In movies, the camera becomes involved in two variables that do not exist in still photography: it moves the film, and it itself moves. The transport of the film might seem to be a simple matter, yet this was the last of the multiple problems to be solved before motion pictures became feasible. The mechanism that moves the film properly through the camera is known as the "pull-down mechanism" or "intermittent motion mechanism." The problem is that film, unlike audiotape or videotape, cannot run continuously through the camera at a constant speed. Films are series of still pictures, twenty-four per second, and the intermittent motion mechanism must move the film into position for the exposure of a frame, hold it in position rock steady for almost 1/24 second, then move the next frame into position. It must do this twenty-four times each second, and it must accomplish this mechanical task in strict synchronization with the revolving shutter that actually exposes the film.

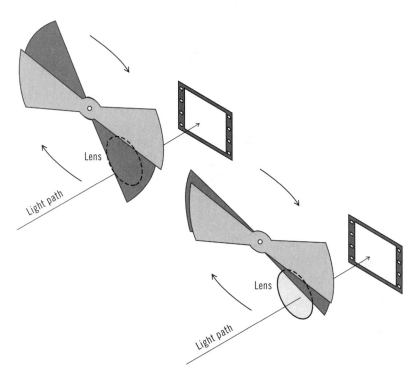

Figure 2-20. THE VARIABLE SHUTTER. In still photography, the shutter is simply a spring-loaded metal plate or fabric screen. In motion-picture photography, however, the time of exposure is limited by the 24-frame-per-second standard speed. The variable shutter allows some leeway in exposure time. Although it revolves always at the same 24 fps speed, the size of the "hole" and therefore the time of the exposure can be varied by adjusting the overlapping plates.

In the U.S., Thomas Armat is usually credited with inventing the first workable pull-down mechanism in 1895. In Europe, other inventors—notably the Lumière brothers—developed similar devices. The pull-down mechanism is literally the heart of cinema, since it pumps film through the camera or projector. The key to the success of this system of recording and projecting a series of still images that give the appearance of continuous movement lies in what Ingmar Bergman calls a certain "defect" in human sight: "persistence of vision." The brain holds an image for a short period of time after it has disappeared, so it is possible to construct a machine that can project a series of still images quickly enough so that they merge psychologically and the illusion of motion is maintained. Al Hazen had investigated this phenomenon in his book *Optical Elements,* as early as the tenth century. Nineteenth-century scientists such as Peter Mark Roget and Michael Faraday did valuable work on the theory as early as the 1820s. During

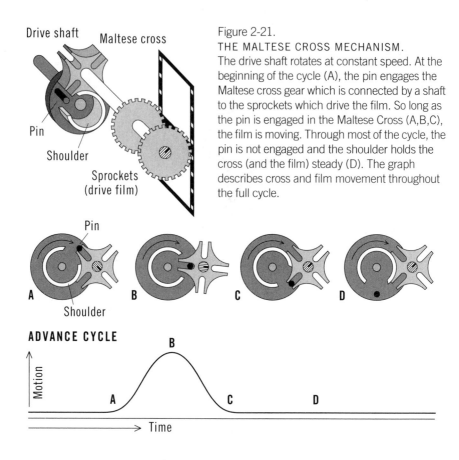

Drive shaft   Maltese cross

Pin

Shoulder

Sprockets
(drive film)

Figure 2-21.
THE MALTESE CROSS MECHANISM.
The drive shaft rotates at constant speed. At the
beginning of the cycle (A), the pin engages the
Maltese cross gear which is connected by a shaft
to the sprockets which drive the film. So long as
the pin is engaged in the Maltese Cross (A,B,C),
the film is moving. Through most of the cycle, the
pin is not engaged and the shoulder holds the
cross (and the film) steady (D). The graph
describes cross and film movement throughout
the full cycle.

Pin

Shoulder

A   B   C   D

ADVANCE CYCLE

Motion

A   C   D

Time

the early years of this century Gestalt psychologists further refined this concept,
giving it the name "Phi-phenomenon."

As it happens, a speed of at least twelve or fifteen pictures per second is necessary, and a rate of about forty pictures per second is much more effective. Early
experimenters—W. K. L. Dickson for one—shot at speeds approaching forty-eight
frames per second to eliminate the "flicker" effect common at slower speeds. It
quickly became evident, however, that the flicker could be avoided by the use of a
double-bladed projection shutter, and this has been in common use since the
early days of film. The effect is that, while the film is shot at twenty-four frames
per second, it is shown in such a way that the projection of each frame is interrupted once, producing a frequency of forty-eight "frames" per second and thus
eliminating flicker. Each frame is actually projected twice.

During the silent period—especially during the earliest years when both cameras and projectors were hand-cranked—variable speeds were common: both the
cameraman and the projectionist thus had a degree of control over the speed of

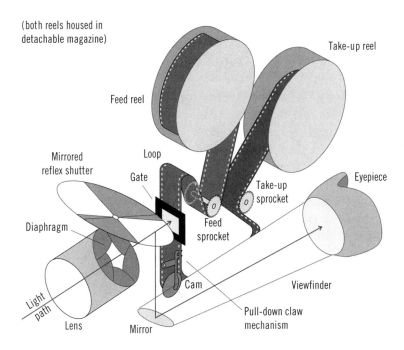

(both reels housed in detachable magazine)

Take-up reel

Feed reel

Mirrored reflex shutter

Loop

Gate

Eyepiece

Take-up sprocket

Diaphragm

Feed sprocket

Light path

Cam

Viewfinder

Lens

Mirror

Pull-down claw mechanism

Figure 2-22. THE REFLEX CAMERA. The feed and take-up reels are housed in a separate magazine which can be changed easily and quickly. The feed and take-up sprockets run continuously. Intermittent motion in this machine is provided by a cam-mounted claw mechanism rather than the more complicated Maltese cross system illustrated in Figure 2-21. The heart of the reflex camera is the mirrored shutter. Tilted at a 45° angle to the light path, this ingenious device permits the camera operator to see precisely the same scene through the viewfinder that the film "sees." When the shutter is open, all light strikes the film. When the shutter is closed, all light is redirected into the viewfinder. The reflex camera has almost entirely replaced earlier systems with separate viewfinders, both in still and motion picture photography.

the action. The average silent speed was between sixteen and eighteen frames per second, gradually increasing over the years to twenty and twenty-two frames per second. Twenty-four frames per second did not become an immutable standard until 1927 (although even now it is not entirely universal: European television films are shot at twenty-five frames per second in order to synchronize with the European television system, whose frequency is twenty-five frames per second). When silent films are projected at "sound speed," as they often are nowadays, the effect is to make the speeded-up action appear even more comical than it was originally.

The effect of frequency is not to be underestimated. Because we grow up inundated with motion-picture and television images in the 24 fps to 30 fps range (or 48 fps to 60 fps projected), we learn to accept this moving-picture quality as standard, when it is in fact just adequate. One of the most effective ways to increase image quality is to increase frequency, which you can prove to yourself by visiting a Showscan or Imax installation. Both of these proprietary technologies for museum and theme park shows use higher frequencies. (Imax also uses wider stock.) When the U.S. standard for HDTV (high-definition television) was adopted in 1994, increased frequency was a major element of the prescription.

The genius of the device Armat invented is that it alternately moves the film and holds it steady for exposure in such a way that there is a high ratio between the amount of time the film is held still and the amount of time it is in motion. Obviously, the time during which the frame is in motion is wasted time, photographically. The sequence of operations is described in Figure 2-21. Considering the smallness of the frame, the fragility of the film, and the tremendous forces to which the tiny sprocket holes are subjected, the motion picture camera and projector are formidable mechanisms indeed. The Maltese Cross gear itself is an eloquent emblem of nineteenth-century mechanical technology.

The speed of the camera introduces another set of variables that can be useful to filmmakers, and it is in this area that cinema finds its most important scientific applications. By varying the speed of the camera (assuming the projector speed remains constant), we can make use of the invaluable techniques of slow motion, fast motion, and time-lapse (extreme fast motion) photography.

Film, then, is a tool that can be applied to time in the same ways that the telescope and the microscope are applied to space, revealing natural phenomena that are invisible to the human eye. Slow motion, fast motion, and time-lapse photography make comprehensible events that happen either too quickly or too slowly for us to perceive them, just as the microscope and the telescope reveal phenomena that are either too small or too far away for us to perceive them. As a scientific tool, cinematography has had great significance, not only because it allows us to analyze a large range of time phenomena but also as an objective record of reality. The sciences of anthropology, ethnography, psychology, sociology, natural studies, zoology—even botany—have been revolutionized by the invention of cinematography. Moreover, filmstocks can be made that are sensitive to areas of the spectrum outside that very limited range of frequencies, known as "colors," that our eyes perceive. Infrared and other similar types of photography reveal "visual" data that have hitherto been beyond our powers of perception.

The terms "slow motion" and "fast motion" are fairly self-explanatory, but it may nevertheless be useful to describe exactly what happens in the camera. If we can adjust the speed of the pull-down mechanism so that, for example, it shoots 240 frames per second instead of the standard 24, then each second of recording time will stretch out over ten seconds of projected time, revealing details of motion that would be imperceptible in real time. Conversely, if the camera takes, say, three frames per second, projected time will "happen" eight times more

Figure 2-23. TIME-LAPSE PHOTOGRAPHY. Because film can compress (and expand) time, as a scientific tool it serves purposes similar to the microscope and telescope. (*Courtesy Archive Films. Frame enlargements.*)

Figure 2-24. Slow motion is occasionally useful in narrative films, as well. This frame from the sequence in extreme slow motion that climaxes Michelangelo Antonioni's *Zabriskie Point* (1969) captures some of the ironic, lyrical freedom of the explosion fantasy. (*Sight and Sound. Frame enlargement.*)

quickly than real time. The term "time lapse" is used simply to refer to extremely fast motion photography in which the camera operates intermittently rather than continuously—at a rate of one frame every minute, for example. Time-lapse photography is especially useful in the natural sciences, revealing details about phenomena like phototropism, for example, that no other laboratory technique could show.

It doesn't take many viewings of slow- and fast-motion films made with primarily scientific purposes in mind before it becomes obvious that the variable speed of the motion picture camera reveals poetic truths as well as scientific ones. If the slow-motion love scene has become one of the hoariest clichés of contemporary cinema while the comedic value of fast-motion early silent movies has become a truism, it is also true that explosions in extreme slow motion (for example, the final sequence of Antonioni's *Zabriskie Point,* 1969) become symphonic celebrations of the material world, and time-lapse sequences of flowers in which a day's time is compressed into thirty seconds of screen time reveal a natural choreography that is stunning, as the flower stretches and searches for the life-giving rays of the sun.

The camera itself moves, as well as the film, and it is in this area that cinema has discovered some of its most private truths, for the control over the viewer's perspective that a filmmaker enjoys is one of the most salient differences between film and stage.

There are two basic types of camera movement: the camera can revolve around one of the three imaginary axes that intersect in the camera; or it can move itself from one point to another in space. Each of these two types of motion implies an essentially different relationship between camera and subject.

In pans and tilts, the camera follows the subject as the subject moves (or changes); in rolls, the subject doesn't change but its orientation within the frame is altered; in tracks (also known as "dollies") and crane shots, the camera moves along a vertical or horizontal line (or a vector of some sort) and the subject may be either stationary or mobile. Because these assorted movements and their various combinations have such an important effect on the relationship between the subject and the camera (and therefore the viewer), camera movement has great significance as a determinant of the meaning of film.

The mechanical devices that make camera movement possible are all fairly simple in design: the tripod panning/tilting head is a matter of carefully machined plates and ball-bearings; tracking (or traveling) shots are accomplished simply by either laying down tracks (very much like railroad tracks) to control the movement of the camera on its mount, or using a rubber-tired dolly, which allows a bit more freedom; the camera crane that allows a cinematographer to raise and lower the camera smoothly is merely a counterweighted version of the "cherry-pickers" that telephone company linesmen use to reach the tops of poles. (See Figure 3-60.)

As a result, until relatively recently, technical advances in this area were few. Two stand out. First, in the late 1950s, the Arriflex company developed a 35 mm movie camera that was considerably lighter in weight and smaller in dimension than the standard Mitchell behemoths that had become the favored instruments of Hollywood cinematographers. The Arriflex could be hand-held, and this allowed new freedom and fluidity in camera movement. The camera was now free of mechanical supports and consequently a more personal instrument. The French New Wave, in the early sixties, was noted for the creation of a new vocabulary of hand-held camera movements, and the lightweight camera made possible the style of cinéma-vérité Documentary invented during the sixties and still common today. Indeed, one of the cinematographic clichés that most identified

PAN   **TILT**   **ROLL**

Figure 2-25. PAN, TILT, AND ROLL. The pan is by far the most common of these three elementary movements. The roll, since it disorients and doesn't provide any new information, is least common.

the 1990s was the quick-cut, jittery, hand-held exaggeration exploited in so many television commercials. The more things change, the more they remain the same.

For nearly fifteen years, hand-held shots, while inexpensive and popular, were also obvious. Shaky camera work became a cliché of the sixties. Then, in the early seventies, a cameraman named Garrett Brown developed the system called "Steadicam" working in conjunction with engineers from Cinema Products, Inc. Since then, this method of filming has gained wide popularity and has significantly streamlined the filmmaking process. In terms of economic utility, it ranks right up there with ultrafast lenses, since laying tracks is the second most time-consuming activity in film production (and the Steadicam eliminates them).

In the Steadicam system, a vest is used to redistribute the weight of the camera to the hips of the camera operator. A spring-loaded arm damps the motion of the

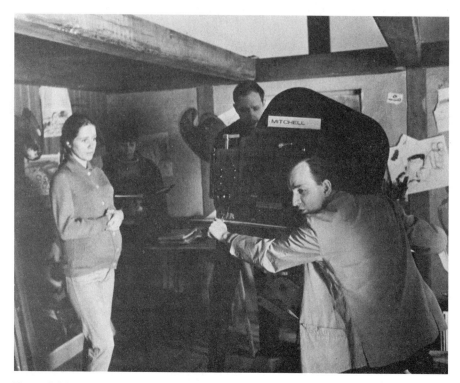

Figure 2-26. Ingmar Bergman with bulky Mitchell camera on the set of *Hour of the Wolf* (1966), Liv Ullmann to the left.

camera, providing an image steadiness comparable to much more elaborate (and expensive) tracking and dolly shots. Finally, a video monitor frees the camera operator from the eyepiece, further increasing control of the hand-held walking shot. Steadicam operators are among the unsung artistic heroes of the film profession. Most are trained athletes; the work they do is a prodigious combination of weightlifting and ballet. Ironically, the better they do it, the less you notice.

Even a lightweight camera is a bulky device when placed on a standard crane. In the mid-seventies, French filmmakers Jean-Marie Lavalou and Alain Masseron constructed a device they called a "Louma." Essentially a lightweight crane very much like a microphone boom, it allows full advantage to be taken of lightweight cameras. The Louma, precisely controlled by servo-motors, enables the camera to be moved into positions that were impossible before and frees it from the presence of the camera operator by transmitting a video image of the scene from the viewfinder to the cinematographer's location, which can be simply outside a cramped room, or miles away, if necessary.

Devices such as the Kenworthy snorkel permit even more minute control of the camera. As the Louma frees the camera from the bulk of the operator, so the

Figure 2-27. Stanley Kubrick "hand-holding" a small Arriflex: the rape scene from *A Clockwork Orange* (1971). Malcolm McDowell wears the nose.

snorkel frees the lens from the bulk of the camera. There are now a number of devices that follow the Louma and Kenworthy principles—and one that represents a quantum leap for the freedom of the camera. Not satisfied with having liberated the camera from tracks and dollies, Garrett Brown developed his "Skycam" system in the mid-1980s.

With hindsight, the Skycam is an obvious offspring of the Steadicam and the Louma. The system suspends a lightweight camera via wires and pulleys from four posts erected at the four corners of the set or location. The operator sits off-set, viewing the action on a monitor and controlling the movement of the camera through controls that communicate with the cable system via computer programs. Like the Steadicam before it, the Skycam is often most effective when it is least obvious. But on occasion, especially covering sports events, the Skycam provides exhilarating images that are otherwise impossible. Peter Pan never had it so good.

With the advent of these devices, most of the constraints imposed on cinematography by the size of the necessary machinery have been eliminated, and the camera approaches the ideal condition of a free-floating, perfectly controllable

Figure 2-28.
THE STEADICAM.
Springs damp the motion
of the camera. The
harness provides
cantilevered balance.

artificial eye. The perfection of fiber optics technology extended this freedom to the microscopic level; the travels through the various channels of the human body that were science fiction when they were created by means of special effects in 1967 for the film *Fantastic Voyage* could, by the mid-seventies, be filmed "on location" for the documentary *The Incredible Machine.*

The Filmstock

The fundamental principle on which all chemical photography is based is that some substances (mainly silver salts) are photosensitive: that is, they change chemically when exposed to light. If that chemical alteration is visible and can be fixed or frozen, then a reproducible record of visual experience is possible.[*]

Daguerreotypes were made on metal plates and required long periods of exposure, measured in minutes, in order to capture an image. Two developments in the technology of photography were necessary before motion pictures became

---

[*] The discussion of photochemical filmstock that follows also applies, the necessary changes being made, to all-electronic photography, which we'll discuss in greater detail in Chapter 6.

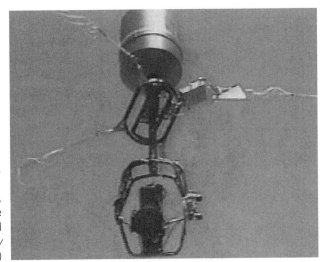

Figure 2-29.
THE SKYCAM.
Suspended by four wires,
the camera and the
winches are controlled
remotely. (*Courtesy
Skyworks, Inc.*)

possible: a flexible base to carry the photographic emulsion, and an emulsion sensitive or "fast" enough so that it could be properly exposed within a time period something like 1/20 second. The speed of standard, popular emulsions is now such that 1/1000 second is more than adequate exposure time under normal conditions.

Not all image-fixing is chemically photographic, however. Television images are electronically produced (although photosensitive and phosphorescent chemicals play a part) and systems used in photocopying (Xerox) machines are also quite different from traditional chemical silver-salt photography. The silver scare of early 1980 when, for a brief period, the price of the metal quintupled, focused renewed attention on non-silver means of photography.

Sony introduced the first all-electronic snapshot camera, the Mavica, in 1989. They were a few years ahead of the market; digital cameras did not find consumer acceptance until the late nineties. In 1992 Kodak (who have the most to lose when photography moves from chemistry to electronics) found a transitional formula: a compromise called Photo CD. The well-established and easy-to-use chemistry-based film is still used to take the picture. Then the commercial photofinisher transfers the image from film to fully digitized files on a version of a CD-ROM, which is returned to the customer just as quickly as his paper prints used to be. The customer inserts the disc in any CD-ROM reader that meets the Photo CD standard and views his snapshots on his monitor or television set.

As color laser and ink-jet printers drop in price and move into the home, the photo buff is able to make his own paper prints, and the darkroom home photo workshop can be replaced by computer software. Already, business software like Adobe Photoshop offers more flexibility than the most advanced photo labs at a

Figure 2-30. Shooting a simple automobile scene can be a time-consuming task. Lights, camera, reflectors, diffusers, and other paraphernalia are all mounted on the car for this scene from *Not a Pretty Picture* (1976). Director Martha Coolidge is at right. (Compare the simple studio rear projection arrangement in Figure 2-57.) (*Photo: Jack Feder.*) Below, the scene as it appeared in the film.

cheaper price than any basement darkroom. The camera itself has been the last link in the chain to be digitized; the progression is inexorable. Photo-chemistry, now well into its second century, is about to be replaced. Indeed, as a consumer technology it has enjoyed a record run of more than one hundred years that may be surpassed only by digital computers. The mechanical wax or vinyl record, second in the consumer technology record book, lasted almost as long before it was replaced by CDs in the late 1980s.

Negatives, Prints, and Generations

Since the salts on which chemical photography is based darken when exposed to light, a curious and useful quirk is introduced into the system. Those areas of the photograph that receive most light will appear darkest when the photograph is

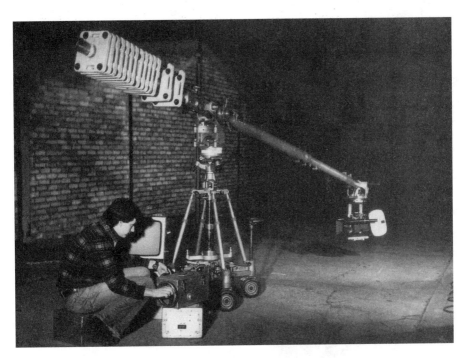

Figure 2-31 THE LOUMA CRANE. The operator controls the movement of crane and camera via servo-mechanisms while observing the image the camera is taking by television monitor. The crane is capable of very precise changes in direction. A zoom motor attached to the camera can also be remote-controlled. (*Photo: P. Brard.*)

developed and put through the chemical baths that fix the image permanently. The result is a negative image in which tones are reversed: light is dark and dark is light. A positive print of this negative image can easily be obtained by either contact printing the negative or projecting it on similar filmstock or photographic paper. This makes possible the replication of the image. In addition, when the negative is projected the image can be enlarged, reduced, or otherwise altered—a significant advantage. Reversal processing permits the development of a direct, projectable positive image on the "camera original"—the filmstock in the camera when the shot is made. Negatives (or reversal positives) can also be printed directly from a reversal print.

The camera original is considered to be first generation; a print of it would be second generation; a negative or reversal copy of that, in turn, is third generation. With each successive step, quality is lost. Since the original negative of a film is usually considered too valuable to use in producing as many as two thousand

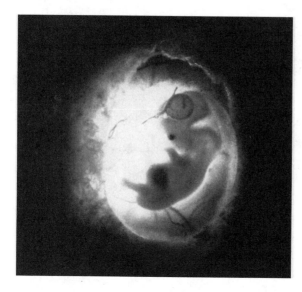

Figure 2-32. An early example of endoscopic fiber optics cinematography: a human fetus in the womb. From *The Incredible Machine*, 1975 (*PBS*).

prints that might be required for a major release of a feature, the print you see in a theater is often several generations removed from the original:

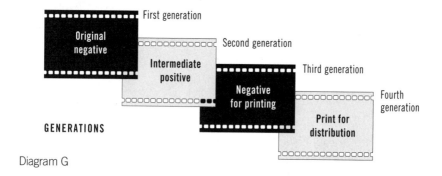

First generation

Original negative

Second generation

Intermediate positive

Third generation

Negative for printing

Fourth generation

Print for distribution

GENERATIONS

Diagram G

If complicated laboratory work is required, then several more generations may be added. "CRI" stock (color reversal intermediate), developed especially to bridge the intermediate positive stage, lessened the number of generations in practice. When large numbers of prints and laboratory work were not needed, reversal stocks provided a very useful alternative. In the 1970s, when film was still the medium of choice for television news, and before the all-electronic newsroom became commonplace, the reversal stock that a television newsman shot at 4 pm, might have been developed at 5 and gone directly into the film chain, still wet, for broadcasting at 6. Amateur cinematographers almost always use reversal films such as Kodachrome or Ektachrome.

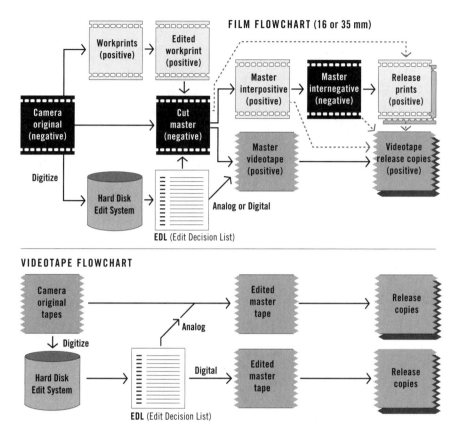

Figure 2-33. STOCK, PROCESSING, GENERATIONS. Most of the production systems commonly in use today are outlined in this flowchart. American theatrical films usually follow the path of the solid line, which means that the print audiences see is fourth generation. European theatrical films often are produced along the path of the dotted line: audiences see a second generation print of better quality. A third system, not shown, interposes a "Reversal Intermediate" between the negative and the print. Although 16 mm film production can follow the same patterns, it is also common to use Reversal originals, which can be screened directly. The addition of tape to the equation allows for an even greater variety of inputs and outputs. When the tape is digital the release copies are equivalent to first generation.

This is a broad outline of the basic choices of filmstock available to the film-maker. In practice, the variety is much greater. The Eastman Kodak company has very nearly a monopoly position in the professional filmstock market in the U.S. (even if it has some distant challengers in the amateur and still film markets) and is dominant abroad as well. But Kodak enjoys that monopoly partly because it produces a large number of very useful products. And while the professional film-maker is effectively limited to Eastman Kodak raw materials, there is a variety of processing techniques available (see the discussion of color below). Yet all these processes reveal basic similarities, since they all must deal with the particular chemistry of the filmstock Kodak supplies.

One of the main reasons the company holds such a strong position in the industry is this close connection between stock and processing. A private laboratory will invest hundreds of thousands of dollars in equipment to process a particular stock. Naturally, such large investments require a degree of financial caution by the labs, especially when the technology is developing rapidly and the useful life of the equipment may be no more than six or eight years. Eastman's 5254 stock, for example, introduced in 1968, was technically superior to color stocks that had existed before then, but it lasted only six years before it was replaced by 5247 in 1974 with an entirely different chemistry. 5247 then was replaced by the EXR stocks (5296, 5293, 5248, 5245).

For these reasons and others, Kodak still enjoys a monopolistic position that is in some ways similar to the situation of IBM in the computer industry before the microcomputer revolution of the early 1980s. It was George Eastman who developed the first flexible, transparent roll filmstock, in 1889. Like IBM in its heyday, Eastman's company has largely defined the languages and systems that must be used by the great majority of their customers. Film is an art, but it is also an industry. Kodak's revenues from filmstock each year are approximately 1.5 times the box-office revenues of the American film industry.

But like IBM, Kodak may be in danger of disappearing from the scene if it cannot make the transition from the chemical technology of the nineteenth century to the digital technology of the twenty-first. Photo CD is a good start, but it merely extends the life of Kodak's chemical franchise. Eventually all photography will be digital, and the company has many more competitors in the disc and tape fields than in filmstock; moreover, there is far less variation among brands in this area than in photochemical film.

While economic and logistical decision still play a large part in the choice of filmstock and process, there are other, more esthetic, decisions that are integrally involved in these choices. The esthetic variables of filmstock include: gauge, grain, contrast, tone, and color. Intimately involved with these variables, especially the first two—although it is not truly a function of the filmstock used—is the aspect ratio, or frame size of the film when projected.

Aspect Ratio

The ratio between the height of the projected image and its width—the aspect ratio—is dependent on the size and shape of the aperture of the camera (and of the projector) and, as we shall see, on the types of lenses used. But it is not solely a function of the aperture. Early in the history of film, an arbitrary aspect ratio of four to three (width to height) became popular and was eventually standardized

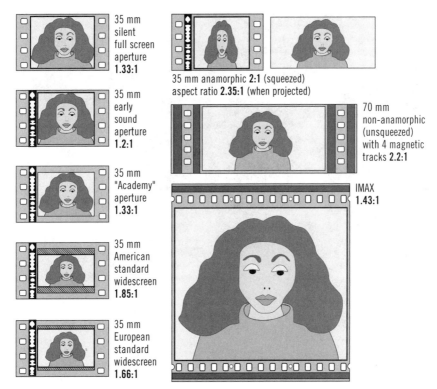

Figure 2-34. ASPECT RATIOS. Standard and widescreen systems.

by the Academy of Motion Picture Arts and Sciences (so that it is now known as the "Academy aperture" or "Academy ratio"). This ratio, more often expressed as 1:1.33 or simply as the 1.33 ratio, while it was undeniably the most common, was never really the sole ratio in use.

Filmmakers—D. W. Griffith is especially noted for this—often masked off part of the frame to change the shape of the image temporarily. When sound was developed and room had to be made on the edge of the filmstock for the soundtrack, the square ratio was common for a while. A few years later the Academy shrank the amount of space within the potential frame that was actually used in order to regain the 1.33 ratio, and this standard gradually developed a mystique, even though it was the result of an arbitrary decision.

Some film textbooks connect the 1.33 ratio with the Golden Section of classical art and architecture, a truly mystical number expressive of a ratio found everywhere in nature, often in the strangest places (in the arrangement of the seeds of a sunflower, for example, or the shape of a snail's shell). The Golden Section is derived from the formula $a/b = b/(a + b)$, where a is the length of the shorter side of the rectangle and b is the length of the longer. While it is an irrational number,

Figure 2-35. The Golden Mean as a sunflower displays it. (*JM*)

this Golden Mean can be closely approximated by expressing the ratio of height to width as 1:1.618. This is very close to the most popular European widescreen ratio in use today, but it is certainly a far cry from the 1.33 ratio of the Academy aperture. While the Academy ratio, arbitrary as it is,[*] really only dominated for twenty years or so (until 1953), it was during this time that the television frame was standardized on its model; and that, in turn, continues to influence film composition. Widescreen HDTV, however, has an aspect ratio of 16:9 (or 1.777:1), much closer to the Golden Mean.

Since the 1950s, filmmakers have been presented with a considerable range of screen ratios to choose from. Two separate methods are used to achieve the widescreen ratios in use today. The simplest method is to mask off the top and bottom of the frame, providing the two most common "flat" widescreen ratios: 1.66 (in Europe) and 1.85 (in the U.S.). Masking, however, means that a much smaller portion of the available film frame is used, resulting in diminished quality of the projected image. In the 1.85 ratio, 36 percent of the total frame area is wasted.

The second method of achieving a widescreen ratio, the anamorphic process, became popular in the mid-fifties as "CinemaScope." The first anamorphic process was Henri Chrétien's "Hypergonar" system, which was used by Claude

---

[*] Cynics will note that the Academy aperture is an expression of Pythagoras' theorem, but that is an abstract ideal while the Golden Mean is a natural, organic one!

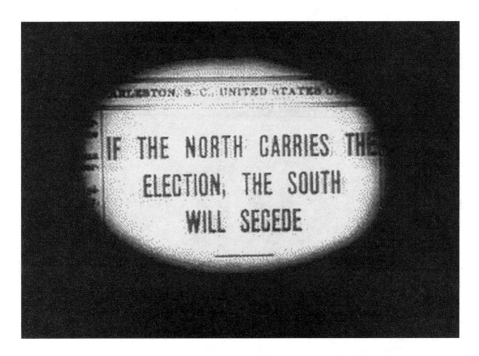

Figure 2-36. D. W. Griffith often masked the image to focus attention, as in this shot from *The Birth of a Nation*. (*Frame enlargement.*)

Autant-Lara in 1927 for his film *Construire un feu*. In the same year, Abel Gance, working with André Debrie, developed a multiscreen system not unlike Cinerama for his epic *Napoléon*. He called this three-projector system Polyvision. A year previously, for their film *Chang*, Merian C. Cooper and Ernest B. Schoedsack had experimented with "Magnascope," which simply enlarged the entire image, much as a magnifying glass would.

An anamorphic lens squeezes a wide image into the normal frame dimensions of the film and then unsqueezes the image during projection to provide a picture with the proper proportions. The standard squeeze ratio for the most common anamorphic systems (first CinemaScope, now Panavision) is 2:1—that is, a subject will appear in the squeezed frame to be half as wide as in reality. The height of the subject is unchanged. Using nearly all the area of the frame available, the earlier anamorphic process obtained a projected image aspect ratio of 2.55; this was later altered to 2.35, which is now standard, to make room for an optical soundtrack.

While the anamorphic system is considerably more efficient than masking, since it utilizes the full frame area available, anamorphic lenses are much more sophisticated optical devices, much more expensive, and more limited in variety than spherical (nonanamorphic) lenses. This results in certain practical limitations

Figure 2-37. Two tripartite screen arrays from the restoration of Abel Gance's *Napoléon* (1927), showing how multiple views can create a single psychological impression. (*MOMA/FSA.*)

placed on the cinematographer using an anamorphic system. In addition, although it seems as if an anamorphic negative contains twice as much horizontal information as a standard negative, the unsqueezing process does amplify grain and inconsistencies along with the image. In other words, the anamorphic lens simply stretches a normal amount of information to fill a screen twice as wide.

The age of widescreen began in September 1952 with the release of *This Is Cinerama*, a successful spectacle whose subject was, in fact, the system that was used to shoot it. Employing stereophonic sound, Cinerama, the invention of Fred Waller, used three cameras and three projectors to cover a huge, curved screen. Like many widescreen systems, it had its roots in a World's Fair exhibit, Waller's "Vitarama," which was used at the 1939–40 Fair in New York and later evolved into the Flexible Gunnery Trainer of World War II.

In 1953, the first CinemaScope film, Twentieth Century Fox's *The Robe*, was released. An anamorphic process rather than a multiprojector extravaganza, CinemaScope quickly became the standard widescreen process of the 1950s. Techniscope, developed by the Technicolor company, employed an interesting variation on the anamorphic process. The Techniscope negative was shot with spherical lenses masked to give a widescreen ratio. The camera employed a two-hole pull-down mechanism rather than the standard four-hole, thus halving film-stock costs. The negative was then printed through an anamorphic lens, providing a standard anamorphic four-hole pull-down print for projection purposes.

While filmmakers had experimented with widescreen systems for many years, it was the economic threat that television posed in the early fifties that finally

Figure 2-38. *This Is Cinerama.* This is an artist's conception of the view of the giant screen from the audience. It does a good job of evoking the experience. Note the upturned heads.

made widescreen ratios common. Having bequeathed the arbitrary 1.33 ratio to the new television industry, film studios quickly discovered that their most powerful weapon against the new art was image size. Because it was so unwieldy, Cinerama quickly fell into disuse. Single camera systems, like CinemaScope and later Panavision, became dominant. Cinerama also engendered the short-lived phenomenon of "3-D" or stereoscopic film. Again the system was too inflexible to be successful and was never more than a novelty attraction, although it made a very brief comeback in the 1980s. What was undoubtedly the best film shot in the two-camera 3-D process, Hitchcock's *Dial M for Murder* (1954), wasn't released in 3-D until 1980.

Ironically, 3-D attempted to exploit an area of film esthetics that was already fairly well expressed by two-dimensional "flat" film. Our sense of the dimensionality of a scene depends, psychologically, upon many factors other than binocular vision: chiaroscuro, movement, focus are all important psychological factors. (See Chapter 3.) Moreover, the three-dimensional technique produced an inherent distortion, which distracted, drawing attention from the subject of the film. These are the twin problems that holography, a much more advanced system of stereoscopic photography, will have to overcome before it can ever be considered a feasible alternative to flat film.

The development of the various trick processes of the 1950s had some useful results, however. One of the systems that competed with CinemaScope in those

Figure 2-39. *The Robe*. Victor Mature and friends set against a large landscape and a larger drama. (*MOMA/FSA*.)

years was Paramount's answer to Fox's process. VistaVision turned the camera on its side to achieve a wide image with an eight-sprocket-hole pull-down (more precisely, a "pull-across"). The frame, then, was twice the size of a normal 35 mm frame and used all the image area available without tricky anamorphic lenses. Release prints were made in normal 35 mm configurations. (Technirama, a later development, combined this technique with an anamorphic taking lens with a 1.5 squeeze ratio).

Today, filmmakers have at their disposal the array of aspect ratios—some for photography, some for distribution prints, some for both—outlined in Figure 2-34. Digital photography, by its very nature, allows all sorts of variations on these themes. When the image is digital any aspect ratio and any vertical and/or horizontal compression scheme can be applied. Similarly, resolutions vary over a wide range. About the only thing that doesn't change in digital photography is the lens: it's still necessary to use curved pieces of glass or plastic to focus the light waves.

Grain, Gauge, and Speed

The development of fast filmstocks (and faster lenses) has given filmmakers welcome freedom to photograph scenes by "available light," at night or indoors. Whereas huge, expensive arc lights were once standard in the industry and greatly restricted the process of filmmaking, fast color and black-and-white filmstocks now give film almost the same sensitivity that our eyes have. The exposure speed of a filmstock is closely linked with its definition or grain, and varies inversely: what is gained in speed is generally lost in definition. Faster films are grainier; slower films give sharper, fine-grain images.

8   Super8   16   35   70   IMAX

Figure 2-40. GAUGE. These six samples of standard film gauges are reproduced life-size. The 35 mm image is four sprocket holes high. The soundtrack is the thin line to the right of the left-hand sprockets. The 16 mm frames and the 8 mm and Super-8 mm frames are each one sprocket high. In addition, 8 and 16 mm release prints have only one row of sprockets. The 16 mm soundtrack is to the right of the image. (There are no soundtracks on the 8 and Super-8 mm samples.) The smaller sprocket holes of Super-8 mm film provide an image area approximately 35 percent larger than regular 8 mm stock. The 70 mm and IMAX samples offer 10 and 30 times the image area of the standard 35 mm frame, respectively. IMAX runs horizontally through the camera and projector. The frame is 15 sprocket holes wide.

35mm

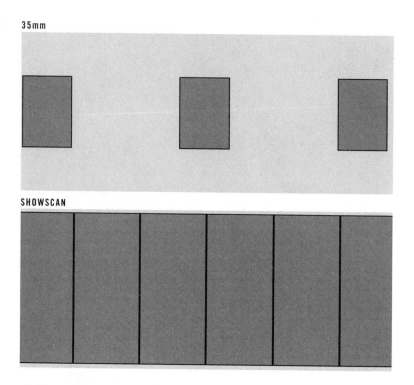

SHOWSCAN

Figure 2-41. VISUAL DENSITY: SHOWSCAN. This telling illustration derived from a Showscan® marketing brochure demonstrates graphically the superior acuity of that process, which delivers about ten times as much visual information (represented by the shaded areas) as conventional 35 mm film. Both strips represent about 1/8 second of viewing. The 70 mm 60 fps Showscan film is photographed at 1/125-second per frame; the 35 mm 24 fps standard film is shot at 1/50-second per frame, so the Showscan image is also sharper. From another point of view, this illustration shows just how little information the standard medium of film communicates. (*Courtesy Showscan.*) Compare Figure 2-42.

Grain is also a function of the gauge or size of the filmstock. A standard frame of 35 mm film has an area of slightly more than half a square inch. If it is projected onto a screen that is forty feet wide, it has to fill an area that is 350,000 times larger than itself—a prodigious task; a frame of 16 mm film (since the stock is a little more than half as wide as 35 mm, the area of the frame is four times smaller), if it were to fill the same screen, would have to be magnified 1.4 million times. The graininess of a filmstock, which might never be noticeable if the frame were enlarged to the 8 x 10-inch size that is a standard in still photography, will be thousands of times more noticeable on a motion picture screen.

The distance between the observer and the image is another factor to consider. From the back row of a very large theater with a small screen, the image of a 35 mm movie might appear in the same perspective as an 8 x 10 print held one foot

35mm

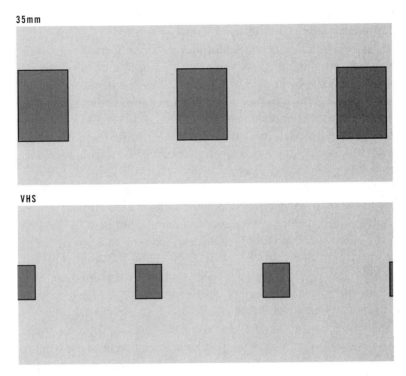

VHS

Figure 2-42. VISUAL DENSITY: VIDEO VERSUS FILM. We have extrapolated the Showscan illustration to suggest the difference between 35 mm film running at 24 frames per second and 525-line American/Japanese video running at 30 fps (or 625-line European video running at 25 fps). The dimensions of the video frames have been calculated to illustrate the poorer resolution of standard video. It is remarkable that we can construct a visual experience with so little information!

in front of the observer. In that case, the grain would appear to be more or less equivalent.

The standard width for motion-picture stock has been 35 mm. Introduced many years ago as suitable only for the amateur filmmaker, 16 mm stock became a useful alternative in the 1960s, as filmstock and processing became more sophisticated. It was used in television film work, especially in Europe, and it is still usable for shooting feature films. The "super 16" format, developed in the early seventies, measurably increased the area of the frame and thus the defini- tion of the image. Both regular and super 16 mm formats are still popular in the world of independent filmmaking. Also, 8 mm film, which had been restricted entirely to amateur use until the 1970s, found some applications in commercial filmmaking for a while, especially in television news and industrial filmmaking. Whatever problems of definition and precision exist in 35 mm are multiplied by a factor of four in 16 mm and by a factor of sixteen in 8 mm, since we are concerned with areas rather than linear dimensions.

By the same arithmetic, a wider filmstock will greatly ameliorate those problems. Hence 70 mm filmstocks are valuable for productions that need a feeling of panoramic detail and power on a large screen. While the possibilities of the wider stocks are intriguing, the increased sophistication of the 16 mm and 8 mm gauges had a greater effect on filmmaking in the 1970s and 1980s because they were so inexpensive: 16 mm stock is two to four times cheaper than 35 mm and therefore opened up filmmaking to a much larger number of potential filmmakers. It not only made it possible for more people to afford to make films, it also meant that more films could be made for the same money, so that professional filmmakers were less reliant on the vagaries of the venture capital market.

Of course, videotape offers still greater economies, but most professional filmmakers are still wedded to chemistry, which continues to maintain its mystical esthetic attraction. Tape has been a viable alternative for filmmakers since the early 1970. And since the videotape revolution of the early 1980s, tape has been the medium via which most viewers experience "films." Yet, the creative personnel in the industry still prefer the physicality and gestalt of old-fashioned film.

Although it didn't survive, the VistaVision of the 1950s suggested two profitable lines of development: first, that the film itself, if it were larger, would permit widescreen photography without loss of clarity. This led to the development of commercial 65 mm and 70 mm stocks.* (Wide stock had been experimented with as early as 1900.) Second, that the system used for photographing the film did not have to be the system used for distribution and projection. Since the 1960s, it has been common to shoot on 35 mm stock while releasing 70 mm prints to those theaters that are equipped to show them. This practice resulted in a slight increase in image quality, but much less than if the film had been shot on wide stock, as well. The main advantage of releasing in 70 mm was the more elaborate stereophonic soundtrack that stock allows. In the 1980s, 70 mm shoots were rare, due to the significant expense (combined with the increased quality of 35 mm stock). Although some films were released in 70 mm in the 1980s, *Far and Away* (1992) was the first U.S. film shot on 70 mm since *Tron* (1982).

Color, Contrast, and Tone

Until the 1970s, the theory persisted that black-and-white film was somehow more honest, more esthetically proper, than color film. Like the idea that silent film was purer than sound film, or the notion that 1.33 was somehow the natural

---

* Wide-stock movies are shot on negative that is actually 65 mm wide; release prints are 70 mm; the additional 5 mm area is used for the stereophonic soundtrack.

Figure 2-43. CONTRAST RANGE. This series of photographic prints displays a wide range of contrasts from very subtle, narrow grays to nearly pure black and white.

ratio of the screen dimensions, this theory of black-and-white supremacy seems to have been invented after the fact, more an excuse than a premise.

This is not to suggest that black-and-white wasn't a great medium for film artists for many years: certainly it was, and it continues to attract the attention of a few ambitious filmmakers, most notably Martin Scorsese (*Raging Bull*, 1980), Woody Allen (*Manhattan*, 1979; *Zelig*, 1983), and Steven Spielberg (*Schindler's List*, 1993). *Pleasantville* (1998) made tension between black-and-white and color its basic esthetic principle. Black-and-white communicates significantly less visual information than color film, and that limitation can have the effect of involving us more deeply in the story, dialogue, and psychology of the film experience instead of the spectacle. From the artist's point of view, the constraint of black-and-white poses a challenge to communicate more with composition, tone, and mise-en-scène.

Yet filmmakers were experimenting with color, as with sound, from the earliest days of cinematography; only the complicated technology of color film held them back. Between 1900 and 1935, dozens of color systems were introduced and some gained moderate success. Many of the "black-and-white" films of the twenties, moreover, used tinted stock to provide a dimension of color. Eastman's Sonochrome catalogue of the late twenties listed such elegant shades as Peachblow, Inferno, Rose Dorée, Candle Flame, Sunshine, Purple Haze, Firelight, Fleur de Lis, Azure, Nocturne, Verdante, Acqua Green, Argent, and Caprice!

It was 1935, however, before the Technicolor three-strip process opened up color photography to the majority of filmmakers.[*] This system used three separate

---

[*] The first Technicolor three-strip film was *La Cucaracha* (1935); the first Technicolor feature was *Becky Sharp*, also in that year.

Figure 2-44. HIGH CONTRAST. Blacks and whites are extreme values; the range of grays between is limited. Ingrid Thulin, Jörgen Lindström in Ingmar Bergman's *The Silence* (1963).

strips of film to record the magenta, cyan, and yellow spectrums. In processing, separate relief matrix films were made from each of these negatives, and then were used to transfer each color to the release print in a process very similar to color ink printing. The three-strip system was soon replaced by the "tri-pack" system, in which all three negatives were combined in layers on one strip.

In 1952 Eastman Kodak introduced a color negative material with a system of masking that improved color renditions in the final print, and Technicolor negatives quickly became obsolete. The Technicolor dye-transfer printing process remained in use, however, since many cinematographers felt that the dye-transfer technique produced better and more precise colors than Eastman's chemical development. The difference between an Eastman chemical print and a Technicolor dye-transfer print is even today evident to professionals. The Technicolor print has a cooler, smoother, more subtle look to it than the Eastman print. Moreover, the dye-transfer print will maintain color values for a far longer time.

Technicolor closed the last of its dye-transfer labs in the U.S. in the late 1970s. The system was regularly employed in China (where Technicolor built a plant

Figure 2-45. LOW CONTRAST. No pure blacks or whites; grays predominate. Romy Schneider in Luchino Visconti's "The Job" (*Boccaccio 70*, 1963).

soon after the recognition of China by the U.S.) until 1992. At almost the same time that the dye-transfer process was being phased out in the Western world, film archivists and technicians were becoming aware of significant problems with the Eastmancolor process. The colors fade very quickly and never in the same relationship to each other. Unless Technicolor dye-transfer prints, or expensive three-strip black-and-white color records have been preserved, most color films of the fifties, sixties, seventies, and eighties will soon deteriorate beyond help—if they haven't already. (Technicolor retooled for dye transfer in the U.S. in 1995 in response to the challenge.)

We think of film as a permanent medium, but that's true more in theory than in practice. You can rent a print today of Michelangelo Antonioni's *Red Desert* (1964), for example, but it's highly unlikely that you'll see the same film that so impressed filmgoers with its visual elan back then. You're likely to wonder what all the fuss was about. (You'll have to trust me: *Red Desert* was a breathtaking exercise in the psychology of color.) You may catch a screening of Terrence Malick's *Days of Heaven* (1978) somewhere, but chances are it won't be in 70 mm, the exquisite colors have faded, of course, and you're likely to walk out yawning.

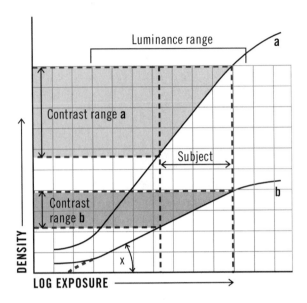

Figure 2-46. GAMMA. The curved line here is called the "characteristic" of a film emulsion. A perfect emulsion would have a characteristic curve which was a straight line. That is, for every equal increase in exposure there would be an equal increase in the density of the negative obtained. No emulsion, however, has such a curve, and most emulsions in use today show a similarly curved line. The area in which the curve is relatively flat is the usable contrast range of the emulsion. More important, the slope of this curve (x) is a measure of the "contrastiness"—or potential contrast—of the emulsion. The emulsion represented by curve a, for example, has a greater potential contrast than that of curve b. In other words, emulsion a will better be able to distinguish between two similar luminance values. The gamma of an emulsion, precisely, is equal to tan x (the tangent of the angle of the slope).

(Trust me again, *Days of Heaven* was an exuberant portrait of the American Midwest, dense with eidetic imagery.)

Preservation problems are not confined to color and format: if you haven't seen a silver-nitrate print (or at least a 35 mm print newly struck from the nitrate negative) of classics like *Citizen Kane* or *The Big Sleep*, you are liable to underestimate seriously the power of the imagery of these films. Indeed, most of the print material now available for films from the 1920s, 1930s, and 1940s is in such poor condition that generations of film students are sentenced to look at film history through a glass, darkly. As we've noted, this is not true of Technicolor classics from the late 1930s and 1940s. New prints of these films come very close to reproducing the original look and feel.

Since the advent of colorization in the mid-1980s, there's an additional problem to deal with: every time you turn on an old movie on television you have to check the history books to see if what you're watching is the original. Newly col-

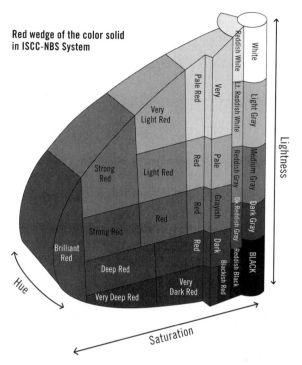

Figure 2-47. The "Color Wedge" graphically illustrates the relationships among the three major variables of color theory. This is a section of the full color solid which covers the entire spectrum.

orized black-and-white films don't look much worse than badly faded original-color films (or poorly preserved black-and-white television prints), but that's not the point. Martin Scorsese and others have united to protest the practice of colorization. It seems to me they don't go far enough: it's just as necessary to restore the magnificent black-and-white nitrates of the 1930s and 1940s and the faded Eastmancolor of the 1950s, 1960s, and 1970s.

Film is subject to these geriatric problems because it is a chemical technology. As electronics replaces chemistry, preservation of the artist's original intent will be much less problematic. Already, laserdiscs have proved a boon to film lovers; once this technology is fully digitized, color, tone, and contrast, too, will be preserved—potentially—forever. Whether or not we can restore the original visuals to the faded relics of the past remains to be seen. "Re-colorization" is an intriguing concept, but color is a distinctly psychological phenomenon: one man's blue is another woman's green (but if you're gay, it may be teal), and memories fade faster than Eastman stock.

Before 1952, black-and-white was the standard format, and color was reserved for special projects. Between 1955 and 1968 the two were about equal in popularity. Since 1968, when much faster, truer color stock became available, color has become the norm and it is a rare American film that is shot in black-and-white. The reasons for this have as much to do with economics as with esthetics. The popularity of color television made it risky for film producers to use black-and-white, since the resale value to television was affected.

If we limit ourselves for the moment to a discussion of black-and-white photography, we can better isolate two other dimensions of filmstock that are significant: contrast and *tone. When we speak of "black-and-white," we are not really talking about a two-color system, but rather about an image deprived entirely of color values. What remains in the "black-and-white" picture are the related variables of contrast and tone: the relative darkness and lightness of the various areas of the image, and the relationship between the darks and the lights.

The retina of the human eye differs from film, first in its ability to accommodate a wide range of brightnesses, and second in its ability to differentiate between two close shades of brightness. Film is a limited medium in both respects. The range of shades of brightness, from pure white to pure black, that a particular filmstock can record is technically referred to as its "latitude." Its ability to differentiate between close shades is called the "gamma" of the film stock. The fewer the number of shades that the stock can separate, the cruder the photograph will be. At its most extreme limit, only black and white will be seen, and the film will represent all the shadings in between as either one or the other. The more ability the stock has to discriminate, the more subtle the tone of the photography. Figure 2-46 shows this graphically: a low-contrast photograph is one in which the scale of tonal values is very narrow. Tone and contrast are closely associated with grain, so that the best range of tonal values is seen in filmstocks with the finest grain and therefore the highest resolution power.

Advances in processing techniques have greatly expanded the latitude of standard filmstocks. Although a particular stock is designed to produce the highest-quality image within certain chemical parameters such as development time, it had become common practice by the late sixties to "push" film in development when greater sensitivity was needed. By developing for a longer time than the standard, a laboratory can effectively stretch the latitude of the stock to make it two or even three times more sensitive than its exposure rating might indicate. Grain increases when this is done, and with color stocks there are extra problems with color rendition, but Eastman Color Negative, for example, has enough inherent latitude so that it can be pushed one stop (doubled in sensitivity) or even two stops (quadrupled) without significant loss in image quality. The greatest loss in sensitivity, as one might expect, occurs at the point in the contrast scale where there is least light available—in the shadows of a scene, for example.

A more sophisticated way to cope with this problem is the technique of flashing. First used by cinematographer Freddie Young for Sidney Lumet's 1967 film *A

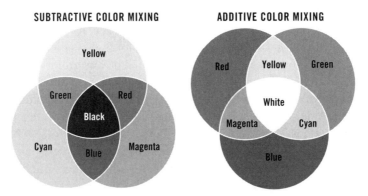

Figure 2-48. PRIMARY COLOR THEORY. For psychological reasons all colors of the visible spectrum can be reproduced by the combination of three so-called "primary" colors. The "additive" primaries are red, blue, and green. The "subtractive" primaries are magenta (red-blue), cyan (blue-green), and yellow. All the colors of the spectrum together produce white light, just as complete absence of color yields black. If both magenta and yellow are subtracted from a beam of white light, the result is red. If both red and green beams are added together, the result is yellow, and so on. There is no mathematical reason for this to be; it's a psychological conundrum.

Deadly Affair, flashing entails exposing the film, before or after the scene is shot, to a neutral density gray light of a predetermined value. By in effect boosting even the darkest areas of the image into that area of the gamma scale where differentiations between close shades are easily made, flashing extends the latitude of any filmstock. It also has the potential advantage of muting color values and thereby giving the filmmaker some measure of control over the color saturation of the image. In 1975 the TVC labs introduced a chemical process called Chemtone (developed by Dan Sandberg, Bernie Newson, and John Concilla) that was a much more sophisticated version of flashing. Chemtone was first used on such films as *Harry and Tonto* (1974), *Nashville* (1975), and *Taxi Driver* (1976).[*]

Contrast, tone, and exposure latitude are all important factors in the matter of film lighting. With the advent of high-speed color filmstock and the techniques of pushing, flashing, and Chemtone, the technology of cinematography reached a point, after more than three-quarters of a century, where film might approximate the sensitivity of the human eye. It is now possible for filmmakers to shoot under almost any conditions in which they can see. But this was hardly the case during the first seventy-five years of film history.

---

[*] The theory behind flashing is very similar to the theory behind the Dolby noise reduction system. See Figure 2-50. (Of course, now all of this is done digitally.)

The earliest black-and-white emulsions were "monochromatic"—sensitive only to blue, violet, and ultraviolet light. By 1873, a way had been found to extend the spectrum of sensitivity to green, the color to which our eyes are most sensitive. This was the so-called Orthochromatic film. Panchromatic film, which responds equally to all the colors of the visible spectrum, was developed in 1903, but it was not until more than twenty years later that it became standard in the film industry. Among the first films to use panchromatic stock were Robert Flaherty's *Moana* (1925) and Cooper and Schoedsack's *Chang* (1926). Without panchromatic film, warm colors, such as facial tones, reproduced very poorly, so the filmmaker had need of a light source in the blue-white range. Besides the sun itself, the only source of this kind of light was the huge, expensive arc lamp. As black-and-white stock became more sensitive and panchromatic emulsions were introduced, cheaper and more mobile incandescent lamps became usable; but when filmmakers began working with color, they had to return to arc lamps—both because the color stock was much slower and because it became necessary, once again, to maintain strict control of the "color temperature" of the light source.

Color temperature, or hue, is only one of the variables that must be calculated for color stock in addition to brightness, tone, and contrast. The others are saturation and intensity. The range of visible hues runs from deep red (the warmest) to deep violet (the coolest), through orange, yellow, green, blue, and indigo. The saturation of the color is a measure of its amount—the same hue of a color can be either weak or strong; the intensity, or lightness, is a measure of the amount of light transmitted (color shares this element with black-and-white).

As with contrast and latitude in black-and-white photography, the filmmaker has only limited parameters within which to work in color. The source of the light used to illuminate the subject, until recently, had to be rigidly controlled. We make unconscious adjustments for the color temperature of a light source, but the filmmaker must compensate for these variations directly. A color stock balanced for 6000° Kelvin (the color temperature of an overcast sky) will produce an annoyingly orange picture if used with standard incandescent light sources with a color temperature of 3200°K. Likewise, a stock balanced for 3200°K will produce a very blue image when used outdoors under a 5000°K or 6000°K sky. As amateur photographers know, filters can be used to adjust for these imbalances.

The Soundtrack

Before examining the post-production phase of filmmaking—editing, mixing, laboratory work, and projection—we should investigate the production of sound.

Ideally, the sound of a film should be equal in importance with the image. Sadly, however, sound technology in film lags far behind not only the development of cinematography but also the technology of sound recording that has developed independently from film.

The recording of sound is roughly parallel to the recording of images: the microphone is, in effect, a lens through which sound is filtered; the recorder compares roughly with the camera; both sound and picture are recorded linearly and can be edited later. But there is one significant difference: because of the contrasting manners in which we perceive them, sound must be recorded continuously, while pictures are recorded discretely. The concept of "persistence of vision" does not have an aural equivalent, which is one reason why we don't have "still sounds" to compare with still pictures. Sound must exist in time.

A corollary of this is that we cannot apply sound recording devices to aural information in the same way we can apply cinematography to visual information. Film can stretch or compress time, which is useful scientifically, but sound must exist in time, and it is pointless to compress or stretch it. Sound was digitized as early as the 1970s. Digital recordings can be played back at a faster or slower rate, but generally when we change the speed of a recording we change the quality of the sound as well.

The union of sound and image, the original dream of the inventors of cinematography, was delayed for technological and economic reasons until the late 1920s. So long as image was recorded in a linear, discontinuous mode and sound was recorded in a circular, continuous mode, the problem of synchronization of sound and image was insurmountable. Lee DeForest's audion tube, invented in 1906, made it possible for the first time to translate sound signals into electrical signals. The electrical signals could then be translated into light signals that could be imprinted on film. Then the two prints—sound and image—being parallel, could easily be "married" together so that they were always and forever synchronous, even if the film broke and had to be spliced. This was essentially the German Tri-Ergon system that was patented as early as 1919. This optical sound system has existed more or less unchanged to the present.

For twenty years after the sound film was born in 1926, filmmakers were hampered by the bulky and noisy electromechanical equipment necessary to record sound on the set. Even though portable optical recorders were soon available, recording on location was discouraged. In the late forties, however, the technology of film took another quantum leap with the development of magnetic recording. Tape is easier to work with than film, more compact, and, thanks to transistors, the recording devices themselves are now small and lightweight. Magnetic tape, in general, also produces a much better quality signal than an optical soundtrack does. Today, magnetic recording has entirely replaced optical recording on the set, although the optical soundtrack is still more common than the magnetic soundtrack in theaters. There is good reason for this: optical soundtracks can be printed quickly and easily along with image tracks, while magnetic soundtracks must be recorded separately. Developments in optical soundtrack technology, moreover, suggest that some of the advantages that magnetic recording now enjoys over optical recording might be matched: variable-density and variable-hue optical soundtracks could eliminate the effects of rough handling, providing a higher fidelity, and could also be adapted to stereophonic and multiphonic systems. Because of its advantages in handling, editing, and mixing, however, magnetic tape remains the medium of choice on the set and in the laboratory.

The microphone, the lens of the sound system, acts as the first gate through which the signal passes. Unlike the optical lens, however, it also translates the signal into electronic energy, which can then be recorded magnetically on tape. (Playback systems work exactly the reverse: magnetic potential energy is translated into electrical energy which is further translated into physical sound by the loudspeaker.) Since sound is being recorded on a tape physically separate from the filmed image, there must be some method of synchronizing the two. This is accomplished either by a direct mechanical linkage, or by electrical cable connections that carry a timed impulse, or by a crystal sync generator, which produces a precisely timed pulse by using crystal clocks. This pulse regulates the speeds of the two separate motors, keeping them precisely in sync. The sound record is then transferred to magnetically coated film, where the sprocket holes provide the precise control over timing that is necessary in the editing process. Finally, the print of the film that is projected carries the signal, usually in the optical mode, but sometimes magnetically. Stereophonic and "quintaphonic" sound systems common to 70 mm systems almost always use magnetic tracks.

The variables that contribute to the clear and accurate reproduction of sound are roughly comparable to the variables of filmstock. The factor of amplitude can be compared to the exposure latitude of filmstock: the amplitude is the measure of the strength of a signal. Tape, recorder, and microphone working in concert should be able to reproduce a wide range of amplitudes, from very soft to very loud.

Next in importance is the frequency range, directly comparable to the scale of hues reproducible in color film. The normal range of frequencies to which the ear responds is 20 to 20,000 Hertz (cycles per second). Good high-fidelity recording equipment can reproduce this range adequately, but optical playback systems have a much more limited range of frequency response (100 to 7,000 Hertz, on the average).

The recording medium and the equipment should also be able to reproduce a wide range of harmonics, those subtones that give body and life to music and voices. The harmonics of sound can be compared to the tonal qualities of an

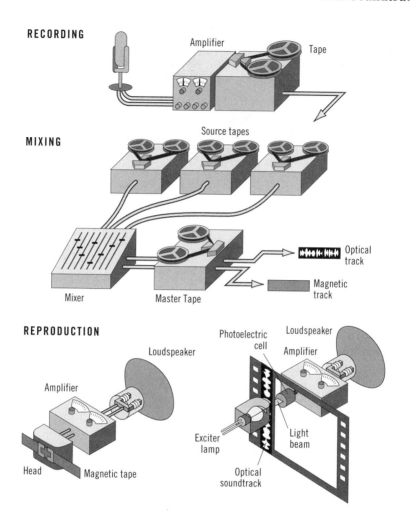

RECORDING

MIXING

REPRODUCTION

Figure 2-49. SOUND. Tracks from several sources (A) (dialogue, music, and effects, for example) are mixed to produce a master tape (B) which is then used to produce the actual soundtrack, which is usually optical, sometimes magnetic. The magnetic track is read by the electromagnetic head which senses variations in the magnetic signal (C). The optical soundtrack is read by a photoelectric cell which senses variations in the amount of light transmitted through the soundtrack. The exciter lamp is the uniform light source.

image. The signal should be free from wow, flutter, and other kinds of mechanical distortion, and the equipment should have a satisfactory response time: that is, the ability to reproduce sounds of short duration without mushiness. This is the "resolution" of the sound signal.

While stereoscopic images are subject to special psychological and physical problems that significantly reduce their value, stereophonic sound is relatively free of these problems and therefore highly desirable. We are used to hearing sound from every direction. Although we engage in selective attention to sounds, we don't focus directly on a sound the way we focus on an image. Film sound should have the ability to reproduce the total aural environment.

In the 1970s, the assimilation of multitrack recording techniques developed in the music industry expanded the horizons of the art of film sound—for example, such highly sophisticated soundtracks as Coppola's *The Conversation* (1974) and Altman's *Nashville* (1975), produced on an eight-track system. The application of Dolby techniques of noise reduction and signal enhancement in the mid-seventies greatly increased the potential fidelity of film sound as well. Roughly comparable to the flashing of filmstock, the Dolby electronic circuitry reduces the background noise inherent in even the best tape stock, thereby significantly enhancing the latitude. It does this by selecting out the area of the sound spectrum in which the noise occurs and boosting the signal level in that area during recording. When the signal is reduced to normal levels during playback, the noise is reduced along with the audio signal.

For years film sound technology had lagged behind home audio technology. Many films were released with monophonic tracks long after stereo became the standard for records. Beginning in the 1980s, however, theater owners began to pay more attention to quality sound reproduction. Dolby and Sony led the way with ingenious schemes for recording multitrack sound on basic filmstock. George Lucas's THX system set the standard for advanced sound systems. By the mid-1990s sophisticated sound reproduction had become a major marketing advantage for theater chains.

Post-Production

Film professionals divide the process of their art into three phases: preproduction, shooting, and post-production. The first phase is preparatory—the script is written, actors and technicians hired, shooting schedules and budgets planned. In another art, this period of preparation would be relatively uncreative. But Alfred Hitchcock, for one, regarded this period of the film process as paramount: once he had designed the film, he used to say, its execution was comparatively boring. Moreover, in this most expensive of arts, intelligent and accurate planning often spells the difference between success and failure. It must be clear by now that making films is a complicated business—so much so that modern systems design has had a measurably positive effect on the process. The elaborate, carefully orga-

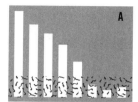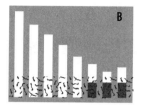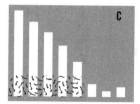

Figure 2-50. THE DOLBY EFFECT. A certain amount of basic surface noise is inherent in any recording medium (A). It presents no problem when the level of the recorded signal is high enough, but it masks out the weaker parts of the signal. The Dolby system boosts the weaker signal during recording (B), then reduces it to its proper level during playback, thus reducing the recorded surface noise along with it (C).

nized systems Stanley Kubrick created for his film projects, for example, were one of the more intriguing aspects of his work.

Nearly all the discussion in this chapter on film technology has so far centered on the second phase of film production: shooting. Yet there is a sense in which this area of the process can be seen as preparatory, too. Shooting produces the raw materials that are fashioned into finished products only in the third stage of the process. Editing is often regarded as the fulcrum of film art, since it is in this process that film most clearly separates itself from competing arts. The theory of film editing will be discussed in Chapters 3 and 5; here we will outline the practice and describe the equipment involved. Three jobs generally proceed more or less concurrently during post-production: editing; sound mixing, augmentation, and looping (or ADR); and laboratory work, opticals, and special effects. A film could conceivably be edited, mixed, and printed within a few hours; assuming both the sound track and the picture in their raw state were satisfactory, the editing would be simply a matter of splicing a few takes end to end. But very few films are this simple, and post-production work often takes longer than the actual shooting of the film. Although it is called "post-production," the work often begins during the shoot and runs concurrently.

Editing

The shot is the basic unit of film construction; it is defined, physically, as a single piece of film, without breaks in the continuity of the action. It may last as long as ten minutes (since most cameras only hold ten minutes of film); it may be as short as 1/24 second (one frame). Hitchcock's *Rope* (1948) was shot to appear as if it were one continuous take, and most of Miklós Jancsó's films are composed of full-reel shots (ten or twelve per film), but the standard fictional feature is comprised of as many as five hundred or a thousand separate shots. Each of the shots must be physically spliced with cement or tape to the shots that precede and follow it.* The craft of editing consists of choosing between two or more takes of the same shot, deciding how long each shot should last and how it should be punctuated, and matching the soundtrack carefully with the edited images (or vice versa, if the soundtrack is edited first).

In America, until the mid-sixties, this work was accomplished on an upright editing machine generically known by the major brand name, Moviola. Another, much more versatile configuration—the horizontal, or flat-bed, editing table— had been pioneered by the UFA studios in Germany in the twenties and was widely used throughout Europe before World War II. Because the film rested horizontally on plates in the table configuration rather than vertically on reels, it was much easier to handle. The development after the war of the revolving prism to replace the intermittent-motion pull-down mechanism further enhanced the versatility of the editing table, allowing speeds up to five times the normal twenty-four frames per second.

During the sixties, partly due to the influence of documentary filmmakers who were among the first to recognize its great advantages, the editing table (Steenbeck and Kem were two important brand names) revolutionized the process of montage. The more modern editing tables also permitted instantaneous comparison of as many as four separate picture and sound tracks, thereby vastly shortening the time needed to make a choice of shots. Documentarians, who often have huge amounts of footage to examine while editing, saw the advantages immediately. The editors of the film *Woodstock* (1970), for example, were confronted with hundreds of hours of footage of that epochal concert. Even using split-screen techniques as they did, it was necessary to edit that raw material down to four hours, a feat that would have been very difficult indeed without the speed and multiple abilities of the editing table. A normal fictional feature might be shot at a ratio of ten to one (or more): that is, ten feet of film shot for every foot finally used.

Of course, the mechanics of the editing process are greatly simplified if the images are digitized. CBS introduced the first computerized editing system in the mid-seventies. The price was $1 million. By the late eighties, microcomputer-based editing systems like the Avid, twenty to fifty times cheaper, were revolutionizing the art of editing once again. By the mid-1990s, computer-based editing dominated this tedious and time-consuming art. (After the digitized film is edited on the computer, the actual negative is cut and spliced to match—unless, of course, the final cut is going straight to digital videotape.)

Interestingly, the software programs adopted the metaphor of the editing table, so conversations between editors sound much the same as they did in the past.

---

* This is true even if the film has been edited digitally. The Edit Decision List provides a map for physically cutting and splicing the negative.

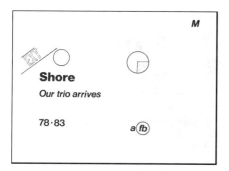

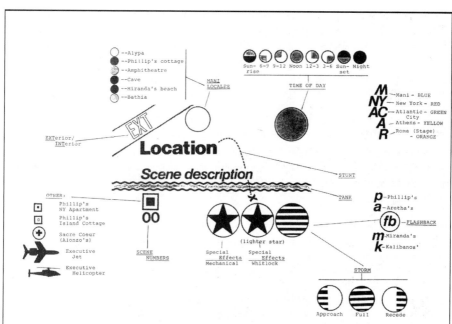

Figure 2-51. PREPRODUCTION. These storyboard sketches by Leon Capetanos for Paul Mazursky's *Tempest* (1982) suggest the structure of the sequence. The key follows. (*Courtesy Paul Mazursky.*)

Figure 2-52A. Flatbed editing tables, such as the Steenbeck pictured here, permitted comparisons between as many as three or four picture and sound tracks. This particular table is set up for one picture track and two soundtracks. (*W. Steenbeck and Co.*)

Despite the versatility and flexibility of computer-based editing, digitization does add several layers of complexity, and editors now must worry about "timecodes" (which match the digital images to the film frames) and "Edit Decision Lists" (which record the various editorial choices), as well as all the technology of microcomputers. So there are still some oldtimers who maintain they can do a better job on an old-fashioned table: feeling the stock as it runs through their fingers, and sensing rhythms from the whirring reels.

Mixing and Looping

The editing of a soundtrack differs somewhat from the editing of images. First, for various reasons, the sound recorded on the set at the same time as the picture may not be usable. While a bad take of the picture is totally useless and must be reshot, a bad take of the sound can be much more easily repaired or replaced. In the process called post-dubbing, or looping, a few seconds of film are formed into a loop that is projected in a sound studio and repeated many times so the actors can catch the rhythm of the scene and then mouth their dialogue in synchronization with the image. This is then recorded and spliced into the original soundtrack. During the eighties, this process began to be glorified in credits with

Figure 2-52B. Computer editing suites, such as the Avid, shown here, try to mimic the physical setup of the old editing tables. Comparisons are quicker and much more flexible.

the acronym "ADR," for "additional dialogue recording," but the method has remained the same since the advent of talkies.

This process was formerly much more common than it is today because sound recording techniques have been vastly simplified by the introduction of magnetic tape. On-location recording has become the rule rather than the exception. It remained the practice in Italy, however, to post-dub the entire film. Federico Fellini, for one, was renowned for occasionally not even bothering to write dialogue until after the scene had been shot, directing his actors instead to recite numbers (but with feeling!).

Post-dubbing has generally been a useful technique for translating films into other languages. Usually, a soundtrack produced this way has a noticeable deadness and awkwardness to it, but the Italians, as might be expected, since their practice is to post-dub all films, have produced some quite passable foreign-language dubbing jobs.

Once the tedious job of dubbing has been completed, the soundtrack can be mixed. This process has no real equivalent with images for, although split-screen techniques and multiple exposures can present us with more than one image at a time, those multiple images are seldom combined. Matte techniques and rear projection (see below) offer more directly comparable equivalents to sound mixing, but they are relatively rarely used. This may change, as computers become as essential to film editors as they are to writers. Once it's as easy to edit digital images as it now is to edit digital sounds, the editor may become a "mixer" as well,

Figure 2-53. CEL ANIMATION. Classical animation uses the cel technique for efficiency and accuracy. The image is divided into layers of movement and each of those layers is drawn on a separate transparent sheet called a "cel" (from "celluloid"). Thus, the stationary background need be drawn only once for a scene, simple movements can be executed rapidly, and special attention can be paid to isolated, complex movements. In this scene from R. O. Blechman's *The Life and Times of Nicholas Nickleby* (1982), four cels (A-D) are overlaid on the background (E). The elements are divided into groups according to the action. (*Designed by Seymour Chwast/Push Pin Studios. Courtesy of The Ink Tank.*)

combining picture elements within the frame with the same ease he or she now joins shots end to end.

By 1932, sound technology had developed to the point where rerecording was common, and it was possible to mix as many as four optical tracks. For many years, mixing consisted simply of combining prerecorded music, sound effects (a crude term for a sophisticated craft), and dialogue. However, in the 1960s the multiple-track magnetic recorder greatly expanded the potential of sound mixing.

Figure 2-54. EARLY COMPUTER ANIMATION. Since animation involves managing large quantities of data, computers have proven invaluable. The early programs, of varying degrees of sophistication, could take simple cels though their animated paces, as in this compressed history of evolution from Carl Sagan's *Cosmos* (1980). The drawing moves continuously and smoothly from stage to stage, a wonder at the time. The difference between these stick figures and the lifelike herds of dinosaurs integrated seamlessly into the live action in *Jurassic Park* measures the explosive growth of computing power in the 1980s. (*James Blinn, Pat Cole, Charles Kohlhase, Jet Propulsion Laboratories Computer Graphics Lab.*)

A single word or sound effect was easily spliced in (this was difficult with optical soundtracks), the quality of the sound could be modified, reinforced, or altered in many different ways electronically, and dozens of separate tracks could be combined, with the sound mixer in total control of all the esthetic variables of each track.

In the nineties the art of sound mixing and editing was quickly digitized. Digital tape recorders joined their analog predecessors on the set, while mixing and editing moved to the computer. Since the audio industry had converted to the digital distribution format of the CD in the 1980s, it isn't surprising that the art of film sound is now thoroughly digital. As with digital film editing, the old metaphors have been retained, and—yes—there are oldtimers who still think they can do a better job with analog pots and panels. Yet, by the early 1990s, this formerly arcane technology was familiar to most kids with computers, who quickly filled up hard discs with their own attempts at audio art.

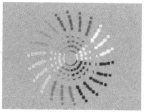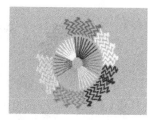

Figure 2-55. MATHEMATICAL ANIMATION. Beginning in the 1960s, John Whitney and others first explored abstract computerized animation with oscillographic compositions like this. They established a style of mathematical imagery that has become a common thread of contemporary design, as the power of the microcomputer brought similar tools to every desktop. These frames are from a recent effort, "Moon Drum," 1992. (*Frame enlargements, courtesy John Whitney.*)

Special Effects

"Special effects" is a rather dull label for a wide variety of activities, each of which has direct creative potential. The craft of special effects rests on three premises: (1) film need not be shot continuously, each frame can be photographed separately; (2) drawings, paintings, and models can be photographed in such a way that they pass for reality; (3) images can be combined.

The first premise makes possible the art of animation. The precursors of animation were the Zoetrope and the age-old "flip book," in which a series of drawings were bound together so that if the pages were flipped quickly the image appeared to move. But animation is not dependent on drawings, even though most animated films are cartoons. Models and even living figures can be animated by photographing frames individually and changing the position of the subject between frames. This animation technique is called "pixillation." As for cartoon animation, the cel technique in which various sections of the cartoon are drawn on separate transparent sheets (cels) makes the process much more flexible than one might at first think. Approximately 14,400 separate drawings must be made for a ten-minute animated film, but if the background remains constant then it can be painted on a separate cel and the artist need draw only those subjects that are meant to be seen in motion.

Since the 1960s, computer video techniques have made animation even more flexible, since a computer can be programmed to produce a wide variety of drawings instantaneously and to change their shape accurately and with proper timing. Until the late eighties, computer animation was the province of the professional. Now, as with so many of the hitherto proprietary techniques of the film industry, animation has become a familiar tool to scores of thousands of office workers who routinely add animations to their "desktop presentations."

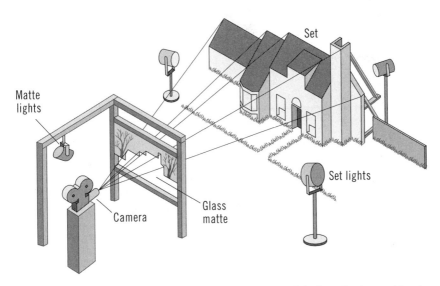

Figure 2-56. GLASS SHOTS. The bottom part of the glass is left clear; the top part has been painted. The glass is situated far enough from the camera so that both it and the set are in focus. Set lights and matte lights are adjusted to balance. The camera is mounted on a solid base to prevent vibration.

The second premise yields a series of special effects known as miniature or model shots and glass shots. The success of miniature photography depends on our ability to run the camera at faster than normal speeds (called "overcranking"). A two-inch wave, traveling at normal speed but photographed at four times normal speed, will appear to be approximately four times larger when it is projected at the standard rate (and therefore slowed down by a factor of four). The rule of thumb in miniature photography is that the camera speed be the square root of the scale; that is, a quarter-scale model will require a camera speed twice normal. In practice, the smallest miniatures that work are 1/16-size, and even 1/4-size miniatures present some problems of verisimilitude.

Glass shots are possibly the simplest of special effects. The technique involves placing a glass several feet in front of the camera and in effect painting over the area of the scene that must be changed. The effect depends of course on the talent of the painter, but surprisingly realistic examples of this simple technique exist.

The third premise is possibly the most fruitful for contemporary filmmakers. The simplest way to make use of the idea is to project another image—the background—on a screen behind the actors and the foreground. Thousands of Hollywood taxi rides were filmed this way by the aid of rear projection, introduced in 1932. (See Figure 2-57.) The advent of color made rear projection obsolete, how-

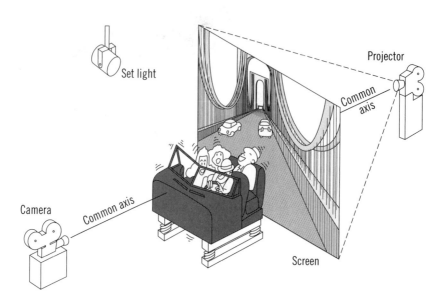

Figure 2-57. REAR PROJECTION. Camera and projector are interlocked so that the projector projects a frame at precisely the same time the camera takes one. The actors in the car mock-up in front of the screen are lit in such a way that the translucent screen behind them does not reflect; it only transmits the light from the projector. Note the springs which support the car mock-up in order to simulate movement.

ever. Color photography required a greater amount of light on the subject, which tended to wash out the rear-projected image. More important, the color image provides more visual information, which makes it much more difficult to match foreground and background. Two techniques were developed to replace rear projection.

Front projection utilizes a directional screen composed of millions of tiny glass beads that act as lenses, which enable the screen to reflect as much as 95 percent of the light falling on it back to the source. As can be seen in Figure 2-58, this requires that the source be on the same axis as the camera lens, a position that also eliminates shadows on the screen. This positioning is achieved by using a half-silvered mirror set at a 45° angle. Front projection was perfected for Stanley Kubrick's *2001: A Space Odyssey* (1968). (That film, in fact, remains a catalogue of modern special effects.)

Glass shots and rear and front projection are techniques that combine images and are accomplished on the set. Matte shots and blue screen (or traveling matte) shots, however, are produced in the laboratory. Stationary matte shots produce an effect similar to the glass shot. In the laboratory, the film is projected on a white card and the artist outlines the area to be matted out and paints it black.

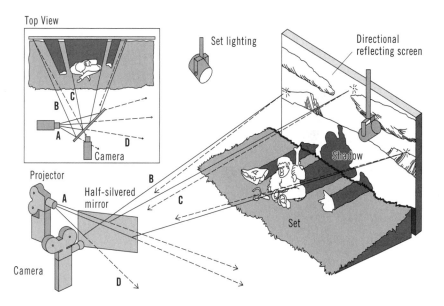

Figure 2-58. FRONT PROJECTION. The essential element of the front projection system is the half-silvered mirror, which both transmits and reflects light. This makes it possible for the projector to project the background image onto the screen behind the set and actor along precisely the same axis that the camera views the scene. Thus, the camera cannot see the shadows which the actor and set cast on the screen. Set lighting is adjusted so that it is just bright enough to wash out the background image which falls on the actor and set. The screen is highly directional, reflecting a great deal more light from the projected image along the axis than off to the side and thus providing a bright enough image. The projected scene travels from the projector (A), is reflected off the half-silvered mirror onto the screen (and set and actor) (B), and then back into the camera, through the mirror (C). Some of the light from the projector is also transmitted through the mirror (D). See the final effect below.

Figure 2-59. Front projection from *2001*. Kubrick and his staff of special effects technicians perfected the system for the film. (*Frame enlargement.*)

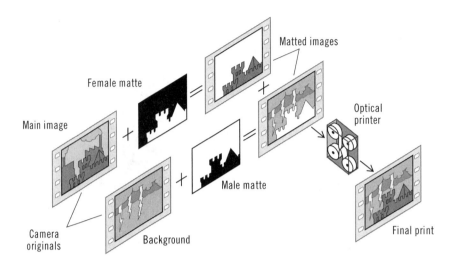

Figure 2-60. MATTES. Both male and female mattes are derived from the main image. In the stationary matte technique they are drawn; in the traveling matte system, diagramed here, the mattes are derived optically.

This black outline (see Figure 2-60) is then photographed, and the film, after it is developed, is packed together with the original shot in the projector and a copy is made in which the proper area is matted out in each frame. The scene to be added to this area (together with a reversal of the first matte) is then printed onto the copy of the original scene, and the print is developed.

Traveling matte shots replaced front and rear projection shots and came into use when color film began to dominate the industry. The process, essentially, is this: a deep blue screen is placed behind the foreground action, and the scene is photographed. Because the background color is uniform and precise, "male" and "female" mattes can be made by copying the film through filters. A blue filter would let through only the background light, leaving the foreground action blank and producing a "female" matte; a red filter would block out the background and expose only the foreground, producing a black silhouette, the "male" matte. The female matte can then be used, as in the stationary matte technique, to block out the blue background when a copy of the original film is made, the male matte will block out precisely the right areas of the background scene that has been chosen, and the matted background and matted foreground can then be combined. This is a difficult and exacting process in film, but the technique has been carried over to television, where it is called "chroma key," and there it can be achieved electronically simply by pressing a button. It has become a basic tool of television, used constantly in news and sports to integrate the announcer with the action.

Figure 2-61. A matte shot from *2001*. The scenery of the moon was matted in. The images on the tiny screens below the windows were rear-projected. (*Frame enlargement.*)

Figure 2-62. A model shot of the moon landing station from *2001*. The small portholes in the model spherical landing capsule as well as the bright rectangular areas to the left and right were matted with live-action scenes to increase the illusion of the model. Most of the exquisite detail is lost in this reproduction. (*Frame enlargement.*)

Here, as just about everywhere else in post-production, computer programs are rapidly replacing the meticulous and painstaking mechanical techniques developed by filmmakers over the years to adjust and modify the images their cameras have captured. Combining foregrounds and backgrounds by matting is now something that any accomplished desktop publisher can do. And filmmakers themselves have taken the next logical step, actually modeling or transforming at will the images they have shot. These transformations are called "morphs"; they were introduced to general audiences in James Cameron's *Terminator 2* (1991) (although they had been used to great effect in television commercials before then). Within eighteen months, similar software was available to anyone with a Macintosh for less than $100.

Opticals, the Lab, and the Post House

Traditionally, the laboratory has performed two basic jobs for the filmmaker: the first is to adjust the image so that it more closely approximates what the filmmaker had in mind while shooting; the second is to add a number of effects called "opticals," usually for purposes of punctuation.

In color work, the role of the laboratory is critical. While the brain automatically and unconsciously corrects for variations in lighting and color, film does not. The laboratory technician must "time" the print, adjusting the colors of various scenes shot at different times and under widely varying conditions to conform to some agreed-upon standard. As we have already noted, some compensation can be made for differences in the color temperature of the light source during filming, yet timing is almost always necessary. At the same time, the lab might have to correct for under- or overexposure by over- or underdeveloping the filmstock. To save footage that might otherwise be unusable, the film can also be flashed at this point. Some methods of flashing have been tried (notably by Gerry Turpin for *Young Winston*, 1973) that add a wash of color to the print at this point. This is a return to one of the oldest devices in film history, for black-and-white films of the twenties were often printed on tinted stock to add emotional value to a scene.

In addition to timing the print and correcting for exposure differences, the laboratory also executes a number of punctuational devices known collectively as "opticals," including fades, wipes, dissolves, freezes, and masks. These are discussed in detail in the next chapter. A number of other optical effects are available. Ghosts (visual echoes achieved by double-printing frames), multiple images (split-screen and the like), and superimpositions (double exposures) are the most common.

Finally, the laboratory is equipped to enlarge or reduce the size of the image. The whole film might be enlarged or reduced so that it can be released in a different gauge, or a single shot might be altered by enlarging part of it on the optical printer, the machine on which most of these effects are accomplished. When a Panavision print is prepared for television, for example, a technique known as "pan and scan" is used so that at least the major part of the action shows up within the 1.33 television frame. As the film is printed down to the Academy aperture, artificial cuts and pans from one side of the widescreen image to the other are added on the optical printer.

When they are accomplished mechanically and optically, nearly all these laboratory effects add extra generations to the printing process and therefore affect the quality of the image. This is one reason the laboratory has largely been replaced by the "Post House"—an all-digital center for post-production.

When the second edition of this book was completed in 1981, the techniques and vocabulary of the film editor, sound mixer, and special-effects technician were as arcane and mysterious to the average reader as the professional lingo of printers and publishers then was. Now, the remarkable microcomputer revolution of the past twenty years has made fades and flip wipes as familiar as fonts and folios. The work of the filmmaker—like that of the publisher—is no longer so mysterious. Indeed, it is so easy for newcomers to accomplish these effects that they may wonder what all the fuss was about.

Yet, as far as the filmmakers themselves are concerned, the revolution has only begun. All of this difficult work is so much easier when you're dealing with a digitized image that the transformation from chemically based cinematography to electronic imaging seems irresistible. The art of film, as we have known it, is now embarked on a relentless morph to digital cinematography and worlds beyond.

Video and Film

The technologies of television and videotape will be discussed in more detail in Chapter 6, but here we can examine the marriage that has taken place between film and television. For many years the relationship was subdued, but that has now changed. In nearly every stage of film production, from preparation to shooting to post-production, video now serves useful functions.

The most obvious advantage of videotape over film is that tape is immediately available for review; it need not be processed first. In addition, whereas the camera operator is the only person who has a clear view of the image while a film is being shot, a video image can be instantaneously transmitted to a number of monitors. As a result, videotape has found a number of applications on the set. It frees the operator from the camera, as in the Louma process described above. In normal cinematography, a video camera can be attached to a film camera by means of a semireflecting mirror, and can see the same image the operator sees. The director (and other technicians) can then observe on a monitor elsewhere on the set the precise image being shot. If the scene is taped, it can immediately be played back so that actors and technicians can check to make sure the take went as planned, thus greatly reducing the need for additional takes.

As we've seen, video has its most revolutionary effect in the editing process. Digital editing is ideally quicker and simpler than the physical splicing of film. A film can be transferred easily to disk for editing with one section of the computer's memory being reserved for frame numbers. Once the file has been edited satisfactorily, the frame numbers can be recalled, providing a foolproof guide for the actual splicing of the film. Computer technology allows an editor to put together a sequence of shots instantaneously, ask the computer to remember the sequence, then "recut" it just as quickly, compare the two versions, and recall the one that is most effective. The problem of storage and retrieval of thousands of pieces of film is vastly simplified. Disk storage of the electronic signal offers immediate random access to any shot.

While film-to-tape transfer has been in wide use in television almost since its inception (a production is shot on film, then transferred to tape for exhibition), the reverse process (shooting on tape for transfer to film) is only now finding applications. Before the development of videotape, the only means of preserving a live television show was to film it as it appeared on a monitor—the "kinescope." Anyone who has seen one of these records is familiar with their poor quality. But a much sharper video image, especially produced for tape-to-film transfer and enhanced by electronic techniques, can provide quite a serviceable film image. As long ago as 1971, Frank Zappa shot *200 Motels* on videotape using a system that offered 2,000 lines of resolution, significantly greater than even today's HDTV and a serious competitor to 35 mm film.

With hindsight, we now understand that the development of electronic techniques of recording images and sounds was a necessary prelude to the true revolution: digitization. Once these remarkable evocations of reality are quantified, they reach a level of abstraction that allows us to manipulate them as we will, effortlessly. Both the technical and moral equations of filmmaking change radically. Most of the techniques we have discussed in this chapter are vastly simplified in the electronic digital world we have now entered. Morally, this profound new technical power means that we can no longer place the same trust in the images and sounds as we have done for the past hundred years. Once filmmakers have near total control over the recording, they are no longer dependent on reality as the source of the images and sounds. What we see is not necessarily what they shot, but rather what they wanted to shoot, or imagined that they might have shot, or determined, later, that they should have shot.

Figure 2-63. VIDEOASSIST.
Directors increasingly rely on video on the set, sometimes even using the monitor instead of the camera eyepiece to frame a shot. Video playback permits an immediate review of the shot, saving time and money. The monitor is often the hub of the set, with cast and crew rushing to gather round to see the immediate results of their work. (A) An Aaton VR42 black-and-white CCD videoassist installed on an Aaton XTR Plus camera. (B) A view of the inside of the video-tap. (*Courtesy Abel Cine Tech.*)

Projection

One final step remains before the chain of film technology is complete: projection. This is, in a way, the most crucial step, since all the work done in the earlier stages must funnel through this one before a film reaches an observer. Ironically, the film projector is the single piece of film equipment that has changed least during the past fifty years. Except for the addition of the optical or magnetic head, which reads the soundtrack, and adapters necessary to project anamorphic prints, the projector is basically the same machine used in the early 1920s. Indeed, some projectionists think antique machines from the thirties work better than many manufactured today.

Any projector is, simply, a camera that operates in the reverse mode: instead of taking a picture, it shows it—but this one difference is significant. The amount of light necessary to record an image is easily obtained, while the even larger amount of light necessary to project a picture must be provided by a source small enough to fit behind the lens of the projector, and it must be able to enlarge the 1/2-square-inch 35 mm frame 300,000 times or more to fill the screen. Until the 1960s, the light source of commercial projectors was a carbon arc lamp that could provide the intense light of 5000° or 6000° K that is necessary. An arc of high-voltage current between two carbon rods was the direct source. The difficulty with the carbon arc lamp (the same sort used to illuminate sets in earlier days) was that the carbon rods were consumed in the process and had to be continually

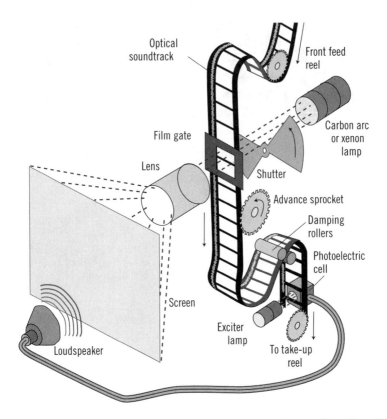

Figure 2-64. STANDARD PROJECTOR. The smaller sprocket wheels pull the film off the feed reel and feed it to the take-up reel. The main sprocket advances the film intermittently. It is connected to the Maltese Cross gear (see Figure 2-21). A series of rollers damps the intermittent motion of the film before it reaches the sound head, so that the soundtrack can be read continuously and smoothly.

adjusted. In addition, the lamps needed powerful ventilation systems. Carbon arc lamps were replaced by xenon lamphouses, which last longer, need not be continually adjusted, and don't require special ventilation.

While a film negative runs only once through a camera and once through an optical printer, the print of a film is subjected to far more stress, normally being run thirty-five or forty times per week in a commercial movie theater. This is the second salient difference between camera and projector: the latter must treat the film more gently. Because so few advances have been made in projector design, however, prints are subjected to much unnecessary damage. The result is that you very seldom see a film exactly the way its authors intended. A writer can be fairly sure that his publisher and printer will represent his intentions to his reader; a filmmaker has no such assurance from distributors and exhibitors. Damage to the

Figure 2-65. MODERN FLATBED PROJECTOR. The feed and take-up reels have been replaced by angled rollers which feed the film from large open reels installed on the platters to the left. Fewer reel changes means projectionists can handle several theaters at once; hence, the multiplexes. (*Courtesy Magnasync Moviola Company.*)

film means that splices will be made excising parts of the film. Cuts are also made simply to shorten the running time (as well as to eliminate politically or sexually objectionable material). A reader knows if a copy of a book has been altered: page numbers will be missing. A film viewer seldom knows just what relationship the print he is seeing bears to the original. Film is often thought to be a permanent medium: on the contrary, it is exceptionally fragile.

There are better ways to do this job. In the 1970s, the Hollogon Rotary projection system—the first radical redesign of projection machinery in seventy-five years—promised a considerable advance. The Hollogon system utilized a revolving twenty-four-sided prism like those used in high-speed cameras and modern editing tables to reduce strain on the print. Instead of a complicated system of sprocket wheels, pull-down mechanisms, damping rollers, and sound heads, the Hollogon projector consisted simply of two continuously revolving wheels, constantly in sync. As the frame image moved around the picture wheel, it was kept optically steady on the screen by the multifaceted prism.

Besides keeping the projector in working order, the projectionist has two other responsibilities: to keep the image in focus and, through a proper combination of lenses and masks, to show the film in the proper aspect ratio. Standards are as slack here as elsewhere in projection. Although scientifically precise means of focusing are readily available (and at one time were usually found in projection booths), the average contemporary projectionist prefers to improvise, relying on the naked eye. Generations have grown up not knowing what a well-focused film looks like.

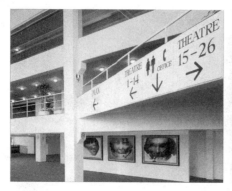

Figure 2-66. Opened in Brussels in 1988, the modestly-named "Kinepolis" holds the multiplex record to date with 25 theaters equipped for 35 mm and 70 mm, plus an IMAX theater. The total seating capacity is 8,000, exceeding even Radio City Music Hall, the last great movie palace of the thirties. Kinepolis is at the center of a massive entertainment complex which includes a theme park, water rides, and a "mini-Europe" constructed of scale models, together with restaurants and boutiques. (*Courtesy Kinepolis and Sonja Coudeville.*)

The problem of masks is even more acute. Few theaters keep a complete range of masks and concomitant lenses on hand. Many theaters have only the contemporary standard 1.85 American widescreen mask and the basic anamorphic lens. If a 1.66 film arrives—or, even worse—a movie in the Academy aspect ratio, the projectionist shows it with whatever mask is at hand. Heads are lopped off with abandon, and whatever composition the director originally had in mind is a matter of conjecture. Finally, there is sound: significant strides have been made here in recent years. Now, most first-run theaters are equipped to handle stereophonic or six-track sound, Dolbyized tracks, magnetic tracks, and the THX sound system.

Multiplexed cinemas, with tiny theaters (albeit better economics) have exploded in numbers since the 1970s. When you combine the lack of advances in projection with the fact that most audiences now see films in rooms not much larger than their living rooms on screens closer in size to their television sets than to the cinema screens of years past, it is a wonder that theatrical film has survived at all.

Projection has been the last area of film production to succumb to digitization, but even here video is superseding celluloid. The substantial costs of prints for a wide release make it inevitable that theatrical movies will be delivered digitally via broadcast once the necessary bandwidth is available. Call it "Nickelodeon-on-demand." The first public trials of digital projection were held in the spring of 1999 shortly after the release of the fourth Star Wars film.

It is clear that filmmaking is not (as ads directed to amateur photographers have tried to convince us for years) simply a matter of looking through the viewfinder and pressing the button. Filmmaking requires a degree of technical knowledge and expertise far surpassing that of any other art. While it is true that there are certain areas in which the technology of film has not yet caught up with the aspirations of filmmakers, it is equally true that there are areas where the technology offers a potential that cinéastes have yet to explore. The technology and the esthetics of film are interlocked: where one pulls, the other must follow. So a full understanding of the technological limitations and interconnections is necessary before one can begin to comprehend the ideal world of film esthetics that is the subject of the following chapter.

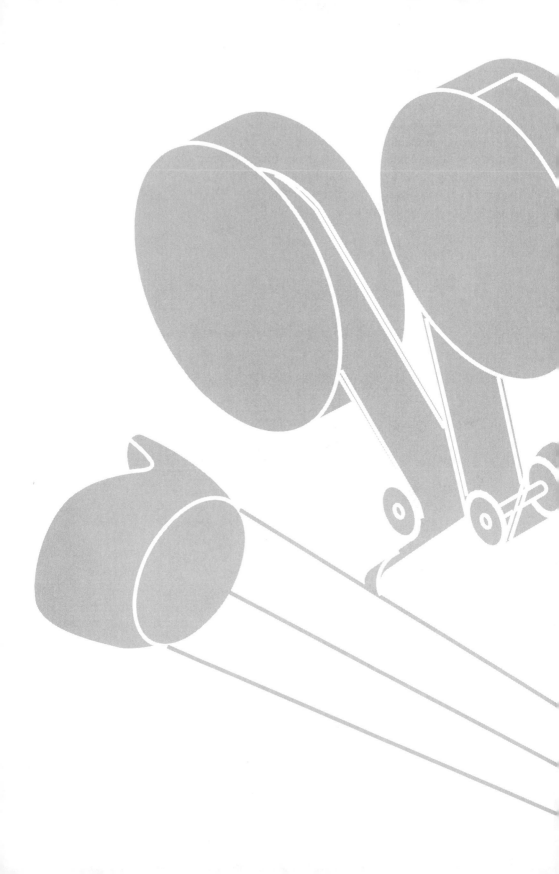

3

THE LANGUAGE OF FILM: SIGNS AND SYNTAX

Signs

Film is not a language in the sense that English, French, or mathematics is. First of all, it's impossible to be ungrammatical in film. And it is not necessary to learn a vocabulary. Infants appear to understand television images, for example, months before they begin to develop any facility with spoken language. Even cats watch television. Clearly, it is not necessary to acquire an intellectual understanding of film in order to appreciate it—at least on the most basic level.

But film is very much *like* language. People who are highly experienced in film—highly literate visually (or should we say "cinemate"?)—see more and hear more than people who seldom go to the movies. An education in the quasi-language of film opens up greater potential meaning for the observer, so it is useful to use the metaphor of language to describe the phenomenon of film.

In fact, no extensive scientific investigation of our ability to comprehend artificial sounds and images has yet been performed, but nevertheless we do know through research that while children are able to recognize objects in pictures long before they are able to read, they are eight or ten years of age before they can comprehend a film image the way most adults do. Moreover, there are cultural differences in the perception of images. In one famous 1920s test, anthropologist William Hudson set out to examine whether rural Africans who had had little contact with Western culture perceived depth in two-dimensional images the same way that Europeans do. He found, unequivocally, that they do not. Results varied—there were some individuals who responded in the Western manner to the test—but they were uniform over a broad cultural and sociological range.

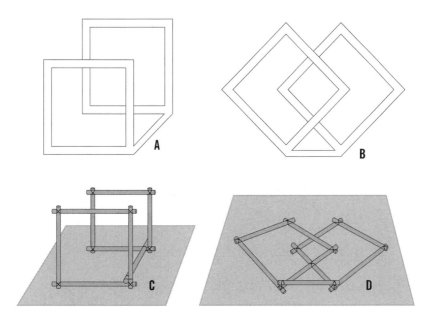

Figure 3-1. CONSTRUCTION-TASK FIGURES. Subjects asked to reconstruct these figures in three dimensions using sticks or rods, respond in different ways. People from Western cultures, trained in the codes and conventions that artists use to convey three-dimensionality in a two-dimensional drawing, see A as three-dimensional and B as two-dimensional. The operating code for three-dimensionality here insists that the dimension of depth be portrayed along the 45° oblique line. This works well enough in A, but not in B, where the oblique lines are not in the depth plane. Subjects from old African cultures tend to see both figures as two-dimensional, since they are not familiar with this Western three-dimensional code. Figures C and D illustrate the models of A constructed by Western and African observers, respectively. (*From "Pictorial Perception and Culture," Jan B. Deregowski. © 1972 by Scientific American, Inc. All rights reserved.*)

The conclusions that can be drawn from this seminal experiment and others that have followed are two: first, that every normal human being can perceive and identify a visual image; second, that even the simplest visual images are interpreted differently in different cultures. So we know that people must be "reading" these images. There is a process of intellection occurring—not necessarily consciously—when we observe an image, and it follows that we must, at some point, have learned how to do this.

The "ambiguous trident," a well-known "optical illusion," provides an easy test of this ability. It's safe to say that the level of visual literacy of anyone reading this book is such that observation of the trident will be confusing to all of us. It would not be for someone not trained in Western conventions of three-dimensionality.

Similarly, the well-known optical illusions in Figures 3-3 and 3-4 demonstrate that the process of perception and comprehension involves the brain: it is a men-

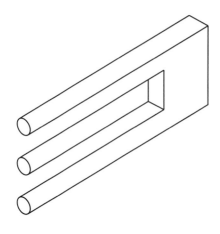

Figure 3-2.
THE AMBIGUOUS TRIDENT. The illusion is intriguing only because we are trained in Western codes of perspective. The psychological effect is powerful: our minds insist that we see the object in space rather than the drawing on a plane.

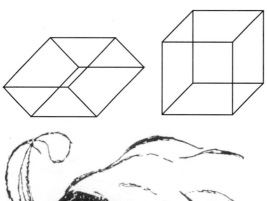

Figure 3-3.
THE NECKER CUBE. Devised in 1832 by L. A. Necker, a Swiss naturalist. The illusion depends, once again, on cultural training.

Figure 3-4. "My Wife and My Mother-in-law," by cartoonist W. E. Hill, was published in *Puck* in 1915. It has since become a famous example of the phenomenon known as the multi-stable figure. The young woman's chin is the old woman's nose. The old woman's chin is the young woman's chest. (*New York Public Library.*)

tal experience as well as a physical one. Whether we "see" the Necker Cube from the top or the bottom or whether we perceive the drawing in Figure 3-4 as either a young girl or an old woman depends not on the physiological function of our eyes but on what the brain does with the information received. The word "image," indeed, has two conjoined meanings: an image is an optical pattern; it is also a mental experience, which is probably why we use the word "imagine" to describe the mental creation of pictures.

So there is a strong element of our ability to observe images, whether still or moving, that depends on learning. This is, interestingly, not true to a significant extent with auditory phenomena. If the machines are sophisticated enough, we can produce recorded sounds that are technically indistinguishable from their originals. The result of this difference in mode of the two systems of perception—visual and auditory—is that whatever education our ears undergo in order to perceive reality is sufficient to perceive recorded sound, whereas there is a subtle but significant difference between the education necessary for our eyes to perceive (and our brain to understand) recorded images and that which is necessary simply to comprehend the reality that surrounds us. It would serve no purpose to consider phonography as a language, but it is useful to speak of photography (and cinematography) as a language, because a learning process is involved.

The Physiology of Perception

Another way to describe this difference between the two senses is in terms of the function of the sensory organs: ears hear whatever is available for them to hear; eyes choose what to see. This is true not only in the conscious sense (choosing to redirect attention from point A to point B or to ignore the sight altogether by closing our eyes), but in the unconscious as well. Since the receptor organs that permit visual acuity are concentrated (and properly arranged) only in the "fovea" of the retina, it's necessary for us to stare directly at an object in order to have a clear image of it. You can demonstrate this to yourself by staring at the dot in the center of this page. Only the area immediately surrounding it will be clear. The result of this foveated vision is that the eyes must move constantly in order to perceive an object of any size. These semiconscious movements are called "saccades" and take approximately 1/20 second each, just about the interval of persistence of vision, the phenomenon that makes film possible.

The conclusion that can be drawn from the fact of foveated vision is that we do indeed read an image physically as well as mentally and psychologically, just as we read a page. The difference is that we know how to read a page—in English, from left to right and top to bottom—but we are seldom conscious of precisely how we read an image.

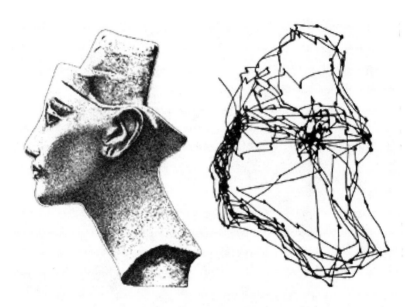

Figure 3-5. SACCADE PATTERNS. At left, a drawing of a bust of Queen Nefertiti; at right, a diagram of the eye movements of a subject viewing the bust. Notice that the eye follows regular patterns rather than randomly surveying the image. The subject clearly concentrates on the face and shows little interest in the neck. The ear also seems to be a focus of attention, probably not because it is inherently interesting, but rather because it is located in a prominent place in this profile. The saccadic patterns are not continuous; the recording clearly shows that the eye jerks quickly from point to point (the "notches" in the continuous line), fixing on specific nodes rather than absorbing general information. The recording was made by Alfred L. Yarbus of the Institute for Problems of Information Transmission, Moscow. (*From "Eye Movements and Visual Perception," by David Noton and Lawrence Stark, June 1971. Copyright © 1971 by Scientific American, Inc. All rights reserved. Reproduced by permission.*)

A complete set of physiological, ethnographic, and psychological experiments might demonstrate that various individuals read images more or less well in three different ways:

❑ physiologically: the best readers would have the most efficient and extensive saccadic patterns;

❑ ethnographically: the most literate readers would draw on the greatest experience and knowledge of a wide variety of cultural visual conventions;

❑ psychologically: the readers who gained the most from the material would be the ones who were best able to assimilate the various sets of meanings they perceived and then integrate the experience.

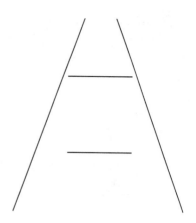

Figure 3-6. THE PONZO ILLUSION.
The horizontal lines are of equal length, yet
the line at the top appears to be longer than
the line at the bottom. The diagonals suggest perspective, so that we interpret the
picture in depth and conclude, therefore,
that since the "top" line must be "behind"
the "bottom" line, further away, it must thus
be longer.

The irony here is that we know very well that we must learn to read before we can attempt to enjoy or understand literature, but we tend to believe, mistakenly, that anyone can read a film. Anyone can *see* a film, it's true. But some people have learned to comprehend visual images—physiologically, ethnographically, and psychologically—with far more sophistication than have others. This evidence confirms the validity of the triangle of perception outlined in Chapter 1, uniting author, work, and observer. The observer is not simply a consumer, but an active—or potentially active—participant in the process.

Film is not a language, but is *like* language, and since it is like language, some of the methods that we use to study language might profitably be applied to a study of film.

Yet, since film is not a language, narrowly linguistic concepts can be misleading. Ever since the beginning of film history, theorists have been fond of comparing film with verbal language (partly to justify the serious study of film), but it wasn't until a new, larger category of thought developed in the fifties and early sixties—one that saw written and spoken language as just two among many systems of communication—that the real study of film as a language could proceed. This inclusive category is known as semiotics, the study of systems of signs.

Semioticians justified the study of film as language by redefining the concept of written and spoken language. Any system of communication is a "language"; English, French, or Chinese is a "language system." Cinema, therefore, may be a language of a sort, but it is not clearly a language system. As Christian Metz, the well-known film semiotician, pointed out: we understand a film not because we have a knowledge of its system; rather, we achieve an understanding of its system because we understand the film. Put another way, "It is not because the cinema is language that it can tell such fine stories, but rather it has become language because it has told such fine stories" [Metz, *Film Language*, p. 47].

For semioticians, a sign must consist of two parts: the signifier and the signified. The word "word," for example—the collection of letters or sounds—is a signifier; what it represents is something else again—the "signified." In literature, the relationship between signifier and signified is a main locus of art: the poet is building constructions that, on the one hand, are composed of sounds (signifiers) and, on the other, of meanings (signifieds), and the relationship between the two can be fascinating. In fact, much of the pleasure of poetry lies just here: in the dance between sound and meaning.

But in film, the signifier and the signified are almost identical: the sign of cinema is a short-circuit sign. A picture of a book is much closer to a book, conceptually, than the word "book" is. It's true that we may have to learn in infancy or early childhood to interpret the picture of a book as meaning a book, but this is a great deal easier than learning to interpret the letters or sounds of the word "book" as what it signifies. A picture bears some direct relationship with what it signifies, a word seldom does.[*]

It is the fact of this short-circuit sign that makes the language of film so difficult to discuss. As Metz put it, in a memorable phrase: "A film is difficult to explain because it is easy to understand." It also makes "doing" film quite different from "doing" English (either writing or speaking). We can't modify the signs of cinema the way we can modify the words of language systems. In cinema, an image of a rose is an image of a rose is an image of a rose—nothing more, nothing less. In English, a rose can be a rose, simply, but it can also be modified or confused with similar words: rose, rosy, rosier, rosiest, rise, risen, rows (ruse), arose, roselike, and so forth.

The power of language systems is that there is a very great difference between the signifier and the signified; the power of film is that there is not.

Nevertheless, film is *like* a language. How, then, does it do what is does? Clearly, one person's image of a certain object is not another's. If we both read the word "rose" you may perhaps think of a Heritage rose you picked last summer, while I am thinking of the one Laura Westphal gave to me in December 1968, or the prop for "The Interface," the short film we shot in 1995. In cinema, however, we both see the same rose, while the filmmaker can choose from an infinite variety of roses and then photograph the one chosen in another infinite variety of ways. The artist's choice in cinema is without limit; the artist's choice in literature is circumscribed, while the reverse is true for the observer: the great thing about literature is that you can imagine; the great thing about film is that you can't.

---

[*] Pictographic languages like Chinese and Japanese might be said to fall somewhere in between film and Western languages as sign systems, but only when they are written, not when they are spoken, and only in limited cases. On the other hand, there are some words—"gulp," for example—that are onomatopoeic and therefore bear a direct relationship to what they signify, but only when they are spoken.

Figure 3-7. LOGOS. The concept of the logotype has been with us since medieval times, when guildsmen stamped their work with a proprietary mark. In the twentieth century, the logo became a crucial mark of corporate identity. The telephone company was unusually lucky. Founded by Alexander Graham Bell, the "Bell System" was born with a name that echoed its most identifying feature and was also easily pictured. The early years of the corporate consciousness often traded on signatures, like Ford's, or seemingly more personal script, Coca-Cola. (Even the ribbon treatment is protected.) International Business Machines—as they were once known—began the trend to acronyms. Esso (a nice derivation of S. O.—Standard Oil) decided in the 1960s that that nonce-word wasn't modern enough; they were reborn as Exxon, on the theory that x's are somehow more contemporary (although they remained Esso in Europe). Scores of major corporations followed their lead, attempting to reinvent themselves, if in name only. The trend peaked in the mid-seventies, when NBC, owner of one of the most memorable musical logos, paid over $700,000 for a nice red and blue "N" only to discover that a public television station in Nebraska already had the same logo (for which they had paid next to nothing). Interestingly, only two of the major film studios developed animated logos, MGM and Fox. Although numerous producers of the thirties and forties used their signatures on their films, only Alfred Hitchcock developed a memorable personal logo.

Film does not suggest, in this context: it states. And therein lies its power and the danger it poses to the observer: the reason why it is useful, even vital, to learn to read images well so that the observer can seize some of the power of the medium. The better one reads an image, the more one understands it, the more power one has over it. The reader of a page invents the image, the reader of a film does not, yet both readers must work to interpret the signs they perceive in order to complete the process of intellection. The more work they do, the better the balance between observer and creator in the process; the better the balance, the more vital and resonant the work of art.

The earliest film texts—even many published recently—pursue with short-sighted ardor the crude comparison of film and written/spoken language. The standard theory suggested that the shot was the word of film, the scene its sentence, and the sequence its paragraph. In the sense that these sets of divisions are arranged in ascending order of complexity, the comparison is true enough; but it breaks down under analysis.

Assuming for the moment that a word is the smallest convenient unit of meaning, does the shot compare equivalently? Not at all. In the first place, a shot takes time. Within that time span there is a continually various number of images. Does the single image, the frame, then constitute the basic unit of meaning in film? Still the answer is no, since each frame includes a potentially infinite amount of visual information, as does the soundtrack that accompanies it. While we could say that a film shot is something like a sentence, since it makes a statement and is sufficient in itself, the point is that the film does not divide itself into such easily manageable units. While we can define "shot" technically well enough as a single piece of film, what happens if the particular shot is punctuated internally? The camera can move; the scene can change completely in a pan or track. Should we then be talking of one shot or two?

Likewise, scenes, which were defined strictly in French classical theater as beginning and ending whenever a character entered or left the stage, are more amorphous in film (as they are in theater today). The term "scene" is useful, no doubt, but not precise. Sequences are certainly longer than scenes, but the "sequence-shot," in which a single shot is coterminous with a sequence, is an important concept and no smaller units within it are discrete.

It would seem that a real science of film, as in physics, would depend on our being able to define the smallest unit of construction. We can do that technically, at least for the image: it is the single frame. But this is certainly not the smallest unit of meaning. The fact is that film, unlike written or spoken language, is not composed of units as such, but is rather a continuum of meaning. A shot contains as much information as we want to read in it, and whatever units we define within the shot are arbitrary.

Therefore, film presents us with a language (of sorts) that:

❑   consists of short-circuit signs in which the signifier nearly equals the signified; and

❑   depends on a continuous, nondiscrete system in which we can't identify a basic unit and which therefore we can't describe quantitatively.

The result is that, as Christian Metz says: "An easy art, the cinema is in constant danger of falling victim to this easiness." Film is too intelligible, which is what makes it difficult to analyze. "A film is difficult to explain because it is easy to understand."

Figure 3-8. A rose is not necessarily a rose. (A) James Rosenquist's roses: *Dusting Off Roses.* 1965. (*Lithograph, printed in color, composition: 25 15/16" by 21 11/16." Collection, Museum of Modern Art, New York. Gift of the Celeste and Armand Bartos Foundation. Photograph © 1995 The Museum of Modern Art, New York.*) (B) The rose from "The Interface." (C) The white rose and the red, from the credits to Olivier's *Richard III.*

Denotative and Connotative Meaning

Films do, however, manage to communicate meaning. They do this essentially in two different manners: denotatively and connotatively.

Like written language, but to a greater degree, a film image or sound has a denotative meaning: it is what it is and we don't have to strive to recognize it. This may seem a simplistic statement, but the fact should never be underestimated: here lies the great strength of film. There is a substantial difference between a description in words (or even in still photographs) of a person or event, and a cinematic record of the same. Because film can give us such a close approximation of reality, it can communicate a precise knowledge that written or spoken language seldom can. "Film is what you can't imagine." Language systems may be much better equipped to deal with the nonconcrete world of ideas and abstractions (imagine this book, for example, on film: without a complete narration it would be incomprehensible), but they are not nearly so capable of conveying precise information about physical realities.

By its very nature, written/spoken language analyzes. To write the word "rose" is to generalize and abstract the idea of the rose. The real power of the linguistic languages lies not in their denotative ability but in this connotative aspect of language: the wealth of meaning we can attach to a word that surpasses its denotation. If denotation were the only measure of the power of a language, for example, then English—which has a vocabulary of a million or so words and is the largest language in history—would be more than three times more powerful than French, which has only 300,000 or so words. But French makes up for its "limited" vocabulary with a noticeably greater use of connotation. Film has connotative abilities as well.

Considering the strongly denotative quality of film sounds and images, it is surprising to discover that these connotative abilities are very much a part of the film language. In fact, many of them stem from film's denotative ability. As we have noted in Chapter 1, film can draw on all the other arts for various effects simply because it can record them. Thus, all the connotative factors of spoken language can be accommodated on a film soundtrack while the connotations of written language can be included in titles (to say nothing of the connotative factors of dance, music, painting, and so forth). Because film is a product of culture, it has resonances that go beyond what the semiotician calls its "diegesis" (the sum of its denotations). An image of a rose is not simply that when it appears in a film of *Richard III*, for example, because we are aware of the connotations of the white rose and the red as symbols of the houses of York and Lancaster. These are culturally determined connotations.

In addition to these influences from the general culture, film has its own unique connotative ability. We know (even if we don't often remind ourselves of it consciously) that a filmmaker has made specific choices: the rose is filmed from a certain angle, the camera moves or does not move, the color is bright or dull, the rose is fresh or fading, the thorns apparent or hidden, the background clear (so that the rose is seen in context) or vague (so that it is isolated), the shot held for a long time or briefly, and so on. These are specific aids to cinematic connotation, and although we can approximate their effect in literature, we cannot accomplish it there with the precision or efficiency of cinema. A picture is, on occasion, worth a thousand words, as the adage has it.

When our sense of the connotation of a specific shot depends on its having been chosen from a range of other possible shots, then we can say that this is, using the language of semiotics, a *paradigmatic* connotation. That is, the connotative sense we comprehend stems from the shot being compared, not necessarily consciously, with its unrealized companions in the paradigm, or general model, of this type of shot. A low-angle shot of a rose, for example, conveys a sense that the flower is for some reason dominant, overpowering, because we consciously or unconsciously compare it with, say, an overhead shot of a rose, which would diminish its importance.

Conversely, when the significance of the rose depends not on the shot compared with other potential shots, but rather on the shot compared with actual shots that precede or follow it, then we can speak of its *syntagmatic* connotation; that is, the meaning adheres to it because it is compared with other shots that we do see.

These two different kinds of connotation have their equivalents in literature. A word alone on the page has no particular connotation, only denotation. We know what it means, we also know potentially what it connotes, but we can't supply the particular connotation the author of the word has in mind until we see it in context. Then we know what particular connotative value it has because we judge its meaning by conscious or unconscious comparison of it with (1) all the words like it that might fit in this context but were not chosen, and (2) the words that precede or follow it.

These two axes of meaning—the paradigmatic and the syntagmatic—have real value as tools for understanding what film means. In fact, as an art, film depends almost entirely upon these two sets of choices. After a filmmaker has decided *what* to shoot, the two obsessive questions are how to shoot it (what choices to make: the paradigmatic) and how to present the shot (how to edit it: the syntagmatic). In literature, in contrast, the first question (how to say it) is paramount, while the second (how to present what is said) is quite secondary. Semiotics, so far, has concentrated on the syntagmatic aspect of film, for a very simple reason: it is here that film is most clearly different from other arts, so that the syntagmatic category (editing, montage) is in a sense the most "cinematic."

Film draws on the other arts for much of its connotative power as well as generating its own, both paradigmatically and syntagmatically. But there is also another source of connotative sense. Cinema is not strictly a medium of intercommunication. One seldom holds dialogues using film as the medium. Whereas spoken and written languages are used for intercommunication, film, like the nonrepresentational arts in general (as well as language when it is used for artistic purposes), is a one-way communication. As a result, even the most utilitarian of films is artistic in some respect. Film speaks in neologisms. "When a 'language' does not already exist," Metz wrote, "one must be something of an artist to speak it, however poorly. For to speak it is partly to invent it, whereas to speak the language of everyday is simply to use it." So connotations attach to even the simplest statements in film.

There is an old joke that illustrates the point: Two philosophers meet; one says "Good morning!" The other smiles in recognition, then walks on frowning and thinking to himself: "I wonder what he meant by that?" The question is a joke

Figure 3-9. ICON. Liv Ullmann in Ingmar Bergman's *Face to Face* (1975). This image is what it is.

when spoken language is the subject; it is however, a perfectly legitimate question to ask of any statement in film.

Is there any way we can further differentiate the various modes of denotation and connotation in film? Borrowing a "trichotomy" from the philosopher C. S. Peirce, Peter Wollen, in his highly influential book *Signs and Meaning in the Cinema* (1969), suggested that cinematic signs are of three orders:

❑   The Icon: a sign in which the signifier represents the signified mainly by its similarity to it, its likeness;

❑   The Index: which measures a quality not because it is identical to it but because it has an inherent relationship to it;

❑   The Symbol: an arbitrary sign in which the signifier has neither a direct nor an indexical relationship to the signified, but rather represents it through convention.

Although Wollen didn't fit them into the denotative/connotative categories, Icon, Index, and Symbol can be seen as mainly denotative. Portraits are icons, of course, but so are diagrams in the Peirce/Wollen system. Indexes are more difficult to define. Quoting Peirce, Wollen suggests two sorts of indexes, one technical—medical symptoms are indexes of health, clocks and sundials are indexes of

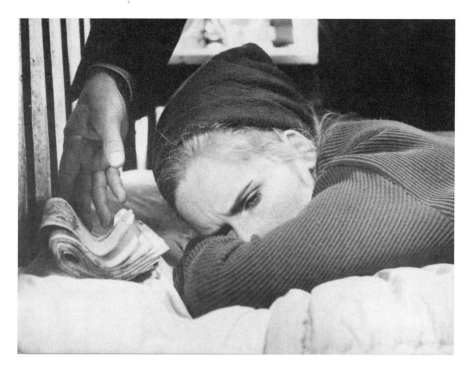

Figure 3-10. INDEX. Liv Ullmann in Bergman's *Shame* (1968). The offer of money—the roll of cash on the pillow—is an index of prostitution and, hence, of Eva's shame.

time—and one metaphorical: a rolling gait should indicate that a man is a sailor. (This is the one point where the Peirce/Wollen categories verge on the connotative.) Symbols, the third category, are more easily defined. The way Peirce and Wollen use it, the word has a rather broad definition: words are symbols (since the signifier represents the signified through convention rather than resemblance).

These three categories are not mutually exclusive. Especially in photographic images, the iconic factor is almost always a strong one. As we have noted, a thing is itself even if it is also an index or a symbol. General semiotic theory, especially as it is put forth in Christian Metz's writings, covers the first and last categories—icon and symbol—fairly well already. The icon is the short-circuit sign that is so characteristic of cinema; the symbol is the arbitrary or conventional sign that is the basis of spoken and written language. It is the second category—the index—that is most intriguing in Peirce and Wollen's system: it seems to be a third means, halfway between the cinematic icon and the literary symbol, by which cinema can convey meaning. It is not an arbitrary sign, but neither is it identical. It suggests a

Figure 3-11. SYMBOL. Bergman often uses coffins and corpses as symbols in his films. Here, Ullmann again in *Face to Face* …

third type of denotation that points directly toward connotation, and may in fact not be understandable without the dimension of connotation.

The index seems to be one very useful way in which cinema can deal directly with ideas, since it gives us concrete representations or measurements of them. How can we convey the idea of hotness cinematically, for instance? In written language it's very easy, but on film? The image of a thermometer quickly comes to mind. Clearly that is an index of temperature. But there are more subtle indexes as well: sweat is an index, as are shimmering atmospheric waves and hot colors. It's a truism of film esthetics that metaphors are difficult in cinema. Comparing love with roses works well enough in literature, but its cinematic equivalent poses problems: the rose, the secondary element of the metaphor, is too equivalent in cinema, too much present. As a result, cinematic metaphors based on the literary model tend to be crude and static and forced. The indexical sign may offer a way out of this dilemma. Here film discovers its own, unique metaphorical power, which it owes to the flexibility of the frame: its ability to say many things at once.

The concept of the index also leads us to some interesting ideas about connotation. It must be clear from the above discussion that the line between denotation

Figure 3-12. … and Max von Sydow in *Hour of the Wolf* (1966).

and connotation is not clearly defined: there is a continuum. In film, as in written and spoken language, connotations if they become strong enough are eventually accepted as denotative meanings. As it happens, much of the connotative power of film depends on devices that are indexical; that is, they are not arbitrary signs, but neither are they identical.

Two terms from literary studies, closely associated with each other, serve to describe the main manner in which film conveys connotative meaning. A "metonymy" is a figure of speech in which an associated detail or notion is used to invoke an idea or represent an object. Etymologically, the word means "substitute naming" (from the Greek *meta*, involving transfer, and *onoma*, name). Thus, in literature we can speak of the king (and the idea of kingship) as "the crown." A "synecdoche" is a figure of speech in which the part stands for the whole or the whole for the part. An automobile can be referred to as a "motor" or a "set of wheels"; a policeman is "the law."

Both of these forms recur constantly in cinema. The indexes of heat mentioned above are clearly metonymical: associated details invoke an abstract idea. Many of the old clichés of Hollywood are synecdochic (close shots of marching feet to represent an army) and metonymic (the falling calendar pages, the driving

Figure 3-13. METONYMY. In *Red Desert* (1964), Michelangelo Antonioni developed a precise metonymic of color. Throughout most of the film, Giuliana (Monica Vitti) is oppressed psychologically and politically by a gray and deathly urban industrial environment. When she manages to break away from its grip on several occasions, Antonioni signals her temporary independence (and possible return to health) with bright colors, a detail associated with health and happiness not only in this film but in general culture as well. In this scene, Giuliana attempts to open her own shop. The gray walls are punctuated with splotches of brilliant color (the attempt at freedom), but the shapes themselves are violent, disorganized, frightening (the relapse into neurosis). In all, a complicated set of metonymies.

wheels of the railroad engine). Indeed, because metonymical devices yield themselves so well to cinematic exploitation, cinema can be more efficient in this regard than literature can. Associated details can be compressed within the limits of the frame to present a statement of extraordinary richness. Metonymy is a kind of cinematic shorthand.

Just as, in general, our sense of cinema's connotations depends on understood comparisons of the image with images that were not chosen (paradigmatic) and images that came before and after (syntagmatic), so our sense of the cultural connotations depends upon understood comparisons of the part with the whole (synecdoche) and associated details with ideas (metonymy). Cinema is an art and a medium of extensions and indexes. Much of its meaning comes not from what we see (or hear) but from what we don't see or, more accurately, from an ongoing

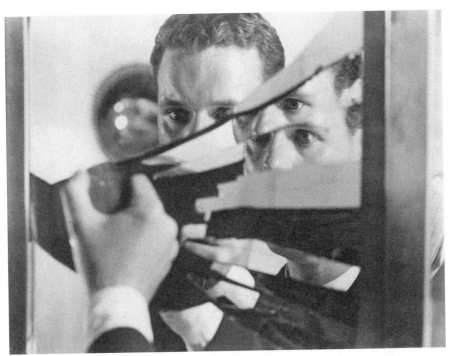

Figure 3-14. METONYMY. In Claude Chabrol's *Leda* (1959), André Jocelyn portrays a schizo-phrenic character. The image in the cracked mirror is a simple, logical metonymy.

process of comparison of what we see with what we don't see. This is ironic, considering that cinema at first glance seems to be an art that is all too evident, one that is often criticized for "leaving nothing to the imagination."

Quite the contrary is true. In a film of strict denotation, images and sounds are quite easily and directly understood. But very few films are strictly denotative; they can't help but be connotative, "for to speak [film] is partly to invent it." The observer who adamantly resists, of course, can choose to ignore the connotative power of film, but the observer who has learned to read film has available a multitude of connotations.

Alfred Hitchcock, for example, made a number of very popular films in a career that spanned more than half a century. We could ascribe his critical and popular success to the subjects of his films—certainly the thriller strikes a deep responsive chord in audiences—but then how do we account for the failed thrillers of his imitators? In truth, the drama of film, its attraction, lies not so much in what is shot (that's the drama of the subject), but in how it is shot and how it is presented. And as thousands of commentators have attested, Hitchcock was the master par excellence of these two critical tasks. The drama of filmmaking in large part lies in the brainwork of these closely associated sets of decisions. Highly "liter-

Figure 3-15. SYNECDOCHE. Giuliana in *Red Desert*, again, this time surrounded and nearly overwhelmed by industrial machinery, a "part" that stands for the "whole" of her urban society. It isn't this ship or the dockside ganglion of pipes that oppress her, but the larger reality they represent.

ate" filmgoers appreciate Hitchcock's superb cinematic intelligence on a conscious level, less literate filmgoers on an unconscious level, but the intelligence has its effect, nevertheless.

One more element remains to be added to the lexicon of film semiotics: the trope. In literary theory, a trope is a "turn of phrase" or a "change of sense"; in other words, a logical twist that gives the elements of a sign—the signifier and the signified—a new relationship to each other. The trope is therefore the connecting element between denotation and connotation. When a rose is a rose is a rose it isn't anything else, and its meaning as a sign is strictly denotative. But when a rose is something else, a "turning" has been made and the sign is opened up to new meanings. The map of film semiotics we have described so far has been static. The concept of the trope allows us to view it dynamically, as actions rather than facts.

As we have noted in earlier chapters, one of the great sources of power in film is that it can reproduce the tropes of most of the other arts. There is also a set of tropes that it has made its own. We have described the way they operate in general in the first part of this chapter. Given an image of a rose, we at first have only its iconic or symbolic denotative meaning, which is static. But when we begin to

Figure 3-16. SYNECDOCHE. Juliet Berto in Godard's *La Chinoise* (1967) has constructed a theoretical barricade of Chairman Mao's "Little Red Books," parts that stand for the whole of Marxist/Leninist/Maoist ideology with which the group of "gauchistes" to which she belongs protect themselves, and from which they intend to launch an attack on bourgeois society.

The terms "synecdoche" and "metonymy"—like "Icon," "Index," and "Symbol"—are, of course, imprecise. They are theoretical constructs that may be useful as aids to analysis; they are not strict definitions. This particular synecdoche, for example, might be better classified as a metonymy in which the little red books are associated details rather than parts standing for the whole. (The decision itself has ideological overtones!) Likewise, although this image seems easiest to classify as Indexical, there are certainly elements of the Iconic and Symbolic in it.

expand the possibilities through tropes of comparison, the image comes alive: as a connotative index, in terms of the paradigm of possible shots, in the syntagmatic context of its associations in the film, as it is used metaphorically as a metonymy or a synecdoche.

There are undoubtedly other categories of film semiotics yet to be discovered, analyzed, propagated. In no sense is the system shown in the chart below meant to be either exhaustive or immutable. Semiotics is most definitely not a science in the sense that physics or biology is a science. But it is a logical, often illuminating system that helps to describe how film does what it does. Film is difficult to explain because it is easy to understand. The semiotics of film is easy to explain because it is difficult to understand. Somewhere between lies the genius of film.

Syntax

Film has no grammar. There are, however, some vaguely defined rules of usage in cinematic language, and the syntax of film—its systematic arrangement—orders these rules and indicates relationships among them. As with written and spoken languages, it is important to remember that the syntax of film is a result of its usage, not a determinant of it. There is nothing preordained about film syntax. Rather, it evolved naturally as certain devices were found in practice to be both workable and useful. Like the syntax of written and spoken language, the syntax of film is an organic development, descriptive rather than prescriptive, and it has changed considerably over the years. The "Hollywood Grammar" described below may sound laughable now, but during the thirties, forties, and early fifties it was an accurate model of the way Hollywood films were constructed.

In written/spoken language systems, syntax deals only with what we might call the linear aspect of construction: that is, the ways in which words are put together in a chain to form phrases and sentences, what in film we call the syntagmatic category. In film, however, syntax can also include spatial composition, for which there is no parallel in language systems like English and French—we can't say or write several things at the same time.

So film syntax must include both development in time and development in space. In film criticism, generally, the modification of space is referred to as "mise-en-scène." The French phrase literally means "putting in the scene." The modification of time is called "montage" (from the French for "putting together"). As we shall see in Chapter 4, the tension between these twin concepts of mise-en-scène and montage has been the engine of film esthetics ever since the Lumières and Méliès first explored the practical possibilities of each at the turn of the century.

Over the years, theories of mise-en-scène have tended to be closely associated with film realism, while montage has been seen as essentially expressionistic, yet these pairings are deceptive. Certainly it would seem that mise-en-scène would indicate a high regard for the subject in front of the camera, while montage would give the filmmaker more control over the manipulation of the subject, but despite these natural tendencies, there are many occasions when montage can be the more realistic of the two alternatives, and mise-en-scène the more expressionistic.

Take, for example, the problem of choosing between a pan from one subject to another and a cut. Most people would say that the cut is more manipulative, that it interrupts and remodels reality, and that therefore the pan is the more realistic of the two alternatives, since it preserves the integrity of the space. Yet, in fact, the reverse is true if we judge panning and cutting from the point of view of the observer. When we redirect our attention from one subject to another we seldom actually pan. Psychologically, the cut is the truer approximation of our natural

Figure 3-17. TROPE. An ant-covered hand from Dali and Buñuel's surrealist classic *Un Chien Andalou* (1928). Another very complex image, not easily analyzed. Iconic, Indexical, and Symbolic values are all present: the image is striking for its own sake; it is a measure of the infestation of the soul of the owner of the hand; it is certainly symbolic of a more general malaise, as well. It is metonymic, because the ants are an "associated detail"; it is also synecdochic, because the hand is a part that stands for the whole. Finally, the source of the image seems to be a trope: a verbal pun on the French idiom, "avoir des fourmis dans les mains," "to have ants in the hand," an expression equivalent to the English "my hand is asleep." By illustrating the turn of phrase literally, Dali and Buñuel extended the trope so that a common experience is turned into a striking sign of decay. (I am indebted to David Bombyk for this analysis.) (*MOMA/FSA.*)

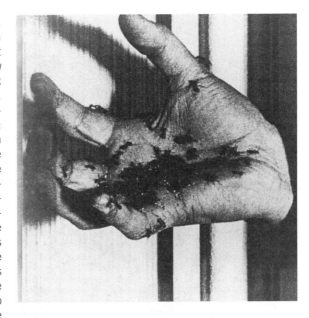

perception. First one subject has our attention, then the other; we are seldom interested in the intervening space, yet the cinematic pan draws our attention to just that.*

It was André Bazin, the influential French critic of the 1950s, who more than anyone developed the connections between mise-en-scène and realism on the one hand, and montage and expressionism on the other. At about the same time, in the middle fifties, Jean-Luc Godard was working out a synthesis of the twin notions of mise-en-scène and montage that was considerably more sophisticated than Bazin's binary opposition. For Godard, mise-en-scène and montage were divested of ethical and esthetic connotations: montage simply did in time what

---

* It has been suggested that the zip pan, in which the camera moves so quickly that the image in between the original subject and its successor is blurred, would be the most verisimilitudinous handling of the problem. But even this alternative draws attention to itself, which is precisely what does not happen in normal perception. Perhaps the perfect analogue with reality would be the direct cut in which the two shots were separated by a single black frame (or better yet, a neutral gray frame), which would duplicate the time (approximately 1/20 of a second) each saccadic movement of the eye takes!

Figure 3-18. METONYMIC GESTURE. Max von Sydow suffers in Ingmar Bergman's *Hour of the Wolf* (1967)...

mise-en-scène did in space. Both are principles of organization, and to say that mise-en-scène (space) is more "realistic" than montage (time) is illogical, according to Godard. In his essay "Montage, mon beau souci" (1956) Godard redefined montage as an integral part of mise-en-scène.

Setting up a scene is as much an organizing of time as of space. The aim of this is to discover in film a psychological reality that transcends physical, plastic reality. There are two corollaries to Godard's synthesis: first, mise-en-scène can therefore be every bit as expressionistic as montage when a filmmaker uses it to distort reality; second, psychological reality (as opposed to verisimilitude) may be better served by a strategy that allows montage to play a central role. (See Chapter 5.)

In addition to the psychological complexities that enter into a comparison of montage and mise-en-scène, there is a perceptual factor that complicates matters. We have already noted that montage can be mimicked within the shot. Likewise, montage can mimic mise-en-scène. Hitchcock's notorious shower murder sequence in *Psycho* is an outstanding example of this phenomenon. Seventy separate shots in less than a minute of screen time are fused together psychologically into a continuous experience: a frightening and graphic knife attack. The whole is greater than the sum of its parts (see Figure 3-21).

Figure 3-19. … and in the same director's *Shame* (1968). Gesture is one of the most communicative facets of film signification. "Kinesics," or "body language," is basically an Indexical, metonymic system of meaning. Here, von Sydow's pose conveys the same basic meaning in each film: the hand covers the face, shields it from the outside world; the knees are pulled up close almost in the fetal position, to protect the body; the ego has shrunk into a protective shell, a sense further emphasized in the shot from *Shame* by the framed box of the wooden stairway von Sydow is sitting on. Texture supports gesture in both shots: both backgrounds—one exterior, one interior—are rough, barren, uninviting. The differences between the shots are equally as meaningful as the similarities. In *Hour of the Wolf*, von Sydow's character is relatively more open, relaxed: so is the pose. In *Shame* the character (at this point in the narrative) is mortified, a sense emphasized by both the tighter pose and the more distanced composition of the shot.

Codes

The structure of cinema is defined by the codes in which it operates and the codes that operate within it. Codes are critical constructions—systems of logical relationship—derived after the fact of film. They are not preexisting laws that the filmmaker consciously observes. A great variety of codes combine to form the medium in which film expresses meaning. There are culturally derived codes—those that exist outside film and that filmmakers simply reproduce (the way people eat, for example). There are a number of codes that cinema shares with the

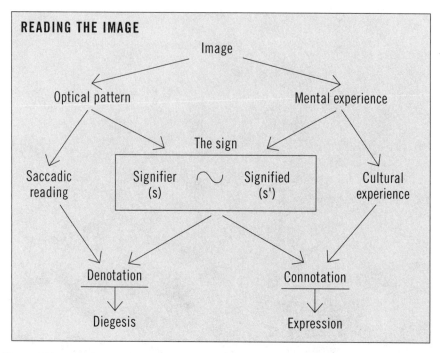

Diagram H. READING THE IMAGE: The image is experienced as both an optical and a mental phenomenon. The optical pattern is read saccadically; the mental experience is the result of the sum of cultural determinants, and is formed by it. Both optical and mental intellection combine in the concept of the sign, where signifier (s) is related to signified (s'). The signifier is more optical than mental; the signified, more mental then optical. All three levels of reading—saccadic, semiotic, and cultural—then combine with each other in various ways to produce meaning, either essentially denotative or essentially connotative.

other arts (for instance, gesture, which is a code of theater as well as film). And there are those codes that are unique to cinema. (Montage is the prime example.)

The culturally derived codes and the shared artistic codes are vital to cinema, naturally, but it is the unique codes, those that form the specific syntax of film, that most concern us here. Perhaps "unique" is not a completely accurate adjective. Not even the most specifically cinematic codes, those of montage, are truly unique to cinema. Certainly, cinema emphasizes them and utilizes them more than other arts do, yet something like montage has always existed in the novel. Any storyteller is capable of switching scenes in midstream. "Meanwhile, back at the ranch," is clearly not an invention of cinema. More important, for nearly a century film art has had its own strong influence on the older arts. Not only did something like montage exist prior to 1900 in prose narrative, but also since that time, novelists, increasingly influenced by film, have learned gradually to make their narratives even more like cinema.

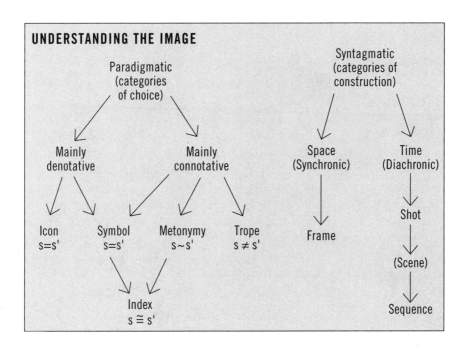

Diagram I. UNDERSTANDING THE IMAGE: We understand an image not only for itself, but in context: in relation to categories of choice (paradigmatic) and in relation to categories of construction (syntagmatic). The categories of choice are variously denotative or connotative, and each variety, none of whose boundaries are sharply defined, is characterized by the relationship between signifier and signified. In the iconic image, signifier is identical with signified. In symbols the signifier is equal to the signified, but not identical. In metonymies and synecdoches, signifier is similar in some way to signified, while in tropes, the signifier is not equal to (distinctly different from) the signified. Here the relationship is considerably more tenuous. In indexes, signifier and signified are congruent.

Syntagmatic relationship (categories of construction) operate either in space or in time: synchronic phenomena happen at the same time, or without regard to time, while diachronic phenomena happen across time, or within it. (Here, the words "synchronic" and "diachronic" carry their simplest meanings. They are also used with more specific definitions generally in semiotics and linguistics, in which case synchronic linguistics is descriptive, while diachronic linguistics is historical.)

Finally, we must note that many of the concepts expressed in this chart are true for sounds as well as images, although usually to a considerably lesser extent. While it is true that we do not read sounds saccadically, we nevertheless focus psychologically on particular sounds within the total auditory experience, just as we "block out" unwanted or useless noise. While sound must seem, in general, far more denotative and iconic than image, it is nevertheless possible to apply the concepts of symbol, index, metonymy, synecdoche, and trope, if the necessary changes are made.

The point is, simply, that codes are a critical convenience—nothing more—and it would be wrong to give them so much weight that we were more concerned with the precise definition of the code than with the perception of the film.

Taking the shower scene in *Psycho* once again as an example, let's derive the codes operating there. It is a simple scene (only two characters—one of whom is barely seen—and two actions—taking a shower and murdering) and it is of short duration, yet all three types of codes are evident. The culturally derived codes have to do with taking showers and murdering people. The shower is, in Western culture, an activity that has elements of privacy, sexuality, purgation, relaxation, openness, and regeneration. In other words, Hitchcock could not have chosen a more ironic place to emphasize the elements of violation and sexuality in the assault. Murder, on the other hand, fascinates us because of motives. Yet the dimly perceived murderer of *Psycho* has no discernible motive. The act seems gratuitous, almost absurd—which makes it even more striking. Historically, Jack the Ripper may come to mind, and this redoubles our sense of the sexual foundation of the murder.

Since this particular scene is so highly cinematic and so short, shared codes are relatively minor here. Acting codes hardly play a part, for instance, since the shots are so brief there isn't time to act in them, only to mime a simple expression. The diagonals that are so important in establishing the sense of disorientation and dynamism are shared with the other pictorial arts. The harsh contrasts and backlighting that obscure the murderer are shared with photography. The musical code of Bernard Herrmann's accompaniment also exists outside film, of course.

In addition, we can trace the development of the use of the culturally derived codes in cinema and allied arts: Hitchcock's murder scene might be contrasted with the murder of Marat in his bath (in history, in the painting by Jacques-Louis David, and in the play by Peter Weiss), the bathtub murder scene in Henri-Georges Clouzot's *Les Diaboliques* (1955), or that in *The Last of Sheila* (1973), written by Stephen Sondheim and Anthony Perkins (who played in *Psycho*), or the direct homages to *Psycho* in Mike Hodges's *Terminal Man* (1974) or Brian DePalma's *Dressed to Kill* (1980), or even the shot-by-shot remake of *Psycho* by Gus Van Sant (1998).

As we have already noted, the specifically cinematic codes in Hitchcock's one-minute tour de force are exceptionally strong. In fact, it's hard to see how the montage of the sequence could be duplicated in any other art. The rapid cutting of the scene may indeed be a unique cinematic code.

Hitchcock manipulates all these codes to achieve a desired effect. It is because they are codes—because they have meaning for us outside the narrow limits of that particular scene: in film, in the other arts, in the general culture—that they affect us. The codes are the medium through which the "message" of the scene is

Figure 3-20. Mise-en-scène or montage? A crucial scene in Bergman's *Face to Face*, this was shot from a hallway giving a "split screen" view of two rooms. Instead of cutting from the action in one to the action in the other, Bergman presented both simultaneously while keeping the action in each separate. The cross-cutting dialectic of montage is thus made an integral element of mise-en-scène. (*Frame enlargement.*)

transmitted. The specifically cinematic codes together with a number of shared codes make up the syntax of film.

Mise-en-Scène

Three questions confront the filmmaker: What to shoot? How to shoot it? How to present the shot? The domain of the first two questions is mise-en-scène, that of the last, montage. Mise-en-scène is often regarded as static, montage as dynamic. This is not the case. Because we read the shot, we are actively involved with it. The codes of mise-en-scène are the tools with which the filmmaker alters and modifies our reading of the shot. Since the shot is such a large unit of meaning, it may be useful to separate a discussion of its components into two parts.

Figure 3-21. Hitchcock's spellbinding shower murder in *Psycho* (1959) has become notorious over the years for its vertiginous editing, yet the bathroom murder was not a new idea. (*From Psycho. © 1974. Ed. by Richard J. Anobile. Frame enlargement.*)

Figure 3-22. Several years earlier Henri-Georges Clouzot's *Diabolique* had shocked audiences with an altogether quieter but no less eerie murder scene. (Paul Meurisse is the victim.) (*Walter Daran. Time/Life Picture Agency. © Time Inc. Frame enlargement.*)

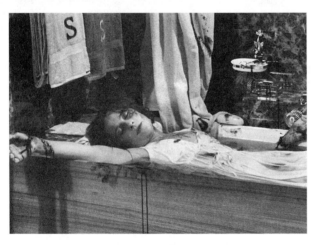

Figure 3-23. *Psycho*'s star, Anthony Perkins, cowrote the script for Herbert Ross's *The Last of Sheila* (1973). Joan Hackett attempted suicide in an elegant shipboard bath.

THE BATHTUB/SHOWER CODE

Figure 3-24. Murder isn't the only activity that takes place in tubs. In Godard's poetic essay *Pierrot le fou* (1965), Jean-Paul Belmondo relaxed in a tub as he shared some thoughts on the painter Velázquez with his daughter. (*l'Avant-Scène. Frame enlargement.*)

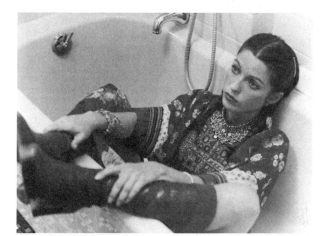

Figure 3-25. In Jean-Charles Tacchella's *Cousin, cousine* (1975), Marie-France Pisier settled into an empty tub in contemplation.

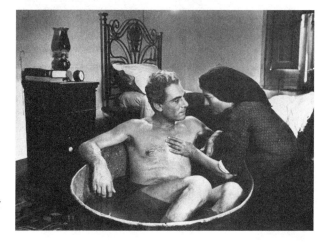

Figure 3-26. Gian Maria Volonté found some surcease from exile in a remote Italian village in an old-fashioned tub. Irene Papas assisted in Francesco Rosi's *Christ Stopped at Eboli* (1979).

Figure 3-27. In the late seventies, the bath became a focus of contemporary California life with the rise in popularity of the hot tub. Stacey Nolkin took a call in *Serial* (1980).

Figure 3-28.
Ghostbusters II (1989).
The bath fights back;
Sigourney Weaver wins.
(*Frame enlargement.*)

Figure 3-29. In a variant,
Kevin Kline as President
showers in Ivan
Reitman's *Dave* (1993).
Weaver is surprised.
(*Frame enlargement.*)

Figure 3-30. The bathtub code extends as far back as Jacques-Louis David's *The Death of Marat* (1793), shocking because of its intimate realism. (*Oil on canvas. 65" by 50 1/2". Royal Museum of Fine Arts, Brussels.*)

The Framed Image

All the codes that operate within the frame, without regard to the chronological axis of film, are shared with the other pictorial arts. The number and range of these codes is great, and they have been developed and refined in painting, sculpture, and photography over the course of thousands of years. Basic texts in the visual arts examine the three determinants of color, line, and form, and certainly each of the visual codes of film fits within one of these rubrics. Rudolf Arnheim, in his highly influential study *Art and Visual Perception,* suggested ten areas of concern: Balance, Shape, Form, Growth, Space, Light, Color, Movement, Tension, and Expression. Clearly, a full exposition of the codes operating in the film frame would be a lengthy undertaking. We can, however, describe briefly the basic aspects of the syntax of the frame. Two aspects of the framed image are most important: the limitations that the frame imposes, and the composition of the image within the frame (and without necessary regard to it).

Since the frame determines the limit of the image, the choice of an aspect ratio suggests the possibilities of composition. With the self-justification that has been

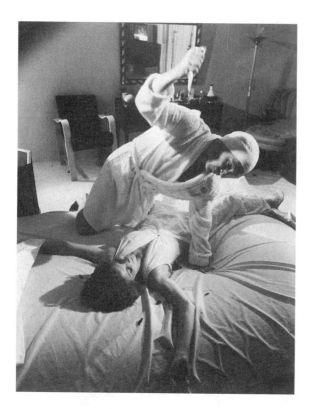

Figure 3-31. *Psycho* itself spawned a number of homages. Here, George Segal (just out of the bath) in Mike Hodges's *Terminal Man* (1974)....

endemic to the elusive subject of film esthetics, early theoreticians waxed eloquent over the value of the Academy aperture, the 1.33 ratio. When widescreen ratios became popular in the 1950s, the classical estheticians bemoaned the destruction of the symmetry they perceived in the Academy aperture, but, as we demonstrated in Chapter 2, there was nothing sacred about the ratio of 4:3.

The question is not which ratio is "proper" but rather which codes yield themselves to exploitation in which ratios? Before the mid-fifties, it seems, interiors and dialogue dominated American and foreign screens. After the introduction of the widescreen formats in the 1950s, exteriors, location shooting, and action sequences grew in importance. This is a crude generalization, but there is some useful truth to it. It's not important whether there was a cause-and-effect relationship between the two historical developments, only that wide screens permitted more efficient exploitation of action and landscape codes.

CinemaScope and Panavision width ratios (2.33 and above) do make it more difficult, as the old Hollywood estheticians had suggested, to photograph intimate conversations. Whereas the classic two-shot of the 1.33 screen size tended to focus attention on speaker and listener, the very wide anamorphic ratios cannot

Figure 3-32. … and Angie Dickinson in Brian De Palma's *Dressed to Kill* (1980). (Compare the hands here and in Figure 3-33.)

avoid also photographing the space either between them or beside them and therefore calling attention to their relationship to the space surrounding them. This is neither "better" nor "worse"; it simply changes the code of the two-shot.

The filmmaker can also change the dimensions of the frame during the course of the film by masking the image, either artificially or naturally through composition. This has been an important aspect of the syntax of frame shape ever since D. W. Griffith first explored its possibilities.

Just as important as the actual frame size, although less easily perceived, is the filmmaker's attitude toward the limit of the frame. If the image of the frame is self-sufficient, then we can speak of it as a "closed form." Conversely, if the filmmaker has composed the shot in such a way that we are always subliminally aware of the area outside the frame, then the form is considered to be "open."

Open and closed forms are closely associated with the elements of movement in the frame. If the camera tends to follow the subject faithfully, the form tends to be closed; if, on the other hand, the filmmaker allows—even encourages—the subject to leave the frame and reenter, the form is obviously open. The relationship between the movement within the frame and the movement of the camera is one of the more sophisticated codes, and specifically cinematic.

Hollywood's classic syntax was identified in part by a relatively tightly closed form. The masters of the Hollywood style of the thirties and forties tried never to allow the subject to leave the frame (it was considered daring even if the subject did not occupy the center of the 1.33 frame). In the sixties and seventies, film-

Figure 3-33. The Academy aperture two-shot. Spencer Tracy and Katharine Hepburn in George Cukor's *Pat and Mike* (1952). More intimate and involving than…

makers like Michelangelo Antonioni were equally faithful to the open widescreen form because it emphasizes the spaces between people.

Most elements of compositional syntax do not depend strictly on the frame for their definition. If the image faded at the edges like a vignette (which itself is one of the minor devices of the framing code), such codes as intrinsic interest, proximity, depth perception, angle of approach, and lighting would work just as well as they do in frames with sharply defined limits.

The filmmaker, like most pictorial artists, composes in three dimensions. This doesn't mean necessarily that he is trying to convey three-dimensional (or stereoscopic) information. It means that there are three sets of compositional codes: One concerns the plane of the image (most important, naturally, since the image is, after all, two-dimensional). One deals with the geography of the space photographed (its plane is parallel with the ground and the horizon). The third involves the plane of depth perception, perpendicular to both the frame plane and the geographical plane. Figure 3-40 visualizes these three planes of composition.

Naturally, these planes interlock. No filmmaker analyzes precisely how each single plane influences the composition, but decisions are made that focus attention on pairs of planes. Clearly, the plane of the frame must be dominant, since

Figure 3-34. ... the widescreen two-shot. Jean-Claude Brialy and Anna Karina in Jean-Luc Godard's *A Woman Is a Woman* (1961). The still life on the table is carefully composed, both to fill the middle space of the frame and to connect the characters.

that is the only plane that actually exists on the screen. Composition for this plane, however, is often influenced by factors in the geographical plane since, unless we are dealing with animation, a photographer or cinematographer must compose *for* the frame plane *in* the geographical plane. Likewise, the geographical plane and the plane of depth perception are coordinated, since much of our ability to perceive depth in two-dimensional representations as well as three-dimensional reality depends on phenomena in the geographical plane. In fact, perception of depth depends on many important factors other than binocular stereoscopic vision, which is why film presents such a strong illusion of three-dimensional space and why stereoscopic film techniques are relatively useless.*

---

* If so-called 3-D film techniques simply added the one remaining factor to depth perception, there would be no problem with them. The difficulty is that they actually distort our perception of depth, since they don't allow us to focus on a single plane, as we do naturally, and since they tend to produce disturbing pseudostereoscopic and pseudoscopic stereoscopic images.

Figure 3-35. Michelangelo Antonioni was well known for his sensitivity to architectural metaphor. This naturally masked shot from *Eclipse* (1962) both isolates Alain Delon and Monica Vitti and calls attention to the comparison to be made between Vitti and the portrait on the wall behind her.

Figure 3-41 illustrates some of the most important psychological factors strongly influencing depth perception. Overlapping takes place in the frame plane, but the three others—convergence, relative size, and density gradient—depend on the geographical plane. We've already discussed in Chapter 2 how various lens types affect depth perception (and linear distortion as well). A photographer modifies, suppresses, or reinforces the effects of lens types through composition of the image within the frame.

Here are some other examples of how the codes of the compositional planes interact:

Proximity and proportion are important subcodes. Stage actors are forever mindful of them. Obviously, the closer the subject, the more important it seems. As a result, an actor in the theater is always in danger of being "upstaged" by other members of the company. In film, of course, the director has complete control over position, and reverse angles help to redress the balance.

Figure 3-42, a classic shot from *Citizen Kane* (1941), gives us a more sophisticated example of the significance of proximity and proportion. Kane enters the room at the rear; his wife is in bed in the midground; a bottle of sleeping medicine looms large in the foreground. The three are connected by their placement in the frame. Reverse the order and the medicine bottle would disappear into the background of the shot.

Figure 3-36. Antonioni was obsessed with widescreen composition. This shot from *Red Desert* demonstrates his architectural formalism. (*Frame enlargement.*)

One of the aspects of composition that differentiates Baroque from late Renaissance painting is the shift from the "square" orientation of the geographic plane to the oblique. There were several reasons for this—one was the quest for greater verisimilitude: the oblique composition emphasized the space of the painting, whereas the symmetrical Renaissance compositional standard emphasized its design. The net effect, however, was to increase the psychological drama of the design: geographical obliques translate into the plane of the frame as diagonals, which are read as inherently more active than horizontals and verticals. Here, as in the earlier examples, there is a relationship between compositional factors in separate planes.

Eventually the geographic and depth planes "feed" information to the plane of the frame. This is truer in painting and photography, which don't have the ability film does to move physically into the pictorial space, but it is still generally true in cinema as well. The frame plane is the only "real" plane. Most elements of composition, therefore, realize themselves in this plane.

The empty frame, contrary to expectations, is not a tabula rasa. Even before the image appears, we invest the potential space of the frame with certain qualities, ones which have been measured scientifically: our natural tendency to read depth into the two-dimensional design, for instance. Latent expectations determine intrinsic interest. Figures 3-43 and 3-44 demonstrate this. In 3-43, both verticals are precisely the same length, yet the left-hand line looks much longer. This is because we read the angles at top and bottom as representative of corners, the left receding, the right intruding. If both lines *seem* to be equal, we then calculate

Figure 3-37. This shot from Jean Renoir's *Boudu Saved from Drowning* (1932) isolates the forlorn figure of Boudu, about to jump into the Seine, by vignetting the image. The masking has a literal function as well: Boudu (Michel Simon) is seen through a telescope in this shot. (*l'Avant-Scène. Frame enlargement.*)

that the line on the left must be longer, since it is "farther away." In Figure 3-44, which stairway ascends and which descends? The "correct" answers are that *A* ascends and *B* descends. The trick is in the verbs, of course, since stairs always go both up and down. But since Westerners tend to read from left to right, we see stair *A* ascending and stair *B* descending.

So, even before the image appears, the frame is invested with meaning. The bottom is more "important" than the top, left comes before right, the bottom is stable, the top unstable; diagonals from bottom left to top right go "up" from stability to instability. Horizontals will also be given more weight than verticals: confronted with horizontal and vertical lines of equal length, we tend to read the horizontal as longer, a phenomenon emphasized by the dimensions of the frame.

When the image does appear, form, line, and color are impressed with these latent values in the frame. Form, line, and color also have their own inherent values of weight and direction. If sharp lines exist in the design of the image, we tend to read along them from left to right. An object with a "light" inherent significance (Mrs. Kane's medicine bottle) can be given "heavy" significance through shape.

Figure 3-38. CLOSED FORM. The notorious stateroom scene from *A Night at the Opera* (Sam Wood, 1935) must be the zenith of Hollywood-style closed form! The brothers are cramped in the frame, as well as in the stateroom.

Figure 3-39. OPEN FORM. Macha Meril in Godard's *A Married Woman* (1964). The taxi is moving to the left out of the frame, Meril is walking to the right out of the frame and looking back toward the left; the car in the background is moving diagonally up out of the frame. The design elements of the shot conspire to make us aware of the continuous space beyond the limits of the frame. (*French Film Office*.)

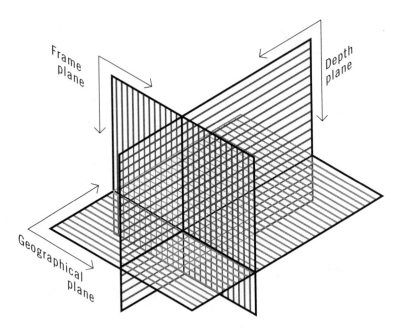

Figure 3-40. THE THREE PLANES OF COMPOSITION: The plane of the image; the geography of the photographic space; the axis of depth perception.

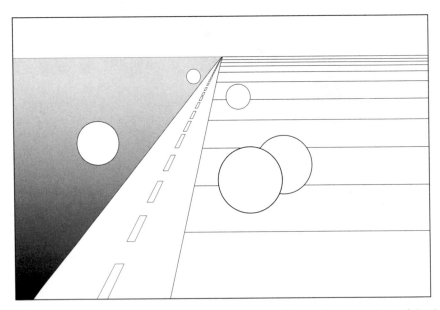

Figure 3-41. CONVENTIONS OF DEPTH PERCEPTION. Four major conventions of depth perception are illustrated here: convergence (the boundaries of the road), relative size (the near and far balls), density gradient (of shade on the left, of lines on the right), and overlapping (the balls on the right).

Figure 3-42. Dorothy Comingore (in shadow), Orson Welles, and Joseph Cotten in Welles's *Citizen Kane* (1941). It is not the material of the shot but its design that tells the story. (*Sight and Sound.*)

And color, of course, adds an entirely new dimension. Hitchcock begins *Marnie* (1964) with a close shot of his heroine's bright yellow pocketbook. The other color values of the scene are neutral. The sense is of the pocketbook carrying the woman rather than vice versa, just the effect Hitchcock wants, considering that the yellow bulge contains the money Marnie had just stolen and that her life, as we later see, is dominated by her kleptomania. Before we learn any of this narratively, we "know" it. (*Marnie* is also an excellent example of other types of color dominance, since the subject of the film is color symbolism: Marnie suffers from rosophobia.)

Elements of form, line, and color all carry their own intrinsic interests, significant weights that counteract, reinforce, counterpoint, or balance each other in complex systems, each read against our latent expectations of the frame and with the senses of composition in depth and planar design combined.

Multiple images (split screen) and superimpositions (double exposures, et cetera), although they are seldom used, can multiply the intrinsic weights by factors of two, three, four, or more. Texture, although it is not often mentioned when speaking of film esthetics, is also important, not only in terms of the inherent texture of the subject but also in terms of the texture—or grain—of the image. One illustration will suffice: we have learned to associate graininess with enlargement,

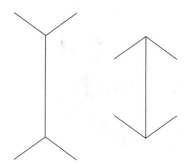

Figure 3-43.
THE MÜLLER-LYER ILLUSION. Both verticals are the same length, yet the left-hand line looks much longer. We read the angles at top and bottom as corners, the left receding, the right intruding. If both lines seem to be equal, we think the line on the left must be longer, since it is "further away."

Figure 3-44.
UPSTAIRS/DOWNSTAIRS ILLUSION. Which stairway ascends and which descends? Since Westerners tend to read from left to right, we see stair A ascending and stair B descending.

A   B

and with documentary. The filmmaker therefore has this code at his command. A grainy image signifies a "truthful" one. The grain of enlargement and its significance as a barrier to comprehension provided the basic metaphor of Antonioni's 1966 film *Blow-up.*

Perhaps the most important tool the filmmaker can use to modify the meanings of form, line, and color, and their intrinsic interests, is lighting. In the days when filmstock was relatively insensitive (before the 1960s), artificial lighting was a requisite, and filmmakers made a virtue of necessity, as always. The German Expressionists of the twenties borrowed the code of chiaroscuro from painting to dramatic effect—it allowed them to emphasize design over verisimilitude. The classical Hollywood cinematographic style wanted a more natural effect and so developed a system of balanced "key" lights and "fill" lights (see Figure 3-50) that provided thorough but not overt illumination and therefore presented a minimal barrier between observer and subject. At its best, this sophisticated system was capable of some extraordinary, subtle effects, yet it was inherently unrealistic; we seldom observe natural scenes that have both the very high light level and the carefully balanced fill that mark the Hollywood style (and that is perpetuated today in both theatrical and television productions).

The development of fast filmstocks permitted a new latitude in the code of lighting, and today most cinematographers work for verisimilitude rather than classic Hollywood balance.

Needless to say, all the lighting codes that operate in photography operate in film as well. Full front lighting washes out a subject; overhead lighting dominates it; lighting from below makes it lugubrious; highlighting can call attention to

Figure 3-45. Mischa Auer in Orson Welles's *Mr. Arkadin* (1955): a typically tilted Welles composition. That the line of the table moves down from left to right disorients us even further. The observer in the frame strains, stretches his neck to see. The low angle of the shot increases our sense of foreboding. Most important, the trope of the magnified eye is doubled and redoubled with typically Wellesian irony by the echoing circles of the top hat and the light above. The "cheat" here is that the magnifying glass is positioned for our use, not Auer's. (*l'Avant-Scène. Frame enlargement.*)

details (hair and eyes most often); backlighting can either dominate a subject or highlight it; sidelighting is capable of dramatic chiaroscuro effect.

Aspect ratio; open and closed form; frame, geographic, and depth planes; depth perception; proximity and proportion; intrinsic interest of color, form, and line; weight and direction; latent expectation; oblique versus symmetric composition; texture; and lighting. These are the major codes operating within the static film frame. In terms of the diachronic shot, however, we have just begun.

The Diachronic Shot

Filmmakers use a wealth of terminology in regard to the shot. The factors that now come into play include distance, focus, angle, movement, and point of view. Some of these elements also operate within the static frame, but all are more appropriately discussed as dynamic qualities. Shot distance is the simplest variable. So-called "normal" shots include the full shot, three-quarter shot, medium shot (or mid-shot), and head-and-shoulders shot—all defined in terms of the

Figure 3-46. Multiple exposure is one of the most unnatural codes of cinema (we seldom see two images at the same time in real life) but it can also be one of the most meaningful. Here, three multiple exposures from various films by Orson Welles, in increasing order of complexity. The first, from *Citizen Kane*, simply connects Susan Alexander (Dorothy Comingore) with her image in the press, a common use of the double exposure code.... *(l'Avant-Scène. Frame enlargement.)*

Figure 3-47. ... The second, from *The Magnificent Ambersons* (1942), suggests two levels of reality.... *(l'Avant-Scène. Frame enlargement.)*

Figure 3-48. ... The third, from *The Lady from Shanghai* (1947), is from the famous mirror sequence in that film: will we survive the nightmare? *(l'Avant-Scène. Frame enlargement.)*

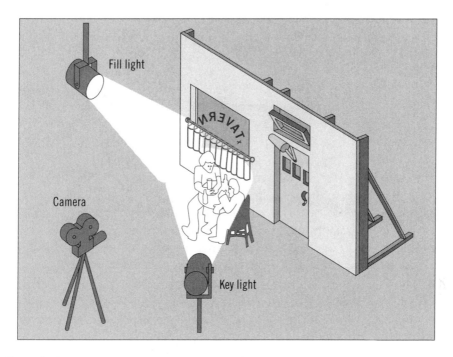

Figure 3-49. KEY LIGHTS AND FILL LIGHTS. The key light, usually at a 45° angle to the camera-subject axis, provides the main source of illumination. The smaller fill light softens the shadows in this classic Hollywood lighting technique.

amount of subject viewed. Closeups, long shots, and extreme long shots complete the range of distances.

Note that none of these terms has anything to do with the focal length of the lens used. As we saw in Chapter 2, in addition to being defined in terms of the distance of the camera from the subject, shots are also named for their lenses. Note, too, that in practice these terms are loosely used. One person's closeup is another's "detail shot," and no Academy of film has (so far) sat in deep deliberation deciding the precise point at which a medium shot becomes a long shot, or a long shot metamorphoses into an extreme long shot. Nevertheless, within limits, the concepts are valid.

A film shot mainly in closeups—Carl Dreyer's *The Passion of Joan of Arc* (1928), for example—deprives us of setting and is therefore disorienting, claustrophobic. The effect can be striking. On the other hand, a film shot mainly in long shot—many of Roberto Rossellini's later historical essays, for instance—emphasizes context over drama and dialectic over personality. The code of shot distance is simple, but to a large extent it controls which of the many other codes of film we may use.

Focus is the next most important variable in the syntax of the shot. There are two axes in the determination of focus: the first choice is between deep focus, in which foreground, middle ground, and background are all relatively sharp focus, and shallow focus, in which the focus emphasizes one ground over the others. Shallow focus obviously allows the filmmaker greater control over the image. Deep focus, on the other hand, is one of the prime esthetic hallmarks of mise-en-scène. (It is much easier to "put things in the scene" when all three grounds are in focus, since the scene is then much larger, more accommodating.) (See Figures 2-18 and 2-19.)

The second axis of focus is the continuum between sharp and soft focus. This aspect of the shot is related to texture. Soft focus is generally associated with so-called romantic moods. Sharp focus is more closely associated with verisimilitude. These are generalizations that specific instances often contradict. (As always, the rules are made to be broken.) Soft focus is not so much romantic as it is mollifying. It smoothes out the identifying details of an image and distances it.

Surely focus is a function of the still frame as well as of the diachronic shot. It is intimately associated with the compositional planes, since it permits concentration on a single ground. But it also tends toward movement. By maintaining relatively shallow focus and changing focus during the shot, the filmmaker can shift the intrinsic interest of the frame from one ground to another, which in a way parallels the effect of the pan, zoom, or tracking shot but does so within the frame and without moving the camera.

Focus changes within the shot are of two basic sorts: follow focus, in which the focus is changed to permit the camera to keep a moving subject in focus; and rack focus, in which the focus is changed to direct attention away from one subject and toward another in a different ground. Follow focus was one of the basics of the Hollywood style, admired for its ability to maintain attention on the subject. Rack focus is one of the hallmarks of the modern, intrusive style. Focus, then, is one of the codes that connect the codes of composition with those of movement.

The third aspect of the diachronic shot—angle—also reaches back toward static composition and forward toward the movement of the shot. Because the relationship between camera and subject exists in three-dimensional space, there are three sets of separate angles that determine the shot.

We have already discussed one of these, the angle of approach (squarely symmetrical or oblique), in the previous section. To understand the relationships among the three types of angle, it may be useful to visualize the three imaginary axes that run through the camera (Figure 2-25). The pan axis (vertical) is also the axis of the angle of approach; it is either square or oblique. The tilt axis (horizontal from left to right) determines the elevation of the shot: overhead, high-angle, eye-level, and low-angle are the basic terms used here. It goes without saying that high-angle shots diminish the importance of the subject while low-angle shots

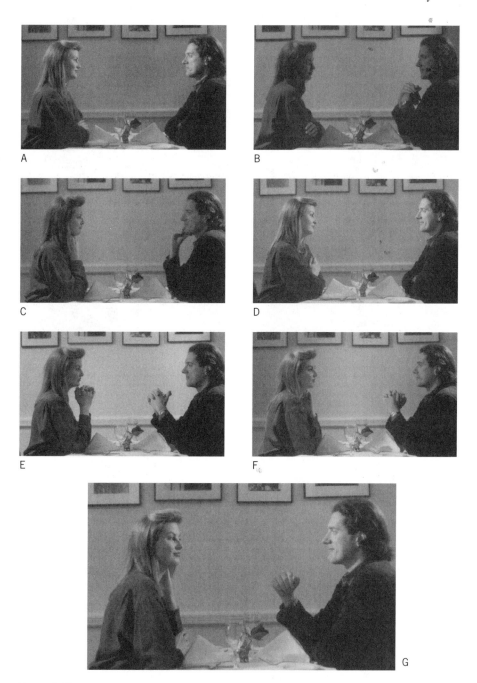

Figure 3-50. LIGHTING COMBINATIONS FROM "THE INTERFACE":
(A) Key light. Two key lights were used here. (B) Back light. (C) Fill light. (D) Key light and fill light. (E) Back light and fill light. (F) Key light and fill light. (G) The final composition: key, fill, and back lights.

Figure 3-51. HOLLYWOOD LIGHTING. Margaret O'Brien and Judy Garland in Vincente Minnelli's *Meet Me in St. Louis* (1944). The set is vibrantly, thoroughly lit. There are only the faintest hints of shadows, even in the back room, which is out of focus. Since this was a Technicolor film, the lighting is even stronger than it might have been for black-and-white.

emphasize its power. Interestingly, the eye-level shot, the least obtrusive, is not always so easily defined. The Japanese filmmaker Yasujiro Ozu is well known for the constant low-angle of his style, yet Ozu wasn't really trying to distort the basic design of his image: he was merely shooting from the eye level of a Japanese observer seated on a tatami mat. "Eye level," of course, depends on the eye of the beholder. Even in European and American cinema, the subtle differences among eye levels, although not immediately remarkable, can have significant effects over the course of a film.

The third angle variable, roll, is determined by the movement of the camera around the last remaining axis, the horizontal that parallels the axis of the lens. Possibly because this axis represents the metaphysical bond between the observer (or camera) and the subject, possibly because roll destroys the stability of the horizon, the camera is very seldom revolved around this axis. The only common roll movement that comes to mind is that sometimes used to mimic the movements of the horizon as seen from the boat in heavy seas. Roll movement (or the oblique horizon of a static shot) is the only change of camera angle that does not

Figure 3-52. HIGHLIGHTING. Jean-Pierre Melville's and Jean Cocteau's *Les Enfants terribles* (1950). The eyes are specially lit.

significantly alter our focus of attention. To pan or to tilt is to change images; to roll is simply to alter the original image.

The camera not only revolves around these three axes, it is also moved from one point to another: hence "tracking" shots (also called trucking or dolly shots) and "crane" shots. The zoom shot, as discussed in Chapter 2, mimics the effect of a track in or track back, but not precisely. In the zoom, since the camera does not move, the relationships among objects in different planes remain the same; there is no sense of entering into the scene; our perspective remains constant, even if the image is enlarged. In the track, however, we do move physically into the scene; the spatial relationships among objects shift, as does our perspective. Although the zoom is often an inexpensive alternative to the tracking shot, its effect is strangely distancing: we seem to move closer without getting any nearer, and that is disorienting, since we have no such experience in real life for comparison.

Just as debates have evolved between proponents of deep focus and shallow focus, and between champions of mise-en-scène and montage, so, too, the moving camera has its adherents and detractors. Because it continually changes our perspective, the tracking shot significantly increases our perception of depth. More important, the moving camera has an inherent ethical dimension. It can be used in two essentially different ways (like focus shifts, pans, and tilts): either to follow the subject or to change it. The first alternative strongly emphasizes the centrality of the subject of the film; the second shifts interest from subject to cam-

Figure 3-53. Backlighting is one of the more interesting lighting codes taken from painting. Here, a relatively early example from painting, Constance Marie Charpentier's *Mlle Charlotte du val d'Ognes* (c. 1801). The light source highlights the subject's hair and the folds of her dress. Although there is no perceivable light source from the front, details are nevertheless evident and the shadows are soft and elegant. (*Oil on canvas, 60 1/2" by 50 5/8", The Metropolitan Museum of Art, The Mr. and Mrs. Isaac D. Fletcher Collection. Bequest of Isaac D. Fletcher, 1917.*)

Figure 3-54. Jean-Luc Godard is one filmmaker who has been intrigued by this code. By the time of *Weekend* (1968), from which this shot comes, he had abstracted the backlit shot to the extreme of silhouette. The lighting is harsh, bold, and overwhelms the subject. In order to search out detail in the shot we have to work, which makes us feel, faced with the bright window, not unlike voyeurs—exactly the effect Godard wants. Jean Yanne and Mireille Darc in *Weekend* (1968). (*Frame enlargement.*)

Figure 3-55. Woody Allen achieved an entirely different feel in this equally harshly backlit shot from *Manhattan* (1979). The silhouettes of Diane Keaton and Allen are instantly recognizable at a cocktail party in the garden of the Museum of Modern Art.

Figure 3-56. In addition to widescreen architectural composition, Antonioni was fascinated by the focus code. Here, in *Red Desert*, Monica Vitti enters the frame out of focus (just like her character). (*Frame enlargement.*)

era, from object to filmmaker. As André Bazin has pointed out, these are ethical questions, since they determine the human relationships among artist, subject, and observer.

Although some estheticians insist that the moving camera, because it calls attention to the filmmaker, is somehow less ethical than the stationary camera, this is as specious a differentiation as the earlier dichotomies between mise-en-scène and montage and between deep and shallow focus. A tracking or crane shot need not necessarily shift interest from subject to camera; it can, rather, call attention to the relationship between the two, which is arguably both more realistic and more ethical, since there is in fact a relationship.

Indeed, many of the best and most lyrical tracking shots are the cinematic equivalents of making love, as the filmmaker courts, then unites with his subject; the track becomes the relationship, and the shot a synthesis of filmmaker and subject, greater than the sum of its parts.

F. W. Murnau and Max Ophüls loom large in the history of the moving camera. Their use of it was, essentially, humanistic—to create a lyrical celebration of their subjects and to involve their audiences more deeply. Stanley Kubrick, a contemporary filmmaker closely identified with tracking shots, also uses camera movement to involve his audience, but in a colder, more intellectual way. Michael Snow, an important abstract filmmaker and artist, explored in great depth—in a series of three seminal films—the significatory potential of the moving camera.

A. Sylvia Bataille in Jean Renoir's *Partie de campagne* (1936).

B. Bibi Andersson, Gunnar Björnstrand, Liv Ullmann in Bergman's *Persona* (1966).

C. Renée Longarini, Marcello Mastroianni in Fellini's *La Dolce Vita* (1959).

D. Giulietta Masina in Fellini's *La Strada* (1954).

E. Masina in Fellini's *Nights of Cabiria* (1957).

F. Masina in Fellini's *Juliet of the Spirits* (1965).

Figure 3-57. SHOT COMPOSITION. In practice, shot distance is much more idiosyncratic than the terminology suggests. Both A and B, for example, are somewhere in between closeups and detail shots. Both give us half a woman's face, yet in A the face takes up nearly the whole frame while in B it is part of a three-shot. The aspect ratio of the frame is an important consideration, too. Both C and D are, more or less, mid-shots, yet C, in the scope ratio, has an entirely different effect from D, in the standard Academy ratio. C includes a lot more action than D; D is more like a closeup in effect. Composition is a major element, as well. Shots E and F both must be classified as long shots—same actress, same director. In each, Giulietta Masina takes up three-quarters of the height of the frame, more or less. Yet in E, Fellini has composed a shot in which the other design elements—the road, the statues, the horizon—work to focus attention on Masina. Psychologically, the image of her is more impressive here. In F, composition (and her posture) works to de-emphasize her presence. (*All shots, l'Avant-Scène. Frame enlargements.*)

Figure 3-58. A typical low-angle shot from Yasujiro Ozu's *The End of Summer* (1961). The angle doesn't seem so striking because the subjects are seated on the floor. (*New Yorker Films.*)

Wavelength (1967) is an obsessive zoom, lasting forty-five minutes, which takes us from an image of a rather large New York loft in its entirety to, in the end, a detail shot of a photograph hanging on the wall at the opposite end of the large room. The potential of the simplest pan from left to right and back again is explored in ↔ (1968–69, also called *Back and Forth*). Snow set up his camera in an empty classroom, then panned continuously and quickly over a sector of about 75° and in periods ranging from fifteen cycles per minute to sixty cycles per minute. *La Région Centrale* (1970–71), Snow's masterwork lasting more than three hours, gives us an obsessive "map" of the complete sphere of space that surrounds the camera on all sides. Snow constructed a servomechanism control head for his camera, set it up in a remote and rocky region of northern Quebec, and controlled its patterns of movement from behind a hill. The camera swoops, swirls, gyrates, twirls, tilts, zigzags, sweeps, arcs, and performs figure eights in a multitude of patterns while nothing is visible except the barren landscape, the horizon, and the sun. The effect is the thorough liberation of the camera from both subject and photographer. The global space that surrounds it becomes raw material for Snow's complex patterns of movements. Movement is all.

The liberated, abstract quality of Snow's images leads us directly to a consideration of the last of the five shot variables: point of view. Unlike the first four, this is more a matter of metaphysics than of geometry. The point of *La Région Centrale*, for example, is that is has no point of view, or rather that its point of view is abstract and global. Most narrative films, however, do show some sort of subjec-

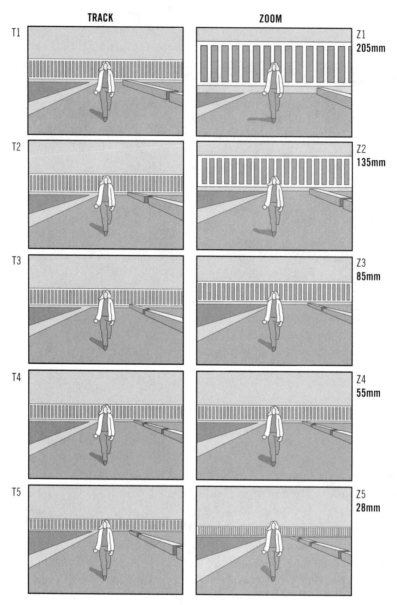

Figure 3-59. TRACKING VERSUS ZOOMING. These ten frames from parallel tracking and zoom shots illustrate the significant differences between the two techniques. In both series, the woman is walking towards the camera, covering a distance of approximately fifty yards between frame 1 and frame 5. The track was shot first, with a 55 mm lens. (Thus frames T4 and Z4 are identical.) The zoom was then shot to correspond to the track. The relationship between subject and background is dramatically different in the zoom. As the lens changes from telephoto (205 mm) to wide-angle (28 mm) focal lengths, depth perception changes from suppressed to exaggerated, and perspective undergoes a slight moderation as well. In the tracking shot, the distance between subject and camera is constant from one frame to another, and the building is far enough in the background so as not to change greatly between frames. In the zoom, the distance between subject and camera is constantly changing, and the relative size of the background building is magnified in the telephoto shots and distanced, or minimized in the wide-angle frame. Notice, too, that the angle of the shadow changes in the zoom. See Figure 2-10.

Figure 3-60. THE MOVING CAMERA. On the set of Jean-Luc Godard's *One Plus One* (1968). The typical camera at right is a "prop" in the film. (The red and black flags are not standard equipment.) The camera platform is counterbalanced by weights out of the frame. In the middle ground can be seen tracks laid for a camera that is barely visible at the extreme left. In the foreground, a third camera is mounted on a special truck.

tive point of view. This varies from the objective point of view of long shots, deep focus, and static camera, to the more subjective approach of closeups, shallow focus, and moving camera. We've already noted that the moving camera has an ethical aspect to it. The question of point of view is at the heart of this ethical code, and critics and semioticians are only now beginning to investigate the phenomenon specifically. Considering the structure of the artistic experience we set up in Chapter 1, the ethics of film—the quality and shape of the relationships among filmmaker, subject, artwork, and audience—is elemental: all other ideas about film must stem from it and relate back to it.

Point of view is easier to describe in prose narrative: novels are either narrated by someone in the story—the first-person narrator—or by someone outside it—the omniscient narrator. The first-person narrator may be either a major or a minor figure in the events; the omniscient narrator is sometimes developed as a separate character, sometimes characterless, except insofar as he represents the character of the author. In its totality, film can fairly well duplicate these fictional models.

Most films, like most novels, are told from an omniscient point of view. We see and hear whatever the author wants us to see and hear. But when we come to

Figure 3-61. ROLL. Pans, tilts, and tracks are common enough cinematic codes, but rolls are relatively rare. The reason is obvious: pans, tilts, and tracking shots mimic common, everyday movements, but we seldom "roll" our heads (tilt them sideways), so this is often a striking perspective. While shots are often made at a rolled angle (see the illustrations from Orson Welles films in Figures 3-42 and 3-45) the movement of rolling is unusual. Here, Fred Astaire performs an entire dance routine in one unedited shot, gradually moving up the wall, across the ceiling, and down the opposite wall, in Stanley Donen's *Royal Wedding* (1951). The precisely choreographed routine was accomplished on a set mounted within a drum. The furniture and the camera were secured. As Astaire moved from floor to wall, from wall to ceiling, the set turned and the camera turned with it.

Figure 3-62. Stanley Kubrick used a similar apparatus for many unusual shots in *2001: A Space Odyssey*. This particular shot was a setpiece to show off the device. The flight attendant walked full circle, supposedly using Velcro slippers on the special path. (*Frame enlargement.*)

the first-person mode—which has proved so useful in prose fiction because of the resonances that can be developed between events and the character or persona of the narrator who perceives them—problems arise in film. It's easy enough to allow a film character to narrate the story. The difficulty is that we see what is happening as well as hear it. In the novel, in effect, we only hear it. As we've

Figure 3-63. Murnau's set for *Sunrise* (1927). The long tram ride has earned a place in film history. In this case, the tracking shot is purely verisimilitudinous: there is no other way to ride a tram than on tracks! (*MOMA/FSA.*)

Figure 3-64. Max Ophüls was unusually fond of the moving camera. This is a still from a long lyrical, and very complex crane shot in *La Ronde* (1950). Anton Walbrook at left, Simone Signoret on the carousel. (*MOMA/FSA.*)

Figure 3-65. If the tracking shot was logical and realistic for Murnau, lyrical and romantic for Ophüls, it became, by 1968, a tool of intellectual analysis (as well as a grand joke) for Jean-Luc Godard. This frame comes from the middle of the seven-minute-long tracking shot of the traffic jam in *Weekend*. Godard's camera moves slowly and inexorably past a seemingly endless line of stopped autos. Drivers and passengers honk incessantly, argue with each other, fight, stop for an impromptu picnic, play ball from car to car (as here), or test their gear on trailer-mounted sailboats. The poplar trees that line the road at regular intervals divide this magnificent continuous shot into segments that function as separate framing devices. (*Frame enlargement.*)

Figure 3-66. Michael Snow's *Wavelength* (1967) treated the tracking shot as a structural law, the subject of the film. This is a frame from about the middle of the forty-five minute zoom. By the end of the film, Snow's camera has moved into a closeup of the middle of the photograph tacked to the wall above the chair. The image? Waves, of course! (*MOMA/FSA. Frame enlargement.*)

noted earlier, Robert Montgomery's *Lady in the Lake* (1945) is the most famous example of rigid adherence to the first-person rule applied to cinema—and the most obvious demonstration of its failure.

In *Stage Fright* (1950), Alfred Hitchcock discovered, to his chagrin, that the first-person point of view in film is fraught with problems even when it is used perfunctorily. In that film, Hitchcock had one of his characters narrate a flashback—and lie. Audiences saw the lie on screen, and when they later found out that it was false they reacted angrily. They weren't able to accept the possibility that the *image* would lie, although they would have been quite willing to believe that the *character* had lied. The screen image is vested with an immutable aura of validity.

By the early 1940s, Hollywood had evolved a very smooth, efficient, and clearly understood idiom of point of view. The establishing shot—a long shot—established place, often time, and sometimes other necessary information. Hitchcock was a master of the establishing shot. The opening pan and track of *Rear Window* (1954), for example, tells us where we are, why we are there, whom we are with, what is going on now, what has happened to get us there, who the other characters of the story are, and even suggests possible ways the story might develop—all effortlessly and quickly and without a spoken word! Paragraphs of prose are condensed into seconds of film time.

Figure 3-67. Michael Snow's ultimate pan/tilt/roll machine, with camera, set up to shoot *La Région Centrale*. Snow operated the camera from behind the rock at right so as not to appear in the picture. (*MOMA/FSA.*)

The Hollywood dialogue style is equally efficient: we normally begin with a shot of both speakers (an establishing two-shot), then move to a montage of one-shots as each of the participants variously speaks and listens. Often these are "over-the-shoulder" shots, an interesting use of the code, since it suggests the speaker's point of view but is also physically separate from it. The shot of the first character from (approximately) the second character's point of view is usually termed a reverse-angle shot. The rhythms of this insistent and intimate shot-countershot technique are often intoxicating: we surround the conversation.

This is the ultimate omniscient style, since it allows us to see everything from the ideal perspective. More contemporary techniques, which tend to emphasize the separateness and individuality of the camera, may allow us to "see every-thing," but always from a separate, distinct point of view. Antonioni's camera, for instance, often holds on a scene that a character has either not yet entered or already left. The effect is to emphasize environment over character and action, context over content. We might call this the "third-person" point of view: the camera often seems to take on a personality of its own, separate from those of the characters.

In either omniscient style—the Hollywood or the modern—the point-of-view shot (abbreviated "POV") has its uses. And soundtrack narration is often able to strengthen the sense of the character's perspective of events. Yet the psychologi-cally insistent, ever-present image attenuates this perspective. In print we need not always be "looking" at a scene: writers don't always describe or narrate, they often explain or theorize. In film, however, because of the presence of the image,

Figure 3-68. Grace Kelly and James Stewart in Hitchcock's *Rear Window* (1954). Stewart, a photographer, is immobilized in his apartment on Tenth Street in Greenwich Village. The "CinemaScope" picture windows of the building across the courtyard intrigue him. (Look closely!) He becomes deeply involved in the stories they tell. A metaphor for filmmaking? Certainly a study in "point of view." (*MOMA/FSA.*)

there is always the element of description—even when the soundtrack is used concurrently for explanation, theorizing, or discussion. This is one of the most significant differences between prose narrative and film narrative. Clearly, the only way to circumvent this insistent descriptive nature of the film image is to eliminate it entirely, in which case the soundtrack can duplicate the abstract, analytical potential of written language. Jean-Luc Godard experimented with just this technique in his highly theoretical films of the late sixties. Sometimes the screen is simply black, while we listen to the words on the soundtrack.

Sound

While the fact of the image is a disadvantage of a kind in terms of point of view in film narrative, the fact of sound—its ever-presence—is a distinct advantage. Christian Metz identifies five channels of information in film: (1) the visual image; (2) print and other graphics; (3) speech; (4) music; and (5) noise (sound effects). Interestingly, the majority of these channels are auditory rather than visual. Examining these channels with regard to the manner in which they communicate, we discover that only two of them are continuous—the first and the fifth. The other three are intermittent—they are switched on and off—and it is easy to conceive of a film without either print, speech, or music.

Figure 3-69. Gregory Peck drowns his interlocutor in a glass of milk—and we share the view-point and the experience—in this memorable pov shot from Hitchcock's *Spellbound*. (*Frame enlargements.*)

The two continuous channels themselves communicate in distinctly separate ways. We "read" images by directing our attention; we do not read sound, at least not in the same conscious way. Sound is not only omnipresent but also omnidi-rectional. Because it is so pervasive, we tend to discount it. Images can be manip-ulated in many different ways, and the manipulation is relatively obvious; with sound, even the limited manipulation that does occur is vague and tends to be ignored.

It is the pervasiveness of sound that is its most attractive quality. It acts to real-ize both space and time. It is essential to the creation of a locale; the "room tone," based on the reverberation time, harmonics, and so forth of a particular location, is its signature. A still image comes alive when a soundtrack is added that can cre-ate a sense of the passage of time. In a utilitarian sense, sound shows its value by creating a ground base of continuity to support the images, which usually receive more conscious attention. Speech and music naturally receive attention because they have specific meaning. But the "noise" of the soundtrack—"sound effects"—is paramount. This is where the real construction of the sound environment takes place.

But "noise" and "effects" are poor labels indeed for a worthy art. Possibly we could term this aspect of the soundtrack "environmental sound." The influence of environmental sound has been felt—and noticed—in contemporary music, espe-cially in that movement known as "musique concrète." Even recorded speech has been affected by this new ability. In the great days of radio, "sound effects" were limited to those that could be produced physically. The advent of synthesizers, multitrack recording, and now computer-manipulated digitized sound has made it possible for the sound effects technicians, or "Foley artists," as they are now called, to recreate an infinite range of both natural and entirely new artificial sounds. Much of the best modern sound drama (which has appeared mainly on records, and public interest radio stations) has recognized the extraordinary potential of what used to be known simply as sound effects. Contemporary music also celebrates this formerly pedestrian art.

Film, too, has recognized sound's new maturity. In the early days of the sound film, musicals, for instance, were extraordinary elaborate visually. Busby Berkeley conceived intricate visual representations of musical ideas to hold an audience's interest. Now, however, the most powerful film musical form is the simple concert. The soundtrack carries the film; the images are dominated by it.

We can conceive of nonmusical cinema in this vein as well. In England, where radio drama lasted longer than in the U.S., a tradition of aural drama was maintained from the *Goon Shows* of the 1950s through *Monty Python's Flying Circus* of the 1970s.

In the U. S. much of the best comedy has been almost exclusively aural since the days of vaudeville: beginning with the masters Jack Benny, George Burns, and Fred Allen, this exuberant if unsung tradition has given us Nichols and May, Mel Brooks, and Bill Cosby; the complex "cinematic" constructions of the Firesign Theatre and Albert Brooks; and the "new commentary" of Billy Crystal, Whoopi Goldberg, Jerry Seinfeld, and Steven Wright. Much of this recent comedy extends the boundaries of the old vaudeville tradition: aural artists have moved into more complex modes.

In cinema, Francis Ford Coppola's fascinating *The Conversation* (1974) did for the aural image what *Blow-up* (1966) had done for the pictorial image eight years earlier. While the soundtrack can certainly support greater emphasis than it has been given, it cannot easily be divorced from images. Much of the language we employ to discuss the codes of soundtracks deals with the relationship between sound and image. Siegfried Kracauer suggests the differentiation between "actual" sound, which logically connects with the image, and "commentative" sound, which does not. Dialogue of people in the scene is actual, dialogue of people not in the scene is commentative. (A filmmaker sophisticated in sound, such as Richard Lester, often used commentative dialogue of people who were in the shot, but not part of the action of the scene.)

Director and theorist Karel Reisz used slightly different terminology. For Reisz, who wrote a standard text on editing, all sound is divided into "synchronous" and "asynchronous." Synchronous sound has its source within the frame (the editor must work to synchronize it). Asynchronous sound comes from outside the frame.

Combining these two continuums, we get a third,[*] whose poles are "parallel" sound and "contrapuntal" sound. Parallel sound is actual, synchronous, and connected with the image. Contrapuntal sound is commentative, asynchronous, and

---

[*] I am indebted to Win Sharples Jr, "The Aesthetics of Film Sound," *Filmmakers Newsletter* 8:5, for this synthesis.

Figure 3-70. The title frame from Orson Welles's tour de force establishing track at the beginning of *Touch of Evil* (1958). In a few minutes, we know all that we need to know. (*Frame enlargement.*)

opposed to or in counterpoint with the image. It makes no difference whether we are dealing with speech, music, or environmental sound: all three are at times variously parallel or contrapuntal, actual or commentative, synchronous or asynchronous.

The differentiation between parallel and contrapuntal sound is perhaps the controlling factor. This conception of the soundtrack as working logically either with or against the image provides the basic esthetic dialectic of sound. The Hollywood sound style is strongly parallel. The programmatic music of thirties movies nudged, underlined, emphasized, characterized, and qualified even the simplest scenes so that the dullest images as well as the most striking were thoroughly pervaded by the emotions designed by the composers of the nearly continuous music track. Erich Wolfgang Korngold and Max Steiner were the two best-known composers of these emotionally dominating scores.

In the experimental 1960s and 1970s, contrapuntal sound gave an ironic edge to the style of film music. Often the soundtrack was seen as equal, but different from, the image. Marguerite Duras, for example, experimented with commentative soundtracks completely separate from the image, as in *India Song* (1975). In the 1980s, Hollywood returned to programmatic music. John Williams, composer of the soundtracks for many of the blockbusters of the late 1970s and 1980s from

Jaws (1975) and *Star Wars* (1977) to *Home Alone* (1990) and *Jurassic Park* (1993), has defined the musical themes of a generation, just as his notable predecessors had done. But music is still used commentatively as well. Rock, for example, offers filmmakers a repertoire of instant keys to modern ideas and feelings, as George Lucas's *American Graffiti* (1973), Lawrence Kasdan's *The Big Chill* (1983), or any of the films of John Hughes demonstrated clearly.

Ironically, music—which used to be the most powerfully asynchronous and commentative element of the soundtrack—has now become so pervasive in real life that a filmmaker can maintain strict synchronicity of actual sound and still produce a complete music track. The ubiquitous Walkman radio and Boom Box have made life a musical.

Montage

In the U.S., the word for the work of putting together the shots of a film is "cutting" or "editing," while in Europe the term is "montage." The American words suggest a trimming process, in which unwanted material is eliminated. Michelangelo once described sculpture similarly as paring away unneeded stone to discover the natural shape of the sculpture in a block of marble. One edits or cuts raw material down. "Montage," however, suggests a building action, working up from the raw material. Indeed, the classic style of Hollywood editing of the thirties and forties, revived in part in the eighties—what the French call découpage classique—was in fact marked by its smoothness, fluidity, and leanness. And European montage, ever since the German Expressionists and Eisenstein in the twenties, has been characterized by a process of synthesis: a film is seen as being constructed rather than edited. The two terms for the action express the two basic attitudes toward it.

Whereas mise-en-scène is marked by a fusion of complexities, montage is surprisingly simple, at least on the physical level. There are only two ways to put two pieces of film together: one can overlap them (double exposure, dissolves, multiple images), or one can put them end to end. For images, the second alternative dominates almost exclusively, while sounds lend themselves much more readily to the first, so much so that this activity has its own name: mixing.

In general parlance, "montage" is used in three different ways. While maintaining its basic meaning, it also has the more specific usages of:

❏ a dialectical process that creates a third meaning out of the original two meanings of the adjacent shots; and

❏ a process in which a number of short shots are woven together to communicate a great deal of information in a short time.

This last is simply a special case of general montage; the dialectical process is inherent in any montage, conscious or not.

Figure 3-71. To end *The Passenger* with a long, majestic, and mysterious track up to and through a window, Antonioni set up this complex apparatus—sort of a combination of a Steadicam, Skycam, and overhead track. The operator guided the camera, suspended from a crane, up to the window grill, which grips then opened while attaching the camera to the crane so that it could move out into the courtyard.

Découpage classique, the Hollywood style of construction, gradually developed a broad range of rules and regulations: for example, the practice of beginning always with an establishing shot, then narrowing down from the generalization; or, the strict rule of thumb for editing dialogue scenes with master shots and reverse angles. All the editing practices of the Hollywood grammar were designed to permit seamless transitions from shot to shot and to concentrate attention on the action at hand. What helped to maintain immediacy and the flow of the action was good; what did not was bad.

In fact, any kind of montage is in the end defined according to the action it photographs. Still pictures can be put together solely with regard to the rhythm of the succeeding shots. Diachronic shots, inherently active, demand that the movements within the shot be considered in the editing. The jump cut, where the natural movement is interrupted, provides an interesting example of the contrasting ways in which découpage classique and contemporary editing treat a problem.

In Hollywood cinema, "invisible cutting" was the aim, and the jump cut was used as a device to compress dead time. A man enters a large room at one end, for instance, and must walk to a desk at the other end. The jump cut can maintain tempo by eliminating most of the action of traversing the long room, but it must do so unobtrusively. The laws of Hollywood grammar insist that the excess dead time be smoothed over either by cutting away to another element of the scene (the desk itself, someone else in the room) or by changing camera angle sufficiently so that the second shot is clearly from a different camera placement. Simply snipping out the unwanted footage from a single shot from a single angle is not permitted. The effect, according to Hollywood rules, would be disconcerting.

Modern style, however, permits far greater latitude. In *Breathless* (1959), Jean-Luc Godard startled some estheticians by jump cutting in mid-shot. The cuts had no utilitarian value and they were disconcerting. Godard himself seldom returned to this device in later films, but his "ungrammatical" construction was absorbed into general montage stylistics, and jump cuts are now allowed for rhythmic effect. Even the simple utilitarian jump cut has been streamlined: edited from a single shot (single angle), it can be smoothed by a series of quick dissolves.

The lively 1960s films of Richard Lester—especially his musicals *A Hard Day's Night* (1964), *Help!* (1965), and *A Funny Thing Happened on the Way to the Forum* (1966)—popularized jump cuts, rapid and "ungrammatical" cutting. Over time, his brash editorial style became a norm, now celebrated every night around the world in hundreds of music videos on MTV. Because these video images now dominate our lives it's hard to understand how fresh and inventive these techniques seemed in the 1960s. Because this style is now so pervasive in music videos, Lester must be counted as—at least in one sense—the most influential film stylist since D. W. Griffith. Except for morphs, there are few techniques of contemporary music videos that Richard Lester didn't first try in the 1960s. (But then, there isn't much about contemporary music that the Beatles and their colleagues didn't first explore in the 1960s.)

It's important to note that there are actually two processes going on when shots are edited. The first is the joining of the two shots. Also important, however, is determining the length of any individual shot, both as it relates to shots that precede and follow it and as it concerns the action of the shot. Découpage classique demands that a shot be cut so that the editing doesn't interfere with the central action of the shot. If we plot the action of each shot so that we get a rising then a falling curve, Hollywood grammar demands a cut shortly after the climax of the curve. Modern directors like Michelangelo Antonioni, however, reversed the logic, maintaining the shot long after the climax, throughout the period of aftermath. The last shot of *The Passenger* (1975) is an excellent example.

The rhythmic value of editing is probably best seen in the code of "accelerated montage," in which interest in a scene is heightened and brought to a climax through progressively shorter alternations of shots between two subjects (often in chase scenes). Christian Metz pointed to accelerated montage as a uniquely cinematic code (although Charles Ives's antagonistic brass bands provided an illustration of this kind of cross-cutting in music). Accelerated montage points in the direction of a second type of editing.

Montage is used not only to create a continuity between shots in a scene but also to bend the time line of a film. "Parallel" montage allows the filmmaker to alternate between two stories that may or may not be interrelated, cross-cutting between them. (Accelerated montage is a special type of parallel montage.) The flashback and the flash-forward permit digressions and forecasts. "Involuted"

Figure 3-72. Robert Altman's magnificent satire of the film industry, *The Player* (1992), begins with a reel-long tracking shot which is the equal of Murnau's, Welles's, or Godard's: establishing the location, setting up the action, introducing the characters, passing by small incidental dramas, tossing off inside jokes, peering in windows, and, postmodernly talking about its antecedents at the same time that it pays homage to them, even while Altman's own shot surpasses those of his predecessors, distanced with insouciant wit, as if to say, "long tracking shots, like long sentences, separate the players from the rest." (*Frame enlargement.*)

montage allows a sequence to be narrated without particular regard for chronology: an action can be repeated, shots can be edited out of order. Each of these extensions of the montage codes looks toward the creation of something other than simple chronology in the montage itself, a factor very little emphasized in classic découpage continuity cutting.

Possibly the most common dialectic device is the match cut, which links two disparate scenes by the repetition of an action or a form, or the duplication of mise-en-scène. Stanley Kubrick's match cut in *2001: A Space Odyssey* (1968), between a prehistoric bone whirling in the air and a twenty-first-century space station revolving in space, is possibly the most ambitious match cut in history, since it attempts to unite prehistory with the anthropological future at the same time as it creates a special meaning within the cut itself by emphasizing the functions of both bone and space station as tools, extensions of human capabilities.

The codes of montage may not be as obvious as the codes of mise-en-scène, but that doesn't mean that they are necessarily less complex. Few theorists have gone further than differentiating among parallel montage, continuity montage, accelerated montage, flashbacks, and involuted montage. In the 1920s, both V. I. Pudovkin and Sergei Eisenstein extended the theory of montage beyond these

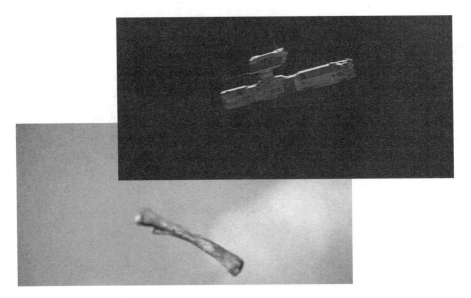

Figure 3-73. Kubrick's transcendent match cut. (*Frame enlargements.*)

essentially practical concerns. Pudovkin identified five basic types of montage: contrast, parallelism, symbolism, simultaneity, and leitmotif. He then developed a theory of the interaction between shots variously called "relational editing" or "linkage." Eisenstein, on the other hand, saw the relationship between shots as a collision rather than a linkage, and further refined the theory to deal with the relationships between elements of individual shots as well as the whole shots themselves. This he called the "montage of attractions." Both theorists are discussed in greater detail in Chapter 5.

In the late sixties, Christian Metz attempted to synthesize all these various theories of montage. He constructed a chart in which he tried to indicate how eight types of montage were connected logically. There are a number of problems with Metz's categories, yet the system does have an elegance all its own and it does describe most of the major patterns of montage. More important, despite its idiosyncrasies and occasional confusions, it remains the only recent attempt to comprehend the complex system of montage.

Note that Metz is interested in narrative elements—syntagmas—that can exist within shots as well as between them, an important refinement since, as we have already indicated, the effects of many types of montage can be accomplished within a shot without actually cutting. If the camera pans, for example, from one scene to another, those two scenes exist in relationship to each other just as they would if they were cut together.

Metz's grand design may seem forbidding at first glance, but it reveals a real and useful logic when studied. He begins by limiting himself to autonomous segments of film. These must be either autonomous shots—which are entirely independent of what comes before and after them—or what he calls "syntagmas"—units that have meaningful relationships with each other. (We might call these "scenes" or "sequences," but Metz reserves those terms for individual types of syntagma.) At each stage of this binary system, a further differentiation is made: the first bracket differentiates between autonomous shots and related shots, clearly the primary factor in categorizing types of montage. Either a shot is related to its surrounding shots, or it is not.

The second bracket differentiates between syntagmas that operate chronologically and those that do not. In other words, editing either tells a story (or develops an idea) in chronological sequence, or it does not. Now, on the third level, the differentiations branch out. Metz identifies two separate types of achronological syntagmas, the parallel and the bracket. Then he differentiates between two types of chronological syntagmas: either a syntagma describes or it narrates. If it narrates, it can do so either linearly or nonlinearly. If it does so linearly, it is either a scene or a sequence. And finally, if it is a sequence, it is either episodic or ordinary.

The end result is a system of eight types of montage, or eight syntagmas. The autonomous shot (1) is also known as the sequence shot (although Metz also places certain kinds of inserts—short, isolated fragments—here). The parallel syntagma (2) has been discussed above as the well-known phenomenon of parallel editing. The bracket syntagma (3), however, is Metz's own discovery—or invention. He defines it as "a series of very brief scenes representing occurrences that the film gives as typical examples of a same order or reality, without in any way chronologically locating them in relation to each other" [Metz, p. 126].

This is rather like a system of allusions. A good example might be the collection of images with which Godard began *A Married Woman* (1964). They all alluded to modern attitudes toward sex. Indeed, Godard in many of his films seemed to be particularly fond of the bracket syntagma, since it allows film to act something like the literary essay.

The descriptive syntagma (4) merely describes. The relation between its elements is spatial rather than temporal. Almost any establishing sequence (such as the one already discussed in *Rear Window)* is a good example of the descriptive syntagma. The alternate syntagma (5) is very much like the parallel syntagma except that the parallel syntagma offers two separate scenes or sequences that do not have a narrative connection, while the alternate syntagma offers parallel or alternating elements that do. The effect here is of simultaneity, as in chase scenes in which the montage alternates between shots of pursuer and pursued.

If events do not happen simultaneously, they happen one after the other, in linear sequence, and this brings us to Metz's remaining three categories of montage: the scene (6) and two types of sequence—episodic (7) and ordinary (8). There has always been a great deal of confusion in the vocabulary of film criticism

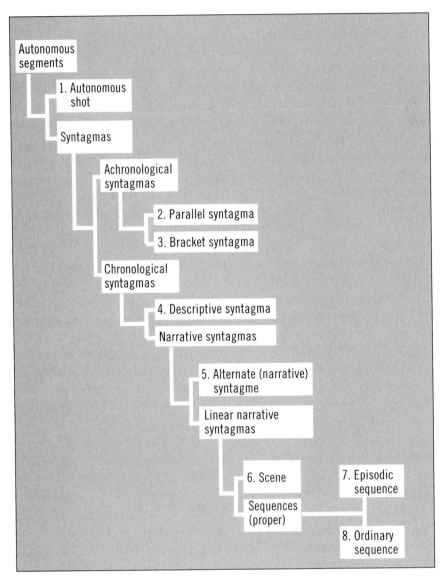

Diagram J. METZ'S SYNTAGMATIC CATEGORIES.

between the concepts of scene and sequence, and Metz's elaborate system is valuable for the precise definitions he offers. Metz takes his definition of scene from theatrical parlance. In the scene, the succession of events—the linear narrative—is continuous. In the sequence, it is broken up. It is still linear, it is still narrative, it is still chronological, it is still related to other elements, but it is not continuous.

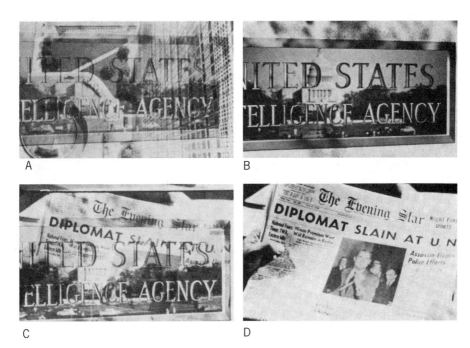

Figure 3-74. This sequence of four shots is a double dissolve from Alfred Hitchcock's *North by Northwest* (1959). At first it seems no more than a highly economical transition from the previous scene at the UN building, in which Roger Thornhill (Cary Grant) has been mistaken for a murderer, to a conference at the CIA in Washington, at which this turn of events is discussed. Hitchcock segues from his striking overhead shot of the antlike Thornhill running away from the slab of the UN Secretariat (barely visible in A) to the building nameplate in B. Since Hitchcock has had the foresight to use a mirrored surface for the sign, it can reflect the Capitol building, thus identifying the city as well as "company" and neatly saving an extra shot. He then dissolves to the newspaper headline in D, which tells us that (1) time has passed, (2) Thornhill has been identified, and (3) he has so far eluded capture. The newspaper is being held by the head of the intelligence agency. Hitchcock pulls back from the paper and goes on with the conference scene.

At the same time, however, there is some rich metaphorical information in this elegant little dissolve, for, if we analyze these still images, we can see that the CIA imposes itself on the UN, that the Capitol is a reflection of the CIA (or that the intelligence agency has superimposed itself over the seat of government), and finally, that the CIA gives birth to the newspaper headlines that include, in addition to the one conveying the necessary information: "National Fears Tieup" and "Nixon Promises West Will Remain in Berlin." (*Frame enlargements.*)

Metz's last differentiation, between the episodic sequence and the ordinary sequence, is a bit arbitrary. In the episodic sequence the discontinuity is organized; in the ordinary sequence it is not. A good example, then, of the episodic sequence is the one in *Citizen Kane* in which Orson Welles portrays the progressive deterioration of Kane's marriage by a set of successive episodes at the breakfast table. In fact, we might call this a "sequence of scenes," and this is a major characteristic of the episodic sequence—that its elements are organized so that each of them seems to have an identity of its own.

Some of these differentiations might still not be clear. For most film viewers, the concepts of the bracket syntagma and the descriptive syntagma are so close that differentiation may seem specious. Parallel syntagma and alternate syntagma present the same difficulty, as do episodic and ordinary sequences. Yet, despite its problems, Metz's system remains a helpful guide to what is, as yet, relatively uncharted territory: the ever-shifting, complex, and intricate syntax of film narrative. Whether or not his eight categories seem valid, the factors of differentiation that he defines are highly significant and bear repeating:

- ❏ Either a film segment is autonomous or it is not.
- ❏ Either it is chronological or it is not.
- ❏ Either it is descriptive or it is narrative.
- ❏ Either it is linear or it is not.
- ❏ Either it is continuous or it is not.
- ❏ Either it is organized or it is not.

We have only to describe the punctuation of cinema to complete this quick survey of the syntax of mise-en-scène and montage. Because punctuation devices stand out and are simply defined, they often take pride of place in discussions of cinematic language. They are useful, no doubt, as are, well, commas, for example, in written language.

The simplest type of punctuation is the unmarked cut. One image ends, another begins. The "fade" calls attention to the ending or the beginning, as does the "iris" (a favorite of early filmmakers that has now fallen into disuse). The "wipe," in which one image removes another in a dizzying variety of ways (flips, twirls, pushovers, spirals, clock hands), was a favorite in the thirties and forties. Optical houses offered catalogues of scores of patterns for wipes. Now it is used in film only for nostalgic effect, although it has found new life in television, where electronic special-effects generators permit new variations on the theme, sometimes shifting the preceding image so it looks like a page of a book is being turned, in three dimensions.

"Intertitles" were an important mark of punctuation in the silent cinema and are still used on occasion today. The "freeze frame" has become popular since it was used to such effect by François Truffaut in *The 400 Blows* (1959). (Truffaut, by the way, was the C. S. Lewis of film punctuation.) Filmmakers in the 1960s and 1970s modernized some of the old forms, fading to colors instead of black (Ingmar Bergman) or cutting to blank, colored frames (Godard). Focusing in and out (the effect of going slowly in focus at the beginning of the shot, or out of focus at the end) paralleled fading, and Antonioni was fond of beginning a shot on an out-of-focus background before an in-focus subject moved into the frame.

Figure 3-75. Truffaut's land-mark freeze frame brings *The 400 Blows* to an abrupt and quizzical stop. (*MOMA/FSA.*)

All these various marks are periods. End points. A fade out/fade in may suggest a relationship, but it is not a direct link. The dissolve, however, which superimposes fade out and fade in, does connect. If there is a comma in film amongst this catalogue of periods, it is the dissolve. Interestingly, the dissolve serves a multitude of purposes: it is commonly employed to segue or lead into a flashback; it is also used in continuity montage with the jump cut, while at the same time it can represent the passage of long periods of time, especially when it is sequential. It is the one mark of punctuation in cinema that mixes images at the same time that it conjoins them.

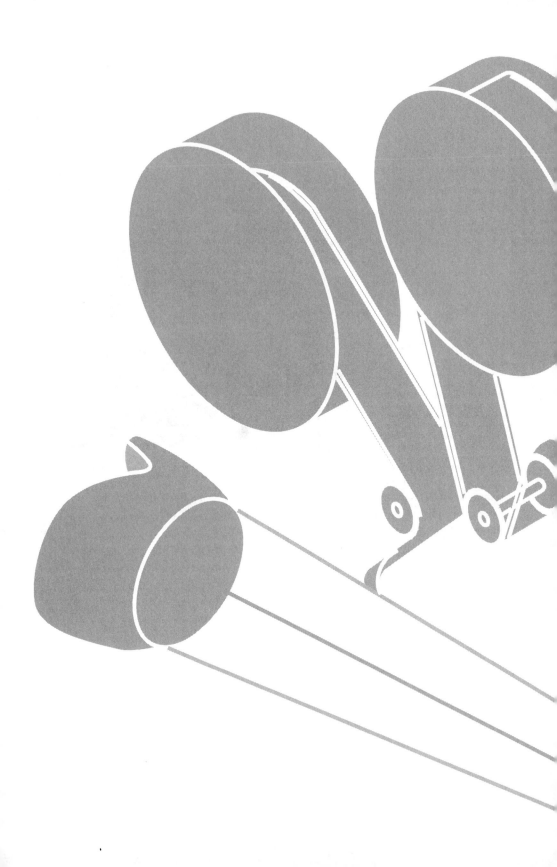

4

THE SHAPE OF FILM HISTORY

Movies/Film/Cinema

French theorists are fond of making the differentiation between "film" and "cinema." The "filmic" is that aspect of the art that concerns its relationship with the world around it; the "cinematic" deals strictly with the esthetics and internal structure of the art. In English, we have a third word for "film" and "cinema"—"movies"—which provides a convenient label for the third facet of the phenomenon: its function as an economic commodity. These three aspects are closely interrelated, of course: one person's "movie" is another's "film." But in general we use these three names for the art in a way that closely parallels this differentiation: "movies," like popcorn, are to be consumed; "cinema" (at least in American parlance) is high art, redolent of esthetics; "film" is the most general term with the fewest connotations.

This history of movies/film/cinema is rich and complex, although it spans only a century. Film history is a matter of decades and half-decades. Partly this is a result of the explosive nature of the phenomenon of film—as a medium of communication it was immediately apprehensible to large numbers of people; partly it is a matter of the geometric progression of technology in the twentieth century coupled with economic cycles, which demanded that film develop or die.

At the same time that we speak of three approaches—movies, film, and cinema—we should remember that within each approach there is a corresponding spectrum of function, ranging from documentary and nonfiction on the left, through the massive commercial narrative cinema that occupies the middle ground, on to avant-garde and "art" film on the right. The major part of this historical discussion will dwell on the middle ground, since it is here that the politics and economics of film have had their most significant effect.

Interesting parallels exist between the history of the art form of the novel during the course of the past three hundred years and the development of film during the past one hundred years. Both are, above all, popular arts that depend on large numbers of consumers to function economically. Each began with roots in journalism—that is, as a medium of record. Each developed through an early stage marked by invention and freshness, and soon reached a commanding position in which it dominated other arts. Each evolved a complex system of genres that served a wide range of audiences. Finally, each entered into a later period of consolidation, identified by a stronger concern for elite, esthetic values over those of popular entertainment, as it was challenged by a new medium (film for the novel, television for film).

Just as novels have fed films, providing a rich lode of material, so now films feed television. Indeed, it may no longer be possible to make explicit differentiations among these three forms of narrative entertainment. Commercially, the novel, movies, and television are more closely intertwined than ever before.

The development of film differed, however, in two important respects from the precedent of the novel. Before prose narrative could reach a wide popular audience, it was necessary for a culture of literacy to develop. Film had no such prerequisite. On the other hand, film is highly technological. Although the novel depends on the technology of printing, that technology is comparatively simple, and the development of the form of the novel has been affected only in minor ways by technological developments. We can speak of the history of the novel as being audience-intensive—that is, it is closely linked with the development of its audience's capabilities—while the history of film is technology-intensive—it does not depend on audience capability so much as technical capability.

All histories of film mark the obvious division between silent and sound periods. While any structure more complex than this simple bifurcation is arbitrary, it is useful to attempt greater precision. Each of the eight periods outlined below has its own coherence. Although we tend naturally to identify these periods by esthetic differences ("cinema"), it is interesting to note that they are defined rather by economic developments ("movies").

❏ The period of film's prehistory includes the development of all the precursors of the Cinématographe as well as the evolution of certain aspects of the other arts that have a significant effect when applied to film (the qualities of Victorian melodrama, for example, or the values of the photographic portrait).

❏ The years between 1896 and 1912 saw cinema evolve from a sideshow gimmick into a full-fledged economic art. The end of this period is marked by the advent of the feature-length film.

❏   The years 1913 to 1927 comprise the silent feature period.

❏   Between 1928 and 1932, world cinema was in a state of transition. This interval holds no unusual esthetic interest for us, but it does suggest itself economically and technologically as a significant stage.

❏   The period from 1932 to 1946 was the "Golden Age" of Hollywood; during this era, the movies had their greatest economic success.

❏   Immediately after World War II, film began to confront the challenge of television. The years 1947 to 1959 were characterized by this response, concurrent with a growing internationalism. Esthetically, if not economically, Hollywood now no longer dominated.

❏   The growth of the New Wave in France in the early sixties signaled the beginning of the seventh period of film history, 1960–80. Technological innovations, a new approach to the economics of film production, and a new sense of the political and social value of film combined to form numerous "new wavelets" in Eastern Europe, Latin America, Africa, Asia, and eventually even the United States and Western Europe.

❏   1980 seems as good a point as any to mark the end of the "New Wave" period of world film history and the beginning of what we might call "postmodern" film. During this present era, movies are best seen as part of a varied panoply of entertainment and communications media clearly dominated by television in all its forms. As a member of the group that includes audio recordings, videotapes, and discs, and various types of print as well as broadcast, satellite, and cable television, film no longer exercises the economic leverage it once did. Movies still serve as prestigious models for these other forms of media, but increasingly film must be understood in this broad context. Theatrical feature filmmaking is simply one of the numerous facets of this new media world.

Indeed, we now need a new term to indicate the generalized production of audiovisual communications and entertainment. Whether this unnamed but pervasive form is produced on filmstock or magnetic tape or disc, analogically or digitally; whether it is distributed through theaters, via broadcast, "narrowcast," cable, satellite, disc, or tape—our core experience of it amounts to the same thing. Now, when we speak about movies/film/cinema we usually mean to infer all of these various media forms.

Contemporary film can be seen as a synthesis of the forces that have each at one time or another seemed to dominate the cinematic formula. It is most important to an understanding of film history, however, to see how each of these social, political, economic, cultural, psychological, and esthetic factors involves the others in a dynamic relationship. Film history is best comprehended as the product of a wide range of contradictions. This can be seen on every level, from the most specific to the most general.

An actor's performance, for example, is the result of the conflict between the role and the actor's own persona. At times the personality dominates, at times the character, but in either case the sum is a third thing, a logical conclusion—performance—which then becomes one of the elements involved in the larger unit, the film. A particular film, likewise, is the product of a number of oppositions: director versus screenwriter, the ideal of the script versus the practical realities of shooting, shadow versus light, sound versus image, character versus plot, and so on. Each film then becomes an element in the larger systems of oppositions: genre contrasts with the individuality of scripts; studio styles are in logical opposition to personal directorial styles; thematic tendencies contrast with the concrete physical reality of the medium. Finally, each of these larger elements is involved in one or more contradictions that together give the general history of film its overall shape and substance.

What should be remembered is that in very few cases are phenomena in film history correctly described in terms of simple cause and effect. For the purposes of discussion, the brief survey of film history that follows has been organized according to the three principal forces involved: economics, politics (including psychology and sociology), and esthetics. But none of these factors is clearly and ultimately dominant. If film is essentially an economic product, nevertheless there have been numerous filmmakers who have worked without any conceivable regard to the realities of the marketplace and have managed to survive. If certain types of film are best seen in terms of their political and social effects, it should be remembered that the causes of these effects may not be political at all, but rather highly personal and esthetic.

In short, our aim should not be to decide, simplistically, "what caused what" in the history of film, but rather to gain an understanding of "what is related to what." For every interesting phenomenon in film history, there are several plausible explanations. It's not so important which of these explanations is true, as it is to see how they relate to each other and to the world around them.

Like any art, only more so because of its all-encompassing and popular nature, film reflects changes in the social contract. That is why it is useful to look first at the economic and technological foundations of the medium (what economists and historians call its "infrastructure"), then to discuss some of the major political, social, and psychological implications of the art (its "structure"), and finally to conclude with a survey of the history of film esthetics (its "superstructure").

Any one of these three aspects of film history could easily serve as the organizing principle for a hefty volume. What follows is only the barest outline of some of the major issues involved. Moreover, film has not developed independently of the other arts and media. Its history should be seen in context with the growth of the other media (see Chapter 6) and in relationship to developments in the older arts (see Chapter 1).

"Movies": Economics

More so than most of the other technological innovations that form the panoply of modern electric and electronic modes of communication, film was a communal invention. Unlike the telephone, telegraph, or even wireless, film depended on a whole series of small inventions, each attributable to a different inventor. Even single concepts had multiple authors.

In the U.S., Thomas Edison is usually given major credit for inventing the movies, and indeed, much of the important work of development was performed in his New Jersey laboratories. But considering Edison's demonstrated talents and obvious understanding of the problems involved in producing a workable camera/projector system, what is surprising is that he personally didn't achieve more. An Englishman, William Kennedy Laurie Dickson, was the chief experimenter working on the project for Edison. He demonstrated a crude system of projection as early as 1889, but Edison seems to have conceived of movies as more a personal than a communal experience. He was more interested in producing a private viewing system than one to project an image for the entertainment of large groups. He called his individual viewer the "Kinetoscope." It was in production in the early 1890s—one of the first short programs was the famous *Fred Ott's Sneeze*—and it soon became a common fixture of side shows and carnivals.

The Kinetoscope inspired a number of European and American inventors and businessmen to apply their talents to the solution of the remaining problems. In England, the Frenchman Louis Augustin Le Prince and the Englishman William Friese-Greene both developed workable portable camera/projection systems in the late 1880s, although nothing came of them.

The key to the main problem of projection for a large audience was the intermittent motion mechanism. Louis and Auguste Lumière in France and Thomas Armat in America came up with this device in 1895. Armat sold out to Edison. The Lumières went into production and, on December 28, 1895, in the basement of the Grand Café, number 14 Boulevard des Capucines, Paris, showed the first projected films to a paying audience. During the next year, the Lumière Cinématographe was demonstrated in most major European cities. Edison's first formal public performance of large-screen communal cinema took place on April 23, 1896, at Koster and Bial's Music Hall, 34th Street and Sixth Avenue, New York.

The Lumières' decision to concentrate on the projection of film for large groups had a far-reaching effect. If the development of the technology had progressed along the lines Edison had laid down, the result would have been a medium much more like television, experienced privately, eventually in the home. This quite different mode of distribution and exhibition would undoubtedly have affected the types of films produced. As it happened, Edison's Kinetoscope rather quickly yielded to the Lumières' Cinématographe (and Edison's very similar Kinetograph projector) and the future of public, communal cinema was assured for at least the next 80 years. It is only recently, with the development of videocassettes and discs and home players, that the private, individualized Kinetoscope mode has been revived.

During the next year or two, a number of competitors joined the field. The Italian Filoteo Alberini had taken out several significant patents before 1896; in Germany, Max and Emil Skladanowsky developed their Bioskop; in England, Robert W. Paul was projecting films (with his version of the Edison machine) within weeks after the Lumières' premiere. In 1896 and 1897, the use of the Cinématographe, Edison's Kinetograph, and similar machines spread widely.

It soon became evident that there was considerable potential profit in the invention. In the U.S., Dickson left Edison's employ to form (with partners) the American Mutoscope and Biograph Company, which not only produced a better peepshow machine (the Mutoscope) than Edison's Kinetoscope but a better projector as well. The Biograph Company was soon to dominate American film. J. Stuart Blackton, of English origins like Dickson, formed the Vitagraph Company. Both the Biograph and the Vitagraph offices were located near New York's theatrical neighborhoods (Biograph on East 14th Street near Fifth Avenue, Vitagraph in the Chelsea district), which gave them easy access to stage actors—who would surreptitiously spend an afternoon filming before reporting to work in the theater.

In France, Georges Méliès, a stage magician, saw the illusionary power of the medium and entered production, while Charles Pathé began a ruthless campaign to dominate the fledgling industry. Pathé was fairly successful. Unlike his competitors, Pathé was able to find large amounts of capital backing, which he used to establish a near monopoly, vertically integrated. He controlled the French film industry from the manufacture of equipment to the production of films (in his large studio at Vincennes) to distribution and exhibition, and his influence was widely felt in other countries as well, during the early years of this century. As a result, French film dominated world screens in the years prior to the First World War. Before 1914, Pathé commonly distributed twice as much film in the U.S. alone as did the whole American industry. For other, more esthetic reasons, Italian influence in those years was also widespread.

By 1905 the concept of the film theater was established. In 1897 the Lumières had opened the first establishment devoted strictly to the showing of movies. In 1902 Thomas L. Tally's Electric Theatre (prophetically located in Los Angeles) became the first American film theater. Within a few years, the concept spread

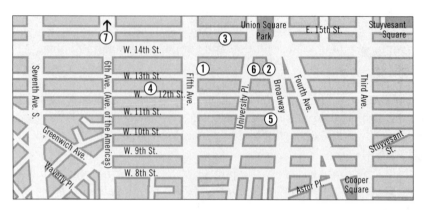

Figure 4-1. FILM IN GREENWICH VILLAGE. Much of the early history of the film industry centered in New York's Greenwich Village neighborhood, long a literary and artistic center. W. K. L. Dickson first visited Thomas Edison in his office at his dynamo at Fifth Avenue and Thirteenth Street (1). The American Mutoscope and Biograph Co. set up shop in an office building at 841 Broadway (2), then moved to a brownstone on Fourteenth Street east of Fifth Avenue (3). Griffith often shot on West Twelfth Street (4). The old St. Denis Hotel (5), where Alexander Graham Bell demonstrated his first working telephone system in 1877, has provided office space for numerous filmmakers. New Line Cinema's first office was located above a bar and grill at University Place and Thirteenth Street (6). Edison's first public performance took place a few blocks north on Sixth Avenue (7). Such filmmakers as Mel Brooks, Paul Mazursky, Brian DePalma, Susan Sarandon, and Tim Robbins have chosen to live in the area at one time or another (although most eventually moved to L.A.) Even today, these streets are regularly filled with filmmakers shooting on location, and the old loft buildings on Broadway have become a mecca for the new multimedia companies.

rapidly. By 1908 there were more than five thousand "Nickelodeons" across the country ("nickel" because that was the price of admission; "odeon" from the Greek for a small building used for the presentation of musical and dramatic programs). The last link in the chain—manufacture, production, distribution, exhibition—was complete. No company or individual had complete control over the system, however.

Thomas Edison set out to rectify that oversight. In 1897 he had begun a long series of suits against interlopers. Armat, who felt he had been double-crossed by Edison, started his own legal proceedings. Biograph, who had some important patents of their own, prepared countersuits. In all, more than five hundred legal actions were instituted during the first decade of the film industry. These were temporarily resolved with the foundation in January 1909 of the Motion Picture Patents Company, a monopoly consortium of the nine major producers—Edison, Biograph, Vitagraph, Essanay, Selig, Lubin, Kalem, Méliès, and Pathé—with the distributor George Kleine.

All patents were pooled, Edison received royalties on all films produced, and George Eastman agreed to supply his filmstock only to members of the company.

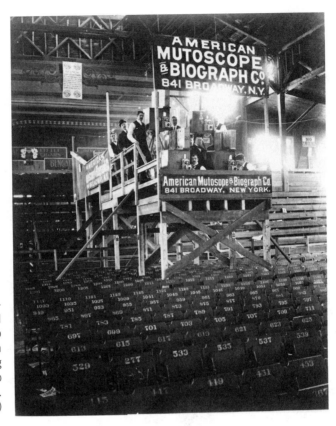

Figure 4-2. The American Mutoscope and Biograph Co. set up to film a stage event. With four cameras rolling they are not likely to miss anything. (*MOMA/FSA.*)

(Pathé had had the foresight to monopolize Eastman's filmstock in France years earlier.) No distributors who handled films of other companies were permitted to distribute Patent Company films. Most of the distributors were soon merged in their own trust, the General Film Company. But several distributors understandably rebelled against these blanket monopoly agreements. The solution was to produce their own films, and several renegade production companies sprang up, the most important being Carl Laemmle's Independent Motion Picture Company ("Imp"), which would later become Universal Studios.

Antitrust suits replaced patent suits, and the American film industry was off on another ten-year round of legal battles. Eventually the Motion Picture Patents Company was ruled an illegal trust, but by that time most of the original members of the company had gone out of business. None of them survived the twenties. By 1912 the Patent Company and the General Film Company controlled more than half of the ten thousand exhibition outlets—Nickelodeons—in the country, but this still left the independents room to maneuver.

Their greatest weapon against the trust was not the legal fight but rather an innovation in film form. The trust and the Nickelodeons were geared to one- and

Figure 4-3. Biograph's brownstone headquarters on Fourteenth Street between Fifth Avenue and Union Square, circa 1905. The building is long gone, but in the mid-1970s, Lillian Gish and Blanche Sweet assisted in the dedication of a plaque on the site. (*MOMA/FSA.*)

two-reel films (a reel was then approximately ten minutes in length). The independents, borrowing a concept pioneered by Italian and French filmmakers, introduced the longer, "feature" film. Within a few years, the Patent Company and its short films were obsolete.

Ironically, D. W. Griffith, the filmmaker who had done most to ensure the success of Biograph, the most important of the trust components, was also the first American, after his break with Biograph, to explore the potential of the feature film form.[*] The unprecedented financial success of *The Birth of a Nation* (1915) ensured the future of the new form. It also set the pattern for the "blockbuster," the film project in which huge sums of money are invested in epic productions with the hope of even huger returns. *The Birth of a Nation,* costing an unprecedented and, many believed, thoroughly foolhardy $110,000, eventually returned

---

[*] Europeans had already produced epic features before this: *Quo Vadis?* (1912) and *Cabiria* (1914) in Italy, *Germinal* (1913) and *L'Enfant de Paris* (1914) in France. Griffith was only following their lead—albeit more lucratively.

Figure 4-4. *Puck's* view of the fantasy world of early Hollywood, 1913. *(Collection of the New-York Historical Society.)*

$20 million and more. The actual figure is hard to calculate because the film was distributed on a "states' rights" basis in which licenses to show the film were sold outright. The actual cash generated by *The Birth of a Nation* may have been as much as $50 million to $100 million, an almost inconceivable amount for such an early film. The focus of film activity had clearly moved out of the Nickelodeon into the legitimate theater, to the detriment of the trust companies.

The urge to monopolize, however, was irresistible. The Great War immobilized film production in the European countries, and the dominance of France and Italy was soon overcome. Through a series of mergers the new independent American companies moved quickly to supply world markets and consolidate their position at home.

Adolph Zukor acquired Paramount Pictures Corporation, a distribution and exhibition company, and merged it with his own production organization (Famous Players in Famous Plays) and another company, owned by Jesse Lasky. Carl Laemmle founded the Universal Film Manufacturing Company around the nucleus of Imp. William Fox, an exhibitor and distributor, formed his own production company in 1912, later to become Twentieth Century Fox. Marcus Loew, a successful theater owner, acquired Metro Pictures Corporation (whose chief executive was Louis B. Mayer) in 1920, then merged it with Goldwyn Pictures (founded by Samuel Goldfish—later Goldwyn—and Edward Selwyn) to form Metro-Goldwyn-Mayer in 1924. The four Warner brothers, exhibitors and distributors, started producing films in 1912. Their company later absorbed First National (which had also started in distribution) and the last of the trust companies to survive, Vitagraph.

By 1920, the "independents" had achieved an informal, low-profile oligopoly that would have been the envy of the more belligerent trust companies. Each of them controlled a major section of the industry, each was vertically integrated, active in every link of the film "chain": production, distribution, and exhibition. Not until the late forties was this de facto monopoly challenged successfully in court. Even then the majors were required only to divest themselves of their theater chains. They were allowed to maintain control over distribution, the heart of the system. All five companies survive today and still control the film industry (although MGM played only a minor role throughout the 1970s and 1980s and nearly died in the 1990s).

One of the modern production/distribution organizations, however, had different roots. United Artists was formed in 1919 by Charles Chaplin, Mary Pickford, Douglas Fairbanks, and David W. Griffith as a corporate shelter for their own activities.

Surrounding this constellation of six major companies in the twenties, thirties, and forties were a number of minor producers, the "poverty row" companies. Several of them, such as Republic and Monogram, specialized in B pictures,

Figure 4-5. Founding moguls Adolph Zukor, Carl Laemmle, and Samuel Goldwyn. (*MOMA/FSA.*)

which found a niche as the second halves of double bills. By the mid-fifties, the market for such "Programmers" had all but disappeared and the companies that supplied them went out of business. They were in a sense replaced by such independent low-budget producers as American International Pictures in the 1950s, Roger Corman's New World in the 1960s, and New Line in the 1980s, all specializing in "exploitation" films mainly directed to the youth market.

One poverty row company that survived to become a "major" was Columbia Pictures, which evolved in 1924 out of an earlier company founded by Harry Cohn, a vaudeville performer and song-plugger; his brother Jack; and a friend, Joe Brandt. Like United Artists, one of the "little two" for many years, Columbia moved to the ranks of the majors in the late forties. By the late fifties it was one of the more significant producers of international features.

During the thirties and forties RKO, which had been formed by a series of mergers to provide an outlet for the RCA sound system that was in competition with Western Electric for the market in the new technology, was also considered one of the "Big Five." Disney, Selznick, and Goldwyn all released through RKO at its peak. In 1948 Howard Hughes bought most of the stock. In 1953 RKO ceased production and its studios were sold to Desilu for television production.

A powerhouse since the 1940s because of its domination of the animation niche, Disney created its own distribution arm, Buena Vista, in the 1950s, then moved to center stage in the 1980s with an ambitious and successful program of "live-action" features. Michael Eisner and Jeffrey Katzenberg joined the studio in 1984 with a mandate to produce and distribute mainstream features. The Touchstone Pictures brand name was established in 1984 to position the company in the adult marketplace. It was immediately successful and was joined by the Hollywood Pictures brand in 1989. Throughout the 1980s and into the 1990s, the Disney brands ranked among the most successful in Hollywood.

A

B

C

D

E

Figure 4-6. EARLY HOLLYWOOD STUDIOS. A. Independent Studios (1925). B. The famous Paramount main gate (1939). C. An early mixed media company (1913). D. Metro bungalow (1918). E. "Warner Brothers West Coast" (c. 1928). F. Doug and Mary hoisting the sign (1922). G. The back of Columbia (1935), still a great billboard gallery today. H. The original RKO radio beacon (1940). I. An RKO movie palace in the thirties. (*Hollywood: The First Hundred Years. Courtesy Bruce Torrence.*)

National cinemas in Europe were also subject to monopoly pressures. The French organizations—Pathé and Gaumont—continued to dominate national distribution after World War I. In Germany, the formation in 1917 of Universum Film A.G. ("UFA," with one-third of its capital supplied by the state) effectively merged the major film companies. The Soviet film industry was nationalized in 1919. In Great Britain, the U.S. companies supplied the majority of the product, but exhibition was controlled by British interests. Gaumont-British and Associated British Picture Corporation (who also produced through their subsidiary British International Pictures) controlled 300 theaters each (out of a total of 4,400) in 1936. In Italy, the continued growth of what had once been one of the world's most successful cinemas was esthetically damped by the Fascist regime, although it continued to produce films popular at home if not abroad. When the Nazis took power in Germany in 1933, the influence of German cinema on world screens effectively came to an end.

It was not only the debacle of World War I and the rise of Fascist governments in Italy and Germany that assured the international dominance of the American corporations. More important, perhaps, were the industrial aspects of the American system of production. In Europe, the concept of cinema as art had appeared early and developed in tandem with the concept of cinema as business. The *film d'art* movement in France dated from 1908. Its earliest successes, many starring Sarah Bernhardt in the re-creation of her stage roles, pointed toward the creation of the feature film. *Film d'arte italiana* followed quickly. After the war, avant-garde experiments liberally punctuated French cinema, and theorists began to treat the medium more seriously, as coequal with literature and the fine arts.

In the U.S., however, "cinema" was "movies" plain and simple. Even the earliest production companies—Biograph and Vitagraph especially—considered their studios to be factories, involved in the production of a commodity rather than the creation of an art. D. W. Griffith's company of actors and technicians began wintering in Los Angeles in 1910. Other companies soon followed. Independents appreciated the isolation of the West Coast, where they were insulated to some extent from the strongarm tactics of the Patent Company. By 1914 the locus of filmmaking had shifted from New York to Hollywood. The Los Angeles area provided much sunshine, good weather, and a wide variety of contrasting locales—in short, the raw materials of filmmaking—together with an attractive labor pool. The film industry located in Hollywood for the same reasons that the auto industry located in Detroit: proximity to raw materials and labor.

Three thousand miles from the cultural capital of the nation, American filmmakers were even more effectively isolated from prevailing artistic influences. Moreover, the men who established the major production companies had minimal experience of established literary culture. They were for the most part first- or second-generation immigrants from Germany, Poland, or Russia who had started

Figure 4-7. The fantasy world Hollywoodland development in the Hollywood Hills in 1924. The giant promotional sign (upper right) gave the city its iconic landmark (once the suffix fell down). (*Hollywood: The First Hundred Years. Courtesy Bruce Torrence.*)

out as merchants, had moved into sideshow film exhibition, and from there to film distribution. They became film producers mainly to provide products for their theaters.

More important, the tremendous popularity of film demanded quick expansion in the industry, which, in turn, required large amounts of capital investment. The "moguls" turned to the banks and became increasingly dependent on them. By the time they were forced to retool for sound, they were deeply in debt. Film historian Peter Cowie has written, "By 1936 it was possible to trace major holdings in all eight companies to the two powerful banking groups of Morgan and Rockefeller." Similar relationships between banking interests and film companies were developing in European countries—especially Germany, where the Deutsches Bank took effective control of UFA after World War I.

In recent years, banks have continued their fascination with the film industry. New York-based investment bankers Allen & Co. have long been associated with Columbia Pictures; the French bank Crédit Lyonnais found itself in the early 1990s owning a bankrupt MGM after bankrolling the purchase of the venerable studio.

European national cinemas had to contend with the overpowering flow of product from the American factories. Great Britain was most vulnerable in this respect. Although there was an upsurge in British production immediately following World War I, it was cut short by the unstable economic conditions of the early twenties. In 1927, Parliament passed the Cinematograph Act, which forbade "block booking" (the standard practice of requiring an exhibitor to take a year's worth of product from a single studio) and imposed a nominal 5 percent quota to guarantee that British exhibitors would show at least a few British-made films each year.

By this time, however, the American companies had already invested in British branches and were able to recycle their British funds by producing "quota quickies" themselves. Even when they farmed out the business to native British producers, they imposed a contract limit of £6,000 per film and kept the films as short as the law permitted (6,000 feet—a little more than one hour). The German and French governments instituted similar safeguards, with similar lack of success.

The American companies clearly dominated the world market from 1920 on. As the films flowed out, the artists flowed in as the studios widened their search for new talent. In one of the earliest instances of the "brain drain," European filmmakers made their way to Hollywood. Ernst Lubitsch was one of the first to arrive. He was followed later in the twenties by several fellow German directors: Fritz Lang, F. W. Murnau, Paul Leni, and E. A. Dupont among them. (Another wave, led by Billy Wilder, arrived in the thirties as refugees from Nazism.) The two most important Swedish directors of the time, Mauritz Stiller and Victor Sjöström, both immigrated to Hollywood. Stiller brought his star, Greta Garbo, with him. Indeed, many of the most successful American stars of the silent film era were European émigrés, Garbo and Rudolph Valentino being the most prominent.

With the switch to sound, the demand for foreign-born filmmakers grew. It was common practice before 1932, when the postdubbing technique came into practice, to shoot a major film in parallel versions (usually English, French, Spanish, and German). Native directors were useful for the foreign-language versions. Many of the most effective contract directors of the thirties were émigrés, including William Dieterle (German), Edgar Ulmer (Austrian), Robert Florey (French), and Michael Curtiz (Hungarian), as well as Lubitsch, Murnau, and Lang. (Sternberg and Stroheim, both Austrians, had emigrated as children.)

By the mid-twenties, silent film was well established as a major form of entertainment. No longer were films shown in storefront Nickelodeons or on the bottom half of vaudeville bills. Now they commanded ornate pleasure domes of their own. The picture palaces accommodated thousands of patrons at a time, rather than scores. Possibly the most elaborate of these ornate constructions were the theaters operated by Roxy Rothapfel in New York, which was still the capital of exhibition, if not of production. The Roxy opened in 1927, to be followed in 1932

Figure 4-8. The Warner Brothers/First National/Vitaphone studios in Burbank, California, August 1931, one of the best-equipped film production plants at the time. The large, hangar-like buildings are sound stages. To the rear can be seen a number of standing sets—western towns, New York City streets, and the like—on the back lot. In the foreground, to the left, are administration offices and technical support facilities. (*Marc Wanamaker/Bison Art Ltd.*)

by Radio City Music Hall, the ultimate movie cathedral, and one of the few still standing (although it no longer shows movies on a regular basis).

All the important technical modifications that the film process has undergone—the addition of sound, color, and widescreen—were first demonstrated to the public at the International Exposition in Paris in 1900, albeit in primitive forms. Color films, for example, were mostly handpainted, hardly a commercially viable process. Sound could be produced by the primitive nonelectronic phonograph, but synchronization was very difficult and sound level was problematic. Lee De Forest's invention of the audion tube in 1906 (see Chapter 6) pointed the way to the workable electronic sound amplifier. By 1919 the German Tri-Ergon process had been patented and film sound was a distinct possibility. In the late 1920s, confronted with the growing public interest in radio and responding to what may have seemed like a saturated market for silent films, the production companies turned hesitantly to sound.

By 1932 the technological shakedown period for sound was over and the outlines identifying the Hollywood system were clear. Except for the manufacture of equipment and filmstock, the studios exerted complete control over the film process, from production to distribution to exhibition. The system of block booking and the close ties between most of the studios and large theater chains meant that nearly any film that the studio chose to produce would be shown—not a disadvantage artistically. At its peak, MGM, the most powerful of the studios, produced forty-two feature films a year on twenty-two sound stages and one hundred acres of backlot standing sets.

The studios operated as efficiently run factories. Properties were acquired; scriptwriters set to work remodeling them for production; set design and costume design departments turned out the required physical elements of the production. Technicians were on salary, working regular shifts, as were actors and directors. Today, it is unusual if a director makes more than one film per year. Between 1930 and 1939, Michael Curtiz shot 44 films, Mervyn Leroy 36, and John Ford 26. After the film was shot, the raw material was turned over to the post-production department for editing, mixing, and dubbing. Studio executives made the final artistic decisions. The most prestigious directors sometimes were allowed to be involved in post-production, but few indeed could follow a film from inception to premiere.

The result was that studios developed individual styles that often superseded the weaker styles of the filmmakers. MGM was noted for its glossy production values and middlebrow subject matter. Even though it was produced independently by David O. Selznick (and released through MGM), the 1939 epic *Gone With the Wind* is the epitome of the MGM style. Romantically melodramatic, expensively produced, with a lush score, it treats epic subject matter while doing relatively little to illuminate its themes.

Paramount, which employed more than its share of émigrés, exhibited a European sensibility, both in terms of design and subject matter. Universal specialized in horror films, Republic in Westerns. Warner Brothers, a major competitor of MGM and Paramount but leaner and hungrier, developed—quite unintentionally—a reputation for realism. Why? To save money, the Warner brothers often filmed on location.

In this tightly organized production system, individual contributors—whether directors, cinematographers, screenwriters, or designers—could not easily assert themselves. Not only did the mass of films exhibit a studio style, they also displayed a surprising degree of intellectual conformity. We can discern a difference between MGM's gloss and Paramount's sophistication, but there is no significant contrast in terms of the political and social consciousness each evinced. Always concerned with the essential commodity value of the films they produced, the moguls of the golden age of Hollywood preferred to make films that were *like* other films—not different from them.

As a result, very few of the thousands of films produced during these years strike us as unique. The study of Hollywood is more a matter of identifying types,

Figure 4-9. Radio City Music Hall, one of the great Art Deco movie palaces built in the thirties. (*MOMA/FSA.*)

patterns, conventions, and genres among a great many films than of intently focusing on the qualities of each individual movie. This doesn't make Hollywood films necessarily any less interesting than more personal works of cinematic invention. In fact, because these films were turned out on an assembly-line basis in such massive numbers, they are often better indexes of public concerns, shared myths, and mores than are individually conceived, intentionally artistic films.

As the studios moved into the forties, these qualities became even more striking. Actively involved in propaganda and education even before the United States entered the war, the major studios displayed their particular styles even in such propaganda instruments as *Freedom Comes High* (Paramount) and *You John Jones* (MGM).

Hollywood thrived during the war. In 1946, its best year, box-office grosses amounted to $1.7 billion. In a sense, World War II had delayed the moment of truth for the Hollywood film factories by making impossible the introduction of commercial television, which had been successfully demonstrated in the thirties. In addition, the war effectively limited competition from European countries. In the twenties, Germany had been a major competitor, producing films that were not only popular but also carried with them the cachet of art. In the thirties, a

Figure 4-10. Throughout most of the thirties and forties, Warner Brothers films were noticeably more realistic in style—gutsier—than the films of the competing studios. Here, a scene from one of Warner's best-known socially conscious movies, Mervyn Leroy's *I Am a Fugitive from a Chain Gang* (1932). Star Paul Muni leans against the post. (*MOMA/FSA.*)

handful of French directors gained widespread respect for that nation's industry. Great Britain, despite the pressure of English-language films from Hollywood, produced 225 films in 1936, the second-highest output in the world. The war ended these threats even though it also closed many export markets, hurting some small companies.

The effect of television when it did come in the early 1950s was devastating. Television grew out of radio rather than film, and naturally employed radio people. Instead of realizing that they could just as easily produce film product for television as for theatrical distribution, the studios tried to fight. For years, they refused to capitalize on their huge backlog of product. Indeed, with very unbusinesslike shortsightedness, they often destroyed old films rather than pay for storage. The effect of this strategy was to allow television production companies time to develop, seriously weakening the tactical position of the studios. The same thing had happened forty years earlier, when the trust companies had proved unwilling or unable to move from Nickelodeon shorts to theatrical features.

The process of adapting to the new conditions was slow and painful, but it need not have been. It was fifteen years or more before the studios began dimly to understand how best to operate in the new environment. Aging owners and

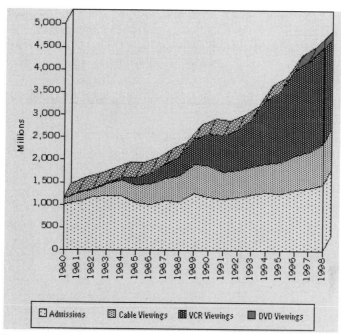

Figure 4-11. FILM AND THE VIDEO REVOLUTION IN THE EIGHTIES AND NINETIES. Film viewing changed radically beginning in the early eighties. Despite the hype and the explosion of multiplex and megaplex screens, most films are now viewed most often on a television screen, not in a theater. The little sliver on the top right represents DVD viewings. In another ten years expect this track to dominate. The theatrical admissions figures are precise; the video viewings are conservatively extrapolated from video sales. (*Sources: MPAA, NCSA, JM.*)

production heads rigidly clung to the old methods of mass production in studio complexes with enormous overhead costs. Psychologically, this may have been due to their shared roots long ago as exhibitors. Although exhibition was always the weakest link in the Hollywood monopoly chain, it held a peculiar fascination for the founders.

In 1946, a ruling under the antitrust laws required Paramount Pictures (and by implication the other studios) to divest themselves of their theater chains. The studios appealed, but to no avail, entering into a consent decree in 1951. This wasn't as drastic a change as it might seem. Since the studios were still permitted to maintain their distribution arms, they continued to exert actual if not legal control over exhibition. Had the studios analyzed their situation more carefully the antitrust decision would have had a salutary effect. They would simply have tightened their belts and shifted their attention from the theatrical market to the new, increasingly profitable television channels. This did not happen immediately (although today the major studios, having seen the light, are responsible for most network programming).

As their assets shrank and as the original founders died off or retired, the studios were merged into the developing interindustrial conglomerates of the fifties and sixties or sold outright. Television producers filled the vacuum: Desilu bought the RKO studios, Revue took over the Republic soundstages. At the same time, more sensible independent distributors were making quiet fortunes serving as middlemen between the aggressive television networks and the paralyzed film studios.

Eliot Hyman was probably the most astute of these traders. He first bought the Warner Brothers backlist, traded in it for a while, then sold it to United Artists. He then acquired rights to a good number of Fox films. By 1967 his company, Seven Arts, was in a position to purchase Warner Brothers outright.

In the early fifties, Howard Hughes had sold RKO to the General Tire and Rubber company who liquidated it, and Universal had been acquired by the American subsidiary of the Decca Records organization. The Music Corporation of America (MCA), originally a talent agency, acquired the Paramount backlist, profits from which helped it finance the purchase of Decca and, with it, Universal.

Paramount was absorbed into Charles Bluhdorn's conglomerate work of art, Gulf + Western Industries, in 1966. Shortly thereafter, United Artists was taken over by Transamerica Corporation, a typical multinational conglomerate of the period who owned at the time, in addition to United Artists and its subsidiaries, Budget Rent-a-Car, Transamerica Computer Services, Pacific Finance Loans, Occidental Life Insurance Co., Transamerica Insurance Co., Cinegraphics, Inc., Transamerica Airlines, a capital fund, an investors fund, a relocation service, a title insurance company, a microfilm service, a moving and storage company, and a real estate/tax service.

In 1969 Warner Brothers–Seven Arts was merged with Steven Ross's Kinney National Services, which later became Warner Communications, Inc. Kinney's (and Ross's) fortune had been built in funeral parlors and parking lots, but like the moguls of old, Ross showed a surprising affinity for the business, building Warner into a powerhouse entertainment conglomerate. In 1989 he merged Warner with Time Inc., producing the largest media company in the world.

In 1969 a controlling interest in Metro-Goldwyn-Mayer, formerly the most powerful and prestigious of studios, was acquired by Kirk Kerkorian, a Las Vegas real-estate dealer. Kerkorian appeared to be interested in MGM mainly for its brand name, which he immediately applied to the hotel he was building. The company turned to low-budget features, with little success. In 1974 MGM was effectively liquidated, the studio sold, and the distribution organization closed. Throughout the 1970s MGM was best known as the owner of the MGM Grand Hotel in Las Vegas (named for the 1932 MGM movie).

In 1979, perhaps regretting his earlier decision to shift MGM's capital assets from the film industry to the gambling industry, Kerkorian attempted to buy a controlling interest in Columbia Pictures Industries. The deal fell through (there was talk of antitrust prosecution), and shortly thereafter it was announced that the MGM company, with the permission of its stockholders, would split in two, the original company to continue running the casino operations (now extended to Reno and Atlantic City) while the "new" company re-entered film production and distribution.

The low-budget strategy MGM's film company adopted did not pay off, and Kerkorian embarked on a new round of dealmaking. In 1981 he purchased the remnants of United Artists from a chastened Transamerica. In 1985 he sold the company to Ted Turner, only to buy it back shortly thereafter, minus the film library, which Turner kept, and the real estate, which went to Lorimar. In 1989 Kerkorian sold the remnants yet again, this time to Pathé, a European entity controlled by Italian entrepreneur Giancarlo Paretti and backed by the Dutch branch of Crédit Lyonnais. Paretti soon found himself in both legal and financial troubles. Crédit Lyonnais took control of MGM, feverishly attempting to save its by now considerable investment. By 1993 the company was back in business under the stewardship of respected industry executive Frank Mancuso, formerly of Paramount. In 1996 Kerkorian returned for yet another round, purchasing the company (with partners Mancuso and Seven Network Ltd. of Australia) for the third (or was it fourth?) time. The price was $1.3 billion. MGM will hold the record for Hollywood stock deals for quite a while. By late 1997 Mancuso had purchased enough rights so that the company controlled the world's largest film library. A year later, MGM sold ten percent of its stock to the public. Kerkorian had found yet another way to harvest golden eggs from the tired goose. (Mancuso left in 1999.)

The MGM saga was certainly the most humiliating, but it was only one of a long series of financial stories that kept Hollywood's increasingly profitable restaurants buzzing from the late 1970s through the turn of the century. Indeed, in "the industry," the deal had become both more important and more entertaining than the product, and the biggest and best deals involved studios, not movies, a fact that was not lost on the increasingly powerful talent agencies, as we shall see.

In 1977 David Begelman, then head of production at Columbia, was charged with embezzling $60,000 in a sordid case that received wide publicity coverage and that engendered much talk about various shady business practices in Hollywood (none of which were new). Alan J. Hirschfield, then president of Columbia, attempted to fire Begelman on ethical grounds and was himself dismissed. Many observers felt that the management of Columbia Pictures Industries cared more for Begelman's fabled knack for making profitable pictures than for Hirschfield's moral stance. Begelman was eventually convicted and fined—and hired as head of production at MGM. Hirschfield also landed on his feet, as president of Twentieth Century Fox.

Early in 1978 the five chief executives of United Artists resigned en masse in a dispute with parent Transamerica over management prerogatives and executive compensation. Arthur Krim and Robert Benjamin had taken over the moribund distribution company in the early fifties and molded it into one of the leading film companies of the sixties and seventies. Then in 1967 they had sold it to Transamerica. Now they regretted their decision. Together with president Eric Pleskow, treasurer William Bernstein, and production chief Mike Medavoy, they formed Orion Pictures Corp., an entity that was something more than just another production company but less than a full-fledged studio. Their unprecedented agreement with Warner Communications at the time allowed them full control over the marketing and advertising of their films through the Warner distribution system. Orion became the first new major player in Hollywood since the thirties. Meanwhile, without the experienced Krim team, UA quickly ran into trouble. The disaster of Michael Cimino's *Heaven's Gate* (1980) effectively put that studio out of business only three years after the Orion group had left.[*]

Within sixteen months Orion had been joined at this new power level by the Ladd Company, formed when Alan Ladd Jr and some of his associates left Twentieth Century Fox after several financially successful years. As the television networks reentered feature film production and distribution in 1979 and 1980 (they had failed at this in the late sixties) and as new, more powerful production companies like Lorimar and EMI joined the Hollywood ranks at levels of power slightly lower than Orion and the Ladd Company, the control structure of the American film industry appeared to be changing.

The founding of Orion and the Ladd Company (even though it lasted only a few years) signaled the shift of control from the corporate organizations to powerful individuals. This change had been in the works since the 1960s when the old studio system began breaking down. With major talent no longer under long-term contract, each film had to be a new deal. Power shifted to agents, packagers, and a few studio executives who had established invaluable networks of personal relationships.

Within a few years after the five principals of Orion had left United Artists, that studio was essentially out of business. When Orion itself was on the ropes in the early 1990s, Mike Medavoy, its chief of production, soon surfaced as a major figure at TriStar, bringing his stable of talent contacts with him. As Orion sank, TriStar rose in the Hollywood heavens—for a while. Within a few years, Tri-Star was

---

[*] These events were chronicled with great flair in three interesting books: Peter Bart's *Fade Out: The Calamitous Final Days of MGM* recounts the trials and tribulations of that formerly prestigious studio with great relish; David McClintick's *Indecent Exposure* chronicles the Begelman affair; and Steven Bach's *Final Cut* tells the United Artists story.

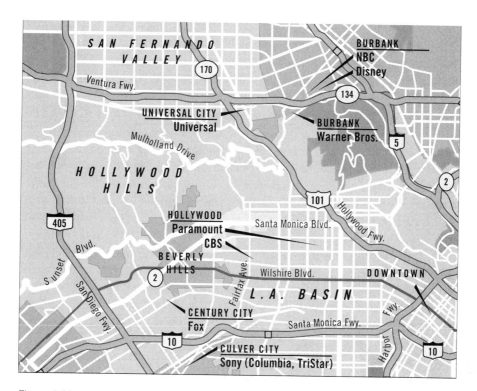

Figure 4-12. "HOLLYWOOD" TODAY. Los Angeles today is a vast suburban sprawl covering the Basin to the south of the Santa Monica mountains (Mulholland Drive) and the San Fernando Valley to the north: a city built after the invention of the automobile and impossible without it. There remains a tiny kernel of an early twentieth-century eastern city tucked behind the modern skyscrapers of the new "downtown." You can shoot for, say, Cleveland, on Hill Street or Broadway in the old L.A., and filmmakers still do. If you drive out Wilshire Boulevard from downtown, past the once-distant suburb of Hollywood, through trendy West Hollywood and placid Beverly Hills, past Twentieth Century Fox's greatest achievement— the Century City office development—around Westwood into Santa Monica, you understand the historical development of a city that invented itself on the model of its beloved industry. Today, only one major studio is actually situated in Hollywood. The others, like L.A. itself, are spread out in a wide ring on both sides of the hill.

caught up in the troubles of its sister studio, Columbia. Medavoy left in 1994, ending—at least temporarily—one of the longest careers of any modern studio chief. The growth of minor "studios" and "mini-majors" in the 1980s further spread the power base (even if companies like Cannon and Carolco had life spans on the order of desert flowers).

One of the minors thrived and survived. New Line Cinema had been founded by Bob Shaye in offices above a seedy bar on University Place in Greenwich Village in 1967. Growing slowly from imports and pickups, by the late 1970s New Line was ready to enter production. Two series of gory horror films, *Friday the 13th* and *Nightmare on Elm Street,* helped the company grow throughout the 1980s. By 1990 it was regarded as a candidate for admission to the select group of studios that dominate Hollywood. Ted Turner acquired New Line in 1993. Shaye and his veteran team remained in charge, and the company continued to grow, even after Turner's merger with Time Warner.

In the 1980s Shaye's feat was duplicated by two other New Yorkers—Bob and Harvey Weinstein. They founded Miramax in 1979 as a distribution company. It quickly developed into a key player in the film industry and has remained so for twenty years. The Weinstein brothers began by cannily acquiring saleable art films and making them profitable through inventive marketing. By the late 1980s Miramax owned the best foreign film Oscar, having won it four years running. In 1989 they began to venture into production while continuing their string of import successes with products like *The Crying Game* (1992), *The English Patient* (1997), and the films of Roberto Benigni. The Weinsteins cashed out in 1993, selling Miramax to Disney, but continuing to run it as an independent subsidiary in New York, maintaining their image as Hollywood renegades. Bob works behind the scenes, while Harvey plays the role of the cigar-chomping mogul of yore better than anyone left alive in Hollywood. In 1999 the company pulled down ten Oscars, including Best Picture for *Shakespeare in Love,* beating the establishment favorite, Dreamworks' *Saving Private Ryan.* The Weinsteins were accused of buying the award with an expensive promotional campaign, but it was more likely that their comedy beat the widescreen war drama because it worked better on VHS—and these days far too many of the Academy members see their movies that way rather than in proper theaters.

From the 1960s through the 1980s the U.S. television networks tried several times to establish film-production arms—without much success. Only TriStar, created in 1982 as a joint venture of Columbia, CBS, and HBO, had much of a life. Coca-Cola had bought Columbia in 1982 in a deal that earned minority shareholder New York investment banker Allen & Co. a reputed $40 million on a $2.4 million investment. Allen & Co. head Herbert Allen Jr, long a financial éminence grise in Hollywood, parlayed his involvement into numerous lucrative deals with Coca-Cola and others.[*]

---

[*] It is one of the haunting themes of Hollywood's long history that the moguls, old and new, despite their pomp and panache, have never been able to escape from the control of the "Eastern Bankers." Even today, at the turn of the century, four of the seven majors (Columbia/Tri-Star, Warner, Fox, Paramount) have to answer ultimately to New York, where Sony, Time Warner, News Corp., and Viacom maintain their headquarters; Universal reports to Montreal (where Seagram is headquartered), New Line talks to New York; and the once-grand MGM must report—at least in part—to Las Vegas and Australia. Only Disney remains locally owned and operated.

Apparently the "synergies" between movies and soft drinks weren't there. By 1989 Coke was ready to sell. Allen's friend super-agent Michael Ovitz found a willing buyer in Sony, the most creative force in the postwar electronics industry, who were now turning their attention to software and had just the year before purchased CBS Records. It wasn't long before the other shoe dropped: in 1990 Ovitz and Allen arranged the sale of MCA for a sum in excess of $6 billion to Sony's arch-rival Matsushita.

By 1990 six of the eight organizations that could call themselves Hollywood studios were in foreign hands.[*] Only Paramount and Disney remained wholly U.S.-owned. This state of affairs may be sobering to aging cultural critics who railed against American cultural imperialism back in the 1970s.

With a sense of the grand and profligate gesture which endeared it to the Hollywood community, Sony immediately hired producers Peter Guber and Jon Peters—fresh from their *Batman* triumph—to head the studio. To do so, Sony had to buy out their contract with Warner and purchase their production company, which added hundreds of millions to the purchase price. (Matsushita, conservative as always, left Universal management in place.) The team was not successful.

Meanwhile, back at the ranch—Century City, to be precise—Twentieth Century Fox was acquired by oilman Marvin Davis in 1981 and sold to Australian media baron Rupert Murdoch in 1985. With Barry Diller at the helm, Fox became a major force in television during the late 1980s.

At the end of the decade, after the dust had settled, two Hollywood studios were on a shared deathbed (MGM and UA), one was self-destructing (Orion), and all except Paramount and Disney had changed ownership at least once. It wasn't for want of trying. Rumors surfaced regularly about Disney. And Paramount chief Martin S. Davis, who had refocused Gulf + Western after the death of Charles Bluhdorn, changing its name to Paramount Communications to reflect a concentration on media, had tried unsuccessfully for the Time Inc. prize.

Davis finally made a deal in 1994, selling the larger Paramount to Sumner Redstone's smaller, tightly held Viacom, but not until after a protracted contest with former Paramount head—and Davis's arch-nemesis—Barry Diller.[†]

This battle set off another round of feverish dealmaking. Sony stuck with Columbia for the time being, but Matsushita, always more conservative, bailed

---

[*] Columbia/Tri-Star is owned by Sony, a Japanese company; Toshiba, another Japanese company, had a significant stake in Warners (reduced in 1998); MGM and UA, for what they are worth, are part-owned by Australians; Fox is owned by Rupert Murdoch's News Corp. (Murdoch became a U.S. citizen in the 1980s for business reasons, but News Corp. is still Australia-based.) Since 1995, the major stake in Universal has been owned by the Canadian-based Bronfman's family's Seagram Company, Ltd. Before that it belonged to Matsushita.

out of Universal in 1995, selling its stake to the Bronfman family's Seagram Company Ltd. Less than two months later, Disney's Michael Eisner announced the purchase of Capital Cities/ABC, creating the second-largest media conglomerate in the world. For years, Disney had been mentioned as a CBS acquisition target, but the network, weakened by ten years of Lawrence Tisch's management, was in no position to be a purchaser.

Days after Eisner's announcement, CBS was sold to Westinghouse. Foiled by the cable interests on his board, Ted Turner had lost his bid for the Tiffany network. Six weeks later, Turner decided to stop trying to buy a network and, instead, put on his sales hat, arranging a $7.5 billion deal with Time Warner, the largest media conglomerate, noting, perhaps ironically, "I'm tired of being little all the time. I'm nearing the end of my career. I want to see what it's like to be big for a while."

The investment bankers and corporate CEOs weren't the only ambitious players during the mid-1990s. The death of Frank Wells, Eisner's second in command at Disney in a helicopter crash in April 1994, started an interesting subplot to the boardroom dramas of the time. Jeffrey Katzenberg, who had come with Eisner to Disney ten years earlier, was hurt when he was passed over for the vacant job. He resigned angrily in August. Within a few days he was in business with old friends David Geffen and Steven Spielberg. They announced with great fanfare that they intended to build the first new Hollywood studio in fifty years. They would call it (Spielberg's hand is apparent) "Dreamworks SKG."

Others had tried this before (Francis Coppola several times), but the breadth of the experience and talent of these three would-be moguls meant their effort would be taken more seriously. Almost immediately they took in a major investment from Microsoft cofounder Paul Allen, allying Dreamworks with hip new media. In late 1995, after toying with the idea of a radical move to eastern Long Island (where Spielberg and—increasingly—other movers and shakers spend R&R time) they made a deal for the old Hughes Aircraft plant near the Los Angeles airport, thus assuring themselves of an impressive physical presence on the Hollywood scene. (Hughes had built his famous *Spruce Goose* in a hangar that was slated to house six sound stages.) By 1999 environmental concerns led them to scotch the plan: the Hughes plant is situated near rare wetlands.

Since the beginning of his career, Spielberg had been tied closely to Universal because of his loyalty to longtime studio bosses Sid Sheinberg and Lew Wasserman. With his mentors increasingly isolated by Matsushita management,

---

† The founding moguls must have smiled from on high: for the first time since they departed, a Hollywood studio had been sold to someone who had grown up in the business. Redstone began his career in the 1950s operating his father's drive-ins in the Boston area.

Spielberg was finally ready to make a move. With Spielberg gone from the lot, Universal was a less attractive property. Matsushita sold it in less than a year.

Meanwhile, after several setbacks, éminence grise Barry Diller was making moves in the East. Arguably the most influential industry executive of the 1980s, Diller had done well at Paramount (where Eisner and Katzenberg trained) before moving to Fox to build an effective new television network for Rupert Murdoch—a feat that had not been equaled before. When in 1992 it became clear that despite its size News Corp. was a family business, leaving no room for his own advancement, Diller quit. After a lengthy tour of the new media industry he bought into QVC, a cable shopping channel, intending to use it as a base for expansion.

After losing a bidding war for Paramount to Sumner Redstone's Viacom, Diller moved out of QVC, acquiring shares in Silver King, a Florida-based chain of television stations. In December 1995 he announced the purchase of Home Shopping Network, erstwhile competitor to QVC, and the acquisition of Savoy Pictures Entertainment Inc., a publicly traded film production company. In the fall of 1997 Diller bought a couple of cable networks and most of the television programming division of Universal for $4.1 billion, a deal intended to give him the mass he needed to found his own network. At about this time he realized he was weak on the Internet side. The newly-renamed USA Networks, Inc. bought 47 percent of Ticketmaster from Paul Allen in 1997, acquiring the rest the next year, and merged it with acquisition CitySearch in 1998, then selling shares of the subsidiary to the public. In 1999 Diller bid unsuccessfully for Internet portal Lycos: the Lycos shareholders thought USA Networks wasn't Internet enough for them. At the end of the century Diller was still struggling to find the right combination of elements for his vision of the studio of the future.

Despite this unprecedented financial upheaval, there has been no discernible change in the product that Hollywood manufactures. At the turn of the century the corporate entities that own the studios believe in synergy. They are horizontally (rather than vertically) integrated organizations. In addition to studios, they also own paperback book publishing companies, record companies, television production companies, theme parks, sports franchises, chains of video stores, stadiums, and the occasional wild animal preserve. (They've sold the toy companies.) A property, once acquired, can now be exploited in five or more media: films, books, records, broadcast television, and videodisc and tape. Yet the print divisions of Time Warner deal with the film division as if it were still a separate company; Columbia doesn't hire any more musicians under contract to Sony Music than they did previously; and there is no profitable connection between Twentieth Century Fox and Rupert Murdoch's tabloid newspapers (except that they inspired his tabloid television journalism).

Paradoxically, despite the concentration of media ownership in a few hands, the artists who actually produce the product have no less freedom. This is a tricky concept, about which we'll have more to say in Chapter 7, but for now let us note that in the history of Hollywood there have always been those "Eastern Bankers," and, as Steven Spielberg has put it so succinctly, "Whatever they are paying you, it is not enough." The moguls who founded the American film industry expressed their personalities and left their imprints. The businessmen who have bought (and sold and bought and sold again) their creations have not. Long after the balance sheets and income statements of the most-recently merged entertainment mega-company have passed into insignificance, the films which contributed so mightily to the profits (or losses) will be remembered.

For many years now, the people who run the studios have often been former talent agents—people trained in putting together "packages" of stars, script, and financing—so it should be no surprise that since the mid-1970s the locus of power in Hollywood has been the talent agencies themselves. For years, the William Morris agency dominated, then power shifted to ICM, formed by Morris renegades. Since the mid-1980s, CAA (Creative Artists Agency), led until 1995 by Michael Ovitz, has generally been regarded as the hot agency, followed close behind by ICM, led by Jeff Berg, and Morris. A former San Fernando Valley High School classmate of financier, convicted felon, and born-again community worker Michael Milkin, Ovitz had almost as much influence in the 1980s in his domain as Milkin had on Wall Street. Indeed, when he agented the Columbia and Universal deals, Ovitz was invading Milkin's own territory.

When in 1995 Ovitz acceded to Michael Eisner's blandishments and accepted the number two position at Disney, many people thought it was a step down. After all, Ovitz had just turned down a similar position at Universal. (CAA's second in command, Ron Meyer, accepted that job.) A year later, Ovitz was gone from Disney—albeit with a huge severance payment.

Since they no longer have players and technicians under contract, the studios have shifted to concentrate on distribution. To a lesser extent, they also operate as financiers. The real work of film production is now split up among a number of independent producers, many of whom are also directors or stars as well—what the Hollywood jargon calls "hyphenates."

The studios arrived at this point by a process of trial and error, even though the structure of the post-television film market could easily have been predicted early on. Television was clearly designed to fulfill cinema's function as the mass entertainment medium. If theatrical film was going to survive, it would have to shift to serving specialized audiences. This is, in fact, what has happened. The movie palaces have been replaced by more intimate theaters seating an average of fewer than two hundred patrons. These small theaters are bunched together in "multiplexes" to provide a wider choice as well as to cut overhead expense.

There are now more than twice as many nominal movie theaters in the U.S. as there were in the early 1970s. More important, more than half of Hollywood's income now comes from ancillary rights, mainly video. Yet this great increase in the number of distribution channels hasn't had the effect one might have predicted. Despite a brief flirtation with the new freedom in the late sixties, the studios have been loath to exploit these possibilities. Instead, they turned increasingly in the seventies to the blockbuster film (usually of the action genre), presold through books and aided by massive saturation television advertising, absorbing huge amounts of capital in the process. This practice continued throughout the 1980s. Indeed, a young moviegoer today would be surprised to discover that there once was a time when successful films did not immediately engender a raft of sequels.

Internationally, the death of the old studio system had positive effects, simply because—for a while—it opened up world markets to more strenuous competition. In the early fifties, the French and the Italian governments established quasi-official export sales organizations (Unifrance, Unitalia) that were instrumental in softening up markets for those countries' films (Unifrance having been much more active than its Italian counterpart). The growth of film festivals in most major film-producing countries was effective in this respect as well.

Two important factors in the film production equation in many countries have been government subsidy plans and television coproduction. The model for this new method of finance was the Swedish Film Institute, founded in 1963 to distribute monies collected from a 10 percent tax on all cinema admissions, partly on the basis of gross receipts, partly on the basis of quality. The Swedish plan encouraged the vigorous growth of an exportable film industry in a very small country. The French subsidy system has had a marked effect on that country's film industry. In 1993 French subsidies totaled $350 million distributed to 150 French pictures made that year. The money came from a box-office tax—mostly on American pictures, which increasingly dominate French screens, despite the subsidy system to which they contribute by their very popularity.

European film production was aided, too, in the fifties and the sixties by American location productions abroad, designed to take advantage of lower costs. This temporary internationalism came to an end in 1970, as prices equalized and as the American companies found themselves in a monetary bind. The British film industry, which had depended heavily on American capital in the sixties, was nearly decimated by the withdrawal. But film's loss was television's gain. The best British filmmakers now work in television (or in Hollywood).

By 1980 the American companies had regained effective control of the world's screens, challenged only occasionally and weakly by European conglomerates such as Lord Grade's ITC or Polygram. The extraordinary success of the French pay-television company Canal Plus in the eighties and nineties suggested that it might become an international force, but we still await a major French player in the world media game. Similarly, Italian magnate Silvio Berlusconi was able to put together a European entertainment octopus in the 1980s, but never ventured into the main arena of world markets, preferring the lesser challenge of Italian politics instead. The heartening, albeit brief, success of the English start-up Goldcrest Films in the 1980s suggests that opportunities still exist for small companies, despite the domination of the conglomerates.[*]

As the videotape industry exploded in the 1980s, the film industry thrived on the additional income. This time Hollywood avoided most of the mistakes it had made when television arrived in the early 1950s, embracing the new technology as a new profit center. Most of the major studios quickly set up their own video-cassette distribution companies, sometimes in partnership with television companies (RCA-Columbia, CBS-Fox). Yet Hollywood didn't control the development of the cassette business. Cassettes became established as a major entertainment medium in the 1980s because a few enterprising individuals far away from Hollywood figured out that people might want to rent a tape for an evening (rather than purchase it outright). As a result, the film distributors missed out on billions of dollars in income that might have been theirs if they had devised an effective "sell-through" strategy at the beginning of the cassette business.

Yet the dollars that did flow their way funded a number of independent entrepreneurs who, by 1990, provided a fertile training ground for young filmmakers. Of the 529 films the industry information source Baseline listed as having been released in 1992, only 330 were theatrical issues; most of the rest were Direct-to-Video productions. This low-cost genre had taken over for the B movies and Programmers of the thirties and forties.

A different challenge awaits the film industry at the turn of the century as the multimedia revolution gains speed. Videocassettes are a distribution medium, and not much more; the cassette business as we know it today requires Hollywood film product. The multimedia business now just beginning, however, competes with film as a production medium as well as borrowing from it. It is the first new production medium since broadcast network television, and as such it may draw valuable talent, capital, and customers from the venerable feature film industry.

With discs, the potential exists for a system of distribution as precise and flexible as that enjoyed by the print media, as the technologies of film and video continue to merge. As entertainment and as information channels, both movies and television have, until now, been characterized by limited access: in the U.S., five to seven studios have controlled film distribution; four commercial networks and

---

[*]   The Goldcrest story was told in meticulous detail in *My Indecision Is Final*, by Jake Eberts and Terry Ilott.

one public network have controlled access to television. The digital revolution and the Internet, together with the newly attained maturity of cable television (see Chapter 6), now present a remarkable multiplicity of access channels.

Will Hollywood continue to dominate American entertainment? Or will the power centers shift from the studios' San Fernando Valley to the computer industry's Silicon Valley—or even back to the publishing industry's Hudson Valley, where the film industry was born more than a century ago?

"Film": Politics

The economics of film determines its infrastructure—its foundations—and therefore its potential. The politics of film determines its structure: that is, the way it relates to the world. We understand film, experience it, and consume it from two different perspectives. The "sociopolitics" of film describes how it reflects and is integrated with human experience in general. Film's "psychopolitics" attempts to explain how we relate to it personally and specifically. Because film is such a widespread popular phenomenon, it plays a very important part in modern culture, *socio*politically. Because it provides such a powerful and convincing representation of reality, film also has a profound effect on members of its audience, *psycho*politically. The two aspects are closely interrelated, yet the differentiation is useful, since it focuses attention on the difference between the general effect of film and its specific personal effect.

Whichever way we look at it, film is a distinctly political phenomenon. Indeed, its very existence is revolutionary. In his landmark essay on the subject, "The Work of Art in the Age of Mechanical Reproduction," the critic Walter Benjamin wrote:

> One might generalize by saying: the technique of reproduction detaches the reproduced object from the domain of tradition…. It substitutes a plurality of copies for a unique existence. And in permitting the reproduction to meet the beholder or listener in his own particular situation, it reactivates the object reproduced. These two processes lead to a tremendous shattering of tradition…. Both processes are intimately connected with the contemporary mass movements. Their most powerful agent is the film. Its social significance, particularly in its most positive form, is inconceivable without its destructive, cathartic aspect, that is, the liquidation of the traditional value of the cultural heritage [*Illuminations,* p. 221].

Benjamin's prose is a bit abstruse, but the points he makes are basic to an understanding of the way film (and other mechanically reproduced arts) function in society. The most significant difference, Benjamin is saying, between film and the older arts is that the new art can be mass-produced, reaching the many rather than the few. (This is the sociopolitical aspect.) This has a revolutionary effect: not only is the art available on a regular basis to large numbers of people, but it also meets observers on their home grounds, thereby reversing the traditional relationship between the work of art and its audience. These two facts about film— (1) that it is plural rather than unique; (2) that it is infinitely reproducible— directly contradict romantic traditions of art and therefore invigorate and purify. (This is the psychopolitical aspect.)

Film has changed the way we perceive the world and therefore, to some extent, how we operate in it. Yet while the existence of film may be revolutionary, the practice of it most often has not been. Because the channels of distribution have been limited, because costs have prohibited access to film production to all but the wealthiest, the medium has been subject to strict, if subtle, control.

In America between 1920 and 1950, for example, the movies provided the main cultural format for the discovery and description of our national identity. (Television quickly replaced movies after 1950.) Historians argue whether the movies simply reflected the national culture that already existed or whether they produced a fantasy of their own that eventually came to be accepted as real. In a sense, the point is moot. No doubt the writers, producers, directors, and technicians who worked in the large studio factories during the great age of Hollywood were simply transferring materials they had picked up in "real life" to the screen. No doubt, too, even if those materials weren't consciously distorted toward political ends, the very fact that the movies amplified certain aspects of our culture and attenuated others had a profound effect.

Thus, two paradoxes control the politics of film: on the one hand, the form of film is revolutionary; on the other, the content is most often conservative of traditional values. Second, the politics of film and the politics of "real life" are so closely intertwined that it is generally impossible to determine which is the cause and which is the effect.

This discussion mainly involves American movies. The relationship between politics and film is no less intriguing in other contexts, but it was the homogeneous factory system of the studios that most subtly reflected (or inspired) the surrounding political culture. Because Hollywood movies were mass-produced, they tended to reflect the surrounding culture—or, more accurately, the established myths of the culture—more precisely than did the work of strongly individual authors. Indeed, many of the most notable auteurs in film history stand out precisely because their work goes against the establishment grain, politically: Chaplin, Stroheim, Vidor, Eisenstein, Renoir, Rossellini, Godard, for example.

The basic truism of film history is that the development of the art/industry is best seen as a product of the dialectic between film realism and film expressionism: between film's power to mimic reality and its power to change it. The earliest film artists—the Lumière brothers and Georges Méliès—succinctly demonstrated this dichotomy between realism and expressionism. Yet, underlying the dialectic of mimesis/expression is another, more basic, premise: that the definition of film style depends on the film's relationship with its audience. When a filmmaker decides on a realist style, he or she does so to decrease the distance between viewer and subject; the expressionist style, on the other hand, looks to change, move, or amuse the observer through the technique of film. Both these esthetic decisions are essentially political, since they insist on relationships (among filmmaker, film, subject, and observer) rather than idealized abstract systems. In this way, too, film is inherently and directly political: it has a dynamic relationship with its audiences.

To summarize, every film, no matter how minor it may seem, exhibits a political nature on one or more of these three levels:

❏ ontologically, because the medium of film itself tends to deconstruct the traditional values of the culture;

❏ mimetically, because any film either reflects reality or recreates it (and its politics);

❏ inherently, because the intense communicative nature of film gives the relationship between film and observer a natural political dimension.

A political history of film, then, might very well be three times as complex as an esthetic history, since we should trace the development of all three political facets. We have space to examine only a few of the most salient features of film politics.

Ontologically, the best evidence we have that film has radically altered traditional values lies in the phenomenon of celebrity. Previously, heroic models for society were either purely fictional creations or real people of accomplishment (whom we knew only at one remove). Film fused the two types: real people became fictional characters. The concept of the "star" developed—and stars are quite different from "actors." The most important role Douglas Fairbanks played was not Robin Hood or Zorro, but "Douglas Fairbanks." (In fact, Douglas Fairbanks was played by Douglas Ullman—his original name.) Likewise, Charles Chaplin played, not Hitler or Monsieur Verdoux, but always "Charlot," the tramp, and Mary Pickford (with Chaplin and Fairbanks the United Artists, the preeminent stars of their day) was forever typecast as "Little Mary, America's sweetheart." When she tried in the late twenties to change her public image, her career came to an end.

Early film producers seem to have been well aware of the potential phenomenon of stardom. They insisted that their actors work in anonymity. In 1912, however, the first fan magazines appeared, identifying "the Biograph Girl" and "Little Mary." A few years later, having been liberated from anonymity, Chaplin and

Figure 4-13AB. STARS. Both Fairbanks (left) and Chaplin (right) are "out of character" in these publicity shots, but because they had become celebrity personalities by this time, even off the set they carried with them the aura of stars. (*MOMA/FSA.*)

Pickford were vying to see which of the two would be the first to sign a million-dollar contract. Clearly, Little Mary and Charlot had struck responsive chords in audiences. The complex relationship between stars and the public has been a prime element of the mythic, and hence political, nature of film ever since.

"Stars" act out their personas through nominal character roles. "Celebrities" appear mainly as "themselves" and are known, in Daniel Boorstin's apt phrase, "for their well-knownness." We tend to downplay the significance of this phenomenon, yet stars are extraordinary psychological models of a type that never existed before.

We can trace the development of the phenomenon of celebrity back to the lecture circuits of the nineteenth century, where intellectual heroes such as Charles Dickens and Mark Twain (a "character," by the way, created by Samuel Clemens) played themselves to adoring audiences. Yet, until the "age of mechanical reproduction," these celebrities reached few people. The public outpouring of grief over the death of Rudolph Valentino in 1926, after his short and undistinguished career as a film actor, exceeded in intensity and dimension the reaction to any similar public death up to that time. It was only after politicians became celebrities that victims of assassination elicited such universal mourning.

Although studio moguls tried to construct stars of this magnitude artificially, they seldom succeeded. Stars were—and still are—the creation of the public: political and psychological models who demonstrate some quality that we collec-

Figure 4-14AB. Humphrey Bogart (left) as Philip Marlowe in *The Big Sleep* (Howard Hawks, 1946). (*MOMA/FSA.*) Jean-Paul Belmondo (right) as Michel Poiccard mimicking Bogart in *Breathless* (Jean-Luc Godard, 1959). The driving force of the film is the relationship between film and life.

tively admire.* Clark Gable was objectively no more physically attractive than dozens of other young leading men of the thirties, yet there was something in the persona he projected that touched a responsive chord. Humphrey Bogart was not an extraordinary actor and certainly not handsome by Hollywood standards, yet he became a central role model not only for his own generation but also for their children. As the actors became stars, their images began to affect audiences directly. Star cinema—Hollywood style—depends on creating a strong identification between hero and audience. We see things from his point of view. The effect is subtle but pervasive.

Nor is this phenomenon peculiar to Hollywood. In the sixties, European cinema demonstrated some of the same mystical power of identification. When Jean-Paul Belmondo models himself on Humphrey Bogart in Jean-Luc Godard's *Breathless* (1960), he is announcing a second generation of celebrity, one that demonstrates a historical consciousness. Marcello Mastroianni became the epitome of existential European manhood. At his death in 1996 he was treated like a

---

* Few film critics and historians have written cogently about stars. David Thomson's *Biographical Dictionary of Film* offers a wealth of intelligent and telling sketches. Richard Schickel's *His Picture in the Papers* is a thoughtful introduction to the subject. See also *Celebrity,* edited by James Monaco, and *Stars,* by Richard Dyer.

national hero. Jeanne Moreau was the model for wise, self-assured European womanhood, Max von Sydow and Liv Ullmann the Swedish versions of the two models. Yves Montand served as the essentially Gallic Bogart. More recently, Gérard Depardieu has become an icon of his generation.

But these people are actors as well as stars, so the effect is muted. There are occasions in their careers when individual roles supersede star personas. As American films came back to life in the sixties, a new generation of stars like the Europeans developed, displaying critical intelligence as well as powerful personas. Politically, this is an important advance. At its most deleterious, the Hollywood star system worked psychologically to outlaw roles that did not fit its own images. It was acceptable to act like Bogart, Gable, or John Wayne, but until the late 1960s there was no male star who was not a tough guy (like this trio) or sophisticated and urbane (like Fred Astaire or Cary Grant). Because we can now be critical of celebrities, contemporary audiences enjoy a wider range of types.

To a large extent, at least in nations in which film is dominant, the cinema helps to define what is permissible culturally: it is the shared experience of the society. Because its role models are so psychologically powerful, those roles for which it provides no models are difficult for individual members of society even to conceive, much less act out. Like folktales, films express taboos and help to resolve them. The cause-and-effect relationship is, as we noted, not very clear, but it is interesting to note that the quasi-revolutionary mores of the 1960s in America were predated by more than five years by the two major star personas of the 1950s—Marlon Brando and James Dean—both of which were notably rebellious. More specifically, Jean-Luc Godard's film *La Chinoise,* which portrayed a group of revolutionary students from the University of Paris at Nanterre, predated the uprising of May–June 1968 by precisely a year and, indeed, students from Nanterre were in the vanguard during the aborted real revolution, just as they had been in Godard's fictional rebellion.

In the age of mechanical reproduction fiction has a force it never had before.

Because it is so much more pervasive, television has taken over a large part of the folktale function of cinema. In Haskell Wexler's *Medium Cool* (1969), an incisive, brilliant analysis of the relationship between media and politics, a group of Black militants challenge a television reporter: "You put him on the six-, the ten-, *and* the twelve-o'clock news," they demand for one of the characters, *"then* he be real!" The function of media in determining the validity of an action, person, or idea was one of the central truths of radical politics in the sixties and has remained so into the age of the sound bite.

This unusual ability of film to "validate" reality is its most important mimetic political function. For example, one of the most telling social criticisms provided by the Black Power movement of the 1960s was its historical analysis of the inherently racist characterizations to which Blacks had been subjected as a matter

Figure 4-15. James Dean in a publicity still for *Rebel Without a Cause* (Nicholas Ray, 1955). Within a year, he was dead in an auto accident at the age of twenty-four, completing the legend. Although he only made three major films before his death (*East of Eden* and *Giant,* as well as *Rebel*), Dean touched a responsive chord in audiences of the fifties, and the outpouring of grief at his death was reminiscent of the hysteria surrounding Rudolph Valentino's death thirty years earlier. There is even a film about the effects of his death on some teenagers in a small southern town: James Bridges's *September 30, 1955* (1977). (*MOMA/FSA.*)

of course throughout the history of film and television. In this respect, too, the media faithfully reflected the values of the society. But they also exaggerated the real situation. In general (there were some exceptions), films pictured Blacks in servile roles. More important, Blacks were used only to play Blacks—that is, in roles in which race was a significant element. One of the great accomplishments of the Black Power movement of the 1960s was to begin to crack that barrier. Black lawyers, doctors, businessmen—even heroes—are now validated by the media (if only intermittently). Yet it is still rare for a casting director to hire an African-American to play a role that isn't specified as "Black."

As with so many other aspects of our culture, progress in racial politics seems to have been in a state of suspension for thirty years.[*] On the face of it, there were no more—or better—roles for African-Americans in the 1990s in mainstream films than there were in the 1970s. One of the brighter developments of the past few years has been the new group of African-American directors who have established themselves on the fringes of Hollywood. Yet there is nothing to connect the interesting work of filmmakers like Spike Lee, Matty Rich, and John Singleton with the first wave of Black film 25 years earlier; they are not building on the work of the previous generation, they have had to start over again.

---

[*] I personally date the beginning of this deep freeze from 1971, when Don McLean first sang about "the day the music died," on *American Pie.*

A

B

C

Figure 4-16. (A) Brando in the fifties. *A Streetcar Named Desire* (Elia Kazan, 1951). Brando, too, projected an image of rebellion that caught the public imagination of the fifties. But in twenty years the sexual energy had modified to produce the quirky, desolate image of... (B) Brando in the seventies. Here in *Last Tango in Paris* (Bernardo Bertolucci, 1972). The eyes, the look, the gestures, the relationships with women were similar, but more seasoned after twenty years. (C) Brando in the nineties (*The Island of Dr. Moreau*, 1996). He was the first of the great stars to develop an image as a thoughtful actor as well as a personality, and also one of the first to become a caricature of himself.

Racism pervades American film because it is a basic strain in American history. It is one of the sad facts of film history that the landmark *The Birth of a Nation* (1915) is generally hailed as a classic despite its essential racism. No amount of technical expertise demonstrated, money invested, or artistic effect should be allowed to outweigh the essential racist tone of *The Birth of a Nation*, yet we continue in film history as it is presently written to praise the film for its form, ignoring its offensive content.

This is not to imply that Griffith's masterpiece was anomalous. Until the late fifties, racial stereotypes were pervasive in film, then in television. There had been

Figure 4-17. The riots surrounding the Democratic Party convention in Chicago 1968 formed the background for Haskell Wexler's *Medium Cool* (1969). Immersing himself and his crew in reality, Wexler crafted a moving essay about the passivity that television inculcates. In a famous line, one of Wexler's crew shouts to him, "Look out, Haskell. It's real!" as the tear-gas canisters start popping around the filmmakers—as well as their subjects.

liberal acts of conscience before—films such as King Vidor's *Hallelujah* (1929) or Elia Kazan's *Pinky* (1949)—but even these were almost without exception marked by subtle condescension. It was not until the late sixties that Blacks began to take on nonstereotypical roles in American film.

We are speaking here of Hollywood. A thriving if limited African-American film industry, separate and unequal, dated from the 1920s, producing films about Blacks, by Blacks, for Blacks. But, of course, general audiences rarely saw these films.

Native Americans were as poorly served until very recently. Since they were integral to the popular genre of the Western, they were seen on screen more often than Blacks, but the stereotypes were just as damaging. There were a few exceptions in this regard. Possibly because the battle had already been won against the Indians, films were occasionally produced that portrayed them in a positive, human light. Thomas Ince's *The Indian Massacre* (1913) is an early example, John Ford's *Cheyenne Autumn* (1964) a later instance.

Despite their rapidly increasing influence in U.S. culture, Asian-Americans have been relatively quiet on the film front. Bruce Lee in the 1970s and his son Brandon in the 1990s both dominated the martial-arts genre before their eerily similar early deaths. Wayne Wang has had singular success dealing with Asian-American topics since *Chan Is Missing* (1981), *Dim Sum: A Little Bit of Heart* (1985), and *Eat a Bowl of Tea* (1989). With *The Joy Luck Club* (1993), from the popular Amy Tan novel about immigrant mothers and their American daughters, he reached a wider audience. *Smoke* (1995), about a Brooklyn cigar store, marked a move into general subjects.

Ang Lee has had perhaps the most unusual career. Born in Taiwan, he attended NYU film school, then returned home to direct *The Wedding Banquet* (1993) and *Eat Drink Man Woman* (1994), two unusual films about cultural attitudes social traditions. Without skipping a beat, back in the west he scored with *Sense and Sensibility* (1995) and the cold psychological drama *The Ice Storm* (1997). The trans-cultural resonances are quite intriguing.

The image of women in American film is a more complex issue. It seems likely that in the twenties movies did much to popularize the image of the independent woman. Even sirens such as Clara Bow and Mae West, while serving as male fantasies, were at the same time able to project a sense of independence and a spirit of irony about their stereotyped roles. Moreover, the image of women in films of the thirties and forties, on the whole, was very nearly coequal with that of men. A sensitive feminist can detect numerous stereotypical limitations in the films of that period, it is true, but for most of us to compare the thirties in film with the sixties or seventies or eighties is to realize that despite the awakened consciousness of contemporary women, cinematically we have only recently regained the level of intelligence of the sexual politics of even the mid-thirties. Actresses like Katharine Hepburn, Bette Davis, Joan Blondell, Carole Lombard, Myrna Loy, Barbara Stanwyck, Irene Dunne, and even Joan Crawford projected images of intelligence, independence, sensitivity, and egalitarian sexuality the likes of which we have rarely seen since.

All this ended in the early fifties with the advent of the personas projected by stars Marilyn Monroe (the child-woman seductress) and Doris Day (the virginal girl-next-door). Of the two, the image projected by Day and similar actresses was to be preferred. She never achieved real independence, but she was often more than simply a male fantasy, like Monroe. It wasn't as if actresses of the caliber of the earlier stars didn't exist. Sidney Lumet's *The Group* (1966), for example, starred not one but eight young actresses, at least seven of whom showed talent. Yet only Candice Bergen achieved real success thereafter—and it took her more than twenty years. With the advent of the "buddy" film in the late sixties (the most popular early example of which was *Butch Cassidy and the Sundance Kid*, 1969), what few major roles there were for women very nearly disappeared.

The sexual politics of the past thirty years in American movies is one clear area in which film does not simply reflect the politics of reality. This may have been true to a certain extent in the fifties, when our national culture was intent on

Figure 4-18. Lucia Lynn Moses in *The Scar of Shame* (1927), produced by the Colored Players Film Corp., and directed by Frank Peregini. (*MOMA/FSA.*)

coaxing women who had gained a measure of independence during the war back into the home. But it was certainly a false picture of the real world in the seventies, eighties, and nineties when millions of women were raising their own consciousness, if not their spouses'.

For instance, one of the first films of the seventies that was praised for its "feminist" approach was Martin Scorsese's *Alice Doesn't Live Here Anymore* (1975); yet that film presented us with a woman who, when deprived of the creature comforts of domesticity, couldn't survive on her own and, in the end, happily submitted to the role of helpmate once again. Why otherwise intelligent critics regarded *Alice* as in any way feminist is difficult to say, unless it was simply that the situation had deteriorated so drastically that any film that gave a woman a central role, no matter what its politics, had to be regarded as an advance.

Despite a lot of hype, the feminist position in film didn't advance much in the seventies or eighties. Such vaunted women's films as *An Unmarried Woman, The Turning Point,* and *Julia* (all 1978) did, it's true, use women as central characters, but with no discernible raised consciousness. Martin Ritt's drama *Norma Rae* (1979) gave Sally Field a powerful, Oscar-winning role as protagonist but dealt more with union politics than sexual politics.

Ironically, the film of that period that showed the most sophisticated understanding of sexual politics was Robert Benton's *Kramer vs Kramer* (1979), in which the woman (Kramer, played by Meryl Streep) was, if not actually the villain, then certainly the source of the problem, and the focus was almost entirely on the sensitive and painful reaction of the man (Kramer, Dustin Hoffman) to a classic feminist-inspired situation of the seventies. No film in recent years has shown this

Figure 4-19. "America's Sweetheart," Little Mary Pickford (c. 1920): sausage curls, gingham, and cute puppies. (*Marc Wanamaker/Bison Art Ltd.*)

Figure 4-20. Judy Garland as Dorothy (1939): pigtails, more gingham, and childhood fantasies: America's second-generation sweetheart. (*Bison Art Ltd.*)

sensitivity and concern for a woman's point of view. Indeed, if we are to judge from Hollywood's evidence, the main benefit of the contemporary women's movement has been to free men from male stereotypes. This is true, but it is not anywhere near the whole truth.

In the eighties, the "new women's movie" (I hesitate to call it feminist film) quickly became an accepted genre, but without any real emotional or political clout. Such modern-day "women's movies" as *Steel Magnolias* (1989), *Fried Green Tomatoes* (1991), *Nine to Five* (1980), or *Thelma & Louise* (1991), for all their virtues, don't tell us much about sexual politics. The first two deal with women in their own world, while the last two simply let them play the buddies the men usually play, celebrating the newly acceptable character of the liberated woman without extending the dialogue and without challenging accepted mores.

So what else is new? From the mid-1970s through the end of the century sexual politics in America and Europe, like politics in general, has existed in a state of suspended animation. The same issues were discussed on the twenty-fifth Earth Day as on the first. The same problems confront what we continue to call, inappropriately, "minorities" now as then. The struggle continues to continue.

Yet, despite the fact that we can't point to a continuity of progress, the situation of women in film now is better than it was thirty years ago. There is an indefinable sense that the balance between men and women is shifting. More important,

Figure 4-21. Clara Bow, the *IT* girl, projected a powerful sexual image in the twenties, but with a sense of humor that made her acceptable to still-puritan American audiences. "S.A."—sex appeal—has powered the industry since.

it is now no longer unusual for an actress to be able to prolong her career as female lead well into her fifties: Jane Fonda, Shirley MacLaine, Tina Turner, Goldie Hawn, and Barbra Streisand suffered no decrease in earning power as they matured. And Susan Sarandon was past forty before she realized the full range of her talent. Sarandon is the first American actress in a long while to combine sexuality with mature intelligence in an ongoing star persona, just as Meryl Streep has carved a position for herself as a commanding "actor's actor."

Indeed, here women have taken the lead in redefining our attitude toward aging. The generation that came of age in the 1960s, the "War Babies" and the "Baby Boomers," have decided to maintain a level of sexuality well into their fifties and sixties that was unheard of thirty years ago.

Figure 4-22. After twenty-five years of independent, witty, strong women stars like Katharine Hepburn, Rosalind Russell, and Bette Davis, American film returned to raw "S.A." in the early fifties. Marilyn Monroe's remarkable career saw her portray male fantasies on screen while she boldly explored the boundaries of fifties-style eroticism off-screen. Her nude calendar poses would have been considered pornographic at the time. This is a shot from her last photo session, six weeks before her death. Bert Stern was the photographer. (*Used with permission.*)

At the same time, paradoxically, Generation X clasped to its bosom a retrograde sexual mythology that echoed the worst of the 1950s. Madonna refashioned the Marilyn Monroe sex kitten into a campy Valkyrie whose armor was her underwear. *Truth or Dare* was a stage most of us leave behind as high-school sophomores. Actresses like Sharon Stone, Demi Moore, Kim Basinger, and Drew Barrymore are used and abused on a regular basis. Like their male predecessors in the 1980s—Sean Penn, Rob Lowe, Matt Dillon, Patrick Swayze—this new generation of actresses plays on less admirable Hollywood traditions. It is not enough to suggest that these roles may be ironic; we all know what they are selling. In the 1990s, sex disintegrated into a commodity, and a vaguely boring one at that. Hard-core "porn" like *Deep Throat* and *The Devil in Miss Jones*—films which caused a furor when they were released in the early seventies—is now available on numerous cable networks in every living room and keeps most suburban video stores in profits. Since *Flashdance* (1983) and *Dirty Dancing* (1987), sex for teens and preteens has been a profitable Hollywood sideline, and many theatrical fea-

Figure 4-23. During the same period, Doris Day's roles were just as limited—and limiting—even if she was the girl-next-door foil to Monroe's sex kitten.

tures exploit their soft-core assets by releasing more explicit "video cuts" to the cassette market.[*]

Perhaps this is progress; perhaps it is necessary to pass through this phase to rediscover romance and nonpornographic eroticism; perhaps the AIDS epidemic requires more "virtual sex." In any case, it seems like the turn of the century is a good time to re-view *Fellini Satyricon*, and to remind ourselves that Clara Bow, the "It" girl of the twenties who introduced the idea of sex appeal, played her role with a wit and directness that revealed both a greater sense of self and a more powerful sensuality than we find in any storeful of current video cuts.

Sexual politics in film is closely connected with what we might call the "dream function" of the movies. Much of the academic criticism of the late seventies and eighties focused on this aspect of the film experience. The strong identification we make with cinematic heroes is simply observed evidence that film operates on our psyches not unlike dreams. This is the inherent aspect of film politics: how do we interrelate with films? Since the early days, filmmakers have been in the business of selling fantasies of romance and action—or, to use the contemporary syn-

---

[*] This marketing trend grew through the 1990s and reached its nadir in 1999 as teenage sexual fantasies were replaced by *Beavis-and-Butthead*-inspired preteen bathroom humor in films like *South Park: Bigger, Longer & Uncut* and *Austin Powers: The Spy Who Shagged Me* as Hollywood zeroed in on the lucrative preadolescent male market. The trend came to be known as "gross-out humor."

Figure 4-24. The sixties saw only a little improvement over the fifties in women's roles. On the whole, men dominated the American screens of the decade, as the buddy film celebrated male bonding. Here, Paul Newman and Robert Redford go out with guns blazing in *Butch Cassidy and the Sundance Kid* (1969), perhaps the apotheosis of Buddy films.

onyms, sex and violence. In this respect, film is not much different from literature. Popular films, like popular novels, depend on the motivating forces of these twin libidinal impulses.

The issue is complex: film satisfies the libido not only by giving a kind of life to fantasies, but also more formally—the style of a film, its idiom, can be either romantic or active, sexual or violent, without any regard to its content. In addition, it is far from clear what precise effect this particular function of film has on the people who experience it. Does it take the place of real experience? Or does it inspire it?

This is a particularly interesting conundrum when expressed in terms of political action. A film in which the hero wins the day may simply convey to audiences that "business is being taken care of"—that there is no need to act—while a film in which the hero loses may be taken as a sign that action is futile. How can a political filmmaker, then, create a structure in which the audience is involved, but not to such an extent that the characters serve as surrogates? How can it be made clear that action is both possible and still necessary in real life? There are no simple answers.

Figure 4-25. It wasn't until 1991's *Thelma & Louise* that the buddy theme was feminized in a hit movie. The film about two gun-toting women renegades caused a media sensation as audiences argued about its potential as a feminist statement. Here Geena Davis and Susan Sarandon take off with the pedal to the metal.

The question of surrogate action is more easily explained in terms of romance and sex. Here the characters are clearly surrogates for the audience and there is no real intent to suggest that the drama of the film be carried over into real life. In fact, the verisimilitude of the film experience suggests the opposite: that the experience of the film can to a great extent replace the experience of reality. We speak of film "fans" and film "buffs," but there is also a subculture of film "addicts": people with such a strong need for the dream experience of film that it might very well be physiological as well as psychological. These profound effects of film have not as yet been studied in sufficient detail. Much of the most interesting work in film theory during the next few years will concern such topics.

The libidinal effect of film as dream also has a more practical aspect. Ever since Edison's Kinetoscope loop the John Rice–May Irwin *Kiss* (1896), movies have excited outpourings of moralism, which in turn have led to censorship. While in Continental countries film censorship has most often been political in nature, in the U.S. and Britain it has been anti-sexual and puritanical, a vestige of native puritanism and Victorian attitudes toward sex.

In 1922, in response to supposed public moral outrage at a recent spate of sex scandals involving film actors (notably the Fatty Arbuckle affair), Hollywood founded the Motion Picture Producers and Distributors of America organization (the MPPA), colloquially known as the "Hays Office" after its first president. The Hays Office performed no formal censorship, preferring to counter bad publicity with good, but gradually guidelines were issued. The first production code dated

A

B

C

D

Figure 4-26. While the eighties and nineties did not see a return to the independent wit and depth of character the women of the thirties and forties showed, the period was remarkable in one respect: as the actresses of the sixties and seventies aged, led by Jane Fonda and Barbra Streisand, they continued to play romantic leads throughout their forties well into their fifties. For the first time since perhaps the eighteenth century, middle-aged women were allowed to retain their sexuality, even flaunt it. (Of course, American men had aged gracefully and sexily on the screen ever since Fairbanks.) (A) Tina Turner at 54. (B) Goldie Hawn at 49. (C) Susan Sarandon at 51 as the sexy star in *Twilight* (1998). (D) Trumping all of her contemporaries, erstwhile sixties singer Nancy Sinatra posed for a classic *Playboy* photo spread in 1995 at the age of 54.

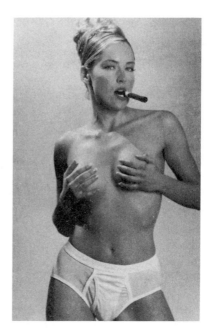

Figure 4-27. That we haven't yet regained the sexual political equilibrium of the 1940s is certainly more our own fault than Hollywood's. Despite thirty-five years of "sexual revolution" and twenty-five years of an active feminist movement, sexuality in the nineties was, more often than not, sour and dysfunctional, as suggested here in this Sharon Stone publicity shot. After eight hundred years of Romance, the flesh remains willing but the lyric spirit is weak. Perhaps it is time to build new temples for Euterpe, Erato, and Thalia.

from 1930. When Joseph Breen joined the MPPA in 1934, the code began to be strictly enforced. (The Catholic Legion of Decency was founded the same year and exerted a marked puritanical influence until the early sixties.)

The code made absurd demands on filmmakers. Not only were outright acts of sex and violence strictly prohibited, but also a set of guidelines was laid down (and strictly enforced) that prohibited the depiction of double beds, even for married couples, and censored such expletives as "God," "hell," "damn," "nuts"—even "nerts." The effect was profound.

One of the greatest surprises awaiting a student of film first experiencing pre-code movies is the discovery that in the late twenties and very early thirties films had a surprisingly contemporary sense of morality and dealt with issues, such as sex and drugs, that were forbidden thereafter until the late sixties. The effect is curiously disorienting. We have grown up with late thirties, forties, and fifties Hollywood through the wide exposure of the films (usually recensored) on television. To experience some of the realistic films from the precode era is to discover a lost generation. One of the last vestiges of precode relevance, for example, was the cycle of Gangster films—*Public Enemy* (1931) and *Scarface* (1932) among them—that attempted to treat political issues directly.

In Britain, self-censorship by the British Board of Film Censors dates from 1912. Interestingly, the British system of censorship has had a less marked effect than the American code. Until 1951, British films were rated U, A, or H (for Universal, Adults, and Horrific—prohibited to children under sixteen). The object has

Figure 4-28. Edison's John Rice–May Irwin *Kiss* (1896), where it all began. (*Frame enlargement.*)

been to protect young children from undue exposure to extreme violence (which is what "horrific" meant), an unobjectionable aim. In 1951, as sex became more important in film, H was replaced with X.

The American code was useful to producers throughout the Hollywood period. Although it set up maddeningly arbitrary rules, it also freed the studios from any ethical pressure to deal with relevant political and sexual subjects or even to treat milder subjects with a degree of sophistication. Hollywood settled comfortably in the mid-thirties into a style of filmmaking that generally eschewed relevance in favor of the highly prized, often hollow, fantasy "entertainment values" of the Golden Age.

It was not only the direct proscriptions of the code that were significant. The code also had a general chilling effect on an industry that was particularly suscep-tible to economic pressure. In addition, this vulnerability yielded another type of censorship. The studios produced nothing that would offend powerful minorities in the audience. They were also very eager to please when the political establish-ment made suggestions. The lawlessness of the Prohibition era, for example, led to a cycle of protofascist movies in the early thirties—*Star Witness* (1931), *Okay America* (1932), and *Gabriel Over the White House* (1934) are examples.

During World War II, naturally, Hollywood rose to the occasion, not only by producing thousands of training and propaganda films (the most famous example being Frank Capra's *Why We Fight* series), but also by quickly erecting in fiction films a myth of the conflict that played no small part in uniting the country behind the struggle.

A perfect example of this is Delmer Daves's *Destination Tokyo* (1943), which displays the usual varied ethnic group united against the common enemy. As leader, Cary Grant stops in mid-picture to write a letter home to his wife in the Midwest. The sequence takes a good ten minutes. As Grant writes, justifying the war, documentary shots illustrate his lecture, the gist of which is that the Japanese and the Germans are racially despicable, while our allies, the Chinese and the Russians, are genetically destined to win and historically peace-loving people very much like ourselves! Later, this didn't fit very well with the mythology of the Cold War. By design or accident, many of the prints of *Destination Tokyo* available at the height of the Cold War lacked this powerful sequence.

As World War II came to an end, there were occasional realistic treatments of combat that could almost be called antiwar in approach. *The Story of G.I. Joe* and *They Were Expendable* (both 1945) are two notable examples.

After the war, Hollywood dutifully followed along as the national myths of the Cold War developed. In the quasi-documentary spy films produced by Louis de Rochemont (*The House on 92nd Street,* 1945; *13 Rue Madeleine,* 1947; *Walk East on Beacon,* 1952), we can trace a smooth progression as Commies replaced Nazis as villains, without any alteration of the style or the structure of the films.

During the fifties, the Cold War mentality was pervasive. There were cycles of Spy films and films glorifying Cold-War institutions like the Strategic Air Command and the FBI. But more abstractly, we can also discern Cold-War psychology in the popular genre of science fiction during the 1950s. *Invasion of the Body Snatchers* (1956) is perhaps the prime metaphor for the political paranoia of those years, while *Forbidden Planet* (1956) provides a more sophisticated approach. In the latter film, the monsters are not insidious, implacable, otherworldly beings against whom there is no defense short of complete mobilization, but rather creatures of our own ids, reflections of our own elemental fears. Once the characters of *Forbidden Planet* learn to deal with their own subconsciouses, the monsters evaporate.

Obviously, the purges and the blacklisting that occurred at the urging of House Un-American Activities Committee in the late forties had a deeply disturbing effect. But this in itself is not enough to explain the widespread, nearly unanimous ideology exhibited by Hollywood films in the 1950s. Filmmakers were seized by the same paranoia that held the rest of the country in its grip. It was as if, having found a spirit of unification and purpose in the war against fascism, we desperately desired another enemy of equal danger to bring us together. When Cold-War myths disintegrated in the sixties, coincidentally, forces for social change were partially liberated. American films reflected these changes as well.

In Europe, the effects of World War II on film were, paradoxically, positive. In quiet, more sensible, and reasonable propaganda of films like *In Which We Serve* (Noël Coward, 1943), English filmmakers found a sense of purpose. As the documentary techniques of Grierson and his associates were applied to fiction,

England discovered a national cinematic style for the first time. Politically conscious, historically intelligent, that style was reborn for a brief period in the late fifties and early sixties as the so-called Angry Young Men of the theater had their effect on film.

In Italy, the long drought of fascism was ended by a flood of politically active, esthetically revolutionary films known collectively as Neorealism. Rossellini's *Rome, Open City* (1945) and *Paisan* (1946), De Sica's *Bicycle Thief* (1948) and *Shoeshine* (1946), Visconti's *Ossessione* (1942) and *La Terra Trema* (1947) set standards that inspired filmmakers around the world for decades.

But the political relevance that marked both British and Italian cinemas during the forties did not survive long in the fifties. Not until the late sixties was it revived, in a series of French and Italian muckraking films that had proven political effect. The main exponents of this style were Constantin Costa-Gavras (*Z*, 1969; *State of Siege*, 1973) in France and Francesco Rosi (*Salvatore Giuliano*, 1962; *The Mattei Affair*, 1972) in Italy. There were very few examples of this muckraking style of cinema in the U.S. The most notable example was *The China Syndrome* (1979), released only weeks before the near-meltdown at Three Mile Island mimicked its plot.

Since 1980, the relationship between politics and film has become increasingly skewed (as has the bond between politics and real life). The muckraking tradition continues to exist, but it has been almost twenty years since any European or American film has had a direct effect on real politics. Oliver Stone has established a unique niche for himself in Hollywood as the industry's last remaining politico, but his investigations of contemporary issues (*Talk Radio*, 1988; *Natural Born Killers*, 1994; and especially *Wall Street*, 1987) are overshadowed by his more popular historical panegyrics (*Platoon*, 1986; *JFK*, 1991; *Nixon*, 1995) obsessed with the events of thirty years ago. Perhaps the mixture of his obsessions simply mirrors our own, stuck at the end of the century between two political worlds—"one dead, the other powerless to be born."

Like all forms of mass entertainment, film has been powerfully mythopoeic even as it has entertained. Hollywood helped mightily to shape—and often exaggerate—our national myths and therefore our sense of ourselves. It has likewise had a profound effect abroad. For the New Wave in France in the early 1960s, the phenomenon of American filmic cultural imperialism was an important subject of study. As recently as 1976, for example, only 40 percent of West German box-office receipts was garnered by American films. By 1992 that figure had more than doubled, to 83 percent. American cinema is nearly as dominant in England, Italy, and France, and these are all major film-producing nations. American films consistently garner 50 to 60 percent of the French market. In smaller countries in Europe, and especially in emerging nations, the situation is even more unbalanced. In 1975, for example, 18 percent of Dutch film income went to native producers. By 1991 that figure had been reduced to 7 percent. (It should be noted that American market share can vary significantly depending on the particular films in release in a given year; American market dominance does not necessarily advance inexorably.)

At present, the overwhelming dominance of American films in the world marketplace is being challenged from several directions. Some countries have instituted quota systems. In the 1970s, Third World filmmakers worked to counteract Hollywood myths with their own, while a number of other filmmakers attempted a more radical approach, questioning the very premise of the Hollywood film: entertainment. This approach, sometimes called dialectical film, involved reconceiving the entertaining consumer commodity as an intellectual tool, a forum for examination and discussion.

This is a view of film that not only admits the relationship between film and observer but also hopes to capitalize on it to the viewer's benefit by bringing it out into the open. Like the plays of Bertolt Brecht (see Chapter 1), these films want to involve their observers intellectually as well as emotionally. It is necessary, then, that the viewers participate intellectually in the experience of the film; they must work, in other words. As a result, many people who don't understand the dialectical ground rules are turned off. Waiting for the film to do all the work, to envelop them in the expected heady fantasies, they find that dialectic films— Jean-Luc Godard's work, for example—are boring.

Although it certainly doesn't guarantee an increase in market share, this approach, when properly understood, offers one of the more exciting possibilities for the future development of film:

- ❏ Ontologically, the power of film to deconstruct traditional values is enhanced and put to use.

- ❏ Mimetically, film becomes not simply a fantastic reflection of reality, but an essay in which we can work out the patterns of a new and better social structure.

- ❏ Inherently, the political relationship between the film and the observer is recognized for what it is and the observer has, for the first time, a chance to interact, to participate directly in the logic of the film.

Hollywood film is a dream—thrilling, enthralling, but sometimes a political nightmare. Dialectic film can be a conversation—often vital and stimulating.

Figure 4-29. LUMIÈRES' REALITY. *Leaving the Factory* (1895): the fact of existence. (*MOMA/FSA. Frame enlargement.*)

"Cinema": Esthetics

When we consider the variety of forces that must conspire to get a film made, all the demanding economic, political, and technological factors (so few of which individual poets, painters, or musicians need consider), it's a wonder that any "art" survives the arduous process of moviemaking. Yet, as film has been a primary channel for the expression of our politics in the twentieth century, so too has it proved the main arena for the expression of our esthetics. Because it's such a public medium, it is—intentionally or not—about how we live together. Because it's such an expansive, encompassing medium, it offers heady and unrivaled opportunities for the expression of esthetic ideas and feelings.

One way to get a feel for the shape of cinema history is to identify the esthetic dialectic that seems to inform each period of its development. These neat binary oppositions may appear simplistic when applied to such a rich and complex medium of expression, but they offer convenient handles. Out of their personal struggles with these ideas, the most public artists of the century created a rich heritage.

Figure 4-30. MÉLIÈS'S FANTASY. *The Kingdom of the Fairies* (1903): the expressive narrative. (*MOMA/FSA. Frame enlargement.*)

It's impossible, of course, to offer a comprehensive history of film styles and filmmakers in a single volume (much less an individual chapter). What follows is just a sketch. The story is very much a matter of individuals, and individual efforts; we've tried to note the most significant in the pages that follow.

Creating an Art: Lumière Versus Méliès

The first dichotomy of film esthetics is that between the early work of the Lumière brothers, Auguste and Louis, and Georges Méliès. The Lumières had come to film through photography. They saw in the new invention a magnificent opportunity to reproduce reality, and their most effective films simply captured events: a train leaving the station at Ciotat, workers leaving the Lumière photographic factory. These were simple yet striking protofilms. They told no story, but they reproduced a place, time, and atmosphere so effectively that audiences paid eagerly to view the phenomena. On the other hand, Méliès, a stage magician, saw immediately film's ability to change reality—to produce striking fantasies. His *Voyage to the Moon* (1902) is the best-known example of Méliès's thoroughly cinematic form of illusion, and one of the most elaborate early films. Significantly, many of Méliès's films had the words "nightmare" or "dream" in their titles. The dichotomy represented by the contrasting approaches of the Lumières and Méliès is central to film and is repeated through the years that followed in a variety of guises.

At the same time in the U.S., Thomas Edison's company was turning out simpler films, which seldom exhibited the ingrained cinematic sense of his French contemporaries. *Fred Ott's Sneeze* and the John Rice–May Irwin *Kiss* are two prototypical examples of Edison's diffident approach.

In 1897, Edwin S. Porter, a salesman, joined Edison's company. For the next eleven years, he was the most important filmmaker on the American scene. After an apprenticeship filming newsreel footage, Porter produced in 1903 two films— *The Life of an American Fireman* and *The Great Train Robbery*—that are milestones of film history. Porter is known for his fluid parallel editing (indeed, he is often considered the "inventor" of film editing), and while it is true enough that both of these films are inventive, his reputation as one of the fathers of film technique raises the first serious problem in the history of film esthetics. Porter's later films never fulfilled his early promise. Moreover, other filmmakers were exhibiting much the same fluency at the same time in England and France. In fact, the memorable parallel editing of *The Life of an American Fireman* may have been partly accidental, since one of Porter's aims in making the film was to use some leftover footage he had discovered in the Edison factory. Yet Porter is praised in standard film histories as an innovator. One of the major difficulties with film history to date is this uncontrollable urge to discover "firsts," to create a sort of *Guinness Book of World Records* in film.

The truth is that it would have been difficult for Porter (or someone else) *not* to have "discovered" the potential of the cut. It is inherent in the physical nature of film; even for this, supposedly the most cinematic of devices, there are models in the other arts, and any intelligent practitioner of the art should have been able to make the necessary logical jump. Porter's parallel cutting, Griffith's closeups, tracking, and panning were all devices that cried out to be discovered and used; judged by the standards of the established arts, they were hardly innovative. In film, however, it was very easy to set records if you were among the first to play the game.

In England in the early years of the century, Robert W. Paul and Cecil Hepworth were doing more interesting work than Porter. Hepworth's *Rescued by Rover* (1905) is a better illustration of the potential of editing than the American classics. In France in the latter half of the decade, Ferdinand Zecca (at Pathé) and Louis Feuillade (at Gaumont) were actively exploring numerous film possibilities, and Max Linder (Pathé) became the first successful film comedian. Émile Cohl was beginning to explore the possibilities of the animated film. In Italy, Filoteo Alberini was shooting some of the earliest historical dramas. Clearly, the first period of film history is the story of European accomplishments.[*]

D. W. Griffith first entered films as an actor in 1907. During the succeeding six years he directed hundreds of one- and two-reelers for Biograph and in the process established a reputation as the leading film artist of the day. Griffith was particularly effective with actors and theatrical devices—especially lighting. He used closeups, tracks, pans, and parallel editing with great aplomb. He made films that were emotionally profoundly affecting, even if they nearly always operated within the conventions of Victorian melodrama. He certainly deserves his reputation as the "father" of the feature film. Yet there are a number of serious problems with his work.

It is not necessary to compare Griffith's work in film with developments in the other arts of the period: Picasso in painting; Conrad, Joyce, and Dreiser in the novel; Strindberg, Chekhov, and Shaw in the theater. That comparison is certainly unfair, since film was still a fragile enterprise that depended very much on its popular audience. Yet other filmmakers at about the same time were doing fresh and interesting work, unhampered by the clichés of the nineteenth-century theater. A good part of Griffith's reputation as the patriarch of film art is due to a kind of esthetic inferiority complex, which marked film history until at least the 1960s.

Griffith, who had begun his career in the theater, wanted very much to make films that were "respectable." He wanted to liberate film from its lower-class, "bad object" status. Yet much of the vitality and power of film lay in just that renegade status. By 1911, Mack Sennett, who had begun by acting and writing for Griffith, was making his first comedies, which show a sense of freedom and a gusto that are also evident in the best of Griffith, but which he often seems to be working against. Griffith's art looked backward; Sennett's looked forward, toward Dada and Surrealism.

The problem with Griffith's reputation is twofold: we don't yet take cinema seriously enough, and so we tend to denigrate slapstick; and at the same time we take film too seriously, and so we yearn for the respectable father, the role that Griffith played so well. Similar attitudes reveal themselves in the study of American literature, where we tend to overemphasize writers who offer a neat parallel with British literature and neglect native American work as not quite respectable. When the balance is redressed, Griffith's reputation will benefit, since we will be able to accept the faults with the successes. We will also understand better why his early promise led to the grandiose schemes of later years and eventually to failure.

Central to both Griffith's melodrama and Sennett's farce was the concept of the chase, still today a dominant element of popular film. Dating from the early

---

* This period is wonderfully documented in Kevin Brownlow's and David Gill's 1995 six-part series *Cinema Europe: The Other Hollywood.*

Figure 4-31. THE SENNETT CHASE. The Keystone Kops in riotous action on the streets of old Los Angeles: a ballet of sight gags.

examples of Porter and Hepworth, with antecedents in the conventions of Victorian theater, the chase was the single great element of narrative dramaturgy that film did not share with theater. It brought theater out of the proscenium arch (real or ideal) and into the world, and it became a quintessential model of the battle between protagonist and antagonist that drives all dramatic narrative.

When Griffith is at his best, in such films as *The Lonedale Operator* (1911), *The Musketeers of Pig Alley* (1912), the closing sequence of *Intolerance* (1916), or *Way Down East* (1920), the chase is often the device (real or metaphorical) that allows him to free himself from the stasis of Victorian sentiment to discover the power inherent in melodrama. Likewise, Sennett's reeling chases through the bleak streets of early Los Angeles provide some of the most inventive cinematic moments of early film history.

The Silent Feature: Realism Versus Expressionism

The spectacle, melodrama, and sentiment we associate with Griffith were the commercial hallmarks of the silent feature, as the successful career of Cecil B. DeMille attests. We can also divine at least the last two elements in the phenomenal popularity of Mary Pickford's films during the late teens and twenties. (Her husband, Douglas Fairbanks, commanded the first!) But esthetically, it was the Sennett tradition that flowered eloquently during these years.

Figure 4-32. D. W. Griffith: *The Musketeers of Pig Alley* (1912). Lillian Gish as "the girl." Famous for its documentary image of New York, *The Musketeers of Pig Alley* was one of Griffith's most popular Biograph films. It was shot on location on West Twelfth Street and at the Biograph studios on East Fourteenth Street, in September 1912. (*MOMA/FSA. Frame enlargement.*)

Silent film in the U.S. is primarily a matter of comedy. Charles Chaplin, Buster Keaton, Harold Lloyd, Harry Langdon, and Mack Sennett and Hal Roach as producers dominate the period. The personas invented by Chaplin, Keaton, and Lloyd are among the most memorable and meaningful creations in film history. Sennett had built his earliest films around a simple structural idea: there was no moral to his stories; they were simply collections of gags. The great comic actors of the late teens and twenties added a dimension of commentary that raised the slapstick film from the level of mechanical competence to the level of metaphor and meaning. Interestingly, Chaplin reveals nearly as much Victorian sentiment as Griffith but expresses it in contemporary terms.

All the silent comedians translated a basically political problem—how can the individual cope with industrial civilization and power politics?—into physical terms. Audiences responded, and still respond, with visceral understanding. If Lloyd was the most mechanical and abstract of the silent comedians, Chaplin was the most human and political, but all of them to varying degrees made the connection between mechanics and morality. Probably the quintessential example of the styles and concerns of silent comedy is Chaplin's masterpiece *Modern Times*

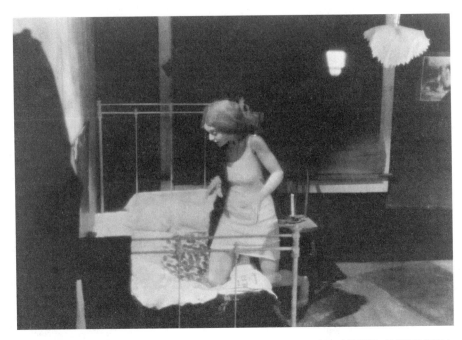

Figure 4-33. Zasu Pitts and a bed of gold coins: von Stroheim's *Greed* (1923). (*MOMA/FSA.*)

(although made in 1936 it has no dialogue, only music), a film about machines and men that remains relevant today.

Apart from the comic tradition, the most interesting esthetic force operating in American cinema in the twenties was the exploration of the possibilities of film realism. Erich von Stroheim, struggling against the developing commercial trend, managed to complete only a small number of films. More often than not, his conceptions were drastically reedited by studios, but he nevertheless had a profound influence on the course of American cinema. *Foolish Wives* (1921), *Greed* (1923), and *The Wedding March* (1928)—all savaged by studio heads—nevertheless survive as legends and object lessons on the vital power of realist techniques such as deep focus, complex mise-en-scène, and location shooting. Filmmakers are still exploring the potential of these devices. Stroheim was among the first to recognize that the observer of a film had to be given freedom to operate in concert with the creator.

Nor was Stroheim alone during the twenties in exploring the possibilities of the camera as communicator rather than manipulator. Working outside the Hollywood system, Robert Flaherty became the first notable documentarist with such films as *Nanook of the North* (1922) and *Moana* (1926). F. W. Murnau, who had had a successful career in Germany in the early twenties, arrived in America in

Figure 4-34. German Expressionist chiaroscuro: Robert Wiene's *Raskolnikow* (1923). The play of light and shade was a major code. (*MOMA/FSA.*)

1926. *Sunrise* (1927) and *Tabu* (1929, 1931, with Flaherty) remain fine examples of how theatricality can be fused with realism. To a lesser extent, King Vidor's *The Big Parade* (1925) and *The Crowd* (1928), as well as the later *Our Daily Bread* (1934), stand as examples of political realism.

While in America in the twenties film was rapidly industrializing, in Europe it was a business that was also seen as an art. Filmmakers in general worked more closely with established painters, musicians, and playwrights than the Americans did, not just because they found themselves in the same towns, but also because the new medium appealed to the avant-garde movement that was then establishing itself.

In London, the Film Society was founded in 1925 to promote the art of film. In France, Louis Delluc became the first important esthetic theorist of film, and such filmmakers as Abel Gance, Jean Epstein, Germaine Dulac, René Clair, Luis Buñuel and Salvador Dali, Man Ray, and Marcel Duchamp provided practical examples of film as art while the commercial cinema produced little of value. In Germany, UFA set about consciously raising the esthetic standards of German film. The result was one of the major efflorescences of talent in cinema history: German Expressionism.

Figure 4-35. Asta Neilsen was Europe's first star—like Mary Pickford, a savvy businesswoman as well as a celebrity. Here she is seen with Conrad Veidt in *Der Reigen (Richard Oswald, 1920). (Courtesy Cinegraph Hamburg.)*

Writer Carl Mayer, designer/painters Hermann Warm, Walter Röhrig, and Walter Reimann played significant roles in the movement, as did directors Robert Wiene (*The Cabinet of Dr. Caligari,* 1919), Fritz Lang (*Dr. Mabuse,* 1922; *Metropolis,* 1927), Murnau (*Nosferatu,* 1922; *The Last Laugh,* 1924), and Paul Leni (*Waxworks,* 1924, and in Hollywood *The Cat and The Canary,* 1927). Meanwhile, G. W. Pabst (*The Joyless Street,* 1925) explored realist alternatives. As fascinating as this period of film history is, only Lang and Murnau proved to be major artists, and only Lang survived to produce any considerable body of work.

While German Expressionism had a far greater effect worldwide, interesting, productive traditions were developing in Sweden and Denmark as well during the teens and early twenties. Swedish directors Mauritz Stiller and Victor Sjöström shared backgrounds in the theater. From its earliest days through the career of Ingmar Bergman, Swedish film has been closely associated with the the-atrical world. Stiller at first specialized in witty comedies (*Love and Journalism,* 1916; *Thomas Graal's Best Film,* 1917) before moving on to more literary projects (*Gösta Berling's Saga,* 1924) and finally emigrating to Hollywood with his star,

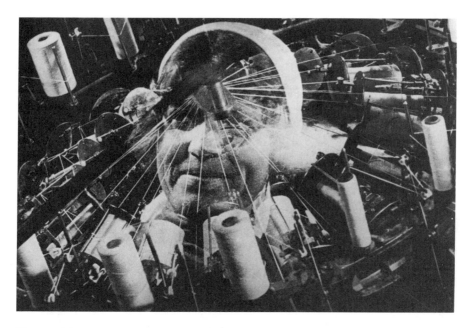

Figure 4-36. Dziga Vertov's *Man with a Movie Camera* (1929): idiosyncratic kino-pravda. (*MOMA/FSA. Frame enlargement.*)

Greta Garbo. Sjöström, an actor, is best known for his poetic social commentary (*The Outlaw and His Wife*, 1917; *Körkalen*, 1921).

Danish director Carl Theodor Dreyer's career spanned more than fifty years, although he directed relatively few films. His *Passion de Jeanne d'Arc* (1928) has become one of the standard masterpieces of world film, as have *Vampyr* (1932) and *Gertrud* (1964). Dreyer's cinema is notable for its transcendental simplicity and fascination with cruelty, humiliation, and suffering.

The twenties were also the great age of Soviet cinema. Lev Kuleshov and Vsevolod Meyerhold had established separate but parallel theories that were taken up and greatly elaborated on by Sergei Eisenstein (*Strike*, 1924; *Potemkin*, 1925; *October*, 1927), V. I. Pudovkin (*Mother*, 1926; *The End of St. Petersburg*, 1927), and Alexander Dovzhenko (*Arsenal*, 1929; *Earth*, 1930). These films remain major landmarks in the history of cinema, especially *Potemkin*, probably the clearest example of Eisenstein's influential theories of montage.

Eisenstein saw film as a dialectical process, and his technique in *Potemkin* demonstrates the effectiveness of that approach. Using "types" rather than fully developed characters, he created a forceful, incessant logic for this story of the 1905 mutiny of the crew of Battleship Potemkin. The Odessa Steps sequence (see Figures 5-1 to 5-4) is one of the most famous examples of his celebrated montage

Figure 4-37. Action and composition in Jean Renoir's *The Rules of the Game* (1939). (*l'Avant-Scène. Frame enlargement.*)

technique, building both drama and significance purely through the juxtaposition of shots.

At the same time, Dziga Vertov was developing his theory of "film-truth" in such films as *Kino-Pravda* (1922–25), *Kino-Eye* (1924), and *Man with a Movie Camera* (1929). As the Germans had investigated the expressiveness of artificial setting and mise-en-scène, so the Soviet revolutionary filmmakers explored the powerful expressive intelligence of montage. Their theories, among the most important in cinema, will be discussed in the following chapter.

Hollywood: Genre Versus Auteur

By the early thirties, American cinema had achieved a position of dominance on world screens. Between 1932 and 1946, the history of film is, with two exceptions, the history of Hollywood. The exceptions are the group of directors in France sometimes linked together under the rubric "Poetic Realism," and the beginnings of the British documentary tradition with John Grierson and his group in England. Grierson, who made only one film himself, acted as producer, organizer, and herald for the British documentary tradition in the thirties, a movement whose effect on the future development of British cinema was more important than the actual films that issued from it. Although not associated with Grierson, Humphrey Jennings produced possibly the most enduring examples of this genre during the war: *Listen to Britain* (1942), *Fires Were Started* (1943), and *A*

Figure 4-38. In the early thirties Howard Hawks made the classic gangster film *Scarface* for producer Howard Hughes before moving on to other genres. Ann Dvorak and George Raft starred.

Diary for Timothy (1945) are all documentary personal statements from a former poet and painter.

As Alfred Hitchcock dominated British fiction film in the 1930s, so Jean Renoir towered over the French film scene of that decade. Less appreciated then than now (when he is regarded as one of the acknowledged masters of world cinema), Renoir created a new fusion of modes that combined the humanism of such silent artists as Chaplin with realist technique in an extraordinary series of films: *Boudu Saved from Drowning* (1932), *Toni* (1934), *The Crime of M. Lange* (1935), *Grand Illusion* (1937), and *The Rules of the Game* (1939). The influence of his humane, socially sensitive, drolly comic style is still being felt.

At the same time in France, a number of other strong and very personal styles were developing: Marcel Pagnol directed a series of popular, lyrical, and diffident studies of French provincialism. René Clair, whose reputation has suffered with the years, directed several amusing, if lightweight, films. Marcel Carné was responsible for a number of highly theatrical witty dramas, culminating in *Children of Paradise* (1944). Jacques Prévert was his frequent collaborator. Most memorable, perhaps, are the two major films made by Jean Vigo before he died at the

Figure 4-39. Lauren Bacall, Humphrey Bogart: *The Big Sleep* (Howard Hawks, 1945): a more balanced relationship between women and men than is common today. (*MOMA/FSA.*)

age of twenty-nine: *Zero for Conduct* (1933) and *L'Atalante* (1934) are fresh and direct products of Vigo's clear-eyed, virtuoso cinema.

There were few such clearly identifiable personal signatures in Hollywood at the time. Alfred Hitchcock, who had matured in England, became the most obvious of the Hollywood auteurs after his arrival in 1940. He dominated the genre of the thriller for half a century.

He should have; he invented it. In a number of films made during his first years in America, Hitchcock further refined the basic sense of political paranoia with which he had experimented in England in the 1930s. *Foreign Correspondent* (1940) was a film of subtle reversals and correspondences that pointed toward the future. *Saboteur* (1942) was the first of his films to spread the American landscape before us in a coast-to-coast chase. In it he developed some interesting ideas about the relationship between the individual and the state in wartime. *Shadow of a Doubt* (1943), from a script by the playwright Thornton Wilder, contrasted small-town life with the criminal personality and is generally regarded as one of the major films of the Hitchcock canon. *Spellbound* (1945) seems simplistic today but was one of the earliest introductions of Freudian concepts in American film. *Notorious* (1946) paired Cary Grant and Ingrid Bergman in an intensely personal exploration of the effects on a relationship of the paranoia engendered by war.

Figure 4-40. Joel McCrea as Sullivan the successful director, sets out with Veronica Lake to suffer in Preston Sturges's cutting satire on Hollywood, *Sullivan's Travels.*

Also during this period: Josef von Sternberg left his mark in a series of visually elaborate romances (*The Blue Angel, Morocco,* 1930; *Shanghai Express,* 1932; *The Scarlet Empress,* 1934). Busby Berkeley invented a peculiarly cinematic form of musical (*Gold Diggers of 1935,* 1935; *The Gang's All Here,* 1943). John Ford made the form of the Western sing with new resonance (*Stagecoach,* 1939; *My Darling Clementine,* 1946) and extended many of the metaphors of that essentially American genre in other directions in the scores of other films he directed.

Howard Hawks left his imprint on a wide variety of genres, his films always impressive for their wit, good nature, and richness of texture. Among them were so-called Screwball Comedies (*Twentieth Century,* 1934; *Bringing Up Baby,* 1939; *His Girl Friday,* 1939), dramas (*To Have and Have Not,* 1944), and Westerns (*Red River,* 1948; *Rio Bravo,* 1959). Hawks's *The Big Sleep* (1946) is a classic Film Noir detective story, based on Raymond Chandler's novel and starring Humphrey Bogart and Lauren Bacall. It is also a near-perfect model of all that is best in the Hollywood film. Chandler, Hawks, Bogart, and screenwriters William Faulkner, Leigh Brackett, and Jules Furthman combined talents to produce a tightly woven fabric of their various concerns and styles. It is significant that the film, despite being the product of a number of artistic personalities, nevertheless impresses with its unity. As entertainment it has few equals in the Hollywood canon. The electric Bogart-Bacall relationship merges with Hawks's witty mise-en-scène; Chandler's laconic, poetic existentialism; and the tough, rich, humorous dialogue and elegantly complicated plot provided by the screenwriters (under Hawks's direction). The result is richly resonant entertainment.

But *The Big Sleep*, like all of Hollywood's best films, is more as well, almost unconsciously. Hawks's gallery of women is unmatched for the depth of characterization and, more important, the strength and the intelligence they exhibit. (And this from a director known best for his treatment of male friendships!) The balanced tension between the men and the women in the film gives it a special psychological relevance. At the same time, *The Big Sleep* is representative of the Hollywood style in a less admirable way: most of the directly political material of Chandler's novel has been cut out so that the film is, in this respect, a pale shadow of its original source. It was nearly thirty years before *Chinatown* (1974), written by Robert Towne and directed by Roman Polanski, explored on the screen the same subjects of decay and corruption that Raymond Chandler discussed in nearly all his novels, including *The Big Sleep*, but which were only hinted at in the many film versions of his stories made in the 1940s.

Hitchcock, Ford, Hawks, von Sternberg, and a few others may have been able to maintain a recognizable personal signature from film to film during the great age of Hollywood. For the most part, however, Hollywood cinema was the product of numerous craftspeople: directors, actors, cinematographers, writers, designers, producers. Directors such as William Wellman, Lewis Milestone, Leo McCarey, and John Huston display personal styles, no doubt, and are proper studies of auteurist critics, yet the structure of the Hollywood system was such that even powerful directorial personalities were more often than not submerged in a sea of studio styles, actors' styles, producers' requirements, and writers' idiosyncrasies.

One of the most interesting exceptions to this rule was Preston Sturges. A playwright in the twenties, he, like so many of his colleagues, migrated from New York to Hollywood with the advent of sound. He enjoyed a successful career as screenwriter during the 1930s. *Easy Living* (1937, directed by Mitchel Leisen) is probably the best of his scripts from this period. He began directing in 1940, and for almost a decade was able to maintain a remarkable measure of control over his films, writing all his own scripts and working regularly with the same group of actors. His eccentric, pointed satire is best represented by *The Lady Eve* (1941), *Sullivan's Travels* (1942), and *The Miracle of Morgan's Creek* (1944).

Another writer-director with a mordant wit, Billy Wilder (born in Vienna in 1906) was the most successful of the émigrés from Europe (as well as the most prolific). He arrived in Hollywood in 1934, fleeing Nazism in Europe. His writing

Figure 4-41. GENRES: THE MUSICAL. At Warner Brothers in the thirties, Busby Berkeley made the elaborately choreographed geometric dance routine famous, but it was not solely his invention. Here a scene from the first Fred Astaire–Ginger Rogers musical, RKO's *Flying Down to Rio* (1933, directed by Thornton Freeland). It combines the vivid star work of the Astaire–Rogers team with the pas de milles made famous in Berkeley's work. The choreographer was Dave Gould. (*MOMA/FSA*.)

partnerships with Charles Brackett (1938–1950) and later I. A. L. Diamond helped him to become the most American of immigrant directors, with a long string of critical and commercial hits. Although he is famed for his cynicism, his work reveals a deeper, brighter wit in the service of real social wisdom. From the films noirs of the forties (*Double Indemnity*, 1944; *The Lost Weekend*, 1945; *Sunset Boulevard*, 1950) through the romances and comedies of the fifties (*Sabrina*, 1954; *The Seven-Year Itch*, 1955; *Some Like It Hot*, 1959) and culminating in the sixties with *The Apartment* (1960) and *The Fortune Cookie* (1966), Wilder was responsible for an unrivaled number of American cultural touchstones.

It was this dialectic between auteur and genre that drove the classic Hollywood cinema: the clash between an artist's sensibility and the defined mythic structures of the popular story types. Probably the most important of these genres was the Western, since it embodied so many of the myths—the frontier, individualism, the land, and law and order versus anarchy—upon which the national psyche of the United States still depends. Musicals were probably second in popularity, whether the geometric exercises of Berkeley's Warner Brothers series or the sophisticated, light comedies of Fred Astaire at RKO.

Comedy remained strong in the thirties, as the Broadway writers of the twenties were imported en masse to provide dialogue for sound films. Again, it was the performers who led the way, as it had been in the silent era. The Marx Brothers, Mae West, and W. C. Fields (who had begun in silents) produced some of the most intriguing comic personas, the Marxes setting a mode of illogic that was to last through the nineties. The quick patter and insouciance of Broadway in the twenties gave rise to the Screwball Comedy, the genre that probably best identifies the 1930s on American screens. Gangster films, Horror films, Historical Romances, and embryonic Thrillers were also important genres of the time.

In the forties, the mood changed. War films, of course, were added to the genre catalogue. Beginning in the mid-forties, that peculiar blend of urban cynicism, downbeat subject matter, and dark shadows known as "Film Noir" made its appearance, as post-war cynicism added dark and foreboding colors to the American palette.

Throughout the classic Hollywood period, the genres refined themselves; by the end they were nearly self-parodies. Yet they proved engrossing in two respects: on the one hand, by their nature, genres were mythic. To experience a Horror film, a Gangster film, or a Screwball Comedy was cathartic. The elements were well known: there was a litany to each popular genre. Part of their pleasure lay in seeing how those basic elements would be treated this time around. On the other hand, individual examples of a genre were also often specific statements. For the more knowledgeable observer, there was an equal interest in the multiple clash of styles in the film—styles of the studio, the director, the star, the producer, occasionally even the writer or designer or cinematographer. Genres offered myriad combinations of a finite number of elements.

In the middle of this often confusing forest of genres, styles, auteurs, and stars stands the monument of Orson Welles's *Citizen Kane* (1941), possibly the most important American movie ever made. (It was voted as such by the American Film Institute's panel of critics in 1998.) Welles's classic belongs to no specific genre, but it operates like genre films by tapping mythic resonances and shaping them to dramatic ends. The saga of Charles Foster Kane, media baron and politician, public figure and private man, is an emblem of American life in the first half of this century. Moreover, Welles—with the aplomb of a master—shapes his narrative in exuberant cinematic terms. It was as if this stranger to Hollywood, child of New York theater and radio, had viewed objectively all the various strands of film technique of thirties Hollywood and woven them all together. His notorious ego, which he exerted as cowriter, producer, director, and star, also makes Welles's film a prime example of auteurship.

Figure 4-42. Tim Holt, Ann Baxter, Joseph Cotten, Dolores Costello, and Agnes Moorehead with "The Original Morgan Invincible" in Welles's *The Magnificent Ambersons* (1942). A less startling film than *Citizen Kane* (1941), *Ambersons* was no less perceptive about the American condition and—in its commentary on the effect of the automobile on American society— strangely prophetic. In his first two films, Welles investigated the two major factors—the media and the automobile—that defined twentieth-century American life. (*MOMA/FSA*.)

His second film, *The Magnificent Ambersons* (1942), was never released in the version he had prepared, and Welles never again matched his success with *Citizen Kane*. This union of the strong auteur and strong genre elements was a singular phenomenon, as well as the greatest tour de force in film history.

Neorealism and After: Hollywood Versus the World

Television was not the only challenger the Hollywood studios faced during the late forties and fifties. Cinemas in other countries were maturing and reorganizing after the paralysis of fascism and the war. The 16 mm equipment perfected for use during the war permitted an alternate system of distribution that grew slowly but steadily, coming of age in the sixties. Film festivals and film societies bloomed, providing effective promotional tools for filmmakers who did not have the resources of the Hollywood business combines behind them. Recognizing film as an export commodity, France, for example, built the Cannes festival into the major international marketplace and established the Unifrance promotion organization.

This more fluid economic environment allowed major artists, even in small countries, to find an international market. If Hollywood had to battle television economically to survive the fifties, it had to contend esthetically with a worldwide flowering of new talent during the late forties, fifties, and sixties. The old genres remained, a few new ones were added; the old Hollywood hands grew older. But in Europe and Asia a new type of cinema was coming to the fore: personal, inventive, nongeneric, and speaking directly to the contemporary experience.

The first group of these films appeared in Italy just at the end of the war, the product of the Neorealist movement. Cesare Zavattini, a critic and writer, had established the ground rules for Neorealism and was responsible for the scripts of several important films (*Shoeshine*, 1946; *Bicycle Thief*, 1948; *Umberto D*, 1952). Vittorio De Sica, who had been a leading romantic star of the thirties, directed these three scripts (and several others by Zavattini), thereby making an important contribution to Neorealism, before falling back into more commercial, less interesting work in the mid-fifties. Luchino Visconti directed one of the earliest Neorealist films (*Ossessione*, 1942), a classic during the height of the movement (*La Terra Trema*, 1948), as well as one of the latest examples of the style (*Rocco and His Brothers*, 1960), although most of his work was closer in style to his first love, opera, than to Neorealism.

Most important was the work of Roberto Rossellini (*Rome, Open City*, 1945; *Paisan*, 1946; *Germany—Year Zero*, 1947; *Stromboli*, 1949), for he was the only one of the three major directors to build on the experience of Neorealism. His work throughout the fifties and in television, to which he turned in 1960 (*The Rise to Power of Louis XIV*, 1966; *Acts of the Apostles*, 1968; *Socrates*, 1970), established the foundation for materialist cinema, the direct descendant of Neorealism.

Rome, Open City remains one of the major landmarks of film history. Secretly planned during the German occupation of Rome, the film was shot soon after the Allies took the city. The conditions under which it was shot add much to its sense of urgent realism. The story of a resistance leader and a priest who are arrested and killed by the Gestapo, *Rome, Open City* is marked by an urgency and intensity that are directly related to the time and place in which it was filmed. Rossellini shot with whatever filmstock he could find, often leftover portions of reels. Working under such conditions there was no possibility that the film could be given a professional gloss, even if Rossellini had wanted to do so. Professional actors Anna Magnani and Aldo Fabrizi worked with a cast that was otherwise entirely nonprofessional. The result was an authenticity of performance that is rivaled only in true documentaries. The style of the film was highly influential. Ever since, the elements of realist film technique have been an integral part of world film esthetics.

The Neorealists were working for a cinema intimately connected with the experience of living: nonprofessional actors, rough technique, political point,

Figure 4-43. Aldo Fabrizi as Don Pietro in Rossellini's monumental Neorealist document *Rome, Open City* (1945). (*MOMA/FSA. Frame enlargement.*)

ideas rather than entertainment—all these elements went directly counter to the Hollywood esthetic of smooth, seamless professionalism. While Neorealism as a movement lasted only a few years, the effects of its esthetics are still being felt. In fact, Zavattini, Rossellini, De Sica, and Visconti defined a set of ground rules that would operate for the next fifty years. Esthetically, Hollywood never quite recovered.

Meanwhile, back at the Southern California ranches, business proceeded much as usual. There was room in Hollywood neither for the political commentary of Neorealism nor for the personal, non-genrestyle that was developing throughout Europe. While there were occasional surprises, such as Frank Capra's *It's a Wonderful Life* (1947), which was the most interesting of his series of populist sentimental dramas and a crisp, direct lesson in the benefits of cooperative social and economic organizations, the political mood of Hollywood, as we noted earlier, was reactionary.

The most intriguing esthetic result of this dark, paranoiac mood was the cycle of Films Noirs of the late forties and early fifties. A vaguely defined genre (as the name announces, it was first defined by the French), Film Noir is one of the more complex and intelligent Hollywood styles. Part detective story, part gangster, part urban melodrama, Film Noir was identified most easily by its dark and pessimistic undercurrents. While many examples of the genre had Cold-War overtones, this was not necessarily a condition: if the genre had a literary source it was in the detective novels of Dashiell Hammett and Raymond Chandler, both of whom evinced sympathies with the Left.

One of the earlier examples of Film Noir was Hawks's *The Big Sleep* (1946), from Raymond Chandler's novel. Combine the weary cynicism of Chandler's hero Philip Marlowe with the Freudian aspects of another memorable Film Noir, Raoul Walsh's *White Heat* (1949), and you have a good model for the genre. Combine the titles for those two films and you have, interestingly, *The Big Heat* (1953), one of Fritz Lang's most deeply fatalistic movies and a central film of the genre.

Jacques Tourneur's *Out of the Past* (1947) is one of the most neglected and most beautiful Films Noirs, Nicholas Ray's *They Live by Night* (1948) one of the best remembered. Jules Dassin's *The Naked City* (1948) and John Huston's *The Asphalt Jungle* (1950) make eloquent use of the urban settings that were such an important element, as does Sam Fuller's *Pickup on South Street* (1953), a film that also shows how Cold-War psychology could be adapted to the form of the Film Noir. Carol Reed's *The Third Man* (1950) established the genre in a European postwar context and connected it to the American tradition via its stars, Orson Welles and Joseph Cotten. Welles's *Mr. Arkadin* (1955) gives us the essence of the mood of the genre. Robert Rossen's short career included two outstanding Films Noirs: *Body and Soul* (1947) with John Garfield, and, later, *The Hustler* (1961) with Paul Newman.

The definition of Film Noir can be stretched to include most of the films of the "tough guy" directors who came to the fore in the 1950s: Samuel Fuller (*House of Bamboo,* 1955; *China Gate,* 1957; *Shock Corridor,* 1963), Robert Aldrich (*Kiss Me Deadly, The Big Knife,* both 1955), Phil Karlson (*Kansas City Confidential,* 1952; *The Phenix City Story,* 1955; and a later example: *Walking Tall,* 1974), and Don Siegel (*Riot in Cell Block 11,* 1954; *Crime in the Streets,* 1956). Visually, Siegel took the genre to its extremity in *Escape from Alcatraz* (1979), a film made with so little light that it must have set a record for the dark genre. Robert Benton's *The Late Show* (1977) gave us Art Carney's version of the gumshoe antihero thirty years on. Benton returned to the genre twenty years later with the elegant, well-aged *Twilight* (1998).

The urban, downbeat, detective genre had been a staple of American television from Jack Webb's *Dragnet* of the early fifties to *Kojak* and *Columbo* in the seventies. While the eighties and nineties saw a regular progression of theatrical films that were direct descendants of the old genre, it was television writer-producers who brought it new life. In the eighties, Michael Mann colorized Film Noir in the sty-

Figure 4-44. John Ford's two favorite Western stars: John Wayne and Monument Valley, as they appeared in one of Ford's most intriguing Westerns, *The Searchers* (1956). A "revisionist" Western, *The Searchers* critically examined elements of the Western myth that had hitherto been taken for granted as truths. Wayne's Ethan Edwards is a hero in the contemporary mold: lonely and obsessive as well as heroic, neurotically compulsive as well as faithful. The underlying text of racism was brought to the surface in *The Searchers*. Westerns would never be the same afterwards. (*MOMA/FSA*.)

listically influential series *Miami Vice,* while Steven Bochco honored the long tradition at the same time that he satirized it in the inventive *Hill Street Blues*. In the nineties, Dick Wolf formalized and intellectualized it with his analytical homages *Law and Order* and *Crime and Punishment*, while Bochco took it to new television extremes with *NYPD Blue*. Clearly, Film Noir has been a fertile genre for filmmakers throughout the last half of the twentieth century.

Two other popular genres of the fifties, the Western and the Science Fiction film, also exhibited the downbeat mood of Film Noir, each in its own way. The Western began to treat more serious and more pessimistic themes; the Science Fiction film developed a number of objective correlatives for the cultural paranoia of the decade.

Delmer Daves, one of the more underrated of Hollywood craftsmen, directed *Broken Arrow* in 1950, the first Western since silent days to allow Indians some measure of self-respect. He was also responsible for *3:10 to Yuma* (1957). John

Figure 4-45. Yasujiro Ozu's *Tokyo Story* (1953). With character-istic Japanese clarity, sensitivity, and respect, Ozu's films most often deal with family relation-ships between genera-tions. The old couple of *Tokyo Story* find on a visit to their children in the capital that the younger generation, busy with their own endeavors, no longer has much time for their parents. (*New Yorker Films.*)

Sturges made a number of classic Westerns, including *Gunfight at the O.K. Corral* (1957), *Last Train from Gun Hill* (1958), and *The Magnificent Seven* (1960). Anthony Mann developed a cult reputation with such films as *Winchester 73* (1950), *The Far Country* (1954), and *The Man From Laramie* (1955). Two of the first "adult" Westerns were Fred Zinnemann's *High Noon* (1952) and George Stevens's *Shane* (1953). John Ford weighed in with *The Searchers* (1956), possibly his best Western, and *Two Rode Together* (1961). Henry King directed *The Gunfighter* (1950), Henry Hathaway *From Hell to Texas* (1958). Arthur Penn's first film was *The Left-Handed Gun* (1958).

The sixties saw such significant Westerns as Marlon Brando's *One-Eyed Jacks* (1961), John Huston's *The Misfits* (1961), David Miller's *Lonely Are the Brave* (1962), and a number of films by Sam Peckinpah, notably *Ride the High Country* (1962) and *The Wild Bunch* (1969). In Italy, meanwhile, the "Spaghetti Western" had come of age. Sergio Leone reworked the elements of the genre in films like *A Fistful of Dollars* (1964) and *The Good, The Bad, and The Ugly* (1967), starring an American, Clint Eastwood.

In the seventies, the Western fell into decline as an increasingly urbanized America lost its zest for the wide-open spaces. We can mark the beginning of this eclipse with Robert Altman's iconoclastic and atmospheric *McCabe and Mrs. Miller* (1971). The long Western drought, broken only by Terrence Malick's remarkable *Days of Heaven* (1978), came to an end in the early 1990s with two surprising Oscar winners, Kevin Costner's *Dances with Wolves* (1990), a poor movie but a great project, and Clint Eastwood's *Unforgiven* (1992). These revisionist homages serve as elegies to the genre.

Figure 4-46. Victor Sjöström comes to terms with his past in Bergman's *Wild Strawberries* (1958). Sjöström, one of the fathers of Swedish film, capped his career with this film. It was not by accident that Bergman chose a fellow director to play the central role of Professor Isak Borg, for *Wild Strawberries* also marked an important stage in Bergman's own struggle with his past.

Science Fiction films of the fifties were telling psychoanalytic documents: paranoid fantasies of moving blobs, invading pods, reified ids, and metamorphoses. Among the most important were: *The Thing* (1951, Christian Nyby), *The Day the Earth Stood Still* (1951, Robert Wise), *Invasion of the Body Snatchers* (1956, Don Siegel), *Forbidden Planet* (1956, Fred Wilcox), *The Incredible Shrinking Man* (1957, Jack Arnold), *The Fly* (1958, Kurt Neumann), and *The Time Machine* (1960, George Pal). The genre was reborn in 1968 with Stanley Kubrick's magnificent *2001: A Space Odyssey*, arguably the most influential film of the past forty years, since it gave rise to the strongest genre of the 1970s and 1980s. From *Star Wars* to *Star Trek*, from *E.T.* to *Jurassic Park*, the Science Fiction genre has strangely reigned supreme since the late 1970s.

The Musical, like the Western, benefited greatly from the technologies of color and widescreen and enjoyed a renaissance during the fifties under the sponsorship of producer Arthur Freed at MGM. Vincente Minnelli directed *An American in Paris* (1951) and *Gigi* (1958). Stanley Donen worked with Gene Kelly in *On the Town* (1949) and *Singin' in the Rain* (1952) and with Fred Astaire in *Royal Wedding*

Figure 4-47. Like Bergman's films of the period, Federico Fellini's also reflect a basically introspective nature. *8 1/2* (1962) examines the existential dilemma of a film director, Guido (Marcello Mastroianni), who is not unlike Fellini. The film begins at a spa where the diaphanous, quasi-mythical Claudia Cardinale offers Guido the purifying waters. It is an image of innocence that constantly recurs in Fellini's films....(*l'Avant-Scène. Frame enlargement.*)

(1951) and *Funny Face* (1957, produced by Roger Edens for Paramount). Astaire also starred in Rouben Mamoulian's *Silk Stockings* (1957, produced by Freed). Mamoulian had been responsible for one of the very first significant Hollywood Musicals, *Applause* (1929). In just a few films he left an indelible mark on the genre. His films were characterized by a rare wit and a sophisticated sense of pace.

While the Broadway Musical has continued to thrive throughout the past thirty years, the film Musical has almost entirely disappeared. Martin Scorsese's *New York, New York* (1977) and Francis Coppola's *The Cotton Club* (1984) stand as ambitious exceptions. Although Stephen Sondheim continued through the seventies and eighties to produce the best American musical theater this side of Gershwin, few of his plays have been translated to the screen, and none successfully since his first (*A Funny Thing Happened on the Way to the Forum*, 1966). Although during the past thirty years the Broadway theater has been invigorated by the advent and continued success of the Black Musical (from *Ain't Supposed to Die a Natural Death* to *Jelly's Last Jam*), this inviting new strain of the art has been ignored by Hollywood. Although more people have seen *Les Misérables* (or *Cats*) in theaters than go to most movies, the ersatz English musicals haven't made money on the screen. Why? Well, for one thing, Musicals don't lend themselves to sequels.

Despite the continued dominance of genres, a few American directors of the late forties and fifties managed to convey a strong sense of personal style in their films. Among these auteurs were Elia Kazan (*Gentleman's Agreement*, 1947; *Viva*

Figure 4-48. ... *La Dolce Vita* (1959) had ended with this image of unreachable innocence. At the seashore, the journalist Marcello (Mastroianni, again) found it impossible to communicate with this young woman. (*l'Avant-Scène. Frame enlargement.*)

Zapata!, 1952; *On the Waterfront*, 1954; *East of Eden*, 1955), Otto Preminger (*Laura*, 1944; *The Man with the Golden Arm*, 1955; *Anatomy of a Murder*, 1959), Nicholas Ray (*Johnny Guitar*, 1954; *Rebel Without a Cause*, 1955; *Bigger Than Life*, 1956) and Douglas Sirk (*All That Heaven Allows*, 1955; *Written on the Wind*, 1956). Both Ray and Sirk were taken up as heroes by the generation of younger European film-makers in the next two decades: Ray by the French in the sixties for his existential bent, Sirk by the Germans in the seventies for his rabid sentimentalism.

Despite these interesting currents and eddies in the flow of Hollywood product, American film experienced a slow but steady decline throughout the fifties. Real innovations in cinema were occurring elsewhere as the art split into popular and elite factions, the latter served by the growing number of "art" houses.

World audiences were discovering the Asian cinema for the first time. Japanese cinema had a long tradition to draw on, including one of the more interesting styles of silent film in which "reciters" were used to describe and explain the action—a device borrowed from Kabuki theater. Filmmakers outside Japan were unaware of these accomplishments until the success of Akira Kurosawa's *Rashomon* at the Venice Film Festival of 1951. Although it was Kurosawa's Samurai films that gained the most attention, he made many films in modern settings as well. Among his most important films are *Ikiru* (1952), *Seven Samurai* (1954), *Throne of Blood* (a version of *Macbeth*, 1957), and *Yojimbo* (1961).

Kurosawa's success led to the export of other Japanese films in the 1950s. Kenji Mizoguchi, whose career dated from 1922, directed a number of films in the fifties that became classics of the world repertory: *The Life of Oharu* (1952),

Ugetsu Monogatari (1953), *Sansho the Bailiff* (1954), *Chikimatsu Monogatari* (1954), and *Princess Yang Kwei Fei* (1955) among them.

The last of the Japanese triumvirate to be "discovered" in the West was Yasujiro Ozu, possibly the most interesting of the group. An unusual stylist, Ozu contemplated locales and seasons with a very un-Western sensitivity and tranquility, whereas the films of Kurosawa are much more easily understood by Westerners. Among Ozu's most important films are the "season" series: *Late Spring* (1949), *Early Summer* (1951), *Early Spring* (1956), *Late Autumn* (1960), *Early Autumn* (1961), and *An Autumn Afternoon* (1962), as well as *Tokyo Story* (1953), his most popular film in the West.

Like Japan, India has long had a prolific film industry. The staple of Indian cinema is the lengthy, highly stylized Musical, which still remains to be introduced to the world market. In the late fifties, however, one filmmaker—Satyajit Ray—began producing films with more universal appeal. The Apu trilogy (*Pather Panchali*, 1955; *Aparajito*, 1957; *The World of Apu*, 1959) was immediately appreciated in the West, and Ray became a favorite of film festivals and art houses with such films as *The Music Room* (1958), *Kanchenjunga* (1962), *Days and Nights in the Forest* (1970), and *Distant Thunder* (1973).

During the 1950s England gave world screens the series of priceless Alec Guinness comedies (*The Man in the White Suit, The Lavender Hill Mob*, both 1951; *The Horse's Mouth*, 1959), which were followed by the Peter Sellers comedies of the sixties (*I'm All Right Jack*, 1959; *Only Two Can Play*, 1961; *Heavens Above!*, 1963) and the Music-Hall low-comedy series of *Doctor...* and *Carry On ...* farces. German cinema didn't recover from the destruction of the war and Nazism until 1970.

In the fifties, French screens were dominated by what the young critic François Truffaut termed the "cinéma du papa," an overly literary and—Truffaut thought—stultifying style, but the New Wave was about to break and at least three independent, contrasting auteurs—Jean Cocteau, the poet; Jacques Tati, the comedian; and Robert Bresson, the ascetic esthete—were producing interesting work. Cocteau completed *Orpheus* in 1950 and *The Testament of Orpheus* a decade later. Tati directed and starred in *Mr. Hulot's Holiday* (1953) and *Mon Oncle* (1958). Bresson, a meticulous craftsman, finished *Diary of a Country Priest* (1950), *A Man Escaped* (1953), and *Pickpocket* (1959).

At about the same time Max Ophüls, whose career had begun in Germany in the early thirties and wound its way through France and Italy to Hollywood in the fifties, returned to France to produce three films that were highly influential: *La Ronde* (1950), *The Earrings of Madame de...* (1953), and *Lola Montès* (1955). Ophüls is best known for these ironic love stories and for his long, fluid, exhilarating tracking shots, which were the hallmark of his style. (See Figure 3-64.)

The movement of film esthetics toward personal art and away from collectively produced genres reached a climax in the middle fifties with the coming of

Figure 4-49. Fellini was obsessed with this imagery (and the emotions it represents) throughout the 1950s. In *La Strada* (1954) and *The Nights of Cabiria* (1957), he had built whole films around it as it was personified by his wife, Giulietta Masina, here shown as Gelsomina in *La Strada*. (See also Figure 3-57.) (*l'Avant-Scène. Frame enlargement.*)

age of two profoundly idiosyncratic filmmakers: Ingmar Bergman and Federico Fellini. These two, together with Alfred Hitchcock, whose work in the fifties represents the summit of his career, dominated film esthetics in the late fifties and prepared the way for the cinéma d'auteur, which became the rule rather than the exception in the sixties. Interestingly, all three deal in one way or another with the anxiety that also motivated the popular genres of the period and that the poet W. H. Auden had declared the characteristic emotion of the age.

For Bergman, angst was expressed in psychoanalytic and religious terms; for Hitchcock, anxiety was a matter of stylized paranoia of everyday life; for Fellini, angoscia was a social problem as much as it was personal.

Bergman began making films in the mid-forties, but it wasn't until *Smiles of a Summer Night* (1955), *The Seventh Seal* (1957), *Wild Strawberries* (1958), and *The Virgin Spring* (1959) that he gained world renown. *The Seventh Seal* was especially effective in this respect. Its symbolism was immediately apprehensible to people trained in literary culture who were just beginning to discover the "art" of film, and it quickly became a staple of high school and college literature courses. Based on Bergman's own play, *The Seventh Seal* starred Max von Sydow, who was to become the main actor in Bergman's extraordinary repertory company of the 1960s. Antonius Blok, a medieval knight returning from the Crusades, undergoes a series of encounters with death. Sweden is ravaged by the plague. Each of the real encounters—with a group of strolling players, a witch-burning, flagellating peasants—is paralleled by a symbolic encounter with the black-clad figure of death, with whom Blok is engaged in a running chess game, the stakes of which are life itself.

Images of stark blacks and whites effectively convey the medieval mood of the film, which is further enhanced by Bergman's visual and dramatic references to medieval painting and literature. Unlike Hollywood "movies," *The Seventh Seal* clearly was aware of elite artistic culture and thus was readily appreciated by intellectual audiences. Bergman's best work lay ahead in the sixties, after the religious symbolism had been exorcised and he was able to concentrate on more personal, less symbolic situations. *Wild Strawberries,* one of his best films, points in this direction.

Federico Fellini had first entered the film world during the Neorealist period of the late forties. He first directed a film in 1950. *La Strada* (1954) had nearly as profound an effect on world screens as *The Seventh Seal* had a few years later. *Nights of Cabiria* (1956) was also widely hailed, while *La Dolce Vita* (1959) marked the opening of a new period in cinema history. A sprawling, widescreen, three-hour fresco of life among the upper classes in the Rome of the late 1950s, *La Dolce Vita* contrasts ironically with *Rome, Open City.* Fellini's film takes the form of the Renaissance peripatetic epic poem, stringing a series of tableaux and adventures together, uniting them by the figure of Marcello (Marcello Mastroianni), a gossip columnist. The "sweet life" is empty and meaningless, but the film about it is a rich and ironic tapestry of manners and morals. Fellini sharply prefigured the mood of the "swinging sixties," and the film was very successful outside of Italy, even in the U.S.

A generation older than Bergman and Fellini, Alfred Hitchcock remains the one director to have made exceptionally personal films working entirely within the genre factory system. He had, in a sense, not one but four careers (in silent film, in sound film in Britain, in Hollywood in black and white in the forties, and since 1952 in color), any one of which would guarantee his position in the history of cinema. Arguably, his most representative films (and many of his best) date from the 1950s, the period in which he consolidated his position, becoming the one director whose name was known to every filmgoer (and television viewer) in America. In *Rear Window* (1953), *Vertigo* (1958), and *North by Northwest* (1959) he constructed three masterpieces of anxiety—as perceptual, as psychosexual, and as psychopolitical, respectively.

The last of these, *North by Northwest,* was exceptionally prescient: an emblem for America in the sixties and seventies. Roger O. Thornhill (Cary Grant) is mistaken one afternoon for a mysterious Mr. Kaplan and chased, north by northwest, across most of the nation by foreign agents. Kaplan, it turns out, is the fictional invention of a government agency—Hitchcock suggests strongly that it is the CIA (see Figure 3-74)—which is quite happy to find a real person acting out the imaginary role. The film ends with a spectacular chase across the foreheads of the fathers of the country at Mount Rushmore. As Grant runs for his life, the national symbols stare ahead, unblinking and unseeing. A pleasant and witty thriller directed with consummate skill, *North by Northwest,* written by Ernest Lehman, took on new dimensions of meaning a decade after it was released, when the antagonism between the people of the U.S. and its government came out into the open.

This period, in which film as art established its precedence worldwide, came to a notable climax. The year 1959, give or take six months, was an annus mirabilis: an extraordinary conjunction of talents bloomed. In France, Truffaut, Godard, Chabrol, Rohmer, Rivette, and Resnais all made their first films—the New Wave was established. In Italy, Fellini took a new path with *La Dolce Vita,* and Michelangelo Antonioni with *L'Avventura.* In England, the Angry Young Men of the theater were moving into film production. In America, the personal, independent cinema was established as a viable path with the release of John Cassavetes's *Shadows.*

The New Wave and the Third World: Entertainment Versus Communication

The New Wave in France signaled a new attitude toward film. Born after the development of the sound film, these filmmakers had a sense of film culture and film heritage; the movies they made exhibited that sense. Claude Chabrol, François Truffaut, Jean-Luc Godard, Eric Rohmer, and Jacques Rivette had all written for *Cahiers du Cinéma* in the 1950s and been influenced by the theories of André Bazin. Louis Malle and Alain Resnais did not begin as critics, but nevertheless exhibited parallel attitudes.

Truffaut's early classics, *The 400 Blows* (1959), *Shoot the Piano Player* (1961), and *Jules and Jim* (1962), were the first great popular successes of the group. In each of those three disparate films he displayed a virtuosity, humanity, and depth of feeling that quickly won audiences worldwide. After that early period Truffaut retreated to more abstract concerns, beginning a series of films that were studies in genre: *The Soft Skin* (1964), *Fahrenheit 451* (1966), and *Mississippi Mermaid* (1969) attempted, as he put it, "to explode genres by combining them." This was a cinema that came close to insisting that viewers shared with the filmmaker an understanding of past forms and conventions. The story of alter ego Antoine Doinel (played throughout by Jean-Pierre Léaud) that begins with *The 400 Blows,* continued through four other films over the next twenty years, as Truffaut followed the character to middle age. One of these, *Stolen Kisses* (1968), remains a romantic icon of the 1960s. In the seventies, Truffaut turned to more introverted genre studies. Two films stand out: *The Wild Child* (1970), in which he investigates language and love, and *Day For Night* (1973), his paean to his own love and language: cinema.

Figure 4-50. The challenge and the grandeur of the wide open spaces of the Western had become a paranoid nightmare by the late 1950s. Here advertising-man-in-the-gray-flannel-suit Roger Thornhill (Cary Grant) runs for his life through desolate midwestern cornfields, chased by a faceless assassin flying a crop-duster—an ecological portent! Thornhill's suit and tie are peculiarly but aptly out of place in the heart of the country in Hitchcock's. *North by Northwest.* Compare Figure 4-44.

Truffaut died—dramatically and arbitrarily—of a brain tumor in the American Hospital at Neuilly in 1984. He was only 52.

Like his friend Truffaut, Godard also began with a number of personal versions of genre films: the Gangster film (*Breathless,* 1960), the Musical (*A Woman Is a Woman,* 1961), two Films Noirs (*Le Petit Soldat,* 1960; *My Life to Live,* 1962)—even a star-filled Hollywood melodrama (*Contempt,* 1963). His first film, *Breathless,* was a refreshingly iconoclastic study that immediately marked him as one of the most innovative and thoughtful members of the new generation of filmmakers. Ignoring the established conventions of narrative, which even such personal filmmakers as Bergman and Fellini more or less observed, Godard operated on a number of levels simultaneously. *Breathless* was at one and the same time a Gangster story and an essay *about* Gangster films.

Michel Poiccard, played by Jean-Paul Belmondo, kills a cop, meets up with an American woman named Patricia (Jean Seberg), hangs out in Paris for a while, evading the police, and is eventually betrayed by Patricia and shot down. Poiccard is fascinated by the image of Humphrey Bogart as he knows it from the old Hollywood films. He invents a pseudonym for himself. He isn't so much a gangster as he is a young man acting out the role of gangster that he has learned from American films. Patricia, for her part, is compared visually by Godard to a number of

Figure 4-51. Antoine Doinel (Jean-Pierre Léaud) and friend escape to the broad boulevard of the Champs-Élysées in Truffaut's poignant *The 400 Blows.*

artistic images of women, notably those by Picasso. She is not so much a character, the "moll," as she is an esthetic image of woman on the model of the paintings in the film. Even the death of Michel which closes the film is played at one remove, Michel doing his best to die a heroic death as he has learned it from the movies, while Patricia persists in her emotional isolation, never quite understanding the potential drama of the plot.

As Godard's career progressed, he turned more and more to the essay form, eventually abandoning fictional narrative altogether. In an extraordinary series of films in the mid- and late sixties, he established an approach to filmmaking that has had worldwide influence. *A Married Woman* (1964), *Alphaville, Pierrot le Fou* (both 1965), *Masculine-Feminine, 2 or 3 Things That I Know About Her* (both 1966), *La Chinoise* (1967), and *Weekend* (1968) explored cinema as personal essay conscientiously and with exhilaration.

In these films, Godard set up a direct communication with the viewer, using the conventions of genre to his own ends and avoiding the distractions of the well-made, absorbing dramatic experience. In the late sixties, Godard withdrew into an even more personal, political cinema under the shelter of the "Dziga-Vertov Group" for a series of films that lacked all pretense as finished products and were meant clearly as works in progress. The result of this period of cinematic contemplation was *Tout va bien* (1972). Godard then turned his attention to video before returning to theatrical screens with *Sauve qui peut la vie* in 1980, which marked the beginning of a series of reprises that included *First Name: Carmen*

Figure 4-52. Charles Aznavour as Charlie Kohler in Truffaut's *Shoot the Piano Player*, an essay in genres. Like most of the New Wave, Truffaut was fascinated by American films. Here he combined elements of Film Noir and the Western and Gangster films with a notably French philosophical attitude. The mixture of cultures was exhilarating.

(1983, woman as hero), *Détective* (1985, the genre film), *Hail Mary* (1985, Godard as the enfant terrible again), and *New Wave* (1990, an essay on cinema).

Unlike Truffaut and Godard, Claude Chabrol confined his attention to one genre. Strongly influenced by Hitchcock, the subject of a study he wrote with Eric Rohmer, Chabrol redefined the Hitchcockian universe in French terms and contributed, beginning in the late sixties, a fine series of parodic thrillers that effectively satirized bourgeois values as they celebrated them. *Les Biches* (1968), *La Femme infidèle* (1969), *Le Boucher* (1970), *Just Before Nightfall* (1971), and *Red Wedding* (1972) stand out. After a fallow period, Chabrol returned to form in the mid-eighties with new explorations of the genre, including *Cop au vin* (1985) and *Story of Women* (1988).

Eric Rohmer brought to cinema familiarity with a literary culture hundreds of years old. His series of "Moral Tales"—including *La Collectionneuse* (1967), *My Night at Maud's* (1968), *Claire's Knee* (1970), and *Chloë in the Afternoon* (1972)—demonstrated that many of the literary pleasures of narrative, setting, and reasoned analysis could be derived from film. In the 1980s Rohmer began a new series he called "Comedies and Proverbs," revolving around quirky characters who all manage to

Figure 4-53. American and French culture meet for the first time in the New Wave on the Champs Élysées in *Breathless*. Michel Poiccard (Jean-Paul Belmondo), a devotee of Bogart and the Gangster mythos, falls for *New York Herald Tribune* newspapergirl Patricia Franchini (Jean Seberg), the archetypal American girl in Paris in the early sixties. Maybe it was the t-shirt. (*l'Avant-Scène. Frame enlargement.*)

survive and focusing on the women's point of view (*Pauline à la plage*, 1983; *Le Rayon vert*, 1986). A third series, "Tales of Four Seasons," began in 1990 with *Conte de printemps* and ended in 1998 with *Conte d'automne*. At the end of the century the 79-year-old director was experimenting with DV: a digital screening of his short "Cambrure" at the Cannes Film Festival in May 1999 preceded by several weeks the landmark digital projection of George Lucas's *The Phantom Menace*.

While Rohmer's cinema was influenced by the novel, Jacques Rivette's was informed by stage drama. The last of the *Cahiers* group to come to prominence, Rivette was obsessed with the structures of dramatic narrative. In *L'Amour fou* (1968), *Out One* (1971), and *Céline et Julie vont en bateau* (1973) he examined the phenomena of duration and psychological intensity that shape our fictional world.

Alain Resnais brought some of the avant-garde complexity of the new French novel to cinema. Usually working in close collaboration with novelists (several of whom—Alain Robbe-Grillet and Marguerite Duras, for example—later turned to filmmaking themselves), Resnais explored the function of time and memory in narrative with stunning effect in such films as *Night and Fog* (1956, Nazi concentration camps), *Hiroshima, mon amour* (1959, the atomic bomb), *Last Year at*

Marienbad (1962, memory as esthetic abstraction), *La Guerre est finie* (1965, the Left coming to terms with history), and *Je t'aime, je t'aime* (1968, the music of time). In the 1970s Resnais summarized his fascination with the relation of narrative and memory in three remarkable films: *Stavisky...* (1973), an essay on the 1930s rogue celebrity with a score by Stephen Sondheim; *Providence* (1977), a super-postmodern investigation of the function of writing with a script by David Mercer; and *Mon Oncle d'Amérique* (1979), a provocative, humorous essay on the theories of biologist Henri Laborit.

Like Rohmer, Resnais continued directing well into his seventies. *La Vie est un roman* (1983) covered 70 years in the life of a chateau and its three sets of occupants. *Smoking/No Smoking* (1993), based on a play by Alan Ayckbourn, presented a set of different life scenarios for one set of characters. *On connaît le chanson* (1997) was a musical homage to the work of Dennis Potter.

Louis Malle, like Resnais trained as a technician, was the most eclectic member of the New Wave: *The Lovers* (1968) was a highly romantic drama, *Zazie dans le Metro* (1960) a Screwball Comedy, *India* (1969) an idiosyncratic Documentary, and *Lacombe, Lucien* (1973) one of the best of the then current cycle of films about the Nazi occupation of France. Malle moved to the U.S. in the seventies. *Pretty Baby* (1978), with quasi-child-actor Brooke Shields as a prostitute proved controversial. *My Dinner with Andre* (1981) became one of the rare popular art films of the eighties. He achieved further popular success with *Au Revoir, les enfants* (1987), his personal memoir. Malle died of cancer in November 1995.

Agnès Varda brought a documentary sensibility to the New Wave. Her *Cleo from 5 to 7* (1961) was a touchstone of the early New Wave. *Le Bonheur* (1965) remains one of the more interesting experiments in color prior to 1968 and an unusual romantic essay. *Daguerreotypes* (1975) was a witty and insightful homage to Varda's neighbors in the rue Daguerre, and *Vagabond* (1985) her best-received work. In *Jane B. par Agnès V.* (1988) Varda found a novel way to discuss the themes of feminism and independence in an essay about her old friend actress Jane Birkin.

The New Wave had been fascinated by Hollywood cinema, but in the 1960s little of major interest was happening in America. The masters of the 1930s and 1940s were winding down and the new generation, which has dominated the Hollywood scene ever since, had not yet arrived. Hitchcock continued with *Psycho* (1960), *The Birds* (1963), *Marnie* (1964), and *Topaz* (1969), all interesting films if not as important as his major work in the fifties. Hawks and Ford made minor contributions. One good thing did happen in the 1960s: George Axelrod (*How to Murder Your Wife*, 1965) and Blake Edwards (*The Pink Panther*, 1964) restarted the comic engine that drives American culture. Edwards was also responsible for two of the romantic classics of the decade (*Breakfast at Tiffany's*, 1961; *Days of Wine and Roses*, 1962). While Axelrod returned to screenwriting, Edwards continued

Figure 4-54. The guests cast shadows, but the trees don't in this epistemological garden from Resnais's *Last Year at Marienbad*, a study in memory. Compare 4-49. (*Frame enlargement.*)

through the seventies and eighties to produce a string of popular hits which gained grudging respect from the critics, most notably *S.O.B.* (1981), his personal attack on Hollywood.

Generally, however, the sixties were years of transition in American cinema. Esthetically, the most interesting developments in the U.S. were taking place underground, where a strong avant-garde tradition was bearing fruit in the films of Kenneth Anger, Ron Rice, Bruce Baillie, Robert Breer, Stan Vanderbeek, Stan Brakhage, Gregory Markopoulos, Ed Emshwiller, Jonas and Adolfas Mekas, James and John Whitney, Jordan Belson, and others. Aboveground, Andy Warhol's Factory produced a number of "Underground" films that had some curious commercial success.

Hollywood felt the first thrust of the television esthetic as a number of directors trained in television turned to film. Among the most prominent were Arthur Penn (*Bonnie and Clyde*, 1967; *Alice's Restaurant*, 1969; *Night Moves*, 1976), Sidney Lumet (*The Group*, 1966; *Dog Day Afternoon*, 1975; *Network*, 1976; *Just Tell Me What You Want*, 1980), John Frankenheimer (*The Manchurian Candidate*, 1962), Martin Ritt (*Hud*, 1963; *Sounder*, 1972; *The Front*, 1976; *Norma Rae*, 1979), and Franklin Schaffner (*The Best Man*, 1964; *Patton*, 1969). Of this group, Lumet stands out and continued to produce a varied body of work through the eighties and nineties (*Prince of the City*, 1981; *Power*, 1986; *Q&A*, 1990; *Night Falls on Manhattan*, 1997; *Gloria*, 1999, a remake of the John Cassavetes film).

Perhaps the most influential development in the U.S. was seen not on movie screens but on television. The perfection of lightweight, adaptable 16 mm equip-

Figure 4-55. Olga Georges-Picot and Claude Rich on the beach in Alain Resnais's *Je t'aime, je t'aime* (1968), one of Resnais's most vigorous studies in time and memory. This scene, repeated many times throughout the film in varying versions, is the focal point of Rich's science-fiction odyssey through his past. Resnais uses the fiction of a journey by time machine to experiment with the repetition of scenes and the disjuncture of narrative. The result is as close to music as film gets. (*French Film Office.*)

ment in the late fifties and early sixties made possible a new style of documentary, so different from the traditional, highly "worked," and often semifictional style as to deserve a new name: Direct Cinema. Filmmakers became reporters, with nearly as much freedom as print journalists, and television was the place to view their work. Robert Drew headed a group, Drew Associates, that produced a number of important films for television. Working with him were Richard Leacock and Donn Pennebaker, as well as Albert and David Maysles, all to become major figures in the movement. *Primary* (1960) was the first major result of Direct Cinema techniques. Pennebaker's *Don't Look Back* (1966) was a portrait of Bob Dylan. The Maysles brothers adapted the techniques to theatrical release in a series of films they called "nonfiction features," most notably *Salesman* (1969), *Gimme Shelter* (1970, about a Rolling Stones concert), and *Grey Gardens* (1975).

Thirty years later both Pennebaker and Albert Maysles were still going strong. (David Maysles died in 1987.) Pennebaker found new audiences with *The War Room* (1992), an inside look at the Clinton presidential campaign, and *Moon Over Broadway* (1997), about the making of a musical. Maysles scored with *Christo in Paris* (1991), his profile of the artist, and *Concert of Wills: Making the Getty Center*

Figure 4-56. Audrey Hepburn as Holly Golightly parties in Blake Edwards's romantic classic of the early sixties, *Breakfast at Tiffany's*. As a romantic icon of the fifties and sixties, Hepburn's only peer was Shirley MacLaine.

(1998), a revealing portrait of the architects and bureaucrats responsible for the gargantuan new museum in Los Angeles.

The principal theory of Direct Cinema was that the filmmakers not involve themselves in the action. Gone were the well-phrased narrations of earlier documentaries. The camera was all-seeing: hundreds of hours of film were shot to capture a sense of the reality of the subject.

Frederick Wiseman, trained as a lawyer, brought this technique to perfection in a well-received series of studies of institutions for public television, among them *Titicut Follies* (1967, about a mental institution), *High School* (1968), *Hospital* (1970), *Primate* (1974), and *Meat* (1976).

In France during the sixties, a parallel style of new documentary was developing. Called "cinéma vérité," it differed from Direct Cinema in that it admitted that the presence of the camera made a difference and indeed traded on that fact. *Chronique d'un été* (1960), by anthropologist Jean Rouch and sociologist Edgar Morin, was the first and still classic example of cinéma vérité. Because cinéma vérité and Direct Cinema both measurably expand the boundaries of the permissible in film, they have had a profound effect out of all proportion to the number of films actually identified as being in those styles.

The traditional Musical, for example, has been superseded by the filmed concert, which in its turn has become a dramatic event. More important, our sense of what is "correct" in narrative has been drastically altered as the profusion of nonfiction films has prepared us for the rhythms of real time. We no longer insist on Hollywood's découpage classique.

In the late forties, the French critic Alexandre Astruc had composed a manifesto in which he called for a cinema built around the "caméra-stylo" ("camera-pen"), which would be just as flexible and personal as literature (see Chapter 5). To a large extent, his wish was fulfilled in the fifties, as cinema shifted from assembly-line product to personal statement. What he did not foresee was that the flexibility of the caméra-stylo would also lead to a new level of film realism: the new equipment encouraged the filmmaker to get closer to the world around him, film on location rather than in the studio, and shoot actualities rather than actors. Direct Cinema and cinéma vérité were only two evidences of this radical change in attitude. Cinema had become a medium with a wide range of applications.

In England there was a brief burst of prosperity in the sixties. In 1958, John Osborne, the major figure of the stage renaissance taking place at that time, formed Woodfall Films in collaboration with the director Tony Richardson. Much of the best British cinema of the sixties was closely connected with the vital theater of that period. Tony Richardson began with two adaptations of plays by John Osborne—*Look Back in Anger* (1959) and *The Entertainer* (1960)—and continued with an adaptation of Shelagh Delaney's *A Taste of Honey* (1961) before turning to Alan Sillitoe's novel *Loneliness of the Long Distance Runner* (1962). Richardson won an Oscar for *Tom Jones* (1963), from Henry Fielding's eighteenth-century novel.

Karel Reisz directed one of the more interesting "kitchen-sink" films, *Saturday Night and Sunday Morning* (1960, also written by Sillitoe), then turned to *Morgan* (1966) and *Isadora* (1968) before moving to the U.S., where he directed *The Gambler* (1974) and *The French Lieutenant's Woman* (1981). John Schlesinger's more interesting films include *A Kind of Loving* (1962), *Billy Liar* (1963), *Darling* (1965, written by Frederic Raphael), and *Sunday, Bloody Sunday* (1971, written by film critic Penelope Gilliatt). In the U.S. he directed *Midnight Cowboy* (1969), one of the landmarks of 1960s U.S. cinema, and *Marathon Man* (1976), then he returned to England for *Yanks* (1979). Lindsay Anderson may have been the most ambitious director of this group: his films included *This Sporting Life* (1963, from a novel by David Storey), *If . . .* (1968), *Oh Lucky Man* (1973), and *In Celebration* (1975, from the Storey play), and the scathing *Britannia Hospital* (1982).

All of the earlier films of these directors shared an interest in working-class subjects, although as they matured, all four turned toward more middle-class concerns. With few exceptions, their later films share little of the passion of the early years.

Anderson, Reisz, and Richardson were associated with the Free Cinema documentary movement in the fifties. The Documentary tradition continued to have an effect on British cinema in the sixties. Peter Watkins's strident *The War Game*

Figure 4-57. Frederick Wiseman's *Welfare* (1975). Wiseman's films combine the insistent, relentless shooting techniques of Direct Cinema with a lawyer's sense of social structures in order to investigate the inner workings of significant contemporary institutions. (*Zipporah Films.*)

(1966), about the effects of atomic war, was considered too convincing to be broadcast on the BBC. Kevin Brownlow and Andrew Mollo's *It Happened Here* (1963) documented an equally fictitious historical event: the German occupation of Britain during the Second World War.

More interesting in England during the sixties was the work of several American exiles. Joseph Losey, blacklisted in Hollywood, directed a number of mediocre films, but those written by Harold Pinter—*The Servant* (1963), *Accident* (1967), and *The Go-Between* (1971)—managed to capture the playwright's droll, warped view of bourgeois society.

Stanley Kubrick had made several interesting minor films in the U.S. before he settled in England. *Dr. Strangelove* (1963) remains a superb satire of the Cold-War mentality; its significance increases with each passing year. *2001: A Space Odyssey* (1968) is a masterful blending of cinematography with scientific and religious theory. It set the style for decades of popular and remunerative Science Fiction. *A Clockwork Orange* (1971), a striking symphony of violence, remains perhaps the most prescient film about the future that we now inhabit. *Barry Lyndon* (1975) was not only a superbly accurate evocation of time and place (eighteenth-century Europe), but also adventurous in narrative style: a very expensive commercial

Figure 4-58. Julie Christie, George C. Scott in Richard Lester's *Petulia* (1967). Not highly popular when it was released, *Petulia* is now generally regarded as one of the landmark films about America in the sixties. Returning from fifteen years in Europe, Lester was able to see us as we could not see ourselves, and the jaundiced vision of the hip society he projected held more truth than the counterculture myths of the time.

proposition, it nevertheless eschews all the Hollywood rules of pace. *The Shining* (1980) was Kubrick's attempt to succeed at a highly profitable, if ethically suspect, genre, while *Full Metal Jacket* (1987) brought him back to the subject of war. He had just finished *Eyes Wide Shut*, a study in sexual obsession—a subject he hadn't treated since *Lolita* (1962)—when he died suddenly in March 1999.

Richard Lester began his career directing television in Philadelphia, moved to London in the mid-fifties, and became involved with Peter Sellers and the Goon Show people. He first gained attention as a director with The Beatles films (*A Hard Day's Night*, 1964; *Help!*, 1965) and was castigated by many critics thereafter for his supposedly frenetic editing style. Little did they know he would turn out to be the most stylistically influential director since Welles, as any glance at MTV in any of the scores of countries in which it airs will attest.

Lester's *A Funny Thing Happened on the Way to the Forum* (1965) remains one of the best film adaptations of stage musicals. *Petulia* (1967), shot in San Francisco, was as prescient as it was sharply ironic—one of the two or three best American films of the period. *How I Won the War* (1967) and *The Bed-Sitting Room* (1968) are among the few English-language films to employ Brechtian techniques successfully. These latter two films were commercially unsuccessful. Lester was inactive

Figure 4-59. Neville Smith, Ann Zelda, and Charles Gormley in Maurice Hatton's witty, sardonic investigation of the British film scene of the postmodern period, *Long Shot* (1979).

for more than five years, finally returning to the cinema with less ambitious, commercially safer projects such as *The Three Musketeers* (1973), *Juggernaut* (1974), *Robin and Marian* (1978), and *Superman II* and *III* (1980, 1983).

When sources of funding dried up in the late sixties, British filmmakers had two choices: to leave the country, or to turn to television. Directors like John Boorman and Peter Yates came to the U.S., where they established themselves as effective craftsmen. Ken Loach (*Poor Cow,* 1967; *Kes,* 1969; *Family Life,* 1972) had always considered television as important as cinema. His films demonstrate sophisticated refinements of realist techniques, as do his television efforts (notably the series *Days of Hope,* 1976).

Maurice Hatton, like Loach, chose to stick close to his English roots. His first feature, *Praise Marx and Pass the Ammunition* (1968), is one of the rare films that combine politics with humor successfully. Hatton's *Long Shot* (1979) applied the same mordant wit to the moribund British film industry. A film about the difficulties of remaining a filmmaker in Britain in the late 1970s, *Long Shot* was made entirely independently—a remarkable economic as well as artistic achievement. After *American Roulette* (1988) Hatton found it ever more difficult to produce independently in Britain. He was at work on a long-planned documentary when he died suddenly in 1997.

Ken Russell and Nicolas Roeg were among the few British filmmakers to survive the withdrawal of American capital in the late sixties. Russell, who first gained attention with a series of unusual biographies of musicians done for the

BBC, continued in feature films to specialize in cinematic biography, although his approach became progressively more eccentric (*The Music Lovers,* 1970; *Mahler,* 1974). His lurid, pop art, comic strip style was probably shown to best advantage in *Tommy* (1975). Roeg, a former cinematographer, produced several films that are stunningly photographed although less interesting in other respects (*Walk-about,* 1971; *Don't Look Now,* 1973; *The Man Who Fell to Earth,* 1976).

During the late 1970s, a new generation of British filmmakers—most of them trained in television commercials—found commercial success in the international market. After *Bugsy Malone* (1976), an unusual and ingratiating musical about children, for children, but also for adults, Alan Parker filmed *Midnight Express* (1978), far more lucrative, and as exploitative as his earlier film had been charming. He achieved some success in the U.S. with *Fame* (1980), the very model of the modern musical, and *Mississippi Burning* (1988). *The Commitments* (1991), about a fictitious Irish rock group, further extended Parker's claim to be the Vincente Minnelli of modern times.

Similarly, Ridley Scott tested the waters with the romantic *The Duellists* (1977), then delivered the highly manipulative (and profitable) *Alien* (1979). Scott achieved cult status with *Blade Runner* (1982), everyone's favorite Science Fiction Film Noir, and *Thelma & Louise* (1991), the women's road movie for the nineties.

For a while in the early 1980s, the remarkable success of Goldcrest Films (*Gandhi,* 1982; *Local Hero,* 1983; *The Killing Fields,* 1984) suggested that there might be a future for the British film industry, but the hope proved illusory as Goldcrest self-destructed in 1987 due to a combination of mismanagement and underfinancing.

In Italy, Fellini and Antonioni, two influential masters, held sway throughout the sixties. Fellini completed several major films, including *8 1/2* (1962), *Juliet of the Spirits* (1965), and *Fellini Satyricon* (1969), before turning his attention to television, where he produced a series of semiautobiographical essays that eventually culminated in the theatrical films *Roma* (1972) and *Amarcord* (1973). In the eighties, Fellini sailed pleasantly into old age with *And the Ship Sails On* (1983), *Ginger & Fred* (1984), and *Intervista* (1987), having given the world a panoply of celebrations of the life force that are as invigorating as they are audacious. He died in 1993, the same year that Cinecittà closed.

Antonioni came into his own with *L'Avventura* (1960), the first film of a trilogy that included *La Notte* (1961) and *L'Eclisse* (1962), which redefined basic concepts of film narrative. *Red Desert* (1964) and *Blow-Up* (1966) continued his experiments with narration and perception in an existential setting. *Zabriskie Point* (1970) was his essay on the America of the 1960s. *The Passenger* (1975) was the epitome of Antonioni's very special cinema, a film redolent of existential angst, constructed in long, periodic, hypnotic rhythms.

Figure 4-60. Harrison Ford in the futuristic Film Noir, *Blade Runner*, which set a downbeat style for the eighties.

Luchino Visconti's latter films (*The Damned*, 1970; *Death in Venice*, 1971; *Conversation Piece*, 1975) were as languorously decadent as his earlier Neorealistic films had been alert and pointed. "The Job" (from *Boccaccio 70*, 1962; see Figure 2-45) and *The Leopard* (1963) were more successful if less remarkable.

Pietro Germi, who had been one of the leading directors of the Neorealist movement (*In the Name of the Law*, 1949), but who had never had much success outside of Italy, established an international comic style for the sixties with two assured comedies of manners, *Divorce Italian Style* (1961) and *Seduced and Abandoned* (1963).

Pier Paolo Pasolini, poet and theorist, turned to film in the sixties and completed *Accattone* (1961), *The Gospel According to St. Matthew* (1964), *The Hawks and the Sparrows* (1966), and a number of other symbolic exercises before his death in 1976. Francesco Rosi, one of the most underrated of modern Italian directors, directed a number of intriguing political films, including *Salvatore Giuliano* (1962), *Le Mani Sulla Città* (1963), *The Mattei Affair* (1972), *Lucky Luciano* (1973), and *Christ Stopped at Eboli* (1979).

Of the next generation of Italian filmmakers, Bernardo Bertolucci was the first to attract attention with *Before the Revolution* (1964), *The Conformist* (1970), and *Last Tango in Paris* (1972). Bertolucci quickly fell into a Visconti-like fascination

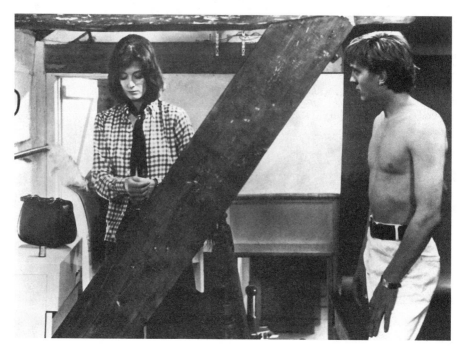

Figure 4-61. Vanessa Redgrave, David Hemmings. A typical, highly designed shot from Antonioni's *Blow-Up* (1966). The plot of the film concerned the mystery of images. (*MOMA/FSA.*)

with the shapes and surfaces of bourgeois decadence, which he ostensibly criticized. *Last Tango in Paris* achieved a certain international reputation for its clever combination of star (Marlon Brando) and frank sex. It marked a turning point in sexual mores. In his five-hour epic *1900* (1976) Bertolucci seemed to return to his earlier epic social vision. *Luna* (1979), whose subject was incest, follows the *Tango* line, but Bertolucci returned to the epic form in *The Last Emperor* (1987), which was a major international success. *The Sheltering Sky* (1990) was also well regarded.

Marco Bellocchio, who shared Bertolucci's spotlight in the 1960s, received far less international attention with his ideological satires—*Fists in the Pocket* (1965), *China Is Near* (1967), *In the Name of the Father* (1971), and *Slap the Monster on Page One* (1973).

In the seventies, Lina Wertmüller took center stage for a brief moment with a series of sardonic sex comedies flavored with a suspicion of politics, including *Love and Anarchy* (1972), *The Seduction of Mimi* (1973), *Swept Away* (1974), and *Seven Beauties* (1975).

While directorial stars such as these rose with regularity on the Italian horizon, there were a number of less spectacular directors whose work never received its

Figure 4-62. In the seventies and eighties Bernardo Bertolucci ventured outside of Italy to create "world-films" like *The Last Emperor*, gorgeously photographed and epic in scope.

international due. Most of their films had strong social implications; the political melodrama pioneered by Rosi and Costa-Gavras has been most successful in Italy. Some of the directors in this group were: Mario Monicelli (*The Organizer,* 1963), Giuliano Montaldo (*Sacco and Vanzetti,* 1971), Elio Petri (*Investigation of a Citizen above Suspicion,* 1970; *The Working Class Goes to Heaven,* 1971), Gillo Pontecorvo (*The Battle of Algiers,* 1965; *Burn,* 1968), Gianni Amico (*Tropici,* 1968; *Ritorno,* 1973), Nelo Risi (*Diary of a Schizophrenic Girl,* 1969), and Ermanno Olmi (*Il Posto,* 1961; *Un Certo Giorno,* 1969; *Durante l'estate,* 1971).

Olmi's *The Tree of the Wooden Clogs* (1978), a deeply felt, mesmeric three-hour evocation of peasant life at the turn of the century, is one of the more outstanding films from Italy during the past twenty-five years. Like *1900* and the Taviani brothers' *Padre, Padrone* (1976), *The Tree of the Wooden Clogs* is representative of a newly rediscovered Italian fascination with peasant habits and rhythms. Fellini's *Amarcord* and Rosi's *Christ Stopped at Eboli* should also be included in this interesting genre.

In Sweden, Ingmar Bergman completed a regularly spaced string of films, working with what amounted to a repertory group of actors and technicians. From this period dates his finest cinema: *Through a Glass Darkly, Winter Light,* and *The Silence*

Figure 4-63. Ermanno Olmi's *The Tree of the Wooden Clogs*, filmed with a kind of anthropological perspective, set a style for such investigations in the eighties.

form the trilogy in which Bergman exorcised God from his consciousness (1961–63). *Persona* (1966) remains possibly his most imaginative and daring film. The series of films with Liv Ullmann and Max von Sydow (*Hour of the Wolf,* 1967; *Shame,* 1968; *The Passion of Anna,* 1969) forms one of the more striking accomplishments in the cinema of the sixties. In the seventies, Bergman withdrew to firmer ground. His television series *Scenes from a Marriage* (1973), however, compared with his best work. In 1976, after a Kafkaesque encounter with tax authorities, he left Sweden to try his luck elsewhere, returning for the elegiac *Fanny and Alexander* (1982).

Younger Swedish directors found an international audience in the sixties, as well. Jörn Donner (*To Love,* 1964), Bo Widerberg (*Elvira Madigan,* 1967), Vilgot Sjöman (*I Am Curious–Yellow,* 1967), and most notably Jan Troell, whose trilogy of emigration and resettlement—*The Emigrants, The New Land* (both 1970), and *Zandy's Bride* (1974)—brought a new freshness of vision and historical perspective to a classic theme.

In Eastern Europe, the state film schools nurtured a new wave of talent in the sixties: in Poland, Roman Polanski (*Knife in the Water,* 1962), who left to become an international director of facile, often empty, vaguely supernatural Thrillers; Jerzy Skolimowski (*Walkover,* 1965; *Barrier,* 1966; and in London, *Deep End,* 1970); and Krzysztof Zanussi, whose quiet, searching studies of scientists and engineers (*Behind the Wall,* 1971; *Illumination,* 1973) are unique in world cinema.

Figure 4-64. Liv Ullmann, Max von Sydow, and money in Jan Troell's *The New Land* (released 1973).

In Hungary, Miklós Jancsó earned a reputation as one of the foremost Structural filmmakers, intent on the relationship between camera and subject rather than the subject itself (*The Red and the White,* 1967; *Winter Wind,* 1969; *Electreia,* 1974). Marta Meszarós gained an international festival following with a number of precisely realized essays, mainly on the roles of women, including *Nine Months* (1976), *Women* (1977), and *The Heritage* (1980).

Perhaps the most significant development in Eastern Europe was the Czech Renaissance which flowered unexpectedly for a few brief years in the middle sixties. Milos Forman (*Loves of a Blonde,* 1965; *The Fireman's Ball,* 1967), Ivan Passer (*Intimate Lighting,* 1966), Jirí Menzel (*Closely Watched Trains,* 1966), and Vera Chytilová (*Daisies,* 1969) evolved a vivid humanist realism, invested with humor and respect for their subjects, which was cut horribly short by the Soviet invasion of the country in 1968 and the subsequent return to Stalinism. Forman and Passer moved to the United States, where they did interesting work, but never on the level of their earliest films, although Forman had some notable popular successes. *One Flew Over the Cuckoo's Nest* (1975) won all five top Academy awards. (The same year, Forman was appointed co-director of the Columbia University film program.) His *Hair* (1979) was a notable modern musical, and *Ragtime* (1981)

Figure 4-65. The finish line, a moral as well as physical goal, in *Chariots of Fire*. (Hugh Hudson,1981). David Puttnam's production heralded a minor renaissance in British film.

a respectful mounting of the Doctorow novel. He scored multiple Oscars again in 1984 with *Amadeus*.

As for the Soviet Union, the strict state control of the art instituted during the earliest days of the Stalinist period stifled what was once one of the world's leading cinemas. In the days before glasnost, only a few films escaped. Sergei Paradzhanov, Armenian by birth, gained international acclaim with *Shadows of Our Forgotten Ancestors* (1964) and *Sayat Nova* (1969). When he joined the growing civil rights movement, he was imprisoned and sent to a labor camp, ostensibly for homosexuality, in January 1974. The sentence resulted in an international cause célèbre. After the end of the Brezhnev regime, Paradzhanov was able to complete several additional celebrations of Georgian and Armenian folklore before his death in 1990. Andrei Tarkovsky became known in the West when his lyrical *My Name Is Ivan* (1962) won an award at the Venice Film Festival. His allegorical *Andrei Roublev* (1966) was also well received in the West, to which Tarkovsky eventually immigrated and where he died in 1986.

Dušan Makavejev, the best-known Yugoslav filmmaker (*Love Affair, or the Case of the Missing Switchboard Operator,* 1967), ran into censorship problems as well because he mixed politics with sex in an intriguing but officially unacceptable way. *WR: Mysteries of the Organism* (1971) was banned in Yugoslavia.

The 1960s and 1970s saw the extension of film culture beyond the boundaries of the U.S., Japan, and Europe into the developing countries collectively known as the Third World. Often rough and angry, Third World cinema was also sometimes

Figure 4-66. A series of surrealistic blackout sketches, Buñuel's *The Discreet Charm of the Bourgeoisie* (1972) is droll, good-natured satire. Here, a dinner party ends in discreet embarrassment as the guests are machine-gunned.

vital and relevant. Like the nonfiction filmmakers of the West, Third World cinéastes generally saw film as a powerful medium of communication, a medium they employed with passion.

The most productive Third World movement of the time was the Brazilian Cinema Nôvo, which got under way in the early sixties and, although slowed by the right-wing military junta that took power in 1964, nevertheless survived, partly because of the symbolic stylization most of the films employed. Glauber Rocha (*Barravento*, 1961; *Antonio das Mortes*, 1969) was the most visible of the group. Other important directors included: Ruy Guerra (*Os Fuzis*, 1964), Nelson Pereira dos Santos (*How Tasty Was My Little Frenchman*, 1971), Joaquim Pedro de Andrade (*Macunaima*, 1969), and Carlos Diégues (*Os Herdeiros*, 1971), all of whom share to some degree Rocha's commitment to political allegory.

Mexico, like Brazil, produces more than fifty features per year. For many years Mexican cinema was dominated by the imposing figure of Luis Buñuel. Buñuel, who had made two important surrealist films with Salvador Dali in Paris in the late twenties (*Un Chien Andalou*, 1928; *L'Âge d'or*, 1930), spent the next twenty years on the fringe of the film industry before finding a home in Mexico in the late forties. He directed a number of essentially commercial films during the next ten years.

But it was not until he returned to his native Spain in 1961 to film his first feature there, *Viridiana*, that he finally achieved the worldwide attention that was his due. Although Buñuel was born in 1900, the center of his career lay in the sixties. Making films mainly in France, he produced a masterful series of surrealist allegories (*Diary of a Chambermaid*, 1964; *Belle de Jour*, 1967; *The Milky Way*, 1969; *Tristana*, 1970; *The Discreet Charm of the Bourgeoisie*, 1972; *Phantom of Liberty*, 1974) that assured his position in the international pantheon of the art film. Buñuel's more personal Mexican films are: *Nazarín* (1958), *The Exterminating Angel* (1962), and *Simon of the Desert* (1965), antireligious allegories all.

In the early 1970s, the new Chilean cinema made a brief but welcome impact on world screens before it was cut short by the military putsch of 1973. Four films of special interest were produced during the Allende years: *Valparaiso, Mi amor* (1970) and *Praying Is Not Enough* (1972), directed by Aldo Francia, and *The Jackal of Nahueltoro* (1969) and *The Promised Land* (1973), directed by Miguel Littín. Committed, passionate, direct, expressive, and lyrical, Chilean cinema would have been rewarding had it survived. Of special interest was the three-part documentary *The Battle of Chile*, produced outside the country after the coup, mainly from footage shot before.

In Cuba, the Cuban Institute of Cinematic Art and Industry (ICAIC) nurtured an active and interesting cinema throughout the 1960s and 1970s. Several admired films available outside Cuba included *Memories of Underdevelopment* (Tomás Gutiérrez Alea, 1968), a New Wave-like exploration of the psychological condition of Cuban intellectuals at the time of the revolution; *Lucia* (Humberto Solas, 1969), a widely praised three-part study of Cuban womanhood; and *First Charge of the Machete* (Manuel Octavio Gomez, 1969), a stylized depiction of the uprising of 1868.

Other Latin American countries contributed to the repertory of Third World classics on a more limited scale. Notable were *Blood of the Condor* (Bolivia, Jorge Sanjines, 1969) and *The Hour of the Furnaces* (Argentina, Fernando Solanas and Octavio Getino, 1968).

English-language Canadian cinema has always suffered from the proximity of the United States. It wasn't until 1974 that a native English-language Canadian feature (Ted Kotcheff's *The Apprenticeship of Duddy Kravitz*) was able to gross enough in Canadian theaters to pay its own way. French-language cinema, however, enjoyed some success in the sixties and early seventies. Claude Jutra's *A Tout Prendre* (1963) was a landmark film, as was his *Mon Oncle Antoine* (1971), one of the first Québecois films to enjoy some popularity outside Canada.

A few English-language Canadian films also escaped the long border, most notably Irvin Kershner's *The Luck of Ginger Coffey* (1964); Paul Almond's *Act of the Heart* (19/0),

Don Owen's *Nobody Waved Goodbye* (1964); Allan King's *Warrendale* (1967) and *A Married Couple* (1969), two influential documentaries; and Donald Shebib's *Goin' Down the Road* (1970). The avant-garde filmmaker Michael Snow, who has often worked in the U.S., is one of the best known Canadian filmmakers. His most important films are *Wavelength* (1967), ↔ (also called *Back and Forth*, 1969), and *La Région Centrale* (1970)—this last shot in northern Quebec. (See Figures 3-66 and 3-67.)

The business (although not necessarily the art) of Canadian film experienced explosive growth starting in 1978 and 1979 when tax laws made it profitable to invest in Canadian productions. By selling public subscriptions in the stock of the film (much as if the movie were a new manufacturing venture), Canadian producers pioneered a form of financing which became standard operating procedure in the 1980s. Most of the films produced under this system were unexceptionable internationalist grist, but a few, like Darryl Duke's *Silent Partner* (1979) attracted critical attention as well, and the tax breaks that were granted to investors who lost money on Canadian productions at least resulted in a large number of Canadian actors and technicians being able to work at home—for a while.

While Toronto and Vancouver became established as hospitable production centers during this period, they quickly became extensions of Hollywood. Meanwhile, Canadian filmmakers—producers, directors, actors—moved in large numbers to Los Angeles, where they found considerable success. Perhaps the most notable émigré has been Ivan Reitman (*Animal House*, 1978; *Twins*, 1988; *Dave*, 1993), whose *Ghostbusters* (1984) became an icon of 1980s culture around the world.

Australian cinema came of age in the late 1970s. Although there was an honorable tradition of Australian film, productions seldom made the ocean crossing (even if, occasionally, Americans and Europeans journeyed to Australia to exploit its natural wonders). An active government program instituted in the mid-seventies, however, soon resulted in a number of interesting Australian talents coming to international attention at festivals, then in commercial distribution. The most commercial of the new group was Peter Weir, whose apocalyptic fantasies, *The Last Wave* (1978) and *Picnic at Hanging Rock* (1977), provided fashionable metaphors for the peculiar, stereotyped psychology that non-Australian audiences like to think characterizes the edge of the world. Phillip Noyce's *Newsfront* (1977) was an unusual film, part documentary, part fiction, that described the lives of newsreel cameramen during the forties and fifties. Fred Schepisi's *The Chant of Jimmie Blacksmith* (1978); Gillian Armstrong's *My Brilliant Career* (1978), based on an autobiographical novel about a young woman's fantasies of civilized success while growing up in the wild outback at the turn of the century; and Bruce Beresford's *Breaker Morant* (1980), about an incident in the Boer War, all led to international careers. All now work part-time in the States. Weir directed *Witness* (1985) and *Dead Poets Society* (1989), as well as the remarkable *The Truman Show* (1998). It

Figure 4-67. Judy Davis and Sam Neill in Gillian Armstrong's *My Brilliant Career*, one of the new wave of Australian films to garner worldwide attention in the late seventies.

amounts to an interesting body of work. Noyce was responsible for *Patriot Games* (1992) and *Sliver* (1993). Schepisi shot *Plenty* (1985), *Roxanne* (1987), and *Six Degrees of Separation* (1993). Armstrong is best known for *Mrs. Soffel* (1984), and Beresford for *Tender Mercies* (1982) and *Driving Miss Daisy* (1989).

The African cinema has so far produced at least one filmmaker of international standing, Ousmane Sembène, whose films were regularly seen in Europe and the U.S. Among the most important were *Black Girl* (1965), *Mandabi* (1970), and *Xala* (1974). Senegalese, Sembène was a novelist as well as a filmmaker. Film industries of considerable size exist in Algeria, Egypt, Nigeria, and Tunisia. *Countdown at Kusini* (1976), directed by Ossie Davis, was the first Black American–Nigerian coproduction.

Japanese cinema continued to expand its international influence during the sixties and seventies. Kurosawa completed *High and Low* in 1963, *Red Beard* in 1965, *Dodes 'Kaden* in 1970, and *Dersu Uzala* in 1975. Among the more interesting younger directors of the sixties and seventies was Hiroshi Teshigahara, whose *Woman in the Dunes* (1964) quickly became a classic of allegorical cinema and whose *Summer Soldiers* (1971) was a unique cross-cultural attempt at treating the subject of American deserters from Vietnam residing in Japan. Nagisa Oshima may have been the first Japanese filmmaker to have made a complete break with the past. He was certainly one of the most important of the new generation. His films include *Diary of a Shinjuku Burglar* (1968), *Boy* (1969), and *The Ceremony*

Figure 4-68. Ousmane Sembène's *Xala* (1974), from the director's own novel, satirizes and criticizes the growth of a pompous, venal governmental bourgeoisie in emerging African nations. It created a furor when it was released in Senegal. (*New Yorker Films.*)

(1971). His international fame, however, is based on his 1977 succès de scandale, the sexually exploitative *In the Realm of the Senses.*

Southeast Asian cinema blossomed in the sixties and seventies. Filipino blood epics were regularly exported to the U.S. and Europe. Hong Kong cinema gave us the Martial Arts genre, an enormously successful type of film worldwide since the late sixties and seventies. King Hu (*Dragon Gate Inn,* 1966; *A Touch of Zen,* 1969, 1975; *The Fate of Lee Khan,* 1970) made a personal mark.

The New Wave had a practical as well as esthetic effect on French cinema. Godard, Truffaut, Chabrol, and the others had demonstrated that it was possible to make films inexpensively, whether directed toward a commercial audience or toward a minority audience. The spread of cinema into countries that previously could never have afforded the capital expense is one salient result of the new economy of film. Another, perhaps even more telling, is the vigorous eclecticism that sprang up in French cinema in the 1970s. During this period, French film rediscovered a sense of social values that had been lacking since World War II.

Marcel Ophuls's extraordinary historical document, the 4 1/2-hour *The Sorrow and the Pity* (1971), was a landmark of this new awareness. Documenting with panache and intelligence the true nature of French collaboration with their Nazi occupiers during World War II, it had a deep effect on French sensibilities. One of

Figure 4-69. "Neo-New Wave": Jean Eustache's *The Mother and the Whore* (1973): two actors whose careers began in the early days of the New Wave, Bernadette Lafont and Jean-Pierre Léaud, in a rigorous, demanding, witty psychodrama. (*New Yorker Films.*)

the results was a whole cycle of Occupation films during the early seventies, the most interesting of which were Malle's *Lacombe, Lucien* and Michel Mitrani's *Les Guichets du Louvre* (1974). Ophuls's *Memory of Justice* (1976), an investigation into the Nuremberg trials following World War II, was an equally subtle film essay.

Jean Eustache's *The Mother and the Whore* (1973) marked the end of the New Wave, esthetically. Eustache was able, during 3 1/2 hours of intense cinema, to capture, examine, and parody not only many of the conventions of the now old New Wave, but also that particular atmosphere that surrounds and sometimes suffocates French intellectuals. Maurice Pialat, middle-aged when he made his first film, *L'Enfance nue* (*Me,* 1968), became one of the more innovative directors working in commercial cinema. *La Gueule ouverte* (1975), *Nous ne vieillirons pas ensemble* (1972), and *À nos amours* (1983) were absorbing studies of the way we live now. Nelly Kaplan's *A Very Curious Girl* (1969) was also of interest in this respect.

Jean-Louis Bertucelli directed several of the more interesting "new realist" films. *Ramparts of Clay* (1970), *Paulina 1880* (1972), and *Mistaken Love Story* (1974) dealt with a variety of political situations (respectively, Algeria at the point of independence, nineteenth-century feminism, and contemporary sexual politics) with

Figure 4-70. The Jerry Lewis-style open set for Godard's *Tout va bien* (1972) becomes a concrete representation of the structure of a factory organization. The poster declares: "It's right to lock up the bosses, UNLIMITED STRIKE." *Tout va bien* was the practical result of Godard's five-year period of experimentation with film form with his "Dziga-Vertov Group." (*New Yorker Films. Frame enlargement.*)

unusual intelligence. Pascal Aubier, in *Valparaiso, Valparaiso* (1971) and *Le Chant du départ* (1975), extended allegorical techniques to political subjects. At the same time, several filmmakers returned to more traditional, humanistic portraits. Pascal Thomas (*Les Zozos*, 1973; *Don't Cry with Your Mouth Full*, 1974) and Claudine Guilmain (*Véronique, ou l'été de mes treize ans*, 1975) were among the more promising.

Soon after this flurry of activity, French cinema settled down to do what it does best: middle-class romance. Jean-Charles Tacchella's *Cousin, cousine* (1975) was released in the U.S. two years later and broke the foreign-film box-office record of *A Man and a Woman*, a record that had stood for more than ten years. This extraordinary performance was exceeded in 1979 by Edouard Molinaro's *La Cage aux folles*, an amusing if small story about a homosexual ménage.

Bertrand Tavernier also garnered some international success with a quick series of well-mounted melodramas in the late seventies. Tavernier's first successful export was released in 1975 as *The Clockmaker*. The screenwriters for that film were two men named Jean Aurenche and Pierre Bost—precisely the two whom, twenty years earlier, François Truffaut had castigated in his famous essay on the cinéma du papa. The irony was lost on the new generation of filmgoers who responded just as nicely to this current wave of well-made *petits drames* as their parents had to similar fare in the fifties.

Esthetically, the most important French innovator of the 1970s was Jean-Marie Straub, who, with his wife and collaborator Danièle Huillet, developed a type of Materialist cinema that made its mark on the avant garde. Although French by birth, Straub has worked in the German language and mainly with German money. *The Chronicle of Anna Magdalena Bach* (1967), *Othon* (1970), *History Lessons* (1972), and *Moses and Aaron* (1975), his version of Schönberg's opera, are austere experiments in narrative modes and essays in esthetic theory that, although they were never appreciated by general audiences, nevertheless served as an inspiration to the filmmakers of the Neue Kino, the new German cinema that came into being in the late sixties and gained quite an international reputation through film festivals in the seventies.

Alexander Kluge was the first of this informal group to turn to film. *Yesterday Girl* (1966), *Artists Under the Big Top: Perplexed* (1968), *Part-time Work of a Domestic Slave* (1974), and *Strongman Ferdinand* (1975) exhibited a political drive couched in cold wit.

Volker Schlöndorff's cinema is also broadly political in nature, but Schlöndorff exhibits both a greater cinematic facility and less simplistic logic. *Young Törless* (1966) was a version of the Robert Musil psychological novel; *The Sudden Wealth of the Poor People of Kombach* (1971), a Brechtian medieval morality tale. Working with his wife, Margarethe von Trotta, Schlöndorff next made *Strohfeuer* (*A Free Woman*, 1972), a feminist film that enjoyed some commercial success. On her own, von Trotta is best known for broad studies of political themes (*Marianne and Julianne*, 1981; *Rosa Luxemburg*, 1985).

Schlöndorff and von Trotta's *The Lost Honor of Katharina Blum* (1975, from the novel by Heinrich Böll) was a major document of modern German politics and a distinct popular success because it confronted the right-wing, jingoist press lord Axel Springer directly. In 1979 Schlöndorff completed his film version of *The Tin Drum*, Günter Grass's classic postwar novel. Schlöndorff's elegant and inspired version of that parabolic masterpiece met with due international acclaim, including the first U.S. Academy Award ever granted a German film. In a dramatic acceptance speech, Schlöndorff accepted the aptly-named Oscar not only for himself and for the young generation of German filmmakers but also, as he put it movingly, "for Fritz Lang, Billy Wilder, Lubitsch, Murnau, Pabst—you know them all! You welcomed them!"

In the 1970s, Rainer Werner Fassbinder was the best known practitioner of the Neue Kino. Combining careers in the theater, television, and cinema, he completed more than forty films before his death in 1982 at age thirty-seven. His earlier, more political films—*Why Did Herr R. Run Amok?* (1969), *The Merchant of Four Seasons* (1971), for example—may be of greater interest than *The Bitter Tears of*

Figure 4-71. Angela Winkler in Schlöndorff's and von Trotta's *The Lost Honor of Katharina Blum* (1975): the political face of New German Cinema.

Petra von Kant (1972), *Fear Eats the Soul* (1973), and *Fox* (1974). The later films, although more popular, show more of the camp influence of Douglas Sirk and are generally more involuted. After numerous television films, Fassbinder made his first English-language film in 1978: *Despair,* from a screenplay by Tom Stoppard of the novel by Vladimir Nabokov. Despite those impressive literary antecedents, it did not establish him as an international director. In 1979, *The Marriage of Maria Braun* (in German once again) enjoyed considerable success and appealed to more general audiences. *Berlin Alexanderplatz* (1980), his fifteen-hour television series, marked the apex of his brief career.

Werner Herzog is the least classifiable of the group. *Even Dwarfs Started Small* (1970) and *Fata Morgana* (1971) were ineffable experiments, while *Land of Silence and Darkness* (1971) and *Every Man for Himself and God against All* (*Kaspar Hauser,* 1974) are much more lucid, the former a study of the world of the deaf-mute, the latter Herzog's version of the wolf child/noble savage legend. Herzog concentrates on human beings in extreme situations, almost as if he were an experimental anthropologist. *Aguirre, the Wrath of God* (1972) studies an obsessive Spanish explorer in the New World on a trip up an increasingly alien river. Many critics compared it favorably to its not-dissimilar but far more expensive successor *Apoca-*

lypse Now, as a study of the psyche under pressure. *Heart of Glass* (1977) was a hermetic, abstract essay on the mysteries of medieval glassworkers, while *Stroszek* (1977) was a much more accessible portrait of a simpleminded European confronting American culture. *Little Dieter Needs to Fly* (1997), the story of a pilot and prisoner of war, combined many of these themes.

In the 1970s the most underrated of the group of new German directors was probably Wim Wenders. Direct rather than cloying (as Kluge, Herzog, and especially Fassbinder sometimes seemed to be), Wenders made a number of low-key yet intense films in which human concerns rather than style held center stage. Among these were *The Goalie's Anxiety at the Penalty Kick* (1971), which, like *Wrong Movement* (1975), had a script by playwright Peter Handke, *Alice in the Cities* (1974), and *Kings of the Road* (1975). *The American Friend* (1977), an international coproduction that deftly summarized his themes of alienation and American-European cultural intercourse, found an audience in the U.S. Shortly after completing this remarkable film, Wenders was "discovered" by Francis Ford Coppola, who signed him to direct *Hammett* (released 1983)—and also named a San Francisco restaurant after "Wim." The romance didn't last. Little of Wenders's work remained when the film was finally released. But Wenders did get to make his American film, *Paris, Texas* (1984), from a script by Sam Shepard. Wenders later had an international hits with *Wings of Desire* (1987), a wistful elegy, and *Buena Vista Social Club* (1998), a celebration of Cuban music.

Coppola was also instrumental in gaining some critical and popular attention for Hans-Jürgen Syberberg, certainly the most abstruse of the German filmmakers of the 1970s. In 1979 Syberberg's magnum opus, *Our Hitler: A Film from Germany*, seven hours in length, was screened to eager audiences in San Francisco and New York. Entirely lacking in discipline and only at times exhibiting the shadow of intelligence, *Our Hitler* amounted to very little beyond its avant-garde hype.

The renaissance of Swiss cinema was one of the more attractive developments of the seventies. The films of Alain Tanner (*Charles, Mort ou vif*, 1969; *La Salamandre*, 1971; *Retour d'Afrique*, 1973; *The Middle of the World*, 1974) display a unique mixture of traditional dramatic narrative and sophisticated mise-en-scène. *Jonah, Who Will Be 25 in the Year 2000* (1976), a wry, humane, and very wise political allegory, was one of the more important social documents of the 1970s, considering its perceptive comments on the cultural and political fallout of the events of 1968. Claude Goretta's films (*L'Invitation*, 1972; *Pas si méchant que ça*, 1975) were shaggy dog stories of particular charm. Michel Soutter managed to combine a bit of Goretta's charm with Tanner's politics in *James ou pas* (1970), *Les Arpenteurs* (1972), and *L'Escapade* (1973). The films of all three directors were pleasantly reminiscent of the spirit of the early New Wave.

Figure 4-72. Alain Tanner's *Jonah Who Will Be 25 in the Year 2000* remains one of the most significant films of the seventies, a warm, heartfelt investigation of the way we lived then—and the way we still might.

American cinema also saw an explosion of talent in the late sixties and early seventies, but unlike French and German new cinema it was highly commercial. The concept of genre remained strong. Gangsters and Musicals were hard to find in the seventies, but they were replaced by a series of new genres, including the Chase film, the Road film, the Nostalgia film, the Hollywood film (about the golden days of yesteryear), the Martial Arts film (usually imported—*Variety* called this genre "Chop Socky"), the respectable Porn film, and—most profitable of all in the mid-seventies—the Disaster film. Significantly, all of these invented genres were narrower in scope; none offered as wide an opportunity for self-expression as, say, the Western or the Film Noir. While the new genres were of some interest, the most important innovation in the U.S. in the 1970s was the Black film, a wide category that included a great deal of cheap material ("Blaxploitation" in *Variety*'s parlance) but also a number of films of lasting value. By the end of the decade, Black film had almost disappeared from the Hollywood scene, but it was to rise again with renewed energy in the 1990s.

Melvin Van Peebles, deciding that he wanted to be a filmmaker, went to France to accomplish his aim. After making one film there (*Story of a Three-Day Pass*, 1967) he returned to the U.S. and was able, having proved himself abroad, to obtain a Hollywood contract. The result was a fairly weak comedy, *The Watermelon Man* (1969). His third film, however, the independently produced *Sweet Sweetback's Baadasssss Song* (1971) is still the purest Black film, in terms of esthetics, that has yet been made—a shriek of pain that is also an object lesson in Black survival in America. Having conquered Hollywood, Van Peebles turned his attention to the stage in the seventies, playing a major role in the development of the Black musical theater (*Ain't Supposed to Die a Natural Death, Don't Play Us Cheap*), which remains a strong and profitable component of the Broadway repertoire. Apparently bored with the worlds of stage and film, Van Peebles next moved to Wall Street, the place to be in the eighties. He authored *Bold Money: A New Way to Play the Options Market* (1986). In the late eighties, he returned to film, working with his son Mario.

Gordon Parks Sr had been a widely respected photographer for *Life* magazine and an author when he decided to break the race barrier in film. His first film, based on his autobiography, *The Learning Tree* (1968), was a visually stunning essay on his Kansas childhood, but too static for audiences accustomed to regularly timed stimulation. Parks satisfied that commercial requirement with his next film, *Shaft* (1970), which was the founding example of the Black Action genre that was commercially so popular in the early seventies. After a few more similar ventures, Parks returned to a more personal subject with *Leadbelly* (1976), a biography of the Blues singer and a major film in the short history of the new Black cinema.

Bill Gunn was responsible for one of the most original and exciting films of the seventies—*Ganja and Hess* (1973)—which started out as a Black vampire exploitation vehicle but became much more than that. Although it won awards at Cannes that year, the film was shelved by its distributor and has hardly been seen. Novelist (*Rhinestone Sharecropping*), playwright (*Black Picture Show,* 1975), screenwriter (*The Angel Levine,* 1970), and television producer (*Johannas,* 1972; *The Alberta Hunter Story,* 1982), Gunn died in 1989.

In the late sixties, it looked as if a new generation of young American filmmakers would be able, like their European counterparts, to move onward to a more personal cinema. Building on the examples of independent directors like Arthur Penn (*Bonnie & Clyde,* 1967; *Alice's Restaurant,* 1969; *Little Big Man,* 1970; *Night Moves,* 1975) and Frank and Eleanor Perry (*David and Lisa,* 1962; *Diary of a Mad Housewife,* 1972), the younger Americans, many of them trained in film schools, looked toward a cinema that would be less dominated by commercial considerations than Hollywood had been in its great days.

The key film for the new generation was *The Graduate*. Upon its release during the "Summer of Love" in 1967 it was immediately perceived as the emblem of the sixties generation—by then in full revolt against their parents' culture. Directed by Mike Nichols from a screenplay by Buck Henry and Calder Willing-

Figure 4-73. BLACK CINEMA. Bill Gunn and Duane Jones in Gunn's remarkable *Ganja and Hess* (1973), part vampire movie, part anthropological analysis of the myth. (*MOMA/FSA.*)

ham (based on a novel by Charles Webb) *The Graduate* rocketed Dustin Hoffman to stardom. The famous refrain from the Simon & Garfunkel soundtrack hung in the air for more than thirty years:

> Where are you now, Joe Dimaggio?
> A nation turns its lonely eyes to you....
> Woo, woo, woo.[*]

The irony of those lyrics—Joe was, of course, the hero of their parents' generation—was lost on the young audiences of the time. Some would figure it out later, as the Summer of Love drifted into smoky memory, the tie-dyed tees were exiled to the attic, the music died—and they became their parents.

Mike Nichols was several years older than the generation of the sixties that would take command of Hollywood in the years succeeding *The Graduate*. He was a product of the Beatnik years of the fifties, not the Hippie years, and as a child-hood refugee from Nazism was further isolated. He has maintained that outsider status for more than thirty years. It has given him a unique perspective as a film-maker and resulted in several films that will be required viewing for history students of the future trying to understand the postmodern culture of the late twentieth century.

---

[*] "Mrs. Robinson" © 1967 Paul Simon, Charing Cross Music. Used with permission.

Figure 4-74. *The Graduate.* Dustin Hoffman and Anne Bancroft: a learning experience.

Nichols and his partner Elaine May first rose to prominence in 1961 as the creators of the Broadway hit *An Evening with Nichols and May,* a review based on their standup comedy routines. It was the first of his cultural landmarks, announcing a new sophistication and resonance for the art of standup comedy that has become one of the pillars of American culture. In a few years he was directing theater in New York, then landed his first film assignment with *Who's Afraid of Virginia Woolf?* (1966) from the landmark Edward Albee play, starring the reigning Hollywood royal couple of the day, Elizabeth Taylor and Richard Burton. He followed *The Graduate* with *Catch-22* (1970). The Joseph Heller black comedy had been the key novel for the postwar generation that had come of age in the fifties and early sixties. *Carnal Knowledge* (1971), starring Art Garfunkel and Jack Nicholson, extended the discussion of the sexual revolution that had begun in *The Graduate.*

Over the next twenty years Nichols directed some interesting films (*The Fortune*; 1975; *Silkwood*, 1983; *Working Girl*; 1988) but he had fallen out of favor with the critics—essentially because he had no recognizable personal style; he was not an "auteur." In the late 1990s he began working again with Elaine May. They scored big in 1998 with *Primary Colors,* based on the Joe Klein novel about the 1992 Clinton campaign, and debuting just in time for the Monica Lewinsky media circus. John Travolta's resonant portrait of Bill Clinton is likely to remain the definitive character of the 1990s for some time.

Figure 4-75. Emma Thompson and John Travolta in *Primary Colors*. They feel our pain.

Coming from the world of theater, Nichols was not what film critics of the late 1960s were expecting. Everyone knew what had happened in France ten years earlier—when the critics of *Cahiers du Cinéma* had exchanged their typewriters for cameras—and expected history to repeat itself. When precocious film critic Peter Bogdanovich inveigled production funds out of Roger Corman for his first film, *Targets* (1968), and when writers and *Esquire* magazine trend-setters Robert Benton and David Newman sold their script for *Bonnie & Clyde* to Hollywood, everyone thought the American "New Wave" had begun.

Bogdanovich enjoyed some success in the early 1970s echoing his heroes from the Golden Age (*The Last Picture Show*, 1971; *What's Up, Doc?*, 1972; *Paper Moon*, 1973), then lost his bankability. Separately Benton and Newman went on to long and distinguished careers as director and screenwriter, respectively. But few other critics managed to join the movement (Paul Schrader and Andrew Bergman had published their dissertations, Jay Cocks had written for *Time*). The American renaissance was born in film schools, not critical journals.

The films produced by the independent company BBS were among the first to announce a new style: *Easy Rider* (1969, directed by actor Dennis Hopper), *Five Easy Pieces* (1970, Bob Rafelson), *A Safe Place* (1971, Henry Jaglom), *Drive, He Said* (1971, Jack Nicholson). Yet the commercial success of *Easy Rider* led only to the short-lived Youth genre, and even Rafelson, the most accomplished of the group, was only able to complete two films in the next seven years: *The King of Marvin Gardens* (1972) and *Stay Hungry* (1976). Monte Hellman, another director associated with the BBS group, had been responsible for two remarkable Westerns in the mid-sixties (*The Shooting, Ride the Whirlwind*) and made one of the best films of the seventies—and certainly the superior Road film—in *Two-Lane Blacktop* (1970), but was able to put together only one project in the six years that followed. Filmmakers who tried to maintain a personal vision while learning to work within the studio system had better success at getting their films made.

Coming out of NYU film school, Martin Scorsese began with two unusual independent productions (*Who's That Knocking at My Door?*, 1967 and *Mean Streets*, 1973) but then produced two films that, while seemingly independent in style, nevertheless fit Hollywood patterns neatly: *Alice Doesn't Live Here Anymore* (1974) and *Taxi Driver* (1976). *New York, New York* (1977) was an ambitious attempt to rework 1940s Musical style that never found its audience, while *The Last Waltz* (1978), an elegantly filmed record of The Band's farewell concert, achieved some critical and commercial success. Scorsese hit his stride in the eighties with a string of increasingly ambitious and interesting films. As the more famous filmmakers of his generation succumbed to habits, he broke new ground with *Raging Bull* (1980), based on the autobiography of boxer Jake LaMotta, a raw, visceral cry from the heart filmed in black and white. *The King of Comedy* (1983), *After Hours* (1985), *The Color of Money* (1986) and *The Last Temptation of Christ* (1988) followed. It is hard to imagine a more varied group of films: a dark comic essay on celebrity; a shoestring production of a student script; a big-star sequel to a classic film noir (*The Hustler*); and a modern biblical epic based on the controversial novel by Nikos Kazantzakis.

Scorsese's output in the 1990s was equally diverse and exploratory. Yet another collaboration with Robert De Niro, *Goodfellas* (1990) reinvented the Gangster genre mixing equal parts of humor, mundane anxiety, and terror. The two collaborators next turned to a Hollywood-style remake of the Film-Noir classic *Cape Fear* (1991). *The Age of Innocence* (1993), based on the Edith Wharton novel about New York society in the 1870s, provided a canvas for historical accuracy, while *Casino* (1995) offered another platform for De Niro's gangster persona. Scorsese capped this varied suite of movies with *Kundun* (1997), a mesmeric meditation on the early life of the Dalai Lama. Taken together the films of this twenty-year period constitute a series of virtuoso directorial performances. During this period Scorsese was also active in film preservation and history: *A Personal Journey with Martin Scorsese through American Movies* (1995), his four-hour contribution to the British Film Institute's *A Century of Cinema* series, provided a unique perspective, emphasizing the contributions of independent filmmakers.

The model for the new generation of Hollywood directors in the seventies had been Francis Ford Coppola, who went to work for Roger Corman straight out of

Figure 4-76. Daniel Day-Lewis and Michelle Pfeiffer in Martin Scorsese's *Age of Innocence*, an elegant historical treatment of the Edith Wharton novel which exhibited marvelous attention to detail and demonstrated that Scorsese had a mature stylistic range.

film school in the 1960s, achieved some success as a screenwriter, then produced and directed several personal films, including *The Rain People* (1969) and *The Conversation* (1974). In between, he was responsible for one of the most profitable landmarks of the early seventies, *The Godfather* (1972), which along with its sequels (1975, 1991) is regarded by many critics as the most significant American film of recent years. Such a combination of commercial and critical success is extremely rare.

Coppola next spent close to four years and more than $30 million on *Apocalypse Now* (1979), a stunningly conceived and elegantly filmed attempt to wring some meaning out of Joseph Conrad's *Heart of Darkness* set in the context of the Vietnam war. Critics and audiences seemed to agree that the attempt was not entirely successful. Despite its vividly felt metaphors for the malaise of the American experience in Vietnam—perhaps because of its brilliantly constructed images and sounds—*Apocalypse Now* didn't seem to tell us very much about Vietnam. In 1968, when the idea first occurred to Coppola and John Milius, such a film would have had revolutionary impact. More than ten years later, the postwar generation needed more than the nightmare of war; they needed understanding. It may be asking too much of three hours of film to provide such an analysis, but *Apocalypse*, throughout its agonizing production schedule, seemed to promise a great deal that it eventually didn't deliver.

Figure 4-77. In *Peggy Sue Got Married* and *Tucker*, Francis Ford Coppola masterfully captured the look and feel of the sixties and the forties at the same time that he crafted eloquent fables to capture the romantic and adventurous myths of those periods that remain with us today. Here, Peggy Sue (Kathleen Turner) is named Queen of her twenty-fifth high school reunion…

Undaunted, Coppola picked himself up quickly and in the spring of 1980 bought the former Samuel Goldwyn Studios in Hollywood. Ten years earlier he had tried with middling success to found an alternative studio in San Francisco. His challenge to the Hollywood power structure—"American Zoetrope"—succeeded mainly behind the scenes as Coppola supported the budding careers of several younger filmmakers. Renamed more ambitiously "Omni Zoetrope," the new studio had an even shorter life span.

Throughout the eighties he experimented with a wide variety of styles, seldom with box office success. *One from the Heart* (1982) was obsessed with computerized special effects many years before they were advanced enough to become commercial. In 1983 *The Outsiders* and *Rumblefish* from the S. E. Hinton youth novels introduced a remarkable number of actors who would dominate Hollywood for the next few years. 1984's *The Cotton Club*, an ambitious re-creation of a special period in American musical history, fell short. But with *Peggy Sue Got Married* (1986) and *Tucker: The Man and His Dream* (1988), a long-delayed project, Coppola realized two remarkable visions. The former was a perfect elegy to the late fifties and early sixties, an emblem for that generation. The latter was the first 1940s movie to be made since *The Godfather*, and a hymn to American entrepreneurship that will grow in importance as it seasons. In 1990, Coppola completed the Godfather trilogy with *Part III*, which met with much less success than its predecessors.

Figure 4-78. ... while Preston Tucker (Jeff Bridges) watches as the first Tuckers roll off the Chicago assembly line.

In the 1990s Coppola had some success as director of *Bram Stoker's Dracula* (1992) and *The Rainmaker* (1997), from the John Grisham courtroom novel, but chose to spend most of his time producing rather than directing.

In this he was not alone. Although the generation of the 1970s came of age at a time when the director had been declared king of the filmmaking hill by auteurist critics on both sides of the Atlantic, all of the major star directors—Spielberg, Coppola, Scorsese, and Lucas—have spent at least as much time producing (and writing) as directing during the last twenty-five years. Indeed, Lucas—arguably the most influential filmmaker of the period—went twenty-two years between directorial assignments. So much for the auteur theory!

Ironically, one of Coppola's earliest protégés, George Lucas, was able to realize his mentor's corporate dream first. After his debut with *THX 1138*, a Science Fiction film produced by Zoetrope that earned very little at the box office, Lucas turned in 1973 to *American Graffiti*, one of the most popular films of the seventies. He followed it in 1977 with *Star Wars*, the highest-grossing film at the time, which, through its lucrative licensing rights (dolls, games, toys, T-shirts), became the foundation of Lucas's own empire: Lucasfilm Ltd. Lucas then abandoned the director's chair to concentrate on producing and managing his company. With the profits from *Star Wars* he built film production facilities in Marin County north of San Francisco from which he has operated ever since.

Throughout the eighties, Lucas prospected in the *Star Wars* goldmine (two sequels) and, together with Steven Spielberg, established the lucrative and entertaining Indiana Jones franchise. Lucas also became increasing involved in the special-effects business, which continued to grow throughout the eighties, largely due to the success of films like the two series he himself was producing. His company Industrial Light & Magic pioneered digital effects and established the THX standard for theatrical sound.

The *Star Wars* series gives us an extensive and knowledgeable catalogue of Hollywood history. Most of its popular elements have direct antecedents in classics of numerous genres that characterized the Golden Age of Hollywood. *Star Wars* isn't just a Science Fiction film, it's also a Western at times, a War movie, a Historical Romance, and so forth. Considering the many details, styles, and tricks of the trade Lucas borrowed from his illustrious predecessors, or paid homage to, it seems only fitting that these films have earned more than any series of films in American history. Lucas had always envisioned the Star Wars saga as a series of nine films, not unlike the Saturday morning serials he remembered from his youth. In 1993 he announced a schedule of three more *Star Wars* pictures. The first of these, *Star Wars: Episode I—The Phantom Menace*, proved a cultural event of the first magnitude when it premiered in the U.S. on 19 May 1999. Fans lined up days before for midnight screenings, and—confronted with the prospect of mass absenteeism—many Silicon Alley companies declared the day a cultural holiday. After all, most of their techie employees had grown up with the *Star Wars* myth; perhaps it helped them to make their career choices.

Neck and neck with Lucas has been Steven Spielberg. *Jaws* (1975) held first place on *Variety*'s list of all-time highest "grosses" for a while before it was displaced by *Star Wars*. Spielberg's own Science Fiction effort, *Close Encounters of the Third Kind*, released at the end of 1977 seven months after *Star Wars*, also ranked near the top of the list. The film *1941* (1979), an attempt at comedy set in that year and an even more expensive film, failed at the box office, bringing Spielberg down to earth for a moment.

He recovered immediately with *Raiders of the Lost Ark* (1981), the first of the Indiana Jones films, and soared again with *E.T.: The Extraterrestrial* (1982). He hasn't left high orbit yet. The eighties were filled with a string of major and minor successes, from *The Color Purple* (1985) and *Empire of the Sun* (1987) to *Always* (1989) and the Indiana Jones sequels (1984, 1989). Like Coppola and Lucas he has been an active producer as well, responsible for the *Back to the Future* series, the *Gremlins* series, and the landmark *Who Framed Roger Rabbit* (1988), among others. No one has had a greater influence on American popular culture during the past twenty-five years than frequent collaborators George Lucas and Steven Spielberg. In 1993 *Jurassic Park* broke the world-wide box-office record, while the remarkable critical reception of *Schindler's List* proved that Spielberg could compete with the best of the world's "serious" filmmakers. As if to reinforce that newfound respect, Spielberg followed up in 1997 with another double-play: the sequel *The Lost World: Jurassic Park* and the thoughtful, eloquent historical drama

Amistad, based on the famous slave rebellion. The next year for the first time he found a subject where he could combine substance and spectacle: *Saving Private Ryan*, a remarkable World War II epic.

Older by a generation than these three director/impresarios, Robert Altman has survived in uneasy alliance with the studios, somehow managing to make his own films his way. He is one of the most original of contemporary filmmakers. His cinema is adventurous: *M*A*S*H* (1970) set the tone for a generation (and secured Altman's artistic freedom in the process). *McCabe and Mrs. Miller* (1971) was certainly the primary Western of the period, just as *The Long Goodbye* (1972) and *Thieves Like Us* (1974) represented original versions of their genres, the Detective film and Film Noir, respectively.

Altman's greatest achievement of the 1970s was *Nashville* (1975), an extraordinarily original film that touched mythic roots in the Bicentennial consciousness. *Buffalo Bill and the Indians* (1976) also raised some interesting questions about the American way of life. Perhaps Altman's main contribution to the "New Hollywood" has been his method of working. While star directors painstakingly labor over their would-be masterpieces for years on end, Altman churned out movies at the rate of one every nine months during his heyday in the seventies. They seldom made much money, but on average they paid for themselves. Sometimes they were interesting (*A Wedding*, 1978), sometimes they were charming (*A Perfect Couple*, 1979), and occasionally they were abysmally arty (*Quintet*, 1978), but they were almost always infused with a love of the medium and a humane intelligence—and there were so many of them!

Altman broke stride in the eighties, selling his Lion's Gate studio base, turning his attention to the theater and directing a few films based on plays before returning with considerable fanfare with 1992's *The Player*, a tour de force satire of contemporary Hollywood riddled with inside jokes and right on the money. *Short Cuts*, released in 1993, met with mixed reactions, but he was back in form with *Ready To Wear* (1994), a satire on the fashion industry, and *Cookie's Fortune* (1999), an audience-pleasing comedy.

John Cassavetes, who had foreshadowed the independence of contemporary directors with his landmark *Shadows* (1959), returned to independent production ten years later with *Faces* (1968). He followed with *Husbands* (1970), *Minnie and Moskowitz* (1971), and *A Woman under the Influence* (1974), his most popular film, then several examinations of the art of acting seen only by conscientious Cassavetes devotees (among them *The Killing of a Chinese Bookie*, 1976, a film of some interest). Despite a difficult style, dependent on improvisation and intense relationships between actors, Cassavetes was able to finance and complete his films without recourse to studio money. As an accomplished professional actor who was able to maintain a productive parallel life as an independent director, John Cassavetes held a unique place in modern American film history. He died in 1989.

Figure 4-79. In 1993, Steven Spielberg accomplished a remarkable coup, releasing both a monster blockbuster (*Jurassic Park*) heavily dependent on advanced special effects and a lengthy Academy-Award-winning elegy dealing with a difficult subject and dependent mainly on intelligent dialogue. Here, the classical monster threatens, in a surprisingly disjointed film that seemed to have its eye on the sequel—or perhaps its own theme park...

Paul Mazursky was one of the key filmmakers to come of age in the 1970s who managed to live more or less successfully within the studio system. Mazursky concentrated on the human comedy in a long string of interesting films. *Bob & Carol & Ted & Alice* (1969), *Alex in Wonderland* (1970), *Blume in Love* (1973), *Harry and Tonto* (1974), and *Next Stop, Greenwich Village* (1976) all displayed a quiet humor at the same time as they limned contemporary lifestyles. *An Unmarried Woman* (1978) was Mazursky's most popular film, catching the feminist wave at its crest. *Willie and Phil* (1980) was a summary of his concerns and an interesting attempt to comment on its spiritual source, Truffaut's classic *Jules and Jim*. In the eighties, Mazursky continued on track with *Tempest* (1982, an audacious reworking of Shakespeare), *Moscow on the Hudson* (1984, Robin Williams as a Russian immigrant), and *Enemies, a Love Story* (1989), a resonant memory of the shadow the Holocaust cast on New York. Mazursky was an actor and standup comic in the fifties and sixties. His first film was Stanley Kubrick's *Fear and Desire* (1953); he also had a role in Richard Brooks's seminal *The Blackboard Jungle* (1955). In the

Figure 4-80. … while Liam Neeson as Schindler—a greedy man with a warm heart, and therefore an irresistible character—says goodbye to the "Schindlerjuden." Leave it to Spielberg to find a positive character in the midst of the Third Reich.

1990s, he did more acting than directing—although his 1998 HBO biopic *Winchell* was well-received.

One of the more underrated directors of the 1970s, Michael Ritchie—in *Downhill Racer* (1969), *The Candidate* (1972), *Smile* (1975), *Bad News Bears* (1976), and *Semi-Tough* (1977)—combined documentary techniques with fictional structures to achieve an unusual blend. *Prime Cut* (1972) remains a witty metaphor for modern America that is still relevant and that should be more widely appreciated.

No one has been more successful at controlling the content and form of his films than Woody Allen, who, after completing a string of comic successes in the early seventies (*Bananas*, 1971; *Sleeper*, 1973; *Love and Death*, 1975), discovered new resonance and new critical attention in 1977 with *Annie Hall*. He followed this with an ill-advised "serious" mock-European essay in intellectual angst, *Interiors* (1978)—whose main effect was to make it difficult to take Woody's mentor Ingmar Bergman seriously again—but snapped back into form with *Manhattan* (1979). Allen then cruised through the eighties, producing a remarkably consistent body of work whose highlights included *Stardust Memories* (1980), *Zelig* (1983), *Broadway Danny Rose* (1984), *The Purple Rose of Cairo* (1985), *Hannah and Her Sisters* (1986), *Radio Days* (1987), and *Alice* (1990), all of which were informed by Allen's quintessentially New York intellectual sensibility. In 1992 he hit a rough patch when his relationship with Mia Farrow became fodder for the television tabloids, and reality proved much stranger than fiction. But—together again with Diane Keaton (who had brought a unique presence to *Annie Hall*)—he returned to form with *Manhattan Murder Mystery* (1993). *Bullets Over Broadway* (1994) and *Mighty Aphrodite* (1995) were lightweight comedies, but garnered an impressive number of Oscar nominations between them. Allen's first musical comedy *Everyone Says I Love You* (1996) was nearly as popular, but the old angst surfaced again in *Deconstructing Harry* (1997) and *Celebrity* (1998), which both met with decidedly mixed reviews. Nevertheless, Woody Allen has managed over three decades to make his kind of movies his way: a remarkably independent artist in an industry that does not prize that quality.

While Allen, Altman, Bogdanovich, Cassavetes, Coppola, Lucas, Mazursky, Nichols, Scorsese, Spielberg, and Ritchie—the pantheon of American film in the seventies—seemed to rise above the general run of American directors, there are others from this period whose work also has lasted. Alan J. Pakula, Sydney Pollack, John Korty, Philip Kaufman, Hal Ashby, and Mel Brooks all fall into this category.

The documentary fared well in the seventies, too. Besides the filmmakers already mentioned above, Haskell Wexler, Saul Landau, Peter Davis, and Emile De Antonio should be cited. Wexler, an accomplished cinematographer, directed one of the most significant films of the 1960s, *Medium Cool* (1969), which skillfully combined the heartbreak of the 1968 Democratic convention in Chicago with an incisive essay on the relationship between the media and politics.

Landau was responsible for a number of salient nonfiction films (*Interview with President Allende, Report on Torture in Brazil,* both 1971), often working with Wexler. De Antonio specialized in the compilation film, building politically pointed essays out of material shot by other people: *Point of Order* (1963), on the Army-McCarthy hearings, *Millhouse* (1971), about Richard Nixon, and *Painters Painting* (1972), his only nonpolitical film. De Antonio and Wexler combined to film *Underground* in 1976, a film about U.S. political fugitives of the anti-war Weather organization.

Peter Davis's documentary essay about the painful relationship between the U.S. and Vietnam, *Hearts and Minds* (1975), annoyed some viewers because it seemed to be partisan, but remains one of the most remarkable American nonfiction films since 1960. It not only presented much important information visually, but also because it was passionate about its subject it had an emotional as well as intellectual effect on its audiences. Sadly, the film was seen only in the last months of the war, when it was already finally clear, after ten years, that U.S. intervention had been a tragic mistake.

The documentary format also proved to be a comfortable ground for a number of women directors in the seventies: Joyce Chopra, Martha Coolidge, Julia

Figure 4-81. *The Player*, Robert Altman's long-awaited return to form, proved an infectious satire on today's Hollywood, rich with inside jokes but at the same time not dependent on them. Here Studio Exec Tim Robbins gets the message. (*© 1992 Fine Line Features. All rights reserved. Photo by Joyce Rudolph. Courtesy New Line Productions, Inc.*)

Reichert, Amalie Rothschild, Claudia Weill, Nell Cox, Cinda Firestone, Barbara Kopple, and others. Most of these directors found the autobiographical format useful to investigate feminist issues. In 1978 Claudia Weill made an impressive feature debut with *Girl Friends,* an independent production that displayed the sort of direct sensitivity and unvarnished style that marked the independent nonfiction film in the late seventies. In the eighties she reached a wide audience as a director of the landmark television series *thirtysomething.* Chopra, Coolidge, and Reichert followed similar paths, combining the occasional feature with more or less steady work in television. Rothschild, Cox, and Kopple continued to make documentaries.

Among the wealth of nonfiction films made both for theatrical distribution and television airing in the late 1970s three historical studies might be singled out for special attention.

Barbara Kopple's 1976 *Harlan County, U.S.A.* gave us a vivid and moving portrait of the women and men who were still struggling for better working conditions in that mining center forty years after the great labor battles of the thirties earned their county the nickname "Bloody Harlan." Kopple didn't use the real people to make political points, she gave them the freedom to discover their own view of the truth to us and, in the process, ordinary people (albeit with extraordinary stamina, dedication, and humor) became movie stars for a brief time. The film—which won the first of Kopple's two Academy Awards—served as a model for the dramatic documentary style of the late seventies and eighties.

With Babies and Banners (1978, Lorraine Gray, Anne Bohlen, Lyn Goldfarb) documented the story of the Women's Emergency Brigade during the General Motors sit-down strike of 1937 with rare historical footage and affectionate interviews with the same women at a reunion forty years later.

The Wobblies (1979, Stewart Bird, Deborah Shaffer) similarly combined historical footage and contemporary interviews to shed new light on the Industrial Workers of the World and its struggles during the early years of this century. The survivors Bird and Shaffer discovered were by then almost all over eighty. Both films showed how the medium can be used to great effect for historical purposes.

The spirit of vivid historical and political research that these films evinced has continued and even thrived, but since 1980 it has been more a feature of television than of theatrical film, as news-magazine shows have thrived.

The Postmodern Sequel: Democracy, Technology, End of Cinema

It is the salient fact about the 1980s and the 1990s that no new generation of young turks arose to challenge the cinema of the 1970s. Despite the vast changes in the business (and the world) in the past twenty years, with movies it's been more of the same: *Star Wars* then; *Star Wars* now; more *Star Wars* later. Essentially there has been little new to report since the second edition of this book appeared in 1981.

Sequelmania remains the watchword, at least of the American film industry, and every producer's dream is a "franchise" film, one whose situation, storyline, and characters lend themselves to a series. It is unlikely that any producer will beat Albert "Cubby" Broccoli's record: James Bond began in 1962 with *Dr. No*, and has continued for more than thirty-five years and six Bond incarnations. (Only Sherlock Holmes has been played by more actors.) But action series like *48 Hours, Beverly Hills Cop, Lethal Weapon,* and *Die Hard*, and Science Fiction franchises like *Star Trek* and *Aliens* aimed to give Bond a run for his money.[*]

When Hollywood isn't making sequels, it's doing remakes, often of television shows (*The Fugitive, The Beverly Hillbillies*, 1993; *The Flintstones*, 1994; *The Brady Bunch Movie*, 1995; *Mission: Impossible, Sgt. Bilko*, 1996; *Lost in Space*, 1998; *My Favor-*

---

[*] Notable in this group is *Alien*, both because its hero is a woman (Sigourney Weaver) and because it wins the prize for creative series titling: *Alien, Aliens, Alien³, Alien Resurrection.*

Figure 4-82. Woody Allen's black-and-white romantic fantasy of his home town, *Manhattan* (1979), emphasized the mythic elements of New York: bridges and rivers and tow-away zones....

Figure 4-83. ... *Zelig* (1983) was a masterful exploitations of electronic matte techniques, an unusual departure for a filmmaker known for his dialogue, not his special effects. (That's Woody/ Zelig waving behind der Führer.)... (*Frame enlargement*)

Figure 4-84. ... *Manhattan Murder Mystery* (1994) reprised the New York themes once again, after Allen's harrowing brush with reality-based celebrity.

Figure 4-85. Warren Beatty's *Dick Tracy* (1990) was one of the last in a long line of films recycling the comics of the thirties and forties. An ambitious attempt to capture the mood and look of that era (at least as it was portrayed in the comics) the film drew on the talents of both Madonna and Stephen Sondheim, as well as cinematographer Vittorio Storaro.

ite Martian, Wild Wild West, The Mod Squad, 1999), sometimes—surprisingly—of European films (*Three Men and a Baby,* 1987; *Sommersby,* 1992; *Scent of a Woman,* 1992). There is no better evidence that world film cultures are rapidly merging than this unusual interest Hollywood has shown in European hits. There is no more striking evidence of the impoverishment of our popular culture than the endless wave of TV-shows-made-for-movies (unless it's the string of movies converted to Broadway musicals).

European directors now seem to move effortlessly from their own cultures to Hollywood and occasionally back again. Paul Verhoeven did historical dramas and slice-of-life vignettes at home in the Netherlands; in Hollywood, he became a proponent of stylish action-oriented Science Fiction (*Robocop,* 1987; *Total Recall,* 1990), then tried his hand at bold sex (*Basic Instinct,* 1992; *Showgirls,* 1995). In France, Barbet Schroeder was a critic for *Cahiers du Cinéma* and Eric Rohmer's partner; in the U.S., he earned his Hollywood stripes with the complex drama *Reversal of Fortune* (1990). British directors (Alan Parker, Stephen Frears, Michael Apted, Ridley Scott, and Tony Scott) increasingly found work in Hollywood and were joined in the eighties by a number of commuting Australians.

Perhaps one reason for this broadening of the Hollywood purview was the increasing importance of the export market. In the early 1980s the American film

Figure 4-86. Robert Zemeckis's *Who Framed Roger Rabbit* (1988) also paid homage to the comic world, this time by inventing its own, a Toonland now more real to some than its historical predecessors. More inventive than the comic book blockbusters of the eighties, it was also more entertaining. Here, Roger gets the best of his live-action co-star Eddie Valliant (Bob Hoskins).

industry paid tribute to Goldcrest Films, the British production company that seemed to do no wrong—for a few years. Oscars went to *Gandhi* (1982) and *The Killing Fields* (1984). From that time on, the historical stylistic differentiation between American and European films lessened.

The movies that these international crews produced increasingly split into two separate product lines: although Hollywood must pay attention to the Boomer bulge, the large generation in its forties and fifties now moving into middle age, it continues to focus its greatest effort on the thirteen- to twenty-four-year-old market. Two films of the early eighties neatly foreshadowed these markets: Spielberg's *E.T.* (1982), the prototype of the Action-Adventure blockbuster fantasy whose leading characters are children, and Lawrence Kasdan's *The Big Chill* (1983), the model for the contemporary middle-aged, middle-class character dramas that stock the shelves of the video stores.

By far the leading genre of the 1980s and 1990s has been the Action-Adventure film, which, because it relies so little on character and character development, lends itself so well to sequels, and which exploits to the limit the rapidly developing sophistication of Hollywood's now-digitized special effects industry. Characterized by a thin veneer of science fiction and fantasy, which gives the effects specialists the excuse to ply their trade, contemporary Action movies suc-

ceed by exploiting a deeply felt need for visceral excitement and the thrill of violence. A generation of couch potatoes raised by nonstop television has discovered
that widescreen, Surround-Sound, wide-bandwidth action (and stadium seating,
too!) are the best reasons to disconnect from the small screen for a few hours in
favor of the moderately larger one in the local multiplex. The jam-packed activity
of the typical Action movie serves as a paradoxical antidote to the passive malaise
that television inculcates. Of course, it is only a *virtual* alternative reality, like the
feverish video games that are its main competition for the entertainment dollars
of today's teens and preteens.

As it turned out, Paul Verhoeven had started a trend: many recent-day action
movies have been helmed by European emigrés. Verhoeven's cinematographer,
Jan de Bont, has been the most prolific: *Die Hard* (1988), *The Hunt for Red October*
(1990), *Speed* (1994), *Twister* (1996), *The Haunting* (1999). Verhoeven weighed in
again with *Starship Troopers* (1997). But the Dutch don't have a monopoly—German directors have been part of the invasion, too: Wolfgang Petersen (*In the Line
of Fire*, 1993; *Airforce One*, 1997), and Roland Emmerich, director of the monstrous
success *Independence Day* (1996) and the equally monstrous flop *Godzilla* (1998).
The U.K. contributed Tony Scott (brother of Ridley): *Top Gun* (1986), *Enemy of the
State* (1998). Finnish-born Renny Harlin established a rep with *Die Hard 2* (1990)
and *Cliffhanger* (1993). Even the French have tried their hand at this quintessentially American Genre. Jean-Pierre Jeunet managed *Alien Resurrection* (1997), and
Luc Besson contributed his own daydream, *The Fifth Element* (1997).

As the leading Action star of the 1980s and 1990s, Arnold Schwarzenegger
established himself as the model movie persona of the period, eclipsing the more
varied and dimensional actors of the 1970s such as Robert Redford, Jack
Nicholson, and Robert De Niro.

Schwarzenegger began slowly, appearing in the 1976 documentary on weight-
lifters, *Pumping Iron*, later starring in the fantasy swashbucklers *Conan the Barbar-
ian* (1982) and *Conan the Destroyer* (1984) before reaching real prominence with
The Terminator (1984), which also established the careers of director James Cameron and his then wife, producer Gale Ann Hurd. It was here that his unwieldy
Austrian accent was put to good use with simple yet memorable lines like, "I'll be
back." The extensive special-effects work, the spare dialogue, and the would-be
mythical plot combined to set the tone for the genre. The sequel, *T2* (1992, also
Cameron), upped the ante as the first feature to make extensive use of computerized morphing effects.

As a former bodybuilder—a sport more concerned with the image of athleti-
cism than its activity—Schwarzenegger has proved to be a fitting, if ironic, surrogate for us in the virtual world of action on the screen. He has also been admitted
to the country's nobility by virtue of his 1986 marriage to Maria Shriver, niece of

John F. Kennedy. He has killed more than 300 people on screen as his films have grossed well over $1 billion worldwide.

To reach this elevated position in the Hollywood pantheon, Schwarzenegger had to best a formidable competitor—Sylvester Stallone, the actor-writer who was responsible for reinventing the Action genre.* As an actor, Stallone was getting nowhere until he wrote his own script for *Rocky* (1976), a critical and commercial success whose four sequels kept him working into the 1990s. The equally successful Rambo series (beginning with 1982's *First Blood*) took the action from fairly realistic boxing to extensive revenge fantasy. Eschewing the Science Fiction element and its special effects in favor of pure American tough guy, Stallone left the door open for Schwarzenegger and James Cameron to take the development to the next step. In 1993, however, Schwarzenegger fell to earth as *Last Action Hero* flopped, while Stallone returned to box-office form with *Cliffhanger* and the sci-fi comedy *Demolition Man*. The balance of power between the two stars was restored. Over the next few years Schwarzenegger began to pull away again (*True Lies*, 1994; *Eraser*, 1996) as Stallone faded (*Judge Dredd*, 1995; *Daylight*, 1996). At the end of the decade both saw fit to essay character roles, Schwarzenegger as the villain of *Batman & Robin* (1997), Stallone as a voice in the animated *Antz* (1998).

Schwarzenegger and Stallone did have challengers during this period. On the strength of three *Die Hards* and *Armageddon* (1998) Bruce Willis looked like a contender, and so did the team of Mel Gibson and Danny Glover (four *Lethal Weapons* between 1987 and 1998). But all three of these actors don't take the genre seriously enough. (I mean, Gibson even did a *Hamlet*—you know, the play by Shakespeare!)

All of them are quickly being eclipsed by a much younger star: Will Smith. In a tour-de-force career, Smith turned stardom as a teenage rap singer into a successful television series (*The Fresh Prince of Bel-Air*, 1990–96) while trying his hand at serious film roles during hiatus (*Six Degrees of Separation*, 1993). When the series was over he hit the Action-Adventure ground running in *Independence Day* (1996), then kept up the summer movie tempo throughout the late 1990s with *Men in Black* (1997), *Enemy of the State* (1998), and *Wild Wild West* (1999).

If Action movies often seem like fantastic theme-park rides, it is no coincidence. We attend the movies for much the same reasons we take the rides and, increasingly, the theme parks are owned by movie companies, and the films advertise the parks. The trend culminated in yet another celebration of contemporary special-effects technology, Steven Spielberg's *Jurassic Park* (1993), a film whose subject is a futuristic theme park and which, of course, sparked its own spate of

---

* Bruce Lee, the 1970s prototype of the Action hero, died before the genre was properly defined. His son Brandon, a potential 1990s challenger, also died young.

theme-park rides and panoramas—as well as the now inevitable profitable sequel.

The quasi-myths of American comic books continued to interest Hollywood filmmakers, as *Superman* and his sequels were joined by Tim Burton's *Batman* (1989) and its sequels and Warren Beatty's *Dick Tracy* (1990). The latter, with music by Stephen Sondheim, proved to be a thoughtful exploration of the myths of the thirties. The former solidified the reputation of a then young director who had started in the film business as a Disney animator.

Burton had first gained attention with *Pee-Wee's Big Adventure* (1985) and *Beetlejuice* (1988), two campy exercises in making live action conform to the simplicity and constraints of cartoons. As the decade wore on, live action and animation converged, symbolically as well as technically. Now that we had a real live Hollywood actor playing the role of President of the United States, perhaps it was no surprise that the confusion between image and reality increased rapidly. The 1980s prepared us for the digital age of morphs that dawned in the 1990s, since when no image—no matter how apparently authentic—is to be trusted.

This momentous conjunction was marked by Robert Zemeckis's inventive and witty *Who Framed Roger Rabbit* (1988), whose subject was the clash between the two worlds, real acting and cartoon reality. Zemeckis's other films include the *Back to the Future* trilogy (1985, 1989, 1990) and the Michael Douglas vehicle *Romancing the Stone* (1984), all of which display a refreshing postmodernist sensibility, and *Forrest Gump* (1994).

While Steven Spielberg and George Lucas get credit deservedly for founding the contemporary mythology of the movies, directors like Zemeckis and Ivan Reitman have also played a large part. Reitman's *Ghostbusters* (1984) applied humor to horror in a unique and refreshing way. His films with Schwarzenegger (*Twins*, 1988; *Kindergarten Cop*, 1990) contributed to the depth of that star's persona, and his political fable *Dave* (1993) skewered the fragile new political consciousness of the 1990s.

Harold Ramis, who starred in and cowrote *Ghostbusters*, later went on to write and direct the 1990s landmarks *Groundhog Day* (1993) and *Analyze This* (1999).

Reitman first made his mark with *National Lampoon's Animal House* (1978), a film which not only presaged the Boomers' fascination with their youth but also served as a model for contemporary comedy, depending as it did on the character of John Belushi. Reitman also worked with Dan Aykroyd and Bill Murray, who, like Belushi, came out of the television program *Saturday Night Live*. Indeed, most of the comic stars of the 1980s began their careers on that seminal show, from Eddie Murphy and Billy Crystal, who both continue to dominate American film comedy, to Dana Carvey and Mike Myers.[*] The show has been so surprisingly influential in American youth culture that in the early 1990s, almost twenty years

Figure 4-87. James Cameron singlehandledly revived the Disaster genre with his $200 million gamble on *Titanic* (1997). Most of the cast of thousands were digital animations. Six years earlier Cameron had set the code for digital fantasy with *T2*. With this retelling of the epitome of technological failure he set a parallel model for digital reality. *Titanic* is an emblem of our quickening trans-Platonic crossing to the new world of virtuality.

after it began, *Saturday Night Live* skits served as source material for full-length feature films (*Wayne's World*, 1992; *The Coneheads*, 1993).

While younger filmgoers were flocking to multiplexes throughout the 1980s and 1990s for their regular doses of virtual action, postmodern comedy, and sporadic myth, an occasional smaller theater in the 'plex was turned over to those of their elders who still left the house. The revolutionary excitement of the 1960s may have been a memory (celebrated to some degree in the latter-day art-house hit *Cinema Paradiso*, 1990), but the general level of quality remained high. We have already noted the continuing work of the generation of the seventies—Coppola, Scorsese, Altman, Mazursky. No filmmaker of the eighties—except perhaps Spike Lee—has received comparable media attention. This is not surprising; times are different. Now, every colorless technician gets his name above the title, but the true age of the auteur has passed.

---

*   About the only film comedians of the eighties you can name who didn't apprentice at *SNL* were the successful team of Richard Pryor and Gene Wilder—and Wilder later married Gilda Radner, who did. Jim Carrey, the most expensive comic star of the 1990s, came to prominence on Keenen Ivory Wayans's *In Living Color*, the then-new Fox network's imitation of *SNL*. Conversely, the most influential comedian of the period, Bill Cosby, never had equal success in film. Robin Williams, a remarkable standup comic, has had greater success with dramatic than with comic roles.

Figure 4-88AB. Ivan Reitman's 1984 *Ghostbusters* was one of the few films outside the Spielberg–Lucas orbit to create a popular mythos. More important, the script by Dan Aykroyd and Harold Ramis successfully defused the *Exorcist*-inspired trend to sadistic horror. Left: the Staypuft monster sashays up Central Park West (the route of Macy's annual Thanksgiving Day parade). Right: the No-Ghost logo was recognizable the world over and imitated widely.

Although their artistic profiles may be lower, the new generation has nevertheless established a reputation of its own. We've already noted the contributions of Reitman and Zemeckis to the youth mythology that Lucas and Spielberg constructed. Action directors like James Cameron and John McTiernan (*Predator*, 1987; *Die Hard*, 1988; *The Thomas Crown Affair* remake, 1999) have also made their mark here, thanks to their imaginative handling of special effects.

Jim Henson was just as influential in molding contemporary myths as George Lucas and Steven Spielberg, although most of his work was done in television. When he turned to film with *The Muppet Movie* (1979), *The Great Muppet Caper* (1981), and *The Muppets Take Manhattan* (1984), he preserved his puppet characters in more substantial vehicles for future generations before his untimely death in 1991.

James L. Brooks is another switch-hitter. He has had a hand in two of the most important television series of the last thirty years: *The Mary Tyler Moore Show* in the 1970s and *The Simpsons* in the 1990s. But he has also made his mark in theatrical film. He started at the top, with a hat-trick of Oscars for *Terms of Endearment* in 1983, as producer, writer, and director. *Broadcast News* (1987) revisited the television news room and *As Good as It Gets* (1997) gave Jack Nicholson and Helen Hunt a broad canvas to paint a quirky romance.

Those filmmakers, like Brooks, who preferred to speak to adult audiences developed a mix of nostalgia and contemporary social comedy which has proved durable. Barry Levinson is a model. After working as a screenwriter for Mel

Figure 4-89. In the ten years before his untimely death, Jim Henson was able to translate his world, originally invented for television, to the movies in a series of musical films which are all as thoughtful as they are charming. He made taking the kids to the movies a pleasure in the eighties. Here, Kermit and Miss Piggy pose for a publicity still, surrounded by their talented and colorful supporting cast. It may not be easy being green, but it's a kick to be pink.

Brooks, he made a notable directorial debut in 1982 with *Diner*, set in his native Baltimore in the 1950s. He returned to his hometown twice during the next ten years for *Tin Men* (1987), set a few years later, and the elegiac *Avalon* (1990), which traced his family's history. Interspersed with these looks back were the commercially successful *Good Morning, Vietnam* (1987) and *Rain Man* (1988), character dramas and tours de force for their stars, respectively Robin Williams and Dustin Hoffman. Levinson returned to his native Baltimore in the nineties to produce the admired television series *Homicide*. On the big screen in the nineties he can lay claim to *Quiz Show* (1994) and *Wag the Dog* (1997), two films about the political consciousness of the fifties and the nineties, respectively, that should stand the test of time.

The Marshall family has also excelled with older audiences. Penny Marshall (*Big*, 1988; *A League of Their Own*, 1992; *The Preacher's Wife*, 1996) and her elder brother Garry Marshall (*The Flamingo Kid*, 1984; *Pretty Woman*, 1990; *The Runaway Bride*, 1999) have brought a reasoned sense of comedy to their varied projects. Penny's ex-husband Rob Reiner has displayed a wider range of interests in a prolific body of work, from his debut *This Is Spinal Tap* (1984) to *When Harry Met Sally … * (1989, written by Nora Ephron), *Misery* (1990), *A Few Good Men* (1992), *The American President* (1995), and *The Ghost of Mississippi* (1986). Both Marshalls and

Figure 4-90. Nora Ephron hit her stride with *Sleepless in Seattle*, a remarkable tour de force that proved to be a refreshing hit, revisiting the romantic themes of the forties in the person of Tom Hanks and Meg Ryan.

Reiner enjoyed successful runs in television sitcoms before embarking on feature careers, and returned to acting careers in the 1990s.

Former child actor Ron Howard (*The Andy Griffith Show*) has also established a durable directorial career (*Splash*, 1984; *Cocoon*, 1985; *Apollo 13*, 1995; *EdTV*, 1999).

Essayist, novelist, and screenwriter Nora Ephron, daughter of the screenwriting team of Henry and Phoebe Ephron, finally hit her stride in her fifties with *Sleepless in Seattle* (1993), in which the two main characters are separated by a continent and don't "meet cute" until the final reel—a screenwriter's movie, if ever there was one. She redoubled the resonances with the same two actors (Tom Hanks and Meg Ryan) in *You've Got Mail* (1998), a remake of Ernst Lubitsch's 1940 *The Shop Around the Corner* that managed to capture the burgeoning Internet culture perfectly. These two films will last.

What Ephron, the Marshalls, and Reiner do for adult characters, John Hughes did for teenagers. In an unusually focused group of films in the mid-eighties (*Sixteen Candles*, 1984; *Weird Science*, 1985; *The Breakfast Club*, 1985; *Pretty in Pink*, 1986; *Ferris Bueller's Day Off*, 1986; *Uncle Buck*, 1989), all set in the same Chicago suburb, writer-producer-director Hughes examined the roots of Generation X before anyone realized it existed. He did so with understanding and style, displaying a sensitivity to adolescent concerns and middle-class family life that is as rare as it is precise. His production *Home Alone* (1990, directed by Chris Columbus) exploited the

Figure 4-91. What Henson did for the gradeschoolers in the eighties, John Hughes did for the highschoolers: providing a set of essays on middle-class American adolescence that helped his youngish audiences understand a little more about their confusing world. Uncle Buck (John Candy) is the kids' ideal adult.

raw materials of the earlier films, added gratuitous cartoon violence, but evinced none of Hughes's trademark empathy. It became his biggest box-office hit.

Home Alone was apparently intended to be a comic reverse on the hot genre of the late eighties, paranoid fantasies. Echoing the slang of the period, critic James Pallot has called this pattern "the ... from Hell." Always an undercurrent since *Rosemary's Baby* (1968), this genre became one of the key forms of the 1980s and 1990s with the box-office success of *Fatal Attraction* (1987, the lover from hell). The *Child's Play* series debuted the next year (the toy from hell). John Schlesinger weighed in with the tenant from hell (*Pacific Heights*, 1990). The genre picked up speed in the 1990s after the huge success of Jonathan Demme's *Silence of the Lambs* (1991, the prisoner from hell). The next few years saw a string of paranoid fantasies about husbands, roommates, school friends, nannies, and secretaries (respectively, *Sleeping with the Enemy*, 1991; *Single White Female*, 1992; *Poison Ivy*, 1992; *The Hand That Rocks the Cradle*, 1992; and *The Temp*, 1993). It had been more than thirty years since the Science Fiction films of the 1950s, when a comparable spate of paranoia gripped film audiences.

Counterbalancing this fear was the strain of nostalgia we have already noted. It found one of its most endearing and unusual outlets in the surprising string of

Baseball movies of the late 1980s. Baseball had for a long time been anathema to Hollywood.[*] After all, America's national pastime is notorious for its long periods of apparent inaction and the interior monologues that players and fans alike engage in during the course of a game—hardly the nonstop action that contemporary producers seek. But Barry Levinson's film of the classic Bernard Malamud novel *The Natural* (1984) had captured much of the mythic symbolism and sense of history and tradition that endear the game to its fans. By 1988 the time was right for a Baseball movie renaissance—even as the sport itself was entering a period of decline.

John Sayles was first at bat with his historical study of the Black Sox scandal, *Eight Men Out* (1988). This was followed quickly by former minor-leaguer Ron Shelton's authentic *Bull Durham* and David S. Ward's *Major League*. The series culminated in the critical and commercial success of cleanup hitter Phil Alden Robinson's elegiac *Field of Dreams* (1989). Penny Marshall pitched extra innings in 1992 with *A League of Their Own*.

Amid the action and special effects, the paranoia and nostalgia, the artistic conservatism and slick professional sheen of the 1980s and 1990s, two related trends stand in contrast: the continuing possibilities for independent filmmaking outside the Hollywood orbit, and the renaissance of the Black Film.

Interestingly, the Cannes Film Festival served as a crucial showcase for American independent filmmakers throughout the 1980s. Susan Seidelman's *Smithereens* was shown at Cannes in 1982; Jim Jarmusch's *Stranger Than Paradise* won the Caméra d'or in 1984. Both used the resulting publicity to build careers, Seidelman working within the Hollywood orbit, Jarmusch continuing outside it. Ethan and Joel Coen's *Blood Simple*, an homage to the Film Noir, also screened at Cannes in 1984. They have continued, on the margins of Hollywood, to rework the classic genres (*Raising Arizona*, 1987; *Miller's Crossing*, 1990; *Barton Fink*, 1991; *Fargo*, 1996; *The Big Lebowski*, 1998). Steven Soderbergh's *sex, lies and videotape* drew critical attention at Cannes in 1989.

In the 1990s the Sundance festival served a similar career-building function for numerous new American independent filmmakers. Richard Linklater's *Slacker* (1990) was the talk of the 1991 festival. Kevin Smith's *Clerks* was the hit of the 1994 show, which quickly led to a deal with Miramax. Edward Burns's *The Brothers McMullen* garnered invaluable publicity in 1995 as did Todd Solondz's *Welcome to the Dollhouse* (1995) the next year. The Utah-based festival has also helped pro-

---

[*] I know this from personal experience. I spent most of 1979 and part of 1980 trying to pitch a treatment called "Free Agent" in Hollywood with a singular lack of success. A comedy about the new relationships among players, owners, and fans, it still reads pretty well—and it's still available. Call my agent, Virginia Barber, if you're interested.

mote documentaries. Shortly after winning Sundance, Barbara Kopple's *American Dream* (1990) garnered her a second Academy Award.*

The media attention that festival exposure can generate can make all the difference to a filmmaker's career, and often has unusual side-effects. Former child actor Ben Affleck worked for the newly hot Kevin Smith in *Mallrats* (1995), a failure, and *Chasing Amy* (1997), a hit. Affleck and his friend Matt Damon wrote themselves a Hollywood vehicle, *Good Will Hunting* (1997). Their Academy Awards for screenwriting boosted their bankability as actors. Such are the ways of the new Hollywood.

Throughout the 1980s and 1990s the model for independent filmmakers was John Sayles. An author and screenwriter in the 1970s, he debuted as a director with *The Return of the Secaucus Seven* in 1979, which most critics regard as the "real" *Big Chill*. *The Brother from Another Planet* (1984), *Matewan* (1987), and *City of Hope* (1991), together with *Eight Men Out*, *Lone Star* (1996), and *Limbo* (1999) approach American society from markedly different points of view but share a deft and deeply worked sense of character.

Within Hollywood one of the more independent artists of the 1980s and 1990s was Oliver Stone. In *Platoon* (1986), *Born on the Fourth of July* (1989), *The Doors* (1991), and *JFK* (1992) he reviewed most of the critical issues of the seminal decade of the 1960s: the Vietnam war and its aftermath, the counterculture, and assassinations. In *Wall Street* (1987) he blew the whistle on the 1980s just before the stock market crash. He completed his work on the 1960s with *Nixon* (1995). Only the paranoid conspiracy theories of *JFK* mar this forceful body of work.

The new wave of African-American filmmakers have also benefited from the attention a Cannes appearance brings. Spike Lee's *She's Gotta Have It* was shown at the 1986 festival. Lee continued to bring his films to Cannes thereafter, traditionally irate when they didn't win major prizes. Robert Townsend's *Hollywood Shuffle* was screened at Cannes in 1987. At the 1990 festival, you could find Mario Van Peebles with his father, Melvin, at the Majestic Hotel courting distributors for *New Jack City* (1991). John Singleton's *Boyz N the Hood* was a major topic of conversation at the 1991 Festival.

Mario Van Peebles is the only new African-American filmmaker with roots in the industry. He has worked closely with his father, who could be said to have founded the movement in the 1960s. Robert Townsend made his acting debut in Paul Mazursky's *Willie & Phil* (1980) and worked in stand-up comedy before producing his independent satire on the difficulties facing Black actors, *Hollywood*

---

* Although Sundance has not been very useful to foreign filmmakers, it has helped to widen the market for independent "alternative" features from abroad like *Trainspotting* (1996, Danny Boyle) that share the youth subculture that was the most prominent characteristic of independent film in the 1990s.

Figure 4-92. Steven Soderbergh's *sex, lies and videotape* helped to rekindle interest in the independent film in the late eighties. Andie MacDowell is the woman with the video camera.

Shuffle (1987). While working often in television, Townsend directed his first Hollywood film, *The Five Heartbeats*, in 1991. Keenen Ivory Wayans worked on *Hollywood Shuffle* with Townsend, then made his own spoof of the "Blaxploitation" films of the seventies, *I'm Gonna Git You Sucka*, the next year. In 1990 he was signed by Fox television to produce *In Living Color*, which he had conceived. Reversing the racial ratio of *Saturday Night Live* it offered—for the first time—multiple and varied African-American attitudes to current events and issues. It also provided a launching pad for most of his talented siblings: Damon, Kim, Shawn, and Marlon. The Wayans family certainly holds the current record for a successful show business family, outnumbering the Jacksons.

In 1991 the African-American spectrum broadened with the debuts of two very young independent filmmakers who captured the characters, concerns, and sounds of their neighborhoods on opposite sides of the country: John Singleton's "Hood" was South-Central Los Angeles; Matty Rich came *Straight Out of Brooklyn*.

Clearly, the dominant personality in the Black film renaissance of the 1980s and 1990s was Brooklynite actor-writer-director Spike Lee. His NYU film school student thesis, *Joe's Bed-Stuy Barbershop: We Cut Heads* (1980) was screened in the New York Film Festival New Directors series. His first feature, *She's Gotta Have It* (1986), won acclaim at Cannes, impressed critics with its visual flare, did surprising box-office business, and established the character Lee played, streetwise hus-

Figure 4-93. Oliver Stone, almost unique in the eighties as a Hollywood filmmaker driven by political interests, hit the mark with *Wall Street*, a film that sharply captured the ethical climate of the go-go eighties at the same time that it tellingly portrayed a bunch of lively—and true— characters. Michael Douglas is the lizardly Gordon Gekko.

tler Mars Blackmon, as part of the popular culture. (He appeared in Nike commercials with Michael Jordan, and elsewhere.) *Do the Right Thing* (1989), a polemically charged portrait of contemporary race relations, became a subject of controversy at the same time that critics praised its allusive imagery.

For years, numerous filmmakers, mostly white, had attempted—and failed— to film *The Autobiography of Malcolm X*. Lee succeeded. *Malcolm X*, with Denzel Washington in the title role, was released in 1992. A key film in American culture, it manages to capture the rich tensions in the character of Malcolm X at the same time that it entertains with an involving and dramatic saga. Breathtakingly accurate and evocative performances by Washington and Al Freeman Jr as Elijah Muhammad provide the strong core of the film. Lee attenuates his normally exuberant directorial personality to frame these historic characters with remarkable balance. He catches many of the complexities and ironies that combined to make Malcolm a central hero of the 1960s.

Having accomplished this long-sought dream, Lee broadened his purview during the next few years with documentaries (*Get on the Bus*, 1996; *4 Little Girls*, 1997, about the Montgomery bombing in 1963); more general films about urban New York (*Clockers*, 1995, from the Richard Price novel; *Summer of Sam*, 1999, an elegy for the late seventies); and—yes—a basketball movie: *He Got Game*, 1998, with Denzel Washington). With this wide range of productions under his belt, Spike Lee ranks as one of the major American filmmakers at the turn of the cen-

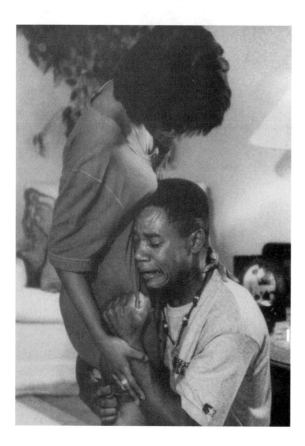

Figure 4-94. Cuba Gooding Jr as Tre Styles comforted by Nia Long (Brandi) in John Singleton's morality play about life in South Central Los Angeles, *Boyz N the Hood* (1991).

tury—and the only member of the pantheon to achieve that rank since the 1970s.

If, as we've already noted, Hollywood developed a more international outlook in the 1980s as the rest of world cinema increasingly came within the esthetic orbit of American movies. Throughout the postwar period, as before, a national artistic identity, usually defined in opposition to the Hollywood style, had been a central tenet of European and Third-World cinemas. Although polemicists and politicians continued to give lip service to this concept, the realities of an increasingly interconnected world culture greatly constrained the independence of national cinemas. If American film found new life in the eighties thanks to infusions of new capital and technological special-effects life-support systems, such wonder drugs were either not available or contra-indicated for less aggressively marketed national film cultures overseas.

As in the U.S., nostalgia predominated in Europe as veteran filmmakers continued along the well-worn tracks laid down for them twenty-five and thirty

Figure 4-95. Clarence Williams III and Eve Plumb talk beans with writer-director-star Keenen Ivory Wayans in *I'm Gonna Git You Sucka* (1988).

years earlier, and younger filmmakers followed dutifully behind. Giuseppe Tornatore's *Cinema Paradiso* (1990) was meant to be an elegy for the Golden Age of the fifties and sixties European film. However, as *The Film Guide* points out, "no, they don't make movies like they used to, and this Oscar-winning Italian-French coproduction spends the better part of three hours proving it."

Because they shared, at least in part, a common language, British filmmakers had long been the prime victims of the Hollywood cultural juggernaut. For a brief moment in the 1980s, however, it looked like an entente had been struck between Los Angeles and London. Producer David Puttnam was at the center of the British campaign throughout the 1980s. He had won Oscars for the manipulative *Midnight Express* (1978) and the unpretentious *Chariots of Fire* (1981). Shortly thereafter, he teamed with Goldcrest Films, whose remarkable success from the release of *Gandhi* in 1982 through *The Killing Fields* (1984) and *A Room with a View* (1986) suggested that commercial films, viable in the Hollywood distribution system, could be produced on a regular basis by British filmmakers. In 1986 Puttnam became head of production at Coca-Cola's Columbia Pictures. By the end of 1987, Puttnam was ousted, and Goldcrest was facing bankruptcy due to under-capitalization and mismanagement. The dream of Hollywood-on-the-Thames was abruptly ended. But the melody lingered on as British directors increasingly found work in America and as British actors continued to win a disproportionate share of Oscar honors.

For those British filmmakers committed to a national cinema, the founding in 1982 of Channel Four, the second independent television network, proved heart-

Figure 4-96. Angela Basset as Betty Shabazz and Denzel Washington as Malcolm in Spike Lee's profound *Malcolm X*.

ening. Within a few years, however, the increased production had been absorbed. Nevertheless, filmmakers like Stephen Frears (*My Beautiful Laundrette*, 1985; *Hero*, 1992), Mike Leigh (*Life Is Sweet*, 1991; *Naked*, 1993; *Secrets and Lies*, 1996) Bill Forsyth (*Local Hero*, 1983), Bruce Robinson (*Withnail & I*, 1987), and Julien Temple (*Earth Girls Are Easy*, 1989) have managed to keep the lines of communication open. Most successful at the acrobatic task of keeping a foot in each camp was Richard Attenborough, whose prestige productions, from *Gandhi* to *Chaplin* (1992), fit well into the Hollywood pattern at the same time that they continued the tradition of British quality cinema.

The most recent British cinematic onslaught was led by versatile actress-writer Emma Thompson and her erstwhile husband, the audacious actor-director Kenneth Branagh. After the prerequisite stint with the Royal Shakespeare Company, Irish-born Branagh intentionally invited comparison with Laurence Olivier by making his film acting/directing debut with a version of *Henry V* (1989). This film, together with an equally fresh and accomplished *Much Ado About Nothing* (1993), brought new life to the Shakespearean film tradition. (His 1996 *Hamlet* suffered from too many production values.) Contemporary dramas like *Dead Again* (1991) and blockbusters like *Wild Wild West* (1999) established his range.

Figure 4-97. Barry Levinson's film of the Bernard Malamud novel *The Natural* captured the baseball myth without much saccharine. Robert Redford was the mystical hero of the Knights.

Thompson starred in most of Branagh's productions and quickly rose to the top tier of film actresses, garnering perennial Oscar nominations. Her most successful work to date has been in the literary films directed by James Ivory: *Howards End* (1992, from the novel by E. M. Forster), for which she won an Oscar as best actress, and *The Remains of the Day* (1993, from the novel by Kazuo Ishiguro), for which she won a nomination. (She also gave us a great Hillary Clinton in *Primary Colors*, 1998).

This work in novel adaptations positioned her to play a central role in the strange Jane Austen craze of the mid-nineties. She collected another Oscar nomination for *Sense and Sensibility* (1995), while her younger sister, Sophie, starred in *Persuasion* (1995) and *Emma* (1996; that's the novel, not the actress), where she was joined by their mother, Phyllida Law. The Thompson family thus had a hand in three of the five Austen projects that hit world screens within two years, missing appearances only in the BBC/A&E miniseries *Pride and Prejudice* (1995) and in Amy Heckerling's *Clueless* (1995), an update of *Emma* (the novel, not the film).

Figure 4-98A. Hollywood turned to France for material all too often in the early 1990s. Here, Anne Parillaud in Luc Besson's international hit of 1991, *La Femme Nikita*....

Why a novelist from the beginning of the nineteenth century found renewed popularity at the end of the twentieth is interesting to contemplate. Perhaps postmodern sexual politics are more like pre-Victorian social mores than we care to admit. Certainly, Austen's novels had proved usable for television miniseries early on. Series of the remaining two of her six works, *Northanger Abbey* and *Mansfield Park*, were made in the early eighties after an earlier version of *Pride and Prejudice* had proved successful in 1979.

While historical novels were grist for the miniseries mills of the seventies and eighties, the form was kept alive on the large screen during this period mainly by the independent work of James Ivory, Ismail Merchant, and Ruth Prawer Jhabvala. Ivory (American) and Merchant (Indian) formed a producing partnership in 1963 to film Polish-Jewish-German-English-Indian Prawer Jhabvala's novel *The Householder*, about the English experience in India.[*] *Shakespeare Wallah* (1963), with a similar theme, brought them some international attention.

In the seventies they turned their attention from Anglo-Indian relations to historical novels, gaining some critical success with Henry James's *The Europeans* (1979) and *The Bostonians* (1984) before moving on to E. M. Forster: *A Room with a View* (1986), *Maurice* (1987), and finally *Howards End* (1992), the recipient of nine Academy Award nominations. It had taken only thirty years of patient work for

---

[*]   Born in Germany of Polish-Jewish parents, Ruth Prawer grew up in England and married an Indian. This background gave her a unique transcultural viewpoint.

Figure 4-98B. ... and Bridget Fonda in the American remake *Point of No Return* (1993). (Nikita continued as a television series in the late 1990s.)

Hollywood to come around to their point of view. Of course this team had fore-shadowed the craze for the English novelist with *Jane Austen in Manhattan* (1980).

The Merchant–Ivory team was challenged in the late 1990s by director John Madden. Coming out of a successful television career he tested the historical waters with *Ethan Frome* (1992), from the novel by Edith Wharton; then drew critical attention with *Mrs Brown* (1997), about Queen Victoria's relationship with her hunting manager. *Shakespeare in Love* (1998) with a witty script by Marc Norman and Tom Stoppard and featuring two young American actors—Gwyneth Paltrow and Ben Affleck—won seven Academy Awards (having been nominated for thirteen).

As we noted earlier, Australians have also learned to commute between home and Hollywood. Notable new talents of recent years include George Miller (*Lorenzo's Oil*, 1993; *Babe*, 1995) who found a world market for his futuristic outback "Western/Road" fantasies *Mad Max* (1979) and *The Road Warrior* (1981), and Jane Campion, who found international critical approbation with *An Angel at My Table* (1990) and *The Piano* (1993).

In France, le cinéma du papa reigns once again as the apprentices of the 1970s have become the journeyman auteurs of the 1980s and 1990s. Adept as ever at bourgeois dramas and comedies (Coline Serreau's *Trois hommes et un couffin, Three Men and a Cradle*, 1985; remade in English as *Three Men and a Baby*, 1987) and occasionally finding international success with policiers or films noirs (Jean-Jacques Beineix's *Diva*, 1980; Luc Besson's *La Femme Nikita*, 1991), French film-makers now find themselves in the humbling position of selling remake rights to Hollywood.

German film in the 1980s and 1990s could not maintain the international following the Neue Kino had developed in the 1970s. With very occasional exceptions (Wolfgang Petersen's epic *Das Boot*, 1981; Michael Verhoeven's political satire *Das Schreckliche Mädchen, The Nasty Girl*, 1990) German cinema has not traveled well, nor have German filmmakers.

The situation has been only slightly better in Italy, despite the supposed economic stimulation of dozens of new television stations, not all of which were owned by Silvio Berlusconi. In addition to Tornatore, Maurizio Nichetti (*Ladri di Saponette, The Icicle Thief*, 1989) developed an international following. Although Giancarlo Paretti tried to buy his way into Hollywood with his purchase of MGM, Italian actors and filmmakers are less in evidence in Hollywood than at any time in recent memory. In 1993, the doors of Cinecittà closed for good.

There has been one bright star, however. The Italian international nova of the 1990s was Roberto Benigni. He set an Italian box-office record with *Johnny Stecchino* (1991), and matched his popularity at home with an equally prominent international standing. He acted in Jim Jarmusch's *Down By Law* (1986) and *Night on Earth* (1996) and starred in Blake Edwards's *Son of the Pink Panther* (1993). His World War II drama-comedy *Life Is Beautiful* (*La Vita è bella*, 1997), which he directed and in which he starred, proved a major international hit and was quickly dubbed a modern classic.

In the 1980s, Spain's Pedro Almodóvar (*Woman on the Verge of a Nervous Breakdown*, 1988) had some success exporting his campy melodramas and achieved an international reputation with films like *Kika* (1993) and *Live Flesh* (1997).

Scandinavian filmmakers have enjoyed a fair degree of prominence in the world market during recent years. Lasse Hallström (*My Life as a Dog*, 1985), Bille August (*Pelle the Conqueror*, 1987), and Gabriel Axel (*Babette's Feast*, 1987) all achieved international reputations. Hallström and August later made the journey to Hollywood (*What's Eating Gilbert Grape?* and *The House of the Spirits*, respectively, both 1993). Perhaps the most interesting director to come out of Scandinavia in many years has been Finland's Aki Kaurismaki, who has displayed a wide range of styles from slapstick comedy to absurdist, deadpan drama (*Ariel*, 1988; *Leningrad Cowboys Go America*, 1989; *The Match Factory Girl*, 1990). With his brother Mika (*Helsinki Napoli All Night Long*, 1988) he represents perhaps the only cinema movement worthy of the name in the nineties (although the Finnish for "New Wave" has not yet entered the international lexicon).

While individual filmmakers based in Asia (Jackie Chan, John Woo) produced films that survived the rigors of export to the West, no movement since the Filipino and Hong Kong action films of the 1970s had a measurable impact on world cinema until the burgeoning of the Chinese "Fifth Generation" during the late 1980s. These filmmakers, who attended Beijing Film Institute after the period of the Cultural Revolution, used the imagery of the medium to cloak political com-

Figure 4-99. Roberto Benigni shares a moment with Giorgio Cantarini and Nicoletta Braschi in *La Vita è bella* (*Life Is Beautiful*, 1997).

mentary. Chen Kaige (*Yellow Earth*, 1984; *Farewell, My Concubine*, 1993) and former cinematographer Zhang Yimou (*Red Sorghum*, 1987; *Ju Dou*, 1989; *Raise the Red Lantern*, 1991; *The Story of Qiu Ju*, 1992) have received considerable attention at Western film festivals, as has Gong Li, the striking actress who was featured in his films.

During this period, Latin American and African filmmakers have generally been limited to their domestic markets. Occasional films succeed internationally (South African Jamie Uys's *The Gods Must Be Crazy*, 1981), but the regular flow that produces the productive conversation between filmmaker and filmgoer has not existed outside of local borders.

By 1980 it was clear that it was no longer possible to make a distinction between what we call film and what we know as video or television. These various forms of audiovisual narrative had been seen as separate—even antagonistic—for more than thirty years. Now they must be regarded as parts of the same continuum. Indeed, we need a new word to embrace both film and tape forms. As video technology continues to grow in sophistication and flexibility, "film"makers increasingly will find the choice of format more a matter of economics and technology than of esthetics.

By 1990 it was apparent that the geographical borders that once helped to define the art (if not the business) of film were disintegrating even more rapidly than the technological lines of demarcation. The aggressive marketing of Ted Turner's CNN and Viacom's MTV, and the rapid expansion of transborder satellite television, first in Europe, then in Asia, presented filmmakers around the world with even greater competition from the Hollywood juggernaut.

Yet at the same time, the technology opened up many more channels to the public, allowing filmmakers a more direct route to their audiences. In fact, a reasonable view of film and television now should see the former as a subset of the latter. The majority of companies that make films also make television programs, and vice versa. In the 1990s, the theatrical-release film industry realized approximately $5 billion in annual sales each year in the U.S., while the network television industry had revenues more than three times as large. Before the late seventies most critics and audiences regarded "made-for-television" productions as notably less prestigious and adventurous than theatrical movies. By the 1980s, this stigma no longer applied. The television films still don't have quite the aura of their more expensive theatrical cousins, but actors and technicians now no longer regard "Movies of the Week" (or "MOWs," in Hollywood parlance) as professional compromises. Made-for-cable movies like HBO productions *Citizen Cohn* (1992), *Barbarians at the Gate* (1993), and *Don King: Only in America* (1997) might easily pass as theatrical features and garner the same quality of publicity that features do. As late as 1979 it was a Hollywood rule that television stars didn't have the weight to carry a feature film. That would be news to Bruce Willis or Will Smith.

Even within the limits of "theatrical" filmmaking, video technology has opened up additional distribution channels. During the late seventies a number of films originally conceived as theatrical productions skipped that stage of distribution to find some measure of success via broadcast or cable television immediately. By the late 1980s, scores of films were produced every year as "Direct-to-Videos." Although their financial upside might be measured at the nation's box offices, their breakeven economics were based wholly on projected video rentals. Replacing the fertile ground of the B movies and Programmers of the thirties and forties (as the telefilms had before them) Direct-to-Videos allow beginning filmmakers to learn their craft, and—more important—ignore the strict rules of content and style that increasingly limit theatrical films whose average cost has risen past $30 million.

In 1992, IRS Media's *One False Move* garnered critical acclaim out of all proportion to its budget and was ranked by several influential critics as one of the best films of the year. Direct-to-Video, the latest variant on an old Hollywood theme, had come of age.

The string of distribution possibilities now looks something like this:

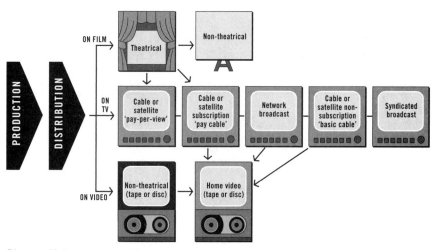

Diagram K. DISTRIBUTION WINDOWS.

One or more of the broadcast stages can easily be skipped with no necessarily significant loss of revenue. In fact, pirating of videotapes and film prints is growing so rapidly that studios are now forced into the tape and disc market almost immediately after a film is released theatrically (and certainly before it has been shown on cable, whose widespread distribution offers video pirates irresistible opportunities).

Network television gets pushed further back in the line, making it necessary for those companies to pour more money and talent into made-for-television product (since that is the one type of movie that they can control). They can no longer depend, as they did in the sixties and seventies, on the broadcast of theatrical films to provide the linchpins of their programming schedules. This is also a prime reason why networks have tried to enter theatrical production.

While commercial filmmakers find themselves confronting a new world of anarchic dimensions, thanks to the unplanned effects of technological developments, independent filmmakers can look forward to dramatically increased possibilities in the new century. As late as 1978, a filmmaker who wished to distribute his or her film had, basically, six choices: the major Hollywood studios. Adjusted for inflation, theatrical box office has continued to decline since the 1970s. The growth of Hollywood in the 1980s and 1990s was fueled first by the rapid expansion of videotape and cable, then by the explosion in the number of independent European television stations hungry for product as one country after another denationalized its television system, and most recently by the proliferation of DBS satellite systems eager to fill their hundreds of channels.

The aggressively marketed technologies of videotape and DVD-Video, cable, and satellite offer refreshing prospects for the independent filmmaker. Theatrical

Figure 4-100. Bill Paxton and Cynda Williams in Carl Franklin's *One False Move*, a direct-to-video production which made a big impression on theatrical audiences and critics.

distribution is now just about as important—or unimportant—to a filmmaker as hardcover publication is to a writer. Expanding cable and satellite services combined with DVD-Video and perhaps even video-on-demand dial-up distribution will require even larger amounts of new product. And tape and disc offer a direct channel to the public very similar to book publication and record production. The conglomerates still have a lot more money to spend hyping a product than the independents, but at least the potential exists for a far more democratic system of distribution.

The increasing viability of e-commerce on the Internet removes the last barrier between filmmakers and their audiences: availability. On the Web everyone has enough shelf space and everything is always in stock. Now when potentially interested customers hear about a movie they know they can get it; they aren't constrained by the limited stock of their local video store. Of course the Web also offers an inexpensive and effective means of publicity as well. The studios realized this immediately. The film industry may have been the last medium to tap into the power of television advertising in the mid-1970s, but it was among the first to realize the power of the World Wide Web: by 1996 every new release had a marketing website. Independent filmmakers can easily afford this kind of marketing. In the summer of 1999 the producers of *The Blair Witch Project*, made on the proverbial shoestring budget, were able to generate considerable buzz for the film by using the Web.

During the 1960s and 1970s the production of film became significantly more democratic as prices were reduced through technological developments. In the 1990s, the process of distribution, once the bottleneck, underwent the same sort of democratization. This wasn't planned. In fact, it was nothing more than a (welcome) side effect of the exploitation of new hardware in a market that had been approaching the saturation point. Nevertheless, it marked an important new stage in the history of film, not only in the U.S. but abroad as well.

Economically, the trend has been—and continues to be—toward greater access. American studios may still dominate the international film market, but at least the potential exists for other countries to join the contest—not by banning American films, which becomes increasingly difficult as technology democratizes the process of distribution, but by challenging American studios on their own ground, understanding the economic multiplier effects of the export of culture, and making collective decisions to engage enthusiastically in the development and export of their own culture.

Technologically, the visual media continue to develop their powers of precision, further opening up the mysterious technological process to new groups of artists. What was once a massive undertaking requiring vast investments of capital is now very close to being that personal, flexible instrument of communication that Alexandre Astruc called the "camera-pen." At the same time, the new technologies of distribution should allow markedly increased access to an ever wider and more varied public—a public, by the way, who will have far greater control over media experiences than they have had in the past.

Esthetically, the confluence of these forces is producing a more varied range of cinematic product. The gap between "elite" and "mass" cultures continues to narrow. And the nineteenth-century concept of the "avant garde" becomes less important with each passing year.

Finally, the sum of these forces suggests that it may be a good time to announce the end of movies/film/cinema—at least as we have known them. From now on, "film" is simply a raw material, one of the possible choices, along with disc and tape, available to the media artist. "Movies" are now an integral part of a new, encompassing art, technology, and industry for which we do not yet have a name, except perhaps "multimedia." And "cinema"? After eighty-five years of dominating the way we view our world—a long, tempestuous, romantic, and rewarding life—cinema has quietly passed on.

For the sequel to this story, proceed to Chapter 7.

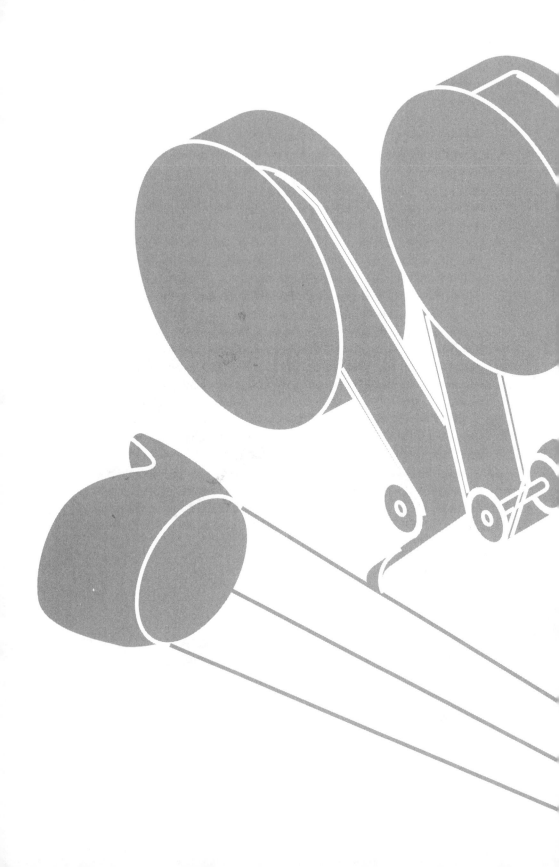

5

FILM THEORY: FORM AND FUNCTION

The Critic

In Mel Brooks's and Ernest Pintoff's funny and insightful short film *The Critic* (1963), we watch abstract animated shapes perform on the screen as we hear the voice of Brooks, an old man, puzzle his way happily through the significance of this "art":

> Vot da hell is dis?!
> Mus' be a cahtoon.
> Op.... Mus' be boith. Dis looks like boith. I remembeh when I was a boy in Russia ... biology.
> Op! It's born. Whatever it is, it's born.... Look out! Too late. It's dead already.... Vot's dis? Usher! Dis is cute! Dis is cute. Dis is nice. Vot da hell is it? Oh. I know vot it is. It's gobbage. Dat's vot it is! Two dollas I pay for a French movie, a foreign movie, and now I gotta see dis junk!

The first shape is joined by a second, and Brooks interprets:

> Yes. It's two ... two *things* dat, dat, dat—they like each other. Sure. Lookit da sparks. Two things in love! Ya see how it got more like?—it envied the other thing so much. Could dis be the sex life of two *things?*

The scene changes again and Brooks's old codger begins to lose interest:

> Vot is dis? Dots! Could be an eye. Could be anything! It mus' be some symbolism. I t'ink ... it's symbolic of ... junk! Uh-oh! It's a cock-a-roach! Good luck to you vit ya cock-a-roach, mister!

As the artistic short comes to a close, the critic passes final judgment:

> I dunno much about psych'analysis, but I'd say dis is a doity pictcha!

The Critic is humorous partly because Brooks manages, in the short space of his three-minute monologue, to touch on a number of vital truths about criticism. "Two dollas" we pay for a movie; what do we get for it? How do we determine cinematic value? How do we know what's "symbolic of junk"? There are others in the audience with Mel Brooks's critic who seem to be enjoying the film. Are values, then, entirely relative? Are there any true universal "rules" for film art? What does film do? What are its limits?

Questions like these are the province of film theory and criticism, two related but not identical activities that have as their common end an increased understanding of the phenomenon of film. In general, theory is the abstraction; criticism is the practice. At the lowest end of the scale, we find the kind of criticism a reviewer practices: more reportage than analysis. The reviewer's function is to describe the film and evaluate it, two relatively simple tasks. At the upper end of the scale is the kind of film theory that has little or nothing to do with the actual practice of film: an intellectual activity that exists primarily for its own sake, and often has its own rewards, but doesn't necessarily have much relation to the real world. Between these two extremes there is much room for useful and interesting work.

A number of important dichotomies govern the work of film theory. The first, the contrast between the practical and the ideal, is suggested by the difference between criticism (practical) and theory (ideal).

Closely associated with this is the contrast between "prescriptive" and "descriptive" theory and criticism. The prescriptive theorist is concerned with what film should be, the descriptive theorist only with what film is. Prescriptive theory is inductive: that is, the theorist decides on a system of values first, then measures actual films against his system. Descriptive theory, in contrast, is deductive: the theorist examines the entire range of film activity and then, and only then, draws tentative conclusions about the real nature of film. Theorists and critics who prescribe are naturally concerned about evaluation; having strong systems of values, they logically measure real films against their requirements and judge them.

The third and most important governing dichotomy is that between theory and practice. The fact is, no filmmaker needs to study the theory in order to practice the art. Indeed, until recently, very few filmmakers had any interest in theory. They knew (or did not know) instinctively what had to be done. Gradually, however, as film art became more sophisticated, a bridge between theory and practice was established. Many contemporary filmmakers, unlike their predecessors, now proceed from strong theoretical bases. Even Hollywood offices are now full of cinema studies Ph.D.s; since the generation of Coppola, Scorsese, and Lucas (film school students all) took charge, advanced degrees have provided an important entree in the studio system.

This is a major change in the way Hollywood does business. Indeed, the Hollywood style, which to a great extent still dominates film history, never produced a codified body of theory. On the face of it, the Hollywood film of the thirties and forties depended on a complex and powerful esthetic system, yet there is no Hollywood theory as such. No art *needs* theory; no artist needs an advanced degree. When academic study becomes a requirement for employment, the very nature of the art changes: it becomes self-conscious and it probably becomes less exciting. You don't have to be a wild-eyed romantic to believe that it's the renegades who break the rules who make the most intriguing art. Formal training ensures a certain level of journeyman competence, but it tends to suppress creativity. We trade off the excitement of genius for the assurance of branded quality. This may explain what has happened to American film since the early seventies.

The old masters, of course, played it by ear. The best that D. W. Griffith (who inspired so many theorists) could come up with was a rather dizzy idea that the "human pulse beat" was the secret metronome of effective filmmaking. In "Pace in the Movies" (*Liberty* magazine, 1926), he wrote:

> The American school ... makes an effort to keep the tempo of the picture
> in tune with the average human heartbeat, which, of course, increases in
> rapidity under such influences as excitement, and may almost stop in
> moments of pregnant suspense.

Much of this sort of after-the-fact cogitation was the result of film's own inferiority complex as the youngest of the arts. Christian Metz suggests that the function of such criticism, psychoanalytically, is to rescue film from its "bad-object" status. More simply, the thinking went: if film can support a weighty system of theory, then it must be just as respectable as any of the other, older arts. This may seem a rather childish motive for film theory, but it was not so long ago that film was commonly regarded by educated people as not to be taken seriously. In the U.S., for example, film did not become a generally accepted subject for study in colleges and universities until about 1970. So the impetus for much of early film theory was to gain a degree of respectability.[*]

Because of this desire for respectability many of the earliest works of film theory were prescriptive—often quite pretentiously so, but sometimes intriguingly elaborate. Continuing the psychoanalytic metaphor, we can think of this as the ascendancy of film's "superego"—its sense of the artistic community's standards of

---

[*] Yes, I know we seem to be arguing both sides of the case: we want film to be accepted in the university but we don't want filmmakers studying too much. As elsewhere in American life during the seventies and eighties, the pendulum swung too far. Many of the truths we discovered in the sixties were dangerously distorted when they were institutionalized. It's the reason we build blank walls around our highways.

behavior and respectability—as it struggled to be treated as an equal, and mastered its natural libidinous impulses. "Standards" were necessary, and film theorists provided them. Now that film theory has matured, it is much less likely to insist on rules and regulations often derived from outside the domain of film itself and instead concentrates on developing its own more flexible and more sophisticated values.

Within any specific film theory, there are a number of oppositions at work. Is the theory mainly esthetic or mainly philosophical? Does it deal with the relationships of parts of cinema to each other, or the parts of a specific film to each other? Or does it concern itself with the relationships between film and culture, film and the individual, film and society?

Sergei Eisenstein, still the most fecund of film theorists, used cinematic terminology to describe the difference between various approaches to film study. In his 1945 essay "A Close-up View" he described "long-shot" film theory as that which deals with film in context, which judges its political and social implications. "Medium-shot" film criticism, meanwhile, focuses on the human scale of the film, which is what most reviewers concern themselves with. "Close-up" theory, however, "'breaks down' the film into its parts" and "resolves the film into its elements." Film semiotics and other theories that attempt to treat the "language" of film, for example, are close-up approaches.

The essential concept here is the classic opposition between form and function. Are we more interested in what a film is (form) or in how it acts upon us (function)? As we shall see, it was quite a while before film theory turned from a focus on the form of the art to the more difficult and meaningful analysis of its function. Gradually, prescription has yielded to more scientific methods of investigation as film theory has become less demanding and more inquisitive.

The Poet and the Philosopher: Lindsay and Münsterberg

The first film theorists, as we have noted, were mainly interested—some more consciously than others—in providing a respectable artistic cachet for the young art. In 1915, just as the feature film was rising to prominence, Vachel Lindsay, at that time a well-known poet, published *The Art of the Moving Picture*, a lively, naïve, often simplistic, but nevertheless insightful paean to the wild, youthful popular art.

The very title of his book was an argumentative proposition: he challenged his readers to consider this sideshow entertainment as a real art. Working on the model of the established narrative and visual arts, he identified three basic types of "photoplays," as movies with pretensions to artistic station were then called:

"The Photoplay of Action," "The Intimate Photoplay," and "The Motion Picture of Splendor," three categories that serve well to triangulate the Hollywood cinema of the next eighty years. In each case, Lindsay had noticed and formulated elements of narrative in which film could not only rival but often surpass the other arts: Action, Intimacy, and Splendor were all strong (sometimes crude), direct values—and still are.

Working intuitively from his lively passion for the movies, Lindsay then further compared the potential of film with the accomplishments of the older arts, discussing film as, in turn, "sculpture-in-motion," "painting-in-motion," and "architecture-in-motion." He concluded his basic outline of the esthetics of film with two chapters, each in its own way surprisingly prescient. At the time he wrote, those few films taken seriously by the cultural Establishment were the ones that mimicked the stage—the "photoplays."

Yet Lindsay understood very early on—after *The Birth of a Nation* (1915) but before *Intolerance* (1916)—that the real strength of film might lie in precisely the opposite direction. In "Thirty Differences Between Photoplays and the Stage" he outlined an argument that was to become a major concern of film theorists throughout the twenties and into the thirties as he explained how the two seemingly parallel arts contrasted. This became the dominant theme as film theorists tried to establish a separate identity for the adolescent art.

Lindsay's last chapter on esthetics, "Hieroglyphics," is even more insightful. With profound insight, he wrote:

> The invention of the photoplay is as great a step as was the beginning of picture-writing in the stone age.

He then goes on to treat film as a language and, although his analysis may be, as he suggests, "a fanciful flight rather than a sober argument," it nevertheless points directly to the most recent stage of development in film theory—semiotics. Quite an achievement in 1915 for an antiacademic poet enamored of the "barbaric yawp" and untrained in the scholarly disciplines!

Nor does Lindsay stop with the internal esthetics of film. The third section of his book is devoted to the extrinsic effects of the "photoplay." Again, the discussion is not so important for its concrete contributions to our understanding of the medium as it is as an early historical marker, yet one of Lindsay's most idiosyncratic theories—always dismissed by later theorists and critics—bears further examination.

Lindsay suggests that the audience should engage in conversation during a (silent) film rather than listen to music. No one took his suggestion seriously; if they had, we might have developed a cinema that was communal and interactive much earlier than we did. Many Third World films (as well as those of Godard) were designed, despite their soundtracks, as first statements in conversation between filmmaker and observer. In short, Vachel Lindsay as poet and passionate lover of film intuited a number of truths that more academic theorists, limited by their rigid systematic thinking, never could have understood.

A year after Lindsay's paean to movies first appeared, it was joined by another major contribution—directly opposed in style, approach, and tone, but just as valuable: Hugo Münsterberg's seminal *The Photoplay: A Psychological Study* (1916). Münsterberg, of German origin, was a professor of philosophy at Harvard and, like his sponsor William James, one of the founders of modern psychology. Unlike Lindsay, the populist poet, Münsterberg brought an academic reputation to his work. He was not a "movie fan" but rather a disinterested academician who only a year before his book was published had little or no experience of the rowdy popular art.

His intellectual analysis of the phenomenon not only provided a much-needed cachet but also remains even today one of the more balanced and objective outlines of film theory. Münsterberg was committed to bridging the gap between professional theory and popular understanding. "Intellectually the world has been divided into two classes," he wrote, "the 'highbrows' and the 'lowbrows.'" He hoped that his analysis of the psychology of film would "bring these two brows together." Sadly, his book was ignored for many years and was only rediscovered by film theorists and students in 1969.

Like Lindsay, Münsterberg quickly understood that film had its own special genius and that its esthetic future did not lie in replicating the kind of work that was better done on stage or in the novel. Like the poet, the professor also understood that film theory must take into account not only implicit esthetics but also explicit social and psychological effects. He calls these two facets the "Inner" and the "Outer" developments of motion pictures, and he begins his study with a discussion of them.

His most valuable contribution, however, predictably lies in his application of psychological principles to the film phenomenon. Freudian dream psychology was a useful tool for many popular theories of cinema from the twenties on. Münsterberg's approach, however, is pre-Freudian (which is one good reason why it was ignored for so long); at the same time he is an important precursor of Gestalt psychology, which makes his approach seem surprisingly contemporary. Freudian film psychology emphasizes the unconscious, dreamlike nature of the experience and therefore concentrates on the passive attitude toward the medium. Münsterberg, in contrast, develops a conception of the relationship between film and observer as interactive.

He begins by describing how our perception of movement in moving pictures depends not so much on the static phenomenon of persistence of vision as on our active mental processes of interpretation of this series of still images. Thirty years later, this active process became known as the Phi phenomenon. Münsterberg had described it (without labeling it) in 1916.

In chapters titled "Attention," "Memory and Imagination," and "Emotions," he then develops a sophisticated theory of film psychology that conceives of film as an active process—a strongly mental activity—in which the observer is a partner with the filmmaker. In a second section, titled "The Esthetics of the Photoplay," he investigates some of the ramifications of this view of the process. In shifting attention away from the passive phenomenon of persistence of vision and toward the active mental process of the Phi phenomenon, Münsterberg established a vital logical basis for theories of film as an active process. At the time, this theory was prescriptive rather than descriptive. During the first thirty or forty years of film theory, the concept of the medium as essentially passive and manipulative was dominant, as it is in film practice. Yet Münsterberg's understanding of the medium as at least potentially interactive would eventually be redeemed.

Curiously, Lindsay's and Münsterberg's books were the last really significant works of film theory produced in the U.S. until quite recently. It seemed as if film theory was beside the point once Hollywood began to dominate film practice. By the early twenties, the focal point of film theory had shifted to Europe and was for fifty years dominated by French, German, and Eastern European thinkers.

Like the British tradition, the American line of development of theory/criticism has been mainly practical—concerned with concrete criticism rather than abstract theory. Ideally, it is not a less valuable tradition because of this practical orientation, but because it is diffuse it is not so easy to describe or to study. Concentrated single volumes of abstract theory lend themselves to analysis much more readily, a fact that should be remembered, since it tends to distort our conception of the shape of developing film theory.

Paradoxically, one of the first signs of the growing vitality of film theory in Europe in the twenties was found in the work of Louis Delluc, who, although he produced several volumes of theory (*Cinéma et cie*, 1919; *Photogénie*, 1920), is best remembered as a practicing daily film critic, filmmaker, and founder of the ciné-club movement. Together with Léon Moussinac, he established film reviewing as a serious undertaking, in direct contrast to the reportage and puff publicity then common. Delluc died in 1924, before his thirty-fifth birthday, but by that time the European tradition of the art film (and the film of art) was solidly established.

Expressionism and Realism: Arnheim and Kracauer

In his useful introduction to the subject, *The Major Film Theories* (1976), J. Dudley Andrew adopted categories derived from Aristotle to analyze the structure of film theory. He approached various theories by four avenues: "Raw Material," "Methods and Techniques," "Forms and Shapes," and "Purpose and Value." We can further simplify the categories if we realize that the two central ones—"Methods and Techniques" and "Forms and Shapes"—are simply opposite facets of the same phenomenon, the first practical, the second theoretical. Each of these categories focuses on a different aspect of the film process, the chain connecting material, filmmaker, and observer. The way in which a theory arranges these relationships to a large extent determines its aim, and is a direct function of its underlying principles. Those theories that celebrate the raw material are essentially Realist. Those that focus first on the power of the filmmaker to modify or manipulate reality are, at base, Expressionist: that is, they are more concerned with the filmmaker's expression of the raw materials than with the filmed reality itself.

These two basic attitudes have dominated the history of film theory and practice ever since the Lumière brothers (who seemed to be obsessed with capturing raw reality on film) and Méliès (who obviously was more interested by what he could do to his raw materials). It is only recently that the third facet of the process, the relationship between film and observer (in Aristotle's terms "Purpose and Value"), has begun to dominate film theory, although it was always implicit in both Realist and Expressionist arguments. The semiotics of film and the politics of film both begin with the observer and work back through the art of the filmmaker to the reality of the raw materials on the other side.

The center of interest has shifted from generative to receptive theories. We are now no longer so concerned with how a film is made as with how it is perceived and what effect it has in our lives. Münsterberg's work (and even Lindsay's) had foreshadowed this shift of emphasis. Moreover, we should remember that all three of these interrelated elements were evident during the practical development of film, even if theory at various points tended to emphasize one to the exclusion of the others.

Expressionism dominated film theory throughout the twenties and thirties. D. W. Griffith described two major "schools" of film practice, the American and the German. The American School, he told his audience, "says to you: 'Come and *have* a great experience!' Whereas the German school says: 'Come and *see* a great experience!'" Griffith's purpose was to suggest that American cinema in the twenties was more active and energetic than German cinema, as indeed it was. Yet although we speak of "German Expressionism" in the twenties and seldom use the word in an American context, nevertheless both of Griffith's schools focus on the essentially Expressionist aim of the "great experience." As Griffith describes his theory of pacing in the movies, it is a tool for the manipulation of the spectators' emotions:

> For a quick, keen estimate of a motion picture give me a boy of ten and a girl of fifteen—the boy for action, the girl for romance. Few things have happened in their lives to affect their natural reactions.

What Griffith and Hollywood wanted were pure reactions to their stimuli; the art of film, accordingly, lies almost entirely in the design of effective stimuli. There is little or no sense of the observer actively involved in the process.

Realism was a common, if subordinate, strain in film practice throughout the first four decades of film history; it didn't come into its own theoretically until the late thirties (in the practical work of the British documentarists led by John Grierson) and the forties (with Italian Neorealism). There were good reasons for this late blooming: first, since Realist theory naturally implied that film itself was of lesser importance (that reality was more important than "art"), this led both filmmakers and theorists toward Expressionist positions. Expressionism not only made the filmmaker more important in the general scheme of things, it was also a natural outgrowth of the early efforts to achieve for film "art" a certain degree of respectability. During the early twentieth century, every one of the other, older arts was moving toward greater abstraction, less verisimilitude—"less matter with more art." Why shouldn't the adolescent upstart, film, move in this direction as well? Moreover, if film was in fact to be considered a mature art, it was necessary to show that the activity of the art of film was just as complex and demanding as, say, the activity of painting. Expressionism, by placing emphasis on the manipulative power of the filmmaker, served this function nicely.

More important, perhaps, is the second reason theories of Expressionism dominated the first fifty years of film theory: there was very little room for private or personal art in film. Because it was so expensive, cinema had to be a very popular form. Theories of Realism demand that we see the observer as a participant in the process. If film is strictly a commodity, how could we justify "making the consumer work" for his entertainment? As a product, film had to be manipulative: the more "effect" the film had, the better value for the money the consumer had spent. In fact, most popular film is still judged by this simple rule: witness the success of such "mind-blowers" as *The Exorcist* (1973), *Jaws* (1975), *Alien* (1979), and *Terminator 2* (1991). In this economic sense, movies are still a carnival attraction—rides on roller coasters through chambers of horror and tunnels of love—and Realism is totally beside the point.

The two standard, most succinct, and colorful texts describing the contrasting Expressionist and Realist positions are Rudolf Arnheim's *Film as Art* (published first in German in 1933 as *Film als Kunst* and translated into English almost immediately) and Siegfried Kracauer's *Theory of Film: The Redemption of Physical Reality* (first published in 1960). Both books are strongly—almost belligerently—prescriptive. Both present "revealed truths" as if film theory were a matter of pronouncements rather than investigations. Yet both remain memorable and have become classics of the literature of film, not only because they each neatly summarize the positions of their respective schools, but also in no small part because they are so sententious: more complex, less determinist theories of film are obviously not so easily remembered.

Arnheim had a distinguished career as a psychologist (he was the author of *Art and Visual Perception: A Psychology of the Creative Eye*, 1954), so it is no surprise to discover that the basic tenets of *Film as Art* are psychological. But unlike his predecessor Münsterberg, he is more concerned with how film is made than with how it is perceived. The thrust of his small volume can be described quite succinctly: he proceeds from the basic premise that the art of film depends on its limitations, that its physical limitations are precisely its esthetic virtues. As he himself summarizes his position in his preface to the 1957 edition:

> I undertook to show in detail how the very properties that make photography and film fall short of perfect reproduction can act as the necessary molds of an artistic medium.

It is a curious proposition, yet in a sense correct, since logically each art must be formed by its limitations. The problem is that Arnheim suggests that it should not exceed those limitations and that technological developments—sound, color, widescreen, and so forth—that do push the limits further out are not to be welcomed. He finds film at its height artistically in the late silent period, a position that, although understandable enough in 1933, he continued to maintain in the 1957 edition.

After listing a number of ways in which film representation differs from reality, Arnheim proceeds to enumerate how each of these differences—these limitations—yields artistic content and form. The gist of his argument is that the closer film comes to reproducing reality, the less room there is in which the artist can create his effects. The success of this theory rests on two assumptions that are certainly problematic:

- ❏ that art equals effect, or expression; that the magnitude of a work of art is directly related to the degree of the artist's manipulation of materials; and

- ❏ that the limitations of an art form only generate its esthetics and do not restrict them.

"The temptation to increase the size of the screen," he writes, for example, "goes with the desire for colored, stereoscopic, and sound film. It is the wish of people who do not know that artistic effect is bound up with the limitations of the medium...." Yet as those new dimensions were added to the repertoire of film art, filmmakers discovered more freedom, not less, and the range of possible artistic effects expanded considerably.

Basically, the difficulty with Arnheim's theory of limitations is that he focuses all too narrowly on the production of film and doesn't take into account the liberating and complicating factor of its perception. Many of the limitations he lists (aside from the technological)—the framing of the image, film's two-dimensionality, the breakup of the space-time continuum by editing—are far less important in terms of how we perceive a film than in terms of how we construct one. By ignoring the total scope of the film process, Arnheim produces a strictly ideal prescription for film art that has less to do with the actual phenomenon of practical film than it might at first appear. In any event, his pure, limited conception of film was quickly overtaken by events as technology developed and practical filmmakers discovered the possibilities of new variables.

The conflict between Realism and Expressionism that colors nearly all film theory is not so direct, explicit, and nicely balanced as it might at first seem. The relationship is more dialectical than dichotomous, so that Realist theory grows out of Expressionist theory just as Expressionist theory had, in its turn, grown out of the urge to build an artistic reputation for film.

Siegfried Kracauer's magnum opus, *Theory of Film: The Redemption of Physical Reality*, coming twenty-seven years after Arnheim's elegant, lean prescription, is in contrast a sprawling, sometimes blunt, often difficult investigation into wide-ranging theories of Realism that had been developing slowly over a period of more than twenty years. Expressionism, because it is self-limiting and self-defining, is relatively easy to outline. Realism, on the other hand, is a vague, inclusive term that means many things to many people. All students of literature have run into the "problem" of Realism before. Is Jane Austen, who wrote precisely about a very narrow segment of society, a Realist? Or is breadth as important as depth to the Realist sensibility? Is Naturalism, rather easily defined as an artistic form based on Determinist philosophy, a kind of Realism, an offshoot from it, or in direct opposition to it? In film, too, "Realism" is a slippery term. The Rossellini of *Rome, Open City* (1945) is a "Realist," but what about the Rossellini of *The Rise to Power of Louis XIV?* Or Fellini? Are politics necessary to Realism? What about acting? Are documentaries always more "realistic" than fiction films? Or is it possible to be a Realist and still be a story teller? The catalogue of questions about the nature of film Realism is endless.

Kracauer covers many of them, but his book is by no means a complete survey of the quirky definitions of the word. It is *a* theory of film, not *the* theory of film. Like Arnheim's essay, it chooses a single central fact of the film experience as crucial, then builds a prescription that leads to a specific conclusion. Like Arnheim, too, Kracauer was writing mainly after the fact. If the great age of film Expressionism was the twenties, then the central period of film Realism was the forties and fifties. The most important Realist trend of the sixties, for instance, occurred in documentary—an area of film activity about which Kracauer has very little to say.

While Kracauer has the reputation of being the foremost theorist of film Realism, he was actually only one among many. André Bazin, for instance, is also generally considered a "Realist," yet although he offered a much richer investigation of the phenomenon during the fifteen years preceding Kracauer's book, his work was never so clearly codified as Kracauer's and therefore hasn't until recently had the direct impact of his successor's.

Throughout most of film history, Realism has been of more interest to practical filmmakers than theoretical critics. Dziga Vertov in the Soviet Union in the 1920s, Jean Vigo in France, and John Grierson in England in the 1930s, Roberto Rossellini, Cesare Zavattini, and the Neorealists in Italy in the 1940s, all developed Realist positions in opposition to Expressionist theories. It was as if the filmmakers reacted against the potential abuse of power of their medium, instead searching for a more "moral" position in Realism.

At the center of Arnheim's theory had been the limitations of the technology and the form of film art. The kernel of Kracauer's theory is the photographic "calling" of film art. Simply because photography and film do come so close to reproducing reality, they must emphasize this ability in their esthetics. This premise is diametrically opposed to Arnheim's. "Film," Kracauer wrote, "is uniquely equipped to record and reveal physical reality and, hence, gravitates toward it." Therefore, he suggests, content must take precedence over form. He then develops what he calls a material esthetic rather than an esthetic of form.

Because theories of art depend so heavily on formalism, then, film becomes for Kracauer a kind of antiart. "Due to its fixed meaning," he concludes, "the concept of art does not, and cannot, cover truly 'cinematic' films—films, that is, which incorporate aspects of physical reality with a view to making us experience them. And yet it is they, not the films reminiscent of traditional art works, which are valid esthetically."

This is the third stage of the psychological development of film as art. After having established itself as respectable in its adolescence, then having joined the community of the arts in its young adulthood by showing how like them it really was, it now moves into maturity, exerting its "ego integrity" by separating itself from the community and establishing its own personal system of values. If film doesn't fit the definition of art, then the definition of art must be changed.

Having celebrated film's uniqueness, Kracauer then makes a crucial logical jump. Since it can reproduce reality so well, he suggests, it *ought* to. It is at this point that his theory is most open to contradiction. It would be just as easy to propose (as Arnheim does in a way) that, since film and reality have such a close and intimate connection, film ought to exercise this mimetic power in the opposite way: by contradicting, molding, forming, shaping reality rather than reproducing it. Nevertheless, after these first significant pronouncements, Kracauer moves on into a more general and more objective study of the medium of film. The logical end point of his primary contention about the close relationship of film and reality would be to elevate the film record, the nonfiction film, and the documentary over the fictional film. Yet Kracauer, as we have noted, pays relatively little attention to strict factual film and instead focuses on the most common type of film: the narrative. He finds the ideal film form to be the "found story." Such films are fiction, but they are "discovered rather than contrived." He continues, explaining the difference between this quasi-fictional ideal form and the fully developed "artwork":

> Since the found story is part and parcel of the raw material in which it lies dormant, it cannot possibly develop into a self-contained whole—which means that it is almost the opposite of the theatrical story [p. 246].

As his theory develops and broadens, it becomes clear that Kracauer has no great objections to form—so long as it serves the purpose of content. And here we get to the heart of Kracauer's true contribution to film theory: film serves a purpose. It does not exist simply for itself, as a pure esthetic object; it exists in the context of the world around it. Since it stems from reality it must also return to it— hence the subtitle of Kracauer's theory: *The Redemption of Physical Reality.*

If this sounds vaguely religious, the connotation is, I think, intended. For Kracauer, film has a human, ethical nature. Ethics must replace esthetics, thereby fulfilling Lenin's prophecy, which Jean-Luc Godard was fond of quoting, that "ethics are the esthetics of the future." Having been divorced from physical reality by both scientific and esthetic abstraction, we need the redemption film offers: we need to be brought back into communication with the physical world. Film can mediate reality for us. It can both "corroborate" and "debunk" our impressions of reality.

This seems an admirable goal.

Montage: Pudovkin, Eisenstein, Balázs, and Formalism

The words "Expressionism" and "Formalism" are often used interchangeably in film criticism to denote those tendencies generally opposed to "Realism." Both Expressionism and Formalism are also labels attached to specific periods of cultural history: Expressionism was the major force in German culture—in theater and painting as well as film—during the 1920s, just as, during the same period, Formalism marked the burgeoning cultural life—both literary and cinematic—in the Soviet Union. Essentially, the difference between the two movements depends on a slight but significant shift of focus. Expressionism is a more generalized, romantic conception of film as an expressive force. Formalism is more specific, more "scientific," and more concerned with the elements, the details that go to make up this force. It is more analytic and less synthetic, and it also carries with it a strong sense of the importance of function as well as form in art.

During the 1920s, the period immediately following the Russian Revolution, the Soviet cinema was among the most exciting in the world, not only practically but theoretically. There is no doubt that the Soviet filmmaker-theorists wanted not only to capture reality but also to change it. Realism, at least esthetically, is not particularly revolutionary: as we have noted, it tends to deny the power of the filmmaker and therefore makes film seem to be less powerful as a tool to effect social change. During this period—before Stalin imposed the doctrine of Socialist Realism (which is neither Realist nor especially Socialist)—two filmmakers, V. I. Pudovkin and Sergei Eisenstein, produced not only a number of exceptional films but also an amorphous body of Formalist theory that had a profound impact on the course of development of film theory. At the same time, the Hungarian writer, critic, and filmmaker Béla Balázs was pursuing a line of Formalist thinking that, although it is less well known than those of Pudovkin and Eisenstein, nevertheless deserves to be ranked with theirs.

Unlike Arnheim and Kracauer, Pudovkin, Eisenstein, and Balázs were practicing filmmakers who wanted to describe their art rather than prescribe for it. Their theoretical work was not compressed into single volumes, but rather spread out in individual essays over many years. It was organic, developing, and ongoing rather than closed, complete, and final. It is thus much less easy to summarize quickly; it is also much more useful and insightful.

Very soon after the revolution of 1917, a filmmaker named Lev Kuleshov was put in charge of a workshop. Pudovkin was one of his students as was, briefly, Eisenstein. Unable to find enough filmstock to fuel their projects, they turned to reediting films already made, and in the process discovered a number of truths about the technique of film montage.

In one experiment, Kuleshov linked together a number of shots made at varying times and places. The composite was a unified piece of film narrative. Kuleshov called this "creative geography." In probably their most famous experiment, the Kuleshov group took three identical shots of the well-known prerevolutionary actor Moszhukin and intercut them with shots of a plate of soup, a woman in a coffin, and a little girl. According to Pudovkin, who later described the results of the experiment, audiences exclaimed at Moszhukin's subtle and affective ability to convey such varied emotions: hunger, sadness, affection.

In his two major works, *Film Technique* (1926) and *Film Acting* (1935), Pudovkin developed from the basic root of his experiments with Kuleshov a varied theory of cinema centered on what he called "relational editing." For Pudovkin, montage was "the method which controls the 'psychological guidance' of the spectator." In this respect, his theory was simply Expressionist—that is, mainly concerned with how the filmmaker can affect the observer. But he identified five separate and distinct types of montage: contrast, parallelism, symbolism, simultaneity, and leitmotif (reiteration of theme).

Here we have the basic premise of film Formalism: Pudovkin discovered categories of form and analyzed them. Moreover, he was greatly concerned with the importance of the shot—of mise-en-scène—and therefore displayed an attitude that we have come to regard as essentially Realist. He saw montage as the complex, pumping heart of film, but he also felt that its purpose was to support narrative rather than to alter it.

Eisenstein set up his own theory of montage—as collision rather than linkage—in direct opposition to Pudovkin's theory. In a series of essays beginning in the early twenties and continuing throughout most of his life, he worked and reworked a number of basic concepts as he struggled with the shape and nature of cinema.[*] For Eisenstein, montage has as its aim the creation of ideas, of a new reality, rather than the support of narrative, the old reality of experience. As a student, he had been fascinated by Oriental ideograms that combined elements of widely different meaning in order to create entirely new meanings, and he regarded the ideogram as a model of cinematic montage. Taking an idea from the literary Formalists, he conceived of the elements of a film being "decomposed" or "neutralized" so that they could serve as fresh material for dialectic montage. Even actors were to be cast not for their individual qualities but for the "types" they represented.

Eisenstein extended this concept of dialectics even to the shot itself. As shots related to each other dialectically, so the basic elements of a single shot—which he called its "attractions"—could interrelate to produce new meanings. Attractions as he defined them included

> every aggressive moment ... every element ... that brings to light in the spectator those senses or that psychology that influence his experience—every element that can be verified and mathematically calculated to produce certain emotional shocks in a proper order within the totality ...
> [*Film Sense*, p. 231].

Because attractions existed within the framework of that totality, a further extension of montage was suggested: a montage of attractions. "Instead of a static 'reflection' of an event with all possibilities for activity within the limits of the event's logical action, we advance to a new plane—free montage of arbitrarily selected, independent ... attractions...." [p. 232]. This was an entirely new basis for montage, different in kind from Pudovkin's five categories.

Later, Eisenstein developed a more elaborate view of the system of attractions in which one was always dominant while others were subsidiary. The problem here was that the idea of the dominant seemed to conflict with the concept of

---

[*]   These essays are collected in *The Film Sense* and *Film Form* and in a number of other volumes.

neutralization, which supposedly prepared all the elements to be used with equal ease by the filmmaker. There are a number of such seeming contradictions in Eisenstein's thought—a good sign that his theory of film was organic, open, and healthily incomplete.

Possibly the most important ramification of Eisenstein's system of attractions, dominants, and dialectic collisional montage lies in its implications for the observer of film. Whereas Pudovkin had seen the techniques of montage as an aid to narrative, Eisenstein reconstructed montage in opposition to straight narrative. If shot A and shot B were to form an entirely new idea, C, then the audience had to become directly involved. It was necessary that they work to understand the inherent meaning of the montage. Pudovkin, whose ideas seem closer in spirit to the tenets of Realism, had paradoxically proposed a type of narrative style that controlled the "psychological guidance" of the audience.

Eisenstein, meanwhile, in suggesting an extreme Formalism in which photographed reality ceased to be itself and became instead simply a stock of raw material—attractions, or "shocks"—for the filmmaker to rearrange as he saw fit, was also paradoxically describing a system in which the observer was a necessary and equal participant.

The simplistic dichotomy between Expressionism and Realism thus no longer holds. For Eisenstein it was necessary to destroy Realism in order to approach reality. The real key to the system of film is not the artist's relationship with his raw materials but rather his relationship with his audience. A hypothetical film that might show the greatest respect for photographed reality might at the same time show little or no respect for its audience. Conversely, a highly Formalist, abstract film expression—Eisenstein's own *Potemkin* (1925), for instance—might engage its audience in a dialectical process instead of overpowering them with a calculated emotional experience.

Eisenstein's basic conception of the film experience was, like his theories, open-ended. The process of film (like the process of theory) was far more important than its end, and the filmmaker and observer were engaged in it dynamically. Likewise, the elements of the film experience that was the channel of communication between creator and observer were also connected logically with each other. Eisenstein's wide-ranging theories of film thus foreshadow the two most recent developments of cinematic theory, since he is concerned throughout not only with the language of film but also with how that language can be used by both filmmakers and observers.

Like Eisenstein, Béla Balázs worked out his description of the structure of cinema over a period of many years. Hungarian by birth, he left his native country after the Commune was overthrown in 1919 and spent time thereafter in Germany, the Soviet Union, and other East European countries. His major work, *Theory of the Film: Character and Growth of a New Art* (1948), summarizes and comments on a

Figure 5-1. As the people of Odessa gather to hail the rebellious soldiers on the battleship *Potemkin* in the harbor, soldiers appear. The crowd runs down the steps in horror as the soldiers fire. A young boy is hit and killed. His mother picks him up in her arms and turns to face the soldiers at the top of the steps....

Figure 5-2. ... As she advances, pleading with them, they prepare to fire. The officer lowers his saber and a volley is fired, cutting down the mother and child. The crowd runs down the steps, trampling those who have fallen....

Figure 5-3. … As they reach the pathway at the bottom, they are attacked by mounted Cossacks. The people are caught in the pincers between the rank of soldiers relentlessly advancing down the steps, and the Cossacks who whip and trample them. Eisenstein cuts between shots of the victims and shots of the oppressors. A woman with a baby carriage is hit near the top of the steps. As she falls, she nudges the carriage over the first step.…

Figure 5-4. … It careens down the steps over corpses, as people watch in terror, until it reaches the bottom step and overturns. (*All stills l'Avant-Scène. Frame enlargements.*)

lifetime of theorizing. Because he had practical experience in the art and because he developed his theory over a number of years, *Theory of the Film* remains one of the most balanced volumes of its kind.

Sharing many of the basic Formalist principles of Eisenstein and Soviet literary critics of the twenties, Balázs manages to integrate these concepts with certain Realist principles. He was fascinated by the "secret power" of the closeup to reveal details of fact and emotion and developed a theory of the true province of film as "micro-dramatics," the subtle shifts of meaning and the quiet interplay of emotions that the closeup is so well equipped to convey. His earliest book on film had been entitled *The Visible Man, or Film Culture* (1924). It made this essentially Realist point strongly and probably influenced Pudovkin.

But while he celebrated the reality of the closeup, Balázs also situated film squarely in the economic sphere of influence. He realized that the economic foundation of film is the prime determinant of film esthetics, and he was one of the earliest film theorists to understand and explain how our approach to any film is molded and formed by the cultural values we share. Predating Marshall McLuhan by many years, he anticipated the development of a new visual culture that would resurrect certain powers of perception that, he said, had lain dormant. "The discovery of printing," he wrote, "gradually rendered illegible the faces of men. So much could be read from paper that the method of conveying meaning by facial expression fell into desuetude." That is changing now that we have a developing, reproducible visual culture that can match print in versatility and reach. Balázs's sense of film as a cultural entity subject to the same pressure and forces as any other element of culture may seem obvious today, but he was one of the first to recognize this all-important aspect of film.

Mise-en-Scène: Neorealism, Bazin, and Godard

Like Eisenstein, André Bazin was engaged in a continual process of revision and reevaluation as his short career progressed from the mid-1940s to his early death in 1958 at the age of thirty-nine. Unlike nearly all other authors of major film theories, Bazin was a working critic who wrote regularly about individual films. His theory is expressed mainly in four volumes of collected essays (*Qu'est-ce que le cinéma?*) published in the years immediately succeeding his death (selected and translated in two volumes: *What Is Cinema?*). It is deeply imbued with his practical, deductive experience. With Bazin, for the first time, film theory becomes not a matter of pronouncement and prescription but a fully mature intellectual activity, well aware of its own limitations. The very title of Bazin's collected essays reveals

Figure 5-5. Eisenstein's *Alexander Nevsky* (1938): the Battle on the Ice. The Russian army is in position to defend against the German invaders. Battle scenes, with their strong visual oppositions, were among Eisenstein's most striking sequences. (*l'Avant-Scène. Frame enlargement.*)

the modesty of this approach. For Bazin, the questions are more important than the answers.

With roots in his background as a student of phenomenology, Bazin's theories are clearly Realist in organization, but once again the focus has shifted. If Formalism is the more sophisticated, less pretentious cousin of Expressionism, perhaps what Bazin is after should be called "Functionalism" rather than simply Realism, for running throughout his argument is the important idea that film has significance not for what it is but for what it does.

For Bazin, Realism is more a matter of psychology than of esthetics. He does not make a simple equation between film and reality, as does Kracauer, but rather describes a more subtle relationship between the two in which film is the asymptote to reality, the imaginary line that the geometric curve approaches but never touches. He began one of his earliest essays, "The Ontology of the Photographic Image," by suggesting: "If the plastic arts were put under psychoanalysis, the practice of embalming the dead might turn out to be a fundamental factor in their creation." The arts arose, he contends, because "other forms of insurance were … sought." That primal memory of embalming lives on in photography and cinema, which "embalm time, rescuing it simply from its proper corruption." This leads to an elegantly simple conclusion:

> If the history of the plastic arts is less a matter of their aesthetic than of their psychology then it will be seen to be essentially the story of resemblance, or, if you will, of realism.

If the genesis of the photographic arts is essentially a matter of psychology, then so is their effect. In "The Evolution of the Language of Cinema," Bazin traces the roots of film Realism back to Murnau and Stroheim in the silent cinema, and quickly and elegantly describes how a series of technological innovations pushed film ever closer, asymptotically, to reality. But while technology was the source of this particular power, it was used for psychological, ethical, and political effects. This tendency blossomed in the movement of Italian Neorealism just at the end of and directly after World War II—a cinematic era for which Bazin felt a great affinity. "Is not Neorealism primarily a kind of humanism," he concludes, "and only secondarily a style of filmmaking?" The real revolution, he thinks, took place more on the level of subject matter than of style.

Just as the Formalists had found montage to be the heart of the cinematic enterprise, so Bazin claims that mise-en-scène is the crux of the Realist film. By mise-en-scène he means specifically deep focus photography and the sequence-shot; these techniques allow the spectator to participate more fully in the experience of film. Thus, Bazin finds the development of deep focus to be not just another filmic device, but rather "a dialectical step forward in the history of film language."

He outlines why this is so: depth of focus "brings the spectator in closer relation with the image than he is with reality." This implies consequently "both a more active mental attitude on the part of the observer and a more positive contribution on his part to the action in progress." No more the "psychological guidance" of Pudovkin. From the attention and the will of the spectator, the meaning of the image derives. Moreover, there is a metaphysical consequence of deep focus: "montage by its very nature rules out ambiguity of expression." Eisenstein's attractions are what they are: they are strongly denotative. Neorealism, on the other hand, "tends to give back to the cinema a sense of the ambiguity of reality." Free to choose, we are free to interpret.

Closely associated with this concept of the value of ambiguity are the twin concepts of the presence and reality of space. Bazin, in a later essay, suggests that the essential difference between theater and cinema lies in this area. There is only one reality that cannot be denied in cinema—the reality of space. Contrariwise, on the stage space can easily be illusory; the one reality that cannot be denied there is the presence of the actor and the spectator. These two reductions are the foundations of their respective arts.

The implications for cinema are that, since there is no irreducible reality of presence, "there is nothing to prevent us from identifying ourselves in imagination with the moving world before us, which becomes *the* world." Identification then becomes a key word in the vocabulary of cinematic esthetics. Moreover, the one irreducible reality is that of space. Therefore, film form is intimately involved with spatial relationships: mise-en-scène, in other words.

Bazin did not live long enough to formulate these theories more precisely, but his work nevertheless had a profound effect on a generation of filmmakers, as did Eisenstein's (but as Arnheim's and Kracauer's prescriptions did not). Bazin laid the groundwork for the semiotic and ethical theories that were to follow. More immediately, he inspired a number of his colleagues on *Cahiers du Cinéma,* the magazine he founded with Jacques Doniol-Valcroze and Lo Duca in 1951. The most influential film journal in history, *Cahiers* provided an intellectual home during the fifties and early sixties for François Truffaut, Jean-Luc Godard, Claude Chabrol, Eric Rohmer, and Jacques Rivette, among others. As critics, these men contributed significantly to the development of theory; as filmmakers, they comprised the first generation of cinéastes whose work was thoroughly grounded in film history and theory; their films—especially those of Godard—were not only practical examples of theory but often themselves theoretical essays.

For the first time, film theory was being written in film rather than print.

This fact itself was evidence that the vision of critic and filmmaker Alexandre Astruc was being realized. In 1948, Astruc had called for a new age of cinema, which he identified as the age of caméra-stylo (camera-pen). He predicted that cinema would "gradually break free from the tyranny of what is visual, from the image for its own sake, from the immediate and concrete demands of the narrative, to become a means of writing just as flexible and subtle as written language."[*] Many earlier theorists had spoken of film's "language"; the concept of the caméra-stylo was significantly more elaborate. Astruc not only wanted film to develop its own idiom, he also wanted that idiom to be capable of expressing the most subtle ideas. Except for Eisenstein, no previous film theorist had conceived of film as an intellectual medium in which abstract concepts could be expressed.

Nearly all theorists naturally assumed that the proper province of the recording medium of film was the concrete. Even Eisenstein's dialectical montage depended thoroughly on concrete images—we might call it a dialectic of objective correlatives. Astruc wanted something more. In an offhand reference to Eisenstein, he noted:

---

[*] *The New Wave,* edited by Peter Graham, contains two essays of note: "The Birth of a New Avant Garde: La Caméra-Stylo," by Alexandre Astruc; and "La Politique des auteurs," by André Bazin; both quoted in this section.

the cinema is now moving towards a form which is making it such a precise language that it will soon be possible to write ideas directly on film without even having to resort to those heavy associations of images that were the delight of silent cinema.

Astruc's caméra-stylo was a doctrine of function rather than form. It was a fitting complement to the developing practice of Neorealism that so influenced Bazin.

It would be more than ten years before Astruc's 1948 vision would be realized in the cinema of the New Wave. Meanwhile, Truffaut, Godard, and the others set about developing a theory of critical practice in the pages of *Cahiers du Cinéma*. Always the existentialist, André Bazin was working to develop a theory of film that was deductive—based in practice. Much of this work proceeded through identification and critical examination of genres. "Cinema's existence precedes its essence," he wrote in fine existential form. Whatever conclusions Bazin drew were the direct results of the experience of the concrete fact of film.

François Truffaut best expressed the major theoretical principle that came to identify *Cahiers du Cinéma* in the fifties. In his landmark article "Une certaine tendance du cinéma français" (*Cahiers du Cinéma*, January 1954), Truffaut developed the "Politique des auteurs," which became the rallying cry for the young French critics. Usually translated as "auteur theory," it wasn't a theory at all but a policy: a fairly arbitrary critical approach. As Bazin explained several years later in an essay in which he tried to counter some of the excesses of the policy:

> The *Politique des auteurs* consists, in short, of choosing the personal factor in artistic creation as a standard of reference, and then of assuming that it continues and even progresses from one film to the next.

This led to some rather absurd opinions on individual films, as Bazin points out, but by its very egregiousness the Politique des auteurs helped to prepare the way for a resurgence of the personal cinema of authors in the sixties who could wield Astruc's caméra-stylo with grace and intelligence. Cinema was moving from theories of abstract design to theories of concrete communication. It was not material Realism or even psychological Realism that counted now, but rather intellectual Realism. Once it was understood that a film was the product of an author, once that author's "voice" was clear, then spectators could approach the film not as if it were reality, or the dream of reality, but as a statement by another individual.

More important than Truffaut's Politique, though much less influential at the time, was Jean-Luc Godard's theory of montage, developed in a series of essays in the middle fifties and best expressed in "Montage, mon beau souci" (*Cahiers du Cinéma* 65; December, 1956). Building on Bazin's theory of the basic opposition between mise-en-scène and montage, Godard created a dialectical synthesis of these two theses that had governed film theory for so long. This is one of the most important steps in film theory. Godard rethought the relationship so that both montage and mise-en-scène can be seen as different aspects of the same cinematic activity.

"Montage is above all an integral part of *mise-en-scène*," he wrote. "Only at peril can one be separated from the other. One might just as well try to separate the rhythm from a melody.... What one seeks to foresee in space, the other seeks in time." Moreover, for Godard, mise-en-scène automatically implies montage. In the cinema of psychological reality that derived from Pudovkin and influenced the best of Hollywood, "cutting on a look is almost the definition of montage." Montage is therefore specifically determined by mise-en-scène. As the actor turns to look at an object the editing immediately shows it to us. In this kind of construction, known as "découpage classique," the length of a shot depends on its function and the relationship between shots is controlled by the material within the shot—its mise-en-scène.

Godard's synthesis of the classic opposition is elegantly simple. It has two important corollaries: first, that mise-en-scène can thus be every bit as untruthful as montage when a director uses it to distort reality; second, that montage is not necessarily evidence of bad faith on the part of the filmmaker. No doubt, simple plastic reality is better served by mise-en-scène, which in the strictest Bazinian sense is still more honest than montage. But Godard has redefined the limits of Realism so that we now no longer focus on plastic reality (the filmmaker's concrete relationship with his raw materials) nor on psychological reality (the filmmaker's manipulative relationship with the audience), but on intellectual reality (the filmmaker's dialectical, or conversational, relationship with the audience).

Techniques like mise-en-scène and montage then cease to be of main interest. We are more concerned with the "voice" of a film: Is the filmmaker operating in good faith? Is he speaking directly to us? Has he designed a machine of manipulation? Or is the film an honest discourse?

(When the first edition of *How To Read a Film* appeared, in 1977, this question of "honest discourse" was simply a nice idea; it's much more important now. The growth of special-effects technology in the eighties and the introduction of digitization in the nineties gave filmmakers powerful new tools for constructing "manipulation machines," and they are using them. As we'll see in Chapter 7, ethical questions now take on added significance.)

Godard redefined montage as part of mise-en-scène. So to do montage is to do mise-en-scène. This presages the semiotic approach that was to develop in the sixties. Godard was fond of quoting the apothegm of one of his former teachers, the philosopher Brice Parain:

THE SIGN FORCES US TO SEE AN OBJECT THROUGH ITS SIGNIFICANCE.

THE SIGN FORCES US TO SEE AN OBJECT THROUGH ITS SIGNIFICANCE.

Figure 5-6. Philosopher Brice Parain chats with Anna Karina about freedom and communication in Godard's *My Life to Live* (1962).

Figure 5-7. MISE-EN-SCENE AS VIEW. Godard in "Camera-Eye" (*Far from Vietnam*, 1967). (*Frame enlargement.*)

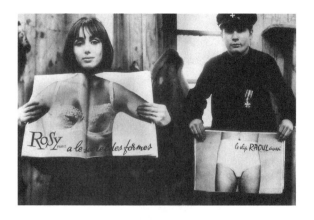

Figure 5-8. "Rosy" and "Raoul," consumer collages, in *Les Carabiniers* (1963).

Figure 5-9. *Le Gai Savoir* (1968). Juliet Berto and Jean-Pierre Léaud in the middle of the dark television studio engage in discussions that aren't broadcast. (*Frame enlargement.*)

Figure 5-10. Juliet Berto, in *Weekend* (1968), is caught between the two unruly forces of the film, sex and energy, a bra ad and the Esso tiger. (*Frame enlargement.*)

Figure 5-11. Recalling the long tracking shot in *Weekend* (see Figure 3-65) past the endless line of stalled autos, this opening sequence from *British Sounds* (1969) objectively follows the construction of a car on the assembly line. The soundtrack is a screech of machinery, as the workers are seen only as parts of the larger machine. The fabrication of the car is as painful as traffic accidents. In both the *Weekend* and *British Sounds* tracking shots, mise-en-scène becomes an ideological tool: it is experienced and thus *felt*, whereas montage is analytical: because it summarizes for us, it does not encourage us to work out our own logic. Montage draws conclusions; mise-en-scène asks questions. (*Frame enlargement.*)

Figure 5-12. In *Vladimir and Rosa* (1971), Godard (left) and his collaborator Jean-Pierre Gorin (right) set up the "dialectic of the tennis court." The elements of the dialectic are, variously: Vladimir (Lenin) and Rosa (Luxemburg), Jean-Luc (Godard) and Jean-Pierre (Gorin), sound and image, American experience and French practice, filmmakers (here) and filmwatchers (also here by implication). (*Frame enlargement.*)

Figure 5-13. An essay on the trial of the Chicago 8, *Vladimir and Rosa* paid close attention to the function of the media. "Bobby X" (Godard/Gorin's character for the real-life Bobby Seale) is gagged and bound in the courtroom (as he was in real life). To demonstrate the absence of Bobby X for the media, the group of revolutionaries in the movie set up a press conference for him. But he can't appear. He speaks from a tape recorder set up on a red chair. Looking for a dramatic *story*, the television cameras are forced to cover a less exciting *idea*: the struggle between sound and image. In this shot, sound finally gets its own image! (*Frame enlargement.*)

Figure 5-14. The tracking shot in the supermarket at the end of *Tout va bien* is equally as long (and as exhilarating) as the earlier shot in *Weekend*. Godard's cameras moves inexorably past a huge rank of twenty-four cash registers, most of them clanging away, as the group of young gauchistes stages a political event in the market: production versus consumption—of images as well as products. (*Frame enlargement.*)

Plastic or material Realism deals only with what is *signified*. Godard's more advanced intellectual or perceptual Realism includes the *signifier*. Godard was also in the habit of quoting Brecht's dictum that "Realism doesn't consist in reproducing reality, but in showing how things *really* are." Both of these statements concentrate the Realist argument on matters of perception. Christian Metz later elaborated this concept, making an important differentiation between the reality of the substance of a film and the reality of the discourse in which that substance is expressed. "On the one hand," he wrote, "there is the *impression* of reality; on the other the *perception* of reality...."

Godard continued his examination of these theoretical problems after he became a filmmaker. By the mid-sixties, he had developed a form of filmed essay in which the structure of ideas usually superseded the classic determinants of plot and character. Most of these films—*The Married Woman* (1964), *Alphaville* (1965), *Masculine-Feminine* (1966), *Two or Three Things that I Know about Her* (1966), for example—dealt with general political and philosophical questions: prostitution, marriage, rebellion, even architectural sociology. By the late sixties, however, he was once more deeply involved in film theory, this time the politics of film. In a series of difficult, tentative, experimental cinematic essays, he further developed his theory of film perception to include the political relationship between film and observer.

The first of these, and the most intense, was *Le Gai Savoir* (1968), in which Godard dealt with the acute problem of the language of film. He suggested that it had become so debased by being used manipulatively that no film can accurately represent reality. It can only, because of the connotations of its language, present a false mirror of reality. It must therefore be presentational rather than representational. While it cannot reproduce reality honestly and truthfully, it *may* be able to produce itself honestly. So that the language may regain some of its force, Godard suggests, it will be necessary for filmmakers to break it down, to engage in what literary critic Roland Barthes called "semioclasm"—the revivifying destruction of signs—we must "return to zero" so that we may begin again.

During the following five years, before Godard turned his attention to video, he completed a number of 16 mm films in which he attempted to return to zero. In *Pravda* (1969) he investigated the ideological significance of certain cinematic devices; in *Vent d'est* (1969) he explored the ideological meaning of film genres; in *British Sounds* (1969) and *Vladimir and Rosa* (1971) he examined, among other things, the relationship of sound and image. Sound, he thought, suffers under the tyranny of image; there should be an equal relationship between the two. Eisenstein and Pudovkin had published a manifesto as early as 1928 declaring that sound should be treated as an equal component of the cinematic equation and allowed to be independent of image. But for forty years film theorists had given only the most perfunctory attention to the element of the soundtrack. Godard hoped the imbalance could be redressed.

Tout va bien and *Letter to Jane* (both 1972) are probably the most important of Godard's theoretical works during this period. The former summarizes what he had learned from his experiments; the latter is, in part, an autocritique of the former.

Tout va bien involves a filmmaker and a reporter (husband and wife) in a concrete political situation (a strike and the worker occupation of a factory) and then studies their reaction to it. From this it builds to an analysis of the entire filmic process of production and consumption. Godard reworked his earlier synthesis of montage and mise-en-scène in economic terms, seeing cinema not as a system of esthetics but as an economic, perceptual, and political structure in which the "rapports de production"—the relationships between producer and consumer—determine the shape of the film experience. The emphasis is not on how cinema relates to an ideal system (esthetics) but rather on how it directly affects us as viewers. Film's ethics and politics therefore determine its nature.

This was not a particularly new idea; Balázs was aware of this dimension of film. In the thirties and forties, the Frankfurt school of social criticism (Walter Benjamin, Theodor Adorno, and Max Horkheimer, mainly) had examined film in this context, most notably in Benjamin's very important essay "The Work of Art in the Age of Mechanical Reproduction." Benjamin had written: "For the first time in world history, mechanical reproduction emancipates the work of art from its parasitical dependence on ritual.... Instead of being based on ritual, it begins to be based on another practice—politics." Benjamin, however, was speaking of an ideal. Godard had to show how commercial cinema had usurped what Benjamin had termed film's unique ability to shatter tradition, tamed it, and made it serve the purposes of a repressive establishment. It was this subliminally powerful idiom that Godard knew had to be broken down.

Letter to Jane, a forty-five-minute essay about the ideological significance of a photo of Jane Fonda (one of the stars of *Tout va bien),* carries out this process in detail. Working with Jean-Pierre Gorin, Godard attempted to analyze the signification of the esthetic elements of the photo. The angle, design, and relationships between components, Godard showed, have delicate but real ideological significance. By the time of *Letter to Jane,* Godard was by no means alone in this dialectic, semiotic approach to film.

Film Speaks and Acts: Metz and Contemporary Theory

While Godard was studying on film the consequences of the idea that "the sign forces us to see an object through its significance," Christian Metz and others were studying in print the ramifications of that dictum. In two volumes of *Essais sur la signification au cinéma* (the first of which appeared in English translated as *Film Language: A Semiotics of the Cinema*), published in 1968 and 1972, and in his major work *Language and Cinema* (1971), Metz outlined a view of film as a logical phenomenon that can be studied by scientific methods. The main points of Metz's thesis have already been discussed in Chapter 3. It will suffice here simply to outline the broad principles of what is the most elaborate, subtle, and complex theory of film yet developed.

Semiotics is a general term that covers many specific approaches to the study of culture as language. With strong roots in the linguistic theories of Ferdinand de Saussure, it uses language as a general model for a variety of phenomena. The approach first took shape in the cultural anthropology of Claude Lévi-Strauss in the fifties and early sixties. This "structuralism" quickly became accepted as a general worldview. Michael Wood described the nature of this intellectual fashion succinctly:

> Structuralism is perhaps best understood as a tangled and possibly unnameable strand in modern intellectual history. At times it seems synonymous with modernism itself. At times it seems to be simply one among several twentieth-century formalisms.... And at times it seems to be the inheritor of that vast project which was born with Rimbaud and Nietzsche, spelled out in Mallarmé, pursued in Saussure, Wittgenstein, and Joyce, defeated in Beckett and Borges, and is scattered now into a host of helpless sects: what Mallarmé called the Orphic explanation of the earth, the project of picturing the world not *in* language but *as* language [*New York Review of Books*, March 4, 1976].

In short, structuralism, with its offspring, semiotics, is a generalized worldview that uses the idea of language as its basic tool.

Metz's approach to film (like all film semiotics) is at once the most abstract and the most concrete of film theories. Because it intends to be a science, semiotics depends heavily on the practical detailed analysis of specific films—and parts of films. In this respect, semiotic criticism is far more concrete and intense than any other approach. Yet at the same time, semiotics is often exquisitely philosophical. The semiotic description of the universe of cinema, in a sense, exists for its own sake: it has its own attractions, and the emphasis is often not on film but on theory. Moreover, semioticians—Metz especially—are noted for being elegant stylists in their own right. Much of the pleasure of reading semiotic studies has to do with

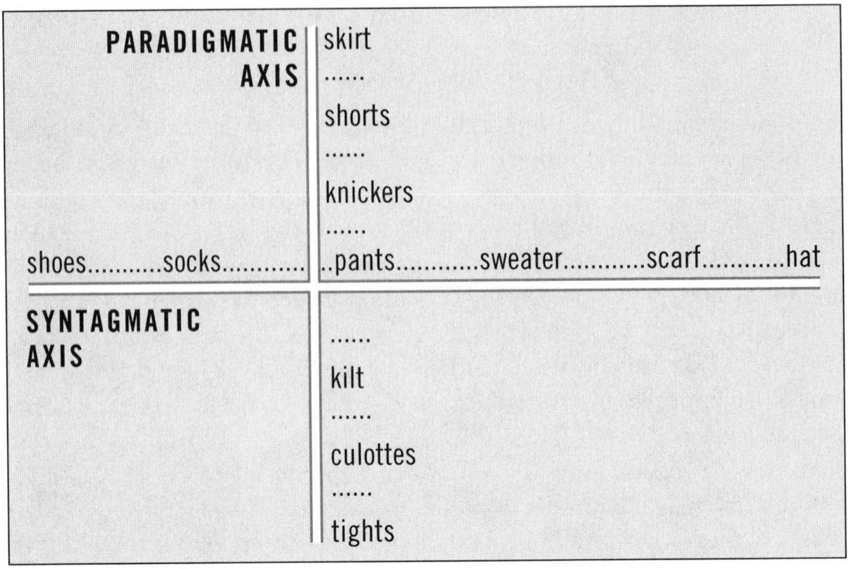

PARADIGMATIC AXIS	skirt
	......
	shorts
	......
	knickers
	......
shoes...........socks............	..pants............sweater............scarf...........hat
SYNTAGMATIC AXIS	......
	kilt
	......
	culottes
	......
	tights

Diagram L. Syntagmatic and paradigmatic structures of clothing.

the pure intellectual creativity and the subtlety of technique of its practitioners. Metz, for example, has a droll, eloquent sense of humor that does much to meliorate his often florid theorizing.

Umberto Eco, next to Metz the most prominent of film semioticians, outlined four stages of the development of the science since the early sixties. The first stage, which according to Eco lasted until the early seventies, was marked by what he calls "the overevaluation of the linguistic mode." As semiotics struggled to achieve legitimacy, it clung tightly to the accepted patterns of the study of linguistics that had preceded it. (In the same way, the earliest stages of film theory had mimicked that of the older arts.)

The second stage began when semioticians started to realize that their system of analysis was not so simple and universal as they would have liked to believe at first.

During the third stage—the early seventies—semiotics concentrated on the study of one specific aspect of the universe of meaning in film: production. The semiotics of the process, of the making of texts, was central here, and political ideology became part of the semiotic equation.

The fourth stage—beginning in 1975—saw attention shift from production to consumption, from the making of texts to the perception of them. In this stage, film semiotics was greatly influenced by the approach to Freudian psychology of the French sage Jacques Lacan.

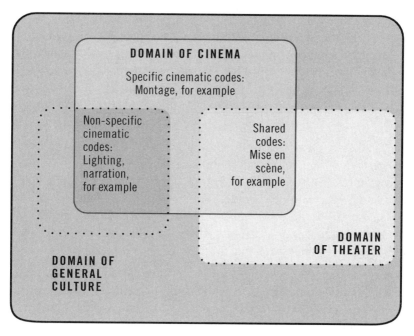

Diagram M. CODE SET THEORY: specific, nonspecific, and shared codes.

Having begun with a quasi-scientific system that purported to quantify and offered the prospect of complete and exact analysis of the phenomenon of film, semiotics gradually worked its way backward to the basic question that has puzzled all students of film: how do we know what we see? Along the way, by rephrasing old questions in new ways, semiotics contributed significantly to the common struggle to understand the nature of film.

We now might want to add a fifth stage—especially in England and the United States: the academic establishment of semiotics. During the past few years, this once elegant system of thought has produced little of real intellectual value. At the same time, it has become a useful tool for academic careerists interested more in publishing before they perish than in increasing our understanding of film theory. Because it is inherently, defiantly abstruse, semiotics is especially dangerous in this regard. In the hands of elegant stylists like Metz, Eco (who later moved on to write popular novels), or Roland Barthes (whose books of essays were their own ends), the tools of semiotics can produce attractive and enlightening discursions. But lesser acolytes can get away with a lot here. Anyone intending to read semiotics should be forewarned: just because you can't understand it doesn't mean it means anything.

Much of Christian Metz's earliest work was concerned with setting up the premises of a semiotics of film. It would seem that the fact of montage offers the easiest comparison between film and language in general. The image is not a word. The sequence is not a sentence. Yet film is *like* a language. What makes film distinctly separate from other languages is its short-circuit sign, in which signifier and signified are nearly the same. Normal languages exhibit the power of "double articulation": that is, in order to use a language one must be able to understand its sounds and meanings, both its signifiers and its signifieds. But this is not true of film. Signifier and signified are nearly the same: what you see is what you get.

So Christian Metz quickly left behind the structures of linguistics that had served as models for all the various semiotic studies of film, literature, and other areas of culture. He turned to the analysis of specific problems. Although he didn't agree that montage was the governing determinant of film language, he felt that the use of narrative was central to the film experience. The motivation of cinematic signs, he felt, was important to define: the difference between denotation and connotation in cinema is important. (See Chapter 3.)

The second important differentiation in narrative, he felt, was between syntagmatic and paradigmatic structures. Both of these are theoretical constructions rather than practical facts. The syntagma of a film or sequence shows its linear narrative structure. It is concerned with "what follows what." The paradigm of a film is vertical: it concerns choice—"what goes with what."

Now Metz felt he had a system of logic that would permit the real analysis of the film phenomenon. Montage and mise-en-scène had been thoroughly redefined as the syntagmatic and paradigmatic categories. These Cartesian coordinates determined the field of film.

Metz next turned, in *Language and Cinema,* to a thorough exposition of the system of codes that govern cinematic meaning. Within the syntagmas and paradigms of film theory, what determines how we acquire meaning from a film? Contemporary mathematical set theory plays an important part in his elaborate structure of codes. Making the differentiation between "film" and "cinema" that we noted earlier, Metz explained that the concept of codes transcends the limits of film. Many codes that operate in film come from other areas of culture. These are "nonspecific" codes. Our understanding of the murder in *Psycho* (1960), for example, does not depend on specifically cinematic codes. The way in which Hitchcock presents that murder, however, is an example of a "specific" cinematic code. Finally, there are those codes that cinema borrows from or shares with other media. The lighting of the shower sequence in *Psycho* is a good example of such a shared code. We thus have our first series of overlapping sets.

The next differentiation of codes follows logically. If some codes are specific to cinema and some are not, then of those specific codes, some are shared by all films and some by only a few, while others are unique to certain individual films. The diagram visualizes this logic:

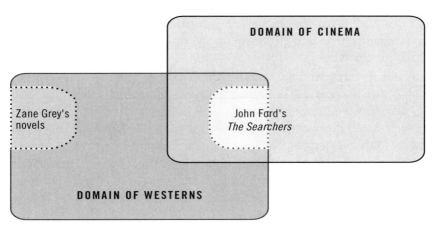

Diagram N. CODE SET THEORY: Generality of codes.

Finally, codes—any codes—can be broken down into subcodes; there is a hierarchy of codes. The system is elegantly simple: film is all the possible sets of these codes; a specific film is a limited number of codes and sets of codes. Genres, careers, studios, national characters, techniques, and every other element ever suggested by previous film theorists, critics, historians, and students can be broken down into code systems.

Codes are the things we read in films.

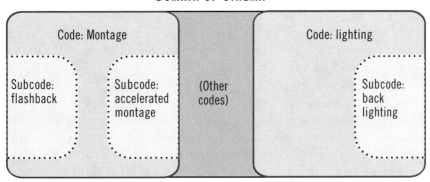

Diagram O. CODE SET THEORY: codes and subcodes.

Along with other semioticians, Metz in the late seventies moved on to a discussion of the psychology of filmic perception, most successfully in his long essay "The Imaginary Signifier," which appeared simultaneously in both French and English in 1975. Drawing on basic Freudian theory as rephrased by Jacques Lacan, he psychoanalyzed not only the cinematic experience but also cinema itself. Because of its great debt to Freud, whose theories are now much less highly regarded in America than they once were, this trend in film semiotics elicited much less interest among English-speaking followers of semiotics than among its French practitioners.

While Metz received the most attention, he was by no means alone in his semiotic pursuits. The movement has been central to French intellectual life for a long time. Roland Barthes, although mainly a literary critic, contributed significantly to the debate in cinema before his death in 1980. Raymond Bellour wrote widely; his two extended studies of sequences from Hitchcock's *The Birds* and *North by Northwest* are of special interest. In Italy, Umberto Eco and Gianfranco Bettetini made significant contributions, and Pier Paolo Pasolini, although as he put it an "amateur" theorist, produced some interesting analyses before his untimely death.

In England, semiotics found an early and receptive home in the journal *Screen* and led to the establishment of the English school of "Ciné-structuralism." Peter Wollen's *Signs and Meaning in the Cinema,* the major argument of which is outlined in Chapter 3, was the most important English-language contribution to the broad outline of semiotic theory.

In the U.S., semiotics had little effect, except to serve as a tool for academics involved in the growth of film scholarship in colleges and universities in the seventies and eighties. Highly intellectualized, abstract theories of cinema have never been popular in America.

The native tradition of the U.S. has been practical criticism, often with a social if not exactly political orientation, stretching from Harry Alan Potamkin and Otis Ferguson in the thirties through James Agee and Robert Warshow in the forties to Dwight Macdonald, Manny Farber, and Pauline Kael in the sixties and seventies. Andrew Sarris, although he doesn't fit into this sociological tradition, had a marked effect on the course of film criticism in the U.S. in the sixties and seventies through his work in popularizing the auteur policy.

There are no younger critics now writing regularly who have yet established critical personas as strong as Sarris's, Kael's, or even John Simon's in the sixties and seventies. Since the rise of television-show criticism in the early eighties, thumbs have replaced theories. That's not to say there aren't a lot of intelligent people writing about film today; there's just no one with an interesting theoretical ax to grind.

The main tradition of American criticism has preferred to see films not so much as products of specific authors but as evidence of social, cultural, and political currents. Especially in the work of Kael, Molly Haskell, and others, this strain of social criticism was modified to include an intensely personal focus. Practically, American criticism is not so far removed from the French theoretical tradition at the moment. Both are strongly concerned with the problem of perception. The difference is that the Europeans, as has been their wont, prefer to generalize and to develop elaborate theories, while the Americans, true to tradition, are more interested in the everyday experience of specific phenomena.

Concurrent with the growth of semiotics on the Continent was a revival of Marxist criticism. The French journals *Cahiers du Cinéma* and *Cinéthique* managed to combine the semiotic and the dialectic traditions in the late seventies. In England, too, semiotics often had a distinctly political cast. In America, much of recent theory sees film as a political phenomenon, albeit abstractly rather than practically.

During the seventies, the developing theory of film in the Third World was also of interest. A major document here was "Toward a Third Cinema," by Fernando Solanas and Octavio Getino (*Cineaste* IV:3, 1970). More a manifesto than a theory, the South American filmmakers' essay suggested that the "first cinema"—Hollywood and its imitators—and the "second cinema"—the more personal style of the New Wave or "author's" cinema—would yield to the "third cinema," a cinema of liberation that would consist of "films that the System cannot assimilate and which are foreign to its needs, or … films that directly and explicitly set out to fight the System." Perhaps that happened somewhere—in Chile for a few years in the early seventies, for example—but with the benefit of hindsight we can discern a lot of wishful thinking in that statement. The world was moving too fast, and the political models of the thirties were no longer viable.

In the U.S. these various currents—semiotic, psychoanalytic, dialectical, and politically prescriptive—each gained their adherents in the 1970s and 1980s as film theory became attractive to academicians. Yet our own native strain of practical criticism continued to develop as well. It centered on a study of narrativity—the ways in which the stories of film are told. Such scholars as Frank McConnell (*Storytelling and Mythmaking in Film and Literature*, 1979) pointed the way to some fertile areas for inquiry.

The great value of such theories of narration is paradoxically that they deflect attention from the specially cinematic qualities of film. If film is seen first as narrative, then we almost immediately infer the corollary, that film is simply one of several different modes of narrative. And that observation, in turn, leads us to consider film in the context of the continuum of media. Both practically and theoretically, this is now a clear necessity.

Throughout the 1980s and 1990s, film criticism—like its subject—reworked the "postmodernist" truths that had revealed themselves in the 1960s and 1970s. As the French tides of Althusserian Marxism and Lacanian Freudian theory began to recede, the semiotic and dialectic discoveries of earlier years gave rise, respectively, to two new variants: cognitive film theory and cultural studies.

Extending the epistemological quest of semiotics, cognitive film theory has sought to explain the way in which a spectator understands a film: how we *read* films. Extending the dialectic sport of contextual analysis first pioneered by the Frankfurt school, cultural studies seeks to understand the relationships between the texts of popular culture and their audiences: how we *use* films.[*]

Both recent trends have found fruitful material for analysis in feminist studies. Since the popular medium of film brightly reflects the general culture in which it thrives, this is no surprise. At the end of the second millennium as Western culture gradually fades into world culture, we find ourselves obsessed with the same topic with which we began this thousand-year journey into literacy and intellectual understanding. Today we call it sexual politics; in the eleventh century we called it Romance. (We still don't understand it. Isn't it nice that it is still mysterious?)

But there may be something more going on here: from the Rice–Irwin *Kiss* to the Playboy Channel, from the phallic lens to hot, round baby spotlights, from the lovemaking of the tracking shot through the voyeuristic reward of the zoom to the rhythmic pulse of montage, movies are sexual. They are not only *about* sexual politics; they *are* sexual politics—subject and object united.

The present course of film theory is away from prescription, toward description. People who think about film are no longer interested to construct an ideal system of esthetics or political and social values, nor do they see their main aim as finding a language to describe the phenomenon of film. These critical tasks were accomplished earlier—with aplomb—by the critics we have discussed in this chapter.

The job of film theory now is truly dialectical. As a fully matured art, film is no longer a separate enterprise but an integrated pattern in the warp and woof of our culture. Cinema is an expansive and far-reaching set of interrelating oppositions: between filmmaker and subject, film and observer, establishment and avant garde, conservative purposes and progressive purposes, psychology and politics, image and sound, dialogue and music, montage and mise-en-scène, genre and auteur, literary sensibility and cinematic sensibility, signs and meaning, culture and society, form and function, design and purpose, syntagmas and paradigms, image and event, Realism and Expressionism, language and phenomenology, sex and violence, sense and nonsense, love and marriage ... a never-ending set of codes and subcodes that raises fundamental questions about the relationships of life to art, and reality to language.

---

[*] I am grateful to Richard Allen for this succinct analysis.

Figure 5-15. Truffaut asks a simple question in *Day For Night*: "Is film more important than life?"

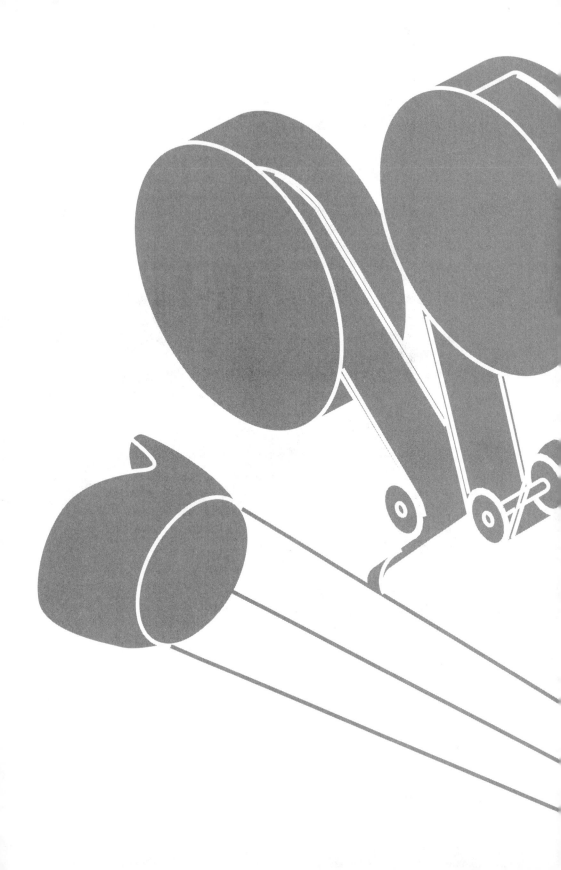

6

MEDIA: IN THE MIDDLE OF THINGS

Community

Despite the rambunctious proliferation of electronic media during the last half of the twentieth century, film, that great nineteenth-century invention, still predominates. As a group, Hollywood producers spend most of their time and make most of their money doing television. In Europe, "film" wouldn't exist if television networks didn't help fund it. The greatest financial success any filmmaker or actor can have is not a theatrical blockbuster but a long-running television series. Even within the feature film business itself, considerably more than half the income from an average production now comes from television and video distribution, not from theaters.

Film is at the hot center of this mix of businesses and technologies; clearly it should be seen in the context of the broader communications and entertainment industry known collectively as "the media." We've alluded to this context throughout; now it's time to examine it in more detail. Video technology is important because of its continuing, ever-growing impact on the art of movies. The history of television and the other electronic media provides the backdrop for the continuing story of film ... and leads inexorably to its future.

One of the more succinct analyses of the differences that define the various techniques of communication known collectively as "the media" lies in a series of pieces written by Samuel Beckett in the 1960s. In *Play, Film, Eh Joe, Cascando,* and *Words and Music,* the playwright/novelist/poet/critic, who wrote in both French and English, captured the essence of each form.

Figure 6-1. George Rose in Beckett's
Eh, Joe (New York Television Theatre,
April 18, 1966. Producer: Glenn
Jordan; director: Alan Schneider).
(*Grove Press, Frame enlargement of
kinescope recording.*)

Play presents three characters immobilized on stage in urns. As the stream-of-consciousness dialogue flows back and forth from one to the other, a sharp, precise spotlight follows the "action"—or comments on it. Beckett's abstract design of the stage focuses our attention on the element of choice that the observer controls in this medium while it emphasizes that physical action is minor. For Beckett, the stage play is deep-focus mise-en-scène, not controlled montage.

Film, on the contrary, develops the dialectic between filmmaker and subject that Beckett sees as essential to that medium. As directed by Alan Schneider and acted by Buster Keaton, *Film* is the silent abstract representation of the drama that goes on not between characters, but between filmmaker and actor. Alone on the screen throughout most of the film. Keaton is nevertheless not alone in the narrative, for the camera is made to appear as a very real presence, and Keaton's struggle to avoid its all-seeing eye is theme of the dramatic design.

Play emphasizes the interaction between and among characters and the relative freedom of the observer to mold the experience. *Film,* on the other hand, emphasizes the solitude of the subject, the drama between subject and artist, and the observer's relative lack of involvement in the process.

Eh Joe, a teleplay, is an equally insightful analysis of the essential elements of television. Lasting about forty-five minutes, the piece contrasts the audio and the video components of the television experience. "Joe," the subject of the play, is seen on the screen in a single sequence shot that progresses over the course of the play from a relatively long shot showing most of the room that is the set, to full shot, to mid-shot, and finally to a long, extremely slow tracking closeup that gradually and inexorably moves from a full head shot to an extreme closeup of eyes, nose, and mouth. On the soundtrack, a woman's voice, speaking to Joe, intones a continuing stream-of-consciousness monologue.

The design of *Eh Joe* subtly emphasizes the two essential elements of television that separate it from film on the one hand and the stage play on the other: the separate, parallel monologue, as it creates the basic atmosphere and tone of the piece, reinforces our sense of the greater significance of sound in television, while the extraordinary, intense sequence shot from long shot to extreme closeup cannily emphasizes the unusual psychological intimacy of this medium.

Cascando and *Words and Music* are both radio plays. The structure of this dramatic form is much simpler than the structures of the stage play, film, and television. Beckett isolates the essential elements of radio art—"words and music," the background noise of civilization. The product of the dynamic between them is the "falling," "tumbling," "cascando" of the radio experience. In each of these analytical pieces, Beckett sets up a dramatic tension, not between characters but between elements of the structure of the various arts: for the stage, audience choice versus the flow of dialogue; for film, the director's control and the subject's integrity; for television, the intense nature of audio versus the psychological intimacy of the image; and for radio, more simply, words and music, information and background.

Beckett's series of analytical plays makes an elegant summary of the esthetic differences between and among media. Politics and technology are also important factors in the media equation. The connotations of the word "media," in fact, suggest that we regard the phenomenon as having a greater latitude than the limits of esthetics would suggest. The media, by definition, are means of communication: all more or less technological systems designed to transmit information without regard to the natural limits of space and time. They have come to be used in a variety of ways that both inform and entertain.

They are, moreover, the primary socializing forces of modern life, as the root of the word "communication" strongly suggests: to "communicate" is to forge a "community."

Print and Electronic Media

Written language is the prototype for all media. For seven thousand years, it has provided a workable and flexible method for getting information from one person to another. But it was not until the invention of movable type by Johann Gutenberg in the fifteenth century that "written" messages could be mass-produced so the author could communicate with a large number of other individuals simultaneously. This "multiple reproducibility" is the prime characteristic of media. Between 1500 and 1800 the production of books developed into a major industry. It was the concept of the newspaper or journal, quickly produced and appearing on a regular schedule, that suggested the second vital element of the media (a corollary of the first)—the open channel of communication. Books are produced in quantity, but they are each singular events, limited to their subjects. Newspapers and magazines are open, in both time and space, to continuing and various uses.

Although print was immediately recognized as a socially revolutionary force, it was not until the nineteenth century and the rise of a massive literate middle class that printing realized its full potential as a medium. It took us collectively a lot longer to learn to read print than to learn to read films. Significantly, the rise of the electronic media in the twentieth century was much more rapid, since no particular skill was required for comprehension.

Print media also benefited from technological advances in the latter half of the nineteenth century. The steam-powered press had been developed by Friedrich König in 1810; rotary presses, which operated continuously rather than intermittently, date from the 1840s through the 1860s. Richard March Hoe is credited with inventing the first rotary press in 1846. Twenty years later, the stereotype printing plate was first patented in England. The combination of steam power, rotary design, and one-piece stereotype plates greatly increased the speed and flexibility of presses. The typewriter, invented by C. L. Sholes in 1867 and first produced by Remington in 1874, and the Linotype typesetting machine, invented in 1884 by Ottmar Mergenthaler, made the preparatory processes much more efficient.

In 1880, the *New York Graphic* printed the first halftone photographs, although it was a decade and more before this important technique gained wide acceptance among newspapers and magazines. Earlier technological developments in printing had been quantitative: they increased the speed and flexibility of the process, but they did not affect its basic nature. The halftone process, on the other hand, was a qualitative advance, making the reproduction of photographs an integral part of the technique of printing. It was at this point, more than a hundred years ago, that the long courtship between print and image began. It is now being consummated in the marriage known as "multimedia."

The basic problem with reproducing photographs in print was that the photographic process produces a continual and infinitely variable range of tones from white through gray to black, while the printing process is essentially "binary"[*]— any given space on a printed page is either white or black; there are no gradations in between. The technique of the halftone solved this problem in an ingenious manner: the continuous space of the photograph was broken up into discrete par-

---

[*] We are using the word "binary" here in its philosophical sense, not its mathematical sense, although the thinking behind the invention of binary digital computers years later has the same flavor.

ticles—as many as two hundred per linear inch—which could be translated into the binary language of print. If 50 percent of a given area was actually printed, then that area would appear a medium gray; if 100 percent was printed, it would be black, and so forth.

In its way, the concept of the halftone was as important in photography as the understanding of persistence of vision was in the development of motion pictures: both utilized basic physiological facts of perception in simple yet powerful ways. Moreover, the concept that underlies the halftone process—the translation of a continuous range of values into a discrete quantified system—was to become one of the most significant and widely effective intellectual devices of the twentieth century: television, phototelegraphy, telemetry, and—most important—computer technology, all rest on this basic "dialectical" concept.[*]

Many of the social and semiotic effects of the electronic revolution were fore-shadowed during the great age of newspapers and magazines in the nineteenth century. It became clear very quickly that the media would provide new versions of reality, a record of history—sometimes even an alternate reality—and that this mediating function would have a profound effect on the organization of life. As economic entities, newspapers and magazines began by selling information and entertainment to their readers, then gradually progressed to a more complex mode in which they also sold advertising space to other economic entities who wanted to communicate with the readership. In other words, publishers of maga-zines and newspapers moved from selling an object to selling a service; the medium that they controlled provided advertisers with a means of access to the general public.

Since about 1930, this service has been refined considerably. Marketing survey techniques enable the publisher to offer a particular audience rather than simply crude space to an advertiser. The advertisers had always been aware generally of the shape of the audience they were reaching, but the rise of the erstwhile science of "demographics" enabled the publisher to pinpoint specific valuable sectors of the general audience. A modern general-interest magazine—*Time*, for example—breaks its readership down into a number of geographic, social, and class sections and then publishes separate (if nearly identical) editions so that it can offer an advertiser a finely tuned audience for its message at the most efficient "cost per thousand." In recent years, the sophistication of the demographic approach has meant that general audience magazines, even those with large circulations, have yielded to smaller, special-interest journals that can offer advertisers smaller but more susceptible audiences for their products.

---

[*] One wonders if Niels Bohr and the other philosophers of quantum theory in physics in the 1920s were influenced, perhaps subconsciously, by the popular tab-loids of the day.

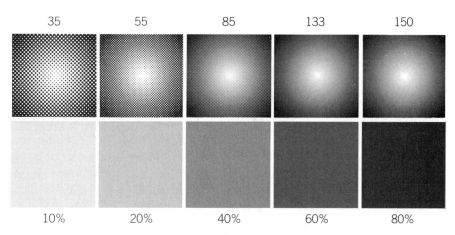

Figure 6-2. HALFTONE SCREENS. The 35 lines per inch and 55 lpi screens are too coarse for anything except special effects. The 85 screen is standard for newspapers. 133 is the most common screen for books. (The halftones in this book use 133.) The 150 lpi screen is used in special applications—such as medical illustrations—where the finest detail is essential.

The shadings at the bottom are used in design. The diagrams in this book, for example, use 20, 40, and 60 percent screens. The shading is accomplished not by changing screen frequency, but by increasing the size of each dot within the pattern. See also Figure 2-2F.

Advertising—crucial to the operation of a capitalist economic system—has had a profound effect on life patterns during the past 150 years. Because the permanent record of the society is kept in the media, it quickly became evident that not only manufacturers but also politicians and public figures had to advertise if their ideas were to be taken seriously by large numbers of people. This led to the development of the publicity and public relations industries, which are closely allied with advertising. Moreover, advertising itself has become such a sophisticated industry that the tail now often wags the dog: ad agencies participate directly in the creation of products, not only identifying opportunities but also sometimes inventing markets for new products where none existed before by establishing a sense of need in consumers.

Caught up in this complex economic system are the secondary, noneconomic functions of the media: the distribution of news, entertainment, and information. The "news hole"—that space in a newspaper or magazine set aside for actual news reports—is often as small as 25 percent of the total space available. In other words, three-quarters of the communicating ability of a print medium in the U.S. is often devoted to advertising.

This veritable deluge is a major factor in determining shared systems of values in contemporary societies. Communication used to take place mainly on a personal level: the largest number of people one was able to reach was determined by the capacity of the meeting place. But the rise of the print media greatly increased the potential for communication. Not only could one reach a far greater number of people, none of whom had to be in the same place at the same time, but also—significantly—communication became for the most part unidirectional: that is, the members of the "audience" now had no chance to interact with the "speaker."

The development of the mechanical and electronic media generally followed the pattern set by the growth of the print media during the preceding 150 to 200 years. There were, however, some significant differences. Unlike the print media, film, radio, television, and records did not require that their audiences be highly trained to perceive and understand their messages. In this sense, at least, it is perfectly true that one does not have to learn to "read" a film. On the other hand, the mechanical and electronic media developed at a significantly higher level of technological sophistication. "Literacy" might not be necessary, but equipment is. Film developed as a public rather than a private experience mainly because of the cost and complexity of the equipment involved in projecting the image. Significantly, it is the only one of the modern media that has maintained a public nature. It may not offer its audiences a chance for interaction with performers (as all public meetings and stage performances had done before it), but it still maintains, at least, the communal sense of the experience.

All the other contemporary media, however, developed as private "enterprises," for an interesting reason. The gradual shift from product to service discernible in the history of the print media is even more pronounced with the electronic and mechanical media. Except for motion pictures, each of the contemporary media began as a product—specifically, in the language of economics, a "consumer durable." Like central heating, refrigerators, gas or electric lighting, or even indoor plumbing and privies, telephones, cameras, record players, radios, television sets, VCRs, and computers once represented major capital investments for consumers.

To sell the devices, manufacturers had to make them simple enough for almost anyone to operate. Then, in most cases, they had to provide something to play on the device—"software." The machine—the receiver or player—was seen in most instances as the major source of profit; the media were provided so that the machine had something to receive or play. Because the machines could be made fairly simply and cheaply and because the initial profit lay in the "hardware," it was thus useful to make the experience of media private so that the greatest number of machines could be sold.

Then, as the machines became widely distributed, hardware margins shrank as markets became saturated and the devices themselves became commodities. (No one today thinks of a telephone or even a VCR as a "major capital investment.") The economic locus shifted first to distributors, then to producers of the software. By the 1980s, international hardware powers began buying up the software pro-

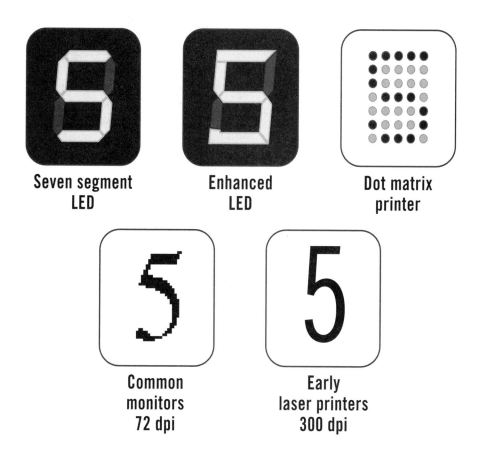

Seven segment
LED

Enhanced
LED

Dot matrix
printer

Common
monitors
72 dpi

Early
laser printers
300 dpi

Figure 6-3. LEDS, DOT MATRIXES, AND BEYOND. The halftone was the first historical instance of the merger of print and visual technology. It set a pattern for future development. By the early seventies, for example, when computer electronic readouts were developed for consumer and professional applications, two versions of simplified alphanumeric representations were standardized.

Above, the seven-segment LED ("light-emitting diode") made possible readable numbers composed of only seven switchable elements, a considerable simplification—and a nice job of analysis. (Notice that in the "enhanced" LED examples the design of the elements has been modified slightly to improve the readability of the numbers.) Such a system wouldn't work for the more complex alphabet, however, so the dot matrix printer was developed to display Roman letters in readable form. The most common version used 35 dots arrayed 5 x 7 to produce all the letters of the alphabet.

The introduction of the graphically oriented Macintosh computer in 1984 and its accompanying Postscript-based LaserWriter printer in 1985 brought a measure of readability to computer screens and printouts, establishing standards of 72 dots per inch for the screen and 300 dots per inch for the printout, levels of resolution just good enough to allow the introduction of simplified versions of modern type fonts. For purposes of comparison, this book was set at a resolution of 2600 dots per inch.

ducers and distributors, as GE purchased NBC; Sony bought CBS Records, Columbia Pictures, and TriStar; Philips won Polygram; and Matsushita acquired MCA. In 1995, Westinghouse acquired CBS, rejoining the television industry they had helped to found 75 years earlier.

There's an interesting corollary to this product/service market development curve: in each case, the medium begins as a professional activity for which a high degree of expertise is necessary, then shifts to a semiprofessional activity as groups of fairly knowledgeable devotees learn the techniques. Finally, it becomes an everyday activity in which anyone can engage with a minimum of training, as the simplified hardware moves into the home.

We have already seen in Chapter 4 how the product/service pattern operated in the development of the motion picture industry. Edison and the other origina-tors of film developed the machinery, then provided films to be played on the machines. Because the machinery and its systems were complex and expensive, there was little chance that projectors could be marketed as consumer durables, and film remained a public rather than private art. Gradually, the center of eco-nomic power in film shifted from the manufacturer of the machinery to the exhibitor (the level of "retail sales"), then to the producer-distributors. In addition, at each stage film businessmen, whether manufacturers, exhibitors, producers, or distributors, naturally attempted to exercise monopoly control—a development later mirrored in the history of network radio and television.

Even before the rise of film, the inventions of the telephone and the amateur camera had foreshadowed this pattern of development. With both, the service and the machinery were intimately connected. Both also provided individual ser-vice rather than broad media of communication, which sets them apart structur-ally from such media as radio, records, and television. Interestingly, radio was considered for a long time simply an adjunct to the telephone—a device that could provide intercommunication, but only on a one-to-one level. Marconi demonstrated the effectiveness of his invention in 1899, but it wasn't until 1920 that "broadcasting"—the widespread dissemination of the signal to reach large numbers of listeners—was seen to be practicable.

The main structural differences among the media are summarized in the chart below. The two economic factors—the "nexus" and the "sales orientation"—determine how media make money. As we have seen, this changes over time. Other factors, such as "access," "control," and "interaction," describe the way we use the media.

By their nature, the early mass media were mainly unidirectional: the moguls made it; we consumed it. Social critics from Aldous Huxley and José Ortega y Gasset to Marie Winn and Neil Postman have described this power and warned us eloquently of its dangers. Since the 1970s, however, the technological watchword has been "interactivity."

| | MEDIA ECONOMICS | | MEDIA POLITICS | | | | |
MEDIUM	Nexus	Sales Orientation	Channels	Access	Interaction	Distribution Flow	Consumer Control
BOOKS	distribution	object	open	good	unidirectional	discrete	yes
NEWS-PAPERS	prod./dist.	object, ad space	open	limited	unidirectional	mosaic	yes
MAGAZINES	distribution	object, ad space	open	limited	unidirectional	semidiscrete	yes
FILM	distribution	entertainment, rights	open	limited	unidirectional	discrete	some
TELEPHONE	network	network access	open	excellent	interactive	continuous	yes
RADIO	distribution	ad time, audience	limited	limited	mainly unidirectional	continuous	no
CB	manufacture	equipment	limited	excellent	interactive	continuous	no
AUDIODISC	prod./dist.	object	open	limited	unidirectional	discrete	yes
AUDIOTAPE	distribution	object	open	good	unidirectional	discrete	yes
TELEVISION	prod./dist.	ad time, audience	closed	none	unidirectional	continuous	no
CABLE	distribution	ads, entertainment	limited	some	unidirectional	continuous	no
VIDEODISC/	distribution	object	open	limited	unidirectional	discrete	yes
VIDEOTAPE	distribution	object	open	good	unidirectional	discrete	yes
CD-ROM	distribution	object	open	good	unidirectional	discrete	yes
INTERNET	network	net access, ad space	open	excellent	interactive	continuous	yes

Nexus: Where does the concentration of economic power lie? *Sales Orientation:* What is the primary product being sold? *Channels:* Are there a limited number of distribution channels? *Access:* How easy is it for someone to gain access to the medium? *Interaction:* Is the medium unidirectional or interactive? *Distribution Flow:* Are the items distributed individually or continuously? *Consumer Control:* Can consumers control the time and location of the experience?

DIAGRAM P. THE POLITICAL AND ECONOMIC RELATIONSHIPS OF MEDIA

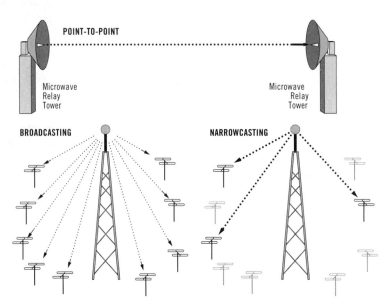

Figure 6-4. BROADCASTING, NARROWCASTING, AND POINT-TO-POINT TRANSMISSION. These various systems of transmission follow the logic of "one to many," "one to a few," and "one to one." What about "many to one"? Online bulletin boards and forums fit that logic.

This trend began in the late sixties. In 1968, the FCC's Carterfone decision opened up the telephone system to competition. About the same time, Philips's audiocassette recorder was introduced, bringing simple and affordable audio recording techniques to the masses for the first time. In the early seventies, the spread of xerography and offset printing opened up publishing to nonprofessionals. In the late seventies, the introduction of the videocassette recorder extended mass recording capability to video.

But all of this was only preparation for the profound microcomputer revolution of the 1980s. Beginning with "desktop publishing" and moving on rapidly to "desktop presentations," by the early nineties, the micro delivered into the hands of children media production power that even professionals had only dreamed about a few years earlier.

Today, anyone can produce a book, film, record, tape, magazine, or newspaper with less training than it takes to fix a leaky faucet. But can these newly empowered producers of media get their work read, seen, or heard by large numbers of people? So long as the work is specialized and directed to a sharply focused audience, this is no problem. But the writer, filmmaker, "tapemaker," or "discmaker" who wants to communicate with the general public often has considerable difficulty. The democratization of distribution is taking longer, although the Internet is beginning to show us how the distribution of complex media can be accom-

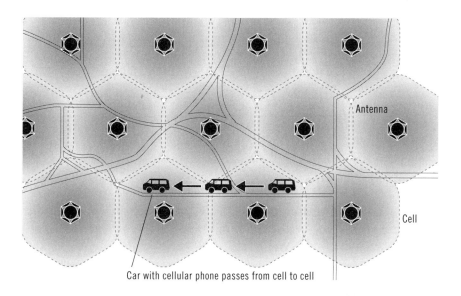

Car with cellular phone passes from cell to cell

Figure 6-5. CELLULAR TELEPHONY. The increasing sophistication of computerized telephone switching systems allowed the commercial introduction of cellular telephony in 1983. Radiotelephones had been in use for many years, but the limited bandwidth of the radio spectrum made them uneconomical. The Citizen's Band radio craze of the mid-seventies pointed to an ingenious solution to the problem, elegant in its simplicity. CB let millions become broadcasters because it radically limited their power, and therefore, their range: thousands could share each channel because they were separated geographically. Similarly, cellular telephony dramatically multiplied the number of channels available by limiting the broadcast range to a few city blocks. The twist? Sophisticated switching systems pass a call signal from one transmitter and channel to another as the caller moves. By the early 1990s in the U.S. car phones were common, and middle-class teenagers prided themselves on their beepers. By the late 1990s personal cell phones were pervasive in the U.S. and even more popular in Europe. The next step? Detach the number from the device and attach it to the person, utilizing similar intelligent networks to shunt a call to whatever device happens to be closest at hand.

plished with the same ease with which we make a telephone call. We'll discuss these developments in further detail in Chapter 7.

As the producers of media gain more freedom, do the consumers benefit? A close examination of the "Relationships of Media" chart leads to some interesting conclusions. Physical items such as books, newspapers, magazines, records, and tapes have considerable advantage over the broadcast media. They are produced and distributed discretely, so the consumer can exercise choice more easily. The consumer also controls the experience of these media: one can listen to a record, read a book, or watch a videodisc as frequently as one likes at whatever speed one prefers.

On the other hand, the salient characteristic of the broadcast media—as opposed to the physical media—is their rigidity. Access is severely restricted, even if cable television, which guarantees a limited amount of public access, and "talk" radio shows, which encourage listeners to phone in, have somewhat expanded opportunities. Moreover, the consumer is locked into the time schedule of the broadcast media and, because the distribution flow is continuous rather than discrete, he has little opportunity to control the experience. Although the advent of VCRs has allowed some "time-shifting," the continuous flow of television broadcasts still dominates the experience; choosing *when* to watch is a far cry from choosing *how* to watch.

Until recently, the number of channels, too, has been strictly limited. Everyone knows the joke about the new cable subscriber who is discouraged to find out that even though he now has eighty channels instead of eight, "there's still nothing on." As we begin to marry computer and television technology, cable systems finally become two-way streets, closer in architecture to a telephone network than to a broadcast network. When video distribution via the Internet becomes a reality, and viewers can order transmission on demand, cable becomes an interactive distribution system and the consumer may have some real measure of control.

Newspapers and magazines present an interesting hybrid case: not only do they combine the sale of ad space and audience with the sale of the object itself, but—more important—they distribute their collections of information and entertainment in such a way that the reader has real power over the experience. The mosaic arrangement of these print media allows the reader the efficient luxury of what in computer terminology is called "real-time access." For instance, a newspaper reader can choose precisely which items he wants to read and can decide as well how long he wants to stay with each one, whereas someone watching television news is locked in to the time scheme of the broadcast and experiences the information precisely the same way as every other viewer.

This is the most significant difference between print and electronic media. Because information in print is coded more strictly than media information, print is still the most efficient medium for communicating abstract information. Partly because the reader has such considerable control over the experience, far more information can be presented, and the structure of the print media makes it available in a more efficient manner: you can't easily thumb through a disc, or skim a film. (Yet.)

The Technology of Mechanical and Electronic Media

Whether the eventual form of transmission is broadcast or physical, all the mechanical and electronic media depend on a single concept: the physics and technology of wave forms. Since our two primary senses—sight and hearing—also depend on wave physics, this is not surprising. Yet until Edison's phonograph, no way had ever been found to mimic or re-create these phenomena.

The phonograph, as Edison conceived it, did not depend on any advanced developments in technology: it was a simple mechanical system involving no chemistry or electronics, nor even any particularly difficult engineering. The essential components are the horn, which amplifies sound waves; the diaphragm, which translates sound waves into physical motion; the stylus, which transmits the physical motion to the recording medium; and the cylinder or disk, the recording medium that accepts and preserves the record of the sound. The governing concept here, as with all the electronic media that followed, is the technique of translating one wave form into another. In this case sound waves, whose medium is air, are translated into physical waves, whose medium is the wax cylinder or disk.

As ingenious as it was, Edison's early phonograph was also a limited instrument. Much quality was lost in the progression of the signal from horn to diaphragm to stylus to wax cylinder, then back again through stylus, diaphragm, and horn. Further improvements had to wait for the development of electronic technology in the early years of the twentieth century. Here, the history of the phonograph merges with the history of radio and telephony.

Both radio and telephony are founded in electrical theory, but there is a significant conceptual difference between them: the telephone transmits its message through a limited channel—the wire—whereas radio performs essentially the same function by using the medium of electromagnetic radiation. Because the nature of the electromagnetic spectrum allows radio signals to be broadcast easily (a radio signal originates at a single point but can be received anywhere within a broad area), radio seems at first to be a more advanced system than telephony, which is "narrowcast" (a telephone signal travels from any single point to any other single point).

Yet, as we shall see, the advantages of the limited-channel telephone system are beginning to be appreciated. The wires of telephony, although difficult and expensive to install compared with radio's easily generated electromagnetic waves, nevertheless offer the prospect of two-way interactive communication, which is more difficult with radio. Cable television is moving rapidly in this direction, as higher-capacity coaxial cable, compression techniques, and—most importantly—fiber-optic cable vastly increase the capacity of this competitor to the august telephone network.

The same technologies are available to telephone companies, who now are beginning to compete on cable television's turf. In the early eighties, the development of cellular "broadcasting" freed the telephone from its wired connection. In the nineties, phone companies and cable companies alike broadened their pur-

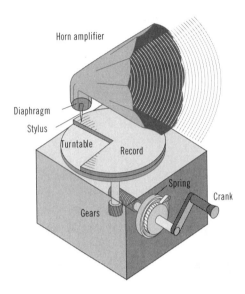

Figure 6-6. THE MECHANICAL PHONOGRAPH. The crank supplies the energy, the main-spring stores it, the gears transmit it. The grooves of the record store the signal, the stylus trans-mits it, the diaphragm translates it from mechanical vibration into sound, the horn amplifies it.

view to include all forms of electronic communication. Interestingly, despite the increasing abstraction of the electronic media, the physical networks built at great cost during the past hundred years remain invaluable assets.[*]

Samuel Morse had patented a telegraph apparatus in 1840. It was a simple device for carrying a signal through wires via electrical energy. It had, however, only two "words": the current was either on, or off. Morse's dot-dash code made useful communication possible, but a more flexible system was needed.

Bell's telephone added a significant dimension to electrical technology: it was the first invention to translate sound waves analogously into electrical waves and back again to sound. Bell began with an amplifying horn similar in principle to Edison's, but he thought to translate the sound waves into an electrical medium rather than a physical medium. This enabled the telephone to transmit its message immediately.

The "microphone" consists of horn, diaphragm, and a collection of carbon granules in direct contact with the diaphragm. As the diaphragm moves in

---

[*]   "Networks" come in many forms. One of the more ingenious strategies of the new long-distance telephone companies competing with AT&T in the 1980s was to contract with the moribund railroads to lay fiber-optic cable along their rights-of-way between cities.

Figure 6-7. Alexander Graham Bell demonstrated his first working telephone system on May 11, 1877, at the Hotel St. Denis at Broadway and Eleventh Street in Greenwich Village, two blocks from where the American Mutoscope and Biograph Co. would set up shop twenty years later and not much farther from Edison's dynamo on Fifth Avenue. The switches required to make the telephone more than an intercom took time to develop. A hundred years later, the building—no longer a hotel, the theatrical center having moved uptown—provided offices for numerous filmmakers and publishers—and later, Silicon Alley new media companies. This edition of *How To Read a Film* was produced here, just down the hall from where Bell rang up the new age.

response to the sound waves that impinge on it, the carbon particles are compressed to a greater or lesser extent so that their electrical resistance varies in response to the acoustic pressure. This variance produces corresponding fluctuations in an electrical current passing through the carbon granules. At the other end of the transmission, a "speaker" translates the electrical signal back into a sound signal by a slightly different process: passed through an electromagnet, the electrical signal varies the intensity of the magnet, which in turn controls the fluctuation of a metallic diaphragm whose movements re-create the sound waves.

By the 1890s, the telephone was in wide use. As important as it was, Bell's microphone-speaker system would have had limited usefulness without the concurrent development of both ingenious switching equipment and amplifying devices. The concept of amplification that allowed the telephone signal to travel greater distances led directly to a host of twentieth-century electronic devices. The theory that developed out of the telephone switching system, which allowed any

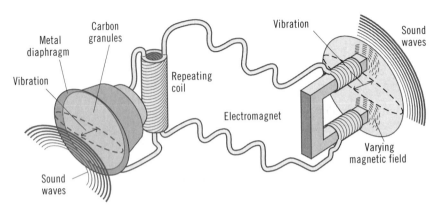

Figure 6-8. THE ELECTRICAL TRANSMISSION OF SOUND. The telephone is the simplest device for translating sound energy into electrical energy, then back again, but the principle described here is the basis for all sound transmission. The key concepts are the carbon granule construction of the microphone (or mouthpiece) which translates sound waves into electric waves, the repeating coil—a simple transformer—which acts as an amplifier, and the electromagnet–diaphragm combination of the loudspeaker (or earpiece) which translates the electrical signal back into sound.

one phone in the system to be connected with any other, directly foreshadowed computer technology and modern systems theory.

Meanwhile, Heinrich Hertz, while conducting experiments that confirmed James Clerk Maxwell's electromagnetic theory, had discovered a way to produce electromagnetic radiation at will. The spectrum of electromagnetic radiation, which runs in frequency from 0 cycles per second as high as 10^{23} cycles per second, includes a wide range of useful phenomena including visible light, heat, X rays, infrared radiation, ultraviolet radiation, and radio waves. It was the radio section of the spectrum that first intrigued inventors.

Two facts were significant about electromagnetic radiation: first, that electromagnetic waves needed no preexisting physical medium (like sound waves)—they could be transmitted through a vacuum; second, that transmitters and receivers could be "tuned" to transmit or receive only waves of a certain frequency. A radio transmitter or receiver could thus be tuned to transmit or receive on any one of a large number of channels, a great advance over the telegraphic/ telephonic systems, whose channels were limited to the number of wires attached to each, and the sophistication of the switching system.

A young Italian, Guglielmo Marconi, was the first of a number of experimenters to perfect a workable system of radiotelegraphy. In 1896 and 1897 he demonstrated his "wireless" telegraph in England, and soon powerful corporations were formed to exploit the commercial value of the invention. Unlike telegraph cables, radio signals were not subject to sabotage: the military value of the invention was seen immediately.

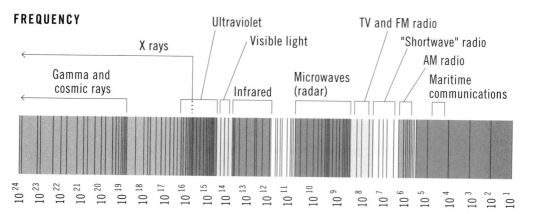

Figure 6-9. THE ELECTROMAGNETIC SPECTRUM. Since the speed of electromagnetic waves is 300,000 kilometers per second, most electromagnetic waves have extremely high frequencies. Even the longest radio waves—with wavelengths measured in kilometers—have frequencies on the order of hundreds of cycles per second. The shortest electromagnetic waves—gamma rays—have wavelengths measured in billionths of a centimeter, frequencies measured in sextillion cycles per second. The most important bands in the spectrum are those occupied by visible light and the radio spectrum, which is further divided arbitrarily into a number of bands allocated for special uses.

Yet, like Morse's system, Marconi's could not carry complex sound signals, only "on-off" code. The telephone translated sound waves into electrical waves that were carried in the medium of the wire, but the "wireless" already depended on a wave system as the medium; how could another wave system (the signal) be carried by the wave system of the medium?

Reginald Fessenden, a Canadian, was one of the first to solve this problem. His idea was to superimpose the signal wave on the carrier wave; in other words, to "modulate" the carrier wave. This is the basic concept of radio and television transmission. Since there are two variables associated with a wave—"amplitude" or strength, and "frequency" or "wavelength"—there were two possibilities for modulation: hence the current AM (Amplitude Modulation) and FM (Frequency Modulation) systems of broadcasting.

At first, Fessenden's theory seemed impractical. Lee DeForest's invention of the "audion" tube in 1906 was crucial. It provided a simple way to modulate the carrier frequency. It was also very useful for the job of amplification. With the audion tube, electronics was born. The system, however, was still fairly crude. It became evident that the carrier frequency and its modulated signal had to be coaxed, filtered, strengthened, and otherwise aided. Edwin H. Armstrong's Regenerative Circuit and Superheterodyne Circuit (1912, 1918) were among the first and most important such devices.

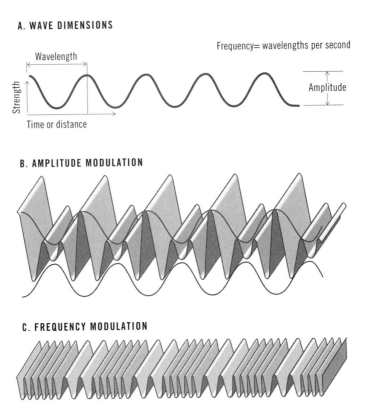

A. WAVE DIMENSIONS

Wavelength

Strength

Time or distance

Frequency= wavelengths per second

Amplitude

B. AMPLITUDE MODULATION

C. FREQUENCY MODULATION

Figure 6-10. WAVE MECHANICS AND SIGNAL MODULATION. Any wave, whether sound, light, or radio, is measured in three dimensions: amplitude, wavelength, and frequency. The amplitude is the strength of the wave. Wavelength and frequency are interconnected. Frequencies are measured in cycles (or wavelengths) per second, known as "Hertz." Therefore, a sound wave with a length of 11 feet will have a frequency of 100 cps; likewise a sound wave 5 1/2 feet long will have a frequency of 200 cps.

To "modulate" a signal means to impose another signal upon it. It's logical that there are two ways to do this: either modulate the amplitude, or modulate the frequency (which is the same thing as modulating the wavelength). AM is illustrated in B: the carrier wave is indicated by the shaded ribbon band. The program signal has been imposed upon it. FM is visualized in C.

The idea that an electronic signal could be modified by circuitry became one of the defining concepts of the twentieth century. DeForest's audion vacuum tube was the workhorse of circuitry until the invention of the transistor in 1948 by John Bardeen, W. H. Brattain, and William Shockley. Much smaller and more reliable than the vacuum tubes, as well as cheaper to produce, the transistors opened up numerous new possibilities in circuitry.

The complexity of the technology took another quantum jump in 1959 with the introduction of the Integrated Circuit. Produced chemically rather than

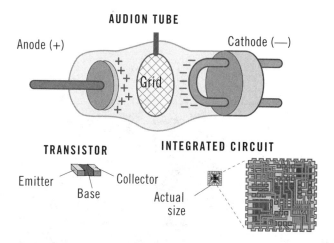

Figure 6-11. ELECTRONIC "VALVES": AUDION TO INTEGRATED CIRCUIT. De Forest's invention was as valuable as it was ingenious. The audion tube amplifies a signal because the grid acts as a continually varying electronic gate. Whatever signal the grid carries is impressed upon the stronger current flowing between cathode and anode. The audion tube was the model for all vacuum tubes—or "valves."

Beginning in the 1950s the transistor (left), drawn here lifesize, began to replace the vacuum tube in most applications. The principle of operation is basically the same, but it is more chemical than physical, and hence the transistor is much smaller and more reliable, both great advantages. The integrated circuit, which combines numerous transistor circuits, is even smaller.

mechanically, the Integrated Circuit did the work of boxes full of earlier electronic equipment. By 1971 this abstract technology had given birth to the silicon-based microchip, on which thousands of circuits could be photographically etched. Gordon Moore, one of the founders of the pioneering Intel corporation, suggested soon after the introduction of the device that the number of circuits that could be printed on a chip would double every eighteen months. This prediction came to be known as Moore's Law and has proved uncannily accurate over the past thirty years. This exponential development rate has been the engine that has powered the microcomputer revolution and the birth of the Information Age.

Just as the developers of cinematography had always wanted to produce sound as well as image, so the early experimenters in radio wanted to broadcast images as well as sound. The difficulty was that, although both sound and light are wave phenomena, we perceive sound waves collectively while we perceive light waves in a sense discretely. The light waves coming from any one point in our field of vision might be as complex as all the sound waves in our "field of hearing."

Because of this added complexity, light waves would have to be analyzed somehow in order to be carried by radio wave forms. The solution to the problem was similar to the one adopted in printing technology: to break down the contin-

Figure 6-12. THE ART OF THE MICROCHIP. Because the circuits are printed, albeit microscopically, microchips reveal the esthetics inherent in their electronic logic, as in this enlargement of a Motorola chip from the mid-nineties. The history of the microcomputer revolution which began in 1977 has been measured in the quantum jumps of chip design, as the number of transistors that a single chip could emulate jumped from 1,000 to 8 million It's a fine irony that the microchip, the most powerful invention of our time, depends after all on the old technologies of photography and printing. This 1995 RISC-based PowerPC 620, designed in collaboration with IBM and Apple, has 7 million transistors. This photomicrograph greatly enlarges the chip, which is less than an inch square.(*Courtesy Motorola.*)

uous image into a sufficient number of discrete particles so that each particle could be transmitted in sequence.

At first, mechanical devices were tried. Paul Nipkow's invention, the "Nipkow disc" (1884), used a spiral array of perforations on a rotating disc to create a rapid scanning movement. As late as the early fifties, the CBS color system utilized this

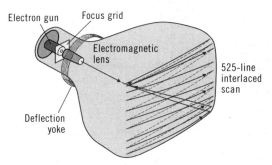

Figure 6-13A. THE CATHODE RAY TUBE. The video display consists essentially, of an electron gun, a focusing arrangement (grid and lens), a deflection yoke, and a screen coated with picture element phosphors. The stream of electrons coming from the gun is focused into a tight beam by the grid and the electromagnetic lens. The deflection yoke causes the beam to scan in regular patterns. In the American television system, the scan consists of 525 lines (there are approximately 400 picture elements on each line). 30 times each second, the beam traces each of these lines (and returns in the "off" mode—indicated by the dotted lines). In order to provide the smoothest picture, however, the scan is "interlaced": that is, all odd numbered lines are scanned in the first half of the frame, then all even numbered lines. Each "frame" comprises two of these "fields."

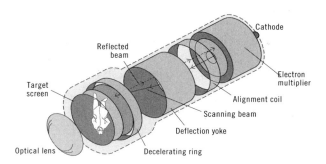

Figure 6-13B. THE IMAGE ORTHICON. Translating an optical image into an electronic signal is more difficult than the reverse operation. In the image orthicon camera tube an optical lens focuses the image on the target screen which is covered with an array of photosensitive diodes which can translate light energy into electrical energy. These various values are then read by the scanning beam which surveys the target screen in the same interlaced pattern as the cathode ray tube. The beam is reflected back into a device called an electron multiplier, an essential part of the system, whose job it is to amplify the very weak signal received from the face of the target screen. The sequential signal—carrying information about the differences in brightness of each of the 210,000 picture elements—is then broadcast to receivers. The Vidicon tube (not shown) was based on the same principle, but was constructed more simply.

mechanical technology. It worked quite well for the color video cameras used in the Apollo moon program in the 1960s and 1970s.

The eventual solution was, however, electronic rather than mechanical. The work of a Russian immigrant to the U.S., Vladimir K. Zworykin, was essential.[*] He developed both the "Iconoscope," a device for receiving an image and translating it into an electronic signal, from which most contemporary television cameras descend, and the "Kinescope," or Cathode Ray Tube, a device for translating the electronic signal back into an image. To produce an image of sufficient quality, it is necessary to break the picture down into at least 100,000 and preferably 200,000 "particles." These particles are called picture elements, or "pixels." Like the dots produced in the printing of photographs by the halftone screen, these picture elements, although separate and discrete, are psychologically understood as composing a continuous picture. In American and Japanese television they are arrayed in a 525-line pattern. In European television, the standard is 625 lines. (As a result, the European image is sharper.)[†]

There are two significant interrelated differences between the halftone system and the television pixel system. First, the dots in a halftone are of different sizes; pixels are all the same size. Second, the halftone dots are either black or white, while pixels have a range of brightnesses. Moreover, unlike the printed photograph, the televised image moves. Therefore, the phenomena of persistence of vision and the Phi phenomenon come into play, as they do in film. Again there is a slight difference between European and American standards. European television operates at twenty-five "frames" per second, American at thirty.

In the iconoscope, image orthicon, and vidicon camera tubes, all of which operate similarly, the image is projected optically onto a surface or screen within the tube covered with the necessary number of picture elements in the proper array, each of which can hold an electrical charge. These charges are read by an electron beam, focused and controlled by an electromagnetic lens, which scans the entire array twenty-five or thirty times each second. The signal that results carries a different value of brightness for each of at least 200,000 pixels, twenty-five or thirty times each second. At least six million values must be recorded and transmitted every second. The television signal is obviously much more complex than the radio signal.

To produce an image on its screen, the Cathode Ray Tube (CRT), the other essential component of the system, essentially reverses the process. The screen of

---

[*] Philo T. Farnsworth was doing similar work independently at the same time, or perhaps even before but didn't have the industrial power of RCA behind him, as Zworykin did.

[†] In neither case are all the lines visible, and many other factors contribute to the resolution of the image. The slower frame rate of European television means that the amount of information transmitted in both systems is about the same.

STANDARD 3-LENS COLOR SYSTEM

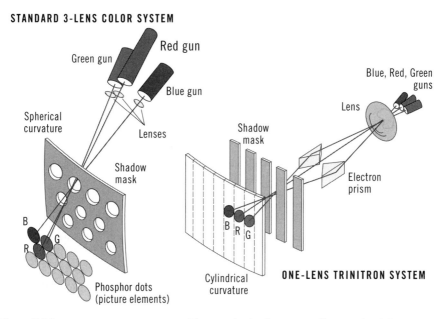

Figure 6-14. COLOR VIDEO SYSTEMS. The standard color system, illustrated at left, consists of three separate electron guns, three lenses, and a shadow mask which effectively blocks the electron beam from the blue gun, for example, from striking any but the blue phosphors arranged on the surface of the screen. Precise focus is crucial—so exacting in fact, that the force of gravity can deflect any color signal beam enough during its short journey from the gun to the screen to throw the color off.

The Trinitron system, developed by the Sony Corporation, gets around this difficulty by aligning all color phosphors vertically, so that when the beam is pulled down slightly by the force of gravity it will nevertheless strike a dot of its own color. In addition, the prism system of the Trinitron allows all three beams to be focused through the same lens and deflection coil. The principle is that the larger the lens and coil, the more precise the focusing. A single lens can be larger than three separate lenses.

the CRT is covered with a phosphorescent coating, any particle of which produces light when struck by a high energy beam of electrons. A "gun" at the opposite end of the tube produces this beam, varying its intensity according to the brightness value of the signal. The beam is controlled by a magnetic lens like the one in the camera tube that sweeps across 525 (or 625) lines thirty (or twenty-five) times each second. In reality, the system is more complex. Just as a film projector shutter splits the light beam not only between frames but also in the middle of each frame to decrease the flicker effect, so the CRT electron gun actually divides each sweep into two components: it first sweeps the even-numbered lines, then returns to the top of the picture to sweep the odd-numbered lines, so that the phosphors of the screen surface fade more evenly from top to bottom between these sweeps, or "fields."*

Color television is similar, only three times more complex. Like color printing, it applies color psychology to halftone technology, creating the entire spectrum of color through various combinations of elemental color values. For television these elements are red, green, and blue. Color cameras originally consisted either of three image orthicon tubes that, through a system of mirrors and filters, each read one of the basic colors, or of a single tube whose screen plate is masked in such a way that the picture elements are arranged in three separate sets. Likewise, the picture tube can consist of three separate electron guns, each scanning a different color, or one gun, which scans each color consecutively. Figure 6-14 describes the system of masks, which can be observed by close examination of any color picture tube. (Color was introduced commercially in the U.S. in 1953 and in Europe generally in the late sixties.)

The modern charge-coupled device camera, described in Figure 6-15, has revolutionized video technology, making possible far greater sensitivity. Flat-panel LCD screens (and their competitors) offer similar promise on the display side of the video equation.

Interestingly, the developing technologies of image (film) and sound (radio) crossed paths in 1928, when both sound film and television were introduced. But while the sound film was immediately accepted, commercial television was delayed nearly twenty years. Partly this delay was caused by technical reasons; mainly, it was the result first of economic decisions, then of the interruption of World War II. Whereas film producers and distributors needed sound to counteract the threat of radio as an entertainment and information medium and revive a faltering market, their counterparts in broadcasting were involved with a relatively young medium, radio, which had not yet reached its full economic potential. As a result, there was no reason to rush into television production. Afraid of the additional expense, William S. Paley, owner of CBS, actively campaigned against the introduction of television.

Beginning in 1925, phonograph technology began borrowing from the developing electronics of radio. Amplification and refinement circuitry both in recording and reproducing greatly enhanced the latitude of the phonograph. The intro-

---

* Computer monitors generally do not divide the frame into fields; they are "noninterlaced"—that is, they sweep every line consecutively. They also operate at much higher frequencies than 30 frames per second. These are two of the technical reasons that they are sharper and far more readable than television monitors. The difference gave rise to a major dispute between the two industries over digital television standards.

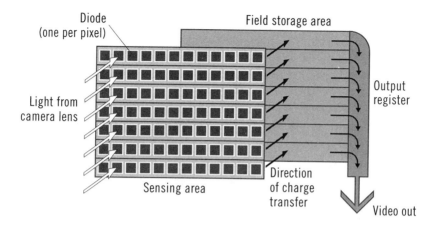

Figure 6-15. THE CHARGE-COUPLED DEVICE. The modern Charge-Coupled Device camera is many times more sensitive than its predecessors. It achieves its edge through a simple yet ingenious architecture. The diodes now are coupled to semiconductor capacitors which store the information until either a line or a whole frame is read. Relieved of their responsibility to communicate their readings instantaneously to the scanning beam, the diodes have far more time to collect information about the image. Moreover, the scanning beam has been eliminated and the charge pattern for an entire frame is transferred simultaneously in parallel for every field, further freeing the capacitor-coupled diodes to do their work. On the display side, the LCD screen uses the same ideas, but the need is far less critical there.

duction of the long-playing record (1948) and stereophonic reproduction (1958) were advances based on radio technology, as was, especially, the development of far more sophisticated "high-fidelity" circuitry during the 1960s. Yet the disc record had one basic drawback as a recording medium: it could not be edited.

In the late 1940s and early 1950s, the perfection of magnetic tape as a recording medium changed this. Besides being a more precise and flexible medium (because it translated the electrical sound signal not into physical waves but into magnetic representations), it was also linear and therefore could be edited. Moreover, it presented the possibility of recording a performance on a number of separate, parallel tracks at the same time, which gave the sound engineer further control over the signal via the technique of "mixing," which was a new form of editing. Finally, because it was nearly as easy to record tape as to play it back, the technique of recording was opened up to wide numbers of individuals, greatly increasing access to the medium. In fact, audiotape (like videotape years later) was marketed first as a do-it-yourself medium rather than as an alternative to the phonograph record.

As a playback medium, compact discs, first introduced in 1982, added little to the technique and experience of sound except the arguable durability of the

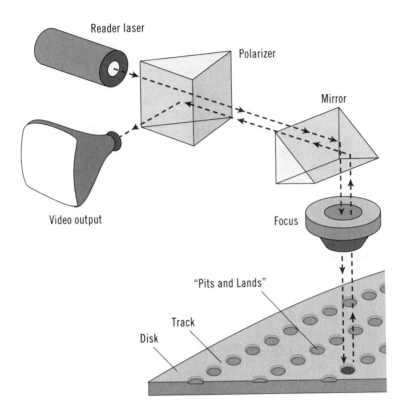

Figure 6-16. LASERDISCS AND CDS. Several videodisc technologies competed in the 1970s. The problem was to encode vast amounts of information on relatively limited areas. The RCA system (not shown) used a physical groove and stylus which at first may seem similar to the standard audio disc, but the information was encoded differently. The stylus did not "bump" along the track but rather read the varying depths of the track as electrical capacitances. The Philips-MCA system, which won the contest after help from JVC, uses a laser reader. No physical stylus touches the disc.

The basic technology is the same for audio CDs and DVDs. The laser reads the pits pressed into the disc medium and recreates waveforms from the information. On a laserdisc, the video signal is still analog. On a CD or DVD it is digital. The illustration here is greatly enlarged. There are billions of pits on a CD and the distance between two adjacent lines of pits is less than 2 micrometers (or about 1/15,000 of an inch). It is the ability of the laser to focus on an area as small as one micrometer that makes this huge data capacity possible.

medium. However, as a recording medium, beginning in the mid-1990s, CDs represented another quantum jump for audio technology: Because the signal recorded on a CD is digital rather than analog it can be manipulated in a great variety of ways—easily, and cheaply. By the turn of the century audiophiles with computers enjoyed a virtual mixing and editing suite that would have cost mil-

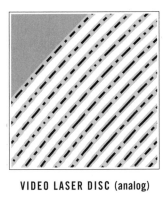

VIDEO LASER DISC (analog)

AUDIO COMPACT DISC (digital)

Figure 6-17. AUDIO CD VERSUS LASERDISC. While the laserdisc represents information in analog format, the audio CD, like the DVD, is purely digital. The pits and "lands" of the disc translate into binary numbers which reflect the sound values of the sampled moments. If a digital recording were "perfect," its sampling rate would be infinite—which is impossible. Current standard CD recordings use a sampling rate of 44,100 Hz. The value that is digitized is one of 65,536 discrete numbers (2^{16}), since the "word" length is only 16 bits. Some veteran audiophiles still insist that neither of these parameters is sufficient to match good analog recording. DVD-Video increases the sampling rate for audio to 96,000 Hz and the word length to 24 bits.

lions to build when the CD medium was born in the early eighties, and the Internet gave them access to hundreds of thousands of recordings—as well as a cheap means of distribution for their own home-made products.

Because the television signal is much more complex than a simple audio signal, it was a good ten years before tape technology was sophisticated enough to accommodate video. Once videotape was introduced in the 1960s, however, it not only changed the shape of commercial television, which had been limited to the choices of either live presentation or film, but also eventually opened up television—at least as a recording medium if not a broadcast medium—to wide numbers of people. The result has been the associated art and business of "video."

Throughout the seventies, Japanese, European, and American electronics companies competed to develop a successful videodisc technology and bring it to market. After many false starts, the first viable videodisc systems went on sale in 1978. But the debut of the videodisc had been delayed for so long that Sony's competing videocassette technology had had enough time to become well established. The laserdisc never did catch up with VHS tapes in the marketplace.

What was surprising about the commercial introduction of videodisc recordings is not that they did the job well, but that they did it at all. Two of the competing systems—the RCA and German TeD systems—used records that consisted of electrical codes carried in a physical groove, which a playback stylus had to follow.

The competing MCA/Philips laser videodisc, which eventually won the market, represented an interesting hybrid technology: its disc carries a visually encoded electromagnetic signal. In effect, it combines some of the best features of tape and disc, analog and digital. Moreover, by introducing laser technology to recording media, it greatly increased efficiency, since light waves are of far higher frequencies than radio waves and thus can carry more information in less space.

Ironically, the laser recording technology first became profitable in the audio market even though audio CDs weren't introduced until four years after laser videodiscs. Despite the far higher resolution and greater flexibility of the laserdisc, tape's lead was almost insurmountable. It was 1991 before laserdiscs became a viable consumer business—and even then the market was limited to film buffs and videophiles.[*] For a while in the mid-eighties it wasn't even possible to buy a laserdisc player, despite the fanatical devotion of the medium's 500,000 or so customers. During this period, the American/European partnership of MCA and Philips sold out the technology to the Japanese trading company Japan Victor Corporation.

The battle of the 1970s between the rival videodisc technologies had been foreshadowed several times before: RCA and CBS both introduced differing versions of the long-playing record in the late forties. Both CBS's 33 1/3 rpm twelve-inch disc (developed by Peter Goldmark) and RCA's 45 rpm seven-inch disc eventually found applications, although the 33 1/3 rpm disc had a more revolutionary effect on the medium. Several years later the two competing giants of the broadcasting oligopoly faced each other again over the question of a color system. RCA's all-electronic system quickly beat out CBS's partially mechanical system (also developed by Goldmark). In each case, just as with videodiscs, the more radical technology was the more successful.

When it came time in the early 1990s to fight the battle of High-Definition Television (HDTV), American and European companies took a more cautious approach. Sony, the dominant innovative force in consumer electronics since the sixties, had pioneered HDTV, demonstrating a widescreen 1,125-line model in conjunction with the Japanese network NHK as early as late 1970s, although it was more than ten years before the system officially debuted in Japan, with sets priced out of reach of most people and with a limited broadcasting schedule. While the Japanese moved ahead, their American and European competitors waited, secure in the knowledge that broadcast television standards required government approval. That had not been the case with the development of the VCR

---

[*] The horizontal resolution of the VHS VCR system is less than 250 lines—far from the ideal of broadcast television. Laserdiscs offer a horizontal resolution of about 425 lines, and DVDs 480 lines. There are other differences that make the laserdisc and the DVD-Video mediums far superior to VHS.

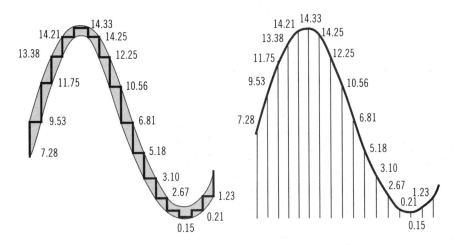

Figure 6-18. DIGITAL VERSUS ANALOG. The theory behind digitization is that everything can be quantified. An analog record of sounds or images (right) mirrors sound or light waves in a continuous—and continuously variable—physical or electronic medium, such as a phonograph groove or electromagnetic signal. A digital record is discontinuous (intermittent) and not continuously variable: it is limited by the number of digits (or decimal places, if you like) used to identify or "quantize" each value. A digital record is made by sampling the audio or video waveform many times each second, converting the sample into whole numbers, and recording those values in numerical form.

While the analog record may appear to be perfect—at any point on the curve you can discern a value, and you can make it as precise as you like—in reality, analog records are subject to deterioration inherent in their media. While the digital record is immune to deterioration—there can be no question about the numbers—in practice, it is limited by both the frequency of the sampling and its precision.

in the seventies, a market that Sony pioneered and the Japanese electronics industry quickly cornered.

Although the Japanese system worked well, the HDTV standard became a major battleground in the trade wars. The Americans and their European allies were not eager to hand over lucrative licensing fees to Japan, Inc. The FCC decided in 1992 that the broadcast HDTV standard they would approve would have to be digital. Since the NHK design was analog (it dated from the 1970s), it was out of the running. Under pressure from the FCC, the four competing finalists—none of them Japanese—merged their technologies and agreed on license fee splits in May 1993.

Trade politics may have been at the root of the FCC's decision to go digital, but it made technical sense, as well. Times had changed; that the American HDTV standard would be digital meant that sets could be easily adapted to the other interactive uses, which seemed imminent. By 1996 when, after lengthy and involved discussions, the FCC finally issued the rule book for the HDTV game in the U.S., the Japanese companies were ready to compete on the digital front. HDTV broadcasting began formally in the U.S. in November 1998, but by that time the set of standards gave broadcasters and set manufacturers so much flexibility that none could agree on a single development path. In addition, the cable companies, who by that time dominated American television, weren't ready to carry the digital signal the "last foot" from the cable tuner to the television monitor.

It wasn't that the market wasn't ready to switch to digital: quite the reverse. Between 1997 and the turn of the century consumers embraced other new digital video products rapidly. In the late 1990s digital still cameras opened a new niche in the home photography market and were soon accompanied by digital video cameras. DVD-Video—a disc format designed to replace VHS tape—was introduced in April 1997 and quickly accepted as superior. (The laserdisc proved an excellent model for productions in the format.) Within eighteen months video stores across the nation were opening DVD sections to compete with tape rentals.[*]

You can see that the history of recording media has been informed by a single overriding aim: how to capture more information in more detail in less space. One way is to shorten the wavelengths used (television versus radio, laserdiscs versus magnetic tape); another is to refine the medium (33 1/3 rpm vinyl versus 78 rpm wax, HDTV versus standard television). While audio and video recording technology was maturing during the latter half of the twentieth century, another form of information technology was developing separately.

Computer memory and information storage began in the 1940s using the venerable vacuum tube, pressed into service from the radio industry. During the next thirty years, computer technicians experimented with a wide variety of media in search of ever greater efficiency and capacity. Because computers were not a consumer product, a number of proprietary information storage technologies were introduced, used for a while, then discarded (although the oldest, the punched card, is still in use). Beginning in the 1960s, magnetic tape proved to be a useful standard for information interchange, although the linear characteristic of tape proved a daunting access barrier. IBM's introduction of the magnetic disc in 1956

---

[*] This is another interesting format wars story. While the HDTV battle was being fought in the headlines, two other consumer-electronics alliances were going head to head over the standard for the successor to CD-ROM. Sony and Philips had been allies since the early days of optical disc technology and indeed shared royalties on every CD sold. The group led by Time Warner and Toshiba wanted a piece of the action. The two groups eventually compromised on the DVD standard. In 1999 the contest was replayed. This time the battle was about the successor to the venerable audio CD. Sony–Philips held out for SACD, based on Sony's contrarian DSD technology; Time-Warner–Toshiba supported DVD-Audio.

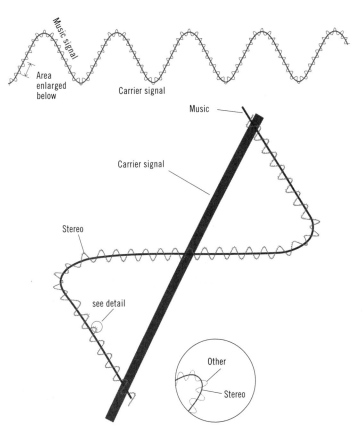

Figure 6-19. MULTIPLEXING. Wave form broadcasting is limited only by the imagination. Just as the carrier wave supplies the base on which the signal is imposed (see above) so the signal itself can be used as a carrier for a second signal, as it is in stereo "multiplexing." That signal, in turn, can be used as the carrier for a third signal (a fourth waveform). Some narrowcast music systems have operated this way, their signal carried piggyback on an FM stereo signal. Data is often transmitted this way. Multiplexing is hard to visualize, but it works.

solved that access problem. With the introduction of the "floppy" disc in 1971 one of the cornerstones of the microcomputer revolution had been laid.

Computer folks were quick to see the information storage capabilities of the new laser recording technology. Within a few years of the introduction of the laserdisc, the technology had been adapted to the recording and storage of bits and bytes as well as images and music. The CD-ROM (for Compact Disc-Read Only Memory), introduced in 1985 by Philips and Sony, heralded the impending union of computers and media, information technology and recording technology.

For their part, audio and video people were beginning to realize that the philosophy of the computer folks had something to offer them: in a word, digitization. Computer technologists had long ago given up on the analog model. The success of the industry had been based on the digital approach to reality. By reducing the world to its most elemental symbols—the 1s and 0s of the binary number system—they were on their way to making that world infinitely manipulable. Why? The simpler the coding system, the easier it is to process. In the early eighties, the audio and video technologists caught the fever.

> Nor mouth had, no nor mind, expressed
> What heart heard of, ghost guessed …
>
> ["Spring and Fall"]

Gerard Manley Hopkins wrote these lines years ago, just as the art of film was beginning. Now audio and video techies and artists could enjoy what their forebears had only dreamed of: complete control of their versions of reality. Once images and sounds were digitized, their representations on screen and through the speaker were limited only by the sophistication of the computer programs that described them. Brice Parain had observed:

THE SIGN FORCES US TO SEE AN OBJECT THROUGH ITS SIGNIFICANCE.

But if the sign is quantified, we can add a corollary:

The significance of the sign is limited only by the imagination of the signer.

And when the images and sounds, whose history we have traced from the earliest photographs and phonographs, are represented in the same medium as the words (and numbers) of literature, a union is possible. This is the subject of Chapter 7.

Radio and Records

Interestingly, there is not all that much difference structurally between radio and television. The esthetic and formal history of television since 1948 in the U.S. is consistent with the history of radio between 1922 and 1948 (although, since the advent of network television, radio has been forced to specialize esthetically). In a sense, it is more useful to speak of "broadcasting," which includes both, than to differentiate too strongly between the two. Both serve the essential socializing function of mediating the world around us. Formerly isolated individuals and communities are brought into relatively intimate contact with a central source (if not with each other). This was a radical shift in cultural patterns. The problem is that these media are unidirectional.

Anyone who has ever watched an infant grow into a child with television as a surrogate mother can testify to the remarkable power of the electronic media. In helping to create new needs (for Barbie Dolls or licensed breakfast cereal on the one hand, or continual fictional stimulation or the omnipresence of a human voice on the other), in inculcating shared values, and in defining the general shape of the culture, television and radio have no equals. The print media, because they do not have a human presence of their own, because the reader controls the experience, and because they must be actively decoded or read, have not a tenth the power of the electronic media; nor does film, which, although it does have a presence and need not, strictly speaking, be decoded, nevertheless stands as a separate experience: it takes place in the movie house, not in the home.

This elemental force may be more clearly seen in contemporary radio than in television, since radio can be apprehended so much more easily (that is, it is not necessary actually to look at it). In this respect, radio still serves as a model for television, a medium which, in contrast to film, puts more emphasis on the sound component than on the image.

The essential purpose of radio is not only to tell stories and convey information but also to create a pervasive aural environment. The ultimate product of this is Muzak, a continuous stream of carefully designed and programmed music constructed to create a specific mood: sound as architecture rather than meaning. Much of contemporary radio, whether talk or music, tends in this direction. Dead space is to be abhorred; what is important, as any disc jockey knows, is the continuous flow. Psychologically, radio serves a "stroking" function: it is artificial but very much needed company. Likewise, much of television is designed to accompany the flow of the day. Visual information, paradoxically, although often useful, is not necessary. There is no particular need to watch a talk show or television news, and most television drama is generally comprehensible without visual input. As a result, it is not uncommon for people to "read" a newspaper and "watch" television simultaneously.

It became clear early in the history of commercial radio that the concept of personality would dominate the medium. Even more than film, radio heightened the effect of celebrity because the "variety" program allowed stars to be free of fictional, artificial roles and to play "themselves." Radio shows were often indistinguishable from their stars. The basic form had been taken over from vaudeville, but the master of ceremonies now dominated the proceedings. Jack Benny, George Burns and Gracie Allen, Fred Allen, Bing Crosby, Edgar Bergen and Charlie McCarthy, and Easy Aces all followed a well-defined form—the basic characteristic of which was a seamless weave of fictional and real elements.

The personas of the stars were simple and easily identified: Benny's stinginess, Gracie's peculiar logic, Fred Allen's homespun sarcasm—and these characteristics formed the skeletons of the shows. In each case, the star was himself as well as an actor in a plot. The radio show itself was quite often an element of the plot, a Pirandellian twist that still intrigues connoisseurs of radio.

A common plot—possibly because it was every writer's nightmare—began with the premise that with just "x" minutes to airtime the star suddenly discovers there is no script for this week's program. Half an hour later, it doesn't matter anymore. Albert Brooks's brilliant parody of the radio comedy form, *The Albert Brooks Show,* uses this plot. During the course of the usually very thin plot, a parade of supporting players, a guest star, a singer, were introduced, did their turn with the star, then moved on. Fred Allen's "Allen's Alley" was probably the most blatant example of this basic technique.

Because there was no visual reality to distract from the story line, radio had a peculiar ability to compress narrative time and space. The cinematic term "montage" isn't applicable because the joints were undetectable. The musical term "segue" is more appropriate: radio segments followed each other continually and easily without a break. On the comedy and variety programs, at least, the star could move from a word of welcome to the audience through a brief scene "in character" with another actor into a commercial announcement and back out into the plot again without skipping a beat. Although it was much less easily accomplished in television, this segue technique was an important model for the new medium, in which "lead-ins" are an essential device.

While dramatic programs had much the same freedom as radio comedies, they were more circumspect in using it. It was felt that some semblance of realism had to be maintained to support the dramatic mood. Radio dramas were of two kinds: "serious" plays, such as could be heard on *Lux Radio Theatre, Inner Sanctum, Suspense,* and—most important—*The Mercury Theatre,* Orson Welles's company; and "serials," by far the dominant dramatic form and radio's most important contribution to dramatic esthetics. Serials (which could as easily be comic as dramatic) dated from the premiere of *Amos 'n' Andy* in 1929. Serials focused attention on continuing characters and allowed dramatic programs to tap the same rich vein of personality as the comedy shows. Such serials as *The Shadow, The Lone Ranger, The Whistler,* and *Sherlock Holmes* presented striking fictional personalities couched in an endless variety of plots. On daytime radio, the genre of the Soap Opera further refined the concept of the serial. Unlike their evening counterparts, these daytime domestic dramas told never-ending stories. Partly as a consequence of their endless, addictive plots, radio Soap Operas lasted well into the television age, not disappearing until the late fifties.

(When television adopted the two forms, the vocabulary became more specific. More narrowly defined, the television "serial" presents a continuing personality in a continuing story, as the radio Soap Operas did, whereas the television "series" presents the same characters in different stories, each complete in itself, following the form of the evening radio serials.)

By the early thirties, the spectrum of radio entertainment was complete; it changed little during the next fifteen years. Comedy and musical variety programs dominated the network schedules; news and sports events took up considerable time; game shows and occasional talk shows, together with soap operas, serials, and occasional serious drama, filled the remainder of the airspace.

In the 1950s, however, the networks turned their attention to the even more profitable medium of television, and radio responded by retreating to a defensible position. Ever since KDKA found the first audience in 1920, the major part of the schedules of non-network, independent local stations had always been dominated by music and talk. As the networks lost interest in radio, this pattern became pervasive.

In addition, as modern marketing techniques began to demand specific audiences for advertisements, radio stations began to specialize instead of offering a mix of various entertainment services. This development was facilitated by the relatively large number of potential radio channels. An American city of any size now counts among its fifteen or twenty radio stations at least one devoted to each of the following major specialties: all-news, talk and call-in, rap, historical rock, middle-of-the-road, country-and-western, and soul music. Larger cities often have stations that play classical music and jazz as well. Although these stations serve small minorities, their audiences are usually "upscale"—that is, heavily weighted in the higher income brackets, and therefore attractive to advertisers.

As a medium, discs have the potential to present as much variety of programming as radio. In actuality, however, the recording industry is essentially a servant of the music industry. Because radio comedy and drama have largely died out, the market for such performances on record is small. Nevertheless, since the death of radio, there have been occasional productions—utilizing the elaborate techniques of mixing and editing that were unavailable to radio in its heyday—that stand out. The albums of the Firesign Theatre, Mike Nichols and Elaine May, Peter Sellers, Albert Brooks, and Steve Martin are examples.

As for music, the influence of modern recording techniques combined with the development of flexible electronic instrumentation has had a profound effect. Both esthetically and economically, music is now more a recording art than a performance art, a development emblematized by the late-Disco/early-Rap device of "playing" records as part of the performance.

The record and radio provided means to package musical commodities so they could be sold more efficiently and, as the technology of recording developed rapidly with the advent of tape and high-fidelity circuitry, it became clear that the record offered musicians an undreamed-of flexibility.

At first, this new latitude resulted only in the gimmickry of double-tracking that characterized much popular music in the 1950s. The records of Les Paul and Mary Ford were landmarks in this respect. Then multiple-track recording systems began to yield more sophisticated results. The remarkable success of The Beatles' *Sergeant Pepper's Lonely Hearts Club Band* album in 1967 marked a turning point. Most of the cuts on that album were so highly "worked" that they couldn't be performed live. From that point on, music has been "built" as often as it has been "played." Jean-Luc Godard investigated this phenomenon in his 1968 film of the Rolling Stones, *One Plus One*.

The development of progressive popular music on record was closely linked with the evolution of radio in the 1960s. FM radio, which provides sound reproduction notably superior to that of AM, had first been developed by Edwin H. Armstrong in 1933. He had foreseen a major conversion of radio to the new, much more faithful system, but David Sarnoff, head of the near-monopoly Radio Corporation of America, decided otherwise. Sarnoff, who was more interested in the marketing of television, felt that FM would compete with television for badly needed capital, and did his best to block the acceptance of the new radio technology. He was successful for a time.

Armstrong managed to start his own experimental FM broadcasts in the late thirties, but television and FM were in competition not only for capital but also for the same high-level frequencies. Originally, channel 1 of the VHF frequencies had been set aside for FM. After the war, the Federal Communications Commission shifted the FM frequencies further up the spectrum, requiring a complete retooling and forcing FM to begin all over again. After long legal battles, Armstrong committed suicide.

For years, FM was effectively dominated by AM networks and independent stations. Almost all FM programming was a duplication of AM transmission. In 1966, however, the FCC handed down a decision requiring owners of FM stations (who in most cases were AM entrepreneurs) to program FM separately from AM. For the first time, the full potential of FM could be realized. The more sophisticated radio medium soon found its proper subject matter in the new progressive rock music, and the two developed rapidly and symbiotically thereafter. Although at first it served smaller audiences than AM, FM attracted more sophisticated listeners and provided an attractive market for advertisers.

By the late seventies, FM had surpassed AM as the leading radio medium for advertising, a remarkable feat in fewer than fifteen years. Since 1980 the two formats have divided the work of radio pretty much according to their capabilities: AM concentrates on talk and news, FM on music. In 1980 the FCC approved a long-awaited system of AM stereo, taking the unusual step of prescribing one of several competing technological systems. The aim was to redress the balance between FM and AM, but the new technology has had a barely measurable effect. Listeners haven't invested in AM stereo, since it simply duplicates the FM stereo they already have.

Ironically, although the FCC required that television sound be FM, American networks and television manufacturers, reacting neurotically to the challenge of FM radio, conscientiously ignored FM's potential for sophisticated television sound. Until the mid-1980s most television receivers were equipped with crude audio systems that would have been embarrassing in even a good-quality AM radio. Even now that television stereo audio is common, it is seldom reproduced with the same fidelity as FM radio, and audio/video component systems haven't caught on with the general public, although they are increasingly popular with buffs who form the market known as Home Theatre.

Television and Video

Television is more like radio than it is different from it. As with radio, the concept of flow is all-important; the product of both media is continuous and continuing, within both the smaller unit of the show and the larger unit of a day's or evening's programming. Moreover, because of the relatively poor quality of the televised image (as compared with theatrical film), television depends heavily on its audio component. The curved screen, the low resolution, the flat contrast, the difficulties of broadcast reception (or cable reception, for that matter) all work to reduce the effectiveness of the television image. The density of visual information is low, which is made up for in part by a density of programming, compressed sequencing, and insistent, busy audio: dead space and dead time are to be avoided at all costs; the flow must continue.

In 1961, Newton Minow, then Chairman of the Federal Communications Commission, gained a certain notoriety when he indicted American television as "a vast wasteland." The phrase stuck. Even now, four television generations later, the "wasteland" is the metaphor of choice for most critics of this entertainment and information medium that is at the center of American life. Perhaps we are blaming the messenger for the bad news. If television had never been invented, radio would have continued its role as the glue that holds our society together, and Newton Minow very likely would have made the same speech in 1961—but about radio.

There is, however, a significant semiotic difference between the two media: the "illustrated radio" which has dominated our lives for half a century demands a different kind of our attention from its pure audio cousin. The very fact that television has an image track as well as a sound track forces producers to choose material with a visual component and lures viewers into a scary evening-long paralysis which is vividly reflected by the phrase "couch potato." Paradoxically, just because the image track of television is so weak, the medium demands our obsession with it. We need to work hard to comprehend it. This is what Marshall McLuhan was getting at when he called television a "cool medium."

"THE SIGN FORCES US TO SEE AN OBJECT THROUGH ITS SIGNIFICANCE."

There are eighty-two broadcast television channels available in each market area of the United States. For various technical reasons, however, fewer than half of these are usable, and, in practice, few cities have more than twelve over-the-air stations available. Moreover, only twelve of the eighty-two are powerful VHF stations; the other seventy, operating on a different frequency band (UHF), are considerably weaker and, with few exceptions, have remained marginal operations. Only seven of the twelve VHF channels are in operation in any one area (and far fewer in most areas outside the major urban centers), a fact that has allowed the commercial broadcast networks—NBC, CBS, ABC, and now also FOX—to dominate the airwaves both economically and esthetically since the commercial birth of television in 1946. Although their power has lessened since the cable revolution of the 1980s, they still clearly dominate the medium.

Cable television has logically developed as a medium of special interests—sports, movies, children's programming, the arts—so the job of socializing our culture still rests mainly with the broadcast networks. Among the cable networks, only MTV—and perhaps CNN—affect our culture in the way that the broadcast networks still do.

Two basic limitations govern the nature of broadcast television and allow networks to dominate: one is the limited number of channels available, the other the limit of time. A television program director has only 168 hours at his disposal each week and his programs, moreover, must be in direct competition with those of the other networks. A newspaper reader can buy several papers and read them all carefully in sequence. A television viewer, however, can watch only one network news program at a time, and while he is watching it he is likely to be missing the others. (Of course, true news junkies tape what they're not watching.)

Because of the inherent limitations of time and channels, the commercial networks still have effective control over the airwaves, subject only to an occasional FCC ruling. Network programming begins at 7 am each day and lasts, with occasional breaks for local shows, until at least 2 am the next day.

Until the Telecommunications Act of 1996, the networks were not allowed to own outright more than a handful of local stations. Over the years, several FCC rulings have been directed to increasing the local affiliates' independence from networks (such as the Prime Time Access rule of the early seventies, which set aside certain hours for non-network programming), but the affiliates' connections with networks are lucrative and they do not disregard the wishes of the networks very often.

At the beginning in the 1950s, the networks themselves produced most of their programming, often in conjunction with advertising agencies (and sponsors) to whom they had sold an entire time block outright.[*] As a rule, they no longer sell blocks of time or whole shows to advertisers, having found it more profitable to market the 13 or 14 percent of each hour reserved for advertising in small pieces ranging from 10 to 120 seconds; 20- and 30-second spots dominate. The price of this time is now more than $500,000 per minute on the most popular shows, so a network's gross revenue for one primetime evening schedule could conceivably approach $20 million.

The price the network can get for advertising time depends on the show's popularity as measured by ratings, the Nielsen rating being the most important. The networks, like contemporary magazines, are not therefore selling time so much as they are selling a particular audience. The result has been a shift from programming in the early 1960s devoted to "Middle America"—middle-aged, middle-class viewers in large towns and rural areas—to programming directed at a younger, more urban, "upscale" audience with more disposable income, just the same sort of shift the magazines have undergone. This strategy allowed ABC to gain parity with CBS and NBC in the mid-1970s.

Ten years later, Barry Diller built the upstart FOX network into a profitable business with the same tactics; the traditional networks had allowed their demographics to skew to middle age; Diller was able to undercut them by appealing to the youthful audience he knew so well from his years in the feature film business. In the 1990s Warner and Paramount were able to carve out profitable slivers of the network pie when their network operations, The WB and UPN, geared their programming almost exclusively to teens and preteens.

Newspapers determine their advertising rates by ratings, too (as measured in circulation) but, significantly, a newspaper's circulation figures, no matter how they are broken down demographically, still reflect on the paper as a whole. In television, each show is rated, so that whereas a newspaper publisher can afford to carry unpopular material, a television programmer must judge the economic potential of each individual program.

Subtle shifts in timing can produce huge increases in revenue, which makes television programming an interesting game to observe, quite apart from the con-

---

[*] The "Fin-Syn" rule limiting networks' financial interests in syndication was promulgated by the FCC in 1970, supposedly to free the affiliates to compete with the networks. In late 1976, NBC consented to the settlement of an antitrust suit that restricted both the number of network-owned programs and the financial interest it might have in entertainment programs owned by others. The other networks concurred later. The networks fought the rule for many years, finally winning their case in 1993. By 1998 they were forcing financial "partnerships" on their producers, with NBC the most aggressive.

tent or value of the shows that are its raw material. As long ago as the 1974–75 season, for example, NBC lost out to CBS in total ratings (for the nineteenth year in a row) by less than a single Nielsen point, yet that slight difference was worth $17.5 million to the winner. In 1976 ABC, with thirty fewer affiliates a perennial also-ran until that time, hired personality Barbara Walters at a then record salary of $1 million per year. All Walters had to do to justify this sum was boost the ratings of ABC News by a single point. If she had increased the Nielsen by two points, ABC would have made a 100 percent profit on the deal.

The networks produce their own news and public affairs programs mainly for the prestige it affords them (even though many news programs draw considerable revenue). News looms large in strategic thinking, since it is the main way that networks differentiate themselves. After all, entertainment programming is produced by others. CBS first established itself as a respectable challenger of NBC through its news coverage of World War II. The rise of ABC to equal ratings status paralleled the increasing prestige of its news operation. All networks produce their own profitable sports programming as well (and late evening and early-morning talk shows), but they rely on outside producers for the bulk of their primetime entertainment product.

The romance of journalism continues to seduce network executives and producers. As television came to maturity in the fifties and sixties, it challenged two established American institutions: the movies and the newspapers. Looking back, we can see that the first generation of broadcasters ceded a large measure of control over their entertainment back to Hollywood. On the news front, however, they maintained economic identities separate from the newspaper business, as well as developing a radically different kind of journalism. By 1974 television had surpassed newspapers, the oldest of the mass media, as the primary means by which most Americans learned of the events of the day.

While they are proprietary producers of news, the networks are mainly distributors of entertainment. The producers of entertainment—most of them subsidiaries of the Hollywood studios—approach programming executives with ideas or outlines for a show. If the executive thinks the show may have potential, he approves expenses for the writing of a few scripts and the making of a pilot, which is often later recycled as a special or theatrical film. The pilot is tested with small audiences. But its success in the tests doesn't in any way guarantee it a spot in the schedule, for the real art of network television lies in the complex game of scheduling.

It is not the gross popularity of each show that matters so much as its share of the audience watching television during its time period, or "slot." If, for example, both ABC and CBS have scheduled comedies for 8 pm Wednesday, NBC might just squeak through to win the period by "counter-programming" with an action show. In addition, a strong show has value as a lead-in (or less frequently as a lead-out) to a program that needs a boost, since television tuners still tend to follow Nielsen's laws of inertia, despite the ubiquity of restless audiences' modern weapon: the remote.

Networks don't sell entertainment, as the Hollywood studios did; they sell audiences, whose size and quality depend almost as much on the talent and luck of the programming executive in placing shows effectively as they do on the inherent value of the shows. The programmer wants a show to fit the "sound" or "look" he is trying to create. We don't watch a show so often as we "watch television." One result is that parts of a show are more significant than the show as a whole. This characteristic is emphasized by the peculiar breakdown of shows into discrete segments by the practice of threading advertisements throughout the time slot rather than bunching them between programs, as is done in some other countries.

The focus of critical attention, then, is the family of programs, each group identified by a particular style or rhythm, an attitude to character, a specific subtext or type of payoff. These characteristics have their roots in film and radio. In the thirties, film genres fit into a similar system yet, despite the practice of the double feature, each film was separate—individually as well as generically identifiable. The concept of genre is much more important to television.

As cable television matured in the 1980s, the rules were reconfirmed rather than revised. Ted Turner started with cable sports programming but had his greatest success with CNN, a fulltime news network that very quickly grew to challenge the broadcast networks' news oligopoly. The multiplicity of channels allowed cable network operators to focus each on an individual special interest, but the genres didn't change. There is no cable—or satellite—channel whose programming doesn't have roots in broadcast network television. (Even C-SPAN's coverage of Congress and public policy echoes the broadcasters' special-event coverage of Watergate in the seventies and the McCarthy and Kefauver hearings of the fifties.) And the few remaining cable networks that still eschew advertising venture only so far as the British dramatic serial popularized in the 1970s by PBS.

We'll have more to say later about the unique position television holds in contemporary life. Meanwhile, let's review the history of this remarkable medium.

"Broadcasting": The Business

Ironically, the commercial potential of broadcasting was demonstrated almost accidentally. Like many other amateur radio operators, Frank Conrad, a resident of Pittsburgh and a researcher for Westinghouse, was in the habit of transmitting program material—music, news, and so forth—as well as conversing with other "hams."

Late in September 1920, the Joseph Horne department store in Pittsburgh ran an advertisement in the Pittsburgh *Sun* that called attention to Conrad's amateur broadcasts and offered for sale an "Amateur Wireless Set" that could receive them. The response was immediate. Westinghouse officials, who had known of Conrad's hobby but had never given it much thought, now perceived the commercial value of broadcasting. As Erik Barnouw put it in his invaluable history of broadcasting, *Tube of Plenty* (1975):

> What had seemed an eccentric hobby, or a form of exhibitionism, or at best a quixotic enterprise pursued by visionaries … was suddenly seen as a sound business concept that could yield rich profits through the sale of receivers.

Conrad was immediately put to work building the first commercial transmitter, which on October 27, 1920, was assigned the call letters KDKA. That station still operates.

At first, despite the immediate success of radio, broadcasting was still regarded as simply a minimal service necessary to instigate the purchase of receivers, where the profit was. The Radio Corporation of America (the descendant of Marconi's original company) joined together with AT&T, Westinghouse, General Electric, and the United Fruit Company (who had discovered early on that radio was useful for communicating with their wide-ranging empire of plantations) to form the RCA group monopoly.

Like the medium itself, the practice of selling commercial time on radio developed almost accidentally. AT&T had been assigned the "radio telephony" sector of the market. In order to become involved in commercial production without breaking their monopoly agreement, AT&T invented what they called "toll radio" in 1922. Instead of broadcasting their own programs, they would simply rent out their studio to whoever wished to broadcast: the studio was likened to a telephone booth, in which the sender of the message pays the bill. WEAF in New York, which later became the cornerstone of the National Broadcasting Company, was the first such toll station. The response was minimal at first, but eventually it became clear that people not only were listening but also would respond to advertising, and the success of commercial broadcasting was assured.

Throughout the thirties, forties, and fifties, this toll system dominated the structure of broadcasting, first in radio, then in television. Although networks and stations did produce much of their own programming, they were essentially in the business of selling time to advertisers. Quite often these advertisers bought large blocks of time and their agencies produced the shows—hence, the *Ipana Troubadours, The A&P Gypsies, The Lux Radio Theatre, The Colgate Comedy Hour,* and so forth.

Gradually it became clear that production simply tied up capital and could more profitably be left to independent entrepreneurs. During the 1960s, the television networks began to concentrate on distribution, themselves producing only news and sports, which required ongoing organizations, and leaving most of the primetime entertainment product to "independent" producers, many of whom, ironically, were subsidiaries of the motion picture studios.

The networks not only did not have to tie up large amounts of capital in production, but they also got away with paying the producers of the shows less than they cost. This strange state of affairs was made possible because the total real value of a successful television program is significantly greater than its one-time production cost. Producers hope to make their profit margin on syndication sales of reruns to independent stations and export sales after the program has received the network imprimatur.

In about 1960, when this system of relying on independent producers had gained currency, the economic nexus of network television also changed. The networks still sold time to advertisers, but it was measured in terms of actual minutes and seconds of commercials broadcast, not hours of programming. Thus, whereas an advertiser in 1952 might buy an hour of primetime on Tuesday evening for the next nine months and then put whatever programming he felt like sponsoring on the air to surround his commercial messages and attract an audience, by 1960 he was reduced to buying thirty seconds of ad time in a specific show produced by independents and controlled by the networks themselves. This new system focused much more attention on the ratings.

In the early days of television, a sponsor might very well finance a show that had a relatively small audience. His aim wasn't necessarily gross ratings points but prestige and influence. Thus, the "Golden Age" of television was marked by such relatively unpopular shows as *Hallmark Hall of Fame, The U.S. Steel Hour,* and *Armstrong Circle Theater.*

But now that networks were controlling programming, the ratings game became all-important. Not only were individual shows carefully ranked (the cost of advertising time within the top-ranked shows could be sold for more than the time in poorly ranked shows), but also each network's yearly average became the index of "success" or "failure." In most years since 1960, the difference in ratings averages between the first and second (and sometimes the third) network has been so small as to be statistically insignificant, but the psychology of ratings has been so obsessive that such meaningless point differences can still make tens of millions of dollars of difference in advertising revenues.

Most observers agree that the quality of network television will not change significantly until the ratings system is either abolished or becomes moribund. It is unlikely that either the FCC or Congress will challenge a system the networks are comfortable with. Yet technological developments are now making the ratings game obsolete. First, if even a significant minority of VCR owners use their machines for what is called "time-shifting," deciding for themselves *when* they want to watch any particular program, the ratings race becomes clouded. Each show is in competition with every other show (as well as prerecorded tapes and discs), and no gross rating assures an advertiser that the show is even watched: it simply proves that someone *recorded* it, maybe to play it back later, maybe not. Moreover, the technology of VCRs even today permits viewers to skip commercials much as they might when reading a magazine or newspaper. The advent of disk-based digital "Personal Video Recorders" in 1999 made this all the more likely since the disk architecture makes it much easier to edit program material.

Finally, the cable revolution of the 1980s irrevocably altered the architecture of the American television industry. (Its sister, satellite television, is now having an even greater effect on European television.) At the beginning of the 1980s, *TV Guide* listed three national networks; at the end of the 1980s, it listed more than thirty. (In the next ten years that number doubled yet again.) Moreover, these new cable networks were all specialized. As a medium, television looked more and more like magazines, where publishers try to attract a special-interest group in hopes of finding a profitable niche market.

As the number of cable networks has continued to grow and been joined in the U.S. by DSS satellite systems that offer even more possibilities, network economic power has declined significantly. However, since nearly all the cable/satellite channels are targeted at special interests it is still the broadcast networks that serve as our public forums—the glue that holds the body politic together.[*]

NBC was formed in 1926 as a subsidiary of RCA, which itself had been erected as a monopolistic shelter corporation for General Electric, Westinghouse, AT&T, and United Fruit. Originally NBC operated two radio networks—NBC Red and NBC Blue—but in 1941 an FCC ruling required NBC to divest itself of one of the two networks. NBC Blue was sold to the manufacturer of Life Savers candies for $8 million and became ABC. CBS was founded in 1927 by the Columbia Phonograph Record Company but was soon sold to a cigar manufacturer, Sam Paley, who turned it over to his son William. By 1950 Paley had built CBS into the most prominent network, and it dominated television ratings for many years.

But it was NBC's programming executive during the early years of television— Sylvester L. "Pat" Weaver Jr (father of the actress Sigourney)—who proved the most inventive of the long line of programming czars to follow. Weaver realized that the "cool medium" was to become a member of the family. During a brief period as president of NBC beginning in 1953, he devised the talk/news/interview/chat format that is still emblematic of the medium. His *Today* and *Tonight* shows continue as the longest-running television shows in history. (His third entry, *Home*, didn't last but set the pattern for the successful daytime shows to follow.) In the early sixties, Weaver championed pay television, long before its time, then took refuge in a safe post in the advertising industry.

---

[*]   This is a strained metaphor, but so is the social phenomenon is describes.

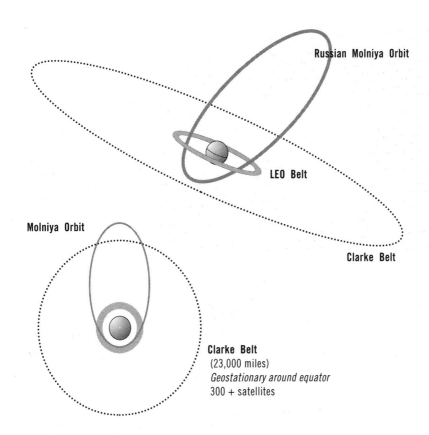

Russian Molniya Orbit

LEO Belt

Clarke Belt

Molniya Orbit

Clarke Belt
(23,000 miles)
Geostationary around equator
300 + satellites

Figure 6-20. SATELLITE PLACEMENT. A satellite in orbit at a height of 22,300 miles is geo-synchronous; that is, it seems to hang stationary overhead since it is moving at the same speed as the surface of the earth. This makes the job of communicating with it much simpler since the earth station antennas needn't move to track it. Although the circumference of this orbit at the equator alone is more than 166,000 miles and VSAT (Very Small Aperture Technology) considerably narrows the necessary angle of separation, the track is already crowded, and nations contend for satellite locations as they do for electromagnetic spectrum frequencies. More than 150 communications satellites are already operating in this orbit. (Note: the map of satellite placement is not drawn to scale.)

Low Earth Orbit ("LEO") satellites also serve communications functions. Although they are useful at any particular location on the surface of the planet only during the brief time they are overhead, several LEO satellites can combine to provide extended periods. There are several ambitious plans to launch large quantities of LEO satellites which would hand-off signals seamlessly from one to another to another—rather the reverse of cellular telephony (the antennas are moving, but the caller remains stationary).

Because much of the territory of the former Soviet Union lies in northern latitudes where equatorial geosynchronous satellites are of little use, Soviet scientists devised the ingenious Molniya orbit. Swinging in a very eccentric ellipse, these satellites are relatively stationary for a useful amount of time while they are at their apogee. (The diagram is not drawn to scale.)

In the early 1960s, CBS president James Aubrey coldly took the "Tiffany" network downscale in search of ratings while Michael Dann, former assistant to Weaver, devised the rules of the programming game that still operate today. Throughout the fifties and sixties, CBS dominated the ratings wars, with NBC usually a close second.

ABC, the perennial also-ran, gained its first ratings victory in 1976 under the leadership of former CBS executive Fred Silverman, with a schedule designed to capture the growing youth market. Silverman was the leading programmer of the seventies, responsible for the likes of *Laverne and Shirley* and *Charlie's Angels*.

When NBC won him away from ABC in 1978, however, Silverman's luck ran out. His three-year tenure as president saw the oldest of the networks sink further into third place. Grant Tinker, former head of MTM productions, proved to be NBC's salvation. With programs like *The Cosby Show* and *Hill Street Blues*, NBC moved into first place where it remained until CBS's resurgence in the 1990s. Thanks to *Seinfeld*, and later *Friends* and *ER*, NBC quickly regained the lead.

The financial benefit of leading the Nielsen charts is multiplied when local stations change network affiliation in search of a winner, as they did during both the ABC and NBC reigns. The thirty-year ratings wars were crucial to the networks financially, no doubt, but while they were jousting with each other, the structure of the industry was changing, inexorably and dramatically.

Coaxial cable technology dates from the early fifties. It was invented to deliver television signals where broadcast reception was poor. As cable moved gradually into major cities in the sixties, cable operators searched for additional sources of programming; urban viewers required more value than just a better signal. Growth was slow, and expensive. The cable industry was fragmented into more than 4,000 small companies, and the capital cost of laying cable was, obviously, enormous. Between 1960 and 1990 the fledgling cable industry had to build a physical network comparable to the telephone network.

Then, in 1975, a regional distributor named Home Box Office had the foresight to offer its premium service to cable system operators across the country via satellite. An instant national network was born, thanks in large part to the "network of networks" the new satellites provided. Focused on feature films, HBO had a profound effect on the film industry as well as the television industry in the late 1970s, as the economics of the business were radically altered.

Many other cable networks followed, each devoted to a niche. Although consumers were required to pay additional fees for premium networks like HBO, they deemed the access to brand-name product from Hollywood worth the extra cost. Cable boomed in the eighties, as penetration grew from less than 30 percent in 1981 to more than 60 percent in 1991. (At the same time, VCR penetration was zooming from less than 8 percent to more than 70 percent.)

Figure 6-21. EMBLEM FOR THE NINETIES. Turner and bride Jane Fonda (with friend) watching his team the Atlanta Braves during the 1992 World Series. Think of the resonances: the rise of the new South, sports champion, eighties entrepreneur, Barbarella, feminist activist, Workout videotapes, Vietnam and the anti-war movement, local politics, 12-meter yachts, Western heroes, satellite television, glamour and romance at age 55, a Hollywood dynasty now into its third generation, the first worldwide television network, the first television cinémathèque, the Gulf War live in your living room, ecological activism, colorization, the Goodwill Games, Workout salons, MGM, baseball and basketball.... The Hollywood myth is not yet dead—even if the Braves did lose that Series. (*Courtesy of the Atlanta Braves.*)

The founding of CNN, a national news network, and MTV, devoted to popular music, both in 1980, marked another milestone in the rapid development of cable's "special interest" approach to television. Within ten years both had become broadly international in scope, primary forces in the development of the New World Culture (if not the New World Order). Just as broadcast network television had homogenized a diverse America in the 1960s and 1970s, so satellite distribution of CNN, MTV, and other cable channels rapidly broke down national cultural barriers, for better or worse.

During this period, European television was also undergoing a radical sea-change as government-controlled, limited television systems were opened to a free-market approach. Cable penetration in some European countries—Belgium, for example—was significant, but in others practically nonexistent. Beginning in the late 1980s, direct-to-home satellite broadcasting (DSB) offered a cheaper, quicker alternative to multifarious but capital-intensive cable systems. During the late 1980s and early 1990s, Rupert Murdoch's Sky Television (later B-Sky-B) accomplished for the U.K. what took numerous independent cable operators thirty years to do in the U.S. Having struggled since World War II against the irresistible power of American popular culture, European nations now felt themselves under bombardment from satellite distribution that no Star Wars defense could be effective against. Yet many observers credited global television distribution with hastening the end of the Cold War.

While all the cable networks taken together seldom garner more than a 20 percent share of the U.S. television audience, that has proved enough to put a serious dent in the profitability of the traditional broadcast networks. Throughout the 1980s and 1990s the broadcast networks continued to lose market share. All three of the traditional networks changed hands at least once. ABC was acquired by Capital Cities Broadcasting, an owner of local stations, in the spring of 1985; Lawrence Tisch wrested control of CBS from an aging William Paley several months later; and at the end of the year GE announced that it would purchase NBC and its parent RCA. Taking advantage of the broadcast shakeup Rupert Murdoch founded Fox Broadcasting in 1986. In 1995 two of the now four commercial networks changed hands again: Capital Cities/ABC merged with Disney, and Westinghouse purchased CBS.

In 1992 ABC, CBS, and NBC all suffered losses for the first time, as they failed to adjust in time to the changing reality. Meanwhile, cable networks with a 1 percent share could be profitable, as they had the additional source of income from license fees from the cable system operators (which traditionally range between 1 cent and 25 cents per month per subscriber).

The system operators, presiding over a limited number of channels, besieged by new networks, and free to choose which to broadcast, increasingly began to challenge the traditional networks for power and influence. By 1991 John Malone, head of TCI (Tele-Communications, Inc.), controlled access to more than nine million American television households as the leading cable system operator. In late 1992 Malone announced he would rewire his systems to accommodate as many as five hundred channels. Malone's announcement, coupled with Hollywood mogul Barry Diller's coincident takeover of the shopping channel QVC (backed by Malone), marked a new interest in "interactive" television.[*] Malone never did get his 500-channel system running, but the challenge to broadcast power continued.

---

[*] After losing his bid for Paramount to Sumner Redstone in 1994, Diller sold out his interest in QVC and acquired, again with Malone's backing, a chain of television stations known as Silver King to serve as the new base for his vision of a fifth broadcast network. Later, he added Home Shopping Network, Ticketmaster, and USA Network to the mix.

Figure 6-22. The serial and series were less important in film than in radio and television. Here, Flash Gordon (Buster Crabbe) and his crew from the popular Universal film serial of the late 1930s, *Flash Gordon*. Film serials were a programming staple in the early days of television and thus became part of the mythic memories of a second generation, as well. In the seventies and eighties they were revived for still a third generation of viewers through the movie homages of directors like George Lucas and Steven Spielberg.

Competing with Malone's vision of hundreds of cable channels was the nascent technology of Video-on-Demand. More like a telephone system than a broadcast operation, and backed mainly by the Baby Bells, Video-on-Demand quickly hit the technology wall. (It depends on digital storage, transmission, and switching of video signals.) Seeing the convergence of television and telecommunications that was approaching, Malone tried to merge TCI with Bell Atlantic in 1993. The deal fell through, but Malone was successful in his second attempt, merging with AT&T in 1998. The eventual combination of the telephone and television industries seemed inevitable, especially after the long-debated Telecommunications Act of 1996 gave both cable and telco interests virtual carte blanche to proceed with mergers and acquisitions. Presented as a liberalization of existing laws intended to increase competition, the Act almost immediately had the opposite effect as five of the seven Baby Bells announced mergers and major companies—now largely freed from ownership constraints—gobbled up hundreds of

Figure 6-23A.
BEFORE. Howard
Morris, Sid Caesar,
Imogene Coca, and
Carl Reiner in a
sketch from *Your
Show of Shows*
(September 1953).
(*NBC.*)

local television and radio stations and scores of smaller chains. Meanwhile, Malone's promise of television bandwidth so wide it would be unsurfable languished, as the cable industry's attention turned to opportunities in Internet service and telephony.

As the founders of television faded from the scene to be replaced by businessmen like Malone and Murdoch and massive conglomerates like Time Warner and Disney, one newcomer kept the entrepreneurial spark alive. Ted Turner had bought a local Atlanta UHF station in 1970 and kept it going with a mixture of movies and sports (he owned interests in two local teams). Shortly after HBO went "on the bird," Turner began national distribution of WTBS (then called WTCG) via satellite, becoming the first of the "superstations"—local stations distributed nationally via satellite.

He became an immediate cable power. He added to the personal myth by winning the America's Cup in 1977 with his yacht *Courageous*. Disregarding industry wisdom, in 1980 he founded CNN—next to MTV the most influential broadcasting operation of the 1980s. He cloned a second news channel, HNN, in 1982 to ward off competition. By 1985 he was taken seriously when he announced he might bid for CBS. (Paley turned to Tisch as a "white knight" to fend off Turner and others.)

Figure 6-23B. AFTER. Morris, Caesar, Coca, and Reiner months later in what appears to be a reprise of the earlier sketch: just add "production values." (June 1954). (*NBC.*)

A year later Turner was more successful in his bid for MGM. He bought the venerable film studio in March 1986, kept its library, and sold the rest (nearly bankrupting his company and losing a measure of control to cable system operators, including the ubiquitous John Malone). By 1988 Turner's strategy became clear: TNT, his fourth cable network, began broadcasting, drawing on the extensive MGM library. Turner had new prints struck for the telecasts, introducing an entire generation to the wonders of old Technicolor and 35 mm black-and-white cinematography. But he didn't stop there: He used developing computer technology to "colorize" many black-and-white classics from the thirties and forties, supposedly to make them more palatable for television audiences. Colorization became a cause célèbre in Hollywood as filmmakers banded together to protect their heritage. Ted Turner continued his rise as a media mogul by marrying into Hollywood royalty in 1991. No one in contemporary times has continued the old traditions of Hollywood glamor, entrepreneurship, and panache so well as Turner … and he did it in Atlanta.

In 1995, after losing out yet again in his bid for CBS (thwarted in large part by the cable interests that now dominated his board), Turner announced that he would sell his company to Time Warner for $7.5 billion. "I'm tired of being little all the time," he declared with laconic wit at the press conference announcing the

Figure 6-24. TODAY. On the morning of January 14, 1952, television came of age, as the NBC announcer intoned: "This is *Today*, the day you are going to live, from the RCA Exhibition Hall on 49th Street in the heart of New York. And here is your communicator, Dave Garroway." From that moment on, television was part of the family.

deal. "I'm nearing the end of my career. I want to see what it's like to be big for a while."

Although the market for television has become much more complex than it was in the 1970s, although the technology certainly exists to provide hundreds of channels and make them interactive, although American families spend almost as much time in front of their television sets as they do at work, it is not yet certain that this brave new world of television will prove to be economically viable. By 1996 the traditional powers in the television business were under attack not only from upstart cable and satellite networks and distributors but also from telephone companies, computer companies—and even Hollywood—as America's entertainment conglomerates jockeyed for position in a market that didn't yet exist.

"Television": The Art

We could roughly define several periods of television history by their genres. The late forties and early fifties are best remembered for their variety series, as the new medium quickly consumed large amounts of aging vaudeville talent, and

Figure 6-25. TONIGHT. Just as important as *Today* in establishing the unique forms of television has been *The Tonight Show*, presided over in its long history by just six hosts. From left to right, Jerry Lester and Morey Amsterdam provided the warmup in the timeslot as the resident comics on *Broadway Open House*. Steve Allen's reign in the fifties brought the level up from burlesque to satire and established the show as an institution. Jack Paar introduced a new personal tone during his short but influential stint. (Sidekick Hugh Downs and frequent guests Dody Goodman and Hermione Gingold are in the background.) All of this was preparation for 29 years of Johnny Carson. Throughout the eighties, the question of succession was grist for the rumor mill. Potential *Tonight Show* hosts came and went—often to their own shows on other networks. When Carson finally retired in 1992, Jay Leno happened to be sitting in the successor's seat. Note the grins: Leno brings us back to Lester.

radio comedy and variety programs were transferred whole to the more profitable medium. This was the era of Ed Sullivan, Milton Berle, Jack Benny, Burns and Allen, Jackie Gleason, and Sid Caesar, who, with Imogene Coca, Mel Brooks, Carl Reiner, and Howard Morris, created one of the earliest and most engaging television programs, *Your Show of Shows*, produced by Max Liebman.

Second to Caesar as an innovator in this period was Ernie Kovacs, who started on local stations in New York and Philadelphia. Kovacs, who died in 1962 perhaps before he had realized his full potential, was easily the most technically inventive television artist of the 1950s. In its perceptive use of the curious technology of the new medium, his work forecast later developments in independent video.

Figure 6-26. Kovacs's famous library sketch. "Eugene" can't quite pour his milk straight into the glass. The camera is tilted so that it is square with the inclined set. (Notice the stagehand mopping up at the right.) (January 1957.) (*NBC*.)

In the mid-fifties, television—as film had before it—turned to more respectable enterprises as it tried to establish a more mature reputation. This period—the adolescence of television—is remembered for its live, nonserial, serious dramas, such as *Philco Playhouse, Studio One, Kraft Television Theatre*, and *Playhouse 90*. The received critical opinion is that this was the "Golden Age" of television drama, yet it can be argued that the stagey quality of these theatrical productions did not use the medium to full effect. During this period television writers and directors achieved some public status. Paddy Chayefsky, Reginald Rose, Tad Mosel, Robert Alan Aurthur, Rod Serling, and Frank D. Gilroy, among others, developed reputations as writers that later stood them in good stead, while directors like John Frankenheimer, Franklin Schaffner, Sidney Lumet, and Arthur Penn later went on to successful careers in feature films.

The introduction of videotape techniques in the early sixties, together with the continuing shift from network production to production by outside agencies, marked an important turning point in television history. During this period, American television developed the mix of standard forms by which we know it today. News and public affairs coverage, the prestigious items, were expanded. Profitable sports coverage became more common and more popular as technical proficiency expanded. Instant replay, slow motion, and stop motion enhanced the impact of professional sports so much that stadiums eventually had to provide live spectators with their own video screens. New leagues were formed in response to the growing interest. Football became the metaphor of choice for politicians. Talk shows, pioneered in the fifties by such personalities as Arthur Godfrey, Dave Gar-

Figure 6-27. Lucy in the knife-throwing sketch. *I Love Lucy* set a style for situation comedy that persisted for forty years. (*CBS.*)

roway, Steve Allen, and Jack Paar, became a dominant television form with the rise of Johnny Carson (1962) and a host of imitators. The mix of talk, game shows, and soap opera was established as the standard for daytime television.

Meanwhile, primetime entertainment had settled into the mix of half-hour comedy and hour-long action/drama series that we recognize today as its basic structure. Television didn't invent these forms. Both types of programs are direct descendants of the dominant radio forms; indeed, we can trace their genesis even further back, to the movies' two-reel comedies and sixty- to seventy-minute action "programmers." But the forms took on new relevance in television.

Jack Webb's *Dragnet* and Lucille Ball's and Desi Arnaz's *I Love Lucy* were basic models in the fifties. Webb established the concept of strong identification with the hero and the importance of location shooting in his seminal, magnificently stylized, "realistic" series about the work of Sergeant Friday of the Los Angeles Police Department. Ball and Arnaz established the basic rules of "situation comedy" production by filming in front of a live audience and shooting with three cameras simultaneously. The three-camera technique dated from the earliest experiments with television in the thirties, but Ball was the first to realize that immediate, "real-time," live television editing (in which the director monitors all cameras and makes instantaneous decisions about which image to use) could be combined with traditional after-the-fact film editing.

Just as many of the best Hollywood films were made in the 1930s, before people were aware that they were inventing narrative forms that would last for sixty

Figure 6-28. The Army–McCarthy hearings in 1954 proved an important turning point for television news/public affairs departments. For the first time, the television vision of the world became a major determining factor in American politics. As the hearings droned on, Senator Joseph McCarthy revealed himself as a sniggling, egomaniacal liar and the once great power he wielded evaporated quickly. Here he is advised by his counsel, Roy Cohn (left). His adversary, Joseph N. Welch, counsel for the Army, gained instant celebrity projecting the image of a wise, good-humored, slightly sardonic judge straight from central casting. (The battle between McCarthy and Welch was more a contest of images than of issues.) Twenty years later, "country lawyer" Senator Sam Irvin projected an image similar to Welch's (and just as popular) as Chairman of the Senate Committee hearings on Watergate. (*From Emile De Antonio's Point of Order. Courtesy New Yorker Films. Frame enlargement from kinescope.*)

years, so much of the best American television dates from the early sixties, when the patterns that were later to become so highly stylized and rigidly defined were first being established. Generally, the action/drama shows organized themselves according to professions. (Jack Webb's influence is important in this respect as well.) Police and Detective genres were action-oriented (as were most Westerns); doctor, lawyer, teacher, and other profession shows were more idea-oriented. Even social workers, nurses, and politicians had their own shows—albeit briefly—in the mid-sixties.

The best of the profession programs were those produced in New York. Herbert Brodkin's *The Defenders* (E. G. Marshall and Robert Reed as lawyers) and David Susskind's *East Side, West Side* (George C. Scott and Cicely Tyson as social workers) stood out. As opposed to the majority of programs produced in Los Angeles, the New York shows were more authentic and thoughtful. They were more likely to use location settings; they were more tightly written, with grittier characteriza-

Figure 6-29. NEW YORK TELEFILMS. George C. Scott and Cicely Tyson in David Susskind's *East Side, West Side* (1963). This episode, #2 "The Sinner," was directed by Jack Smight and photographed by Jack Priestly. Scott's character, Neil Brock, was often impatient, sometimes wrong. He was permitted to fail, as well. The plan was to develop the character throughout the series, but *East Side, West Side* lasted only one season. (*David Susskind. Frame enlargement.*)

tions and more irony; and they availed themselves of the large pool of acting talent in New York, while the Hollywood shows of the time had little to draw on except starlets (of both sexes).[*]

If cops and doctors seem to rule the airwaves still, there may be good reasons for that. As Sonny Grosso, a former New York City detective turned television writer and producer, has pointed out, hospitals and precinct stations are the contemporary clearing houses for dramatic stories. As a result, they make excellent locations for plot-hungry series.

As the 1960s wore on, and as the movie studios began to exert more influence, New York television production all but disappeared. In the late sixties, American television settled into a dull rut: the more sophisticated the ratings game became, the less interesting were the products that acted as lures for massive audiences. During his tenure at CBS, program director James Aubrey set the style for this period: the aim was to aim for the lowest common denominator so as to offend the fewest possible potential members of an audience. To characterize television

---

[*] New York-based profession dramas maintained their edge for more than thirty years, still boasting the same qualities in the nineties: for example, *Law and Order*.

Figure 6-30. *Laugh-In* had little of the Smotherses' political consciousness and lasted longer. A collage of bits and pieces, one-liners, short sketches, blackouts, catch phrases, wordplay, cartoons, set pieces, and running jokes, it set a style considered typical of the sixties. It also gave an unusual opportunity to female performers, including Ruth Buzzi, Judy Carne, Joann Worley, and Goldie Hawn, pictured here, as well as Lily Tomlin. Its most famous guest performer, however, was Richard M. Nixon, who appeared briefly one evening in 1968 to intone the catchline for the show solemnly (and prophetically): "Sock it to me?!" (*NBC.*)

comedy in the mid-sixties, we have only to name the most successful show of those years, Aubrey's *The Beverly Hillbillies.*

During this period, the concept of the "spinoff" gained widespread acceptance. If a show was successful, it was because of the elements of the program rather than its wholeness. As a result, those elements could be duplicated, slightly rearranged, and put together again to form a second successful show. Television began to replicate itself. If *The Beverly Hillbillies* (country folk in the city), then *Green Acres* (city folk in the country). By the mid-1990s the spinoffs had metamorphosed into "knockoffs"—unashamed copies of successful shows. Knockoffs proved especially attractive to the new wannabe networks, rushing to fill their primetime schedules.

In the late sixties, the renaissance of television in the seventies was prefigured by two 60-minute programs—*Laugh-In* and *The Smothers Comedy Brothers Hour* (sic)—both of which dealt in topical humor; both of which, for varying reasons, burned out quickly. *Laugh-In*, although it developed a stable of interesting comic actors, was too much of its time. The Smothers brothers, on the other hand, developed a reputation as political radicals through such acts of network defiance as reading the entire Declaration of Independence on the air.

Figure 6-31. The Smothers Brothers, Dick and Tom (1967). *The Smothers Comedy Brothers Hour* [sic] was not only politically alive and sharply satirical but also stylistically inventive during its short tenure, before it was canceled by nervous CBS executives. (*CBS*.)

In 1970 two programs debuted that set a new style for topical comedy, *The Mary Tyler Moore Show* and *All in the Family* (a remake of the popular British program *'Til Death Us Do Part*). Within five years these two programs were responsible for twelve to fifteen spinoffs and imitations on the network schedules. Since the fifties, programs like these had been referred to as "sitcoms" (situation comedies), but the phrase is misleading. Their real interest, as with the action/drama shows, is their collection of characters, not their situation. There is nothing inherently funny about a lower-middle-class family living in Queens (*All in the Family*), or about a single woman working for a television news program in Minneapolis (*Mary Tyler Moore*). There is, however, something humorous about the characters that Carroll O'Connor, Mary Tyler Moore, and their colleagues fashioned and the ensemble work of the actors. Again, as in radio, personality is the key.[*]

---

[*] *All in the Family* offered a striking lesson in sitcom character. In the pilot show, Jean Stapleton's Edith Bunker was entirely different from the naïve, sweet, dopey "dingbat" who later became famous. This first try at Edith was more intelligent, more sardonic, and—it must have been clear to the producers and writers— entirely too self-confident to last long under Archie's roof. Had this early version of Edith continued, it might have been she that was spun off, not her relative Maude.

The significance of character as opposed to plot, situation, or event is clear even in the action shows, which are ostensibly devoted to event. The most successful detective heroes of the seventies, for example, were *Columbo* (Peter Falk), *Kojak* (Telly Savalas), and Jim Rockford (James Garner) of *The Rockford Files*. It isn't what these characters did that got people to tune in week after week, but what they were. Such extraordinarily quirky characters might be out of place on the stage or in films, but they provided the quintessential television experience. We tuned in week after week to be with them because we knew what to expect.

The basic unit of television is not the show but the series, which gives television an advantage in building character over every other narrative medium except perhaps the novel saga. This is also why television is not so much a medium of stories as of moods and atmosphere. We tune in not to find out what is happening (for generally the same things are always happening), but to spend time with the characters. In the 1990s *Seinfeld* was promoted as a show "about nothing"—as if that were unique. All sitcoms are about "nothing"—nothing but character.

Television is not only better equipped than most other media to deal with subtle development of character; it is also conversely poorly equipped to succeed with other basic dramatic elements. Because it is much less intense than cinema (it gives us less visual and audio information), action and spectacle come off more poorly than in the movie theater. And because it is measurably less intimate than live theater, it can't deal as well with the high drama of ideas and emotions.

There is one factor, however, that prevents American series from reaching their full potential in terms of character: until now, they have been open-ended. A successful series can run nearly forever. The result is that series characters, like Luigi Pirandello's stage characters, can become frozen in the eternal moment, never developing, never changing. A successful program simply has far too great a profit potential to be closed down for esthetic or dramatic reasons, even when it is perfectly clear to everyone, from viewers to actors to executives, that it has outlived its purpose.

The twenty-five-year-old radio/television series *Gunsmoke* was canceled in the mid-seventies not because Kitty, Doc, and Matt Dillon had lost their appeal, but because network executives had decided that Westerns drew a rural, middle-aged audience that wasn't as attractive to advertisers as it might be. Archie Bunker continued as, first his children left the show, then his wife. Producers Norman Lear and Bud Yorkin killed off Edith in the opening episode in 1980, sacrificing her for a few more seasons for the series. *Cheers* ended its eleven-year run in 1993 (a record for a sitcom) nearly as popular as it had been a decade earlier.

Some successful comedies have partially avoided the open-end trap by generating a profusion of spinoffs, each of which altered the situation of the parent show. Two of the supporting players of *Mary Tyler Moore* (*Phyllis* and *Rhoda*) were

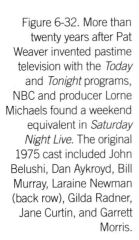

Figure 6-32. More than twenty years after Pat Weaver invented pastime television with the *Today* and *Tonight* programs, NBC and producer Lorne Michaels found a weekend equivalent in *Saturday Night Live*. The original 1975 cast included John Belushi, Dan Aykroyd, Bill Murray, Laraine Newman (back row), Gilda Radner, Jane Curtin, and Garrett Morris.

given shows of their own in the mid-seventies. *All in the Family,* itself a remake, spun off *The Jeffersons* and *Maude,* which in turn spun off *Good Times* (thus a fourth-generation spinoff). Finally, the show spun off *itself* into *Archie Bunker's Place.* In the 1990s *Frasier* spun off from *Cheers* (although it shared none of its parent's elements except the title character).

In fact, of the twenty comedies in the 1975 schedule, all but three were spinoffs or imitations of *Mary Tyler Moore* or *All in the Family* or were produced by Moore (MTM Enterprises) or Norman Lear (Tandem Productions). By the mid-seventies, Lear, an independent, had grown so powerful that he was actually able to challenge the dominance of the networks by stringing together his own ad hoc chain of independent outlets for his parodic soap opera, *Mary Hartman, Mary Hartman,* one of the more significant ratings successes of the mid-seventies and a show originally rejected as too innovative by all the networks. This success in first-run syndication was unheard of at the time but proved a model for the very profitable syndication market of the eighties and ad hoc networks of the nineties.

In the late 1970s television situation comedy sank close to the nadir of the mid-sixties as network programming executives became fascinated with simplistic sexual innuendo and preadolescent humor. Partly this was the result of the success of *Happy Days* and *Welcome Back, Kotter,* which both drew on nostalgia for the fifties teenager lifestyle that appealed, apparently, both to the preteens intent on living a fantasy of those days, and their parents, who remembered them. Television was not alone in exploiting this nostalgia. *Saturday Night Fever* and *Grease* were both highly successful films of the late seventies—both starred John Travolta

Figure 6-33. The miniseries *Roots* (1977), based on Alex Haley's book, not only set ratings records but marked a renewed interest in ethnic heritage that bridged racial divisions.

from *Kotter*. And *Grease* became the longest-running Broadway show up to the time it closed in 1980.

Partly, too, the late-seventies sitcom drew on *Charlie's Angels*, a lightly dramatic hour whose main purpose was to exploit its three female stars who ran around a lot without bras. As a result, such programs gained the sobriquet "Jiggly Shows." They set a pattern for mildly erotic exploitations of sexual fantasies that proved highly lucrative thereafter, often in made-for-television movies that appeared to have "redeeming social value" because they were based on reality. *Baywatch* continued this genre through the 1990s. Efforts like *Three's Company* proved beyond a doubt the validity of programmer Paul Klein's theory of "Least Objectionable Program."

Klein, who was one of the chief programmers for NBC in the late seventies, realized that most people don't watch a specific television program (and thus don't judge individual shows on their worth), they watch television. Hence they are likely to tune in the show that offends them least—and a light sitcom that will only demand half an hour from them and has a couple of pretty girls bouncing around and maybe some jokes (they don't have to be all that good) and some thinly veiled double entendre will probably offend most people least.

We have been speaking, of course, about primetime network television exclusively. Perhaps the central innovation of the 1970s in American television was *Saturday Night Live*, the "experiment" that made the late-night time slot almost as profitable for NBC on Saturday as it was during the week when occupied by the

Figure 6-34. The longest surviving Hollywood icon of the 1940s, Robert Mitchum provided a rock-solid protagonist for the miniseries *Winds of War* (1983) and *War and Remembrance* (1988–89), based on the Herman Wouk novels. More than forty years after it had ended, World War II continued to haunt our collective memory: note the large number of popular miniseries dealing with that period.

venerable Johnny Carson. Like its predecessors, *Your Show of Shows* and *Laugh-In*, *Saturday Night Live* offered a broad canvas to a group of actors to do sketch comedy. Like the Smothers Brothers, the "Not Ready for Prime Time Players" gained an edge by doing topical humor.

Beginning in 1975, the show quickly gained a following among young people. It was, indeed, broadcast live (except when shows were repeated)—a remarkable fact in the late seventies—and this resulted in a spirit of impromptu immediacy that hadn't been seen for almost twenty years in network television. It also provided some of the best humor in America during the period, sometimes relevant, often more than simply witty. It became the last refuge for the vaudeville tradition that had marked the earliest years of the century. For more than twenty years thereafter, as talent came and went, *Saturday Night Live* set the agenda for popular culture. It introduced talent like Chevy Chase, John Belushi, Dan Aykroyd, Gilda Radner, Eddie Murphy, and Mike Myers, who went on to success in feature films.

Two other innovations marked the seventies: the docudrama and the miniseries. The made-for-television movie (or "Movie-of-the-Week,"—MOW in Hollywood parlance) had its roots, ironically, not in television but in film. Starved for product, the networks had turned in the early sixties to the vast backlog of Hollywood movies. Edited for reasons of time and censorship, theatrical films were a major staple of the television diet throughout the decade, especially valuable because they had been premarketed. As the existing product began to run thin and as film producers turned to subjects seemingly unfit for television, the networks turned to producing films themselves.

The trouble with made-for-television films was that, unlike the theatrical product, their telecasts were not supported by massive publicity. The networks discovered an ingenious solution to this problem. Trading on the striking identity between fiction and reality that characterizes the television experience, program executives developed the "docudrama," a made-for-television film based more or less loosely on current events and history, dealing with subjects already well known to viewers and thus in a sense presold.

The Missiles of October (1974), which dramatized the 1962 Cuban missile crisis of John Kennedy's term as president, was among the first of these. *Fear on Trial* (1975) investigated the blacklisting by CBS in the mid-fifties of John Henry Faulk, a well-known commentator, and thus gave the genre a nice self-critical twist. *Brian's Song* (1971) was the true story of a football player's battle with cancer and thus traded not only on the popular fascination with disease but also on the mania for sports. Of course, the godfather of the docudrama was Orson Welles's historic radio program *War of the Worlds* (1938), whose documentary techniques were so lifelike that hundreds of thousands of listeners thought we really were being invaded by Martians.

The second important development of the late seventies was the miniseries, sometimes aptly if awkwardly referred to as the Novel-for-Television. After several experiments with this extended two-part or three-part movie-for-television (*QB VII*, for example) ABC enjoyed extraordinary ratings success with Alex Haley's *Roots*, broadcast in late January 1977 on eight consecutive evenings. The ABC management had thought so little of the cheaply produced series that it had scheduled it during a non-sweep[*] period when it would have the least effect on network and local ratings. *Roots* was an extraordinary hit, however, and seven of its eight episodes were ranked in the top ten television shows of all time (sharing those hallowed precincts with the two parts of *Gone With the Wind*, which had been broadcast for the first time the previous fall, and that January's Super Bowl).

A little more than a year later NBC's *Holocaust*, also taking as its subject a historical tragedy of epic proportions, received controversial critical notices and substantial ratings. The telecast of Francis Coppola's two *Godfather* films together with a

---

[*]   Sweeps periods (generally November, February, and May) are those times of the year when the ratings services measure local television station ratings. To help their affiliates, the networks schedule their most attractive programming during the sweeps periods.

FORMATS

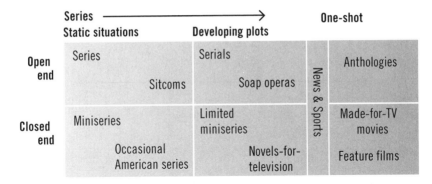

GENRES

Figure 6-35. FORMATS AND GENRES. Over the years, the forms of television broadcasting have been refined and standardized. The variables include continuity, development, and organization (format); and fictional nature, quality, and approach (genre). In recent years, more attention has been paid to hybrid formats and genres: for example, the miniseries, in-between a full series and a one-shot.

few minutes of extra footage re-edited in chronological order during four evenings in November 1977 was also a landmark. By the eighties the miniseries was well established as a television format and the networks were involved in numerous productions of this sort.

In fact, the miniseries simply filled in the continuum between the one-shot hour-and-a-half made-for-television movie and the endless American-style series. A television property (or theatrical film, for that matter) can be couched, now, in numerous forms of various lengths and divisions. What unites all these formats—and separates them from the traditional formats—is their serial style: their stories develop; an end is in sight (even if it is not always reached).

Figure 6-36. Steven Bochco's *Hill Street Blues* (1981–87) set a new style for television drama whose effect was felt well into the nineties. No fewer than fourteen lead characters received screen time in each show. (This is the original cast.)

One effect of the novel-for-television style was to revive the serial format in regular television programming. *Soap* (1977–1981) applied the serial to satirical situation comedy. In 1979, *Dallas*—an evening soap opera—met with worldwide popular success. The more interesting dramatic shows of the eighties and nineties followed this tradition, developing characters from episode to episode.

Chief among these was Steven Bochco's seminal *Hill Street Blues*, which debuted in 1980 and marked the changing of the guard. Perhaps the most innovative narrative in any medium during the eighties, *Hill Street Blues* merged hard-hitting, issues-oriented police drama with absurdist comedy, all set in the context of a continuing set of soap opera stories about a large group of characters. It brought Robert Altman's sense of humor and range to realistic docudrama treatment of relevant political issues. The combination of stylized high comedy with serious intelligence, all set in the context of the most mundane of genres, marked a new level of sophistication in storytelling—one that has yet to be exceeded by practitioners of the feature film.

A product of Grant Tinker's MTM production company, *Hill Street* heralded Tinker's reign as savior of NBC. It was joined in 1982 by another MTM production, *St. Elsewhere*, executive-produced by Bruce Paltrow (father of Gwyneth), which applied the *Hill Street* formula to a hospital setting. In 1985, Bochco himself

Figure 6-37. Bochco's *L.A. Law* (1986–94) applied the formula to a fictional Los Angeles law firm, adding to the mix pungent comment on topical subjects and a droll feel for the city of the eighties. The roster of characters was reduced to twelve: lawyers cost more than cops. (This is the original cast.)

Figure 6-38. The cast of *thirtysomething* (1987–91) in a well-posed publicity shot. While it lacked the bite and irony of Steven Bochco's shows, this series, produced by Ed Zwick and Marshall Herskovitz, was the first major contribution of the "lost" seventies generation.

Figure 6-39. Joshua Brand's and John Falsey's *Northern Exposure* (1990–95) isolated a group of eccentric characters in a small Alaska town.

applied this imaginative and innovative style to a group of lawyers. *L.A. Law* covered hundreds of issues with wit and perception during its long run. It may be remembered as the emblematic television show of the eighties, since it dealt almost as often with business issues as with political issues, and it was business that characterized that decade in America.

You can see what was happening here: television in the eighties, like film in the sixties, was mature enough to develop a self-consciousness. It wasn't enough to make a television show; now it was necessary to couch that program in ironic and sophisticated narrative forms. In the sixties, many of the better journeyman filmmakers came out of television. In the eighties and nineties, many filmmakers found more rewarding work, esthetically and intellectually, in television. The tide had turned. While we are still trained to separate the two forms, artists for quite a while now have considered them two halves of the same coin.

Until the late seventies it was common knowledge that television stars could never carry feature films. Many had tried and failed. But when John Travolta and Henry Winkler successfully made the transition from the smaller screen to the larger, a new era began. Actors moved back and forth between the two forms at will, while many of the brighter young film directors of the seventies (Claudia Weill is an example) found more interested and comfortable artistic lives in television. Writers found the electronic medium most welcoming. In the feature film world, writers are still considered hired guns, with little artistic control, while in

Figure 6-40. Dick Wolf's *Law and Order* (1990–) emphasized ideas over character to such an extent that it was able to maintain its position for five years while changing actors every year. Of the six original leads, four of whom are pictured here, only one remained by 1994. No other prime time series has been able to do that. From left: Chris Noth, George Dzundza, Michael Moriarty, Richard Brooks.

television the writer-producer has become the artistic hero of the day, with real power, as Bochco and many others discovered.

The collision of styles and genres best exemplified by Bochco's work also marked other series of the eighties and early nineties. Michael Mann's *Miami Vice* (1985–89) set a Film-Noir cop show in the colorful pastels of the new capital of Latino America with a hip sound track to match. Glenn Gordon Caron's stylish comedy *Moonlighting* (1985–89) often referenced itself. Edward Zwick's and Marshall Herskovitz's *thirtysomething* (1987–91), while sticking to the basic soap opera mode of narrative, often toyed with stylistic tricks.

By 1990, the pendulum was swinging again. *Northern Exposure*, the creation of Joshua Brand and John Falsey, who had come out of *St. Elsewhere*, reprised the large collection of kooky Altmanesque characters from that series but without the issues. Set in Alaska, and shot entirely on location in Washington State, the show's emotional theme proved as chilly as its locale: an emblem of the AIDS ice age in sexual relations for twenty-somethings. David Lynch's short-lived *Twin Peaks* (1990–91) confirmed this quirky postmodern trend.

More interesting was Dick Wolf's *Law and Order* (also 1990), which paid homage to Jack Webb's pioneering *Dragnet* of thirty years earlier. Shot in New York, and stylized almost to the point of Kabuki theater, *Law and Order* each week devoted its first half hour to three cops investigating a crime and its second half hour to three district attorneys prosecuting that case. The six "characters" were so restrained—they evidenced no private lives whatsoever—that one longed for Sergeant Joe Friday's occasional perfunctory banter with his partner and sidekick about the weekend barbecue. By eschewing character, Wolf was able to concentrate on ideas and issues, producing one intense and involving storyline after another.

Perhaps the most innovative series of the nineties was Steven Bochco's 1991 *Cop Rock*. Like *Law and Order*, it combined cops and attorneys. But unlike Wolf's characterless mouthpieces, these folks had the irresistible habit of breaking into song six or eight times each episode! The series was canceled after a few weeks.

While the hour-long dramas of eighties primetime broke new ground, the half-hour sitcoms were more traditional. Two comedies dominated the period: the long-running *Cheers* (1982–93) and the enormously successful *The Cosby Show* (1984–92). Eschewing both professions and families, *Cheers* set its group of characters in a bar, where they had nothing to distract them from wisecracking.

The Cosby Show showcased the talents of the enormously influential Bill Cosby as the wise and witty head of a middle-class Brooklyn family. It was more important for its sociology than for its humor, as genuine as that was. Having been the first African-American to star in a dramatic series twenty years earlier as the co-star of *I Spy*, Bill Cosby was now ready to take his place in the pantheon of American cultural icons. Black sitcoms had been common throughout the seventies and eighties, ever since Norman Lear's spinoff *The Jeffersons* (1975–85), but the emphasis had always been on race. Cosby, who had refused to "go the chit'lin' route" as a standup comic in the sixties, emphasized the humanity of his character and his family—not their race. As a result, *The Cosby Show* stands as a landmark in the history of American race politics.

As you might expect, much of the action in television during the eighties took place off-network and outside primetime. The programming innovations of the period emphasized the immediacy of the medium, as if in reaction to the wealth of fictional and feature film material offered by the ballooning cable and VCR media. As cable penetration grew from under 30 percent to more than 60 percent during the decade and as VCR ownership exploded from close to zero to more than 75 percent by the early nineties, television consumers were confronted with a cornucopia of filmed entertainment. With the local video store offering a library of five to ten thousand feature films, and two dozen special-interest cable networks providing a weekly feed of thousands of hours of everything from recent features to home shopping, it's a wonder that the traditional broadcast genres of the half-hour sitcom and the hour drama survived at all.

To confront the twin challenges of VCR and cable, broadcasters turned to a style that came to be known as "reality-based programming." If the phrase seems awkward, so does the genre: the relationship between "reality" and the programming is often quite strained. First-run syndication, in which the producers of the programs make deals directly with local stations (or cable systems), became the venue for reality-based programming. As reality shows boomed, so did the first-run syndication market.

The eighties saw a host of new competitors to Johnny Carson in the late-night time slot, some successful (David Letterman, Arsenio Hall), many not (Joan Rivers), and an even greater number of new entries in the tawdry daytime talkshow field that had been pioneered by Phil Donahue in the seventies. While the late-night shows focused on showcasing entertainers plugging new products, the daytime shows engaged in feverish competition for lifestyle sideshow freaks—usually with absurdly convoluted sexual proclivities.

It had all started innocently enough: in the seventies Phil Donahue had gained a good measure of respect for reasoned contributions to the debate on feminist and other political issues; but as the eighties wore on, the daytime talkshow circuit became a circus of logical extremes. In this perhaps it only mirrored the unraveling of intelligence in most areas of American public life. By the mid-1990s, the format had sunk to the level of sleazeball Jerry Springer and smut-nut Howard Stern.

Talkshows weren't the only genre in the reality-based category. In a development unforeseen by even the most aggressive of film educators in the seventies, entertainment itself became a popular subject. Gene Siskel and Roger Ebert, two respected print film critics, pioneered the genre on PBS in 1978. They were soon joined by half a dozen pairs of earnest men expressing opinions and exploiting film clips. *Entertainment Tonight* (1981–) and its imitators covered the business of entertainment in professional detail every evening for millions of buffs.

Rupert Murdoch, who had made his fortune publishing tabloid newspapers, brought this sensibility to television with *A Current Affair* (1986–), one of the first hits of his new Fox network. This traditional mix of gore and sensationalism was soon joined by a host of imitators. In this, the syndicated tabloid shows weren't much different from the average local news shows, which increasingly concentrated on the photogenic subjects of murder, arson, rape, and child abuse.

Even the traditional networks joined the reality-based programming tide as magazine shows became a staple of primetime following the lead of the venerable and profitable *60 Minutes*. By the late 1990s magazine shows were nightly features on most networks—exceeding even the movie programming that had carried the networks through the 1970s. Why? The reality trend was part of the reason; so were the perennial high ratings of *60 Minutes*; but the format became pervasive so quickly because these shows leveraged the existing news departments at the net-

Figure 6-41. Carson in 1968, 1977, and the night of his retirement in May 1992. (*JM*)

works, they were cheap to produce, and—most important—the networks didn't have to pay production fees to others. At a time when, for example, NBC found itself having to write a check to Warner for $850 million to keep its anchor show *ER* (as it did in 1998) and contracts with the sports leagues were denominated in billions, homegrown news productions like the magazine shows were economically irresistible.

One would like to suppose that the popularity of magazine shows represented a hunger for reality, but the "reality" that drove American television in the nineties was more absurd than any fiction. The decade began with Peter Arnett, CNN's star correspondent, on location in Baghdad dumbly describing the bombing that the night-vision cameras were capturing in shades of chartreuse and teal as the Gulf War ejaculated prematurely. Most of the middle of the decade, it seems in retrospect, was taken up with the O. J. Simpson trial, a travesty of justice and media. Then we concluded with a fat cigar and a bang and the year of Monica (1998), which included the actual broadcast of the president's grand jury testimony—a legal travesty that dwarfed O. J. (even though it was tape-delayed). The presidential imbroglio was bookended nicely by the media circuses that fed on the deaths of secondary royalty: Diana (1997) and JFK Jr (1999).[*]

The reality movement found more salutary manifestations in Public Broadcasting. Throughout its early growth in the seventies, PBS had depended heavily on British drama imports. As budgets tightened in the eighties, PBS producers turned

---

[*] Fictional network television in the 1990s was so inconsequential that it is relegated to a footnote. *Seinfeld*, *ER*, and *The Simpsons* dominated. *Law and Order* kept the faith. David E. Kelley's name will be found in the history books but the shows he produced were pale copies of 1980s series. And shows about teenagers, for preteens, and mostly exploiting gross-out humor (*Beavis and Butthead*) constituted the only new additions to the tired repertoire. Grownups in the 1990s were watching the Food Channel, or the Internet.

Figure 6-42. A dramatic shot from Henry Hampton's landmark *Eyes on the Prize*—just one example of the remarkable historical footage the series unearthed.

to homegrown and less-expensive genres. The how-to program became a welcome staple of public television as *The French Chef* pioneer Julia Child was joined by kindred spirits who remodeled old houses, fixed old cars, gardened, and, yes, cooked. After the success of Carl Sagan's *Cosmos* series in 1980, science and nature programs like *Nova* and *Nature* (usually international coproductions) became perennial anchors of the PBS schedule. By the mid-1990s each of these how-to genres had its own cable network.

The documentary, all but banished from the commercial networks, found a welcome home on public television schedules. *Frontline* (1982–) showed that "reality-based" programming could be intelligent, relevant—even wise. Henry Hampton's moving and incisive *Eyes on the Prize* (1987, 1990), a definitive history of the civil rights movement in America, proved the real value of television as a historical medium. Ken Burns's *The Civil War* (1990) attracted record PBS audiences, more than half a million of whom also purchased the videocassette version advertised on the air. For the first time, television was confirmed as a reference medium.

In 1986 Bill Moyers finally abandoned his flirtation with commercial network CBS to settle down as public television's premiere essayist, moving from straight news to politics, from documentary to philosophy, with series like *Joseph Campbell and The Power of Myth* (1988) and *A World of Ideas* (1988–). It's a sad commentary on the history of American television that Moyers may be the only working journalist who can lay claim to the wise heritage of Edward R. Murrow. Let's hope the essay form he has refined over the years proves a model for generations of writer-producers to come.

Just as broadcast television helped to unify the disparate regions of the U.S. in the sixties and seventies, so now satellite broadcasting together with privatized and expanded national television systems are homogenizing Europe and much of the rest of the world. And that homogenized television culture has a distinctly American flavor. In the 1980s popular shows like *Dallas* and *Dynasty* had nearly as many European devotees as American fans. When the Thatcher broadcasting deregulation bill passed the House of Commons in 1989, it called lamely for a 25 percent minimum of British-produced programming.

Until the wave of privatization in the 1980s, European channels were, in the main, reserved as public facilities and operated by state agencies. In Italy, RAI was influential in the 1970s as coproducer of a number of interesting theatrical/television film ventures. Directors like Ermanno Olmi and Roberto Rossellini were sustained by this system. Likewise, the German state networks were instrumental in financing the renaissance in film in that country in the 1970s. (In France, television had both less influence on film and fewer successes on its own.) In most countries of the world, the television and feature film industries are now one and the same.

In France, the great success of the 1980s belonged to Canal Plus (founded in 1984), the pay service that Europeanized the American cable formula of movies and sports, and has built on this strategy to become a leading television force in several countries. In Germany, the largest television market in Europe, private and public channels compete with satellite. In Italy, the first of the European countries to deregulate (in 1975), RAI, the state agency, operates several channels, as does Silvio Berlusconi's powerful Fininvest group. Pay channels were introduced in 1991.

In the U.K., where inventor John Logie Baird had demonstrated the first working television system in the late 1920s, the television industry had always followed a path independent of both the U.S. commercial and continental state-run systems. While publicly funded, the British Broadcasting Corporation was always operated independent of government control. Commercial television was introduced into Britain in 1955, joining the BBC's two channels, which had been in operation since 1936. In 1982 Channel 4, a second independent channel, was introduced with a mandate to serve minorities—esthetic as well as political. During the eighties, Channel 4 proved a boon to British filmmakers: sources of program funding had just increased 33 percent. In 1996 Channel 5, another independent, was added to the mix.

In 1991 the Thatcher government auctioned off the fifteen regional licenses to operate Channel 3, and several changed hands. Meanwhile, the unusual mix of commercial and public television in the U.K. has led to the most creative television industry outside the U.S.—and the only other one with any real international presence.

While cultural critics in France, England, and elsewhere warn against American "cultural imperialism," television executives around the world still find it most profitable to "buy American," and the film/television industry remains one of America's very few export earners.

Both radio and television were closely connected with the military during their infancies. The U.S. Department of Defense now operates numerous television stations and radio transmitters worldwide. Far more powerful is the global syndication network pioneered by NBC, CBS, and ABC and taken over by the Hollywood conglomerates after a 1971 FCC decision ruled that the networks could no longer distribute programs they themselves had not produced. (The "Fin-Syn" ruling was reversed in 1993.)

At its international peak in the late 1970s, *Bonanza* could be seen each week by more than 400 million viewers in 90 countries. The 14-year run of *Bonanza* included 359 episodes. Before its syndication run ended, viewers may have spent more than 143 trillion person-hours exposed to the values of the Cartwright family. In the next decade *Dallas* was almost as widespread, as was *Baywatch* in the 1990s.

These are the numbers for a single program. Hundreds are in distribution. UNESCO once estimated that 100,000 to 200,000 hours of American programming are available for export each year. Warner Brothers has controlled 52 foreign subsidiaries operating in 117 countries, and MCA had 24 subsidiaries dealing with 115 nations. Moreover, many of those national television systems were built outright by the manufacturing arms of the American networks, or else bought their equipment from them. As early as 1972, when satellite distribution was in its infancy, ABC's satellite coverage of the Olympic games was available to 2 billion people in 100 countries. The net result is cultural influence on an unprecedented scale.

As the world economy has developed, entertainment has remained an industry that America dominates. In the sixties and seventies, cultural critics in the U.S. as well as abroad attributed this influence to some nefarious imperialistic impulse. The truth is simpler.

American film and television have been formed by the marketplace ever since their beginnings. Where "art" is often a concern for European film and television producers and directors, it has seldom been allowed to interfere with the process in the U.S. As a result, Hollywood turns out more marketable product, still, than other countries do. Moreover, American actors look like everyone else. If you are Swedish or Italian, Nigerian or Thai, you are more likely to find folks who look like you in an American television show than in, say, a French production. Perhaps most important, the U.S. film industry has been international for many years, drawing on talent where it finds it.

This explanation doesn't make it any less infuriating to you if you are an Australian producer trying to get a show on. As Erik Barnouw pointed out in *Tube of Plenty*, American syndicators effectively undercut native production, offering product at far lower rates than native producers can. The downside to this increasingly homogenized world culture is that we lose the vitality that comes with local color; the upside is that people who laugh at the same jokes may be less likely to shoot each other.

One advantage the Americans have in the world film and television market is the English language. This they share with other countries. During the past twenty years American public television has developed close ties with both public and independent U.K. television. Beginning in the late sixties BBC and ITV prestige series began to have a noticeable effect on world markets, eventually even influencing the developing shape of American television.

Partly this was the result of British traditions of independence, which left the BBC relatively free of the government censorship to which most other state-owned systems had to submit. At the same time, because it was financed through a user license fee (rather than by advertising or tax allotments), British public television was free from the constraints which that system of financing brought to American television, as well as relatively isolated from political censorship. Moreover, while in the U.S. filmmakers thought of television as a training ground, in Britain in the late sixties it also became a refuge for theatrical film directors who could no longer obtain financing for features.

The British series depends less on a single top star and more on ensemble playing: there is a sense of community in most of the best series that is rare in American television. British series are often planned for limited runs, an approach that gave rise to the American miniseries of the late seventies. Finally, the British quickly discovered the similarities between the closed-end television series and the nineteenth-century novel saga, and recycled a number of novels in the new medium.

The twenty-six episodes of the BBC's version of John Galsworthy's *Forsyte Saga* made in 1967 were a major international success and opened world markets to British television. *War and Peace* (1972, twenty episodes and easily the best adaptation of that classic in any medium), Sartre's *Roads to Freedom* (1970, thirteen episodes), and Zola's *Nana* (1968, five episodes) all stood out, but there were many others of considerable impact as well. Kenneth Clark's *Civilization* (1969) and Jacob Bronowski's *The Ascent of Man* (1973) invented the television lecture series, a form which has proven rewarding ever since.

The British dramas of the period were all adaptations of proven material. The BBC left it to the producers of British commercial television (mainly Granada and

Figure 6-43. *Monty Python's Flying Circus* (BBC, 1969–74). Here, the dirty fork sketch. Drawing on the traditions of British Music Hall as modified by the *Goon Show* of the 1950s, the Pythons created an ethereally abstract, yet often sharply pointed satirical style that gained wide audiences.

London Weekend) to come up with original series. *Upstairs/Downstairs* (1971–75, sixty-eight episodes), which chronicled the lives of a well-to-do family and its servants from 1900 to 1930, was a major international success. *A Family at War* (1970–71, fifty-two episodes), the less glamorous saga of a family in Liverpool during World War II poised between middle and working classes, was less popular but more interesting dramatically. Frederic Raphael's *The Glittering Prizes* (1975, six episodes) followed the lives of a group of Cambridge students from the 1950s through the 1970s. All of these series had an international impact.[*]

The most significant British export of that period, however, remains *Monty Python's Flying Circus*. British dramatic series may just be more effective and eloquent versions of a mode of entertainment that is common in the U.S., but British comedy is a radical departure from the American style. *Monty Python,* a half-hour string of skits, animation, wordplay, satire, and silliness, recognized once and for all that the elementary particle of television is the incident, not the show; that comedy can be at least as eloquent, dense, and rewarding as drama; and that "*nobody* expects the Spanish Inquisition."

"TV": The Virtual Family

Because it is a continuing rather than a discrete experience, television has an extraordinary ability to mediate between the viewer and reality. Films may last two or three hours, during which time we live in their world. Television is ongoing, never-ending, whether in the context of a single day's programming or in

---

[*]   Although less innovative in the 1980s and 1990s, the British networks continued to produce exportable drama and comedy.

regard to the series and the serials that are its native forms. Moreover, television happens in our space, in our time. It becomes part of our reality. For an average American family, watching television nearly seven hours a day (according to annual Nielsen surveys), television is the background to everyday life—a background that often overwhelms the foreground. As a consequence, it mediates not only between the viewer and reality but also between reality and fiction. We're all confused.

Because it is both an entertainment and an information medium, sometimes we find it hard to distinguish between the essentially fictional nature of the first and the essentially nonfictional nature of the second. "Reality-based" programming, as we have seen, is often a contradiction in terms. Much has been written about the socializing influence of television—the effect repetitive violence has on children, the tendency of the television world to become the real reality for people addicted to it, and so on.

The sum effect of this powerful medium is that, as Raymond Williams said in *Television: Technology and Cultural Form*, it has made drama a part of life:

> It is clearly one of the unique characteristics of advanced industrial societies that drama as an experience is now an intrinsic part of everyday life, *at a quantitative level which is so very much greater than any precedent as to seem a fundamental qualitative change* [emphasis added].

Drama, which even as late as the heyday of the movies was a separate experience, is now seamlessly integrated into our lives—and dominates many of them. A shooting takes place on the street and people automatically turn to look for the cameras. Often there aren't any. The Vietnam War (1963–75) was filmed, edited, and broadcast the next day; the Gulf War (January, 1991) was offered live as it happened to screens around the world. Real stories are retold as docudramas and "news" is re-enacted because the cameras often miss the first take. But most important, as Williams noted, is the sheer volume of dramatic media to which we are exposed, day in, day out, year after year.

The pervasive influence of television is a question of singular significance. For many years, critiques of television have centered on the issue of subject matter—specifically violence—as it affects viewers. The problem seems especially acute with regard to younger children. There is much evidence to prove that the medium does in fact raise the violence quotient of everyday life. (How could it not when it makes shootings, stabbings, and other acts of violence "as American as cherry pie," as sixties activist H. Rap Brown said thirty-five years ago—and far more common?)

Yet there is also a convincing body of evidence to show that television works as a safety valve, defusing potentially violent personalities. In the late seventies, lawyers for a boy accused of murder in Florida blamed his action in part on his exposure to television violence, and several girls accused of rape in California cited a

Figure 6-44. THE METAMORPHOSIS OF THE TWENTIETH-CENTURY FAMILY. The ideal of the American family in the twenties: Dad and Mom, Junior and Sis in happy reunion around the dinner table, talking with each other and making eye contact. (The poses are cheated for the photo.) Note the four large glasses of milk. Later, in the forties, the nucleus of the nuclear family included the radio. They may be listening to the broadcast and talking less, but they are still making eye contact. By the sixties, the dream was moribund. The nuclear family had become an audience. They can't see each other or hear each other. By the eighties, everyone had their own TV and didn't have to sit together. (*Courtesy Archive Photos/Lambert.*)

Figure 6-45. FIFTIES. What better subject of conversation for the permanent electronic guest in the living room than families? To a significant extent, television families have replaced our own. The strategy thrives, since "drawing room" drama, dependent on dialogue rather than imagery, intimate and psychological, fits the small screen very well. American television families tend to be simple, "nuclear": a mother, father, and a couple of children. The Nelson family, which literally grew up on television, remains the prototype. Ozzie, an ex-bandleader, and his wife Harriet, a singer, starred with their two sons, David and Ricky. David later enjoyed a career in the business; Ricky became a rock star, dying dramatically in a plane crash. Over the next forty years, the Nelson family was often mimicked, never rivaled, for its good-natured gemütlichkeit.

made-for-television movie as their model. These defenses were not successful, but the issue was sharply drawn.

In the 1970s a new line of argument developed. In her 1977 book *The Plug-in Drug,* Marie Winn shifted the focus of censure from the subject matter to the experience of the medium. The problem with television, Winn contended, is not *what* it shows but *how* it shows it. She made a convincing argument that the medium inculcates passivity in children, and suggested that exposure to television might very well affect even the neurological development of small children. Winn discussed the effect of television on language abilities and investigated its relationship to changed states of consciousness, but the crux of her argument—and it remains a powerful one—lay in her critique of the destruction of family life by the presence of television.

For Winn, the box had become a surrogate parent, taking over most of the work of presenting and developing social and ethical values and in the process achieving a much greater degree of authority than the child's biological parents. The title of her book was not meant to be metaphorical. Parents, she says, first use television precisely like a drug, to keep children quiet. Eventually the child becomes addicted and the box becomes a necessary, lifelong habit.

VIRTUAL FAMILIES

Figure 6-46. FIFTIES. The Nelsons' closest competitor in the fifties was the
Anderson family of *Father Knows Best.*
Robert Young (later an equally model
doctor) and Jane Wyatt starred. Elinor
Donohue, Billy Gray, and Lauren Chapin
were the kids. Spending time with the
Nelsons and the Andersons in the fifties,
we had less need of our own families.

Obviously, many children do survive the television experience, but many also are affected deeply by it, and we still don't know to what degree or how, nor do we know what this will mean socially and politically. Much of the discussion of television as a social phenomenon centers on this profound question.

A year after Winn's book appeared, its thesis was made to look positively conservative by ex-adman Jerry Mander's own wide-ranging diatribe against his former meal-ticket. The title of that work was, simply, *Four Arguments for the Elimination of Television.* Mander was serious. He found a ready audience. Fifteen years later, his book was in its twenty-seventh printing. And nothing had changed.[*]

Mander's "Four Arguments"—"The Mediation of Experience," "The Colonization of Experience," "Effects of Television on the Human Being," and "The Inherent Biases of Television"—are convenient classifications for dozens of telling criticisms of the powerful medium that has defined the second half of the twentieth century. Roughly paraphrased, they include: television separates us from reality; television deprives us of choice in experience; artificial light is no good for you; and television is such a weak medium that it distorts reality. Mander presents a

---

[*] Not quite true. By 1992 the average American had thirty or more channels at his command instead of three, the prospect of hundreds more around the corner, and a VCR in case the cable broke down. The average European had a dozen channels to choose from instead of two, and satellites bombarding him with still more signals, and a VCR.

Figure 6-47. THE NOVEL SAGA. The twenty-six-episode British series *The Forsyte Saga* (BBC, 1967), based on the six-book cycle by Victorian novelist John Galsworthy, was an enormous success worldwide. Pictured here sitting for an 1880s-style family portrait are the fifteen major characters. Irene (Nyree Dawn Porter), the heroine, is seated, center. To her left, in the foreground is Soames (Eric Porter), at first the villain of the piece, later its major character. Jo (Kenneth More) is second from the left in the back row, the sensible narrator.

Figure 6-48. SEVENTIES. By the seventies, the ideal was seriously tarnished after ten years of generational conflict. The Bunkers of Queens, New York, and *All in the Family* (Norman Lear and Bud Yorkin, 1971) introduced real family issues and dealt with them with some understanding. Here, Gloria (Sally Struthers), Edith (Jean Stapleton), Archie (Carroll O'Connor), Mike (Rob Reiner), with Betty Garrett.

Figure 6-49. SEVENTIES. In 1973 Craig Gilbert's PBS series *An American Family* portrayed the Louds of Santa Barbara in provocative cinema-vérité style. Living with the family for a year, the filmmakers collected enough drama for a soap opera, including the breakup of the marriage and oldest son Lance's participation in the New York homosexual scene, a taboo television subject at the time. The Louds became national celebrities protesting that the filmmakers focused on the negatives of their family life, ignoring the positives.

VIRTUAL FAMILIES

Figure 6-50. SEVENTIES. The family as self-parody: the Hartman/Shumway clan of M*ary Hartman, Mary Hartman* (Norman Lear, 1976). Part soap opera, part satire, part neurotic psychodrama, *MH, MH* marked a satiric point of no return for the American television family.

Figure 6-51. EIGHTIES. Challenging the mythos of the seventies, the Huxtable clan (pictured here in one of its variations), brought new life to the ideal in the eighties, blurring racial lines in the process. Left to right behind Bill Cosby: Sabrina LeBeauf, Keshia Knight-Pulliam, Lisa Bonet, Malcolm Jamal-Warner, Phylicia Rashad, and Tempestt Bledsoe.

Figure 6-52. NINETIES. *Cosby Show* producers Marcy Carsey and Tom Werner scored again with the realistic working-class family of *Roseanne* (1988–1997). Roseanne and Dan (John Goodman) did a pretty good job raising D. J., Darlene, and Becky.

VIRTUAL FAMILIES

Figure 6-53. NINETIES. As *The Cosby Show* dominated the eighties, so the dysfunctional Simpsons ruled the nineties. The family pendulum has swung back to the "dumb Dad" position. Kids enjoy the postmodern references and thick parody. At least Marge and Homer are still together.

powerful indictment of the ultimate mass medium of the twentieth century. But of all the points he makes, one stands out: most of us now let television lead our lives for us; this seductive and pervasive product has deprived us of intimate contact with reality.

In 1985 social critic Neil Postman joined the battle with *Amusing Ourselves to Death: Public Discourse in the Age of Show Business*, a parallel critique, which focused on the effect of television and our entertainment universe on politics. Postman insightfully differentiated between the two seminal jeremiads of the mid-twentieth century, George Orwell's *1984* and Aldous Huxley's *Brave New World*:

> What Orwell feared were those who would ban books. What Huxley feared was that there would be no reason to ban a book, for there would be no one who wanted to read one. Orwell feared those who would deprive us of information. Huxley feared those who would give us so much that we would be reduced to passivity and egoism. Orwell feared that the truth would be concealed from us. Huxley feared the truth would be drowned in a sea of irrelevance. Orwell feared we would become a captive culture. Huxley feared we would become a trivialized culture.... In *1984*, people are controlled by inflicting pain. In *Brave New World*, they are controlled by inflicting pleasure. In short, Orwell feared that what we hate will ruin us. Huxley feared that what we love will ruin us
>
> [pp. viii–ix].

Postman was writing in 1985. Orwell's dread milestone had come and gone and his prophecy was losing currency. Indeed, Orwell's dark vision of that totalitarian threat was most strikingly commemorated at the beginning of 1984 in

VIRTUAL UNFAMILIES

Figure 6-54. NINETIES. What the Simpsons did for the dysfunctional family, *Seinfeld* (1991–98) did for the dysfunctional non-family, reveling in eternal adolescence, the Boomers' sad gift to Gen X. The singles foursome ran through more lovers in seven years than Homer did doughnuts. (When marriage threatened George, the only way out was to kill off the would-be bride.) Formally, the show succeeded because of its elegant attention to classic comedic styles: Michael Richards's slapstick, Jerry Seinfeld's and Jason Alexander's odd couple, and Julia Louis-Dreyfus's straight-man takes.

Apple Computer's famous Super Bowl commercial introducing the Macintosh. In Apple's Orwellian marketing metaphor, IBM was the totalitarian power and the Macintosh was offered as salvation: "the computer for the rest of us." Talk about trivialization! Even Orwell's own eloquent fear had been neutralized by a Huxleyan device!

From the perspective of the late 1990s, the ascendancy of Huxley is even more apparent. The Soviet Union, a primary object of Orwell's fear, has ceased to exist. The Cold War is over. Even IBM has been transcended by Microsoft.

Meanwhile, the quantity of images and sounds that bombard us has increased exponentially; their producers have ever more powerful tools at their command; the video culture is increasingly homogenized; and the images and sounds themselves continue to move inexorably away from reality and toward fantasy. Someone else's fantasy. The problem, clearly, is not that Big Brother is watching us, but that we are watching Big Brother.

As Mander puts it:

> It causes images in our brain.
> We call this experience, but we can't tell if it is *our* experience
>   or something else.
> It is in our heads, but we didn't create it.
> We don't know if it is real or if it isn't.
> We can't stop the broadcasts.
> We accept whatever comes.
> One vision is equal to the next.
> One thought is as good as the next.
> All information merges.

All experience merges.

We take everything on faith.

One explanation is the same as the next one.

Contradictions do not exist.

We have lost control of our minds.

We are all lost in space.

Our world exists only in memory.

Everything is arbitrary.

[pp 111–112, form added.]

This is a poignant reaction. Indeed, the critiques of all three—Winn, Mander, and Postman—evince a touching personal tone. For it is in our personal lives, in our families, that the power of television has its most immediate effect, well before it begins to distort our politics. Potentially a nourishing and stimulating companion for those who must live alone, or a calming, perhaps restorative, drug for the ill (is there a hospital bed without a television?), the box is often an uncontrollable ogre in any family this side of total dysfunction. It sucks the conversation out of the family like some alien. It destroys time. It replaces parents (or children), husbands (or wives). For too many of us, it does our living for us.

The single most irresistible fact about the television families with whom we spend most of our time is that they don't watch television. If they did, they'd be as boring as we are; we'd turn them off as quickly as we do ourselves.

The most seductive elements of *The Cosby Show*, for example, were the strong relationships between parents and children, and between Cliff and Claire Huxtable, intelligent people with a strong marriage. Roseanne and Dan Connor talked more with each other (and with their children) in the 22 minutes of action in each week's show than most of their fans did in the 10,050 minutes between shows. Mary Tyler Moore did not come home, like most single women, to an empty apartment and an evening of television, but to a kaffeeklatsch of voluble and witty neighbors. Her remade sister, Murphy Brown, had a live-in house-painter, not a television. The twentysomethings of *Friends* hung out at the coffee house, not in front of the tube. Did Harriet ever serve Ozzie, Dave, and Ricky a TV dinner? Would anyone have watched *I Love Lucy* if Lucy and Ethel had spent their afternoons watching soap operas?

Perhaps it needs to be said that none of this is an indictment of the medium itself. The fault lies not in television, but in ourselves, that we abuse it.

In the short history of film and television, the 1970s and 1980s were a period of stasis during which we absorbed the technology and in certain cases refined it. Producers and distributors developed the infrastructure necessary to maximize sales, while most of us consumers willingly went along, rearranging our lives to consume as much as possible.

When the VCR was introduced, its inventors thought it would be used for time-shifting, not realizing that only children would care enough to learn to program the damn things. Instead, it has meant just more to watch. Yet the ideal of time-shifting remains, only it is not so much time that we want to shift, but effort. Much of the social responsibility of watching television can be left to the machines, leaving us time for more active endeavors. When the show has been safely captured on tape it becomes, in a sense, not necessary to watch it. When it's recorded we have control over it.

For more than half a century, first film, then television inculcated that suffocating passivity that so concerned Aldous Huxley and others. But the balance is now shifting. Not because we heeded the warnings of the social critics and took action, but rather because the image and sound technologies that are now maturing bring the powers of production to us.

In 1977 the first edition of *How To Read a Film* concluded with a "Note on Media Democracy" that sketched a future of interactive television, private computers in every home, massive information networks, databanks of programming available on demand, and the like. The future took a little longer than I thought. It always does. But it has finally begun to arrive, and that advent is the subject of Chapter 7.

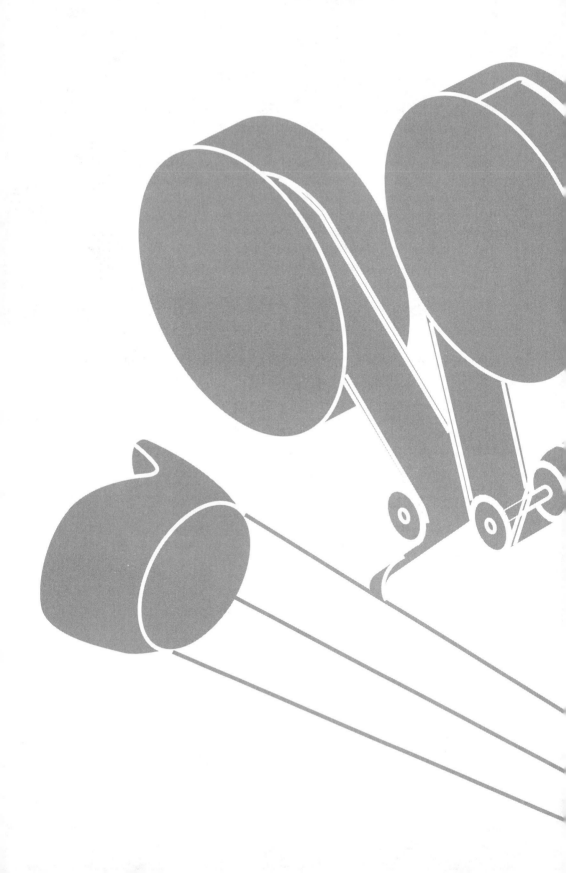

7

MULTIMEDIA: THE DIGITAL REVOLUTION

The Digital Revolution

In the beginning, there was the sign. The sign was spoken and sung. Then it was written, first as picture, then as word. Eventually the sign was printed. The ingenious coding system that was writing allowed ideas and feelings, descriptions and observations to be captured and preserved. The technology of printing liberated these written records from isolated libraries, allowing them to be communicated to thousands, then millions. They are the glue that binds our culture together.

As the scientific revolution took hold in the nineteenth century, we discovered methods to capture images and sounds technologically. Photography, then records and film, reproduced reality without the intervention of words. At least we thought they did. We accepted their representations as if they were real. In fact, they were simply a different set of codes. While far more verisimilitudinous than words, the images and sounds of cinema are still code systems—distillations of reality, sometimes distortions of it, always imaginations of it. That's why it is necessary to learn how to read a film.

Movies and their offspring have defined the twentieth century for us.

But now we find ourselves on the verge of a new phase in the history of media. The languages which we invented to represent reality are merging. Film is no longer separate from print. Books can include movies; movies, books. We call this synthesis "multimedia," or "new media." The technology offers tantalizing promise: instant and universal access to the world's knowledge and art, captured or produced with a versatile set of media tools. But it also brings with it some knotty challenges, both technical and ethical.

The Information Age is quite real. The microcomputer revolution of the 1980s has increased our access to and control over information a hundredfold. As that revolution matures over the next generation, information power will increase by another four or five magnitudes. Within our lifetimes, most of the world's knowledge will be available to many of the world's people instantaneously and at negligible cost. There is no turning back, nor is there any longer any doubt. We now know that we can index everything ever printed and that we can build networks to access this print universe in seconds rather than years. (Similar access to audio and video remains beyond current our capabilities, and we haven't yet thought seriously how to index images and sounds, but this will come, too.)

There is a memorable scene in Godard's *Les Carabiniers* (1963) in which the two soldiers return to their wives after the war with their booty. They have postcards of all the world's wonders which they proudly display, one at a time: the Eiffel Tower, the Great Pyramid, the Empire State Building, the Grand Canyon.... They think these images are deeds to the properties. We laugh at their naïveté as the pile of postcards mounts. The scene is an emblem of the information revolution: we now have the deeds to all the world's intellectual riches. But what will we do with this unimaginable wealth? Perhaps we are just as naïve as Godard's carabiniers: we have been given the keys to the virtual kingdom, but what about the reality that was once its subject?

As we noted in Chapter 1, the virtual world increasingly crowds out the natural world, and the very power that we now have to manipulate these once precious images and sounds devalues them, destroying our faith in their honesty and our appreciation of their art.

When the first edition of this book appeared in 1977, it may have seemed strange that an introduction to film included so much about print and electronic media. At the time, movies and print seemed to have little in common: they were both communication systems, true, but the similarity ended there. Now, as the technologies and distribution systems used to reproduce and disseminate the two converge, we can see how they fit together.

This has happened almost by accident. No one set out in 1960 to find a technological common denominator between books and movies. No Godard fan, noticing his fascination with the clash of words and images, decided to find the link between the two. Nor did a Truffaut aficionado, after having seen *Fahrenheit 451* or having read Truffaut's *Hitchcock*, dedicate years to discovering the technical common bond between the two media which that filmmaker/writer loved equally. The development of semiotics in the sixties and seventies was fortuitous, since it provided a single critical approach to both written language and filmed language, but semiotics was a way of thinking, not a science; there were no semiotics labs funded by governments to discover the basic building blocks of signification.

Rather, as you might expect, the technologies developed more or less independently and for mundane economic reasons. It was only after a decade of furious activity that it became clear that both types of expression, print and film, were going to share a common technology and that—therefore—it would be possible to do both at the same time in the same place. The common technology they now share is digitization.*

In the 1950s, computers were regarded simply as number-crunchers. (In 1952 IBM actually estimated that 18 computers would saturate the entire world market.) The machines of that day were programmed by feeding in decks of punched cards—a medium that dated from the 1890s; they required carefully engineered environments ("computer rooms"); and they were operated by specially trained engineers, who—like priests of old—were exclusively ordained to enter the sanctum sanctorum and approach the electronic oracle.

In the 1960s, it became clear that the CRT screen could provide a more efficient link between the machines and the people who operated them than the punched cards or the paper and magnetic tapes that had become common by that time. Indeed, the engineer at IBM who first thought to connect a television cathode ray tube to a computer may be considered the godfather of multimedia, for once that visual device became the basic input/output channel, the development of a visual metaphor for the logical control process became irresistible. This marriage of technologies was not preordained, and if punched cards and band printers had remained the input/output devices for digital computers, multimedia—to say nothing of the microcomputer appliance itself—might have remained a dream.

In the 1970s, when the development of word processors as basic business tools suggested that computers could be operated by ordinary laypeople, interest increased in a visual control metaphor—or "graphical user interface," as the jargon later tagged it. At the same time, filmmakers and audio technicians became intrigued with the exciting possibilities of applying this new tool to the manipulation of images and sounds. Filmmakers like James and John Whitney used mainframes to produce abstract images for their films as early as 1961. Musicians and audio artists became infatuated with the new Moog synthesizer in the late 1960s. The first digital audiotape recorder was offered for sale by the Lexicon company in 1971. By the late 1970s CBS had developed a machine for digital editing of videotape. The price? $1 million. (It is not known if any were sold. Today you can do a better job with a system that costs less than $3,000.) The elements of multimedia were evolving.

---

* When you consider that digital technology is founded on quantization and binary number theory, which reduces numbers to their basic elements—1s and 0s—the comparison with contemporary physics's quest for quarks is not inappropriate.

Figure 7-1A. John and James Whitney pioneered computer-driven imagery in the 1960s. Here, frames from John Whitney's "Catalog" (1961). (*John Whitney © 1984. Used with permission. Frame enlargements.*)

Figure 7-1B. Jordan Belson's films don't use computer techniques but they do combine optical and mechanical effects with natural phenomena and many other experimental techniques to produce a rhythmic, abstract esthetic. These frames are from Belson's "Samadhi" (1967). (*Jordan Belson © 1989. Used with permission. Frame enlargements.*)

In December 1968 Douglas Engelbart, an employee of the Stanford Research Institute, demonstrated an effective graphical user interface, fulfilling a dream first outlined by physicist Vannevar Bush in his seminal 1946 essay "As We May Think." In the early 1970s researchers at Xerox's Palo Alto Research Center and elsewhere combined the graphics on the now ubiquitous CRT with a separate physical pointing device that they called a mouse. What may have appeared to Engelbart to be the end of a line of technological development now revealed itself as instead the beginning of a fertile and fascinating field of inquiry: the invention of a coherent visual and physical metaphor for the complex and subtle interaction between humans and their first true intellectual tools. Interface design rapidly became a subject of intense interest. It isn't often that a new basic and universal language system is invented.[*] The twentieth century has seen two: first film, now the graphical interface. As new systems of communication, it was only a matter of time before the languages of film and computers merged to give birth to multimedia.

Apple's Macintosh computer, introduced with great fanfare in January 1984, marked the long-anticipated birth of multimedia. As the first microcomputer to

---

[*] Just in time, too, to revive the science of semiotics. By the time the Macintosh was born, the best film semioticians were either dead or writing popular novels. In the early 1980s, as Apple was beginning work on the Mac, the locus of semiotic creativity had shifted from Paris to Cupertino.

commercialize successfully the graphical interface developed at Xerox PARC years earlier, the machine and its software provided a platform sophisticated enough to support the development of new media during the next ten years.*

The company had been founded in 1977 by two young Californians, Steven Jobs and Stephen Wozniak. While Wozniak was regarded as the "techie," Jobs, the "business head," turned out to have the greater impact on the history of technology, for it was he who championed the Macintosh vision of the computer as an appliance, like a toaster, with an interface simple enough for anyone without technical training to operate.

Before the introduction of the Mac, Apple had manufactured machines, like the rest of the nascent microcomputer industry, which required a significant amount of technical expertise to operate. Their success until that time had been due to two factors: the feisty and romantic image they had projected, and the lucky accident that two other young men, Dan Bricklin and Bob Frankston, based in Cambridge, Massachusetts, had written a program called "VisiCalc," which ran only on the Apple II computer. VisiCalc was introduced to the market in 1979, shortly after the machine debuted. Thousands of young MBAs, heady with the financial dreams of the 1980s, rushed out to buy Apples to run this new "spreadsheet" program, a business planning tool.†

The first Macintoshes shipped in 1984 with a painting program as well as word-processing software. Immediately, users could draw on their screens as well as type. Perhaps just as important, the graphic power of the machine was applied to texts as well as images. Writers could actually choose their own fonts and type styles! This was a major advance over the crude representations of the dot-matrix character-based screens of that time. (See Figure 6-3.) The heretofore arcane concerns of publishers and printers—fonts, leading, point sizes, kerning—quickly became common knowledge for a new generation of assistants and middle managers. This social and esthetic sea-change had been foreshadowed in the 1970s when ubiquitous cheap photocopiers allowed almost anyone to be a publisher. Now the Macintosh let anyone design layouts and set type, too.

---

* Xerox itself had attempted to sell a machine with a graphical interface several years earlier, but the "Star" was ahead of its time and overpriced, as was Apple's own Lisa, which predated the Macintosh by a year.

† While Jobs and Wozniak are likely to be remembered in history books for quite a while, throughout the late 1980s and 1990s their competitor and nemesis, Bill Gates, founder of Microsoft, held center stage. Gates had written the first version of Basic for the new microcomputer of the mid-1970s, but his remarkable business success was built on products that were imitations. Seldom a pioneer, Microsoft built its dominating position in the microcomputer industry by applying superior business acumen to ideas and products developed by innovators like Apple, Digital Research Inc., Adobe, and Lotus.

Figure 7-2. The "1984" commercial introducing the Macintosh aired just once during the Super Bowl, January 24, 1984. Ridley Scott directed. (*Courtesy Apple Computer, Inc. Frame enlargements.*)

The "consumer" celebrated in the fifties and sixties was yielding to the "user" of the eighties and nineties. The consumer had been a passive and dutiful partner for the great industrial producers of the first half of the twentieth century; the user was to become an active, independent, and demanding client for the service providers of the next century. Little did we know, as we marched in the streets in the sixties chanting "Power to the People!," that the power would indeed be granted—but in the arts and communications, rather than in politics and economics.

This relationship between the counterculture of the sixties and the microcomputer culture of the eighties is curious but undeniable. Apple understood it early on, and profited by that understanding. The famous Super Bowl commercial that introduced the Macintosh as "the computer for the rest of us" in January 1984 traded heavily on the residue of countercultural yearnings.

Separately from the cultural mystique that it acquired, the microcomputer was also "revolutionary" in the purest sense of the term, since its historical progress is measured geometrically rather than arithmetically. "Moore's Law" suggests that chip density (and by extension computing power) per dollar doubles every 18 months. Gordon Moore, one of the founders of Intel, the dominant chip manufacturer, offered this rule of thumb early on. The history of the microcomputer over the past twenty years bears uncanny witness to its truth. The machine I bought in March 1994 ran 200 times faster than the machine I bought in April 1981, had 200 times the storage capacity, and cost about the same. Those figures are almost exactly what Moore's Law would have predicted. Adjust for inflation, and performance doubles yet again.

This isn't just computer jock talk. Numerically, the information revolution of the 1980s accomplished in fewer than ten years what took the transportation revolution 100 years to achieve before it ended in the 1960s. Put another way, if transportation power had developed at the same speed as information power in the 1980s, the five-hour flight from New York to Los Angeles would now take about a minute and a half. These numbers are so profound that we can only surmise what the cultural and social effects will be. Bob Dylan's phrase from the sixties comes to mind:

> ... something is happening here
> But you don't know what it is
> Do you, Mr. Jones?[*]

While the burgeoning microcomputer industry led the way in the office, the consumer electronics industry took advantage of the microchip revolution in the home.

At the end of the 1970s, people saw movies in theaters, listened to music on records, watched one of the four national television networks (actually getting up out of their chairs to change channels on occasion), used telephones with wires tethering them to the wall, and, if they were so inclined, corresponded with each other using pens, pencils, typewriters, paper, and the U.S. Postal Service.

By the early 1990s, these same folks saw movies mainly at home on videotape, listened to digital music on Compact Discs (more often walking in the street than sitting at home), had their choice of 40 or more cable channels from which to choose (and channel-surfed without leaving their chairs), made telephone calls in their cars or walking around, and, if they were so inclined, corresponded with each other via fax or electronic mail.

A few years later, they could also, if they so chose, buy a camcorder that would let them shoot videotape of near-professional quality. They could install a home theatre with a screen almost as large as the ones at the local sixplex (and with a sound system that was markedly better). They could watch videodiscs, skipping, browsing, freezing, and skimming as they might with a book; install their very own satellite dish; or buy a computer for the kids to play with that had the power of a 1980s IBM mainframe.

Increasingly they chose this last alternative, often for the sake of the children. By 1990, computer literacy was a prerequisite for admission to many colleges and universities. By 1994, nearly 40 percent of American homes had microcomputers and the stage was set for multimedia to weave together most of the technological strands we have just enumerated.

---

[*] "Ballad of a Thin Man," © 1965 by M. Witmark & Sons. Reprinted by permission.

"You say you want a revolution...." Digitization and computerization completed the profound shift in our cultural architecture that had begun in Edison's labs a century earlier. As the Information Age became a reality and knowledge joined labor and capital in the social equation, ideology couldn't keep up. It is more than coincidental that the rise of the microchip accompanied the end of the Cold War, a conjunction that Mikhail Gorbachev himself once pointed out.

Despite the exponential speed of the digital revolution in the eighties, it took more than twelve years after the introduction of the CD-ROM in 1985 before multimedia became a marketable product. The reason? Digitized images and sounds, not to mention movies, made extraordinary demands on processor speed, storage capacity, and communication bandwidth. The digital text for this book, fully formatted, amounts to about 2.5 megabytes. The black-and-white images and diagrams that appear in the book take up an additional 90 megabytes on the DVD-ROM version (although they appear on the disc at greatly reduced resolution; the book versions occupy 750 megabytes). The additional illustrations, color, animation, programming, texts, and movies fill up most of the remaining 4,300 megabytes. In other words, the fully formatted text of *How To Read a Film* occupies less than one-tenth of 1 percent of the disc space required for the multimedia version, while the images and sounds which merely illustrate it consume more than 1,000 times as much real estate.

Some other numbers to think about:

❏   The standard computer screen of the mid-nineties, when multimedia came of age, measured 640 by 480 pixels. If each pixel in a full-screen image was either black or white, 38,400 bytes would be necessary to describe that image.* However, if you have a standard VGA color screen, with a palette of 16 colors, multiply that number by 4; if you have a basic Internet machine with a palette of 256 colors, multiply it by 8; and if you want color approaching the quality of film or television, multiply it by 24. All of a sudden, a single screen occupies nearly a megabyte of storage. You see the disparity: you can store an entire book—or a single decent color image. A picture may be worth a thousand words, but should it cost 150,000? This is not a good deal.

---

*   In the world of microcomputers, a byte is a unit of measurement equal to 8 bits. A bit is a single value, either 1 or 0. The word "bit" is derived from "BInary digiT." If a bit is a letter, then a byte is a word. There is a lot of confusion about bits and bytes, megabits and megabytes, gigabits and gigabytes, most of it stemming from the application of the decimal prefixes (kilo, mega, giga) to a binary system. For example, a kilobit is not 1,000 bits but 1,024 bits (2^{10}). For more detail on this and other digital issues see my *Dictionary of New Media*.

A

B

C

D

Figure 7-3. REMOTES.

(A) Warner-Amex Cable's Qube III cable television "keypad." Introduced in 1977, Qube was the early harbinger of the interactive cable market of the next century. It would have allowed the cable television viewer to select a large variety of programming channels—some of which incurred per-hour charges—and also to "talk back" to the cablecasting network. The technology wasn't ready and the experiment failed. But the keypad remote control changed our experience of the medium in the eighties.

(B) By the nineties, the remote was ubiquitous, not only for television equipment but for audio and other devices, as well. These are the remotes the Monaco family—two adults, three teenagers—used in a small city apartment. The first three at the top (cable box, VCR, and TV) had to be employed as a troika to operate the living room equipment. The largest and smallest in the collection are the Laserdisc player and the Hi-8 camera, respectively. The space in the middle is reserved for the stereo remote: we seem to have lost it. (Not shown: the DVD-Video remote; it's boring.)

(C) We use these remotes in the country for three televisions, two stereos, and an old VCR. Note the wire on the VCR remote, vintage 1984. It is the only one of the complete set of fourteen that never gets lost.

(D) These are the remotes accumulated so far by the Plumlee family—two adults, one two-year-old. Note Anna's toy remote (lower right). By the time she is old enough to channel surf, she'll have the technique down cold.

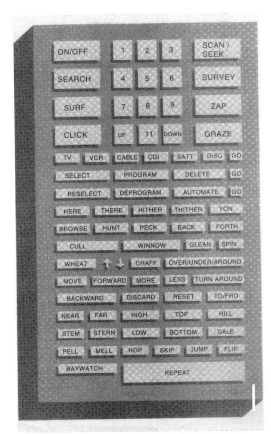

Simplified Remote Control

NEXT CHANNEL

WHAT WAS THAT? GO BACK.

F

E

Figure 7-3. MORE REMOTES.
(E) A "Remote Possibility," as envisioned by Jeff MacGregor for *The New York Times*, October 16, 1994. *(Copyright 1994 by the New York Times Company. Reprinted by permission.)*
(F) The remote reduced to its basic elements.

❏ Now, make that still color image move. Don't even think about 24 frames per second. Try 12—it will almost work. Now you need more than 11 megabytes for each second of jerky movie that you show. A CD-ROM, with its gargantuan storage capacity of 650 megabytes, could hold a minute of film (well, not quite). This is also not a good deal. The old analog world never looked so good. (Maybe this digital thing is a bad idea.)

❏ Finally, assuming that you can find some way to lick the storage problem, remember that you will have to transfer 11 megabytes per second from disc to CPU to screen in order to show your 12-frames-per-second "movie," while the standard transfer rate of CD-ROMs in the late 1980s was 150,000 bytes per second.[*]

You now have some idea of the technical challenges that confronted the digital video pioneers! The solutions they worked out for this seemingly insurmountable problem are ingenious and instructive. For the most part, they were not initially hardware-based. Building chips that could process this amount of information quickly enough and at a reasonable price would have solved only half the prob-

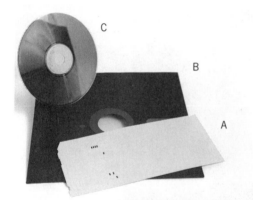

Figure 7-4. STORAGE TECHNOLOGY. (A) The punched card that made IBM successful (1929) held eighty characters on 24 square inches. (B) The 8-inch floppy disk (1971) held 128,000 characters on 50 square inches. (C) The DVD (1997) holds more than 4 billion characters on less than 20 square inches. (D) The singing ring from *The Time Machine* (802,701 AD) holds ... a little bit less, but requires no player, except Yvette Mimieux or Rod Taylor.

lem, since the storage demands were just as astronomical as the demands on the processors. Separate Digital Signal Processor chips (DSPs) are useful—even necessary—but the first stage of multimedia was made possible by software that uses purely mathematical techniques that are as beautiful as they are effective.[*]

---

[*] The calculations: 640 x 480 pixels x 1 bit per pixel = 307,200 bits. 307,200 bits / 8 bits per byte = 38,400 bytes. Four bits of color information yields 16 possible colors (2 to the fourth power). Twenty-four bits of color information yields more than 16 million colors (2 to the 24th power). This is the current standard for realistic digital color. 38,400 x 24 = 921,600 bytes. 921,600 bytes per screen x 12 frames per second = 11,059,200 bytes per second.

[*] By 1996, a decade after CD-ROM had been introduced, manufacturers could produce 24X players at a reasonable cost. (Their transfer rate was twenty-four times the original 150,000 bytes per second.) These machines could handle the raw transfer rates necessary for video as described above, but by this time the compression routines were well established, and necessary for the still greater ambitions of DVD.

Decimal	Binary	Hexadecimal
0	0 0 0 0	0
1	0 0 0 1	1
2	0 0 1 0	2
3	0 0 1 1	3
4	0 1 0 0	4
5	0 1 0 1	5
6	0 1 1 0	6
7	0 1 1 1	7
8	1 0 0 0	8
9	1 0 0 1	9
10	1 0 1 0	A
11	1 0 1 1	B
12	1 1 0 0	C
13	1 1 0 1	D
14	1 1 1 0	E
15	1 1 1 1	F

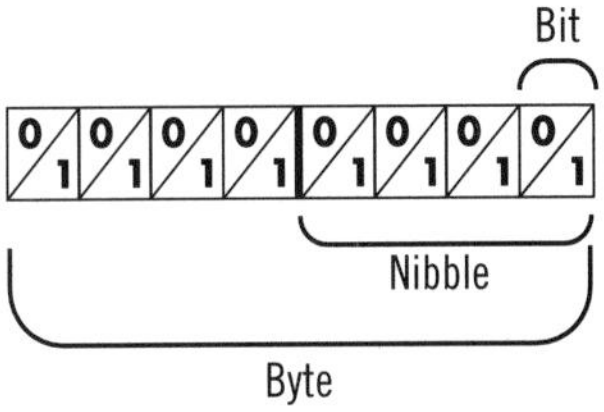

Figure 7-5. DIGITAL CODING. Computer coding is an inventive combination of binary (base 2), hexadecimal (base 16) and decimal (base 10) numbering systems. The theory begins with a binary system, since each circuit can exhibit one of only two states—on or off, 1 or 0. While a binary number system is easy for machines, it is difficult for human beings. By the 1980s, the industry had settled on a standard system which combined binary "bits" (for Binary digITS) into groups of eight, called a byte. Each half of the byte (a nibble) can represent a number up to 16 (2^4) so numbers can easily be represented in hexadecimal notation (where the letters A through F stand for the digits we don't have in the Arabic decimal system). The eight-bit byte permits 256 possible values (2^8) which is a limit sufficient to encode all the letters of the Roman alphabet, both upper- and lower-case, punctuation, numbers, accents, and accented letters.

Although they are too complex to detail here, suffice it to say that these algorithms compress the amount of data required to store and display an image (or that succession of images known as a movie) by recording the difference between successive pixels or frames rather than the individual values of each pixel in each frame. For example, a still image with a large background of a single color would take much less room to store than the same image with a multicolored, variegated background. It is the number of changes that count, not the number of pixels. Similarly, a movie that is slow moving with few cuts requires far less storage than a quickly changing scene with numerous cuts. Only the differences between frames are recorded, not the complete data for each frame. The compression of each still image is known as "spatial compression;" the compression of succeeding frames is called "temporal compression." Both sets of algorithms are necessary to produce economically viable digital video.

These compression techniques can easily reduce storage for a still image by a factor of 10 and storage for a moving image by a factor of 100. So we are back within the limits prescribed by the capacities of current hardware. The main standard for still image compression is known as JPEG (for the group that designed it, the Joint Photographic Experts Group) while the main standard for movies is called MPEG (for Motion Picture Experts Group). The DVD specification is based on MPEG-2 and provides for full-screen, full-motion video. There are many other schemes in use as well. (Oh, yes. There is also a very simple way to reduce the amount of data necessary for a digital movie: reduce the size of the image. That's why most digital movie windows on early multimedia CD-ROMs looked like large postage stamps.)

Although the Voyager Company had demonstrated the possibilities of multimedia as early as 1989 with their release of Robert Winter's *CD Companion to Beethoven's Ninth*, multimedia did not begin to become a market reality until June 1991, when Apple introduced their software technology for movies known as Quick-Time. (Microsoft followed with Video for Windows the next year.) QuickTime was designed as an architecture to support all media types, time-based or not.

One of its aims was to provide a platform-independent technology so that moving images could be shown at the best quality that the hardware on which they were run was capable. As successive versions of the software were issued the architecture supported more features (text, interactivity), more codecs (compression algorithms), and adaptations for use on the Internet (streaming, variable transmission rates).

With QuickTime, new media producers had their first effective tool for integrating audio and video in a text environment, but they were still constrained by the hardware. Their delivery media, the CD-ROM and the Internet, were both limited. CD-ROM was based on technology that was devised in the late 1970s, while Internet transmission was hampered by low modem speeds. DVD, the successor to the CD and designed to have sufficient capacity and speed for digital video, was not marketed until 1997,[*] while high-speed cable modems and DSL Internet connections did not become widespread until the turn of the century.

Developed jointly by Philips and Sony, the laser-based CD was introduced as an audio medium in 1982. Within six years it dominated the recording business, one of the great success stories of twentieth-century consumer electronics mar-

---

[*] As an analog medium Laserdiscs weren't a serious candidate. Philips's other optical disc technology languished throughout the 1980s, adopted only by a coterie of several hundred thousand movie aficionados for their superior resolution and control. As videotape crested, Laserdiscs finally reached the one-million penetration level in the U.S. in early 1991. The so-called RCA rule declares that a consumer product doesn't provide a real market until the installed base reaches one million. Sure enough, just as the Laserdiscs approached that level, the software moved out of the specialty stores and into the video chains.

In the mid-1990s, the VCD format ("Video CD") provided up to 74 minutes of video on a standard CD, compressed with MPEG-1. The medium was popular in Asia—especially for pirated movies—but was not successful elsewhere.

Figure 7-6. One of the first QuickTimes, this team cheer was included on Apple's first demo disk. (*Courtesy Apple Computer, Inc. Frame enlargements.*)

keting. The success of the CD in the audio market brought prices down rapidly, making this physical medium even more attractive for the computer industry which in 1985 adopted CD-ROM as the storage technology of the future.

Ironically, Sony, like Philips, had little success in the multimedia market. During the early 1990s the company brought out at least four versions of a portable CD-ROM player, but neither the Data Discman (in several incarnations), the Bookman, nor the MMCD player was accepted by the public. Success would come, but not until the next generation: DVD.

The audio CD succeeded so quickly because Sony and Philips controlled the technology: a single uniform standard was adopted by all manufacturers. Conversely, until the advent of DVD, CD multimedia development was slowed by a multiplicity of approaches. In addition to the Apple Macintosh and Microsoft MPC formats and Sony's efforts, the list of erstwhile contenders included Philips's CD-I (introduced in 1991), Commodore's CDTV, Tandy's VIS, IBM's Ultimedia, and the game machines of Sega, Nintendo, Sony, and 3DO. Except for CD-I, all were non-starters. Like its imitators, CD-I discs played on an attachment to the television set (priced at about $600 at introduction) controlled by a remote joystick that lacked a keyboard. CD-I was hampered by two major limitations: the poor resolution of the television screen combined with the lack of a keyboard meant that very little could be done with text. CD-I turned out to be little more than a playback medium for still images. The base technology simply hadn't the muscle to support effective video. Although hundreds of companies rushed to market in the early 1990s with CD-ROM-based products (many of them quite ingenious), multimedia remained more a dream than a reality. By 1995 most of the early multimedia producers were out of business. The only successful CD-ROM genres were games and text-centric products like encyclopedias and reference works. Indeed, by 1994 more encyclopedias were sold on disc than in traditional book form.

The original specification for the CD aimed for a product that could deliver more than an hour of digital audio, uncompressed. DVD was designed to have the

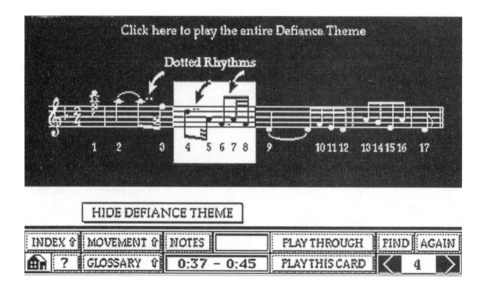

Figure 7-7. Voyager's landmark *Beethoven* disc (1989) marked the start of the multimedia market.

capacity to deliver a standard two-hour feature film on a similar-sized disc. By using a laser with a shorter wavelength engineers were able to fit almost seven times as many bits on the same disc, but as we have seen that is not nearly enough capacity for raw video.[*] Compression technology was necessary for a viable product. Here's where it gets interesting.

Compression algorithms come in two flavors, "lossy" and "nonlossy." As their names imply, nonlossy compression faithfully reproduces every digital value captured from the original, while lossy compression does not: it approximates some values. Furthermore, the very nature of digitization itself implies a loss of values. No matter how high the sampling rate, theoretically values in between the steps are lost. There are still audiophiles who complain about the "coldness" of CD reproduction, preferring the old-fashioned analog vinyl disks, despite their fragility.

---

[*] To return to our earlier equations: 921,600 bytes per screen x 30 frames per second = 27.7 million bytes per second of uncompressed video. 4.7 billion bytes (the capacity of a single layer DVD) / 27.7 million bytes = 170 seconds, or less than 3 minutes of uncompressed video. DVD-Video compression routinely achieves greater than 100:1 ratios, boosting the capacity of a single layer so that there is plenty of room for an entire feature film. (Note: these numbers are simplified. In practice, it's more complicated.) Moreover, the specification allows for double-layer and double-sided discs, so the ultimate capacity exceeds 18 billion bytes.

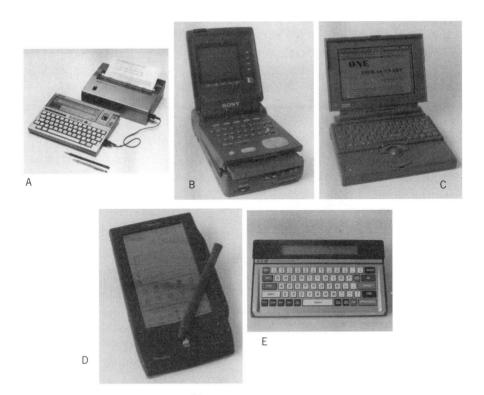

Figure 7-8. THE BOOK "FORM FACTOR." The form that an old-fashioned book takes has been an alluring metaphor for microcomputer designers ever since the visionaries at Xerox PARC first described the ideal "Dynabook" in the early seventies. Sony introduced the Type-corder (A) in 1981, arguably the first laptop computer. It did nothing but word processing with a four-line LCD screen. The typing was recorded on a common microcassette. It worked, but it gained no position in the market, and was quickly superseded by the Radio Shack 100, which had a full operating system. Sony introduced the ingenious Data Discman (B) ten years later. Based on a 3-inch CD disc enclosed in a plastic case and looking like a fat magnetic diskette, the Data Discman (and its successor the Bookman) could store several hundred megabytes of text and display it on a small screen. It was about the size of a large paperback. Sony kept its record of failure in the computer business intact: the Discman didn't catch on.

After years of lagging in the portable computer market, Apple enjoyed huge success with its Powerbook (C), introduced in October 1991. A leading example of sensible ergonomic design, the Powerbook quickly became the status symbol among Hollywood players and others. Barry Diller credited his conversion to digitalism to the Powerbook. Apple was less immediately successful with the Newton (D), its first Personal Digital Assistant, introduced in 1993. Yet PDAs like the Palm Pilot eventually became almost as common as the calculator or cellular phone. As a dedicated communicator and note taker, the Newton marked the beginning of the breakup of individual computer functions on dedicated devices. It had been foreshadowed eleven years earlier by the IXO Telecomputer (E), a tiny device with an even tinier screen that communicated over telephone lines at 300 baud. An interesting idea, far ahead of its time, the IXO failed quickly, superseded by the ubiquitous pager. (*JM.*)

Because it depends on heavy, lossy compression, the DVD format established as a standard late in 1995 for the next generation of optical disc technology compounded these esthetic problems. Most consumers marvel at the picture quality of DVD-Videos. Indeed, the resolution and color fidelity are both far superior to the VHS tape with which a DVD-Video disc is usually compared. The DVD-Video launch was one of the most successful introductions of a consumer electronics product in history.

But, just as CD sound is cold and lifeless for audiophiles, so the digital image is too clean and airless for some videophiles; they continue to prefer analog Laserdisc. As Robert Browning put it, "What's come to perfection perishes."

The problem is ethical as well as esthetic: most of the frames in a DVD-Video simply aren't there; they haven't been recorded. And most of the pixels in the frames that do exist also aren't present. You don't get 100:1 compression for nothing. Filmmakers may very well prefer DVD-Video to VHS for its clarity while at the same time reserving the right to criticize the medium for its supercilious attitude toward fidelity. But then, they are all copies, aren't they?

The fully digital image also presents challenges to distributors. Because copies are exact and there is no generation loss, DVDs present serious piracy problems. Once movies are digitized they are just as easy to duplicate and transmit as digital text. It's only a question of bandwidth.

Yet the call of the digital siren was irresistible to the hardware companies. The MPEG-2 algorithm was adopted by the floundering consumer satellite television industry for its digital second-generation product in the mid-1990s and proved successful. By 1998 the consumer electronics market was flooded with digital cameras, both still and video, and film-based photography was under siege. Sony had tried to market a digital still camera called Mavica as early as 1989. In 1992 Kodak had introduced the Photo CD format to deliver film-based photos digitally. Both had languished. Now, the time was right. From the moment DVD-Video was introduced in April 1997 analog was dead—at least in marketing terms.

The Myth of Multimedia

Considering the formidable technical hurdles involved in digitization, the disorganized marketplace, and serious issues of quality, the seasoned cinephile may be excused for reacting cynically to the multimedia hype of the nineties. Artists have been combining text, images, and sounds since the invention of movies. Edison was the first multimedia artist, and film is the first multimedium. Digitizing the images and sounds gives the viewer a real measure of control over them, which is a useful advance, but didn't the Laserdisc (still an analog device) accomplish much the same end?

From a strictly cinematic point of view, it does. If our aim is simply to control the experience of watching movies, a fully computerized laserdisc (or DVD) player is a decent solution to the problem. Moreover, the existence of a multimedia industry is not going to change the way filmmakers make films in any significant way. As producer Joe Medjuck has pointed out, the artistic strength of Hollywood (and by extension most filmmakers) is linear narrative, which is directly contrary to the interactivity that is the soul of multimedia. Filmmakers tell stories: "First this happens, then this happens, then...." Random access to the parts of a movie can destroy its rhythms, its reasons for being.

From a publisher's point of view, however, the advent of multimedia is a historic event nearly equal to the invention of movable type. For the first time, all media become available to the publisher. Books have always had illustrations. Sometimes a picture *is* worth a thousand words. Moving pictures, then, should be worth 24,000 words per second.

In the 1970s at Xerox PARC, scientist Alan Kay, one of the key figures in the microcomputer revolution, developed a model for the computer of the future that he called the Dynabook. (Remember, this was before there was such a thing as a microcomputer.) Kay envisioned a hand-held computer that had much the same "look and feel" as the book you are now holding (assuming you are reading the book version of *How To Read a Film*). He understood the value of this ancient information format and assumed quite rightly that, as the computer people learned to say years later, "if it ain't broke, don't fix it." Multimedia is an important step in fulfilling the promise of the Dynabook. All that remains is to make it portable, and flexible ... and much faster (and, while we're at it, let's quadruple the resolution).

In a sense, the format is misnamed. Since the main advantage of "multimedia" is that it unifies the various publishing media we have developed over the past hundred years, perhaps "unimedium" would be a better name. This would focus our attention on the job at hand: to produce a unified experience, communicating thoughts and feelings, using whichever information formats work best.

More important, the real value of the format known as multimedia has much less to do with the combination of media for which it is named than it does with its coding system. Another better name for the format would be "digital book." While, as we have seen, digitization creates some serious problems for multimedia movies, it is no less than deliriously liberating for text. The advantages are several, and they are real.

The most important is the ease with which digital text can be retrieved. Most printed nonfiction books have indexes, but digital text allows for "fulltext indexing," which means that every word is retrievable, and this is nearly as useful with

Figure 7-9. At the Digital World multimedia show in 1991, Voyager employees were identified by their contrarian tee-shirts. (This was the show at which Apple introduced QuickTime.) (*Courtesy Colin Holgate, Voyager.*)

fiction as with nonfiction. If the concept of the digital book is extended to the digital library, this unlimited and easy access method becomes a formidable intellectual tool. Commercial electronic indexing was pioneered in the late sixties and early seventies by companies such as Dialog and Lexis long before the CD-ROM and multimedia developments of the nineties. These online databases continue to perform a central function in the world of digital books, even now that they have been joined by "portable" databases on CD-ROM. Even a jukebox full of dozens of CD-ROMs can't approach the capacity of centralized databases, which is one of the reasons online technology will continue to play a role in multimedia publishing. The World Wide Web would be an impenetrable thicket of data were it not for the search engines that drive it.

Fulltext indexing also allows for the electronic variant of cross-referencing that has come to be known as hypertext. In a hypertext document, the user controls the flow of the narrative logic, expanding or contracting the level of detail, going off on tangents at will, or outlining the subject of discussion. With its ubiquitous pointers to relevant information and illustrations, hypertext provides a level of control over the text experience unmatched in print. Hypertext fulfills the dreams of authors who are fond of footnotes[*] (and parentheses) as well as the venerable editors of text commentaries like the Shakespeare Variorum and biblical concordances who had felt the need for a third dimension of textual narrative. Now they have it.

Digital text also offers the reader new control over the experience—a new degree of ownership of the text as well as the book in which it is housed. Digital text is easily copied and moved, sorted and modified. While this is of considerable

---

[*]   Still an effective way to give text a third dimension.

Figure 7-10. The Oxford English Dictionary, one of the world's great publishing enterprises, in its traditional 20-volume book form and on CD. The CD-ROM is easily updatable as well as being easier to search and almost infinitely cheaper to manufacture. (*Courtesy Oxford University Press.*)

benefit to the reader, it poses some serious and interesting problems for the publisher, which we'll discuss shortly.

Digital text still suffers from a lack of screen resolution, and given the choice, a printed book is still the best way to experience a text. With a digital book you can't make marginal notes as easily, turn down the corners of pages, or mark the text as flexibly, but those problems will be solved as we approach the Dynabook, and the control and searchability of the digital book can make up for the rigid linearity of the physical experience.

Perhaps the most valuable feature of digital text from a publisher's point of view is also its most mundane: its price. The cost of producing CDs or even magnetic diskettes is insignificant when compared to the cost of producing even the simplest of books. Moreover, discs—unlike books—can be produced pretty much on demand. It is not necessary to invest in large inventories. Most readers are unaware of the economics of book production, but publishers constantly must confront this painful dilemma.

Most of the cost in printing is front loaded. It takes more time and effort to set up the presses for a print run than it does to do the actual printing. Thus, it is uneconomical to print just a few copies. Publishers are forced under the current technology to print a sufficient number of copies so that the large costs involved in setup can be amortized in such a way that the unit cost is reasonable. More than one publishing house has been destroyed by maintaining excessive inventories, the result of overly ambitious press runs set to make the numbers work rather than serve the market.

The setup cost for a printing of CDs or DVDs is negligible when compared to traditional book printing setup costs. For example, a twenty-volume large-format encyclopedia that might require printing a minimum of a thousand book copies at $150 per set (because if fewer copies were printed the unit cost would be too high) can be produced on a single CD-ROM in a much smaller edition for $1 or $2 per copy. Instead of an investment of $150,000 the publisher needs to spend perhaps $1,500. All kinds of publishing ventures that were uneconomical in print form become possible on disc, greatly expanding the range of publishing.[*]

Indeed, the low cost of digital publishing means that highly capitalized professional organizations may no longer dominate. Electronically sophisticated authors now command the publishing power once reserved to the established publishing houses. With a few hundred dollars worth of software, an author can produce a fully formatted book, replete with illustrations (in color, and in motion). With access to the Internet he or she can make the "book" available to millions, worldwide, instantaneously: a kind of "virtual publishing." What such a cyberauthor can't do better than a commercial publishing house is market this work. For some types of publishing—academic, special interest, private—this may not matter.

It is also not yet clear that universal access to publishing channels is entirely positive. Take it to its logical conclusion: if everything is published, then nothing is focused. The arduous process of production and distribution that pertained for three hundred years provided a filter that, on the face of it, worked. Imagine if there were a thousand times—a hundred thousand times—as many texts to deal with. The great bane of the Internet is logorrhea. We will have to find a new way to separate the wheat from the chaff. While the job of publishing may be increasingly irrelevant, the importance of editing grows each day. The search engines are a start, but much more sophisticated tools are necessary.

There is another aspect to this new world of virtual publishing that needs to be examined. As we noted earlier, because the reader now has such a command of the author's text, the traditional concept of copyright comes into question. Digital publishing is so easy that it leads us beyond traditional self-publishing to what we might call republishing or repurposing. College teachers who succumbed twenty years ago to the siren call of the photocopier, producing limited editions of other people's texts for classroom use have been joined by the rest of us, who can now whip together a little multimedia wedding invitation, for example, from a few

---

[*] It's true that "prepress" costs for multimedia CDs and DVDs can be very high: software development is much more expensive than traditional typesetting and book design. But these costs will drop quickly as publishers learn how to deal effectively with this new format.

riverrun, past Eve and Adam's, from swerve of shore to bend of bay, brings us by a commodius vicus of recirculation back to Howth Castle and Environs.

rivverun, past Eve and Adam's, from swerve of shore to bend of bay, brings us by a commodius vicus of recirculation back to Howth Castle and Environs.

Figure 7-11. On top, text in the Palatino typeface reproduced at a computer screen standard of 72 pixels per inch. Below, the same text as it appears in a book at approximately 2600 dots per inch. (Set 12 points on 14-point leading.)

lines of Gerard Manley Hopkins, a little Lohengrin, and perhaps a David Hockney for the background.

The legal doctrine of copyright has traditionally protected not ideas, but their expression. Because it brings all texts, images, and sounds into a uniform environment, digitization makes it a simple matter not only to reproduce those copyrightable objects with little or no cost barrier, but also to modify them in such a way as to meet the letter of the law, if not its spirit. When does a quotation become plagiarism? When does plagiarism become an homage, a new work of art? These questions have been with us for a long time, but they gain added urgency in the digital age. Aside from laws dealing with physical property, the ownership of intellectual property is a relatively new concept, with its roots in the nineteenth century. It may not last through the twenty-first century.

Sampling—the reuse of other people's music—first became common in the 1980s when professionals gained access to digital editing equipment. By the late 1990s. the availability of cheap CD recorders meant that every high-school kid could dub his own "mix." The development of audio compression formats for the Internet like MP3 made every hard disk a potential pirate jukebox.[*] By 1999, the music industry was in the throes of a revolution: it wasn't just the threat of universal piracy; it was also that musicians could now sell directly to listeners. What had happened slowly in the print world was now spreading at Internet speed through the music world. It is only a matter of time before this is an issue in video as well.

---

[*] If audiophiles think poorly of uncompressed CD, they have nothing but contempt for the lossy compression of MP3. But the vast majority of Internet music hobbyists couldn't care less. After all, the popular music they trade is usually produced with electronic instruments of the same level of quality. We're not talking Stradivarius here—or even Zildjian vs Sabian cymbals.

Expect the next edition of your word-processing software to come with a translator that will modify the borrowed text you select just enough so that no one will be able to identify where it came from. Expect the next edition of your multimedia authoring tool to do the same for movies. You can already buy font design programs that perform a similar function with typefaces. Altsys Fontographer allows you not only to apply slight modifications to a font in seconds, but also to merge two separate and distinct faces. If you combine Hermann Zapf's influential and resonant Palatino with Frederick Goudy's obstreperous Old Style, what do you owe to the designers and producers?

Probably nothing. Current U.S. copyright law is unclear on the copyright status of typeface designs. Since the Copyright Act of 1976, Congress has chosen to "defer" protection of typeface designs. In other words, it has decided not to decide whether these creative enterprises are "works of authorship" and therefore copyrightable. The crux of the matter is whether the design can exist separately from the utility of the product. If it cannot, the Act of 1976 declares, it is not protectable.* This leads to an esthetic paradox that would have bemused architect Louis Sullivan, who insisted in the last century that "form follows function." If you abide by that dictum perfectly, you can't separate the design from the article, so you own no intellectual property rights—according to the Congress of the United States. You've reached design nirvana—and copyright hell.

But clearly you've appropriated other people's work. Just as clearly, your own input has been minimal. Morally, you've transgressed, even if you are not legally liable. Now suppose you spend a certain amount of time, effort, and talent modifying the new typeface. At what point does it become your own work? At what point—if any—is it no longer a plagiarism?

This curious situation is not an isolated anomaly. In 1991, in *Feist Publications v Rural Telephone Service Co., Inc.*, a case with similar implications for the information industry, the U.S. Supreme Court ruled that a factual database that was complete and organized alphabetically, such as a telephone directory, was not protectable under copyright law. The Court decided that it was the editorial labor involved in editing down a complete database that formed the "work of authorship," which was therefore protectable.

Both of these legal rulings would have worked well enough in the mechanical past: type designers made livings because their foundries sold expensive bronze matrixes; the value in any printed list was not that it was comprehensive but that it had been edited down to manageable size. But neither ruling serves us well in

---

* "The design of a useful article ... shall be considered a pictorial, graphic, or sculptural work only if, and only to the extent that, such design incorporates pictorial, graphic, or sculptural features that can be identified separately from, and are capable of existing independently of, the utilitarian aspects of the article." [17 U.S.C. Sec. 101.]

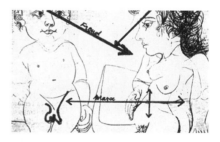

Figure 7-12. With hindsight, the merger of text, images, and sounds was irresistible. Jean-Luc Godard used the technology available in his time. These four shots from *Le Gai Savoir* (1969), combine drawings, print, ads, cartoons, handwriting, and symbols. (*l'Avant-Scène. Frame enlargements.*)

the digital age when fonts are made of infinitely replicatable bits and bytes, and complete databases are the goal, not the bane, of listmakers.

Typefaces are relatively simple intellectual properties, but the same patterns apply to texts, images, and movies. Indeed, the film industry has more experience than any other in handling complex intellectual property rights issues. Film is, of course, a collaborative medium, and any industry lawyer is familiar with the knotty problems of competing claims as to who owns what. Dozens of major contributors can lay claim to various pieces of the intellectual property that is a movie, from the author of the original source material to dozens of filmmakers and actors to numerous distributors in numerous markets. The trouble is that there is little logic to Hollywood rights law, and so the new multimedia industry will have to work out reasonable guidelines without the help of its predecessor.

In the end, if the copyright system is going to survive, it may only be because we apply prodigious amounts of digital processing power to the task of allocating percentages among the hundreds of individuals and companies that may contribute in some way to a multimedia production. The model would be music royalty organizations like ASCAP and BMI, or the British library Public Lending Rights program, that apportion certain amounts of revenue to authors by formula. The only other alternative is to abandon the idea of copyright altogether and return to the system that pertained until the nineteenth century in which the value of a work of art was vested in its physical manifestation, not its abstract intellectual form. In the new world of virtual publishing, where every author is a publisher, this might be conceivable. There's only one problem: so much of intellectual work in the digital age simply has no physical manifestation.

As we watch this new medium struggling to be born—the synthesis of 500 years of print, 150 years of photography, and 100 years of audio recording and movies—we are struck with the contradictions:

- ❏ It has less to do with the new medium of movies than with the old medium of print.

- ❏ That image, sounds, and print are digitized is more important than that they are combined.

- ❏ While digitization vastly increases our control over these media, it also—for the time being—reduces them to abstractions with notably less quality than their analog predecessors.

- ❏ The major advantages of digitization—instant access to information and its comprehensive indexation—have more to do with the rise of networks and their databases than with the combination of media.

- ❏ While digitization vastly increases a reader's power and facility, it poses serious challenges to the concept of copyright on which our current system of authorship is based.

Yet we can sense the rightness of multimedia: this is where we have been headed for hundreds of years. If Sir Walter Scott could have added slide shows to his novels, he would have. If Charles Dickens could have personally narrated his remarkable stories, he would have (and did, to a certain extent, in his lucrative lecture tours). If Daniel Defoe could have included an interactive database of historical statistics with *Journal of the Plague Year*, he would have. If Georges Méliès could have allowed his viewers to interact with *Voyage to the Moon*, he would have. If George Bernard Shaw could have included ancillary texts with *Candida* or *Man and Superman*, he would have (and did, in the published versions of his plays). If Preston Sturges could have spunoff his films as television series, he would have. If Jean-Luc Godard could have written a book that was also a movie, he would have. If François Truffaut could have shot a movie that was also a book, he would have, too.

Text and images and sounds have been separated for hundreds of years only because technology has lagged behind our imaginations. Now it has caught up, and they are united, as they were meant to be: for better, for worse, in sickness and in health....

The Myth of Virtual Reality

There is always a struggle between the artist's aims and the limits of the available technology. But now that the digital revolution is well on the way to providing a common coding system for all forms of media, the tension between desire and capability is yielding to a new controlling dialectic: between ethics and esthetics. This historical development in our intellectual history is not unlike psychologist Erik Erikson's famous dialectics of personal growth. In this case, we reverse the classic biologists' saying: now, "phylogeny recapitulates ontogeny"—the development of the group echoes the development of the individual.

Once images, sounds, and texts are digitized, all things are possible. The struggle between what we want our media to do for us and what they are capable of doing has ended. Or, at least, the struggle is pointless. In the analog world there were strict limits: you could only make a piece of wood or a violin do what it was capable of doing. In the digital world, there are no physical limits: it's only a question of storage capacity, processor speed, and communication bandwidth.* The digital revolution is completing the intellectual revolution that began thousands of years ago when someone first put paint to stone. Cave paintings, like all art since, sought to distill the natural world, to abstract it, to make of it an idea. Now we have no physical barriers between us and the idea.

This new power is intoxicating, but like all power it brings with it the necessity for a strong ethical structure. Godard was fond of quoting Lenin's dictum: ethics is the esthetics of the future. They were both right, but in ways they could not have foreseen. Now that there are no insurmountable technical limits, now that we can make our artistic medium do everything we want, we need to understand the moral limits much better than we have before. In a way, all artists have been adolescents until now, under the thumb of parental technologies. Now they must take on the moral responsibilities of adulthood.

Before we investigate those responsibilities in more detail, we should look at the current business context of virtual reality. Like "multimedia" and "cyberspace,"

---

* Yes, this is a bit of hyperbole, but not much. For the purposes of discussion, let's assume that all the world's texts amount to 100 terabytes (100 million books averaging a megabyte each). Today, you can carry 18 gigabytes in your pocket. (This is the capacity of a two-sided double-layer DVD.) In the past twenty years we have increased storage density by five magnitudes. 100 terabytes equal 100,000 gigabytes. To carry all the world's written knowledge in your pocket, we will need to increase storage density by another five magnitudes. We're halfway there. Perhaps some compromises will have to be made: you may need two or three pockets, or you may have to plug into the Internet for some of it.

"virtual reality" has been one of the catchphrases of the digital revolution. In its narrowest commercial sense, virtual reality intends to apply digital technology to computer games and entertainment to increase the apparent reality of the experience by making it both more verisimilitudinous and more fully interactive. Instead of choosing which room to enter by typing on a keyboard or clicking a mouse, you physically turn left or right: all the fun of walking with none of the aerobic consequences.

Virtual-reality techniques vary in both attitude and ambition. As the century came to a close, virtual-reality engineers and producers were reliving the artistic dialectic that characterized the birth of film a hundred years ago: should the technology be used to reproduce reality or replace it, to capture the world or to invent a new one? It's Lumière versus Méliès all over again, but with a special twist this time, for digital records don't betray their sources. Méliès's fantasies were clearly different from the Lumières' realities. Digital imagery has reached a level of mathematical abstraction that now makes the one indistinguishable from the other. Interestingly, the traditional realists seem to gain more from the new technology than the fantasists: "Telepresence," the application of virtual-reality techniques to reproduce a distant place, will yield significant scientific dividends as machines will go "where no man has gone before."

These classic differences in attitude are accompanied by differences in ambition. At one extreme lies "fully immersive" virtual reality, which attempts a full range of sensory impression, including three-dimensional video, full-range audio, and touch. At the other end of the scale we find basic, yet elegant, applications that simply allow us to control our point of view of standard images.

One of the earliest examples of telepresence was the popularity of "webcams" in the early days of the web: cameras that transmitted live images of the weather or someone's bedroom. The most ingenious of the early webcams was the Telegarden project at the University of Southern California (1995). Web surfers who became members of the project could send commands to operate a robot to plant seeds, water, or fertilize a real garden that had been planted in the Telegarden lab. Anyone could tune in at any time to see how the garden was progressing. The next year NBC installed a number of webcams at more than a dozen venues for the Atlanta Olympic games. The television coverage was so tightly edited (and usually delayed) that the website (operated in conjunction with IBM) became the best way for sports fans to view the contests. In 1997 the landing of the Mars Pathfinder probe drew a record 45 million visits to the Jet Propulsion Laboratory website to view live images from another planet. These early experiments suggest some of the possibilities for telepresence.

As a consumer product, virtual reality means to exploit multisensory perception to increase our involvement. But we mean to take virtual reality in its

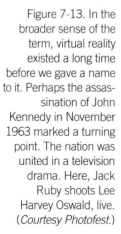

Figure 7-13. In the broader sense of the term, virtual reality existed a long time before we gave a name to it. Perhaps the assassination of John Kennedy in November 1963 marked a turning point. The nation was united in a television drama. Here, Jack Ruby shoots Lee Harvey Oswald, live. (*Courtesy Photofest.*)

broader sense here: as the technological movement toward increased verisimilitude and interactivity that is closely associated with multimedia.

In either sense of the term, virtual reality simply extends a theme that has been part of film history since the beginning. In the early years of this century, movie travelogues provided virtual journeys for homebound would-be travelers. As we've seen, filmmakers have been experimenting with larger screens, 3-D, and stereo sound since the twenties. In 1953, *This Is Cinerama* took us on a collective rollercoaster ride that is still the model for experiential cinema. As a technique to increase verisimilitude, virtual reality continues this tradition. The difference is in its interactivity, the degree of control over the experience that it provides to the viewer.

Here the technology may miss the point. At the 1964–65 New York World's Fair, viewers at the Czechoslovak pavilion could vote to determine plot developments in the movie they were watching. In the late sixties and early seventies, several stage drama experiments offered audiences erstwhile control. The technique did not catch on, for obvious reasons. The National Lampoon satirized audience control with lethal effect in a mid-1970s skit. In their version of *Waiting for Godot*, the always imminent guest shows up only thirty seconds after the play begins. He and Didi and Gogo briefly discuss where to eat. (As I remember it, they decided on Chinese.)

As a technique applied to games rather than cinema, virtual reality shows more promise. The essence of a computer game is its interactivity, so the increased verisimilitude offered by virtual reality is useful to enhance the experience. The basic concept of a dungeons-and-dragons game is a multithreaded matrix of plots, while a battle game depends for its effect on the adrenaline-boosting rhythm of

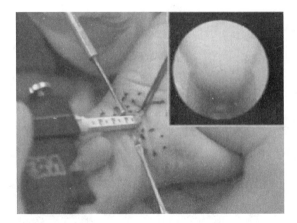

Figure 7-14. Telepresence is one of the faces of virtual reality. Here, a demonstration of carpal tunnel surgical technique shows how the technology permits less invasive surgery. The inset shows the image the surgeon sees.
(*Courtesy 3M Health Care. Frame enlargement.*)

challenges. In both cases, virtual reality enhances the effect. But perhaps its greatest value is with that class of games that duplicate experience, such as flight simulators. Indeed, simulators are less games than they are prototypes for virtual reality experience, and their great promise is educational. Perhaps we are not quite ready yet to trust the training of our surgeons to a virtual-reality lab, but numerous other crafts and techniques can benefit from the simulator approach that has served airline pilots well for many years. Now that these devices have been digitized, we all have access to them. Indeed, the first successes of virtual reality (apart from games) have been in the "how to" business, with CAD programs that allow us to envision—albeit roughly—how the new deck will look if we build it the way we've designed it.

Both key elements of virtual reality—verisimilitude and interactivity—lead to ethical questions.

Digital images and sounds are more true to life only when judged in their own context. No computer screen commercially available today comes close to the resolution of properly projected 35 mm film, to say nothing of superfilm technologies like Showscan and Imax. (Similarly, no electronic screen can match the quality of a well-printed book.) And while the CD has made digital sound the new standard, some audiophiles still prefer the older analog technology, as we have already noted. Are they simply esthetic Luddites?

The acuity of a digitally reproduced sound or image depends on two mathematical factors: the number of samples and the precision—or depth—of each sample. For moving pictures, add a third factor: the frame rate. Theoretically, to match the accuracy of analog reproduction, digital sampling rates would need to approach infinity. Luckily this is not the case in practice. As we have seen in Chapter 2, the invention of film itself depended on limitations of human perception. We only need to exceed those limitations by a measurable margin for error. Moreover, analog techniques of reproduction are themselves far from perfect.

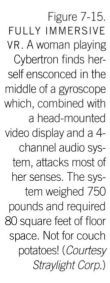

Figure 7-15. FULLY IMMERSIVE VR. A woman playing Cybertron finds herself ensconced in the middle of a gyroscope which, combined with a head-mounted video display and a 4-channel audio system, attacks most of her senses. The system weighed 750 pounds and required 80 square feet of floor space. Not for couch potatoes! (*Courtesy Straylight Corp.*)

Digital models need only match or exceed their analog predecessors—for the time being.

The problem is that they don't, yet. While it is arguable that the audio CD standard is close enough, and it is likely that the 16 million colors available on a high-end computer video driver are sufficiently precise, the resolution of the screen, and the prodigious compromises necessary to store motion pictures still impose significant limitations, despite rapid advances in compression technology.

In the sixties, the story goes, Ingmar Bergman suffered from guilt over the inherent dishonesty of his chosen medium. Bergman brooded over the fact that more than 50 percent of the time his audience was watching a perfectly blank screen. Imagine his distress when confronted with digital imagery, which compounds that singular trick of the movies a thousandfold!

The interactive element of virtual reality presents an additional ethical problem. As we involve the viewer-turned-user in the artistic decision-making process we may abrogate the responsibility of authorship. The very richness of the virtual-reality multimedia environment can be misleading. The more we attempt to duplicate reality, the more freedom we create for the user to manipulate and control this environment, the farther away we seem to get from the point of it all. The closer we come to the full reproduction of reality, the more we lose the dialectic between art and its subject. The term "virtual reality" is, after all, an oxymoron. In physics, what is real is real, what is virtual is not real. The result is that, like David Bowman at the end of *2001*, virtual reality users find themselves in a cage—a beautiful cage, but all the more constricting just because it appears to be open.

Figure 7-16. QuickTime VR, introduced by Apple in 1995, turned movies inside out. Here, the artist gives you the space or the object, and you choose how to view it. If movies are paintings, QuickTime VR is both architecture and sculpture. These frames are from the "Balcony" QTVR, the first released demo of the technology. Thirty-three stills were stitched together into a continuous panorama which the user can navigate at will (*Courtesy Apple Computer, Inc.*)

The comparison with the drug experience is apt. As The Beatles put it:

> Nothing is real
> And nothing to get hung about....*

We've already noted the parallels between psychoactive chemicals and our traditional plug-in drugs. Fully immersive virtual reality is the electronic superdrug. "Strawberry fields forever."

While the philosophy of virtual reality raises these ethical questions, on a more practical level, certain virtual-reality technologies show immediate promise—and in a way we might not have expected.

Apple's QuickTime VR is one of these. Previewed at the Digital World show in June 1994, three years after the debut of the original QuickTime, QTVR and its competitors turn that movie technology on its head. Using the same underlying algorithms that approximate movies in a digital environment, VR permits the user to change point of view, to tour a space at will. The movement of the mouse determines the camera's point of view, and a click of the mouse controls the position of the camera. Panoramic still photographs taken at one or more locations in the subject space are stored on disc. QuickTime VR processes these complete but distorted records to present a properly proportioned still image from the point of view the user has chosen. Users can zoom and pan as they like. If more than one position in the space has been recorded, users can move from point to point. If no 360° panoramic record exists, a separate VR preprocessor will create one from a

---

* "Strawberry Fields Forever," copyright 1967, Northern Songs Ltd. Reprinted with permission.

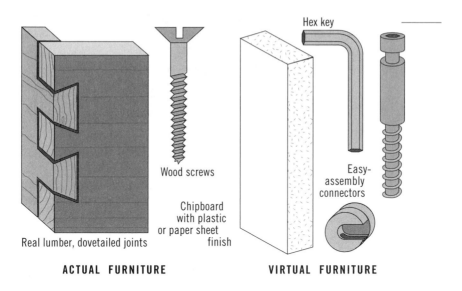

ACTUAL FURNITURE   **VIRTUAL FURNITURE**

Figure 7-17. VIRTUAL FURNITURE. While we might easily assume that virtual reality is a product of developing technology, perhaps there are underlying economic motivations: in an overcrowded world, there isn't enough real reality to go around, so many of us are going to have to make do with synthetic reality. Much the same has happened to furniture in the last 35 years. For many centuries, the world over, furniture was constructed of lumber joined mechanically—rabbet, mortise and tenon, dovetails—and glued. The industrial revolution brought the metal screw to replace the peg, but the basic philosophy of joinery didn't change. That tradition has been superseded in recent years by a method of construction that relies on imitation wood and shifts the burden of construction from the carpenter to the user who—just as in VR entertainment—is provided with an ingenious technology that makes the work of construction appear easier, even though it isn't. The result is a virtual product that appears to meet our criteria—but has an exceedingly short lifespan. Perhaps the same will prove true with VR media.

series of rough stills. The technology also allows the user to track around an object—the reverse of panning around a space.

Now this is hardly the stuff that virtual-reality visionaries dream of. There is no attempt to overwhelm the senses; the user remains in control. The genius of the QuickTime VR technology is in its simplicity. It elegantly and intuitively capitalizes on the singular advantage that digital films have over their analog predecessors: the ability to approximate new images by interpolating old ones, which is the heritage of the compression techniques that had to be developed to deal with the formidable numerical requirements of digital cinema. QuickTime VR is the latest example of a classic pattern in the arts: the limitations of the medium yield its essential utility. The main disadvantage of digital movies has become the engine of a new technology.

Of course, this new technology is not movies; "stillies" might be a better term. It creates a place, not a narrative. It denies both mise-en-scène and montage. It replaces rhythm with atmosphere and character with environment. But as it matures it will serve some of the same needs that film has served. In their own way, "stillies" will take us to other people's worlds just as the movies have done. What this elegantly simple technology will not do is confuse those worlds with our own.

The Myth of Cyberspace

The early visionaries of the digital revolution were almost as fascinated by the communications possibilities of the new technology as they were by its capacity to reproduce reality and fuse together multiple media. At the same time that the microcomputer decentralized power in the office, liberating individual workers from the haughty priests of technology in the computer room, new communications techniques were adapting the telephone network to connect millions of these personal intellectual tools with each other and with centralized databases.

Dialog, the first major online database, opened for business in 1965. It was originally designed by Lockheed as a tool for the space program. Lexis, the first comprehensive professional database, put an entire law library online in 1973. Arpanet, the predecessor to the network of networks that later became known as the Internet, went online in 1969. The British Prestel system opened in 1976, demonstrating that online computer information networks could be useful to consumers as well as professionals. Prestel was never a commercial success, but its television-based cousins, Ceefax and Oracle, became part of British life in the 1980s. The French Minitel system, more technically sophisticated than Prestel, became an integral part of French culture beginning in 1985.

The Minitel system differed radically from its predecessors (with the exception of Arpanet) in that it was a distributed system. Instead of linking tens of thousands of users to one central host computer, it provided a switching network to link them to thousands of smaller, independent hosts. One of the salubrious advantages of this architecture was that it decentralized the costs of development and operations. Thousands of Minitel services quickly sprang up. Many of them hosted chat sessions. In an age before email this new form of instant messaging was all the more unique. The online databases were useful, but that a database was online was important mainly if it was too large or too frequently updated to be effective resident on a local disk.

Communication, as quickly became evident, was the real soul of an online system. Chat proved to be a genuinely new form of human interaction, as a single individual could hold multiple simultaneous separate private conversations. It was a realtime equivalent of old-fashioned written correspondence, but the

Figure 7-18. This is a late model of the French Minitel, first introduced in 1981. To save space, the keyboard folds up. The design goal was to occupy a smaller "foot-print" than a telephone directory. (*JM*)

instantaneous speed combined with the anonymity of typed messages and access to tens of thousands of strangers the world over quickly proved to be an addictive combination. By the late 1980s. the Minitel had been institutionalized in France: thousands of everyday products listed their Minitel numbers as marketers found a new way to build a direct path to their customers. Minitel served as a clear model for the development of the Internet and the World Wide Web: all the elements were there. It worked so well, in fact, that Internet services grew very slowly in France in the 1990s: consumers were satisfied with the older, simpler, and more convenient system.

While Minitel was succeeding during the 1980s, a number of similar American experiments failed, mainly due to misunderstanding of the market for such services. Some, such as Knight-Ridder's and Times-Mirror's experiments, chose to broadcast on television, confusing the medium with its sobriquet, videotext.[*] Not only did this impose a centralized authority on what was meant to be a one-to-one communications medium, it also suffered from the inability of the average television screen to reproduce text. Others, like IBM's and Sears's Prodigy, relied on an outdated network model (again, the massive central host, although this time with subsidiary masters), and a graphics system that was equally out of date. NAPLPS, the North American Presentation Level Protocol Standard, had been devised in the early 1980s as the U.S.'s and Canada's answer to Britain's pioneer-

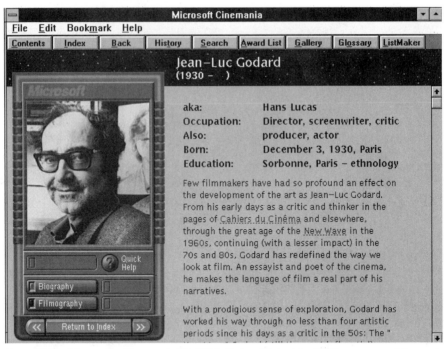

Figure 7-19. Microsoft's *Cinemania* CD-ROM, first published in 1992, was one of the early examples of a multimedia reference work. The keyword indexing is just as valuable as the pictures and sounds.

ing Prestel graphics language and Minitel's Teletel protocol. Prodigy adopted NAPLPS just two years before much more sophisticated graphical user interfaces became ubiquitous on the nation's microcomputers.

The brief history of online graphics is quite interesting. An engineer for the British Post Office named Sam Fedida had come up with the basic concept of Prestel in the early 1970s. The aim was to produce an online system for consumers. From the beginning, basic graphics were to be a part of the service—this at a time when microcomputers didn't exist and time-sharing terminals, their equiva-

---

*   Although a number of terms were in use in the early 1980s as the industry was being formed, English-speakers eventually settled on "videotext" to describe the telephone-based systems like Prestel and Minitel, and "teletext" to describe the video-based systems like Ceefax and Oracle. Of course, it should have been the reverse. Later, videotext lost its final "t." The remaining stub reminded one of disposable paper products—not a felicitous analogy. By the way, the U.S. tried teletext too, with an equal lack of success. Here, the problem was much simpler. In the U.K., where the medium succeeded, all television sets were manufactured with teletext decoders; in the U.S., they were not.

Figure 7-20. Reference works on the Web, such as the Internet Movie Database (www.IMDB.com), offer less bandwidth and independence than CDs, but are capable of being instantly and continuously updated.

lent at that time, were strictly character-based. The Prestel—and later Minitel—graphics character sets were ingenious solutions to the problem of transmitting graphics over telephone lines. (They used the upper-ASCII character set to produce elements for a mosaic graphics format.) The basic colors and shapes greatly added to the effectiveness of the display of characters and simple drawings without attempting the then-arduous task of re-creating photographic imagery.

NAPLPS, ambitiously, attempted to extend the idea to more complex vector graphics. The ambition proved hubristic, as pixel-based graphical user interfaces like the Macintosh quickly established themselves. The engineers at Prodigy (the only ongoing system ever to use NAPLPS), focusing paternally on the graphic responsibilities of the central host computer, had ignored the revolution going on around them. As microcomputers spread, increasing the general wealth of computing power a millionfold, there was no longer any need for NAPLPS—or IBM's mainframes, for that matter.

Although it was not a financial success, Prodigy nevertheless accumulated some two million users during the five years after its introduction in 1988. At the same time in the U.S., Compuserve, the stodgy but profitable online system that had been adopted by the computer industry as its own forum, and America Online, a creative startup, had accumulated three million others between them. By 1993, as microcomputers became easier to use, the online industry dominated the business pages as the "Information Superhighway" had become part of the Clinton administration's national strategy. The "industry in search of a business," as online was known throughout the eighties, had finally found one. As the Internet began its rapid rise, AOL successfully made the transition from a proprietary service. By 1996 AOL was approaching 10 million members and expanding into Europe. In 1997 AOL acquired Compuserve, boosting its audience past 12 million. By the end of the century it was pushing 20 million.

Compuserve had been entirely character-based since it's debut in the late 1970s. AOL stole the lead by integrating client-based graphic elements, updates to which were downloaded and stored locally whenever a user logged on to the network. Pioneer online users in the early 1990s constantly bemoaned the time lost waiting for AOL graphics to arrive. (At about the same time, Compuserve developed the GIF format, a compression algorithm for photos that became ubiquitous.) By the time the Internet started to mushroom in 1995, PCs were powerful enough and modems were fast enough so that graphic elements could be downloaded as needed. It was no longer necessary to store them in advance. World Wide Web pioneers constantly bemoaned the time lost waiting for these graphics, too. At the turn of the century, the industry was still a wild frontier, and the early settlers put up with conditions that would have been unacceptable to their more civilized cousins back east. No other medium established itself so quickly: and no other medium offered so little control to publishers and producers. Imagine television in the early 1950s if every set received the broadcast signal differently, and sometimes not at all. Because so much depends on the browser software, that's still the case with the World Wide Web.

The large, centralized commercial networks like AOL took as their architectural model the television networks of the previous media age. Intending to be general public services, they tried to be all things to all people but quickly felt the weight of this responsibility. Entertainment may be something that we share communally, but information—the heart of these services—is profoundly private. Each of us has different requirements. The model should have been magazine publishing, not broadcast television. In France, it was, partly by accident. For political reasons, the French government had decreed at the beginning that all Minitel services were to be operated by existing print publishers. As a result, many of the early services followed the special-interest model of their print progenitors, and quickly found committed audiences. Service operators in the U.S. had to learn this the hard way.

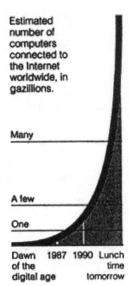

Estimated number of computers connected to the Internet worldwide, in gazillions.

Many

A few

One

Dawn of the digital age   1987   1990   Lunch time tomorrow

Figure 7-21. With a rare display of wit, The *New York Times* ran this graph to accompany a serious story on the growth of the Internet at the beginning of net mania. May 15, 1994. *(Copyright 1994 by the New York Times Company. Reprinted by permission.)*

Partly as a response to this need, by 1994 the Internet had become the online focus of attention in the press. Descendent of the Defense Department's Arpanet, the Internet provided a massive network of interconnected host computers around the world, and therefore what appeared to be a perfect path to an infinite variety of special-interest services. What's more, it was "free," since the government and the universities were still contributing to its upkeep.[*] This transition happened more quickly than anyone familiar with the long history of the Internet could have forecast. Like fax before it, the Net was a technology with more than a twenty-year history behind it when it took off. Most observers credited its metamorphosis from a network of government, scientific, and military networks to an international commercial online medium of unprecedented power to the development of the technology known as the "World Wide Web."

Tim Berners-Lee, an Englishman working at the European Center for Particle Physics ("CERN") in Switzerland first suggested the concept of the World Wide Web in 1989 and developed the basic hypertext technology in 1990. It was based on work he had done as early as 1980. The idea of hypertext linking was not new; but the ambition of linking to anywhere on the Internet had profound implica-

---

[*]   This is one of the more remarkable aspects of Internet history. The government no longer supports the network, but the transition has been seamless and economically painless. The commercial opportunities appear to be so vast, that the telecommunications companies have been more than willing to invest tens of billions to develop the necessary communications infrastructure.

tions. Imagine a library where any book—indeed any page in any book—appears instantly in front of you whenever you think to request it. Now imagine that that page is always from the latest edition, and that it can be illustrated with audio and video as well as with still pictures (and those illustrations do not have to reside on the page; they can exist anywhere). That is the vision of the World Wide Web.

For the first few years, the World Wide Web was mainly a European project—not surprising, since online development had been dominated by French and British projects, while Americans lagged far behind. Then, in September 1993, the National Center for Supercomputing Applications ("NCSA") at the University of Illinois/Urbana-Champaign, released Mosaic, the first fully functional browser (or client software) for the Web. (Marc Andreessen, then a student in his early twenties, is generally given credit for Mosaic.) Within months, interest in the Web exploded, magnifying Internet mania tenfold. In January 1993 1.3 million machines were connected to the Internet; by January, 1996, that number had mushroomed to 9.5 million. Eighteen months after that it had more than doubled to 19.5 million. By July 1999 the count was 56 million.[*]

By mid-1994 hundreds of American corporations had opened "Web sites"; a year later, thousands had. Most of these sites were devoted to marketing information and advertising—anathema to Internet "netizens" just a few months earlier. By mid-1995 no commercial movie opened in the U.S. without its associated Web site. In August 1995 Netscape—the company founded 16 months earlier by Marc Andreessen and Silicon Valley entrepreneur Jim Clark—went public in the most successful initial offering in history until that time. Wall Street valued the company at $2.9 billion.[†] Internet stock mania had begun.

The established media rushed to find a foothold on the Web. Rupert Murdoch's News Corp. took a $2 billion investment from MCI with an Internet fillip. NBC made a deal with Microsoft. By 1996 no major newspaper or television network was without a presence on the World Wide Web. More important, one hundred thousand Web sites had bloomed around the world (as of January 1996), the vast majority operated not by the media giants of broadcasting or print but by individuals, small companies, and public organizations.

---

[*]   Network Wizards, Inc. See WWW.NW.com for current numbers and other useful data on the Web. While you're at it, check out original historical documents at the World Wide Web Consortium (now operated by MIT in association with INRIA) at WWW.W3.org, and NCSA documents at WWW.NCSA.edu.

[†]   After a battle royal with Microsoft for control of the browser market the company was acquired by AOL in November 1998. The announced price was about $4 billion in AOL stock. This was not a very good return on investment for Netscape stockholders. However, by the time the deal was concluded less than four months later, the AOL stock was worth $10 billion to Netscape shareholders.

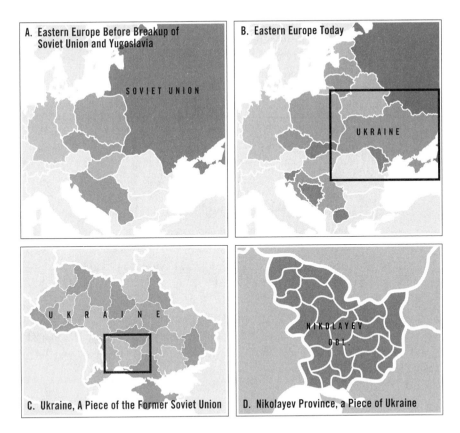

Figure 7-22. POLITICAL FRACTALIZATION. The disintegration of national structures in Eastern Europe in the nineties revealed the political fractalization that created them in the first place. Just as fractal mathematics are used to build complex figures out of small designs, so, in reverse order, larger political units break down into smaller and smaller components until neighbor takes up arms against neighbor.

Search engine companies proved to be almost as valuable as Netscape, the browser company. When Yahoo went public in 1996 they were valued at $300 million. This may not seem like a lot in Internet dollars, but—remember—there were fewer than 30 employees at the time. Because of the vast amount of material available on the Internet, the search engines, which indexed and sorted the world's websites, served as unofficial entry points. As such, they quickly garnered much of the advertising revenue that soon began to flow. By 1998 such magnet sites had been dubbed "portals" and the established media companies rushed to acquire them. In the next 18 months Disney bought Infoseek; Excite was acquired by @Home (with AT&T behind them); Lycos was the target of Barry Diller's USA Networks (although the deal fell through).

By late 1998 it was clear that the Web had established itself not only as major market, but also as the virtual engine of the economy. Priceline, a startup that sold discount airline tickets, had a market value in excess of the total for the top airlines, for example. Although the web was seriously cutting into the limited pie of consumer entertainment time, it had not yet found its share of consumer entertainment dollars. That was about to change. By 1998 every high-school and college student who had the bandwidth (and most did: bandwidth was a major recruiting point for colleges and universities after 1995) was into acquiring and trading MP3 music files. This audio compression technology pointed the way to a media universe where copyright was going to be about as valuable as the paper it was written on. Piracy, a nagging problem for music and video distributors since the late 1970s, was now about to become the norm rather than the exception, thanks to the digitization of the media and the increasing bandwidth of Internet connections.

In just five years the phenomenon of the World Wide Web had had a significant impact on the information industry, advertising, and the entertainment business. But these effects were dwarfed by the Web's potential for "e-commerce." This vast collection of digital ganglia had quickly altered the commercial value of intellectual property. At the turn of the century, with its lure of efficient markets and simplified sales channels, the Web was poised to change the basic way we do business with each other.

You say you want a revolution?

"What Is to be Done?"

In 1980, the second edition of *How To Read a Film* concluded with a note on democracy in the media which observed that, while new technology had extended our power to create media, distribution of print, film, and television was still concentrated in a relatively small number of hands:

> The pervasion of the media has been a common theme in science fiction ever since George Orwell's vision of *1984*: "The instrument, the telescreen, could be dimmed but there was no way of shutting it off completely." But the facts bear repeating: what we still choose to call "reality" is now largely determined for us. It is not only that someone else is telling our stories— it's also the kinds of stories they're telling.

We then suggested that the channels of distribution were about to broaden, too, and listed a litany of imminent technologies from electronic mail to video on demand, from online data services to fiber optic cable, from direct-to-home satellite broadcasting to computers in every home. Many of these innovations are now part of our daily lives. Others are still on the horizon. But one thing is clear: the digital revolution has radically altered the way we deal with reality—no matter who determines it.

My children, who were born after *How To Read a Film* first appeared and who largely grew up before I got around to the third edition, have enjoyed a wealth of media unknown before 1980. They are prodigious consumers of television, video, CDs, computer games, software, and theatrical movies, and—perhaps surprisingly, considering the wealth of new media—are not unfamiliar with the printed word. I may complain at the dinner table about our familial addiction to television (they may dim the telescreen, but there is no way they will shut it off completely), but they may be just as well read as their parents were at their age.

More important than the vast quantities of media they consume is the equally remarkable quantity they produce. They have at their disposal a range of software tools that would have astonished any professional writer, filmmaker, or painter twenty years ago. From the time they were six, they spent almost as much time actively creating as passively consuming.* Shortly after they discovered Hyper-Card, they began a series of illustrated stories. When Apple added sound to the software, so did they. To them this wasn't multimedia; it was fun.

The Orwellian year has come and gone. (We've forgotten who won the Super Bowl, but we remember the commercial.) The warnings about control of the media seem less pointed than they did fifteen years ago. We are now, most of us, so intoxicated with our new power to produce and to distribute media (media of all sorts: multi, uni, ulti, hyper, visual, textual, and traditional) that we could care less who owns the old-fashioned media. A. J. Liebling, the great press critic, noted almost forty years ago that "freedom of the press belongs to those who own one." We are now nearly at the point where we all own one—and a film lab, and a recording studio.

More important, the significant increase in distribution bandwidth during the eighties and nineties resulted in a political equilibrium in the media that is as frustrating as it is welcome. Most points of view get heard. Most people have an acquaintance with the issues of the day. No social or political problem is left untreated in telefilms or talkshows. Most new ideas find their way to the public forum quickly and efficiently. It is no longer us against them. It is them against them. The political and social dialectic has evaporated under the incessant and copious bombardment of more channels, more technologies, more media.

Alain Tanner forecast this state of affairs a long time ago in *Au Milieu du Monde* (1974):

---

* Lest you dismiss this as just a father's boast, I should admit the near balance was only possible because they worked on the computer at the same time that they watched television.

We are in an age of normalization, where exchange is permitted, and nothing changes.

We have democratized the media more quickly and more thoroughly than we ever dared hope. Now we have the power. Do we know how to use it?

Raymond Williams observed in *Communications* (1976):

> In societies like Britain and the United States, more drama is watched in a week or a weekend by the majority of viewers, than would have been watched in a year, or in some cases a lifetime in any previous historical period. It is not uncommon for the majority of viewers to see, regularly, as much as two or three hours of drama, of various kinds, every day. The implications of this have scarcely begun to be considered. It is clearly one of the unique characteristics of advanced industrial societies that drama as an experience is now an intrinsic part of everyday life, at a quantitative level which is so very much greater than any precedent as to seem a fundamental qualitative change.

Of course the numbers have changed since Williams wrote. "Two to three hours" now seems like a frugal budget, and to the experience of broadcast drama we must add news-as-entertainment, video games, tapes and discs, multimedia, and Internet mail, newsgroups, mailing lists, and the Web.

And one implication, at least, is beginning to become clear: we are losing our grounding in reality. We are well on our way to David Bowman's fearful cage. Someone points out that highways are noisy, so we build walls around them, oblivious to the fact that we cut ourselves off visually and morally from our surroundings. We discover that asbestos is carcinogenic, so we spend billions removing it from every public building, without even thinking to calculate the danger (or lack of it) of leaving it quietly in place. We rewrite history so that it won't be offensive. We pay lip service to certain social and political problems we identified more than thirty years ago, but little has changed.

We have the words of science, but not the scientific spirit. We have the rhetoric of commitment, but not the will to act. We are as a society at all times Politically Correct, without paying much heed to the consequences of the loss of a sense of balance—or a sense of humor.

We have, to a large extent, as Raymond Williams intimated, given ourselves over to the fictions and quasi-fictions of the media. And the people who make media are no smarter than we are. Our films and television are technically proficient, relevant, democratic—and dull. Our new technologies are theoretically exciting, but "You say you want a revolution?" There are no revolutions anymore. The culture has been homogenized, and the balance is every bit as problematic as the imbalance we once strove to overcome.

"What is to be done?" We cannot stop the juggernaut that is the contemporary media. It will continue to saturate our lives. New modes of discourse, because they insist that the reader become an active participant in the process, may give us opportunities to find our roots again. But ethics is the esthetics of the future. We must focus on the uses to which our talents and technologies are put. It is no longer sufficient to know how to read a film. Now we must also understand, in a profound way, how to *use* a film.

[Please choose an ending.]

1

And most important, we need to remember that there is still a vestige of reality beyond film, beyond media, beyond multimedia.

In this, we have a guide. Writing in *The New Yorker* in the autumn of 1947 at about the same time George Orwell was sketching his dark vision of the future, essayist E. B. White extrapolated a world of media uncannily like our own. "Preposterous Parables: The Decline of Sport" drolly suggests a nation "in the third decade of the supersonic age" obsessed with games, besieged by loud and multifarious media, and laced breathless with superhighways (the concrete kind).

Because of the fever, "records fell like ripe apples on a windy day," he notes. "Customs and manners changed, and the five-day business week was reduced to four days, then to three, to give everyone a better chance to memorize the scores." In this world, as in our own, no one is content to take in one event at a time, "and thanks to the magic of radio and television nobody had to." What they don't see on the field, they watch on the video scoreboard, or listen to on implanted radios, or watch on pocket televisions. Like the postsurrealist fantasies of artist Bruce McCall, White's parable finds warm comfort in mild absurdity.

As it turns out, this media bubble is about to burst. In White's dream, the Midwest's classic Dust Bowl game of 1975, when a football player is shot by a disgruntled spectator, marks the turning point, beginning a chain of other disasters in the stadiums and on the highways. "All in all, the afternoon of sport cost 20,003 lives. A record," White reports.

> From that day on, sport waned. Through long, noncompetitive Saturday afternoons, the stadia slumbered. Even the parkways fell into disuse as motorists rediscovered the charms of old, twisty roads that led through main streets and past barnyards, with their mild congestions and pleasant smells. It's time for us to hit those twisty roads again.

Figure 7-23. David Bowman's virtual cage at the conclusion to *2001: A Space Odyssey*. (*Frame enlargement.*)

2

And most important, we need to remember that there is still a vestige of reality beyond film, beyond media, beyond multimedia.

In this, we have a teacher. Gertrude Stein, a founder of the modern movement and cogent observer of it, made it clear that "Rose is a rose is a rose is a rose." (She would have found Chapter 3 tedious, perhaps.) For Stein, poetry isn't what gets lost in translation, it is "really loving the name of anything." She is as well remembered for her Paris salon as for her literary art, and rightly so, for everyday life was as important to her as literature. Like so many of her colleagues and friends at the time, from Picasso to Hemingway, her life was a work of art—a separate autobiography. In the Renaissance, the Italian word for this quality was "sprezzatura," a kind of impatience with raw, unformed existence. Stein knew the proper balance between art and life.

We have spent seven chapters investigating the former. Gertrude Stein had the answer to the latter. In one of the great exit lines in history, she exclaimed on her deathbed:

What is the answer?

A few moments passed before she concluded:

What is the question!

That was the answer. Then she was gone.

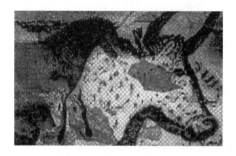 

Figure 7-24. Details from the Main Rotunda of the Lascaux cave paintings, Dordogne, France circa 15,000 BC: very real images, shadows from a pre-Platonic time that bring us back to the beginning. (*Bettman Archives/UPI.*)

3

And most important, we need to remember that there is still a vestige of reality beyond film, beyond media, beyond multimedia.

In this, we have a model. At the height of his career, William Shakespeare quit the playwrighting business to return to his home town. His last play, *The Tempest*, was a conscious envoi to the audiences that had filled the Globe for more than twenty years. It was about theater, his medium, but it is not a celebration so much as an escape. There is a real world outside the theatrical island of the play, and the aim of *The Tempest* and of Prospero (and of Shakespeare, we may infer) is to leave the magic behind and return to that reality. At the end, Prospero asks our leave:

> Now my charms are all o'erthrown,
> And what strength I have's mine own,
> Which is most faint.
> * * *
> Gentle breath of yours my sails
> Must fill, or else my project fails,
> Which was to please. Now I want
> Spirits to enforce, art to enchant;
> And my ending is despair
> Unless I be reliev'd by prayer,
> Which pierces so that it assaults
> Mercy itself and frees all faults.
> As you from crimes would pardon'd be,
> Let your indulgence set me free.
>
> *Exit.*

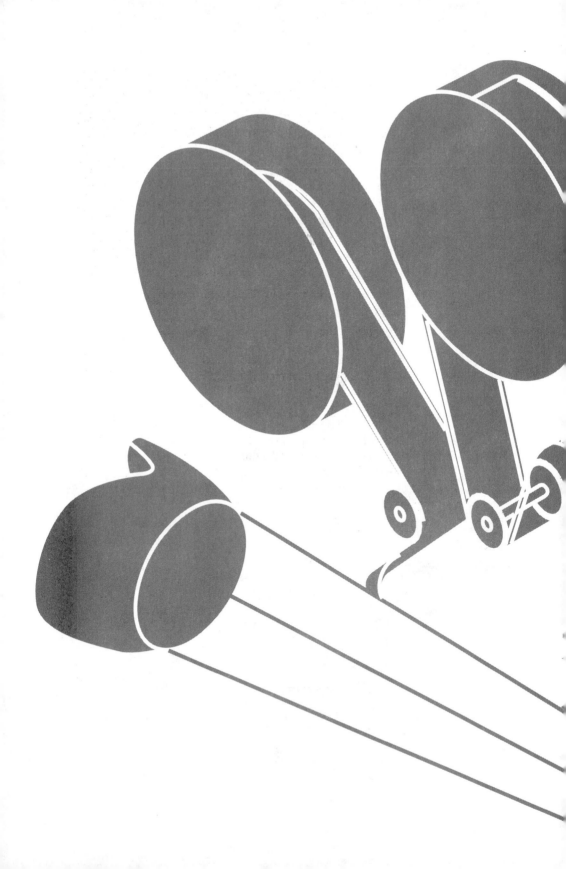

FILM AND MEDIA: A CHRONOLOGY

To 1895: Prehistory

130
Ptolemy of Alexandria discovers the phenomenon of persistence of vision.

1250
Leon Battista Alberti invents forerunner of camera obscura.

1456
August 24. Heinrich Cremer finishes binding the first Gutenberg bibles, first books to be printed with movable type.

1700s
Rise of newspapers and journals.

1800s
Development of widespread literacy in England and elsewhere in Europe, and development as a consequence of mass media culture of books, magazines, and newspapers.

1810
König's steam-powered printing press.

1827
March 16. The first African-American newspaper, *Freeman's Journal*, appears.

1834
Zoetrope, based on an ancient invention, patented.

1839
Daguerreotype and Talbottype announced.

1844

Morse's telegraph.

1846

Hoe's rotary press.

1850

Photographic magic lantern slides come into use.

1867

Sholes invents typewriter, to be exploited by Remington.

1873

Muybridge's experiments begin in photography of motion. He is successful in 1877.

1874

Émile Baudot, French engineer, receives a patent for his 5-unit telegraph code—a great improvement over Morse code, and a foundation for the digital world of a hundred years later.

1876

Bell's telephone.

1877

Edison's phonograph.
Reynaud's Praxinoscope.

1880

New York Graphic prints the first halftone photographs.

1884

Eastman's roll paper photographic medium.
Mergenthaler's Linotype.
The Nipkow disc introduces the concept of scanning.

1886

Henry James hires Scotsman Alexander Pollock Watt to manage his affairs. "He takes 10% of what he gets for me," writes James, "but I am advised that his favorable action...more than makes up for this." Watt thus becomes the first literary agent.

1889

Development of Eastman's flexible roll film medium for photography.
Dickson demonstrates Kinetophone to Edison.

1891

Development of the Kinetoscope private viewer.

1895

December 28. Lumières' first public showing of Cinématographe films at Grand Café, Boulevard des Capucines, Paris.
Max Skladanowsky completes Bioskop projector.

American Mutoscope and Biograph Company founded; originally known as the K.M.C.D. Syndicate (after its founders, E. B. Koopman, Henry N. Marvin, Herman Casler, and W. K. L. Dickson).

1896–1915: The Birth of Film

1896
April 23. Edison's first show at Koster and Bial's Music Hall, New York.
September 2. Marconi demonstrates wireless telegraphy in England.

1897
Edison begins patent infringement suits.
May. Fire at film showing at Bazar de la Charité takes 140 lives.
Edwin Porter joins Edison's company.

1899
James Stuart Blackton founds Vitagraph Company.

1900
At the International Exposition in Paris, prototypical color and sound film systems are demonstrated.
Danish telephone engineer Valdemar Poulsen patents "telegraphone," a wire recording system.

1901
First transatlantic wireless transmission, by Marconi from England to Newfoundland.
Queen Victoria's funeral reported via film.
Fessenden begins experiments in voice transmission.

1902
Méliès's *Voyage to the Moon.*
T. L. Tally's Electric Theatre opens in Los Angeles.
The first Ealing studio is built in the western suburbs of London by Will Barber.
Pathé opens studio at Vincennes.

1903
Porter's *The Life of an American Fireman* and *The Great Train Robbery.*
Biograph moves to an indoor studio on New York's East 14th Street.

1905
Hepworth's *Rescued by Rover.*

1906
DeForest invents Audion vacuum tube.

1907
Griffith begins work in film as an actor.

1908

Émile Cohl (in France) and Winsor McKay (in the U.S.) begin work in animation.
Pathé leads industry in abandoning outright sales of film in favor of rentals.
Film d'art movement begins in France.
June. American Biograph hires D. W. Griffith.

1909

The Motion Picture Patents Company is founded, soon followed by the General
  Film Company (distributors). Patent wars begin.

1910

Griffith and his company begin wintering in Los Angeles. The locus of major film
  activity shifts from New York to Los Angeles within the next few years.

1911

Mack Sennett's first Keystone comedy produced.

1912

Armstrong's regenerative circuit developed.
Warner brothers begin producing films; Fox company and Universal formed.
British Board of Film Censors formed.
First fan magazines appear.

1913

Italian epics *Quo Vadis?* and *Cabiria* suggest value of feature-length films.

1915

Griffith's *The Birth of a Nation* signals beginning of new period in film history.
Vachel Lindsay's *The Art of the Moving Picture* published.

1916–1930: Silent Film, the Births of Radio and Sound Film

1916

Griffith's *Intolerance.*
Münsterberg's *The Photoplay: A Psychological Study* published.

1917

UFA formed in Germany.
Kuleshov's workshop begins in Soviet Union.

1918

Armstrong's Superheterodyne circuit makes radio a commercial possibility.

1919

United Artists formed. Star system dominant in film industry.
General Electric creates Radio Corporation of America to take over monopoly of
  American Marconi Company.
Soviet film industry nationalized.

Tri-Ergon sound-on-film system patented in Germany.
Wiene's *Cabinet of Dr. Caligari*. German Expressionist movement begins.

1920

Thanks in part to World War I, America dominates world film industry.
Immigration of filmmakers to Hollywood starts.
KDKA begins broadcasting in Pittsburgh.

1922

August 28. 5:15 pm. The first radio commercial: Mr. Blackwell, for the Queens-
boro Corp. on AT&T's WEAF in New York.
Lang's *Dr. Mabuse*.
Vertov's *Kino-Pravda*.
Flaherty's *Nanook of the North*.
BBC begins informally in Britain.

1923

Stiller's *Saga of Gösta Berling*, starring Greta Garbo.
Stroheim's *Greed*, forerunner of contemporary realism.
Time—first "newsmagazine"—begins publication.

1924

Columbia Pictures founded, MGM consolidated.
Léger's *Ballet Mécanique*.

1925

London Film Society founded; film study develops in France.
Eisenstein's *Battleship Potemkin*.

1926

August 6. Vitaphone (sound-on-record) premiere: *Don Juan*.
November 15. 8 pm to 12:25 am NBC begins network broadcasting with a pro-
gram from the roof of the Waldorf-Astoria Hotel in New York featuring the New
York Symphony, the New York Oratorio Society, Will Rogers, Weber & Fields,
and Vincent Lopez. Twenty-five stations in 21 cities broadcast the program.
Pudovkin's *Film Technique* published.
Rudolph Valentino dies.

1927

British Cinematograph Act provides for a quota system.
BBC chartered.
U.S. Radio Act creates Federal Radio Commission (later FCC).
Roxy Theatre opens in New York.
April. Fox Movietone News begins, using sound-on-film system.
October 6. Warner Brothers' *The Jazz Singer*, with music and several talking
sequences, first popular sound success.
CBS formed.
January 1. NBC's Blue network begins broadcasting.
German inventor Pfleumer devises magnetic tape system.

1928

RKO Radio Pictures Corporation formed by G.E./Westinghouse/R.C.A. to exploit R.C.A.'s sound patents in film.

Television demonstrated by John Logie Baird in London.

Massive transition to sound leads to increased influence of banking interests in film production.

Crossley Radio Survey ratings begin. First published 1930.

First "all-talking" picture: *Lights of N.Y.*

Dreyer's *Passion de Jeanne d'Arc.*

Vertov's *Man with a Movie Camera.*

Dali and Buñuel's *Un Chien Andalou.*

1929

Hitchcock's *Blackmail*, first British dialogue film.

Mamoulian's *Applause,* one of the first successful musicals.

Marx Brothers' first film, *The Cocoanuts,* presages massive exodus of Broadway talent to Hollywood.

Amos 'n' Andy becomes first popular NBC network series.

Conversion to sound has resulted in nearly twofold increase in box-office admission in two years (1927: 60 million admissions; 1929: 110 million).

Electrical transcription introduced to radio.

1930

Production Code instituted, but laxly enforced.

Necessity of foreign-language versions for export results in second wave of influx of European talent to Hollywood.

Clair's *Sous les toits de Paris*, first French sound film.

Von Sternberg's *Blue Angel,* with Marlene Dietrich.

Disney's first *Silly Symphony.*

U.S. brings antitrust suit against RCA and its patent allies.

Grierson, Rotha, Wright, and Jennings involved in British documentary movement.

1931–1945: The Great Age of Hollywood and Radio

1931

Hecht and MacArthur's play *The Front Page* is filmed by Lewis Milestone. It marks the continued growth in importance of newspapers as a cultural medium.

Wellman's *Public Enemy* marks rise of Gangster genre.

Chaplin's *City Lights* filmed with music-only soundtrack.

Dracula and *Frankenstein,* emblems of the Horror genre.

Murnau and Flaherty collaborate on semidocumentary *Tabu.*

1932

Hawks, Hughes, and Hecht collaborate on *Scarface,* major Gangster film.

Postdubbing techniques put into practice, greatly facilitating the shooting of sound films.

Radio City Music Hall, the ultimate movie palace, opens in the Radio City complex, home of RCA, in Rockefeller Center.

Venice Film Festival—first of its kind—begins.

Lubitsch's *Trouble in Paradise* confirms the Paramount style of sophisticated comedy for the decade.

1933

Astaire and Rogers in *Flying Down to Rio* establish a style of urbane sophistication that marks much entertainment of the 1930s.

Cooper and Schoedsack's *King Kong* evokes racial fears to establish a popular myth.

Busby Berkeley's choreography for *42nd Street* establishes a style for the Musical of the 1930s.

Arnheim's *Film as Art* published.

German film industry under Nazi control.

British Film Institute founded.

Armstrong develops FM radio.

First "Fireside Chats" by President Roosevelt utilize radio medium.

1934

Breen strengthens censorship under Production Code.

Capra's *It Happened One Night,* major early Screwball Comedy, along with Hawks's *Twentieth Century.*

Riefenstahl's *Triumph of the Will* celebrates Nazi mystique.

British government involved in financing documentaries.

Flaherty completes *Man of Aran.*

The Communications Act of 1934 recognizes the interdependency of telephone, telegraph, and radio (and television) broadcasting but treats the older media differently from the new radio industry. Telephone and telegraph are seen as natural monopolies and designated as "common carriers" that must furnish service as requested at rates governed by an organization to be called the Federal Communications Commission. Broadcasting, however, is considered a competitive activity. The principle of public ownership of the airwaves is recognized: the FCC will issue limited licenses to broadcasters and govern the nature of their activities.

1935

Technicolor three-strip process comes into use.

De Rochemont's March of Time series of documentaries begins.

"Audimeter"—device for radio broadcast ratings—invented.

1936

BBC begins television service (to be interrupted by the war).

Cinémathèque Française founded by Henri Langlois, Georges Franju, and Jean Mitry.

Chaplin's *Modern Times.*

Capra's *Mr. Deeds Goes to Town* marks cycle of American populist films.

Renoir's *Le Crime de M. Lange.*
Life magazine debuts.

1937

Renoir's *Grand Illusion.*
Arriflex lightweight 35 mm camera—the first with reflex shutter—introduced.

1938

Eisenstein's *Alexander Nevsky.*
Michael Balcon takes over production at Ealing Studios.
October 31. Welles's *War of the Worlds* radio broadcast.

1939

National Film Board of Canada founded.
Hollywood's greatest year: Selznick's *Gone With the Wind* and MGM's *The Wizard of Oz* (both directed by Victor Fleming) become classics of entertainment fantasy.
John Ford's *Stagecoach*, classic Western.
Renoir's *The Rules of the Game.*
April 30. President Roosevelt appears in a telecast at the World's Fair in New York marking the inauguration of regular television service in the U.S.
June 19. Pocket Books, a new company partly owned by Simon & Schuster, puts ten pocket-size paper-covered books priced at 25 cents each on sale at Macy's and a few Manhattan newsstands. The paperback revolution begins.
August 26. First major-league baseball telecast: a doubleheader between the Brooklyn Dodgers and the Cincinnati Reds.

1940

January 12. First American television network broadcast on WNBT-TV, New York, and WRGB-TV, Schenectady.
August. CBS demonstrates their color television system, developed by Peter Goldmark.
Hitchcock moves to Hollywood.
Murrow's broadcasts from London during the Blitz dramatize news value of radio.

1941

Renoir moves to Hollywood.
Ford's *The Grapes of Wrath*, from Steinbeck novel.
Huston's *The Maltese Falcon* establishes his reputation, Bogart's, and the Detective genre.
Welles's *Citizen Kane*, "the great American movie."

1942

Noël Coward's *In Which We Serve* marks paradoxical revitalization of British film during the war.
Capra's *Why We Fight* series of effective documentary propaganda.

1943

Maya Deren's *Meshes of the Afternoon* marks renewed development of the American avant garde.
First wire sound recorders in use in the military.
Due to antitrust suit, ABC created out of NBC's second network.

Institut des Hautes Études Cinématographiques founded by Marcel L'Herbier.

1944

Technicolor Monopack system first used for features.

1945

Rossellini's *Rome, Open City* and De Sica's *Shoeshine* mark Neorealism.

De Rochemont applies semidocumentary style to fiction in *The House on 92nd Street.*

Murrow reports from Buchenwald.

German tape recorders captured.

The ENIAC (Electronic Numerical Integrator Analyzor and Computer) is completed in November at the University of Pennsylvania.

1946–1960: The Growth of Television

1946

February 14. The War Department announces the development of ENIAC. For the first time, electronic speed is applied to numerical tasks. The device covers 15,000 square feet of the basement of the Moore School of Electronic Engineering at the University of Pennsylvania.

American film industry's best year at the box office: $1.7 billion in receipts.

Cannes Film Festival founded.

Sony Corporation founded by Akio Morita.

Paramount antitrust suit begins.

American television networks begin broadcasting; BBC resumes.

Hawks's *The Big Sleep* presages Film Noir genre.

Wyler's *The Best Years of Our Lives,* popular study of the effects of war.

Hitchcock's *Notorious.*

June 8. Milton Berle's first television show. He will become known as "Mr. Television."

June 19. First television network sponsor: Gillette, for the Joe Louis vs. Billy Conn boxing match.

1947

October 1. The *Philco Radio Hour* with Bing Crosby is the first taped, delayed radio broadcast.

October 20. House Un-American Activities Committee (HUAC) begins hearings on "Communist influence in Hollywood"; nineteen Hollywood personalities are subpoenaed by HUAC to testify about their knowledge of or possible involvement in Communist Party activities.

November 24. At notorious meeting at New York's Waldorf-Astoria Hotel, Eastern bankers inform studio executives that investment funds will be curtailed if the studios do not cooperate with HUAC. The studios quickly capitulate, informing employees that a refusal to cooperate means that they will have their employment terminated.

Actor's Studio founded by Robert Lewis, Cheryl Crawford, and Elia Kazan and run by Lee Strasberg from 1948. The studio was home of the "method," an acting technique based on the concepts of Constantin Stanislavski.

La Revue du Cinéma founded by critic and theorist André Bazin, along with Jacques Doniol-Valcroze. Four years later it is renamed *Cahiers du Cinéma*.

Capra's *It's a Wonderful Life*, last in populist tradition.

The transistor is invented at Bell Labs.

1948

Astruc's essay on "Caméra-Stylo" published.

Howard Hughes buys RKO.

Black radio stations begin broadcasting.

Milton Berle's *Texaco Star Theatre* begins television comedy format.

Ed Sullivan's *Toast of the Town* begins television variety format.

June 21. Goldmark's LP record unveiled.

1949

Donen and Kelly's *On the Town:* new-style Musical.

Stop the Music, first TV quiz show, debuts.

For the first time, more paperback books are sold than hardcovers.

1950

Blacklist in radio and television in full swing.

Eastmancolor stock introduced.

Cocteau's *Orpheus.*

Ophüls's *La Ronde.*

Wilder's *Sunset Boulevard.*

Sid Caesar, Imogene Coca begin *Your Show of Shows.*

1951

Murrow and Friendly begin *See It Now* series.

Paramount signs consent decree on antitrust suit.

Lucille Ball's *I Love Lucy* sets the model for television situation comedy; its success indicates film can work in television.

Jack Webb's *Dragnet* premieres, setting the model for television cop shows.

NBC's *Today* program begins, mixing news and features.

Nyby's *The Thing* among first paranoid Science-Fiction films of the decade.

Kurosawa's *Rashomon* successful at Venice Film Festival.

Cahiers du Cinéma begins.

First coast-to-coast television broadcast via AT&T's coaxial cable.

1952

Community Antenna television, precursor of cable, begins.

Kelly and Donen's *Singin' in the Rain.*

Zinnemann's *High Noon*, "adult" Western.

Decca purchases Universal.

Sony develops stereo broadcasting in Japan.

Cinerama debuts.

Nixon's televised "Checkers" speech.

1953

January 19. Desi Arnaz Jr is born the same day that the episode of *I Love Lucy* in which his fictional alter ego is born is telecast.

RKO liquidated by owner, General Tire Corp.

CinemaScope and 3-D introduced.

Hitchcock's *Rear Window.*

Chayefsky's *Marty* on *Goodyear Television Playhouse* signals the heyday of live television drama.

1954

January 1. NBC broadcasts Festival of Roses parade in color: first network colorcast.

January 1. NTSC standard color broadcasting begins in the U.S.

January. Truffaut's essay "Une certaine tendance du cinéma français" published in *Cahiers du Cinéma.*

Fellini's *La Strada,* international success.

Kazan's *On the Waterfront* reinforces Marlon Brando's position as the emblematic star of the 1950s.

Murrow's *See It Now* broadcast about Senator McCarthy has significant political effect.

Televised Army-McCarthy hearings result in McCarthy's disgrace and beginning of the end for the blacklist.

Disney and Warner Bros. contract to produce for ABC.

1955

Satyajit Ray's *Pather Panchali* introduces Indian film to West.

Commercial (ITV) channel begins broadcasting in U.K.

Nicholas Ray's *Rebel Without a Cause* sets the tone for the late fifties.

James Dean dies.

The Village Voice founded. It will be a major force in the counterculture through the 1960s.

U.S. Census Bureau reports that 67 percent of all U.S. homes have television. TV revenue surpasses radio revenue by the end of the year.

1956

Release of hundreds of pre-1948 feature films to television signals the new relationship between film and broadcasting industries.

Ford's *The Searchers,* his most complex Western.

Bergman's *The Seventh Seal,* internationally successful.

IBM introduces the magnetic disk as a storage medium for computer data.

IBM enters into a consent decree with the Justice Department forcing the dominant computer company to segregate its computer services business from its other operations.

November 30. First use of videotape in television: the West Coast feed of *Douglas Edwards with the News,* CBS.

1957

RKO studios sold to Desilu for television production.

Pocket transistor radios introduced.

1958

Stereophonic records and phonographs first marketed.
Hitchcock's *Vertigo.*

1959

Hitchcock's *North by Northwest.*
Birth of the New Wave: Truffaut's *The 400 Blows,* Resnais's *Hiroshima, mon amour.*
Fellini's *La Dolce Vita,* together with other films released this year, marks a turning point in world cinema.
Cassavetes's *Shadows* suggests the possibility of a more personal American cinema.
Decca/Universal merges with MCA talent agency.
First regular series color broadcasts: *Bonanza,* NBC.
The Integrated Circuit is introduced by Texas Instruments and Fairchild Semiconductor. It will soon empower the "transistor sisters" of the decade.

1960

Godard debuts with *Breathless.*
Reisz's *Saturday Night and Sunday Morning,* first major British working-class film.
Hitchcock's *Psycho.*
Videotape now in general use in broadcasting.
First demonstration of laser device, by Hughes Aircraft Co.
March 1. Haloid Corporation ships the first Xerox photocopier.
Leacock-Pennebaker's *Primary* first major Direct Cinema production, indicates new directions for documentary.
Kracauer's *Theory of Film: The Redemption of Physical Reality* published.
Antonioni's *L'Avventura.*
Rouch's *Chronique d'un été,* first film of cinéma vérité.
In-flight movies introduced on airlines.
Screen Actors Guild strikes Hollywood to gain share of residual rights for films sold to television.

1961–1980: The Media World

1961

Buñuel's *Viridiana* marks his return to Europe.
Bergman begins his trilogy with *Through a Glass Darkly.*
Directors trained in television move into film.
September. NBC introduces theatrical movies into prime-time scheduling with *How To Marry a Millionaire,* on *Saturday Night at the Movies.*

1962

Truffaut's *Jules and Jim.*
Dr. No (Terrence Young) begins James Bond series.
Subscription television experiments begin in California.
Johnny Carson takes over NBC's late-night talkshow; this type of programming grows in importance throughout the next thirty years.

Ernie Kovacs, inventive television comedian, dies at age 42.

Telstar 1 launched.

Fellini's *8 1/2*.

All-Channel rule of the FCC goes into effect, requiring all television sets sold in the U.S. to be equipped to receive UHF.

Young German filmmakers issue "Autorenkino" manifesto at the Oberhausen Short Film Festival.

1963

Kubrick's *Dr. Strangelove*.

Swedish Film Institute founded.

Holography demonstrated, developed by Ein Leith and Juris Upatnieks, based on work by Dennis Gabor in 1947.

American Airlines' SABRE is the first computerized reservation system, and the model for future online systems.

Cleopatra is a notorious financial disaster.

Philips introduces the audiocassette format.

1964

Godard's *A Married Woman* develops cinema as essay.

McLuhan's *Understanding Media* published.

Antonioni's *Red Desert*.

Lester's *A Hard Day's Night* with The Beatles helps establish the new rock music.

April. IBM introduces the 360, founding a new generation of mainframe computers.

1965

Super-8 mm film format introduced for amateur market.

April 6. "Early Bird" satellite, Intelsat I, is launched. It is the first commercial communications satellite and also the first geosynchronous communications satellite.

CBS joins NBC as an all-color network. ABC follows a few months later marking completion of conversion from black and white.

Lockheed's Dialog opens for business, first online database.

Digital Equipment Corporation's PDP-8 is regarded as the first minicomputer.

1966

Godard's *2 or 3 Things I Know About Her*.

Rossellini continues work in television with *The Rise to Power of Louis XIV*.

Bergman's *Persona* and Antonioni's *Blow-Up* draw new intellectual interest to film.

Loach's television film *Cathy Come Home* results in changes in British housing laws.

Gulf + Western buys Paramount.

FCC ruling requires separate programming on FM stations. FM develops rapidly in the next few years, drawing on the new rock music.

1967

The *World-Journal-Tribune*, a New York newspaper that was the result of a merger of no less than seven papers, dies after little more than year.

Seven Arts buys Warner Bros.

Corporation for Public Broadcasting formed to develop Public Television network.

Transamerica Corporation buys United Artists.

New Line Cinema founded in Greenwich Village by Robert Shaye.

Multitrack recording techniques are perfected.

Frederick Wiseman begins his career as documentarist for National Educational Television.

Public Broadcasting Laboratory develops magazine/essay format.

Smothers Brothers introduce a new sophistication and relevance to U.S. television comedy.

BBC's *The Forsyte Saga* becomes a worldwide success over the next few years and establishes the televised novel as a powerful new form.

Flashing techniques are introduced that significantly expand latitude of filmstock.

Penn's *Bonnie & Clyde* sets a pattern of antiheroes that continues through the seventies.

Lester's *Petulia* investigates the newly developing consciousness of the sixties.

Sjöman's *I Am Curious—Yellow* breaks new ground in the depiction of sexual activities and excites censorship furor.

American Film Institute founded.

Nam June Paik exhibits video works at the Howard Wise Gallery, New York.

1968

Film an important arena for discussion during the political events of May and June in France.

Television coverage of "police riots" at the Democratic National Convention in Chicago in August equally influential. "The whole world is watching," the demonstrators chant.

Czech film renaissance cut short by Soviet invasion of Czechoslovakia.

Laugh-In experiments with new form of television comedy.

Kubrick's *2001: A Space Odyssey* pioneers many new special effects techniques, including front projection.

Kodak introduces 5254 color stock.

Fellini produces *A Director's Notebook* for television.

Rohmer reaches international audiences with intellectual *My Night at Maud's*.

Christian Metz's *Essais sur la signification au cinéma* published.

FCC's "Carterfone" decision allows telephone customers to hook up own equipment to Bell lines.

1969

Growth of photocopying and offset as "instant" printing systems available to individuals and small groups continues.

Development of phototypesetting accelerates.

General-interest magazines continue to decline as special-interest magazines experience rapid growth.

Sesame Street premieres, utilizing TV commercial techniques to teach basic skills.

Warner Brothers–Seven Arts purchased by Kinney National Services, Inc.

Kirk Kerkorian purchases MGM for the first time.

Swiss film experiences a renaissance beginning with the production of Tanner's *La Salamandre*.

Peter Wollen's *Signs and Meaning in the Cinema* published.

Hill's *Butch Cassidy and the Sundance Kid* marks the continued decline in women's roles in the sixties and presages a raft of male bonding friendships in films of the seventies.

Hopper's *Easy Rider* marks the explosion of the short-lived genre of youth films.

Peckinpah's *The Wild Bunch* forecasts increasing violence in film.

Glauber Rocha's *Antonio Das Mortes* signals new interest in Third World Cinema.

Costa-Gavras's *Z* sets a new style for political melodrama.

ABC telecasts Harold Robbins's *The Survivors,* first novel-for-television.

November. Vice President Spiro Agnew attacks television news establishment as "nattering nabobs of negativism."

The Defense Department's Arpanet is online, first network of networks, progenitor of the Internet.

1970

The economic recession reinforces the trend toward fewer American films produced each year.

American interests—which had recently provided as much as 90 percent of the capital for the British film industry—pull out precipitously due to the recession. British filmmakers emigrate to the U.S. or turn to television.

Kluge, Fassbinder, Schlöndorff establish Neue Kino on world screens. Television coproduction is an important element.

The Mary Tyler Moore Show marks renaissance of situation comedy.

Ted Turner buys a local UHF station in Atlanta. It will become superstation TBS.

Robert Altman consolidates his reputation with *M.A.S.H.*—later a popular television series.

Wadleigh's *Woodstock* sets a new style for concert musicals.

The growth of film study begins to accelerate in the U.S.

May. MGM auctions its heritage of props and costumes to raise cash for Kerkorian.

Sony sells Portapak half-inch portable videotape system. Video movement begins.

FCC institutes the "Fin-Syn" rule prohibiting television networks from financial control of syndication operations.

1971

Van Peebles's *Sweet Sweetback's Baadasssss Song* signals the establishment of the Black film.

Marcel Ophuls's *The Sorrow and the Pity* (originally a television program) excites new interest in the documentary interview form as personal essay.

Cable television systems, supplying nonbroadcast product, continue rapid expansion.

All in the Family, based on a British series, is Norman Lear's first television success.

FCC institutes Prime Time Access rule, ostensibly limiting networks to three hours of programming per evening in prime time.

November. Intel introduces the 4004, first microprocessor chip.

Computer memory chips can hold 1 kilobit (1,024 bits) of information each.

IBM introduces the "floppy" magnetic disc for data storage.

FCC authorizes "specialized common carriers" to compete with AT&T in providing long-distance private lines to customers.

Word-processing computers begin to have an effect on office procedures.

1972

Quadraphonic disc system introduced. The public response is minimal.

Life magazine ceases regular publication.

Bertolucci's *Last Tango in Paris* is considered a mature treatment of sex, a landmark in changing moral attitudes.

Godard and Gorin finish Dziga-Vertov experiments with *Tout va bien*. Godard turns to video.

Intel's 8008 is first 8-bit microprocessor.

Canada's Anik I is launched, first domestic communications satellite.

FCC approves common carrier satellite services.

Coppola's *The Godfather* becomes the most profitable film of all time, to date.

Xerox demonstrates the Alto graphical user interface.

Nolan Bushnell's Pong arcade game is a success and Magnavox's Odyssey video-game machine invades the home.

1973

Growth of Citizens Band (CB) radio greatly accelerated by first oil crisis.

Warners' *The Exorcist* marks renewed interest in shock effect of film.

Michael Crichton's *Westworld* utilizes computer-generated graphics and presages the problems of virtual reality twenty years hence.

Lexis, a law library online, opens for business.

1974

MGM opts out of film business for the first time, sells studio, sets, and costumes.

Home Box Office, a pay-television channel, is marketed through cable systems.

A Roper poll shows that, for the first time, television is the prime source of news for most people, having surpassed newspapers.

Watergate hearings televised.

Eastman introduces 5247 color stock.

Women begin moving into film and video en masse.

Computer memory chips now hold 4 kilobits.

Bergman directs six-part *Scenes from a Marriage* for television.

Westar, the first U.S. domestic communications satellite, is launched.

1975

January. The Altair 8800 is the first personal computer offered for sale to public.

Dolby film sound system introduced.

French television reorganized into three networks, two of which accept advertising.

Networks agree on self-censorship "Family Time" provision.

HBO begins satellite distribution of its programming for cable system operators to offer at a premium price, establishing the first national cable network.

Altman's *Nashville* released.

Bergman's *Face to Face*.

Jaws sets box office records.

Davis's *Hearts and Minds,* documentary on Vietnam.

FCC requires television set manufacturers to build sets with click-stop UHF tuning comparable to VHF tuning.

Steadicam is used for the first time, by Haskell Wexler on *Bound for Glory.*

Italian television deregulated.

Sony introduces its Betamax 1/2-inch videocassette.

Microsoft Corporation founded by Bill Gates and Paul Allen.

1976

Bergman leaves Sweden.

South Africa is the last nation of any size to begin television service.

By end of 1976, U.S. networks sell all prime advertising time for 1977.

ABC places first in ratings for first time.

Home videotape Betamax cassette system marketed by Sony.

October. British Prestel videotext system begins operations.

Bertolucci's *1900*.

More audiocassettes are sold this year than 8-track cartridges.

During the past eighteen months RCA and AT&T have launched their Satcom and Comstar satellites, respectively, marking the maturity of satellite communications systems.

1977

January 23–30. Alex Haley's *Roots* is broadcast on ABC, setting ratings records. Six of the eight episodes will rank among the top ten television shows of all time.

April 27. Edwin Land of Polaroid Corp. demonstrates Polavision, instant movie system, for immediate sale. It is not successful in the marketplace.

For the first time, NBC News uses more tape than film.

Computer memory chips now hold 16 kilobits of information: 16 times more powerful than five years previously.

Autumn. The David Begelman affair focuses public attention on shady Hollywood business practices.

Critical and commercial success of Woody Allen's *Annie Hall* marks slight shift of film industry away from Hollywood, toward New York.

George Lucas's *Star Wars* is released, quickly becomes highest grossing film of all time.

ABC displaces CBS as leading American network in terms of ratings and advertising revenues. CBS had held the number one position almost without exception since the early fifties. A significant number of NBC and CBS affiliates defect to ABC.

Rise of disco music culminates in popularity of the film *Saturday Night Fever*.

Warner-AMEX's QUBE, the first interactive cable television system, is introduced in Columbus, Ohio. It doesn't last; the technology is not yet powerful enough.

The Apple II microcomputer is offered for sale.

1978

Saturday Night Fever, while highly successful in theaters, nevertheless earns more from soundtrack album sales than from the box office.

January. Orion Pictures Corporation Studio is formed by five former top executives of United Artists. By in effect renting Warners' distribution system, Orion avoids start-up costs of more than $250 million.

April. *Variety* publishes its first "Vidcassette" review, of *Lectric Lady Disco,* which claims to be the first show produced specifically for the home videotape market.

Fred Silverman, formerly head of programming at both CBS and ABC when those networks ranked first in the ratings game, moves to NBC as president.

Releases of *Grease* and *Superman* reinforce blockbuster psychology.

October 4. In a live network broadcast of a television match on CBS, Jimmy Connors uses the expletive "bullshit." No complaints are received.

October 5. In an episode of *Taxi* the word "bastard" is used.

The Times of London is struck. (The paper will not appear again until a year later.)

December. Philips–MCA begin test-marketing their videodisc player in Atlanta and Seattle.

The Aspen Project, under the supervision of Nicholas Negroponte, experiments with random access computer control of recorded images and sounds, and hence establishes the basis for multimedia. A prototype for the Department of Defense, this set of videodiscs allows the user to tour Aspen, CO, virtually driving down every street, choosing which way to turn at every corner.

Gene Siskel and Roger Ebert, popular newspaper film critics in Chicago, appear on first PBS film review show, establishing the critical trend for the eighties.

Congress at Brighton, England, of the Fédération Internationale des Archives du Film (FIAF) establishes the Brighton Project, beginning the trend to a new historicism in film studies.

1979

Canada and Australia emerge as film powers.

February 17. On *Saturday Night Live* (NBC) Gilda Radner performs a parody of singer Patti Smith. The song she sings is dedicated to Mick Jagger and includes the refrain: "Are you woman, are you man/I'm your biggest fucked-up fan." The lyrics are garbled but the refrain is clear. According to *The New York Times* two days later, NBC received 160 calls during and right after the show. "75 found Miss Radner's language 'disgusting;' but 85, the network said, thought she was 'a fabulous and very talented lady.'"

The China Syndrome foreshadows events at Three Mile Island several weeks before they actually occur.

Success of "small" films like *Meatballs, Starting Over, Breaking Away,* and *Kramer vs Kramer* marks shift away from blockbusters, despite *Star Trek: The Motion Picture,* reputed to have cost $40 million, and *Apocalypse Now,* $30 million.

Miramax Films, independent distributor, founded by Harvey and Bob Weinstein.

John Sayles's *The Return of the Secaucus Seven* ignites a resurgence of the American independent cinema.

A Melbourne, Australia, television station offers the first 3-D service.

For the first time in more than twenty years, revenues in the recording industry are down. Several conglomerates move to sell their record companies.

August 15. Francis Coppola's *Apocalypse Now* is finally released, accompanied by an elaborate publicity campaign.

October. The Ladd Company is formed by former top executives of Twentieth Century Fox, continuing the decentralization of Hollywood executive power that began eighteen months earlier with the formation of Orion Pictures Corp.

The Intel Corporation introduces a magnetic bubble memory chip capable of storing 1 million bits of information. Price: approximately $2,000. This technology does not succeed.

C-SPAN and ESPN cable networks founded.

Visicalc, the first spreadsheet program, gives businesspeople a good reason to buy the Apple II microcomputer.

1980

Continued development of word processing equipment suggests new more efficient methods of typesetting for books, newspapers, and magazines.

Large home dish antennas to receive satellite signals are offered to the public at reasonable cost.

Screen Actors Guild strikes Hollywood film and television studios to gain share of future tape, disc, satellite, and other ancillary rights.

Godard returns to feature films with *Sauve qui peut la vie*.

Michael Cimino's *Heaven's Gate* is the biggest financial disaster since *Cleopatra* and marks the beginning of the end for United Artists.

June. CNN cable service launched, challenging networks on their own turf: news.

American Film Marketing Association is founded as independent distributors join the establishment.

Martin Scorsese's *Raging Bull* released in black-and-white, later voted the best film of the 1980s by American critics.

November. Ronald Reagan is first movie actor elected President of the United States.

1981–Present: The Digital World

1981

Microsoft wins the contract to provide operating system software for IBM's personal computer. This gift from IBM will make founders Bill Gates and Paul Allen multibillionaires before the age of thirty.

Xerox introduces the first commercially available microcomputer with a graphical user interface, the Star, but at a price of $16,000 it is not a success.

Computer RAM chips now hold 64 kilobits.

May. Kirk Kerkorian acquires United Artists from Transamerica.

Oilman Marvin Davis purchases Twentieth Century Fox.

August. IBM PC establishes the standard for microcomputers, using Microsoft's DOS operating system, a derivative of CP/M.

FCC approves AM stereo system for U.S.

Paramount's syndicated *Entertainment Tonight* becomes first national entertainment news show.

Grant Tinker becomes head of NBC, to lead company to ratings primacy in the decade.

Lucas's and Spielberg's *Raiders of the Lost Ark* revives the serial style of the 1940s as it establishes a new adventure genre.

August 1. MTV launched, establishing new model for television use. It will become one of the dominant cultural forces of the decade.

Walter Cronkite, last of the authoritative newsmen from the early days of broadcasting, retires.

Steven Bochco's *Hill Street Blues* debuts, refreshing the form of the hour drama and marking the beginning of NBC's rise to the top of the ratings heap.

Francis Coppola sponsors restoration of Abel Gance's *Napoléon*, setting off a minor wave of interest in film preservation.

The Gods Must Be Crazy, a small South African film, garners considerable international attention.

December. Trials of French Minitel system take place in the town of Vélizy.

Cable penetration in the U.S. is less than 30 percent; VCR penetration approaches 8 percent.

1982

Spielberg's *E.T.* sets box-office records. The featuring of "Reese's Pieces" signals the beginning of the product placement business.

Coca-Cola buys Columbia Pictures in a contradiction of the old rule of exhibition that the profit is really at the concessions counter.

TriStar studio established as a joint venture of Columbia, CBS, and HBO, in an attempt to provide an alternative channel of distribution.

The success of *Gandhi* marks the arrival on the scene of Goldcrest Films.

R. W. Fassbinder dies at 37, marking the end of Das Neue Kino.

Sales of audiocassettes exceed sales of records for the first time.

The audio CD format is introduced in Japan.

Disney's *Tron* makes extensive use of computer-generated graphics.

FCC establishes requirements for low-power television (LPTV).

Blade Runner becomes a cult favorite and a model for the Film-Noir Science-Fiction films of the future.

Graduating class of the Beijing Film Institute coalesces into the so-called Fifth Generation of Chinese filmmakers. They had entered in 1978, when nationwide college entrance exams had been reinstituted after the Cultural Revolution.

November. Channel 4 opens in the U.K. with mandate to serve minorities.

1983

Lawrence Kasdan's *The Big Chill* adds a Motown soundtrack to the themes of *The Return of the Secaucus Seven*, marks the cinematic coming of age of the baby boom generation, and serves as the emblematic American film of the decade.

By combining characters with historical footage, Woody Allen's *Zelig* suggests the technical possibilities that lie ten years ahead.

Koyanisqaatsi, no dialogue or narration, score by Philip Glass.

Dragon's Lair is the first arcade video game to use laserdisc technology to provide more realism. Revenue from arcade games now exceeds theatrical film rentals as the locus of power in the American entertainment industry begins to shift from Hollywood to Silicon Valley.

ABC broadcasts *The Day After* in the middle of the 1980s revival of the antinuclear movement, drawing huge ratings and sparking controversy with its graphic depiction of the aftermath of a nuclear war between the U.S. and the Soviet Union. Reminiscent of films like *Fail-Safe* and *Dr. Strangelove* twenty years earlier, *The Day After* serves as an eerie reinforcement of the remake philosophy that characterizes the 1980s.

The Radio Shack 100 introduced, first popular "notebook" computer, especially favored by journalists.

1984

January 24. Apple Computer Inc.'s landmark *1984* commercial is shown during the Super Bowl, introducing the Macintosh.

Computer RAM chips now hold 256 kilobits.

AT&T broken up into eight companies: seven "Regional Bell Operating Companies" (RBOCs) and a long-distance vendor (still called AT&T).

U.S. cable television industry deregulated.

Michael Jackson's *Thriller* (directed by John Landis) is the first music video to list filmmakers' credits.

Criterion's release of *Citizen Kane* and *King Kong* on Laserdisc mark the possibilities of this new medium for cinephiles.

Bill Cosby's *The Cosby Show* debuts.

Canal Plus founded, first French pay-television service.

François Truffaut dies of a brain tumor at the American Hospital in Neuilly.

Michael Eisner and Jeffrey Katzenberg take over at Disney, found Touchstone Pictures, as Disney makes bid to join mainstream distributors.

Ghostbusters establishes a new relation between the movies and popular culture as its iconography becomes part of our colloquial expression.

Garrett Brown's Skycam technology is used for the first time at the Los Angeles Olympics.

William Gibson's *Neuromancer* memorializes this Orwellian year with its dark vision of the social "cyberspace" that awaits us ten years hence.

The release of *Yellow Earth* begins a new wave of Chinese-language films.

The Terminator begins the rise to prominence of Arnold Schwarzenegger as the world's leading movie star that culminates with *Terminator 2* seven years later.

The year turns out to be nothing like Orwell's novel (or the film of it). Indeed, just around the corner, "perestroika" and "glasnost" will mark the beginning of the end of the totalitarian wave Orwell feared.

1985

Sony and Philips introduce the CD-ROM format for data storage.

March. ABC network sold to Capital Cities Broadcasting for $3.5 billion. NBC and CBS change hands shortly after.

May. Fox acquires Metromedia broadcast group.

Rupert Murdoch acquires Twentieth Century Fox from Marvin Davis and installs Barry Diller as head.

French Minitel system commercially introduced.

The colorization technique is introduced by Color System Technologies.

November. Lawrence Tisch owns 24.9 percent of CBS.

December. GE announces it will buy RCA and its NBC subsidiary. (The deal is completed in 1986.)

1986

Changes in the tax code eliminating shelters affect independent filmmakers.

Television sets equipped with stereophonic audio and remote controls are now common.

Nintendo dominates the home video game market, which has largely superseded the arcade game business.

Fox's *A Current Affair* launched, establishing model for tabloid television.

March. Ted Turner buys MGM/UA from Kirk Kerkorian, sells the lot to Lorimar Telepictures and other assets back to Kirk Kerkorian, keeps the film library, and renames it Turner Entertainment Company.

March 1. The Grateful Dead conference is founded on the Well, a pioneering online community.

Spike Lee's *She's Gotta Have It* is a success at the Cannes Film Festival, marking a renaissance in Black film.

My Beautiful Laundrette, A Room with a View, and *Mona Lisa* mark the beginning of a British mini-new wave, while British producer David Puttnam's stormy tenure as head of Columbia Pictures marks new relationship between Hollywood and London's Wardour Street.

Platoon revives the genre of Vietnam films begun in the 1970s that continues into the 1990s.

September. Fox television network begins broadcasting.

1987

Goldcrest Films self-destructs.

David Puttnam leaves Columbia.

Fatal Attraction causes a sensation and sets the model for a new series of paranoid fantasies; the film is released with different endings in different markets, according to the way it tests.

March 1. DVI technology demonstrated at the second Microsoft CD-ROM conference. Although never successful in the market, it is the precursor of digital video.

Theater magnate Sumner Redstone purchases Viacom for a reported $3.4 billion.

Henry Hampton's *Eyes on the Prize,* broadcast on PBS, confirms the value of television as an historical medium.

Lethal Weapon (Mel Gibson, Danny Glover) and *Predator* (Arnold Schwarzenegger) make it clear that Action movies are now the dominant genre in American film.

Computer RAM chips now hold 1 megabit (1,024 kilobits).

1988

Rupert Murdoch's Sky TV begins small-dish satellite-to-home broadcasting in the U.K., obviating the need to build a massive cable infrastructure.

Murdoch purchases *TV Guide* from Annenberg Communications for $3 billion.

January. Sony purchases CBS Records for a reported $2 billion.

February 18. Before this date people ask, "Do you have a fax?" After this date they demand, "What's your fax number?"

September. IBM–Sears joint venture Prodigy, an online service aimed at the general public, opens after reported $500 million investment.

October. Turner founds TNT cable network, devoted to classic movies from his MGM library.

1989

John Cassavetes, Richard Roud, and Leslie Halliwell all die at the age of 59 marking the end of the modern period in film history.

Thatcher broadcasting deregulation bill passes the House of Commons.

Steve Ross merges Warner with Time Inc. The new company is the largest media group in the world.

June. The Chinese Tienanmen Square revolt is broadcast to a world audience.

November. Voyager's release of *CD Companion to Beethoven's 9th,* by Robert Winter, is a landmark in the development of multimedia.

November. Sony purchases Columbia Pictures Entertainment (Columbia Pictures, TriStar Pictures, and Loews Theaters) from Coca-Cola for a reported $3.4 billion, then pays $200 million for the Guber-Peters Entertainment company so that the two principles can run the studio.

November. The fall of the Berlin wall is televised worldwide.

Sony introduces the Mavica, first digital magnetic still camera, but few consumers are ready to switch from film, and it fails quickly. Success comes eight years later.

sex, lies and videotape and *Roger and Me* mark the high point of the resurgent American independent movement that began with *Return of the Secaucus Seven*.

Kenneth Branagh establishes himself as the Shakespearean director of his generation with *Henry V.*

Tim Berners-Lee of the European Center for Particle Physics, releases the specifications that become the basis for the World Wide Web.

1990

Murdoch's Sky TV merges with British Satellite Broadcasting to become B-Sky-B, the largest satellite network in the world.

William S. Paley dies at the age of 90.

United Artists' last film is *Rocky V.*

Boyz N the Hood and *Straight Out of Brooklyn* reinforce the developing revival of Black independent film in the U.S.

Dances with Wolves marks the revival of interest in the Western.

Ken Burns's *The Civil War*, broadcast on PBS, sells well as a set of videotapes, further legitimizing television as an historical medium.

Sega's Genesis, a 16-bit system, takes market share from Nintendo in the video game business.

March. Kirk Kerkorian sells the remainder of MGM to Pathé, controlled by Giancarlo Paretti and funded by Crédit Lyonnais. Paretti is soon out of business and under indictment and the bank is left holding the bag.

November. Matsushita acquires MCA/Universal for a reported $6.1 billion. The majority of Hollywood studios are now owned by foreign companies.

1991

January 16. The Gulf War begins, broadcast live to a worldwide audience as it happens. It lasts almost as long as an Olympics.

BBC begins its television World Service, first in Europe, then in Asia in conjunction with Star satellite system.

Cable penetration in the U.S. is more than 60 percent; VCR penetration exceeds 70 percent.

May. Jim Henson dies suddenly at 53 of a bacterial infection. The deal he had arranged to sell Henson Associates to Disney falls through. His children take control of the company.

June. Apple introduces Quicktime digital audio/video technology.

Ted Turner marries Jane Fonda, joining Hollywood royalty.

MGM reacquires UA.

November 25. HDTV broadcasting begins in Japan after trials of more than ten years.

Auction of British independent television franchises changes the face of U.K. television.

James Cameron's *Terminator 2* marks the maturity of digital special effects and morphing.

Orion files for protection under bankruptcy laws.

Toshiba and C. Itoh invest $1 billion in Time Warner.

Computer RAM chips now hold 4 megabits.

1992

February. Barry Diller resigns from Fox. By the end of the year, after a tour of the computer industry, he will find himself in the home shopping business.

May. Johnny Carson retires from the *Tonight Show* after nearly 30-year run.

Kodak introduces Photo CD product, which—unlike Sony's Mavica—allows consumers (and Kodak) to keep their huge investment in chemical film technology while still enjoying the benefits of digital recording.

The Player marks Robert Altman's return to form as it effectively satirizes the film industry of the eighties and nineties that kept him off the screen.

Cable magnate John Malone announces his company, TCI, is developing a 500-channel cable technology that would allow movies on demand. (Is it a ploy?)

Sony introduces Minidisc player using small CDs and advanced technology.

Beauty and the Beast is the first animated film to be nominated for an Academy Award for best picture.

Major film biographies of American political figures *JFK* and *Malcolm X* are controversial.

Howards End, from the novel by E. M. Forster, will garner nine Academy Award nominations and an Oscar for Emma Thompson, marking the resurgence of the literary film.

1993

Cinecittà closes.

Federico Fellini dies.

Elstree closes.

Fin-Syn rule restricting network financial interest in syndication operations rescinded by the FCC.

Voyager's multimedia CD release of *A Hard Day's Night* is the first digital CD to include an entire film.

Spielberg's *Jurassic Park* sets box-office record while his *Schindler's List* wins Oscars.

August. Apple introduces the Newton, one of the first Personal Digital Assistants.

September. Macintosh and Windows versions of NCSA Mosaic browsers are released; the World Wide Web begins its rapid rise.

Mercury introduces One-2-One, first PCS service, in London.

Murdoch acquires control of Star TV, satellite system which reaches most countries between Israel and Taiwan (including China and India) and thus has a potential audience of 3 billion.

Ted Turner acquires New Line Cinema, a "mini-major" distributor, reinforcing his position in the film industry.

FCC attempts to reregulate the cable industry by instituting a set of rules limiting certain charges, but cable operators find loopholes, raising more prices than they lower.

Computer RAM chips now hold 16 megabits

1994

Both CD-ROM multimedia and online interactive technologies come of age in the U.S. as viable consumer products after many years of development.

After a lengthy battle with Barry Diller's QVC, Sumner Redstone, proprietor of Viacom, acquires Paramount, the last remaining "independent" studio besides Disney.

First review of a multimedia CD in *The New York Times Book Review.*

The Fox network lands a one-two punch on CBS, first by outbidding the older network for National Football League broadcast rights, then by enticing 12 major-market affiliates to switch allegiance.

February. After a high-stakes competition lasting several years, the HDTV Grand Alliance (and by extension, the FCC) chooses a digital HDTV system designed by Zenith and AT&T as the standard for the proposed U.S. system, leapfrogging existing Japanese analog technology and setting the stage for the next stages of digitization.

March. Media magnate Silvio Berlusconi wins Italian parliamentary elections and becomes Prime Minister. He is the first media mogul to head a major country.

March. Digital Satellite System (DSS) direct-to-home broadcasting begins in the U.S.

April. Apple introduces a new line of Power Macintosh computers built around the PowerPC chip (designed by Apple, IBM, and Motorola), first RISC micropro-cessor in the PC environment.

IBM introduces new optical disc storage technology that can increase CD-ROM capacity more than tenfold.

April. Disney top executive Frank Wells dies in helicopter crash.

May. Book-of-the-Month Club offers first CD-ROM title, Ron Mann's *Poetry in Motion*.

May. Godard's still at it. His autobiographical *JLG by JLG* premieres.

August. Jeffrey Katzenberg resigns from Disney in a dispute over succession. Within days, he is in business with Steven Spielberg and David Geffen. The com-pany, intending to be a full studio operation, is later named Dreamworks SKG.

September. Sumner Redstone's Viacom completes purchase of Wayne Huizenga's Blockbuster Video, largest retail video chain.

TCI–Bell Atlantic merger talks fizzle. The first telco-entertainment conglomerate will have to wait.

This year, sales of encyclopedias on CD-ROM exceed sales in print for the first time.

December 22. Berlusconi loses his post as Prime Minister of Italy, under the threat of an indictment, which comes in May. (He is not the first media mogul to be indicted.)

1995

January. Sony/Philips and Toshiba/Time Warner introduce competing technolo-gies for Digital Video Discs, storing 3.7 and 4.8 gigabytes, respectively.

February 2. Before this date, people ask, "Do you have electronic mail?" After this date, they inquire, "What's your email?"

May. Apple releases QuickTime VR technology for simple, inexpensive virtual-reality productions.

June. Edgar Bronfman Jr concludes Seagram's purchase of the 80 percent of MCA/Universal owned by Matsushita. After negotiations with Michael Ovitz fall through, Bronfman hires CAA's number two, Ron Meyer, to head his studio.

July. Michael Eisner announces that Disney will purchase Capital Cities/ABC for $19 billion, more than three times sales. The deal comes as a surprise, since a merger of Disney with CBS had long been rumored and ABC—unlike CBS and

NBC—was not in play. Shortly after, Eisner announces that he has hired Michael Ovitz as his second-in-command.

August. It's thunder stolen by the Disney/ABC deal, Westinghouse announces the purchase of CBS for $5.4 billion. Ted Turner—actively pursuing the former Tiffany broadcast network since the early 1980s—loses out once again, thwarted by the cable interests on his board.

August 9. Netscape's initial public offering, 14 months after the company's founding, is the most successful in history, emblematic of Internet mania. At the end of the first day of trading, the market values the company at $2.9 billion. It has yet to make a profit.

August 24. Microsoft introduces its Windows 95 software after an eighteen-month marketing campaign and with worldwide publicity.

September. If you can't beat 'em, join 'em. Unable to expand by acquisition, Turner sells out to Time Warner for $7.5 billion, noting, perhaps ironically, "I'm tired of being little all the time. I'm nearing the end of my career. I want to see what it's like to be big for a while."

September. The Sony/Philips group essentially concedes to the Time Warner/ Toshiba group on a standard for Digital Video Disc/High Density Compact Disc, assuring a single format for the new medium with a maximum capacity of 18.8 gigabytes. Combining the proposed dual-layer and double-sided technologies assures the backward compatibility the computer industry needs (Sony/Philips) with the high capacity the entertainment industry wants (Time Warner/ Toshiba).

November 27. Moving closer to the Hollywood orbit, Barry Diller announces the purchase of Savoy Pictures Entertainment Inc. and Home Shopping Network for his new venture, Silver King Communications, a chain of television stations.

November 29. A small company named Pixar Animation Studios goes public just a few days after its first production, *Toy Story*, is released by Disney, garnering the top box-office rank for the Thanksgiving weekend. The company is 80 percent-owned by Steven Jobs. By the end of the day the combination of 1995's technology bubble and Hollywood glitz makes Jobs's stake in Pixar worth more than $1 billion—far more than his Apple stock was ever worth. *Toy Story* is the first fully computer-animated feature, but it seems a high price to pay for a small production company with an onerous three-picture deal.

December 13. Spielberg, Katzenberg, and Geffen announce that Dreamworks SKG will take over an old Hughes aircraft plant north of Los Angeles International Airport to build the first major studio lot in more than half a century. It is the site where Howard Hughes built his famous "Spruce Goose," and includes a huge hangar that is slated to house six sound stages.

December 14. NBC sells Microsoft a 50-percent stake in one of its cable channels to create a news network to challenge CNN, further cementing the union between the computer and media industries.

Sense and Sensibility (starring Emma Thompson) and *Persuasion* (with her sister Sophie) together with the BBC/A&E series *Pride and Prejudice* mark the curious Jane Austen craze of the midnineties.

Enhanced CDs, combining audio with multimedia, enter the market.

Computer RAM chips now hold 64 megabits.

1996

Telecommunications Act of 1996. Meant to liberalize the restrictions placed on telecommunications companies over the years (beginning with the Communications Act of 1934), the new code lifts limits on radio and television station ownership, permits cable and phone companies to compete in each other's industries, and frees the "baby Bells" from the constraints imposed by the breakup of the Bell system in 1984. Almost immediately, four of the Regional Bell Operating Companies announce mergers (SBC Communications with Pacific Telesis; NYNEX with Bell Atlantic). At the same time what remains of AT&T splits itself into three new companies and, in the U.K., the merger of British Telecom and Mercury falls apart. Misunderstanding the dynamics of large telecom corporations, the U.S. Congress has given them a license to raid and consolidate when it intended, rather, to increase competition.

March 9. George Burns dies at 100, and with him the traditional vaudeville style of the early years of the twentieth century which gave birth to the dominant form of American mass entertainment.

March 25. Like a scene out of Fellini, a badly crippled Superman is displayed to an international television audience on the annual Oscars telecast. Christopher Reeve had been seriously injured when thrown by a horse the summer before. A few weeks later, Lois Lane (Margot Kidder) is found wandering dazed and injured in Los Angeles. The symbolism is meaningless, as the series had played itself out years earlier.

May 31. Timothy Leary, the erstwhile guru of the sixties, dies peacefully at home in bed surrounded by family. His publicized plan to stage his death on the World Wide Web is unfulfilled.

July 15. MSNBC, first combined cable network/website, begins broadcasting (and netcasting). The deal gets Microsoft on TV and NBC on the Internet.

July 16. After months of lackluster bidding, Crédit Lyonnais sells MGM for $1.3 billion to a group lead by none other than Kirk Kerkorian (who hadn't even been in the running). Kerkorian's group includes Frank Mancuso, MGM's chairman, and Seven Network Group, Ltd., an Australian broadcasting company owned in part by News Corporation. It is the third time Kerkorian has bought the company.

July 19. The Centennial Olympiad opens in Atlanta (and on NBC). The official website, managed by IBM, is an integral part of the event. IBM loses face by failing to deliver the scores as quickly and accurately as promised, but succeeds in demonstrating a new medium: the "Sneak Peak Cam" area of the site offers instant stills grabbed every few seconds from the video world feed from dozens of cameras at nearly every venue. Because NBC has orchestrated its television broadcast to succeed as entertainment (delaying transmission of daytime events to prime time), IBM's site is, as analyst Andrew Monaco points out, "just about the only way you can see the Olympics live." The Sneak Peak Cam ironically fulfills the promise of NBC's failed "Triplecast" at the Barcelona Olympic Games four years earlier and suggests a vital role for the Web as a telepresence medium.

July 27. At the Atlanta Olympics, a Finnish javelin thrower gets a rare "do-over" as her javelin hits the skycam. The event marks the continuing struggle between sports and media.

September 30. British Telecom and MCI agree to merge as Concert, first transatlantic telecommunications company in a deal valued at $23 billion. BT had earlier failed in an attempt to buy its main domestic competitor Cable and Wireless PLC.

October. The introduction of the WebTV receiver begins the merger of broadcast television with multicast Internet. Computer and television manufacturers settle their battle over the new digital television standard by agreeing to differ: computers will use progressive scanning while televisions will offer both progressive and interlaced scanning.

October. Deutsche Telekom convinces Germans, traditionally wary of the stock market, to buy its stock in its first public offering.

October 8. John Calley, highly respected studio executive at Warner in the 1970s, takes the reigns at troubled Sony Pictures Entertainment. He had recently returned to Hollywood from retirement to rescue United Artists.

October 31. Marcel Carné dies at 90, still without the respect from French critics that he thought he deserved for *Les Enfants du Paradis*.

November. DVD players come to market in Japan.

December 20. Marcello Mastroianni dies at 72. His body lies in state on the Campodiglio in Rome. Thousands mourn this epitome of the Italian postwar spirit as the public funeral concludes with the final march tune from *8 1/2*.

December 20. Carl Sagan dies at 62. Over a 25-year period, the Astronomy professor from Cornell had used the popular media—especially television—aggressively and adroitly to share his love of the science, setting a model for mass education.

December 20. Apple buys NeXT Software Inc. for $400 million and Steve Jobs returns to the company he cofounded.

1997

January 12. Thousands celebrate the birthday of HAL, the computer star of *2001: A Space Odyssey*. Later in the year, continuing troubles on the MIR space station suggest Arthur C. Clarke and Stanley Kubrick will prove to be as unsuccessful in their prognostications as George Orwell was.

March. DVD-Video sales begin in the U.S.

March. CBS cuts a deal with Web site SportsLine. Web company gets promotional announcements during CBS sports programming; CBS gets 50 percent of revenue from SportsLine content tied to CBS-covered events and 3 million shares of stock. Over the next three years CBS makes a dozen other deals like this one, trading leftover ad space and time for significant chunks of Internet companies.

March 30. Channel 5 begins broadcasting in the U.K.

April 29. Metromedia announces the sale of its 2,200-film library, along with the remains of Orion Pictures and Goldwyn Entertainment to the new MGM. After the deal is completed, MGM—near death two years earlier—will control the world's largest film library.

July 1. Robert Mitchum dies at 80, leaving Jimmy Stewart as the last remaining Hollywood icon from the great days of the 1940s.

July 2. Jimmy Stewart dies at 89.

July. The landing of the Mars Pathfinder probe proves a significant even in Web history as a record 45 million visits to the Jet Propulsion Laboratory site are recorded. Surfers can watch the J.P.L. scientists at work live via a web cam, or download real-time images from Pathfinder's cameras on Mars.

August 30. The melodramatic death of Diana, Princess of Wales, quickly becomes a media event of supernova proportions, as television networks, newspapers, and magazines fall over each other rushing to condemn the networks, newspapers, and magazines who profited from her celebrity, while the outpouring of grief in the U.K. is hailed as a landmark of the new British sensibility, and the Web is crowded with surfers looking to glean any piece of information about the event or chat about their feelings.

September. Internet growth continues at an extreme rate as surveys show 26 million host computers on the net now, up from 15 million a year earlier.

September 20. Continuing a wave of media mergers and acquisitions, Westinghouse announces the purchase of 98 radio stations from American Radio Systems, bringing its total holdings to 175 stations. (So much for the "competition" promised by the Telecom Act of 1996.)

October. Upstart telecom entrepreneur Bernard Ebbers's Worldcom outbids British Telecom and acquires MCI. A month earlier Worldcom had acquired the Compuserve network.

October 21. Barry Diller is still at it. He announces the purchase of a couple of cable channels and nearly all of Universal's television production facilities for $4.1 billion.

October 28. Paul Jarrico, screenwriter, producer, and hero of the Hollywood Blacklist period, dies at 82 driving home from a ceremony marking the fiftieth anniversary of the HUAC hearings.

October 30. Sam Fuller dies at 85, last of the classical Hollywood auteurs.

December 21. James Cameron's *Titanic* opens. Produced for a record $200 million, this old-fashioned grand-hotel story proves a landmark in the short history of digital filmmaking, as the prodigious technology is used, not to create a striking fantasy, but to re-create historical reality. Roberto Rossellini rests a little easier in his grave, knowing that his dream of thirty years earlier is being fulfilled.

1998

January 21. The Monica Lewinsky soap opera begins. It will dominate the mediasphere for the next thirteen months.

April. Walt Disney, minority owner in new-media creator Starwave Corp., exercises option to acquire the rest of the company from founder Paul Allen. (Through its own joint ventures, Starwave creates content for and produces ABCnews.com, ESPN SportsZone, and other new-media sites.)

May 14. Frank Sinatra dies at 85. Uniquely successful as the paramount singer of his era as well as a prolific and successful film actor, his persona remains the transcendent emblem of popular romantic sentiment for a century that will have to limp along for another nineteen months without him.

June. AT&T announces it will purchase John Malone's Tele-Communications, Inc. for $31.8 billion, uniting the number one long-distance company with the number two cable provider, as C. Michael Armstrong continues to reconstruct the mother of all Bells. A few weeks earlier, Malone had purchased *TV Guide* from Rupert Murdoch ($2 billion in cash and stock) for an affiliate of TCI.

June. NBC buys a 19 percent share of Snap, a news and entertainment Web site created by CNET. NBC also buys 5 percent of CNET. Value: about $64 million.

June 19. Disney joins the rush to the Web, buying a significant stake in Infoseek with the intent of creating a Disney-controlled portal. Disney trades Starwave to Infoseek for $475 million.

August 15. Apple "Interim CEO" Steve Jobs continues his winning streak with the introduction of the i-Mac, a new version of the computer-as-appliance he defined fifteen years earlier. (Over the next few months the bluish machine will earn considerably more than *A Bug's Life*, the concurrent product from Jobs's other company, Pixar.)

August 17. In the climactic episode of the Lewinsky saga, President Clinton testifies before the grand jury via a secure video feed. On September 21, the House Judiciary committee broadcasts the tape of the testimony to the nation. Within a week, the four-hour episode is available on DVD for a price of 2 cents (plus $2 shipping and handling).

October 1. Digital television broadcasting begins in the U.K., via satellite.

October 2. The campfire is out; the last roundup has ended: Gene Autry rides off into the final sunset, Roy Rogers having predeceased him by three months. Don't fence them in.

October 19. The age of the Bills crests as the Microsoft antitrust trial begins. The other Bill will be vindicated at the polls, impeached by the House, tried by the Senate, and acquitted long before this Bill's tribulations end next year. Like the Clinton affair, the Gates trial will depend on videotaped testimony and weak memories.

November 1. Digital television broadcasting begins in the U.S. but no one notices. Due to a slight oversight, cable systems are not ready to carry the signals. HDTV sets still cost $10,000. The first network broadcast, on ABC is Disney's *101 Dalmatians* (the 1996 remake).

November 7. Barnes & Noble, the nation's largest book chain, declares it will buy Ingram Book Group, the largest book wholesaler. (Antitrust concerns will halt the deal within six months.)

November 19. Alan J. Pakula dies at 70 in a freak auto accident as a pipe smashes through his windshield on the Long Island Expressway.

November 23. America Online announces it will buy Netscape for about $4 billion in stock. Don't cry for Netscape shareholders: by the time the deal is concluded months later the AOL stock will be worth $10 billion.

December. Michael Ovitz returns to Hollywood, forming Artists Management Group and riling his former associates at CAA. Meanwhile, his Broadway production company, Livent, is in bankruptcy—but he says that's Garth Drabinsky's fault.

It has been the year of seeing double: two World War II epics (*Saving Private Ryan, The Thin Red Line*); two Elizabethan pageants (*Shakespeare in Love, Elizabeth*); two meteoric disasters (*Armageddon, Deep Impact*); and two buggy digital cartoons (*Antz, A Bug's Life*).

December 1. Freddie Young, last of the founding master cinematographers, dies at 96.

December. It must be some sort of landmark in digital postmodernism: When *A Bug's Life* was released weeks earlier, it featured "outtakes" of the cartoon scenes. Now, a new set of "outtakes" has replaced the originals to attract return customers.

1999

The euro is introduced as the transnational currency of the European Union.

January 7. MGM completes the purchase of the Polygram library from Universal. In a remarkable comeback the once moribund studio now owns rights to more than half the extant Hollywood library.

January 20. Cable Internet service provider @Home announces purchase of portal/search engine Excite for $6.7 billion. Deals this small no longer garner much attention.

February 20. Gene Siskel dies at 53. Since the early 1980s he and his television co-host Roger Ebert have dominated American film criticism.

Rise of ECNs—"Electronic Communications Networks" that provide a virtual marketplace for financial transactions.

March 7. After completing post-production work on *Eyes Wide Shut*, his first feature in twelve years, Stanley Kubrick dies peacefully in his sleep at 70 at his home in Hertfordshire, which he loved.

March 21. Miramax's *Shakespeare in Love* wins the best picture Oscar beating industry favorite Dreamworks SKG's *Saving Private Ryan*, and punctuating a remarkable string of recent Oscars for the outsider ministudio. Some observers think the little film beat the big film because it worked better on video—which is how most Academy members now see most movies.

April 9. The British government blocks Rupert Murdoch's $1 billion purchase (through B-Sky-B) of Manchester United, the premiere British soccer club. Murdoch may console himself with his other sports prize, The Los Angeles Dodgers.

May 7. The British government announces that they will sell 58 percent of the country's gold bullion reserves: the announcement is a milestone of the growing virtual economy.

May 19. *Star Wars: Episode I—The Phantom Menace* debuts. The return of George Lucas to the series after sixteen years is marked by such anticipation in geek circles that some Silicon Valley companies declare a culture holiday. (No one was going to go to work this day anyway.)

May 21. Deutsche Telekom loses its bid for Telecom Italia. The much smaller Olivetti wins the prize. Nationalism plays a part in the decision as the euro is not yet triumphant.

May. The summer movie season will be devoted to gross-out humor as *Austin Powers—The Spy Who Shagged Me* leads the way. The fall television season will follow suit.

June 18. Lucas and Fox test digital projections of *The Phantom Menace* in suburban theaters in New York and Los Angeles. A month earlier 79-year-old Eric Rohmer beat them to it with a digital showing of his short "Cambrure" at the Cannes Film Festival.

June 28. The Secure Digital Music Initiative, a recording industry consortium charged with finding a way to protect the value of the industry's intellectual property against the pirate challenge of MP3 and other digital music formats, announces its specification. Musical hackers are unimpressed.

June. Digital hard-disc-based "Personal Video Recorders" go on the market. Will the 25-year-old dream of time-shifting finally become a reality? And where is the "Secure Digital Film/Television Initiative"?

July 3. Mario Puzo dies at 78. His *Godfather* remains a key element of the late twentieth-century mythos.

July 13. Disney announces it will merge its own Internet holdings with Infoseek and spin off the resulting company. They aren't the first to try this ploy. The idea is to provide a pure Internet play and use the windfall from the hugely inflated sales of stock in such a company to make acquisitions that may help eventually to realize the market valuation!

July 15. Robert A. Daly and Terry Semel announce that they will step down as heads of Warner after nearly twenty years in power.

July 17. Bill Gates is now worth $100 billion, as Microsoft stock passes $500 billion in market value.

September 7. CBS and Viacom announce a $37 billion merger. It is the largest deal yet in the media world. The new company will be the second-largest media group (after Time Warner, but ahead of Disney/ABC). The deal was made possible when the FCC relaxed rules about television station ownership earlier in the summer. For those few who remember that CBS was sold to Westinghouse a mere four years previously for $5.4 billion, the price is shocking. Has the company really increased in value almost seven times in four years? In a word: yes, sort of—at least as measured by the virtual economics of the end of the century. Here's what happened: after Westinghouse acquired CBS in 1995, management set out to divest itself of the old Westinghouse real-industry businesses, which it largely accomplished within three years. In 1997 Westinghouse changed its name to CBS, which made sense, since it had just sold the old Westinghouse businesses and all that was left were the CBS businesses, plus a few media-industry acquisitions. The most valuable of these was Infinity Broadcasting, a chain of radio stations. With Infinity came CEO Mel Karmazin, a rising star who quickly seized power and talked Sumner Redstone into the deal. Basically, the difference between the $5.4-billion CBS and the $37-billion CBS is some radio stations, better "positioning," and Karmazin. If that seems strange to you, then you will probably enjoy Joseph Heller's *Closing Time*, the sequel to *Catch-22*. Although written in the 1980s it catches the fin-de-siècle dizziness perfectly. Musing about a world he doesn't understand, listing one absurdity after another, our old friend Yossarian concludes with the ultimate incongruity:

> Men made millions, producing nothing more substantial than changes in ownership.

"And that's the way it is...."

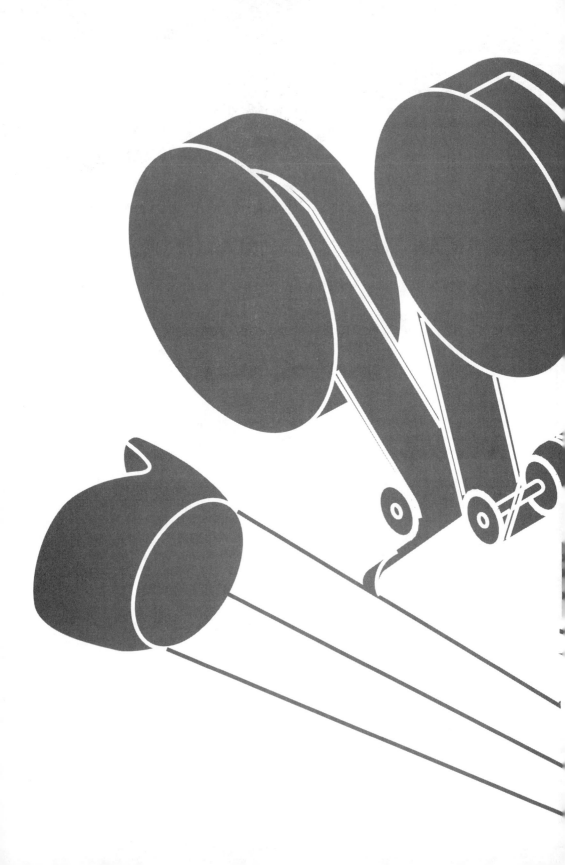

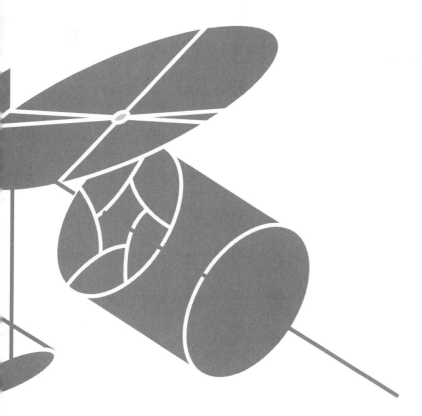

II
READING ABOUT FILM AND MEDIA

This bibliography is designed as an introductory guide to the basic materials available in the field as well as an introduction to further reading on subjects raised in *How To Read a Film.* It is of course by no means comprehensive! Special attention is is paid to classic texts, many of which are out of print.

To make it easier to use, the bibliography has been divided into sections. Part One, "A Basic Library," is divided into seven sections, corresponding to the chapters of *How To Read a Film:*

1. Film as an Art
2. The Technology of Film and Media
3. The Language of Film
4. Film History
5. Film Theory and Practical Criticism
6. Media
7. New Media

Because the Film History section is so extensive, it has been further divided into subsections:

A. The Economics and Politics of Film
B. General Historical Studies
C. Specific Major Periods
D. Genres and Specific Topics
E. National Cinemas
F. Films and Filmmakers

Part Two, "Information," is a guide to research materials, journals, encyclopedias, indexes, and the like. It is organized in six sections:

8. Lists and Encyclopedias
9. Book Bibliographies

10. Guides to Periodical Literature

11. Miscellaneous Guides

12. Journals and Magazines

13. Databases

Titles are listed only once, so it is advisable to check other sections if you don't find what you want immediately. A searchable database is available at Readfilm.com.

Dan Streible of the University of Texas and Curtis Church contributed to the revision of this section. I am especially grateful to Hans-Michael Bock and his colleagues for their help. The version of this bibliography that appears in *Film verstehen*, the German edition of *How To Read a Film*, is more comprehensive thanks to their scholarship and attention to detail.

Part One: A Basic Library

1. FILM AS AN ART

Allen, Don, ed. *The Book of the Cinema*. London: Chris Milsome; New York: Crown, 1979. An illustrated introduction. Includes chapters by Maurice Hatton, Tom Milne, James Monaco, David Robinson, and others.

Andrew, Dudley. *Film in the Aura of Art*. Princeton: Princeton University Press, 1984.

Artaud, Antonin. *The Theatre and Its Double*. New York: Grove Press, 1958.

Auerbach, Erich. *Mimesis: The Representation of Reality in Western Literature*. New York: Doubleday, 1957.

Barsacq, Léon. *Caligari's Cabinet and Other Grand Illusions: A History of Film Design*. New York: New American Library, 1976.

Bluestone, George. *Novels into Film*. Berkeley: University of California Press, 1968.

Brecht, Bertolt. *Brecht on Theatre*. Edited and translated by John Willett. New York: Hill and Wang, 1964.

Fell, John L. *Film and the Narrative Tradition*. Berkeley: University of California Press, 1986.

Fiske, John. *Reading the Popular*. Boston: Unwin Hyman, 1989. Understanding popular culture.

George, Nelson. *Elevating the Game: The History & Aesthetics of Black Men in Basketball*. New York: Simon & Schuster, 1992. In case you thought that the comparison of Michael Jordan and Mikhail Baryshnikov was a stretch.

Gombrich, E. H. *Art and Illusion*. Second ed. Princeton: Princeton University Press, 1961.

Gouldner, Alvin W. *The Dialectic of Ideology and Technology*. New York: Seabury Press, 1976.

Hollander, Anne. *Moving Pictures*. Cambridge, MA: Harvard University Press, 1989. Film is placed within the broader artistic traditions.

Horace. *Ars Poetica*.

Manvell, Roger. *Shakespeare and the Film*. New York: Praeger, 1971.

Manvell, Roger. *Theatre and Film*. London: Tantivy Press, 1980.

Mesthene, Emmanuel. *Technological Change: Its Impact on Man and Society*. New York: New American Library, 1970.

Mumford, Lewis. *Technics and Civilization*. 1934. Reprint. New York: Harcourt, Brace & World, 1966.

Newhall, Beaumont. *The History of Photography*. New York: Museum of Modern Art, 1964.

Nicoll, Allardyce. *Film and Theatre*. London, 1936. Reprint. New York: Arno Press, 1972. An early, standard study.

Pildas, Ave. *Movie Palaces*. New York: Clarkson N. Potter, 1979.

Rohmer, Eric. *Six Moral Tales*. New York: Viking Press, 1980.

Tynan, Kenneth. *Show People*. New York: Simon & Schuster, 1980.

Vardac, A. Nicholas. *From Stage to Screen*. Reprint. New York: Benjamin Bloom, 1968.

Williams, Raymond. *Keywords: A Vocabulary of Culture and Society*. New York: Oxford University Press, 1976.

2. THE TECHNOLOGY OF FILM AND MEDIA

Alton, John. *Painting with Light*. New York: Macmillan, 1949. A classic of its time.

Armes, Roy. *On Video*. New York: Routledge, 1988.

Brosnan, John. *Movie Magic: The Story of Special Effects in the Cinema*. New York: New American Library, 1976.

Campbell, Russell, ed. *Photographic Theory for the Motion Picture Cameraman*. Cranbury, NJ: A. S. Barnes, 1970. Hollywood orthodoxy.

Ceram, C. W. *Archeology of the Cinema*. New York: Harcourt, Brace & World, 1965. The prehistory of film.

Coe, Brian. *The History of Movie Photography*. London: Ash & Grant, 1981.

Dickson, W. K. L., and Antonia Dickson. *History of the Kinetograph, Kinetoscope, and Kinetophonograph*. Twickenham, Middlesex, 1895. Reprint. New York: Arno Press, 1970. By one of the fathers of film.

Ellis, John. *Visible Fictions: Cinema, Television, Video*. New York: Routledge, 1992.

Ellul, Jacques. *The Technological Society*. New York: Vintage, 1964.

Fielding, Raymond, ed. *A Technological History of Motion Pictures and Television*. Berkeley: University of California Press, 1967. A valuable collection of documents.

Kawin, Bruce F. *How Movies Work*. Berkeley: University of California Press, 1992.

Limbacher, James. *Four Aspects of the Film*. New York: Arno Press, 1978. Invaluable for its discussion of color, sound, 3-D, and widescreen processes.

Malkiewicz, J. Kris. *Cinematography*. New York: Van Nostrand Reinhold, 1973.

Maltin, Leonard, ed. *Behind the Camera: The Cinematographer's Art*. New York: Signet, 1971.

Neale, Steven. *Cinema and Technology: Image, Sound, Colour*. London: British Film Institute, 1985.

Newson, Iris, ed. *Wonderful Inventions: Motion Pictures, Broadcasting, and Recorded Sound at the Library of Congress*. Washington: Library of Congress, 1985.

Rosenblum, Ralph, and Robert Karen. *When the Shooting Stops ... the Cutting Begins: A Film Editor's Story*. New York: Viking Press, 1979.

Salt, Barry. *Film Style and Technology: History and Analysis*. Second edition. London: Starword, 1983, 1992.

Schaefer, Dennis, ed. *Masters of Light: Conversations with Contemporary Cinematographers*. Berkeley: University of California Press, 1984.

Smith, Thomas G. *Industrial Light & Magic: The Art of Special Effects*. New York: Ballantine, 1986.

Weis, Elisabeth, and John Belton. *Film Sound: Theory and Practice*. New York: Columbia University Press, 1985.

3. THE LANGUAGE OF FILM

Armes, Roy. *Film and Reality.* New York: Penguin, 1974. A quick survey.

Arnheim, Rudolf. *Art and Visual Perception: A Psychology of the Creative Eye.* Berkeley: University of California Press, 1954. A general text in the visual arts that has much to say about film.

Arnheim, Rudolf. *Visual Thinking.* Berkeley: University of California Press, 1969.

Berger, John. *Ways of Seeing.* London: BBC and Penguin Books, 1972. A book based on Berger's BBC series on advertising and art. Highly recommended.

Bordwell, David, and Kristin Thompson. *Film Art: An Introduction.* Third ed. Reading, MA: Addison-Wesley, 1990. Now classic introductory text.

Bordwell, David, Kristin Thompson, and Janet Staiger. *The Classical Hollywood Cinema: Film Style and Mode of Production to 1960.* New York: Columbia University Press, 1985. One of the more important texts of the 1980s, a highly regarded study of the art and economics of the classical Hollywood studio style.

Braudy, Leo. *The World in a Frame.* New York: Anchor, 1976.

Eidsvik, Charles. *Cineliteracy: Film Among the Arts.* New York: Random House, 1978. Introductory text.

Gessner, Robert. *The Moving Image: A Guide to Cinematic Literacy.* New York: Dutton, 1970. One of the better introductions to the art.

Giannetti, Louis. *Understanding Movies.* Fifth ed. Englewood Cliffs, NJ: Prentice Hall, 1990. Useful basic text. Recommended.

Godard, Jean-Luc. "Montage, mon beau souci." In *Godard on Godard,* edited by Tom Milne, New York: Viking Press, 1972.

Heath, Stephen, and Patricia Mellencamp, eds. *Cinema and Language.* Frederick, MD: University Publications of America, 1983.

Jacobs, Lewis, ed. *The Movies as Medium.* New York: Farrar, Straus and Giroux, 1970. A text composed of articles by various authors.

Kirby, Lynne. *Parallel Tracks: The Railroad and Silent Cinema.* Durham, NC: Duke University Press, 1997. Kirby, a senior producer at Court Television, offers a unique insight into the cultural structures that transportation and communication share.

Nilsen, Vladimir. *Cinema as Graphic Art.* New York: Hill and Wang, 1973. A standard.

Perkins, V. F. *Film as Film: Understanding and Judging Movies.* New York: Penguin, 1972. Highly recommended, it reflects cinematic theory of its time.

Reisz, Karel. *The Technique of Film Editing.* Second enlarged ed. New York: Amphoto/Hastings House, 1968. A "how to" book for film editors, it was aesthetically influential. Recommended.

Scientific American. *Image, Object and Illusion.* Introduction by Richard Held. San Francisco: W. H. Freeman, 1974.

Sharples Jr, Win, "The Aesthetics of Film Sound." *Filmmakers Newsletter* 8:5 (March 1975).

Sobchack, Thomas, and Vivian C. Sobchack. *An Introduction to Film.* Second ed. Boston: Little, Brown, 1987.

Spottiswoode, Raymond R. *A Grammar of Film.* Berkeley: University of California Press, 1950. A classic.

Spottiswoode, Raymond R. *Film and Its Techniques.* Berkeley: University of California Press, 1951. Reprint 1965. Rather out of date, but a classic in its time. Good on technical matters.

Stam, Robert, Robert Burgoyne, and Sandy Flitterman-Lewis. *New Vocabularies in Film Semiotics: Structuralism, Post-Structuralism, and Beyond*. New York: Routledge, 1992. Very useful explanation of current theoretical terminology. Recommended.

Stephenson, Ralph, and J. R. Debrix. *The Cinema as Art*. New York: Penguin, 1965. Still a useful introduction.

Talbot, Daniel, ed. *Film: An Anthology*. Berkeley: University of California Press, 1967. First published in 1959 and still a classic general collection.

Tufte, Edward. *The Visual Display of Quantitative Information*. Cheshire, CT: Graphics Press, 1983. A rigorous, elegant, quirky essay on the grammar of cognitive art and interface. Self-published by the Yale professor, this has become a standard text for visual thinkers. *Envisioning Information* (1990) and *Visual Explanations* (1997) followed, also self-published.

See also Bazin, Eco, Metz, and Wollen entries in Section 5.

4A. FILM HISTORY: THE ECONOMICS AND POLITICS OF FILM

Bach, Steven. *Final Cut: Dreams & Disasters in the Making of Heaven's Gate*. New York: NAL-Dutton, 1986.

Bagdikian, B. H. *Media Monopoly*. Fourth ed. Boston: Beacon, 1992.

Balio, Tino, ed. *The American Film Industry*. Madison: University of Wisconsin Press, 1985.

Balio, Tino. *United Artists: The Company That Changed the Film Industry*. Madison: University of Wisconsin Press, 1987.

Bentley, Eric. *Thirty Years of Treason*. New York: Viking, 1971. The blacklisting period.

Bergman, Andrew. *We're in the Money*. New York: Harper & Row, 1973. The 1930s in America.

Bogle, Donald. *Toms, Coons, Mulattos, Mammies and Bucks*. New York: Viking, 1989. Images of Blacks in American movies.

Brady, John Joseph. *The Craft of the Screenwriter*. New York: Simon & Schuster, 1981.

Ceplair, Larry, and Steve Englund. *The Inquisition in Hollywood: Politics in the Film Community*. New York: Doubleday, 1980.

Corrigan, Timothy. *A Cinema Without Walls: Movies and Culture After Vietnam*. New Brunswick, NJ: Rutgers University Press, 1991.

Cripps, Thomas. *Slow Fade to Black: The Negro in American Film, 1900–1942*. New York: Oxford University Press, 1977. A seminal study.

DeCordova, Richard. *Picture Personalities: The Emergence of the Star System in America*. Urbana: University of Illinois Press, 1990.

Deming, Barbara. *Running Away from Myself: Dream Portrait of America Drawn from the Films of the Forties*. New York: Viking, 1969. Influential, sociologically oriented study.

Dyer, Richard. *Stars*. London: British Film Institute, 1979.

Dyer, Richard. *Heavenly Bodies: Film Stars and Society*. New York: St. Martin's Press, 1986.

Dyer, Richard. *Now You See It: Studies on Lesbian and Gay Film*. London: Routledge, 1990.

Gabler, Neal. *An Empire of Their Own: How the Jews Invented Hollywood*. New York: Crown, 1988.

Gabler, Neal. *Winchell: Gossip, Power, and the Culture of Celebrity*. New York: Knopf, 1994.

Geduld, Harry M. *Birth of the Talkies*. Bloomington: Indiana University Press, 1975.

Goldman, William. *Adventures in the Screen Trade: A Personal View of Hollywood and Screenwriting*. New York: Warner Books, 1983.

Gomery, Douglas. *The Hollywood Studio System*. New York: St. Martin's Press, 1986.

Guback, Thomas H. *The International Film Industry.* Bloomington: Indiana University Press, 1969. Landmark study of international film economics.

Haskell, Molly. *From Reverence to Rape.* New York: Penguin, 1974. Seminal study of women and film. Recommended.

Haskell, Molly. *Holding My Own in No Man's Land.* New York: Oxford University Press, 1997. A breathless 24 years later, Haskell follows up with more precise, reasoned, and thoughtful analysis of the landscape of sexual politics.

Huaco, George A. *The Sociology of Film Art.* New York: Basic Books, 1965. A classic text on the subject.

Jarvie, Ian. *Hollywood's Overseas Campaign: The North Atlantic Movie Trade, 1920–1950.* Cambridge: Cambridge University Press, 1992.

Jones, G. William. *Black Cinema Treasures: Lost and Found.* Denton, TX: University of North Texas Press, 1981. Short history of Black cinema from the 1930s to the 1950s.

Kaplan, E. Ann. *Women and Film: Both Sides of the Camera.* New York: Routledge, 1983.

Kerr, Paul, ed. *The Hollywood Film Industry: A Reader.* London: Routledge & Kegan Paul, 1986.

Kindem, Gorham. *The American Movie Industry: The Business of Motion Pictures.* Carbondale: Southern Illinois University Press, 1982.

Manvell, Roger. *Films and the Second World War.* Cranbury, NJ: A. S. Barnes, 1974.

Mayer, Michael F. *The Film Industries.* Second ed. New York: Hastings House, 1973, 1979. By a lawyer, an influential study of the business of film.

McClintick, David. *Indecent Exposure: A True Story of Hollywood & Wall Street.* New York: William Morrow, 1982. The Begelman affair as an index of contemporary Hollywood.

Monaco, James. *American Film Now: The People, the Power, the Money, the Movies.* Second edition. New York: New York Zoetrope and New American Library, 1984. Includes appendices, bibliography, and charts.

Navasky, Victor. *Naming Names.* New York: Penguin, 1981. The blacklist period.

Paul, William. *Laughing Screaming: Modern Hollywood Horror and Comedy.* New York: Columbia University Press, 1994.

Phillips, Julia. *You'll Never Eat Lunch in This Town Again.* New York: NAL-Dutton, 1992. A newsmaker when it was published, and still a revealing window on Hollywood habits.

Prindle, David. *Politics of Glamour: Ideology and Democracy in the Screen Actors Guild.* Madison: University of Wisconsin Press, 1988.

Puttnam, David, with Neil Watson. *Movies and Money.* New York: Alfred A. Knopf, 1998. The British title is more telling: *The Undeclared War: The Struggle for Control of the World's Film Industry.* Lord Puttnam's view of American cultural imperialism.

Pye, Michael. *Moguls: Inside the Business of Show Business.* New York: Holt, Rinehart and Winston, 1980.

Russo, Vito. *The Celluloid Closet: Homosexuality in the Movies,* New York: Harper & Row, 1981.

Schatz, Thomas. *The Genius of the System: Hollywood Film in the Studio Era.* New York: Pantheon, 1988.

Schickel, Richard. *His Picture in the Papers: A Speculation on Celebrity in America, Based on the Life of Douglas Fairbanks, Sr.* New York: Charterhouse, 1973. A seminal study of celebrityhood and an interesting essay on one of its inventors.

Schickel, Richard. *Intimate Strangers: The Culture of Celebrity.* New York: Doubleday, 1990.

Schivelbusch, Wolfgang. *The Railway Journey: The Industrialization of Time and Space in the 19th Century.* 1977. Berkeley: University of California Press, 1986. Offers interesting comparisons with the history of media.

Schumach, Murray. *The Face on the Cutting Room Floor: The Story of Movie and Television Censorship.* New York: Morrow, 1964. Reprint. New York: Da Capo Press, 1974.

Shindler, Colin. *Hollywood Goes to War.* London: Routledge & Kegan Paul, 1979.

Sklar, Robert. *Movie-Made America: A Cultural History of American Movies.* New York: Random House, 1975.

Sklar, Robert, and Charles Musser, eds. *Resisting Images: Essays on Cinema and History.* Philadelphia: Temple University Press, 1990.

Talbot, David, and Barbara Zheutlin. *Creative Differences: Profiles of Hollywood Dissidents.* Boston: South End Press, 1978. Political activists, past and present: a significant study.

Thompson, Kristin. *Exporting Entertainment: America in the World Film Market, 1907–34.* London: British Film Institute, 1985.

Thomson, David. *America in the Dark.* New York: William Morrow, 1977. Recommended.

Vogel, Amos. *Film as a Subversive Art.* New York: Random House, 1975. Recommended.

Wolfenstein, Martha, and Nathan Leites. *Movies: A Psychological Study.* New York: Atheneum, 1960. Reprint 1970.

Wood, Michael. *America in the Movies.* New York: Basic Books, 1975. An important essay on the politics and style of American movies. Recommended.

4B. FILM HISTORY: GENERAL HISTORICAL STUDIES

Allen, Robert C., and Douglas Gomery. *Film History: Theory and Practice.* New York: Knopf, 1990. Essential guide to film historiography.

Armes, Roy. *A Critical History of British Cinema.* New York: Oxford University Press, 1978.

Bellour, Raymond. *L'analyse du film.* Paris: Albatross, 1979.

Braudy, Leo, and Morris Dickstein. *Great Film Directors: A Critical Anthology.* New York: Oxford University Press, 1978.

Clair, René. *Cinema Yesterday and Today.* New York: Dover, 1972. A personal view.

Cook, David A. *A History of Narrative Film.* Second ed. New York: W.W. Norton, 1990.

Cowie, Peter, ed. *A Concise History of the Cinema.* 2 vols. Cranbury, NJ: A. S. Barnes, 1970. Recommended. Short but useful.

Dickinson, Thorold. *A Discovery of Cinema.* New York: Oxford University Press, 1971. Recommended.

Ellis, Jack C. *A History of Film.* Third ed. Englewood Cliffs, NJ: Prentice Hall, 1990. Textbook.

Everson, William K. *American Silent Film.* New York: Oxford University Press, 1978. A valuable history.

Fell, John L. *A History of Films.* New York: Holt, Rinehart and Winston, 1979. Textbook.

Geduld, Harry M., ed. *Authors on Film.* Bloomington: Indiana University Press, 1972. A farrago of bits and pieces from Tolstoy to James Baldwin. Forty-one items.

Geduld, Harry M., ed. *Filmmakers on Filmmaking.* Bloomington: Indiana University Press, 1967. Thirty pieces by filmmakers ranging from Lumière to Anger.

Gomery, Douglas. *Movie History: A Survey.* London: Wadsworth, 1991.

Hampton, Benjamin. *History of the American Film Industry from Its Beginnings to 1931.* 1931. Reprint. New York: Dover, 1970.

Jacobs, Lewis. *Introduction to the Art of the Movies.* New York: Noonday, 1960. Thirty-six essays written between 1910 and 1960 and arranged chronologically.

Jacobs, Lewis, ed. *The Emergence of Film Art.* New York: Hopkinson & Blake, 1970. Forty-two selections arranged chronologically from Méliès to Mekas.

Jowett, Garth. *Film: The Democratic Art.* Boston: Little, Brown, 1976.

Mast, Gerald. *A Short History of the Movies.* Second ed. Indianapolis: Bobbs-Merrill, 1976.

Montagu, Ivor. *Film World.* New York: Penguin, 1964. A standard work. Still useful.

Pratt, George C. *Spellbound in Darkness: A History of the Silent Film*. Greenwich, CT: New York Graphic Society, 1973. A classic of its time.

Rhode, Eric. *A History of Cinema*. New York: Hill and Wang, 1975.

Robinson, David. *The History of World Cinema*. New York: Stein and Day, 1974.

Rotha, Paul, and Richard Griffith. *The Film Till Now*. New York: Twayne, 1960. First published in 1930, updated several times, this is an early classic of film scholarship.

Sadoul, Georges. *Histoire générale du cinéma*. Paris: Denoël, 1973–75. First published in 1948, this is a classic of film history.

Sarris, Andrew. *"You Ain't Heard Nothin' Yet." The American Talking Film: History and Memory*. New York: Oxford University Press, 1998. Notes from a lifetime of critical thought.

Sklar, Robert. *Film: An International History of the Medium*. New York: Abrams, 1993.

Stanley, Robert H. *The Celluloid Empire: A History of the American Movie Industry*. New York: Hastings House, 1978.

Thompson, Kristin, and David Bordwell. *Film History: An Introduction*. New York: McGraw-Hill, 1994.

Wright, Basil. *The Long View*. New York: Knopf, 1975. A weighty history, but idiosyncratic.

4C. FILM HISTORY: SPECIFIC MAJOR PERIODS

Anbinder, Paul, ed. *Before Hollywood: Turn-of-the-Century American Film*. New York: Hudson Hills Press, 1987.

Anger, Kenneth. *Hollywood Babylon*. Reprint. New York: Delta, 1975. A classic of gossip.

Apra, Adriano, and Patrizia Pistagnesi, eds. *The Fabulous Thirties: Italian Cinema 1929–1944*. Rome: Electa International Publishing Group, 1979.

Barnes, John. *Beginnings of the Cinema in England*. New York: Barnes & Noble, 1976.

Barr, Charles. *Ealing Studios*. Woodstock, NY: Overlook Press, 1980.

Battcock, Gregory, ed. *The New American Cinema*. New York: Dutton, 1967.

Biskind, Peter. *Seeing Is Believing: How Hollywood Taught Us To Stop Worrying and Love the Fifties*. New York: Pantheon, 1983.

Bowser, Eileen. *The Transformation of Cinema: 1907–1915*. New York: Charles Scribner's Sons, 1990. Vol. 2 of Scribner's History of American Cinema series, Charles Harpole, series editor.

Brownlow, Kevin. *The Parade's Gone By*. New York: Ballantine, 1968. Recommended. Early film history.

Brownlow, Kevin. *The War, the West, and the Wilderness*. London: Secker & Warburg, 1979.

Brownlow, Kevin, and John Kobal. *Hollywood: The Pioneers*. London: Collins, 1979.

Brownlow, Kevin. *Behind the Mask of Innocence: Sex, Violence, Prejudice, Crime: Films of Social Conscience in the Silent Era*. London: Jonathan Cape, 1990.

Brownlow, Kevin, and David Gill. *Cinema Europe: The Other Hollywood*. London: BBC, ZDF, and D. L. Taffner, 1995. A six-part television series (available on VHS) surveying the history of silent film in Europe. A model for film-history documentaries. Highly recommended.

Burch, Noel. *Life to Those Shadows*. Berkeley: University of California Press, 1990. The primitive era.

Cameron, Ian, ed. *Second Wave*. New York: Praeger, 1970. Essays on Makavejev, Skolimowski, Oshima, Guerra, Rocha, Groulx, Lefebvre, Straub.

Chanan, Michael. *The Dream That Kicks: The Prehistory and Early Years of the Cinema in Britain*. London: Routledge & Kegan Paul, 1979.

Cowie, Peter. *Fifty Major Filmmakers*. London: Tantivy, 1975.

Cowie, Peter, ed. *Hollywood 1920–1970.* London: Tantivy, 1975.

Doherty, Thomas. *Projections of War: Hollywood and American Culture, 1941–1945.* New York: Columbia University Press, 1993.

Dowdy, Andrew. *The Films of the Fifties.* New York: Morrow, 1973.

Elsaesser, Thomas. *Early Cinema: Space, Frame, Narrative.* London: British Film Institute, 1990.

Eyman, Scott. *The Speed of Sound: Hollywood and the Talkie Revolution, 1926–1930.* New York: Simon & Schuster, 1997.

Fell, John L., ed. *Film Before Griffith.* Berkeley: University of California Press, 1983.

Gelmis, Joseph, ed. *The Film Director as Superstar.* New York: Doubleday, 1970. Interviews with filmmakers of the sixties, all conducted by Gelmis.

Hansen, Miriam. *Babel and Babylon: Spectatorship in American Silent Film.* Cambridge, MA: Harvard University Press, 1992.

Harcourt, Peter. *Six European Directors.* New York: Penguin, 1974. Eisenstein, Renoir, Buñuel, Bergman, Fellini, Godard.

Harvey, Sylvia. *May '68 and Film Culture.* London: British Film Institute, 1978.

Hennebelle, Guy. *15 Ans du cinéma mondial.* Paris: Éditions du Cerf, 1975.

Houston, Penelope. *The Contemporary Cinema.* New York: Penguin, 1963. Recommended. A classic in its time.

Jacobs, Diane. *Hollywood Renaissance.* Rev. ed. New York: Delta Books, 1980. Coppola, Scorsese, Ritchie, and the generation of the seventies.

Kennedy, Joseph P., ed. *The Story of the Films, as told by leaders of the industry to the students of the graduate school of business administration.* Chicago: A. W. Shaw, 1927. Hays, Zukor, Lasky, DeMille, Loew, Fox, Warner, and others. And you thought JFK was the first author in the family.

Kolker, Robert Phillip. *The Altering Eye: Contemporary International Cinema.* New York: Oxford University Press, 1983.

Koppes, Clayton R., and Gregory D. Black. *Hollywood Goes to War: How Politics, Profits and Propaganda Shaped World War II Movies.* Berkeley: University of California Press, 1990.

Koszarski, Richard. *The Astoria Studio and its Fabulous Films: A Pictorial History.* New York: Dover, 1983.

Koszarski, Richard. *An Evening's Entertainment: The Age of the Silent Feature Picture, 1915–1928.* New York: Charles Scribner's Sons, 1990. Vol. 3 of Scribner's History of American Cinema series, Charles Harpole, series editor.

Kuhn, Annette. *Cinema, Censorship, and Sexuality, 1909–1925.* New York: Routledge, 1988.

Leyda, Jay, and Charles Musser, eds. *Before Hollywood: Turn-of-the-Century Film from American Archives.* New York: American Federation of the Arts, 1986. Handsomely illustrated.

McCarthy, Todd, and Charles Flynn, eds. *Kings of the B's: Working Within the Hollywood System.* New York: Dutton, 1975. Anthology of studies of "B" directors.

Monaco, James F. *The New Wave: Truffaut, Godard, Chabrol, Rohmer, Rivette.* New York: Oxford University Press, 1976.

Mordden, Ethan. *The Hollywood Studios: House Style in the Golden Age of the Movies.* New York: Knopf, 1988.

Musser, Charles. *The Emergence of Cinema: The American Screen to 1907.* New York: Charles Scribner's Sons, 1990. Vol. 1 of Scribner's History of American Cinema series, Charles Harpole, series editor.

Parrish, Robert. *Growing Up in Hollywood.* New York: Harcourt Brace Jovanovich, 1976.

Petley, Julian. *Capital and Culture: German Cinema 1933–1945.* London: British Film Institute, 1979.

Polan, Dana. *Power and Paranoia: History, Narrative and the American Cinema, 1940–1950*. New York: Columbia University Press, 1986.

Powdermaker, Hortense. *Hollywood: The Dream Factory*. New York: Arno Press, 1924, 1979.

Pye, Michael, and Lynda Myles. *The Movie Brats: How the Film Generation Took Over Hollywood*. London: Faber & Faber; New York: Holt, Rinehart and Winston, 1979. Comments on Coppola, Lucas, DePalma, Milius, Scorsese, Spielberg, and others.

Ramsaye, Terry. *A Million and One Nights: A History of the Motion Picture Through 1925*. New York: Simon & Schuster, 1926. Reprints 1964, 1986. A very early and classic history.

Ray, Robert B. *A Certain Tendency of the Hollywood Cinema, 1930–1980*. Princeton: Princeton University Press, 1985.

Ryan, Michael, and Douglas Kellner. *Camera Politica: The Politics and Ideology of Contemporary Hollywood Film*. Bloomington: Indiana University Press, 1988.

Saunders, Thomas J. *Hollywood in Berlin: American Cinema and Weimar Germany*. Berkeley: University of California Press, 1994.

Slide, Anthony. *Early American Cinema*. Cranbury, NJ: A. S. Barnes, 1970.

Slide, Anthony. *Early Women Directors: Their Role in the Development of the Silent Cinema*. Cranbury, NJ: A. S. Barnes, 1977.

Taylor, John Russell. *Cinema Eye, Cinema Ear*. New York: Hill and Wang, 1964. A landmark in its approach to film as a serious art; surveys the European scene in the sixties.

Taylor, John Russell. *Directors and Directions: Cinema for the Seventies*. New York: Hill and Wang, 1975. Chabrol, Pasolini, Anderson, Kubrick, Warhol/Morrissey, S. Ray, Jancsó, Makavejev.

Thomson, David. *Overexposures: The Crisis in American Filmmaking*. New York: William Morrow, 1987.

Torrence, Bruce. *Hollywood: The First Hundred Years*. New York: New York Zoetrope, 1982. A remarkable collection of photographs of early Los Angeles.

Wagenknecht, Edward. *Movies in the Age of Innocence*. New York: Ballantine, 1971. Early cinema.

Walker, Alexander. *The Shattered Silents: How the Talkies Came to Stay*. New York: William Morrow, 1979.

Wood, Robin. *Hollywood from Vietnam to Reagan*. New York: Columbia University Press, 1985.

4D. FILM HISTORY: GENRES AND SPECIFIC TOPICS

Aldgate, Anthony. *Cinema & History: British Newsreels and the Spanish Civil War*. London: Scolar Press, 1979.

Altman, Rick. *The American Film Musical*. Bloomington: Indiana University Press, 1987.

Anderson, Gillian. *Music for Silent Films: 1894–1929*. Washington: Library of Congress, 1988.

Balio, Tino. *United Artists: The Company Built by the Stars*. Madison: University of Wisconsin Press, 1976.

Barnouw, Erik. *Documentary: A History of the Non-Fiction Film*. Second revised ed. New York: Oxford University Press, 1993. A basic history. Recommended.

Barrier, Michael. *Hollywood Cartoons: American Animation in Its Golden Age*. New York: Oxford University Press, 1999. An extensive survey.

Barrios, Richard. *A Song in the Dark: The Birth of the Musical Film*. New York: Oxford University Press, 1995.

Barsam, Richard. *Non-Fiction Film: A Critical History*. Bloomington: Indiana University Press, 1992. A good introduction.

Bart, Peter. *Fade Out: The Calamitous Final Days of MGM*. New York: William Morrow, 1990. Instructive insider's view by the veteran producer-journalist, and a deadly accurate view of Hollywood in the 1980s.

Brosnan, John. *Future Tense: The Cinema of Science Fiction*. New York: St. Martin's Press, 1978.

Brosnan, John. *The Primal Screen: A History of Science Fiction Film*. London: Orbit, 1991.

Brown, Royal S. *Overtones and Undertones: Reading Film Music*. Berkeley: University of California Press, 1994.

Brownlow, Kevin. *Behind the Mask of Innocence: Sex, Violence, Crime—Films of Social Conscience in the Silent Era*. New York: Knopf, 1990; Berkeley: University of California Press, 1992.

Buscombe, Edward. *The BFI Companion to the Western*. London: British Film Institute, 1988. Excellent historical essays.

Cavell, Stanley. *Pursuits of Happiness: The Hollywood Comedy of Remarriage*. Cambridge, MA: Harvard University Press, 1981.

Clarens, Carlos. *Crime Movies: From Griffith to* The Godfather *and Beyond*. New York: Norton, 1980.

Colpi, Henri. *Défense et illustration de la musique dans le film*. Lyon: Serdoc, 1963.

Corliss, Richard. *Talking Pictures: Screenwriters in the American Cinema*. New York: Viking, 1973.

Crafton, Donald. *Before Mickey: The Animated Film 1898–1928*. Cambridge, MA: MIT Press, 1982.

Cripps, Thomas. *Black Film as Genre*. Bloomington: Indiana University Press, 1979.

Diawara, Manthia, ed. *Black American Cinema*. New York: Routledge, 1993.

Doane, Mary Ann. *The Desire To Desire: The Woman's Film of the 1940s*. Bloomington: Indiana University Press, 1987.

Doane, Mary Ann, Patricia Mellencamp, and Linda Williams. *Re-Vision: Essays in Feminist Film Criticism*. Frederick, MD: University Publications of America, 1984.

Doherty, Thomas. *Teenagers and Teenpics: The Juvenilization of American Movies in the 1950s*. Boston: Unwin Hyman, 1988.

Durgnat, Raymond. *The Crazy Mirror*. New York: Delta, 1969. About Hollywood.

Dyer, Richard. *Gays and Film*. Rev. ed. New York: New York Zoetrope, 1984.

Dyer, Richard, and Ginette Vincendeau, eds. *Popular European Cinema*. London: Routledge, 1992.

Ellis, Jack C. *The Documentary Idea: A Critical History of English-Language Documentary Film and Video*. Englewood Cliffs, NJ: Prentice Hall, 1989.

Everson, William K. *The Bad Guys*. New York: Citadel, 1964.

Everson, William K. *The Detective in Film*. New York: Citadel, 1972.

Everson, William K. *Classics of the Horror Film*. New York: Citadel, 1974.

Fenin, George N., and William K. Everson. *The Western: From Silents to the Seventies*. Second ed. New York: Grossman, 1973. Recommended.

Fielding, Raymond. *The American Newsreel: 1911–1967*. Norman: University of Oklahoma Press, 1972.

Frayling, Christopher. *Spaghetti Westerns: Cowboys and Europeans from Karl May to Sergio Leone*. Boston: Routledge & Kegan Paul, 1980.

French, Philip. *Westerns: Aspects of a Movie Genre*. New York: Oxford University Press, 1977.

Girgus, Sam B. *Hollywood Renaissance: The Cinema of Democracy in the Era of Ford, Capra, and Kazan*. New York Cambridge University Press, 1998.

Glaessner, Verina, *Kung-Fu: Cinema of Vengeance*. New York: Bounty, 1973.

Grant, Barry Keith. *Film Genre Reader*. Austin: University of Texas Press, 1986.

Grodal, Torben. *Moving Pictures: A New Theory of Film Genres, Feelings, and Cognition*. New York: Oxford University Press, 1999. A theory of genre and its effects on viewers.

Higham, Charles. *Hollywood Cameramen*. Bloomington: Indiana University Press, 1970.

Higham, Charles. *Warner Brothers*. New York: Charles Scribner's Sons, 1975.

Hoberman, J., and Jonathan Rosenbaum. *Midnight Movies*. New York: Harper & Row, 1983.

Hoberman, J. *Bridge of Light: Yiddish Film Between Two Worlds*. New York: Museum of Modern Art, 1991. European and American Yiddish cinema.

Houston, Penelope. *Keepers of the Frame: The Film Archives*. London: British Film Institute, 1994.

Insdorf, Annette. *Indelible Shadows: The Film and the Holocaust*. Cambridge: Cambridge University Press, 1990. Foreword by Elie Wiesel.

Jacobs, Lewis, ed. *The Documentary Tradition: From Nanook to Woodstock*. New York: Hopkinson and Blake, 1971. Ninety-six pieces on documentaries.

Kaminsky, Stuart. *American Film Genres*. Chicago: Nelson-Hall, 1985.

Kaplan, E. Ann, ed. *Women in Film Noir*. London: British Film Institute, 1978. Useful collection.

Kawin, Bruce F. *Mindscreen: Bergman, Godard, and First-Person Film*. Princeton, NJ: Princeton University Press, 1978. A theory of narration.

Kerr, Walter. *The Silent Clowns*. New York: Knopf, 1975. Recommended.

Kitses, Jim. *Horizons West*. Bloomington: Indiana University Press, 1970. One of the first practical applications of semiotic theories.

Kolker, Robert Phillip. *A Cinema of Loneliness: Penn, Kubrick, Scorsese, Spielberg, Altman*. Second ed. New York: Oxford University Press, 1988.

Kuhn, Annette, ed. *Alien Zone: Cultural Theory and Contemporary Science Fiction Cinema*. London, New York: Verso, 1990.

Lawder, Standish D. *The Cubist Cinema*. New York: New York University Press, 1973.

Leyda, Jay. *Films Beget Films*. New York: Hill and Wang, 1965. A study of compilation films.

Lovell, Alan, and Jim Hillier. *Studies in Documentary*. New York: Viking, 1972.

Low, Rachel. *Documentary and Educational Films of the 1930s*. London: Allen & Unwin, 1979.

Low, Rachel. *Films of Comment and Persuasion of the 1930s*. London: Allen & Unwin, 1979.

Maltin, Leonard. *Of Mice and Magic: A History of American Animated Cartoons*. New York: Plume, 1987.

Mamber, Stephen. *Cinéma Vérité in America*. Cambridge, MA: MIT Press, 1974.

Marcorelles, Louis. *Living Cinema*. New York: Praeger, 1972. Study of Direct Cinema and Concrete Cinema.

Mast, Gerald. *The Comic Mind: Comedy and the Movies*. Second Edition. Chicago: University of Chicago Press, 1979.

Meeker, David. *Jazz in the Movies*. Second edition. London: Talisman Books, 1981.

Mellen, Joan. *Big Bad Wolves: Masculinity in American Films*. New York: Pantheon, 1978.

Morin, Edgar. *Les Stars*. Paris: Éditions du Seuil, 1972. A classic work.

Nichols, Bill. *Representing Reality: Issues and Concepts in Documentary*. Bloomington: Indiana University Press, 1992

O'Connor, John E., and Martin Jackson, eds. *American History/American Film: Interpreting the Hollywood Image*. New York: Frederick Ungar, 1978.

Patterson, Lindsay, ed. *Black Films and Filmmakers*. New York: Dodd, Mead, 1975.

Prawer, S. S. *Caligari's Children: The Film as Tale of Terror*. Oxford: Oxford University Press, 1980.

Renan, Sheldon. *An Introduction to the American Underground Film*. New York: Dutton, 1967.

Roddick, Nick. *A New Deal in Entertainment: Warner Brothers in the 1930s*. London: British Film Institute, 1983.

Rosenthal, Alan, ed. *New Challenges to Documentary*. Berkeley: University of California Press, 1987.

Rotha, Paul. *Documentary Film*. London: Faber and Faber, 1939. A classic.

Rotha, Paul. *Documentary Diary: An Informal History of the British Documentary Film 1928–1939*. New York: Hill and Wang, 1973. Recommended.

Roud, Richard. *A Passion for Films: Henri Langlois and the Cinémathèque Française*. New York: Viking Press, 1983. An eloquent homage from one influential cinephile to another.

Rubinstein, Leonard. *The Great Spy Films: A Pictorial History*. Secaucus, NJ: Citadel Press, 1979.

Saleh, Dennis. *Science Fiction Gold: Classic Films of the Fifties*. New York: McGraw-Hill, 1979.

Schatz, Thomas. *Hollywood Genres: Formulas, Filmmaking, Studio System*. Second ed. New York: Random House, 1993.

Schrader, Paul. *Transcendental Style in Film: Ozu, Bresson, Dreyer*. Berkeley: University of California Press, 1972.

Siegel, Scott, and Barbara Siegel. *American Film Comedy: From Abbott & Costello to Jerry Zucker*. New York: Prentice-Hall, 1994. A Dictionary.

Silver, Alain. *The Samurai Film*. Cranbury, NJ: A. S. Barnes, 1975.

Silver, Alain, and Elizabeth Ward, eds. *Film Noir: An Encyclopedic Reference to the American Style*. Woodstock, NY: Overlook Press, 1988.

Sitney, P. Adams. *Visionary Film: The American Avant-Garde 1943–1978*. Second ed. New York: Oxford University Press, 1979. A seminal study. Recommended. (The first edition, 1974, has a chapter on Gregory Markopoulos not in the second edition.)

Sitney, P. Adams, ed. *Film Culture Reader*. New York: Praeger, 1970. From the magazine devoted to New American Cinema.

Smoodin, Eric. *Animating Culture: Hollywood Cartoons from the Sound Era*. New Brunswick, NJ: Rutgers University Press, 1993.

Sobchack, Vivian Carol. *Screening Space: The American Science Fiction Film*. Second ed. New York: Ungar, 1987.

Solomon, Stanley J. *Beyond Formula: American Film Genres*. New York: Harcourt Brace Jovanovich, 1976. An interesting approach.

Staiger, Janet, ed. *The Studio System*. New Brunswick: Rutgers University Press, 1994.

Stam, Robert. *Reflexivity in Film and Literature: From Don Quixote to Jean-Luc Godard*. New York: Columbia University Press, 1992.

Sussex, Elizabeth. *The Rise and Fall of British Documentary*. Berkeley: University of California Press, 1975.

Taylor, John Russell, and Arthur Jackson. *The Hollywood Musical*. New York: McGraw-Hill, 1971.

Telotte, J. P. *The Cult Film Experience: Beyond All Reason*. Austin: University of Texas Press, 1991.

Turan, Kenneth, and Stephen F. Zito. *Sinema: American Pornographic Films and the People Who Make Them*. New York: Praeger, 1974.

Vallance, Tom. *The American Musical*. Cranbury, NJ: A. S. Barnes, 1970.

Waller, Gregory A. *American Horrors: Essays on the Modern American Horror Film*. Urbana: University of Illinois Press, 1987.

Warren, Patricia. *Elstree: The British Hollywood*. London: Elm Tree Books, 1983.

Wright, Will. *Six Guns and Society: A Structural Study of the Western*. Berkeley: University of California Press, 1975.

Youngblood, Gene. *Expanded Cinema*. New York: Dutton, 1970. A classic vision of cinematic forms of "the future."

4E. FILM HISTORY: NATIONAL CINEMAS

Abel, Richard. *French Cinema: The First Wave, 1915–1929*. Princeton: Princeton University Press, 1984.

Aguilar, Carlos, and Jaume Genover. *El Cine español en sus interpretes*. Madrid: Verdoux, 1992.

Anbinder, Paul, ed. *Before Hollywood: Turn-of-the-Century American Film*. New York: Hudson Hills Press, 1987.

Anderson, Joseph L., and Donald Richie. *The Japanese Film: Art and Industry*. Rev. ed. Princeton: Princeton University Press, 1982. A basic text.

Apra, Adriano, ed. *Le Cinéma coréen*. Paris: Centre Georges Pompidou, 1993.

Armes, Roy. *French Cinema Since 1946*. 2 vols. Second enlarged ed. Cranbury, NJ: A. S. Barnes, 1970. A useful monograph. The second volume deals with the New Wave.

Armes, Roy. *Patterns of Realism: Italian Neo-Realist Cinema*. Cranbury, NJ: A. S. Barnes, 1971.

Armes, Roy. *A Critical History of British Cinema*. London: Secker & Warburg, 1978.

Armes, Roy. *Third World Film-Making and the West*. Berkeley: University of California Press, 1987.

Barnouw, Erik, and S. Krishnaswamy. *Indian Film*. Second ed. New York: Oxford University Press, 1980.

Barr, Charles. *Ealing Studios*. Newton Abbot: David & Charles, 1977.

Barr, Charles, ed. *All Our Yesterdays: 90 Years of British Cinema*. London: British Film Institute, 1986.

Behn, Manfred, and Hans-Michael Bock, eds. *Film und Gesellschaft in der DDR: Materialsammlung zu einer veranstaltungsreihe*. Two vols. Hamburg: Metropolis/Cinegraph, 1988–89.

Betts, Ernest. *The Film Business: A History of the British Cinema 1896–1972*. New York: Pitman, 1973.

Björkman, Stig. *Film in Sweden: The New Directors*. Cranbury, NJ: A. S. Barnes, 1976.

Bock, Audie. *Japanese Film Directors*. New York: Kodansha International, 1978.

Bock, Hans-Michael, Michael Töteberg, eds. *Das Ufa-Buch: Kunst und Krisen, Stars und Regisseure, Wirtshaft und Politik*. Frankfurt: Zweitausendeins, 1992.

Browne, Nick, et al., eds. *New Chinese Cinema: Forms, Identities, Politics*. New York: Cambridge University Press, 1994.

Burch, Nöel. *To the Distant Observer: Form and Meaning in the Japanese Cinema*. Berkeley: University of California Press, 1979.

Burton, Julianne. *Cinema and Social Change in Latin America: Conversations with Latin American Filmmakers*. Austin: University of Texas Press, 1986.

Chanan, Michael, ed. *Chilean Cinema*. London: British Film Institute, 1976.

Corrigan, Timothy. *New German Film: The Displaced Image*. Austin: University of Texas Press, 1983.

Cowie, Peter. *Screen Series: Sweden 1*. Cranbury, NJ: A. S. Barnes, 1970. An efficient summary.

Cowie, Peter. *Dutch Cinema: An Illustrated History*. Cranbury, NJ: A. S. Barnes, 1979.

Cowie, Peter. *Finnish Cinema*. London: Tantivy Press, 1975. Second ed. Helsinki: VAPK Publishing, 1990.

Diawara, Manthia. *African Cinema*. Bloomington: Indiana University Press, 1992.

Downing, John, ed. *Film, Politics, and the Third World*. New York: Praeger, 1987.

Durgnat, Raymond. *A Mirror for England*. New York: Praeger, 1971.

Eberts, Jake, and Terry Ilott. *My Indecision Is Final: The Rise and Fall of Goldcrest Films*. London and Boston: Faber & Faber, 1990.

Eisner, Lotte. *The Haunted Screen.* Berkeley: University of California Press, 1974. The German cinema.

Elsaesser, Thomas. *New German Cinema: A History.* London: British Film Institute; New Brunswick, NJ: Rutgers University Press, 1989.

Everson, William K. *The American Movie.* New York: Atheneum, 1963.

Franklin, James C. *New German Cinema: From Oberhausen to Hamburg.* Cambridge, MA: Harvard University Press, 1983.

Hochman, Stanley, ed. *American Film Directors: A Library of Film Criticism.* New York: Ungar, 1974. Arranged as an encyclopedia: 61 directors, filmographies, index of critics and films.

Hull, David S. *Films in the Third Reich.* New York: Simon & Schuster, 1969.

Jacobs, Lewis. *The Rise of the American Film.* New York: Columbia University Teachers College Press, 1939, 1967.

Kanin, Garson. *Hollywood: Stars and Starlets, Tycoons and Flesh-Peddlers, Moviemakers and Money-makers, Frauds and Geniuses, Hopefuls and Has-Beens, Great Lovers and Sex Symbols.* New York: Viking Press, 1974. The title says it all.

Kenez, Peter. *Cinema & Soviet Society 1917–1953.* New York: Cambridge University Press, 1992.

Kinder, Marsha. *Blood Cinema: The Reconstruction of National Identity in Spain.* Berkeley: University of California Press, 1993. CD-ROM available.

King, John. *Magical Reels: A History of Cinema in Latin America.* London and New York: Verso, 1990.

Kracauer, Siegfried. *From Caligari to Hitler: A Psychological History of the German Film.* Princeton: Princeton University Press, 1947. A classic study. Recommended.

Lawton, Ann. *The Red Screen: Politics, Society, Art in Soviet Cinema.* London: Routledge, 1992.

Leiser, Irwin, *Nazi Cinema.* New York: Collier, 1975.

Lent, James A. *The Asian Film Industry.* Austin: University of Texas Press, 1991.

Leprohon, Pierre. *Italian Cinema.* New York: Praeger, 1966.

Leyda, Jay. *Dian Ying: Electric Shadows: An Account of Films and the Film Audience in China.* Boston: MIT Press, 1972. Recommended.

Leyda, Jay. *Kino: History of Russian and Soviet Film.* Third ed. Princeton: Princeton University Press, 1983. Recommended.

Liehm, Antonin J. *Closely Watched Films: The Czechoslovak Experience.* White Plains, NY: International Arts and Sciences Press, 1974. Recommended.

Liehm, Antonin J., and Mira Liehm. *The Most Important Art: Eastern European Films after 1945.* Berkeley: University of California Press, 1977.

Liehm, Mira. *Passion and Defiance: Film in Italy from 1942 to the Present.* Berkeley: University of California Press, 1984.

Litwak, Mark. *Reel Power: The Struggle for Influence and Success in the New Hollywood.* New York: William Morrow, 1986. An interesting outsider's view.

Manvell, Roger. *New Cinema in Europe.* New York: Dutton, 1966. Monograph.

Manvell, Roger. *New Cinema in the U.S.A.* New York: Dutton, 1968. Monograph.

Manvell, Roger. *New Cinema in Britain.* New York: Dutton, 1969. Monograph.

Manvell, Roger, and Heinrich Frankel. *The German Cinema.* New York: Praeger, 1971.

Marcus, Millicent. *Italian Film in the Light of Neorealism.* Princeton: Princeton University Press, 1986.

Mellen, Joan. *Voices from the Japanese Cinema.* New York: Liveright, 1975. A collection of interviews.

Mellen, Joan. *The Waves at Genji's Door: Japan Through Its Cinema.* New York: Pantheon, 1976.

Michalek, Boleslaw, and Frank Turaj, eds. *The Modern Cinema of Poland.* Bloomington: Indiana University Press, 1988.

Mora, Carl J. *Mexican Cinema: Reflections of a Society.* Berkeley: University of California Press, 1989.

Morris, Peter. *Embattled Shadows: A History of Canadian Cinema 1895–1939.* Montreal: McGill-Queens University Press, 1978.

Myerson, Michael. *Memories of Underdevelopment: The Revolutionary Films of Cuba.* New York: Grossman, 1973. Script of the film plus an essay on Cuban cinema.

Nolletti, Arthur, Jr, and David Desser, eds. *Reframing Japanese Cinema.* Bloomington: Indiana University Press, 1992.

Passek, Jean-Loup, ed. *Le Cinéma indien.* Paris: Centre Georges Pompidou, 1983.

Petrie, Graham. *History Must Answer to Man: The Contemporary Hungarian Cinema.* Budapest: Corvina Kiadó, 1978; New York: New York Zoetrope, 1980.

Pick, Zuzana M. *The New Latin American Cinema: A Continental Project.* Austin: University of Texas Press, 1993.

Radvanyi, Jean, ed. *Le Cinéma géorgien.* Paris: Centre Georges Pompidou, 1988.

Radvanyi, Jean, ed. *Le Cinéma d'asie centrale.* Paris: Centre Georges Pompidou, 1991.

Rajadhyaksha, Ashish, and Paul Willemen. *Encyclopedia of Indian Cinema.* London: British Film Institute, 1995.

Ramirez-Berg, Charles. *Cinema of Solitude: A Critical Study of Mexican Cinema, 1967–1983.* Austin: University of Texas Press, 1993.

Ratschewa, Maria, and Klaus Eder. *Der bulgarische film: Geschichte und Gegenwart einer Kinemetographie.* Frankfurt: Kommunales Kino, 1977.

Rayns, Tony. *The New Chinese Cinema: An Introduction.* (with *King of the Children*, by Chen Kaige and Wan Zhi). London and Boston: Faber & Faber, 1989.

Richie, Donald. *Japanese Cinema: An Introduction.* New York: Oxford University Press, 1990. A new edition of this classic first published in 1971.

Sadoul, Georges. *Le Cinéma français: 1890–1962.* Paris: Flammarion, 1962. Classic.

Sarris, Andrew. *The American Cinema: Directors and Directions: 1929–1968.* New York: Dutton, 1968. Sarris's "Pantheon," blurbs on a great number of directors, plus index.

Schnitzer, Luda, Jean Schnitzer, and Marcel Martin. *Cinema in Revolution: the Heroic Era of Soviet Film.* New York: Hill and Wang, 1973. Soviet cinema.

Skvorecky, Josef. *All the Bright Young Men and Women: A Personal History of the Czech Cinema.* Toronto: Peter Martin Associates, 1971.

Slide, Anthony. *The Cinema and Ireland.* Jefferson: McFarland, 1988.

Slide, Anthony. *The American Film Industry: An Historical Dictionary.* New York: Limelight Editions, 1990. Useful reference.

Tam, Kwok-Kan, and Wimal Dissanayake. *New Chinese Cinema.* New York: Oxford University Press, 1998.

Tasic, Zoran, Jean-Loup Passek, eds. *Le Cinéma yougoslave.* Paris: Centre Georges Pompidou, 1986.

Tsivian, Yuri. *Early Cinema in Russian and Its Cultural Reception.* London: Routledge, 1994.

Usai, Pablo Cherchi, et al. *Silent Witnesses: Russian Films, 1908–1919.* London: British Film Institute, 1990.

Youngblood, Denise. *Soviet Cinema in the Silent Era, 1918–1935.* Ann Arbor, MI: UMI Research Press, 1985.

4F. FILM HISTORY: FILMS AND FILMMAKERS

ALLEN, WOODY

Girgus, Sam B. *The Films of Woody Allen.* New York: Cambridge University Press, 1993.

Jacobs, Diane. *But We Need the Eggs: The Magic of Woody Allen*. New York: St. Martin's Press, 1982.

Lax, Eric. *On Being Funny: Woody Allen and Comedy*. New York: Charterhouse, 1975.

Palmer, Miles. *Woody Allen*. New York: Lippincott & Crowell, 1980.

Yacowar, Maurice. *Loser Take All: The Comic Art of Woody Allen*. New York: Frederick Ungar, 1979.

ALTMAN, ROBERT

Kass, Judith. *Robert Altman*. New York: Popular Library, 1978.

Keyssar, Helene. *Robert Altman's America*. New York: Oxford University Press, 1991.

McGilligan, Patrick. *Robert Altman: Jumping Off the Cliff*. New York: St. Martin's Press, 1989.

ANTONIONI, MICHELANGELO

Arrowsmith, William. *Antonioni: The Poet of Images*. New York: Oxford University Press, 1995. With an introduction by Ted Perry.

Brunette, Peter. *The Films of Michelangelo Antonioni*. New York: Cambridge University Press, 1998.

Cameron, Ian, and Robin Wood. *Antonioni*. New York: Praeger, 1969. Monograph.

Chatman, Seymour. *Antonioni, or the Surface of the World*. Berkeley: University of California Press, 1985.

Leprohon, Pierre. *Michelangelo Antonioni*. New York: Simon & Schuster, 1963.

Rohdie, Sam. *Antonioni*. London: British Film Institute, 1990.

BERGMAN, INGMAR

Bergman, Ingmar. *The Magic Lantern: An Autobiography*. New York: Penguin, 1987.

Björkman, Stig, Torsten Manns, and Jonas Sima. *Bergman on Bergman*. Trans. Paul Britten Austin. New York: Touchstone/Simon & Schuster, 1973. Interview.

Kaminsky, Stuart, and Joseph F. Hill, eds. *Ingmar Bergman: Essays in Criticism*. New York: Oxford University Press, 1975.

Simon, John. *Ingmar Bergman Directs*. New York: Harcourt Brace Jovanovich, 1972. Intensive rather than comprehensive.

Wood, Robin. *Ingmar Bergman*. New York: Praeger, 1969. Recommended.

Young, Vernon. *Cinema Borealis: Ingmar Bergman and the Swedish Ethos*. New York: Avon, 1971. One of the more interesting approaches to Bergman. Recommended.

BERTOLUCCI, BERNARDO

Kolker, Robert Phillip. *Bernardo Bertolucci*. New York: Oxford University Press, 1985.

Ungari, Enzo, and Donald Ranvaud. *Bertolucci by Bertolucci*. London: Plexus, 1987.

BOGART, HUMPHREY

Benchley, Nathaniel. *Bogart*. Boston: Little, Brown, 1975. Classic study of a star's career.

BRANDO, MARLON

Manso, Peter. *Brando: The Biography*. New York: Hyperion, 1994.

Schickel, Richard. *Brando: A Life in Our Times*. New York: Atheneum, 1991.

BRESSON, ROBERT

Cameron, Ian, ed. *The Films of Robert Bresson*. New York: Praeger, 1969.

BUÑUEL, LUIS

Durgnat, Raymond. *Luis Buñuel*. Berkeley: University of California Press, 1970.

Mellen, Joan, ed. *The World of Luis Buñuel: Essays in Criticism*. New York: Oxford University Press, 1978.

CAPRA, FRANK

Capra, Frank. *The Name above the Title*. New York: Bantam, 1971. Memoirs.

McBride, Joseph. *Frank Capra: The Catastrophe of Success*. New York: Simon & Schuster, 1992.

CARNÉ, MARCEL

Turk, Edward Baron. *Child of Paradise: Marcel Carné and the Golden Age of French Cinema*. Cambridge MA: Harvard University Press, 1989.

CASSAVETES, JOHN

Carney, Ray. *The Films of John Cassavetes: Pragmatism, Modernism, and the Movies*. Cambridge: Cambridge University Press, 1994.

CHABROL, CLAUDE

Wood, Robin, and Michael Walker. *Claude Chabrol*. New York: Praeger, 1970.

CHAPLIN, CHARLES

Chaplin, Charles. *My Autobiography*. New York: Pocket Books, 1966. Recommended.

Maland, Charles J. *Chaplin and American Culture*. Princeton: Princeton University Press, 1991.

Robinson, David. *Chaplin: The Mirror of Opinion*. Bloomington: Indiana University Press, 1984.

Tyler, Parker. *Chaplin, Last of the Clowns*. New York: Horizon Press, 1972.

CHEN KAIGE

Chen Kaige and Wan Zhi. *King of the Children*. Trans. Bonnie S. McDougall (with *The New Chinese Cinema: An Introduction*, by Tony Rayns). London and Boston: Faber & Faber, 1989.

COCTEAU, JEAN

Fraigneau, André. *Cocteau on the Film*. 1954. Reprint. New York: Dover, 1972. Recorded conversations.

Gilson, René. *Jean Cocteau*. New York: Crown, 1964.

Steegmuller, Francis. *Cocteau: A Biography*. London: Constable, 1986.

COPPOLA, FRANCIS FORD

Cowie, Peter. *Coppola*. London: Faber and Faber, 1990.

Goodwin, Michael, and Naomi Wise. *On the Edge: The Life & Times of Francis Coppola*. New York: William Morrow, 1989.

CUKOR, GEORGE

Lambert, Gavin. *On Cukor*. New York: Capricorn Books, 1973.

McGilligan, Patrick. *George Cukor: A Double Life: A Biography of the Gentleman Director*. New York: St. Martin's Press, 1991.

DEMILLE, CECIL B.

Usai, Paolo Cherchi, and Lorenzo Codelli, eds. *L'eredità DeMille/The DeMille Legacy*. Pordenone: Edizione Biblioteca dell'Imagine, 1991.

DEREN, MAYA

Clark, Vévé A., et al. *The Legend of Maya Deren: A Documentary Biography and Collected Works*. New York: Anthology Film Archives/Film Culture, 1984.

DISNEY, WALT

Eliot, Marc. *Walt Disney ... A Biography*. Secaucus, NJ: Carol Publishing Group, 1993.

Smoodin, Eric, ed. *Disney Discourse: Producing the Magic Kingdom*. New York: Routledge, 1994.

DOVZHENKO, ALEXANDER

Dovzhenko, Alexander. *The Poet as Filmmaker: Selected Writings*. Marco Carynnyk, ed. Boston: MIT Press, 1973.

DREYER, CARL

Bordwell, David. *The Films of Carl Theodor Dreyer*. Berkeley: University of California Press, 1981.

Milne, Tom. *The Cinema of Carl Dreyer*. Cranbury, NJ: A. S. Barnes, 1971.

Skoller, Donald, ed. *Dreyer in Double Reflection*. New York: Dutton, 1973. Translation of Dreyer's *Om Filmen*.

EISENSTEIN, SERGEI

Barna, Yon. *Eisenstein*. Boston: Little, Brown, 1973.

Eisenstein, Sergei. *Notes of a Film Director*. Reprint. New York: Dover, 1970.

Eisenstein, Sergei. *The Complete Films of Eisenstein*. New York: Dutton, 1974.

Eisenstein, Sergei, and Upton Sinclair. *The Making and Unmaking of "Que Viva Mexico."* Bloomington: Indiana University Press, 1970.

Montagu, Ivor. *With Eisenstein in Hollywood*. New York: International, 1967. Reminiscences.

Seton, Marie. *Sergei M. Eisenstein: A Biography*. 1952. London: Dobson, 1978.

FASSBINDER, RAINER WERNER

Rayns, Tony, ed. *Fassbinder*. Second ed. London: British Film Institute, 1976, 1980.

FELLINI, FEDERICO

Bondanella, Peter. *The Cinema of Federico Fellini*. Princeton: Princeton University Press, 1992.

Fellini, Federico. *Fellini on Fellini*. Trans. Isabel Quigley. New York: Delacorte, 1976.

Rosenthal, Stuart. *Cinema of Federico Fellini*. Cranbury, NJ: A. S. Barnes, 1976.

FLAHERTY, ROBERT

Barsam, Richard. *The Vision of Robert Flaherty: The Artist as Myth and Filmmaker*. Bloomington: Indiana University Press, 1988.

Calder-Marshall, Arthur. *The Innocent Eye*. New York: Penguin, 1970.

FORD, JOHN

Anderson, Lindsay. *About John Ford....* London: Plexus, 1981.

Bogdanovich, Peter. *John Ford*. Berkeley: University of California Press, 1978. Interview and filmography, and a modern classic of film writing.

Gallagher, Tag. *John Ford: The Man and His Work*. Berkeley: University of California Press, 1985.

McBride, Joseph, and Michael Wilmington. *John Ford*. Reprint. New York: DaCapo, 1976.

Sarris, Andrew. *The John Ford Movie Mystery*. Bloomington: Indiana University Press, 1977.

Sinclair, Andrew. *John Ford*. New York: The Dial Press, 1978.

FRANJU, GEORGES

Durgnat, Raymond. *Franju*. Berkeley: University of California Press, 1967.

FULLER, SAMUEL

Garnham, Nicholas. *Samuel Fuller*. New York: Viking, 1971.

GANCE, ABEL

Brownlow, Kevin. *Napoléon: Abel Gance's Classic Film*. London: Jonathan Cape, 1983.

GARBO, GRETA

Broman, Sven. *Conversations with Greta Garbo*. New York: Viking, 1992. She speaks.

GODARD, JEAN-LUC

Bellour, Raymond, and Mary Lea Bandy, eds. *Jean-Luc Godard: Son + Image: 1974–1991*. New York: Museum of Modern Art, 1992.

Cameron, Ian, ed. *The Films of Jean-Luc Godard*. New York: Praeger, 1969. Collection of essays.

Godard, Jean-Luc. *Godard On Godard*. Edited by Tom Milne. New York: Viking, 1972.

MacBean, James Roy. *Film and Revolution*. Bloomington: Indiana University Press, 1975. Includes several major essays on Godard. Recommended.

Mussman, Toby, ed. *Jean-Luc Godard*. New York: Dutton, 1968. Collection of essays.

Roud, Richard. *Jean-Luc Godard*. Bloomington: Indiana University Press, 1969. A seminal critical work. Recommended.

Sterritt, David. *The Films of Jean-Luc Godard: Seeing the Invisible*. New York: Cambridge University Press, 1999.

GOLDWYN, SAMUEL

Berg, A. Scott. *Goldwyn: A Biography*. New York: Knopf, 1989.

GREENAWAY, PETER

Lawrence, Amy. *The Films of Peter Greenaway*. New York: Cambridge University Press, 1997.

GRIERSON, JOHN

Hardy, Forsyth. *John Grierson: A Documentary Biography*. London: Faber and Faber, 1979.

GRIFFITH, D. W.

Brown, Karl. *Adventures with D. W. Griffith*. Kevin Brownlow, ed. London: Secker & Warburg, 1973.

Geduld, Harry M., ed. *Focus on D. W. Griffith*. Englewood Cliffs, NJ: Prentice-Hall, 1971.

Gunning, Tom. *D. W. Griffith and the Origins of American Narrative Film: The Early Years at Biograph*. Urbana: University of Illinois Press, 1991.

Henderson, Robert M. *D. W. Griffith: His Life and Work*. New York: Oxford University Press, 1972.

Henderson, Robert M. *D. W. Griffith: The Years at Biograph*. New York: Noonday, 1970.

Schickel, Richard. *D. W. Griffith: An American Life*. New York: Simon & Schuster, 1984.

Wagenknecht, Edward, and Anthony Slide. *The Films of D. W. Griffith*. New York: Crown, 1976.

HAWKS, HOWARD

McBride, Joseph, ed. *Focus on Howard Hawks*. Englewood Cliffs, NJ: Prentice-Hall, 1972.

Wood, Robin. *Howard Hawks*. Revised ed. London: British Film Institute, 1968, 1981.

HERZOG, WERNER

Blank, Les, and James Bogan, eds. *Burden of Dreams: Screenplay, Journals, Reviews, Photographs*. Berkeley: North Atlantic Books, 1984.

Corrigan, Timothy. *The Films of Werner Herzog: Between Mirage and History*. New York: Routledge, 1986.

HITCHCOCK, ALFRED

Durgnat, Raymond. *Strange Case of Alfred Hitchcock*. Boston: MIT Press, 1975.

Modleski, Tania. *The Women Who Knew too Much*. New York and London: Methuen, 1988.

Rohmer, Eric, and Claude Chabrol. *Hitchcock: The First 44 Films*. Trans. Stanley Hochman. New York: Frederick Ungar, 1978.

Spoto, Donald. *The Art of Alfred Hitchcock: Fifty Years of His Motion Pictures*. New York: Hopkinson & Blake, 1976.

Sterritt, David. *The Films of Alfred Hitchcock*. New York: Cambridge University Press, 1993.

Taylor, John Russell. *Hitch: The Life and Times of Alfred Hitchcock.* New York: Berkley, 1977.

Truffaut, François, and Helen Scott. *Hitchcock.* New York: Simon & Schuster, 1966. Landmark book-length interview. Recommended.

Wood, Robin. *Hitchcock's Films Revisited.* New York: Columbia University Press, 1989.

HUSTON, JOHN

Pratley, Gerald. *The Cinema of John Huston.* Cranbury, NJ: A. S. Barnes, 1976.

Ross, Lillian. *Picture.* New York: Avon, 1952. A classic piece of journalism on the filming of John Huston's *Red Badge of Courage.*

Studlar, Gaylyn, and David Desser. *Reflections in a Male Eye: John Huston and the American Experience.* Washington, DC: Smithsonian Institute Press, 1993.

KAZAN, ELIA

Ciment, Michel. *Kazan on Kazan.* New York: Viking, 1973. "Oral history."

Kazan, Elia. *Elia Kazan: A Life.* New York: Knopf, 1988.

KEATON, BUSTER

Dardis, Tom. *Keaton: The Man Who Wouldn't Lie Down.* London: Penguin Books, 1980.

Lebel, J. P. *Buster Keaton.* Cranbury, NJ: A. S. Barnes, 1967.

Moews, Daniel. *Keaton: The Silent Features.* Berkeley: University of California Press, 1977.

Robinson, David. *Buster Keaton.* London: Secker & Warburg, 1970.

KORDA, ALEXANDER

Kulik, Karol. *Alexander Korda: The Man Who Could Work Miracles.* London: Virgin, 1990.

KUBRICK, STANLEY

Agel, Jerome. *The Making of "2001."* New York: Signet, 1970. A chatty compendium in the style of the "non-book" popular in the sixties.

Ciment, Michel, ed. *Stanley Kubrick.* Paris: Éditions Rivages, 1987.

Clarke, Arthur C. *Lost Worlds of "2001."* New York: Signet, 1972. The screenwriter's journal of his experiences.

Dumont, Jean-Paul, and Jean Monod. *Le Foetus astral.* Paris: Éditions Christian Bourgeois, 1970. One of the earliest full-length structuralist studies of a film (*2001*).

Kagan, Norman. *The Cinema of Stanley Kubrick.* New York: Continuum, 1989.

Nabokov, Vladimir. *Lolita: A Screenplay.* New York: McGraw-Hill, 1975. Not strictly about the film, this is Nabokov's original screenplay, which differs considerably from the final film. Comparison is interesting.

KUROSAWA, AKIRA

Prince, Stephen. *The Warrior's Camera: The Cinema of Akira Kurosawa.* Princeton: Princeton University Press, 1991.

Richie, Donald. *Films of Akira Kurosawa.* Berkeley: University of California Press, 1965.

LANG, FRITZ

Eisner, Lotte H. *Fritz Lang.* David Robinson, ed. London: Secker & Warburg, 1976.

LEE, SPIKE

Lee, Spike. *Five for Five: The Films of Spike Lee.* New York: Stewart, Tabori, & Chang/ Workman, 1991.

Lee, Spike. *By Any Means Necessary: The Making of Malcolm X.* New York: Hyperion, 1992.

LENI, PAUL

Bock, Hans-Michael, ed. *Paul Leni: Grafik, Theater, Film.* Frankfurt: Deutsches Filmmuseum, 1986.

LINDER, MAX
Linder, Maud. *Max Linder: Le Dieu du cinéma muet*. Paris: Éditions Atlas, 1992.

LLOYD, HAROLD
Lloyd, Harold. *An American Comedy*. 1928. New York: Dover, 1971.

LOSEY, JOSEPH
Caute, David. *Joseph Losey: A Revenge on Life*. London: Faber and Faber, 1994.

LUBITSCH, ERNST
Eyman, Scott. Ernst Lubitsch: *Laughter in Paradise*. New York: Simon & Schuster, 1993.
Weinberg, Herman. *The Lubitsch Touch*. Third edition. New York: Dover, 1977.

LUCAS, GEORGE
Pollock, Dale. *Skywalking: The Life and Films of George Lucas*. Hollywood: French, 1990.

MALLE, LOUIS
French, Philip, ed. *Malle on Malle*. London: Faber and Faber, 1993.

MAY, JOE
Bock, Hans-Michael, and Claudia Lenssen. *Joe May: Regisseur und Produzent*. Munich: edition text + kritik, 1991.

MINELLI, VINCENTE
Harvey, Stephen. *Directed by Vincente Minnelli*. New York: Harper & Row, 1989.
Naremore, James. *The Films of Vincente Minnelli*. New York: Cambridge University Press, 1993.

MIZOGUCHI, KENJI
Kirihara, Donald. *Patterns of Time: Mizoguchi and the 1930s*. Madison: University of Wisconsin Press, 1992.

MURNAU, F. W.
Eisner, Lotte. *Murnau*. Berkeley: University of California Press, 1973.

OPHÜLS, MAX
Willemen, Paul, ed. *Ophüls*. London: British Film Institute, 1978.

OZU, YASUJIRO
Bordwell, David. *Ozu and the Poetics of Cinema*. Princeton: Princeton University Press, 1988.
Richie, Donald. *Ozu*. Berkeley: University of California Press, 1975.

PABST, G. W.
Rentschler, Eric. *The Films of G. W. Pabst: An Extraterritorial Cinema*. New Brunswick, NJ: Rutgers University Press, 1990.

PASOLINI, PIER PAOLO
Greene, Naomi. *Pier Paolo Pasolini: Cinema as Heresy*. Princeton: Princeton University Press, 1990.

PORTER, EDWIN S.
Musser, Charles. *Before the Nickelodeon: Edwin S. Porter and the Edison Manufacturing Company*. Berkeley: University of California Press, 1991.

POWELL, MICHAEL AND EMERIC PRESSBURGER
Christie, Ian. *Arrows of Desire: The Films of Michael Powell and Emeric Pressburger*. London: Faber and Faber, 1994.
Powell, Michael. *A Life in Movies: An Autobiography*. New York: Knopf, 1987.
Powell, Michael. *Million-Dollar Movie: The Second Volume of His A Life in Movies*. London: Heinemann, 1992.

RAY, NICHOLAS

Ray, Susan, ed. I *Was Interrupted: Nicholas Ray on Making Movies*. Berkeley: University of California Press, 1993.

RAY, SATYAJIT

Seton, Marie. *Portrait of a Director: Satyajit Ray*. Bloomington: Indiana University Press, 1971.

Wood, Robin. *The Apu Trilogy*. New York: Praeger, 1971.

RENOIR, JEAN

Bazin, André. *Jean Renoir*. Edited by François Truffaut. New York: Da Capo, 1992. Recommended.

Braudy, Leo. *Jean Renoir*. New York: Doubleday, 1972. Recommended.

Durgnat, Raymond. *Jean Renoir*. Berkeley: University of California Press, 1975.

Gilliatt, Penelope. *Jean Renoir: Essays, Conversations, Reviews*. New York: McGraw-Hill, 1975.

Leprohon, Pierre. *Jean Renoir*. New York: Crown, 1971.

Renoir, Jean. *My Life and My Films*. New York: Atheneum, 1974.

Renoir, Jean. *Renoir on Renoir: Interviews, Essays, and Remarks*. Cambridge: Cambridge University Press, 1989.

Sesonske, Alexander. *Jean Renoir: The French Films 1924–1939*. Cambridge, MA: Harvard University Press, 1980.

RESNAIS, ALAIN

Armes, Roy. *The Cinema of Alain Resnais*. Cranbury, NJ: A. S. Barnes, 1968.

Monaco, James. *Alain Resnais: The Role of Imagination*. London: Secker & Warburg, 1978; and New York: Oxford University Press, 1979. Includes a chapter on Resnais's "non-films."

Sweet, Freddy. *The Film Narratives of Alain Resnais*. Ann Arbor, MI: UMI Research Press, 1981.

Ward, John. *Alain Resnais or the Theme of Time*. New York: Doubleday, 1968. Recommended.

ROEG, NICOLAS

Izod, John. *The Films of Nicolas Roeg: Myth and Mind*. Houndsmill: Macmillan, 1992.

ROHMER, ERIC

Bonitzer, Pascal. *Eric Rohmer*. Paris: Cahiers du cinéma, 1991.

Crisp, C. G. *Eric Rohmer: Realist and Moralist*. Bloomington: Indiana University Press, 1988.

Rohmer, Eric. *The Taste for Beauty*. Jean Narboni, ed. Cambridge: Cambridge University Press, 1989.

ROSSELLINI, ROBERTO

Bondanella, Peter. *The Films of Roberto Rossellini*. New York: Cambridge University Press, 1993.

Brunette, Peter. *Roberto Rossellini*. New York: Oxford University Press, 1987.

Guarner, José Luis. *Rossellini*. New York: Praeger, 1970.

ROUCH, JEAN

Eaton, Mick, ed. *Anthropology-Reality-Cinema: The Films of Jean Rouch*. London: British Film Institute, 1979.

Stoller, Paul. *The Cinematic Griot: The Ethnography of Jean Rouch*. Chicago: University of Chicago Press, 1992.

SAYLES, JOHN

Sayles, John. *Thinking in Pictures: The Making of the Movie "Matewan."* Boston: Houghton-Mifflin, 1987.

SCHRADER, PAUL

Schrader, Paul. *Schrader on Schrader & other Writings*. Ed. Kevin Jackson. London and Boston: Faber & Faber, 1990.

SCORSESE, MARTIN

Keyser, Les. *Martin Scorsese*. New York: Twayne, 1992.

Thomson, David, and Ian Christie. *Scorsese on Scorsese*. London: Faber and Faber, 1989.

SELZNICK, DAVID O.

Thomson, David. *Showman: The Life of David O. Selznick*. New York: Knopf, 1992.

SJÖSTRÖM, VICTOR

Forslund, Bengt. *Victor Sjöström: His Life and His Work*. Trans. Peter Cowie. New York: New York Zoetrope, 1988. Recommended.

SPIELBERG, STEVEN

Mott, Donald R., and Cheryl McAlister Saunders. *Steven Spielberg*. Boston: Twayne, 1986.

STRAUB, JEAN-MARIE

Roud, Richard. *Straub*. New York: Viking, 1972.

STURGES, PRESTON

Jacobs, Diane. *Christmas in July: The Life and Art of Preston Sturges*. Berkeley: University of California Press, 1992. Highly recommended.

TATI, JACQUES

Maddock, Brent. *The Films of Jacques Tati*. Metuchen, NJ: Scarecrow Press, 1977.

TRUFFAUT, FRANÇOIS

Allen, Don. *Truffaut*. New York: Viking, 1974.

Crisp, C. G. *François Truffaut*. New York: Praeger, 1972.

Insdorf, Annette. *François Truffaut*. Revised edition. New York: Cambridge University Press, 1995. Originally published in 1978, this is a classic work.

Truffaut, François. *Truffaut by Truffaut*. New York: Abrams, 1987.

VERTOV, DZIGA

Vertov, Dziga. *Kino-Eye: The Writings of Dziga Vertov*. Annette Michelson, ed.; Kevin O'Brien, trans. Berkeley: University of California Press, 1984.

VIDOR, KING

Durgnat, Raymond, and Scott Simmon. *King Vidor, American*. Berkeley: University of California Press, 1988.

VIGO, JEAN

Salles Gomes, P. E. *Jean Vigo*. Berkeley: University of California Press, 1971.

Smith, John M. *Jean Vigo*. New York: Praeger, 1972.

VISCONTI, LUCHINO

Nowell-Smith, Geoffrey. *Luchino Visconti*. New York: Doubleday, 1968.

VON STERNBERG, JOSEF

Weinberg, Herman. *Josef Von Sternberg: A Critical Study*. New York: Dutton, 1967.

VON STROHEIM, ERICH

Curtis, Thomas Quinn. *Von Stroheim*. New York: Farrar, Straus and Giroux, 1971.

Koszarski, Richard. *The Man You Love To Hate: Erich von Stroheim and Hollywood*. New York: Oxford University Press, 1983.

Weinberg, Herman. *Stroheim: A Pictorial Record of His Nine Films*. New York: Dover, 1975.

WAJDA, ANDRZEJ

Michalek, Boleslaw. *The Cinema of Andrzej Wajda.* Cranbury, NJ: A. S. Barnes, 1973.

WELLES, ORSON

Bazin, André. *Orson Welles: A Critical View.* New York: Harper & Row, 1978.

Brady, Frank. *Citizen Welles: A Biography of Orson Welles.* New York: Charles Scribner's Sons, 1989.

Cowie, Peter. *The Cinema of Orson Welles.* Cranbury, NJ: A. S. Barnes, 1973.

Higham, Charles. *The Films of Orson Welles.* Berkeley: University of California Press, 1970.

Kael, Pauline. *The Citizen Kane Book.* Boston: Little, Brown, 1972. Includes the script and Kael's important essay on the genesis of the film. Recommended.

McBride, Joseph. *Orson Welles.* New York: Viking, 1972.

Naremore, James. *The Magic World of Orson Welles.* New York: Oxford University Press, 1978.

WENDERS, WIM

Dawson, Jan. *Wim Wenders.* New York: New York Zoetrope, 1977.

Kolker, Robert Phillip, and Peter Beicken. *The Films of Wim Wenders.* New York: Cambridge University Press, 1992.

WILDER, BILLY

Seidl, Claudius. *Billy Wilder: Seine Filme—sein Leben.* Munich: Heine, 1988.

WISEMAN, FREDERICK

Grant, Barry Keith. *Voyages of Discovery: The Cinema of Frederick Wiseman.* Urbana: University of Illinois Press, 1991.

MISCELLANEOUS

Behlmer, Rudy. *America's Favorite Movies: Behind the Scenes.* New York: Frederick Ungar, 1982.

Corliss, Richard, ed. *The Hollywood Screenwriters.* New York: Avon, 1972. Includes filmographies.

Kobal, John. *People Will Talk.* New York: Knopf, 1985. Interviews with stars, directors.

Koszarski, Richard, ed. *Hollywood Directors, 1914–1940.* New York: Oxford University Press, 1976.

MacDonald, Scott. *A Critical Cinema 2: Interviews with Independent Filmmakers.* Berkeley: University of California Press, 1992.

Sarris, Andrew, ed. *Interviews with Film Directors.* New York: Avon/Bard, 1967. A compendium of often important interviews. Recommended.

Schickel, Richard, ed. *The Men Who Made the Movies.* New York: Atheneum 1975. Eight interviews by Schickel based on his television program.

5. FILM THEORY AND PRACTICAL CRITICISM

Adler, Renata. *A Year in the Dark.* New York: Random House, 1969. This "journal" of Adler's year on the *New York Times* provides an interesting mirror of the work of the daily critic.

Agee, James. *Agee on Film.* Vol. 1: *Criticism;* Vol. 2: *Screenplays.* Reprint. New York: Grosset, 1969. Possibly the most important American film reviewer of the early years. Vol. 1 recommended.

Allen, Richard, and Murray Smith, eds. *Film Theory and Philosophy.* New York: Oxford University Press, 1999. A collection of iconoclastic essays challenging current dogma.

Andrew, Dudley. *The Major Film Theories: An Introduction.* Second ed. New York: Oxford University Press, 1976, 1989. The best available one-volume introduction to film theory. Highly recommended.

Andrew, Dudley. *André Bazin.* New York: Oxford University Press, 1978. An important and engaging study of the man and his thought. Highly recommended.

Andrew, Dudley. *Concepts in Film Theory.* New York: Oxford University, 1984. A continuation of *The Major Film Theories.*

Arnheim, Rudolf. *Film as Art.* Berkeley: University of California Press, 1957, 1966. A classic exposition of expressionist theory. Recommended.

Balázs, Béla. *Theory of the Film: Character and Growth of a New Art.* Trans. Edith Bone. 1952. Reprint. New York: Dover, 1970.

Barsam, Richard. *Nonfiction Film Theory.* New York: Dutton, 1980.

Barthes, Roland. *Elements of Semiology/Writing Degree Zero.* Trans. Annette Lavers and Colin Smith. Boston: Beacon, 1968. Essentially a literary critic, Barthes remains basic reading for anyone interested in semiotics. Recommended.

Barthes, Roland. *S/Z.* 1970. Trans. Richard Miller. Preface by Richard Howard. New York: Hill and Wang, 1974.

Barthes, Roland. *Mythologies.* Trans. Annette Lavers. New York: Hill and Wang, 1972.

Barthes, Roland. *The Pleasure of the Text.* 1973. Trans. Richard Miller, with a note on the text by Richard Howard. New York: Hill and Wang, 1975.

Bazin, André. *What Is Cinema?* 2 vols. Selected and translated by Hugh Gray. Berkeley: University of California Press, 1967, 1971. Selections from the multivolume *Qu'est-ce que le cinéma?* Essential.

Bazin, André. *The Cinema of Cruelty.* New York: Okpaku Communications, 1977.

Bellour, Raymond, Thierry Kuntzel, and Christian Metz, eds. *Psychoanalyse et cinéma.* Paris: Éditions du Seuil, 1975. French psychoanalytic semiotics.

Benjamin, Walter. *Illuminations.* Edited by Hannah Arendt. New York: Schocken, 1968. Essays from the 1930s by one of the leading dialectical critics. See especially "The Work of Art in the Age of Mechanical Reproduction." A seminal essay; recommended.

Bettetini, Gianfranco. *The Language and Technique of the Film.* The Hague: Mouton, 1973. A pioneering Italian semiotician.

Bondanella, Peter. *Umberto Eco and the Open Text: Semiotics, Fiction, and Popular Culture.* New York: Cambridge University Press, 1997.

Bordwell, David. *Narration in the Fiction Film.* Madison: University of Wisconsin Press, 1985.

Bordwell, David. *Making Meaning: Inference and Rhetoric in the Interpretation of Cinema.* New York: Oxford University Press, 1989.

Bordwell, David, and Noël Carroll, eds. *Post-Theory: Reconstructing Film Studies.* Madison, WI: University of Wisconsin Press, 1986. The title says it all.

Burch, Noël. *The Theory of Film Practice.* New York: Praeger, 1973. One of the two basic English-language semiotic approaches.

Cameron, Ian, ed. *Movie Reader.* New York: Praeger, 1972. Thirty-three articles on various topics that first appeared in the highly respected magazine *Movie*; includes the *Movie* "Pantheon."

Cavell, Stanley. *The World Viewed: Reflections on the Ontology of Film.* New York: Viking, 1971. Recommended.

Cooke, Alistair, ed. *Garbo & the Night Watchmen.* 1937. London: Secker & Warburg, 1971. A classic anthology from the thirties.

Denby, David. *Awake in the Dark: An Anthology of American Film Criticism 1915 to the Present.* New York: Random House, 1977.

Dovzhenko, Alexander. *The Poet as Filmmaker: Selected Writings.* Edited and translated by Marco Carynnyk. Boston: MIT Press, 1973.

Ebert, Roger, ed. *Roger Ebert's Book of Film.* New York: Norton, 1996. A copious and eclectic collection of Ebert's favorite essays.

Eco, Umberto. *The Semiotic Threshold.* The Hague: Mouton, 1973.

Eco, Umberto. *A Theory of Semiotics.* Bloomington: University of Indiana Press, 1976. A seminal study by an academic who later found fame and fortune as a novelist (*The Name of the Rose,* an international success)—the only scholar who has truly found a way to popularize semiotics.

Eisenstein, Sergei. *Film Sense.* New York: Harcourt, Brace & World, 1947. Essential and basic.

Eisenstein, Sergei. *Film Form.* New York: Harcourt, Brace & World, 1949. Essential and basic.

Eisenstein, Sergei. *Film Essays and a Lecture.* New York: Praeger, 1970.

Ellis, John, ed. *Screen Reader One: Cinema/Ideology/Politics.* London: S.E.F.T., 1977. Selections from an influential journal of the seventies.

Farber, Manny. *Negative Space.* New York: Praeger, 1971. The "outsider" point of view.

Ferguson, Otis. *The Film Criticism of Otis Ferguson.* Ed. Robin Wilson. Philadelphia: Temple University Press, 1973.

Friedberg, Anne. *Window Shopping: Cinema and the Postmodern.* Berkeley: University of California Press, 1993.

Gilliatt, Penelope. *Unholy Fools.* New York: Viking, 1973.

Godard, Jean-Luc. *Godard on Godard.* Trans. Tom Milne. New York: Viking, 1972. Difficult reading, but essential. A thorough anthology of Godard's work as a critic 1952–67.

Greene, Graham. *Graham Greene on Film: Collected Film Criticism 1935–39.* London: Secker and Warburg; New York: Simon & Schuster, 1972. Reprint. New York and Oxford: Oxford University Press, 1980.

Grierson, John. *Grierson on Documentary.* 1947. Edited by Forsyth Hardy. New York: Praeger, 1971.

Hammond, Paul, ed. *The Shadow and Its Shadow: Surrealist Writings on Cinema.* London: British Film Institute, 1978. Important collection of documents.

Harvey, David. *The Condition of Post-Modernity.* Cambridge, MA.: Blackwell, 1989.

Heath, Stephen. *Questions of Cinema.* Bloomington: University of Indiana Press, 1981.

Hillier, Jim, ed. *Cahiers du Cinéma.* Vol. 1: *The 1950s—Neorealism, Hollywood, New Wave.* Cambridge, MA: Harvard University Press, 1985. Selected articles from the highly influential magazine.

Hillier, Jim, ed. *Cahiers du Cinéma.* Vol. 2: *1960–1968—New Wave, New Cinema, Reevaluating Hollywood.* Cambridge, MA: Harvard University Press, 1986. More articles from the highly influential magazine.

Horkheimer, Max, and Theodor W. Adorno. *Dialectic of Enlightenment.* 1944. Trans. John Cumming. New York: Continuum, 1988.

Jameson, Fredric. *Marxism and Form.* Princeton, NJ: Princeton University Press, 1971. Not about cinema. Despite the density of the prose, an important introduction to dialectical criticism. Recommended.

Jameson, Fredric. *The Prison-House of Language.* Princeton, NJ: Princeton University Press, 1972. A useful introduction to semiotics and related areas.

Jameson, Fredric. *Political Unconsciousness.* Ithaca, NY: Cornell University Press, 1982.

Jameson, Fredric. *Signatures of the Visible.* New York: Routledge, 1990. Applications of postmodern materialist theory to readings of particular films.

Jameson, Fredric. *Postmodernism, or the Cultural Logic of Late Capitalism.* Durham, NC: Duke University Press, 1991.

Jay, Martin. *The Dialectical Imagination.* Boston: Little, Brown, 1973. A survey of the Frankfurt School.

Kael, Pauline. *I Lost It at the Movies*. New York: Bantam, 1965. Kael's work in periodicals has been rigorously anthologized, offering a comprehensive survey of the sixties through the eighties that is unrivaled. Succeeding volumes in the series all have titles that echo the sexual connotation: *Kiss Kiss Bang Bang*. New York: Bantam, 1968. *Going Steady*. New York: Bantam, 1971. *Deeper into Movies*. New York: Bantam, 1974. *Reeling*. Boston: Little, Brown, 1976. *When the Lights Go Down*. New York: Holt, Rinehart, & Winston, 1980. *Hooked*. New York: Dutton, 1989. *Movie Love*. New York: Dutton, 1991. *For Keeps*. New York: Dutton, 1994. See also the exchange between Kael and Andrew Sarris on the auteur theory in 1963's *Film Quarterly*, Spring, Summer, and Fall issues (16:3, 16:4, 17:1).

Kael, Pauline. *5001 Nights at the Movies*. Rev. ed. New York: Henry Holt, 1982, 1991. Kael's general guide, most culled from short takes first published in *The New Yorker* magazine.

Kaplan, E. Ann. *Postmodernism and Its Discontents: Theories, Practices*. London: Routledge, 1988.

Kaplan, E. Ann. *Psychoanalysis and Cinema*. New York: Routledge, 1990.

Kauffmann, Stanley. *Figures of Light*. New York: Harper & Row, 1971. Film criticism and the literary sensibility. Other collections: *Living Images*. New York: Harper & Row, 1975. *A World on Film*. New York: Harper & Row, 1966.

Kauffmann, Stanley, and Bruce Henstell, eds. *American Film Criticism: From the Beginnings to Citizen Kane."* New York: Liveright, 1972. A very useful anthology. Wide-ranging and thorough.

Kracauer, Siegfried. *Theory of Film: The Redemption of Physical Reality*. New York: Oxford University Press, 1960. An essential exposition of realist theory. Recommended.

Kuhn, Annette. *Women's Pictures: Feminism and Cinema*. New York: Routledge, 1982.

Kuleshov, Lev. *Kuleshov on Film*. Berkeley: University of California Press, 1975.

Lacan, Jacques. *Écrits: A Selection*. New York: Norton, 1977. An introduction to Lacan's work in English.

Lane, Michael, ed. *Introduction to Structuralism*. New York: Basic Books, 1970. Not specifically about film, but a useful introduction.

Langlois, Henri. *Trois cents ans de cinéma: Écrits*. Jean Narboni, ed. Paris: Cahiers du Cinéma/ Cinémathèque Française, 1986. Collected texts of the famous archivist.

Lapsley, Robert, and Michael Westlake. *Film Theory: An Introduction*. Manchester: Manchester University Press, 1989.

Lindsay, Vachel. *The Art of the Moving Picture*. New York: Macmillan, 1915. The poet examines the young art of movies.

Lopate, Phillip. *Totally Tenderly Tragically: Essays and Criticism from a Lifelong Love Affair with the Movies*. New York: Doubleday, 1998. Collection of film pieces from the veteran essayist.

Lorentz, Pare. *Lorentz on Film*. New York: Harcourt Brace Jovanovich, 1975. The filmmaker as critic.

MacCann, Richard D., ed. *Film: A Montage of Theories*. New York: Dutton, 1966. Forty essays by filmmakers and critics. Recommended.

Macdonald, Dwight. *On Movies*. New York: Berkley, 1971. Macdonald's limited foray into film criticism provides a useful view of the essentially political sensibility confronting the art. A classic of early film criticism.

Mast, Gerald, Marshall Cohen, and Leo Braudy, eds. *Film Theory and Criticism: Introductory Readings*. 1974. Fifth ed. New York: Oxford University Press, 1998. A very useful collection of theoretical texts. Highly recommended.

McConnell, Frank. *Storytelling and Mythmaking: Images from Film and Literature*. New York: Oxford University Press, 1979. An interesting theory of narrativity.

Mekas, Jonas. *Movie Journal: Rise of the New American Cinema 1959–1971*. New York: Macmillan, 1972. The chronicler of the "New American Film" underground and champion of nonnarrative film.

Metz, Christian. *Film Language: A Semiotics of the Cinema*. Trans. Michael Taylor. New York: Oxford University Press, 1974. An English version of the first volume of Metz's two-volume *Essais sur la signification au cinéma*. Paris: Éditions Klincksieck, 1968, 1972. Metz remains the premier theoretician of cinema semiotics. (Be aware that his thought progressed after *Film Language* was written.) Recommended.

Metz, Christian. *Language and Cinema*. Trans. Donna Jean Umiker-Sebeok. The Hague: Mouton, 1974. English version of *Langage et cinéma*. Paris: Larousse, 1971.

Metz, Christian. *The Imaginary Signifier*. Bloomington: Indiana University Press, 1982.

Metz, Christian. *Psychoanalysis and Cinema*. London: Macmillan, 1983.

Metz, Christian. *L'Énonciation impersonelle ou le site du film*. Paris: Méridiens Klincksieck, 1992.

Miller, Mark Crispin, ed. *Seeing Through Movies*. New York: Pantheon, 1990.

Münsterberg, Hugo. *The Film: A Psychological Study. The Silent Photoplay in 1916*. New York: D. Appleton, 1916. Reprint. New York: Dover, 1970. One of the earliest approaches to film psychology.

Neale, Steven. *Genre*. London: British Film Institute, 1980.

Nichols, Bill, ed. *Movies and Methods: An Anthology*. Second ed. Berkeley: University of California Press, 1985. 2 vols. An important anthology of contemporary criticism. Recommended.

Oshima, Nagisa. *Cinema, Censorship, and the State*. Boston: MIT Press, 1992.

Palmer, R. Barton. *The Cinema Text: Methods and Approaches*. New York: AMS Press, 1989.

Pasolini, Pier Paolo. *Lutheran Letters*. 1976. Trans. Stuart Hood. Manchester: Carcanet New Press and Dublin: Raven Arts Press, 1983.

Penley, Constance, ed. *Feminism and Film Theory*. New York: Routledge, 1988.

Potamkin, Harry Alan. *The Compound Cinema: The Film Writings of Harry Alan Potamkin*. Ed. Lewis Jacobs. New York: Teachers College Press, 1978. One of the more important critics of the 1930s.

Pudovkin, V. I. *Film Technique and Film Acting*. 1929, 1937. Reprint. New York: Grove, 1970. Next to Eisenstein, the most important of the Soviet theorists.

Rohdie, Sam, ed. "Cinema Semiotics and the Work of Christian Metz," *Screen* 14:1/2 (Spring/Summer 1973). A landmark collection of essays in English.

Sarris, Andrew. *Confessions of a Cultist*. New York: Simon & Schuster, 1970. With Kael, the most influential of the American critics in the sixties and seventies; popularizer of the auteur theory in America. Other collections: *The Primal Screen: Essays on Film and Related Subjects*. New York: Simon & Schuster, 1973. *Politics and Cinema*. New York: Columbia University Press, 1979.

Silverman, Kaja. *The Subject of Semiotics*. New York Oxford University Press, 1983.

Simon, John. *Movies into Films: Film Criticism 1967–70*. New York: Dial Press, 1971. The critic as hero; best representative of the conservative aesthetic. Also *Private Screenings*. New York: Berkley, 1967.

Solanas, Fernando, and Octavio Getino. "Towards a Third Cinema." *Cineaste* IV:3 1970.

Sontag, Susan. *Against Interpretation*. New York: Delta, 1966.

Sontag, Susan. *Styles of Radical Will*. New York: Farrar, Straus and Giroux, 1970. Important essays on Godard and Bergman.

Sontag, Susan. *On Photography*. New York: Farrar, Straus and Giroux, 1977.

Staiger, Janet. *Interpreting Films: Studies in the Historical Reception of American Cinema*. Princeton: Princeton University Press, 1992.

Thompson, Kristin. *Breaking the Glass Armor: Neoformalist Film Analysis*. Princeton: Princeton University Press, 1988.

Truffaut, François. *The Films in My Life*. New York: Grove Press, 1978.

Tudor, Andrew. *Theories of Film*. New York: Viking, 1973. Useful survey.

Tyler, Parker. *Classics of the Foreign Film*. New York: Citadel, 1962. Influential in its day.

Warshow, Robert. *The Immediate Experience*. 1962. Reprint. New York: Atheneum, 1970. Next to Agee, the most important critic of film's adolescence. Especially useful on film as popular art.

Weinberg, Herman G. *Saint Cinema: Writings on the Film: 1929–1970*. New York: Dover, 1973.

Wollen, Peter. *Signs and Meaning in the Cinema*. Second ed. New York: Viking, 1972. A seminal semiotic study in English. Highly recommended.

Wollen, Peter. *Readings and Writings*. London: Verso, 1982.

Wood, Robin. *Personal Views: Explorations in Film*. London: Gordon Frazer, 1976.

6. MEDIA

Allen, Robert C. *Speaking of Soap Operas*. Chapel Hill, NC: University of North Carolina Press, 1985.

Allen, Robert C., ed. *Channels of Discourse, Reassembled*. Second ed. Chapel Hill, NC: University of North Carolina Press, 1992. Theories and methods of criticism applied to particular shows.

Altick, Richard D. *The English Common Reader: A Social History of the Mass Reading Public, 1800–1900*. Chicago: University of Chicago Press, 1963.

Ang, Ian. *Watching Dallas*. London: Methuen, 1985.

Arlen, Michael. *Living Room War: Writings About Television*. New York: The Viking Press, 1969.

Auletta, Ken. *Three Blind Mice: How the TV Networks Lost Their Way*. New York: Random House, 1991.

Balio, Tino. *Hollywood in the Age of Television*. Boston: Unwin Hyman, 1990.

Barnouw, Erik. *A History of Broadcasting in the United States*. New York: Oxford University Press. Vol. 1: *A Tower in Babel,* 1966. Vol. 2: *The Golden Web,* 1968. Vol. 3: *The Image Empire,* 1970. The standard work on the subject. Highly recommended.

Barnouw, Erik. *The Sponsor: Notes on a Modern Potentate*. New York: Oxford University Press, 1978. A short and pithy analysis.

Barnouw, Erik. *Tube of Plenty: The Evolution of American Television*. New York: Oxford University Press, Second revised ed. 1990. A one-volume revision of *A History of Broadcasting in the United States*. Highly recommended.

Bibb, Porter. *It Ain't as Easy as It Looks: Ted Turner's Amazing Story*. New York: Crown, 1993.

Boddy, William. *Fifties Television: The Industry and its Critics*. Urbana: University of Illinois Press, 1990.

Briggs, Asa. *A History of Broadcasting in the United Kingdom*. 3 vols. Oxford and New York: Oxford University Press, 1961–79.

Brooks, John. *Telephone: The First Hundred Years*. New York: Harper & Row, 1976.

Brown, Les. *Television: The Business Behind the Box*. New York: Harcourt Brace Jovanovich, 1972.

Carey, James W. *Communication as Culture: Essays on Media and Society*. New York: Routledge, 1989. Excellent theory, without the jargon.

Chapple, Steve, and Reebee Garofalo. *Rock 'n' Roll Is Here To Pay: The History and Politics of the Music Industry*. Chicago: Nelson-Hall, 1977. An excellent introduction to the subject.

Compaine, Benjamin M., ed. *Who Owns the Media? Concentration of Ownership in the Mass Communications Industry.* New York: Harmony, 1979, 1980. See especially Thomas Guback's chapter on theatrical film.

Czitrom, Daniel. *Media and the American Mind: From Morse to McLuhan.* Chapel Hill, NC: University of North Carolina Press, 1982.

Dannen, Fredric. *Hit Men: Power Brokers and Fast Money Inside the Music Business.* New York: Vintage, 1991.

Downing, John, et al., eds. *Questioning the Media: A Critical Introduction.* Newbury Park: Sage, 1990.

Feuer, Jane, Paul Kerr, and Tise Vahimagi, eds. *MTM: "Quality Television."* London: British Film Institute, 1984.

Fiske, John. *Television Culture.* London: Methuen, 1987.

Fiske, John, and John Hartley. *Reading Television.* London: Methuen, 1978; New York: Routledge, 1982. A classic.

Flichy, Patrice. *Une histoire de la communication moderne: espace public et vie privée.* Paris: Éditions de la découverte, 1991.

Fornatale, Peter, and Joshua E. Mills. *Radio in the Television Age.* Woodstock, NY: Overlook Press, 1980.

Friendly, Fred. *Due to Circumstances Beyond Our Control.* New York: Random House, 1967. Friendly was at the center of things when the television news business was born. An important memoir.

Frith, Simon. *Sound Effects: Youth, Leisure, and the Politics of Rock 'n' Roll.* New York: Pantheon, 1981.

Frith, Simon, Andrew Goodwin, and Lawrence Grossberg, eds. *Sound & Vision: The Music Video Reader.* London: Routledge, 1993.

Gans, Herbert. *Deciding What's News.* New York: Random House, 1979.

Garnham, Nicholas. *Structures of Television.* Second ed. London: British Film Institute, 1978.

Gitlin, Todd. *The Whole World Is Watching: Mass Media in the Making and Unmaking of the New Left.* Berkeley: University of California Press, 1980.

Gitlin, Todd. *Inside Prime Time.* New York: Pantheon, 1983.

Gitlin, Todd. *Watching Television.* New York: Pantheon, 1986.

Greenfield, Jeff. *Television: The First Fifty Years.* New York: Harry N. Abrams, 1977. A picture book, but Greenfield's text provides a good survey.

Innis, Harold. *The Bias of Communication.* Toronto: University of Toronto Press, 1951, 1973. Seminal.

Kaplan, E. Ann. *Regarding Television: Critical Approaches—An Anthology.* Frederick, MD: University Publications of America, 1983.

Kaplan, E. Ann. *Rocking Around the Clock: Music, Television, Postmodernism, and Consumer Culture.* New York: Routledge, 1987. Analyzing the phenomenon of MTV.

Liebling, A. J. *The Press.* 1960. Revised ed. New York: Ballantine Books, 1975. Classic study by the great press critic.

Leonard, John. *Smoke and Mirrors: Violence, Television, and Other American Cultures.* New York: New Press, 1997. For a decade, Leonard has held forth on CBS's *Sunday Morning* as our premiere television critic. Here's an overview.

MacDonald, J. Fred. *One Nation Under Television: The Rise and Decline of Network Television.* New York: Pantheon, 1990. A good general survey.

Mander, Jerry. *Four Arguments for the Elimination of Television.* New York: Morrow, 1978. An absolutist approach to the problem, but provocative.

Mankiewicz, Frank, and Joel Swerdlow. *Remote Control: Television and the Manipulation of American Life.* New York: Times Books, 1978. Recommended.

Marc, David. *Demographic Vistas: Television in American Culture.* Philadelphia: University of Pennsylvania Press, 1984. Critical insights on programming.

Marc, David. *Comic Visions.* New York: Routledge, 1989.

Mayer, Martin. *About Television.* New York: Harper & Row, 1974.

McArthur, Colin. *Television and History.* London: British Film Institute, 1978.

McLuhan, Marshall. *Understanding Media: The Extensions of Man.* New York: McGraw-Hill, 1964. Controversial and often unintelligible, but seminal.

McRobbie, Angela. *Postmodernism and Popular Culture.* London: Routledge, 1994.

Miller, Jonathan. *Marshall McLuhan.* New York: Viking Press, 1971. The comedian/physician/producer/writer takes on the guru.

Miller, Mark Crispin. *Boxed In: The Culture of TV.* Evanston, IL: Northwestern University Press, 1988.

Monaco, James, et al. *Celebrity: Who Gets It, How They Use It, Why It Works.* New York: Delta Books, 1978. Includes analysis of star images of the seventies.

Monaco, James, et al. *Media Culture: Television, Books, Radio, Records, Magazines, Newspapers, Movies.* New York: Delta Books, 1978.

Mueller, Claus. *The Politics of Communication.* New York: Oxford University Press, 1973.

Naremore, James, and Patrick Brantlinger, eds. *Modernity and Mass Culture.* Bloomington: Indiana University Press, 1991.

Newcomb, Horace. *TV: The Most Popular Art.* New York: Doubleday, 1974.

Newcomb, Horace, ed. *Television: The Critical View.* Fifth ed. New York: Oxford University Press, 1994. This has become a standard, essential anthology.

Newcomb, Horace, and Robert Alley. *The Producer's Medium: Conversations with Creators of American TV.* New York: Oxford University Press, 1983.

Palmer, Tony. *All You Need Is Love: The Story of Popular Music.* New York: Grossman, 1976.

Postman, Neil. *Amusing Ourselves to Death.* New York: Viking Penguin, 1986.

Powers, Ron. *The Newscasters: The News Business as Show Business.* New York: St. Martin's Press, 1977.

Schiller, Herbert I. *Mass Communications and American Empire.* Boston: Beacon Press, 1969.

Schiller, Herbert I. *Culture, Inc.: The Corporate Takeover of Public Expression.* New York: Oxford University Press, 1989.

Schwartz, Tony. *The Responsive Chord: How Radio and TV Manipulate You.* New York: Anchor, 1973.

Shanks, Bob. *The Cool Fire: How To Make It in Television.* New York: Norton, 1976.

Sklar, Robert. *Prime-Time America: Life On and Behind the Television Screen.* New York: Oxford University Press, 1980.

Smith, Anthony. *The Newspaper: An International History.* London: Thames & Hudson, 1979. An introduction.

Smith, Anthony. *Good-bye, Gutenberg: The Newspaper Revolution of the Eighties.* New York: Oxford University Press, 1980.

Smith, Anthony, and Richard Paterson, eds. *Television: An International History.* Second Edition. New York: Oxford University Press, 1998. Basic reference.

Smith, Sally Bedell. *In All His Glory: The Life of William S. Paley.* New York: Simon & Schuster, 1990. A remarkable biography.

Smithsonian Institution. *History of Music Machines.* New York and London: Drake, 1975. Introduction by Erik Barnouw.

Tebbel, John. *The Media in America*. New York: Mentor, 1974. Traces the development of print and electronic media.

Williams, Raymond. *Television: Technology and Cultural Form*. New York: Schocken, 1975. Recommended.

Williams, Raymond. *Communications*. Third ed. London: Penguin, 1976.

Winn, Marie. *The Plug-in Drug: Television, Children, and the Family*. New York: Viking and Bantam, 1977. Influential when it was written, sadly still germane.

Wright, John W., et al. *Edsels, Luckies, and Frigidaires: Advertising the American Way*. New York: Delta Books, 1978. An intriguing collection of historical advertisements.

Wright, John W. *The Commercial Connection: Advertising and the American Mass Media*. New York: Delta Books, 1979. A useful collection of articles, with appendices.

Zook, Kristal Brent. *Color by Fox: The Fox Network and the Revolution in Black Television*. New York: Oxford University Press, 1999.

7. NEW MEDIA

Apple Computer, Inc. *Macintosh Human Interface Guidelines*. Reading, MA: Addison-Wesley, 1992. For anyone interested in the logic of interface design this is the bible.

Augarten, Stan. *State of the Art: A Photographic History of the Integrated Circuit*. New York: Ticknor & Fields, 1983. Now several generations out of date, but still instructive.

Augarten, Stan. *Bit by Bit: An Illustrated History of Computers*. New York: Ticknor & Fields, 1984. An interesting and useful survey of the early history.

Benedikt, Michael. *Cyberspace: First Steps*. Cambridge, MA: MIT Press, 1991.

Brinkley, Joel. *Defining Vision: How Broadcasters Lured the Government into Inciting a Revolution in Television*. San Diego: Harcourt Brace & Company, 1997. The politics and intrigue of the HDTV standard.

Eco, Umberto. *Travels in Hyperreality*. New York: Harcourt Brace Jovanovich, 1986. Includes important essays on culture and media.

Elsaesser, Thomas, and Kay Hoffman, eds. *Cinema Futures: Cain, Abel or Cable? The Screen Arts in the Digital Age*. Amsterdam: Amsterdam University Press, 1998. An international collection of essays on the digital challenge.

Gabler, Neal. *Life The Movie: How Entertainment Conquered Reality*. New York: Alfred A. Knopf, 1998. Gabler's take on the Huxley critique.

Harley, Robert. *The Complete Guide to High-End Audio*. Second edition. Albuquerque, NM: Acapella, 1994, 1998. Harley explains the new technology clearly and concisely.

Harley, Robert. *Home Theater for Everyone*. Albuquerque, NM: Acapella, 1997. A useful introduction to the new maze of digital audio and video.

Hiltzik, Michael. *Dealers of Lightning: Xerox PARC and the Dawn of the Computer Age*. New York: Harper Business, 1999. A thorough history of the microcomputer's nursery.

Johnson, Steven. *Interface Culture: How New Technology Transforms the Way We Create and Communicate*. New York: Harper Edge, 1997. The editor of *Feed* webzine offers his view of new media.

Kelly, Kevin. *Out of Control: The New Biology of Machines, Social Systems, and the Economic World*. Reading, MA: Addison-Wesley, 1994. The *Wired* sensibility.

Levinson, Paul. *Digital McLuhan: A Guide to the Information Millenium*. New York: Routledge, 1999. An approach to McLuhan's thought thirty years on.

Levy, Steven. *Insanely Great: The Life and Times of Macintosh, the Computer That Changed Everything*. New York: Viking, 1994. A good overview of Apple history.

Long, Mark. *The World of Satellite TV: Covering MPEG Digital TV*. Ninth edition. Summertown TN: The Book Publishing Company, 1998. Standard guide to the subject.

Lubar, Steven. *InfoCulture: The Smithsonian Book of Information Age Inventions*. Boston: Houghton Mifflin Company, 1993. Companion volume to the exhibit of the same name and a thoughtful and thorough survey of information technology.

Luther, Arch. *Principles of Digital Audio and Video*. Boston: Artech House, 1997. An excellent technical introduction to the subject.

Luther, Arch. *Video Recording Technology*. Boston: Artech House, 1999.

Negroponte, Nicholas. *Being Digital*. New York: Alfred A. Knopf, 1995. The founder of the Media Lab at MIT and a multimedia pioneer cogitates on the future of the information society.

Nelson, Ted. *Computer Lib/Dream Machines*, 1974. Revised edition. Redmond, WA: Microsoft Press, 1987. A classic text.

Norman, Donald A. *The Design of Everyday Things*. New York: Doubleday, 1988,1990. An early essay on psycho-semiotics that became a classic of interface theory.

Smith, Anthony. *Books to Bytes: Knowledge and Information in the Post Modern Era*. London: British Film Institute, 1993.

Stoll, Clifford, *The Cuckoo's Egg*. New York: Doubleday, 1989. In the mid-1980s astronomer Clifford Stoll was drawn into a year-long Internet espionage saga whose story is told here. A PBS documentary on the subject and many lectures helped to form one of the central myths of network hacking.

Stoll, Clifford. *Silicon Snake Oil: Second Thoughts on the Information Highway*. New York: Doubleday, 1995. An Internet hero realizes that, for all its advantages, the Web presents the same social and political problems as television before it.

Taylor, Jim. *DVD Demystified: The Guidebook for DVD-Video and DVD-ROM*. New York: McGraw-Hill, 1997. A tour de force of technical writing, Jim Taylor's book explains an insidiously complex subject with eloquence and common sense. Must reading for anyone interested in digital media of any sort.

Tognazzini, Bruce. *Tog on Interface*. Reading, MA: Addison-Wesley, 1992. The interface guru tackles specific problems in an enlightening way.

Wallace, James, and Jim Erickson. *Hard Drive: Bill Gates and the Making of the Microsoft Empire*. New York: John Wiley & Sons, 1992. A good overview of early Microsoft history.

Part Two: Information

8. LISTS AND ENCYCLOPEDIAS

FILM

The rise of video has made film reference works viable publishing projects. There are now dozens of choices on the reference shelves of most bookstores. In the sixties such information was hard to come by. Georges Sadoul in France and Roger Manvell and Tim Cawkwell in England pioneered the field of comprehensive film reference. At about the same time, Peter Cowie began his series of annual Film Guides, and Leslie Halliwell in the U.K. and Leonard Maltin in the U.S. brought out the first editions of their popular guides to movies appearing on broadcast television. They had been preceded by more than a decade by Steven Scheuer (1958), a pioneer in the field who is still active.

In the 1980s Ephraim Katz weighed in with his labor of love, *The Film Encyclopedia*, years in the making. He died before the second edition went to press in 1994. Richard Roud's *Cinema: A Critical Dictionary* appeared in 1980. Roud had made his mark as an early champion of Jean-Luc Godard and as the director of the New York Film Festival in the 1960s and 1970s, when that festival led the way in introducing European films to the American market. Although he died in 1989 his influence is still being felt. Also in the 1980s Hans-Michael Bock began his massive work, *CineGraph*, a serial publication which now amounts to thousands of pages. In 1984 film buffs Jay Robert Nash and Stanley Ralph Ross produced their multi-volume idiosyncratic film list, *The Motion Picture Guide*. Their company, CineBooks, was later acquired by News Corp (and briefly owned by Baseline). Under various managements annual updates were produced through 1998 under the management of Jo Imeson and James Pallot.

In the 1990s the focus of film reference shifted to CD-ROM. Microsoft's *Cinemania*, with contributions by Leonard Maltin, Pauline Kael, Baseline, and others, sold almost three million copies before it was put out of print in 1998. CineBooks produced a disc version of *The Motion Picture Guide*, and Blockbuster also sponsored a CD-ROM film reference. As of this writing, all are out of print. The focus has shifted to the Internet where the Internet Movie Data Base (IMDB.com) dominates.

The American Film Institute Catalogue of Motion Pictures Produced in the U.S. Vol. F2: Feature Films 1921–1930 (2 vols.); *Vol. F6: Feature Films 1961–1970. Vol. F1: Feature Films 1911–1920; Vol. F3: Feature Films 1931–1940*. 1971, 1976, 1988, 1993. A continuing series (more than 20 volumes are planned on features, shorts, and newsreels), reputedly complete.

Bawden, Liz-Anne, ed. *The Oxford Companion to Film*. New York: Oxford University Press, 1976.

Bock, Hans-Michael, ed. *CineGraph—Lexikon zum deutschsprachigen Film*. Munich: edition text + kritik, 1984– (serial). Extensive and carefully researched bio-filmographies. Also available online (see below).

Cawkwell, Tim, and John M. Smith, eds. *The World Encyclopedia of Film*. New York: A&W Visual Library, 1972.

Chirat, Raymond. *Catalogue des films français de long métrage*. Multivolume, various publishers. *Films de fiction 1919–1929*. Toulouse: Cinémathèque de Toulouse, 1984. *Films sonores de fiction 1929–1939*. Brussels: Cinémathèque Royale de Belgique, 1975. *Films sonores de fiction 1040–1950*. Luxembourg: Éditions Imprimerie Saint-Paul, 1981.

Directory of Films By and/or About Women. Berkeley: Women's Historical Research Center, 1972. An early feminist classic.

Ebert, Roger. *Roger Ebert's Movie Home Companion*. Kansas City: Andrews & McMeel, 1989– .

Gifford, Denis. *The British Film Catalogue 1895–1985: A Reference Guide*. Second edition. Newton Abbot: David & Charles, 1987.

Halliwell, Leslie. *The Filmgoer's Companion*, New York: Charles Scribner's Sons, 1977. Subsequent regular editions

Halliwell, Leslie. *Halliwell's Film Guide*. London: Granada, 1977. Subsequent regular editions.

Katz, Ephraim. *The Film Encyclopedia*. Second ed. New York: Harper-Collins, 1994. A herculean labor of love by the late film scholar, this has become an essential reference since it was first published in 1980.

Magill, Frank N., ed. *Magill's Survey of Cinema: First Series*, 1980; *Second Series*, 1981; *Silent Films*, 1982; *Foreign Language Films*, 1985. Englewood Cliffs, NJ: Salem Press.

Maltin, Leonard, ed. *Movie and Video Guide*. Annual. New York: New American Library, Signet 1969– . Tens of thousands of entries with capsule descriptions.

Maltin, Leonard, ed. *Leonard Maltin's Movie Encyclopedia*. New York: Dutton, 1994.

Manvell, Roger, and Lewis Jacobs, eds. *International Encyclopedia of Film*. New York: Crown, 1972.

Monaco, James, ed. *Who's Who in American Film Now*. Second ed. New York: New York Zoetrope, 1987. A guide to credits of more than 12,000 actors, actresses, and filmmakers. Based on the Baseline database.

Monaco, James, and James Pallot, eds., with the editors of Baseline. *The Encyclopedia of Film*. New York: Perigee Books; London: Virgin Books, 1991. Based on the Baseline database.

Monaco, James, and James Pallot, eds. *The Movie Guide*. New York: Perigee Books, 1992. *The Virgin International Film Guide*, Second ed. London: Virgin Books, 1993. Based on the CineBooks database.

Monaco, James. *The Dictionary of New Media*. New York: Harbor Electronic Publishing, 1999. An extensive survey of new (and old) media language, with an introductory chapter on the digital revolution.

The New York Times Directory of the Film. New York: Arno Press, 1970, 1974. A computer-generated name index to *Times* film reviews.

Passek, Jean-Loup, ed. *Dictionnaire du cinéma*. Paris: Larousse, 1986.

Pratt, Douglas. *The Laser Video Disc Companion*. Third ed. New York: New York Zoetrope, 1995. An excellent and comprehensive guide to laserdiscs, with interesting commentary on the films.

Pratt, Douglas. *Doug Pratt's Guide to DVD -Video*. New York: Harbor Electronic Publishing, 1999. After 16 years in the disc reviewing business, Pratt knows whereof he speaks. Extensive and knowledgeable.

Roud, Richard, ed. *Cinema: A Critical Dictionary: The Major Filmmakers*. 2 vols. London: Secker & Warburg; New York: Viking, 1980.

Sadoul, Georges. *Dictionary of Films, Dictionary of Filmmakers*. Translated and updated by Peter Morris. Berkeley: University of California Press, 1972.

Scheuer, Steven H., ed. *Movies on TV*. Annual. New York: Bantam Books, 1958– . 20,000 entries. Plot summaries and capsule reviews.

Thomas, Nicholas, ed. *International Dictionary of Film and Filmmakers*. 5 vols. Detroit: Saint James Press, 1991–94.

Thomson, David. *A Biographical Dictionary of Film*. Second ed. London: Secker & Warburg; New York: Morrow, 1981. Excellent essays on star personas. Recommended.

Wakeman, John. *World Film Directors*. New York: H. W. Wilson, 1987. 2 vols. Useful essays on major international figures.

RADIO AND TELEVISION

Brooks, Tim, and Earle Marsh. *The Complete Directory to Prime Time Network TV Shows 1946–Present*. New York: Ballantine, 1979. Subsequent editions.

Brown, Les, ed. *Les Brown's Encyclopedia of Television*. Third ed. Detroit: Visible Ink Press, 1992. An invaluable reference by the dean of American television critics.

Buxton, Frank, and Bill Owen. *The Big Broadcast 1920–1950.* New York: Avon, 1972. A reference guide to radio.

Dunning, John. *On the Air: The Encyclopedia of Old-Time Radio.* New York: Oxford University Press, 1998. A new edition of *Tune in Yesterday.*

McNeil, Alex. *Total Television: A Comprehensive Guide to Programming from 1948 to the Present.* Third ed. New York: Penguin, 1991.

Terrace, Vincent. *The Complete Encyclopedia of Television Programs.* 3 vols. New York: New York Zoetrope, 1985, 1986.

9. BOOK BIBLIOGRAPHIES

Basic Books in the Mass Media. Eleanor Blum. Urbana: University of Illinois Press, 1972. A basic bibliography.

Bibliography of National Filmographies. Harriet W. Harrison, ed. Brussels: FIAF, 1985.

Cinema Booklist. George Rehrauer. Metuchen, NJ: Scarecrow Press, 1972. *Supplement One,* 1974. *Supplement Two,* 1976. The standard bibliographic guide to film literature.

Film Criticism: An Index to Critics' Anthologies. Richard Heinzkill. Metuchen, NJ: Scarecrow Press, 1975.

Literature of the Film. Alan Dyment. London: White Lion Publishers, 1975.

Moving Pictures: An Annotated Guide to Selected Film Literature. Eileen Sheahan. Cranbury, NJ: A. S. Barnes, 1978.

Film: A Reference Guide. Robert A. Armour. Westport, CT: Greenwood Press, 1980.

Literature of the Film. Alan Dyment. London: White Lyon, 1975.

10. GUIDES TO PERIODICAL LITERATURE

Of the seven guides to periodical literature in film, three limit themselves to film magazines, one is mainly devoted to film magazines but includes material from occasional general publications, one concentrates on general magazines, and one covers a wide range of both specialist and general periodicals. Of the three that concentrate on film journals, two are limited to English-language magazines. Each is therefore useful in its own way, although there is considerable overlapping.

International Index to Film Periodicals. Produced by the International Federation of Film Archives (FIAF). 1971 to present. Annual, various publishers. The standard index to film periodicals; covers foreign-language journals as well as English. See also *International Index to Television Periodicals.* FIAF. Four volumes to date, 1979–90.

The Film Index: A Bibliography. Vol. 1: The Film as Art. Vol. 2: The Film as Industry. Vol. 3: The Film in Society. Compiled by the Writers' Program of the Works Project Administration Staff, 1941. Reprint. Millwood, NY: Kraus International Publications, 1985–88. An early classic guide.

The New Film Index. Edited by Richard Dyer MacCann and Edward S. Perry. New York: Dutton, 1975. 540 pp. Covers 38 film magazines in English as well as occasional other journals from 1930 to 1970. Together with the FIAF yearly volumes, comprises a basic research tool.

The Critical Index. John C. and Lana Gerlach. New York: Teachers College Press, 1974. 726 pp. Computer-generated bibliography of articles on film in English, 1946–1973. 22 periodicals covered.

Index to Critical Film Reviews in British and American Film Periodicals; Together with Index to Critical Reviews of Books About Film: 1930–1972. 2 vols. Stephen E. Bowles. New York: Burt Franklin Co., 1975. Approximately 700 pp. The index of book reviews is unique.

A Guide to Critical Reviews, Part 4: Bibliography of Critical Reviews of Feature Length Motion Pictures Released from October 1927 through 1963. James R. Salem. 2 vols. Metuchen, NJ: Scarecrow Press, 1971. 12,000 entries.

Retrospective Index to Film Periodicals 1930–1971. Linda Batty. New York: R. R. Bowker, 1975. Companion to the FIAF yearly indexes listed above. 20 English-language periodicals covered.

Motion Picture Directors: A Bibliography of Magazine and Periodical Articles, 1900–1969. Mel Schuster. Metuchen, NJ: Scarecrow Press, 1973. 418 pp.

Film Literature Index. Albany: State University of New York at Albany, Film and Television Documentation Center, 1973–present. Annual. A subject/author index covering more than 300 film periodicals in various languages and 125 English-language general interest magazines.

Film Review Index. Vol. 1: 1882–1949, 1986; Vol. 2: 1950–1985, 1987. Phoenix, AZ: Oryx.

Film Review Annual. Englewood, NJ: Jerome S. Ozer, 1981–present. Annual.

The New York Times Film Reviews 1913–1968. 6 vols. New York: Arno Press, 1970. A complete reprinting covering more than 17,000 films together with a cumulative index.

The New York Times Film Reviews 1913–1970: A One-Volume Selection. Edited by George Amberg. New York: Quadrangle, 1971. 495 pp.

The Drama Scholar's Index to Plays and Filmscripts: A Guide to Plays and Filmscripts in Selected Anthologies, Series, and Periodicals. Gordon Samples. Metuchen, NJ: Scarecrow Press, 1974. 460 pp.

11. MISCELLANEOUS GUIDES

Cowie, Peter, ed. *International Film Guide.* Yearly, 1964– . London: Tantivy Press. One of the most useful film references with a variety of essays on many topics. Especially useful for its surveys of annual production in many countries. Since 1990, *Variety International Film Guide*. Recommended.

Enser, A. G. S., ed. *Filmed Books and Plays: 1928–1974.* New York: Academic Press, 1974. A list of books and plays from which films have been made.

Gianakos, Larry. *Television Drama Series Programming: A Comprehensive Chronicle, 1959–1975.* Metuchen, NJ: Scarecrow Press, 1979.

Klotman, Phyllis Rauch. *Frame by Frame: A Black Filmography.* Bloomington: Indiana University Press, 1979.

Konigsberg, Ira. *The Complete Film Dictionary.* Second edition. New York: Penguin, 1997.

Marill, Alvin H. *Movies Made for Television: The Telefeature and the Miniseries 1964–1986.* Third ed. New York: New York Zoetrope, 1987.

Monaco, James. *The Connoisseur's Guide to Movies.* New York: Facts On File, 1985. A selective list of 1,400 interesting or significant films.

Powers, Ann. *Blacks in American Movies.* Metuchen, NJ: Scarecrow Press, 1974.

Steinberg, Cobbett. *Film Facts.* New York: Facts On File, 1980.

Thompson, Hilary, et al., eds. *1951–1976 British Film Institute Productions: A Catalogue of Films Made Under the Auspices of the Experimental Film Fund 1951–1966 and the Production Board 1966–1976.* London: British Film Institute, 1977.

Truitt, Evelyn. *Who Was Who On Screen: 1920–1971.* New York: R. R. Bowker, 1974. 480 pp. 6,000 screen personalities.

Van Nooten, S. I., ed. *Vocabulaire du cinéma/Film Vocabulary/Film Woordenlijst,* Sixth ed. The Hague: Netherlands Information Service, 1974. 900 film terms in French, English, Dutch, Italian, German, Spanish, and Danish.

World Radio T.V. Handbook. New York: Billboard Publications. Published yearly.

12. JOURNALS AND MAGAZINES

At one time or another, more than 500 film magazines have been published in the English language alone. As many as 200 survive today. This is a selected list that includes most magazines currently indexed plus a few others that, although small in circulation, have some influence. Be forewarned: most film journals are fragile; some of these may be out of circulation by the time you read this.

American Cinematographer. Hollywood. The leading technical journal.

l'Avant-Scène du Cinéma, 6 rue Gît le coeur 75006 Paris. Venerable periodical that publishes complete screenplays of new films and classics; sometimes bilingual.

Cahiers du Cinéma. Paris. The most influential film journal ever published.

Camera Obscura. Film Studies Program, University of California at Santa Barbara. Feminist film theory.

Cineaste. Edited by Gary Crowdus. New York. Recommended for its eclectic and politically sensitive approach. This quarterly has shown unusual longevity.

Cinema Journal. Theoretical journal of the Society for Cinema Studies. Edited at the University of Illinois at Urbana; published by the University of Texas Press, Austin.

The DVD/Laser Disc Newsletter. Douglas Pratt. Monthly. Founded in 1984, this one-man operation provides the best writing about DVDs and Laserdiscs—and some of the best writing about film, period. New York. WWW.DVDLaser.com. Fax: 516 594 9307.

Film Comment. Edited by Richard T. Jameson. Film Society of Lincoln Center, New York. Bimonthly.

Film Dope. 5 Norman Court, Little Heath, Potters Bar, Hertfordshire EN6 1HY, England. Quarterly. A serial dictionary of film.

Film History: An International Journal. Edited by Richard Koszarski, American Museum of the Moving Image. Accessible historical essays, well illustrated.

Film Quarterly. University of California Press, Berkeley. Quarterly. Long edited by Ernest Callenbach. Now edited by Ann Martin.

Iris. Éditions Analeph, Paris. Theoretical French–English copublication.

Journal of Film and Video. University Film and Video Association.

Journal of Popular Film. Bowling Green State University, Bowling Green, OH. Quarterly.

Literature/Film Quarterly. Salisbury State University, Salisbury, MD.

Premiere. New York. The serious/popular film journal that finally won the acceptance of advertisers.

Quarterly Review of Film & Video. Harwood Academic Publishers, Chur, Switzerland.

SCREEN. John Logie Baird Centre of the Universities of Glasgow and Strathclyde. Quarterly.

Sight and Sound. British Film Institute, London. Monthly. Long edited by Penelope Houston. The BFI's venerable *Monthly Film Bulletin* was folded into *Sight and Sound* in the early 1990s.

Velvet Light Trap. University of Texas Press. Austin, TX. Semiannual.

Wide Angle. Ohio University School of Film. Published by Johns Hopkins University Press, Baltimore, MD.

13. DATABASES

Microsoft Cinemania. Baseline, Roger Ebert, Pauline Kael, Ephraim Katz, Leonard Maltin, James Monaco, et al. CD-ROM. Redmond, WA: Microsoft Electronic Publishing, 1992–97. The combination of data from Maltin, Katz, and *The Encyclopedia of Film* made this the best single CD-ROM reference source for film enthusiasts. Out of print.

The Motion Picture Guide. James Pallot and Jo Imeson, eds. New York: CineBooks, 1992–97. CD-ROM, Annual. Lengthy synopses and credits for more than 30,000 films based on the original 20-volume print edition of the mid-1980s founded by Jay Robert Nash and Stanley Ralph Ross. No multimedia. Annual updates in print form are also available. Much of the material on the disc is available on the Web at WWW.TVGuide.com. Out of print.

Blockbuster Entertainment Guide to Movies & Videos, second edition. Various contributors. Portland, OR: Creative Multimedia, Inc., 1996. CD-ROM. After *Cinemania* and the *Motion Picture Guide,* perhaps the most useful disc was this widely distributed promotional publication for the video store chain, with 23,000 reviews and 10,000 biographies and filmographies gathered from various sources. Out of print.

Lexikon des internationalen films. Katholischen Institüt for Medieninformation and the Katholischen Filmkommission für Deutschland. Munich: Systhema, 1995.

Baseline. A subscription service for professionals in the industry, Baseline carries extensive information on more than 70,000 historical films and television programs, 15,000 companies, 700,000 filmmakers, actors, and technicians, and 5,000 films and television programs in production, news, and other information. The service is available through most major film libraries and directly to thousands of professional subscribers. Parts of Baseline are carried on Nexis. I founded the company in 1982 and left in 1992 to found UNET to concentrate on software and consumer services. In 1999 the Baseline was purchased by BIG Entertainment, operator of several film-related websites.

CineGraph. The online version of Hans-Michael Bock's magnum opus is available at WWW.CineGraph.de. Bock founded CineGraph in the early 1980s to serve as a continuing, definitive encyclopedia of German film. Since 1984 more than 30 sections of *CineGraph – Lexikon zum deutschsprachigen Film* have been published in looseleaf format by editions text + kritik of Munich. For the last several years the work of CineGraph has been supported by the department of cultural affairs of the city of Hamburg. The organization publishes other reference works, operates conferences, and maintains additional databases relating to German-language cinema. It is one of the largest film databases in the world.

Internet Movie Database. WWW.IMDB.com. The IMDB is one of the great success stories of the Worldwide Web. Begun as a set of lists in 1990 by Col Needham in London and others, the database started to take off when it was mounted on the Web at Cardiff University (Wales) in 1993. The database is maintained by hundreds of contributors and scores of editors worldwide. The data is surprisingly accurate, considering the volunteer basis of the enterprise. In 1996 the IMDB became a commercial business, accepting advertising. In 1998 it was acquired by Amazon.

Other Internet sources of information are listed on the website for *How To Read a Film*: WWW.ReadFilm.com.

Topic Index

Concepts, companies, countries, and topics.

People Index

Title Index